INTRODUCTION TO CRIMINOLOGY

INTRODUCTION TO CRIMINOLOGY

By

HAROLD J. VETTER, Ph.D.
Chairman, Department of Psychology
Loyola University
New Orleans, Louisiana

and

JACK WRIGHT, JR., Ph.D.
Director, Law Enforcement and Criminal Justice Program
Delgado College
New Orleans, Louisiana

CHARLES C THOMAS · PUBLISHER
Springfield · Illinois · U.S.A.

Published and Distributed Throughout the World by
CHARLES C THOMAS • PUBLISHER
BANNERSTONE HOUSE
301-327 East Lawrence Avenue, Springfield, Illinois, U.S.A.

© *1974, by* CHARLES C THOMAS • PUBLISHER
ISBN 0-398-03138-X
Library of Congress Catalog Card Number: 74-993

With THOMAS BOOKS *careful attention is given to all details of manufacturing and design. It is the publisher's desire to present books that are satisfactory as to their physical qualities and artistic possibilities and appropriate for their particular use.* THOMAS BOOKS *will be true to those laws of quality that assure a good name and good will.*

Printed in the United States of America
N-1

Library of Congress Cataloging in Publication Data

Vetter, Harold J   1925-
    Introduction to criminology.

    Bibliography: p.
    1. Crime and criminals. 2. Law enforcement.
I. Wright, Jack, 1933-   joint author. II. Title.
HV6025.V47   364   74-993
ISBN 0-398-03138-X

To Roxie and Sherry
with the hope that the society
in which they grow up will be
less darkened by the shadow of
crime.

FOREWORD

IN THE UNITED STATES, until fairly recently, most research and theorizing on crime, criminals, criminal behavior, and the administration of justice was done by sociologists. Criminology was widely regarded by academicians as a branch of sociology. One sociology textbook states in reference to the nature and control of crime, "these subjects fall within the scope of the subdiscipline known as criminology" (Bertrand, 1967). Course offerings in criminology in most American colleges and universities were so meager as to make a separate department of criminology unnecessary.

The past twenty years have brought a great many changes in the scope and content of criminology and in the identity of the criminologist himself. It is no longer accurate to characterize criminology as a "subdiscipline of sociology." Criminology has emerged as an interdisciplinary endeavor which seeks to incorporate the approaches and contributions of the social and behavioral sciences, law, philosophy, and a number of other areas of inquiry as they relate to the systematic study of crime, criminals, criminal behavior, law enforcement, the courts, probation and parole, and corrections. There is a growing consensus that the distinctive task of criminology is to provide a conceptual framework for the integration of ideas generated by various disciplines in the study of crime phenomena.

Society attempts to control crime and delinquency through many agencies, including the police, courts, parole and probation authorities, social casework, and penal institutions. If the study of criminology is to proceed realistically, it must approach the variegated nature of the crime problem in a comparable fashion. Just as no single agency within the criminal justice system can deal effectively with the entire spectrum of criminal and delinquent behavior, no single academic discipline is equal to the task of comprehending or even conceptualizing the complex range of phenomena subsumed under the general term *crime*.

Sociology provides us with some understanding of the social and cultural factors which cause certain kinds of behavior to be defined as prohibited and of the ways in which a society seeks to preserve its values. Psychology aims at the specification of variables which affect the occurrence of behavior and the means whereby the deviant behavior of specific individuals can be modified. Chemistry, physics, biology, and other branches of natural science contribute to *criminalistics,* the generic term for the science and technology of criminal investigation and detection. Studies in criminal law help to explain the operation of the courts in meting out justice. Political science experts address themselves to the analysis of relationships between the criminal justice system and the democratic process. Religion and ethics may furnish insights into contemporary morality and issues involved in conduct that leads to societal disapproval. Social casework can help equip people with methods and skills for dealing with offenders, both in the penal institution and on probation or parole. Each of these disciplines makes a contribution to the body of organized knowledge known as criminology.

As an interdisciplinary endeavor, criminology is increasingly scientific in its orientation and emphases. Many criminologists are attracted to the models, supplied by the behavioral sciences, as a potential framework for the conceptual integration of criminological data and theories. Nevertheless, it would be grossly inaccurate to equate "criminological" with "scientific" in contemporary criminology. Law, to take only one of several possible examples, represents an organized body of fact and theory that has developed its own particular type of systematic inquiry—a methodology no less rigorous than science, despite the fact that the legal mode of inquiry is not scientific. The law is both a focus and a point of departure in criminology, but the specific nature of its concerns, subject matter, and adversary approach to investigation makes it less suitable than behavioral science models as a potential frame of reference for the integration of diverse materials from a variety of disciplines.

We can avoid further preoccupation with identity crises in criminology by simply noting that a criminologist, a term which evokes images ranging from Sherlock Holmes peering through a magnifying glass to a forensic psychiatrist "taking the history" of a sexual offender, is a specialist in any of the disciplines which contribute to the study of crime. Thus, he may be a sociologist, psychologist, psychiatrist, law enforcement official, judge, attorney, or probation officer. His interests may thus extend to urban society, rehabilitative science, social organization, history, fine arts, or literature.

Something should be said about the distinction between "pure" and "applied" criminology. If a researcher attempts to refine and improve an instrument, such as the Social Prediction Scale for delinquents devised by the husband and wife team of Sheldon and Eleanor Glueck, with the objective of gathering further information, this activity is within the province of criminology. Should a judge apply the results of such research as a quide to the sentencing of delinquents, this is public administration (Wolfgang, 1963).

PROFESSIONAL EDUCATION IN CRIMINOLOGY

With regard to the educational preparation of criminologist, Reckless (1967) has stated that it is "well within the bounds of realism to predict that a standardized basic training for criminologists eventually will be developed and that a certificate, diploma, or broad of examination will validate a person's competence as a criminologist." Already, the F.B.I., the Treasury Department, the Border Patrol, large city police departments, juvenile and adult courts, and Divisions of Youth Services and Adult Corrections are seeking graduates with specialized degrees in criminology. Formerly people were recruited who were graduates in fields such as sociology, social casework, and psychology.

The police and the prisons, which have long been areas of societal neglect, have suddenly become the subjects of Congressional concern. They have been the chief recipients of financial support as a consequence of the passage, in 1968, of the Omnibus

Crime Bill and Safe Streets Act, an historic piece of legislation intended to produce an upgrading of the criminal justice system. In response to growing needs for professionally competent people, colleges and universities have set up programs and curricula specifically designed to develop specialists in all phases of criminal justice. Criminology has shared in this growth process: A number of universities have established autonomous departments or schools of criminology, utilizing a variety of patterns of academic organization. Michigan State University has a separate department of police administration within the School of Social Sciences. Harvard University, following the European pattern, provides coursework in criminology in its law school. One of the largest schools of criminology in the United States is located at Florida State University.

Some of the most recent additions to training in the criminal justice system are the School of Criminal Justice of New York at Albany and the City University of New York. In 1965, the Texas legislature created the Institute for Contemporary Corrections and the Behavioral Sciences at the Sam Houston State College at Huntsville. Pennsylvania State University has a Center for Police Administration and Corrections. Southern Illinois University at Carbondale has a center for the study of crime and delinquency. Other major centers in the United States for the study of criminology include: Ohio State University, Indiana University, University of Maryland, University of Pennsylvania, and Washington State University.

The most prominent European programs for the study of criminology include the Institute of Criminology at Cambridge, the Institute for the Prevention of Crime at Rome, and the National Center for Criminology at the Free University of Brussels. The Netherlands has Institutes of Criminology at the University of Amsterdam, University of Groningen, and University of Leyden. In Greece, there is a Center for the Study of Juvenile Delinquency and Social Education at the University of Thessalonia. Sweden has an Institute of Criminology at the University of Stockholm. Finland has an Institute of Criminology at the University of Helsinki, and Denmark's Institute of Criminology is located at the

University of Copenhagen. In Turkey, there is an Institute of Penal Law and Criminology at the University of Istanbul.

REFERENCES

Bertrand, A.L.: *Basic Sociology.* New York, Appleton-Century-Crofts, 1967.

Reckless, W.C.: *The Crime Problem.* New York, Appleton-Century-Crofts, 1967.

Wolfgang, M.E.: Criminology and the criminologist. *Journal of Criminal Law, Criminology, and Police Science, 54:*156-158, 1963.

PREFACE

THIS BOOK IS DESIGNED to acquaint the student and the general reader with the subject matter, terminology, and basic concepts of criminology. It assumes no specialized knowledge or background; all that is taken for granted is a genuine interest on the part of the reader in learning something about the ways in which criminologists pursue the systematic study of crime, criminals, criminal behavior, and the criminal justice system. It also represents the shared convictions of a psychologist and a sociologist that pooling the insights of two disciplines provides a broader perspective on criminality than is afforded by a single discipline.

The Loyola writer would like to express his appreciation for the friends and colleagues who have furnished him with a postgraduate education in criminology: Reed Adams, a painstaking researcher and imaginative theorist; Harry Allen, who introduced him to a strange new form of religious observance; Gary Perlstein, whose innumerable kindnesses include permission to borrow liberally from his astute insights on politics and the law; Cliff Simonsen, an ex-military cop with a talented paint brush and the wit of Alexander Woolcott; Mike Swanson, who may soon be named a one-man criminal justice resource by the state of Georgia; and Jerry Wittman—inventor, raconteur, and nemesis of the blackjack dealers in Reno.

The Delgado writer wishes to acknowledge the influence of the following men, who, in class, or over coffee and other fluids, have influenced his ideas about crime: Chris Roy, an attorney with a sharp mind and a fast right-cross; Virgil Williams, a professor's professor; D. Wood Harper, entrepreneur in sociology; David Knox, a former student who now teaches his professor; Perry Moory, a Damon Runyon sidewalk psychologist; Vernon Fox, who introduced him to the study of criminology; and Tom Bowman, a cigar-chewing civil rights attorney.

Mrs. Farrie Oatis deserves our sincere appreciation for her patience, skill, and indifference to the strain imposed by long hours of manuscript preparation.

Finally, both writers would like to recognize their indebtedness, both professionally and intellectually, to the most knowledgeable criminology faculty in the United States: the murderers, thieves, and drug addicts caged in the Louisiana State Penitentiary at Angola, Louisiana.

H.J.V.   *New Orleans, Louisiana*
J.W.

ACKNOWLEDGMENTS

WE ARE DEEPLY INDEBTED to the following authors, editors, and publishers for extending their kind permission to reproduce or quote from copyrighted works: Reed Adams; Harry Allen; Menachem Amir; CRM Books; Federal Bureau of Prisons; *Federal Probation;* David Feldman; Paul Gebhard; Gilbert Geis; Daniel Glaser; Seymour Halleck; Frank Hartung; Ray Jeffery; *Journal of Criminal Law, Criminology, and Police Science; Kiplinger Magazine;* John MacDonald; Karl Menninger; Ashley Montagu; New Orleans *Times-Picayune; New Yorker Magazine;* Arthur Niederhoffer; Raleigh *Daily Reflector;* Random House; Ronald Press; Jerome Skolnick; *Social Problems;* University of Pennsylvania Press; U.S. Department of Health, Education, and Welfare; U.S. Department of Justice, Federal Bureau of Investigation; Viking Press; Marvin Wolfgang.

CONTENTS

INTRODUCTION TO CRIMINOLOGY

PART I

THE NATURE AND OCCURRENCE OF CRIME IN THE UNITED STATES

Two centuries have transformed the United States from an agrarian, rural society into a nation which is predominantly industrial, urban, and suburban. This transition has confronted the country with challenges and crises undreamed of by the founding fathers. The traditional locus of communal living in the U.S., the neighborhood, has fallen casualty to the increasing suburbanization of our society. Fewer and fewer people are able to regard the neighborhood with any sense of community cohesiveness or continuity. We are told that eight million Americans change their place of residence each year; the moving van has become the identifying symbol of contemporary American life. Gone is the feeling of solidarity which once bound people together as neighbors in mutual interdependence and protection. Many Americans do not know or even care to know the name of the person living next door. The man in the apartment across the hall is not somebody to whom one can turn for help in an emergency, he is rather a stranger to be looked at with fear and suspicion. The norm of urban impersonality is most shockingly exemplified, perhaps, in the tragic slaying of Kitty Genovese in New York, who was murdered under the gaze of more than a score of onlookers. None of them came to her rescue because none of them wanted to "become involved."

Basic changes in the even more fundamental institution of the family have exacerbated the problems of social sanction and control. Discipline and self-restraint, once considered the principal socializing tasks of the family, have passed by default to a variety of public and private agencies. Children, as a result, develop into self-oriented, alienated adults. The search among youth for an alternate, humanistic lifestyle as a reaction to what they consider the objectionable features of a society dominated by materialistic, exploitative values has been captured by James Michener in his novel, *The Drifters*. According to one of his reviewers:

> These young people . . . constitute a "new force in history." By and large they reject a world they never made, the parental, the institutional. They see the parental world as characterized by mean-spirited competition and a gray work ethic; by the quasi-enslavement of large groups (women) and smaller ones (racial or sexual minorities); by reliance upon alcohol; by the routine of "adjustment"; by hypocritical worship, in the West, of a dead Judeo-Christianity; and by the real, and probably suicidal, worship of the Juggernaut technology.
>
> The world they accept, or are working at creating, is not a mere mutation of the old one. It is, even though it borrows much from the history they scorn, "new." It is marked by communal sharing and non-competitiveness; by the rejection of war (though not all of them reject violence); by cunning compromise with, or outright contempt for, work; by a vague ideal of brotherhood, taking no account of sex differences; by reliance upon a whole pharmacopeia of drugs, from pot to heroin; by the quasi-worship of various forms of magic, including sun adoration, amulets and charms, taboo-breaking sex rituals, such nonsense as tarot, astrology and the *I Ching*, high-decibel stimulation the nervous system, and so forth; and by anti-privacy, group-think, and a kind of cheerful rather than an aggressive illiteracy (Fadiman, 1972).

Estrangement and alienation may lead to attack or retreat, to stridently aggressive militancy in seeking to topple the "Establishment," or to a quiet renunciation of a world perceived as abhorrent or irrelevant. In either case, attack or retreat, the response to alienation is a thorough repudiation of parental, i.e. traditional, values.

It is not necessary to indorse the values of the counter-culture to acknowledge that a profound sense of malaise appears to afflict many sectors of contemporary life in these United States. Technological advances and economic achievements have sharpened rather than blunted the tensions within our society and have helped foster social disorganization in the midst of abundance. The implications of this are extremely important if one is to comprehend the phenomenon of societal deviance, of which crime and delinquency are a large and menacing part. As Brown (1971) points out:

> This urbanized, existential society of conflicting values and interests is also characterized by differential means and opportunities. The American dream is usurped by the social reality of frustration and impotence. Success is promised to all, but the avenues to success are closed to many. Differential opportunities within our . . . complex social structure are conducive to deviate behavior. Thus, into the picture comes the authoritative machinery of the state which imposes controls on man's activities.

As we have tried to show in Chapter 1, it is essential to an understanding of criminal behavior that we view it within the broader context of deviance from societal norms. This opening chapter seeks to explore some of the ways in which societies attempt to contain and control deviance by means of sanctions ranging from informal disapproval to the application of the police powers of the state. As criminologists our study necessarily encompasses antisocial attitudes, atypical values, eccentric practices, and unusual behavior of many kinds; all of these phenomena may aid in the illumination of criminal conduct and its determinants.

In Chapter 2, our focus is on the techniques and approaches which criminology employs in its systematic study of crime, criminals, criminal behavior, and the structure and functioning of the criminal justice system. Here we encounter the criminologist as investigator, and we devote considerable attention to the logic of inquiry which underlies his pursuit of answers to basic questions concerning the crime problem.

The final chapter in this section is addressed to a critical examination of the raw materials on which criminological research and theorizing are based: the data which come from a variety of sources within society in general and the criminal justice system in particular. Our primary concern in this chapter is the Uniform Crime Report, a document issued each year by the Federal Bureau of Investigation. Based on information gathered from law enforcement agencies in fifty states, this document reports data on seven major types of serious offense. We have discussed the Uniform Crime Report in considerable detail because many criminologists regard it as the best or most authoritative source of criminological statistics, despite their reservations as to the reliability and validity of the information it presents.

Taken in the aggregate, Chapters 1-3 constitute an introduction to the study of criminology.

REFERENCES

Brown, L.: *The Evaluation of Police-Community Programs.* Washington, D.C., U.S. Government Printing Office, 1971.

Fadiman, C.: *The Drifters*—a review. *Book-of-the-Month Club News,* May, 1971.

Chapter 1
DEVIANCE, SOCIAL CONTROL, AND CRIMINALITY

I
N NEW ORLEANS, LOUISIANA, a young man stations himself in a concrete blockhouse on top of a downtown motel and wages a gun battle with the police until he is slain. In Catonsville, Maryland, a group of antiwar protesters overturn draftboard files and spatter them with animal blood. In Atlanta, Georgia, a young girl is abducted from her motel room and buried underground for eighty hours. In Berkeley, California, the daughter of Randolph Hearst is kidnapped by a group calling itself the "Symbionese Liberation Army."

What do all of these acts have in common? They are acts of deviance. To deviate is to wander, however slightly, from what is considered the most desirable, acceptable, or approved intellectual, physical, or moral choice. The problems of deviance are as ancient as the Pyramids, as contemporary as the morning newspaper, as enduring as man in groups, and as inevitable as death and taxes. Wherever there are rules, there are deviants: people who are unable or unwilling to act according to the normative standard. Before we can approach the problem of crime in American society, we must first address ourselves to the wider problem of deviance, of which crime is a part.

If human beings are to survive, they must live by an agreed-upon set of rules; otherwise, as the English social contract theorist, Hobbes, warned us, the life of man will be "solitary, poor, nasty, brutish, and short." Without laws and rules to govern our actions, man might still be living in caves, fighting animals and each other for survival. But rules, despite their obvious necessity, can be chafing, and man will only follow them so long as they perceive that it is in their best interest to do so.

NORMS AND BEHAVIOR

The concept of "deviance" can only be understood in relation to another concept, norms. Norms determine which human acts are defined as acceptable, proper, desirable, tasteful, and perhaps more important legal. Norms are those acts which are considered "normal" in the ordinary sense of that term, i.e. expected, approved ways of acting and reacting.

Society and Deviant Behavior

Deviance from the norms of society may be in an approved or disapproved direction. An example of approved deviance would be the honor student in college who "overachieves." Societal reaction to deviance is governed by three considerations: the direction of deviance (approved or disapproved), the degree of deviance, and the role and status of the individual within the group. In south Florida a man convicted of killing his wife was sentenced to serve his time only in the summers because more than twenty families would be put out of work if he were in prison "full time." His importance in the continued functioning of the group muted the societal reaction to his deviance. Furthermore, men are more likely to be tolerant of fellow members of their status groups than of strangers and "outgroups."

Normative Functions

Norms serve the function of making interaction between members of a group smooth and unambiguous. In the United States, it is a normative act when two men are introduced to shake hands. This custom evolved out of the ancient practice of clasping open hands to reveal you were not armed. Although its original purpose has faded from modern memory, it persists as a norm governing the introduction of two strangers or as the appropriate greeting for friends. Deviation from this ritual would brand the individual as rude and subject him to social disapproval.

Norms develop a constraining and controlling power over the individual. Deviation from the norms of a group may leave the individual with no guidelines for his conduct, resulting in a feeling of uncertainty and uneasiness. In a complex society, there is safety—both physical and emotional—in following the rules. John Steinbeck (1939) describes the evolution of the rules of society and the feeling of safety that comes with their observance in his novel, *The Grapes of Wrath:*

> And as the world moved westward, rules became laws, although no one told the families. It is unlawful to foul near the camp; it is unlawful in any way to foul the drinking water; it is unlawful to eat good rich food near one who is hungry, unless he is asked to share. And with the laws, the punishments—and there were only two—a quick and murderous fight or ostracism; the ostracism was the worst. For if one broke the laws his name and face went with him, and he had no place in any world, no matter where created. . . The families moved westward, and the technique of building the worlds improved so that the people could be safe in their worlds; and the form was so fixed that a family acting in the rules knew it was safe in the rules.

Sanctions

One method whereby we can determine which acts a society feels most strongly should be observed is to study the *sanctions* or punishments applied to their deviation. If an individual in a society fails to follow a norm, what happens? Failure to observe the handshaking ritual only results in social disapproval. Taking property by breaking into the dwelling of another, however, can result in the offender being locked in a cage for twenty years. The forcing of sexual relations upon an unwilling female can result in the execution of the aggressor by the state.

Generality and Specificity of Norms

All of these examples, however, are taken from the culture of the United States. There are no acts which would be considered deviant in all cultures or even considered deviant in the same culture in different historical periods. (While it is true that no society permits indiscriminate killing of the "in-group" members, whether the act of killing is viewed as deviance depends upon circumstances.) A young man wishing to impress his date in a Hong

Kong restaurant might order a dog from the chef's supply, have it killed and prepared as a delicacy. Such behavior in the United States would be cause of indignant action by the S.P.C.A.—at a dinner in which its members were feasting on the remains of cows, chickens, and pigs.

What is considered appropriate dress varies mercurially. In 1900 a woman was arrested in St. Louis, Missouri for "indecent exposure"—she had stepped off a trolley car and revealed an unstockinged ankle. In contemporary American society, it would take considerably more exposure than an ankle to have a woman labeled "indecent."

Sex and Aggression

Perhaps the greater number of norms attempt to govern and regulate sex and aggression in society. American society does not object to killing; indeed it positively encourages and rewards it in certain circumstances. Young males in our culture are programmed (socialized) to kill when our culture is "threatened" by an out-group (war). Policemen, prison guards, and state executioners are rewarded for killing society's deviants to maintain order. Indeed, the individual who refused to kill for his country (conscientious objector) may be labeled a deviant and placed in prison with murderers (deviants who killed without normative sanction). So the goal of the normative system is to push those persons who "refuse to kill" to kill only when society deems it normative (war, police in the line of duty) and to rehabilitate those deviants who have killed without permission (murderers). They will thus kill only those who threaten our societal values. Under this normative system, one man could kill hundreds of persons, do millions of dollars worth of property damage (to Germany in World War II), and receive the highest "military" honor this country can bestow—the Medal of Honor. Another person, by refusing to go into the armed forces, might be labeled deviant and placed in prison for refusal to kill. The point is to kill only with societal permission and when the object is "in season": Germans in 1940, Koreans in 1950, Vietnamese in 1960.

Norms and Socialization

Norms, or expected ways of behaving, were present in society prior to our birth. Through the socialization process, we internalize these norms and adopt them as our personal guidelines for behavior. The principal agency of socialization, and society's basic unity, is the family. Generally, children adopt the norms, folkways, values, and speech patterns of their parents. Through a series of rewards and punishments, parents prepare their children for life in society. It is inevitable that this training would produce an ethnocentric attitude on the part of the child. *Ethnocentricism* is the belief that one's own culture, or normative system, is the criterion by which all other cultural norms are viewed as appropriate, moral, eccentric, or sinful.

Functional and Dysfunctional Properties of Norms

Ethnocentricism is functional to social groups; it ties the members to their normative system. No social groups or society can remain cohesive if its members are divided in their commitment to the normative system. For individuals to be able to predict the responses of their fellows, agreement on the norms is necessary. The society envisioned by George Orwell in his social science-fiction novel *1984* was highly cohesive and tolerated little deviation. Such societies stifle the imagination necessary for creativity and may become dysfunctional. Police patrol helicopters snooped into people's windows. Telescreens received and transmitted simultaneously, and there was no way of knowing when you were being watched or overheard at a given moment. Children were trained to inform on their parents. The family had become, in effect, an extension of the Thought Police. The essential crime was "thoughtcrime," and for this treasonous act, one could be "vaporized." A totalitarian system attempts to control the individual entirely and to wear an improper expression on one's face was a punishable offense called "facecrime."[1]

---

[1]This offense exists in many totalitarian systems. Florida road gangs once had regulations against "eyeballing," and at one time the Marines had regulations prohibiting "silent contempt."

Deviance can be functional and can reinforce social solidarity by enabling social groups to more adequately define their social norms. The rising crime rate in the United States created a situation in which the three major candidates for President in 1968 all sounded like paraphrases of each other in their call for law and order. Riots caused this country to reaffirm its commitment to change through orderly processes.

Groups who rigidly reject deviants and lack the ability to tolerate dissent may find this posture leads to dysfunctional consequences. Disputes over church doctrines have created over three hundred protestant denominations and sects in this country, fragmenting its influence in the larger society.

While the strengthening of the group norms may be functional for the group immediately, its long run consequences may be detrimental in its relation to out-groups or the larger social world. When Rosa Parks deviated from the seating norms of the Montgomery, Alabama bus system by refusing to move to the rear, the South reacted by reaffirming its belief in segregation of the races. In turn, the nation as a whole responded by reaffirming its belief in democracy by passing national legislation to force southern states to conform to national norms. This national reaffirmation, however, brought to light *de facto*[2] segregation in the North and brought movements to make the ideal culture normative all over the United States.

Deviance may be functional; it affords a safety-valve for discontent. In American culture, there is no socially approved outlet to the sex drive except in marriage. Young persons reach puberty as young as twelve to fourteen years, yet must wait six or seven years before they can economically afford to be in the societally approved marriage state. Widows, bachelors, and married persons separated for long periods are expected to remain as chaste as monks chained to a vow of celibacy. Kinsey's findings in this area revealed an enormous difference in what society expects and the deviance it gets.

---

[2]The black novelist James Baldwin has observed that persons using the term "defacto segregation" do so in a manner that appears to mean "the place got segregated but nobody did it."

FOLKWAYS, MORES, AND LAWS

All norms serve the purpose of regulating and directing human behavior, but they are not all enforced equally. Using the penalty for their violation as criteria, norms may be classified as folkways, mores, or laws.

William Graham Sumner, in his book *Folkways*, referred to expected standards of behavior as folkways, and behavior that is demanded as mores. All mores are folkways, but not all folkways are mores. Folkways, that is those norms which are *preferred and expected*, are enforced through informal sanctions: ridicule, gossip, and possible ostracism by one's peers. Mores, or those standards of behavior which are *demanded*, are enforced by threat of expulsion from the group. Mores are considered essential for the survival of the group or for the continued maintenance of its most central values. In a colony of nudists, for example, if the group permitted the wearing of clothes, their reason for existence would end.

When the mores of a group are backed by the police powers of the state, they have been crystalized into laws. Laws are legislatively enacted rules of behavior, the violation of which results in a jail sentence or fine by the government.

Law evolves as an expression of the moral sentiments of a society and in turn reinforces these same mores. Those persons who flaunt legal norms may find themselves fined, imprisoned, exiled, or executed. Laws are most effective when supported by the mores. For example, the legal requirement that citizens of the United States wear appropriate clothing in public seldom needs enforcement. The population has so internalized this norm that it makes its breach a rarity. However, the United States is not a monolithic culture: It is a federation of diverse subcultures with varying religious and social attitudes held together by a common belief in the democratic processes for decision-making. The values which unite the United States are stronger than the forces which divide it. Given a pluralistic society, seldom would any national legislation be in complete harmony with the mores of all the groups in the society. When the Supreme Court decided in 1954 that "separate but equal" was a misnomer, the order to integrate public schools was an attempt to change the mores and laws, especially of the southern United States. Later, the North was to discover it had practiced a more subtle form of segregation, and the changing of these norms would at times prove more difficult than the visible legal system of the South. When a law is backed by no clear consensus, e.g. the implementation of integration decision in the South, only overwhelming force can bring about its application. (It took an army to enroll one black student in the University of Mississippi.)

If the mores are so powerful, can one legislate against them? If effective law enforcement is dependent upon a firm base in the mores of a group, how can legislation proceed contrary to this foundation? Mores are acceptable patterns of behavior embued with moral sentiment. But, no man steps in the same river twice; both the man and the river have changed. New experiences bring new memories and new· responses. The law cannot change subjective attitudes directly. But the law can change interaction patterns, and in time new social relations will come to seem as natural and desirable as the old ones once so diligently fought to preserve. Indeed, in the United States the law has been the principle agent in both creating segregation and integration of the races (Woodward, 1957). A large body of law grew around the turn of the century which accelerated the trend toward the segregation of the races. A new social order was developed in the South to fill the vacuum left by the destruction of the old one by the Civil War. Laws were passed which prohibited members of different races from using the same lavatories and drinking from the same water fountains. Institution for the aged, orphans, and the blind were segregated. In 1909, Mobile, Alabama passed a curfew law applying exclusively to black people, requiring them to be off the streets by ten p.m. The Oklahoma legislature in 1915 saw fit to provide segregated telephone booths. New Orleans, Louisiana—with a logic fathomed only by those who drafted the ordinance—segregated white and black prostitutes.

For the law to be effective in social change, it must operate with, and not against, the forces of change in society. "Nothing is so powerful as an idea whose time has come." When the law is in harmony with the processes of change, it accelerates that change. The entire trend of national legislation, and judicial decrees, since 1954, has been to speed the process of undoing the normative system of segregation which the law had helped create around 1900.

LAW AS A MEANS OF SOCIAL CONTROL

Social behavior is behavior that affects others; thus social control is the control of social behavior. The means of this control vary with the behavioral situation. Religion, custom, public opinion, and law all control or limit our behavior in varying degrees and in differing circumstances.

What does the law do to aid in social control? It "secures justice, resolves social conflict, orders society, oils the machinery of social intercourse, protects interests, controls social relations" (Howard and Summers, 1965).

Howard and Summers list five conditions necessary for law to accomplish its stated ends.

1. The rules of law must set forth a clearly understandable standard of conduct so that citizens can know what is expected of them.

2. Laws are more effective when they prohibit certain actions rather than when they require duties (such as the "Good Samaritan" law requiring a motorist to stop and give aid at the scene of an accident).

3. The punishment must fit the crime and be in proportion to the "damage" to society. The stringent penalities against marijuana possession have been under attack as the public becomes aware that this "narcotic" is not physically habituating.

4. Law should be in concert with the prevailing moral sentiments of the community it is intended to serve. Compulsory school attendance laws have always been difficult to enforce in Amish communities as these persons do not "believe" in education beyond the eighth grade.

5. Laws must be administered uniformly and with consistent

interpretation. Due process of law is an ideal not always adhered to.

Origin of the Criminal Law

"Law comes with property, marriage and government," writes Will Durant (1954). "The lowest societies manage to get along without it." But the absence of law does not mean an idyllic society free of control. For primitive societies are ruled by a custom as inviolate as any law. The bedrock of any society is custom. The natural selection of custom retains those modes of action which grant to society some measure of order and stability. Should a supernatural sanction be added to the demands of custom, flaunting the norm becomes a sacriledge, for one violates the will of the gods. Even with the arrival of law, custom remains the last "magistrate of men's lives." Only with the coming of private property, which gave the owner economic authority, and the state, which gave the individual a legally defined status, did the "individual" qua "individual" begin to emerge as a distinct reality. As Durant (1954) puts it: "Rights do not come to us from nature, which knows no rights except cunning and strength; they are privileges assured to individuals by community as advantageous to the common good."

Durant (1954) has identified four stages in the development of law: (1) personal revenge; (2) fines; (3) courts; and (4) assumption by the state of the obligation to prevent and punish wrongs.

In primitive societies vengeance is personal, and every man is his own sheriff meting out "justice" according to his ability to enforce it. In the early days of the American West, as is regularly portrayed in films, a cowboy walks into the local saloon, calls out the killer of his brother, dispenses "Justice" with his Colt .45, and rides off into the sunset. The dead man's brother is now obliged to get revenge for this murder (presumably by locating the killer in another saloon) and so on *ad infinitum*. Indeed, Theodore White (1970) attributed some of our modern crime rate to the glorification on television of this primitive philosophy of personal revenge.

This principle of revenge appears in the ancient principle of *Lex Talionis*—the law of equivalent retaliation. Durant (1954) claims that the Abyssinians were so painstaking in measuring out this form of justice that when a boy fell from a tree upon his companion and killed him, the judges decided that the requirements of justice would be satisfied only by the bereaved mother sending another of her sons into the same tree to fall upon the offender's neck. This concept of retaliation has been retained in our modern concept of making penalities proportionate to the gravity of the offense, i.e. "making the punishment for the crime."

The second stage in the development of law was the substitution of damages (fines) for revenge. Replacing "an-eye-for-an-eye" was demanding the equivalent of the damages in gold. This ancient principle persists today in tort actions, as well as criminal cases. Melvin Belli (dubbed the "King of Torts" by his colleagues) once presented a jury with an artificial leg and asked the members how much money they would take in exchange for a limb.

The fines or settlements paid to avert personal revenge required some deliberation and adjudication of offenses and damages. Responding to this need, a third natural development of the law was the formation of courts. For many centuries resort to courts remained optional; should the offended party remain dissatisfied with the verdict, he was still free to seek personal revenge. These courts were not in all cases judgement seats as we know them today but were more often boards of voluntary conciliation.

In many cases disputes were settled by a trial by ordeal. Primitives were practical criminologists and established the rite, not on the theory that some metaphysical jurist would reveal the guilty party, but on the practical grounds that a long standing feud would disrupt the tribe for generations.[3] This early adversary system of justice presaged our own system where the state marshals all its forces against the accused, the defense parries these attacks with all the resources at its command, and out of this conflict truth is supposed to emerge. The contemporary legal duel is a survival of this ancient practice of trial by ordeal.

---

[3] . . . or be dysfunctional to the equilibrium of the social system, as later sociological jargon would describe it.

The fourth advance in the development of law was the assumption by the state of the obligation to prevent and punish wrongs. The state enlarges its domain from merely settling disputes to making an effort to prevent them. To the general body of "common law," derived from the customs of the group, is now added "positive law," derived from the judicial and governmental decrees. Laws, then, "grow up" from custom and are "handed down" from the government.

Other theorists have attributed the genesis of law to the rational processes of a unified society trying to eradicate some wrong, the crystalization of mores, and the conflict of interests between different groups. All of these "explanations" do justice to some laws but not to others. Part of the reason for our lack of knowledge about the origins of criminal law is the preoccupation in law schools with what the law is, neglecting the social origins of law. This situation is being rectified somewhat by the trend among modern schools of law to adopt a "law-science" model.

Definition of Crime

Crime is defined by Perkins (1966) as "any social harm defined and made punishable by law." No matter how reprehensible an act, or omission of an act, may be, it is not a crime unless there is a specific statute which forbids or requires its occurrence. Sutherland and Cressey (1970) have identified four characteristics which distinguish the criminal law from other rules regulating human conduct: politicality, specificity, uniformity, and penal sanction.

POLITICALITY. Only violations of rules enacted by the state are crimes. Fraternal orders, churches, and military all have regulations for their members, but the failure to follow these rules does not necessarily constitute a crime.

SPECIFICITY. If men are to follow the law, it must be stated in such terms that clearly indicate what conduct is expected of them. A statute which punished a commonly understood term such as "robbery" or "rape" is not too indefinite. But a statute which forbade "immoral acts" would not be sufficiently clear, this was the finding in the *State v. Gallegos (1963)*. Any statute which requires or prohibits the doing of an act in terms so vague that men of normal intelligence must guess at its meaning, violates the first essential of due process of law. One of the objections to statutes covering juvenile offenses is that they contain ambiguous terms like "ungovernability" without specifying what is meant by the term.

UNIFORMITY. Justice is represented as blindfolded as she weighs the evidence for guilt or innocence of those who stand before her. This represents the ideal in American jurisprudence: All persons who are adjudged by the law will be treated equally, regardless of social standing. In practice, of course, some persons are more equal than others.

PENAL SANCTION. *Nullum crimen sine lege*—no crime without law—is a guiding principle operating in the field of criminal law. Not only must criminal statutes give citizens "fair warning" of what behavior to avoid, but they should have an idea of the penalities which would accrue to the violation of the criminal law. The goal of punishment is the protection of society, for the first duty of the government is to protect the lives and property of its citizens. No civilized society can long endure which tolerates unrestrained lawlessness. Given the propensities toward unruly or aggressive behavior which are widespread in human societies, laws without penalties would be more honored in the breach than in the observance. As Sorokin (1957) puts it, "One does not educate tigers not to touch a lamb by mere sermons."

Attributes of Criminal Law

Not only does the criminal law define with particularity what conduct is forbidden, but legal scholars have been able to isolate certain general principles from these definitions. The application of these principles to a fact situation can determine whether or not the behavior in question was, or was not, criminal (Hall, 1960).

First, before behavior can be called a crime, there must be voluntary external consequences of "harm." A mental or emotional state is not sufficient. As the folk-saying smugly states: "They can't put you in jail for what you are thinking." The Bible admonishes its readers that if one lusts after a woman, "he has committed adultry in his heart." No earthly court can try you for such erotic fantacies. Even if one walks the streets with the intent of committing a crime, yet changes one's mind before taking action, one would have committed no crime. Intention is not synonymous with action.

Persons acting in concert represent a greater threat to society than does a lone offender; therefore when two or more persons agree to commit a criminal act, it is deemed a "conspiracy" and is a misdemeanor in common law. No further overt act is required to constitute this crime, unless amended by statute. One person cannot commit the offense of criminal conspiracy; "concert" in criminal purpose is the salient factor in the definition of the offense. Simply soliciting someone to engage in a crime, e.g. a prostitute, is a misdemeanor.

Second, the harm must be legally forbidden, is must be prescribed in penal law. Penal law does not have a retroactive effect. A person cannot be punished on a criminal charge for an act which was no offense at the time it was performed. Such laws are prohibited by the Constitution of the United States.

Third, there must be "conduct." A person forced to pull the trigger on a gun which kills someone is not guilty of murder. The intention to kill was not his.

A fourth element in crime is the concept of *mens rea* or "guilty mind." Because of its centrality in determining criminal responsibility, *mens rea* deserves some extended discussion. This concept refers to the mental element in the commission of a crime. To demonstrate *mens rea,* it must be proven that the individual intended to behave in the manner which violated the law. In the *State v. Chicago, Milwaukee & St. Paul R. Co. (1903),* an engineer who failed to stop at a crossing was found not guilty for he did all he could to stop. The fault was due to the brakes not working in a proper manner; the momentum of the train carried it over the crossing. A crime has not been committed where the mind of the person committing the act is innocent. Similarly, a college student, entirely unclothed, *State v. Peery,* 1947, who was seen by coeds passing by his dorm window, was found not guilty of being indecent or lewd for there was no evidence that the defendant had signaled to the witnesses or otherwise tried to direct their attention to himself.

There are, however, offenses which involve no mental element but consist only of forbidden acts or omissions. These are classified as "strict liability offenses." Generally, there can be no crime without criminal intent, but this is by no means a universal rule. With the coming of the industrial revolution and congested urban living, a group of laws called "public welfare offenses" arose in recognition of the wide distribution of harm that would follow the wide distribution of shoddy or toxic goods.

A killing which occurs in the commission of a felony is murder whether such death was intended or not. It is no defense that the defendant did not intend, with malice aforethought, to kill the victim. In *People v. Pulley,* (1964), the defendants, driving a stolen car, attempted to outrun a police car and drove through an intersection causing a fatal accident. They were convicted of second-degree murder. The court reasoned that death here was not a freak coincidence; a predictable risk was set in motion by the original crime.

Essential to the application of the doctrine of *mens rea* is that the actor be capable of forming criminal intent. Thus children under the age of seven (by common law), mental defectives, and persons acting under coercion, intimidation, or in some cases of accident are not held criminally liable as the element of "intent" is missing from the formula determining a crime.

Fifth, *mens rea* and conduct must concur. For example, "Boomer" is angry with his high school friend "L.C." for marrying his former girlfriend "Frumpy May." He searches for the couple with the intent to kill them but is unsuccessful in finding his intended victims. Ten years later. "L.C.", who suffers from color-blindness, runs a red light, and both he and "Frumpy May" are killed instantly when their Volkswagen is demolished by a concrete truck. Ironically, the driver of the truck is the would-be murderer "Boomer". But he is not guilty of the crime of murder. Criminal intent and the harmful conduct did not concur. Fate had delivered the couple into his hands (Roberts, 1956).

Sixth, there must be a casual relationship between the voluntary misconduct and the legally forbidden harm. The harmful consequences must be related to the intentional felonious action. For example, a burglar shoots a policeman. Later the policeman dies in the hospital of pneumonia. If it can be shown that forces set in motion by the shooting (weakening of the policeman, left lying in the cold) were causally related to the final harmful consequences (death by pneumonia), then the offender is guilty of murder. Lastly, there must be a legally prescribed punishment. Citizens must not only be forewarned as to what conduct is forbidden, but must also know the consequences of such action.

Classification of Crimes and Classification of Offenders

Crimes are typically classified as either felonies or misdemeanors. The more serious crimes are termed *felonies* and are punished by a year or more in the state penitentiary. Less serious offenses are regarded as misdemeanors and are generally punished by a year or less in the city or county jail. Exceptions exist, as in the case in North Carolina where the midsemeanants are confined by the State Department of Corrections. The implication of this system of classification for the study of crime point out that petty acts indicate a petty offender. But an act which would be regarded as a misdemeanor in one state can be a felony in another state. Nebraska, for example, punishes first offense marijuana possession as a misdemeanor. In Texas, on the other hand, the same offense can bring up to life imprisonment.

Gibbons (1968) has pointed out that legal labels are inadequate for three reasons: (1) Legal labels reveal nothing about the offender-victim relationship or (2) the social context of the deviant act, and (3) the label is attached at the end of the adjudication process, during which time a "plea-bargain" (pleading guilty for consideration) may have changed the original label. For these reasons, Gibbons sees legal labels as "accurate but deficient" and approaches the study of crime and criminals by assembling particular offenses into patterns of conduct.

Originally, the common law divided those crimes which were "wrong in themselves" *(mala in se)* from those that were "wrong because they were prohibited" *(mala probita)*, i.e. any act forbidden by statute but otherwise did not seem to shock the conscience of the community. Such a classification is anthropologically naive, and as Barnes (1967) comments: "Presently it seems to get its greatest use by misinformed or lethargic courts who insert it as a prop to rationalize preconceived results."

Other classifications of crime include "crime against nature" (Nice, 1965) which, in its broadest sense, includes carnal knowledge of an animal, or when applied to human sexual experience, sodomy, cunnilingus, fellatio, or intercourse (even between legally married persons) in any but the "missionary" position (face-to-face).[4] The reference to these acts as "crimes against nature" do not of course represent an indictment from "nature" herself but a value-judgement on the part of some legislative body as to what is "natural." (If the Kinsey report is accurate, some of these acts are about as statistically "unnatural" as the Grand Canyon).

One of the most recent crime classifications, developed during the trials by the allies of Nazi leaders for war crimes in 1945, is "crimes against humanity." The offenses were seen as being of such magnitude that the offenders were to answer to humanity in general and not to a specific individual country or jurisdiction. European peace groups applied this concept to President Johnson and his staff and tried him in absentia for alleged war crimes in Viet Nam; Johnson et al. were found guilty.

Offenses may be classified as a private wrong, called a "civil injury" or "tort" case, or a "public wrong" which falls under the rubric of criminal law. A public wrong is a violation of public peace for which the community may take action. The punishment imposed is for the protection of the community and not for redress of injury to the individual. Individuals must seek redress in a civil action. When an individual or organization sues another to obtain a remedy for an alleged injury, the case is a civil case. When the state prosecutes an individual or organization for a violation of a legislative statute, the case is normally a criminal

---

[4]This term apparently derived from natives who found the missionary approach to sex unimaginative. And the writers cannot resist recalling H.L. Mencken's definition of a puritan as a man "who has a nagging fear that somebody somewhere is having a good time."

case. The distinction will be discussed in detail in a later chapter.

The same offense may give rise to both civil and criminal actions. Assault and battery may result in a civil action by the victim to obtain damages for the injuries received and also in criminal charges filed by the state to punish the guilty party by fine or imprisonment.

Comparative Criminal Law

The criminal law not only identifies which human acts are to be labeled wrong, but the penalties attached to their occurrence give us a measure of how wrong the society perceives them to be. Sorokin (1937) undertook a herculean task in the history of comparative law when he studied the content and change of the main criminal codes of five countries: France, Italy, Austria, Germany, and Russia. From this analysis, covering a time span ranging from the Barbaric Law to the twentieth century, Sorokin identified over one hundred criminal acts typical for all these societies. He then classified these into nine groups:

Physical person (murder, assault)
Moral person (defamation)
Property
Religion and religious values (blasphemy)
The family (adultry, incest)
Sex crimes (rape, sodomy)
The certainty of evidential means and documents (forgery, perjury)
Social-economic customs and habits (gambling)
The state and political order (treason)

Sorokin rejected the idea that in the course of time the number of the types of action punishable by criminal law increases. He saw changes in the criminal law as following changes in the values of the society in general. An "ideational" (religious) society might punish by deprivation of Christian burial and imposition of anathema and interdiction—reacting to crimes against religion. When the societies under consideration grew more sensate, they decriminalized "sin-crimes," while passing stringent laws protecting property and bodily comforts.

The severity of penal sanctions, according to Sorokin, is related to three factors. The first is ethicojuridical homogeneity. When differences and conflicts arise within groups about what is approved conduct, the severity of punishment imposed by one part of a group on the other increases. The second is periods of cultural transition and crisis. Sorokin found that the punishments of stable, rooted, secure cultures tend to be mild and moderate, while times of social revolution are characterized by cruelty, e.g. the Roman Catholic Inquisition with its attempts to annihilate heretics. The penal laws and oppression of the French Revolution after 1789 or the Russian Revolution after 1917 surpassed all previous records for slaughter, both in magnitude and duration. In France, the establishment of the "Committee of Public Safety" ushered in what is known as the Reign of Terror. Thousands of persons suspected of being royalists were arrested and thrown into prison. After a summary trial, many of these were herded into carts and taken to the public square to be guillotined. Unanimity in France was achieved by the destruction of any forces opposing the Republic. Similarly, thousands were killed by terrorist tactics in the aftermath of the Bolshevik Revolution in Russia.[5]

An ideational culture mentality tends to be more severe because its belief-system is less flexible. Further, the representatives of such a culture may be attempting to discipline a society characterized by former excesses.

Summary

In order to clearly understand the problem of crime, it is necessary to grasp the wider problem of deviance from societal norms. Societies attempt to contain deviance through controls ranging from informal disapproval to the police powers of the state. Antisocial attitudes, conduct norms, eccentricities, odd behaviors may all be studied and are useful in shedding light on criminal conduct. All criminal acts are deviant, but not all deviants are criminal. Therefore, only those deviant acts which legislative bodies

[5]Lorimer (1946) estimates the population loss of the Soviet Union from 1914 to 1926 at 10 million persons and writes: "During the years 1915-23 the Russian people underwent the most cataclysmic changes since the Mongol invasion in the early thirteenth century."

have determined are crimes may legitimately constitute the core subject matter of criminology.

REFERENCES

Barnes, Marian Q. (Ed.): *Clark and Marshall's treatise on the Law of Crimes.* Mundelein, Callaghan, 1967.

Durant, W.: *Our Oriental Heritage.* New York, Simon and Schuster, 1954.

Gibbons, D.C.: *Society, Crime, and Criminal Careers.* Englewood Cliffs, Prentice-Hall, 1968.

Hall, J.: *General Principles of Criminal Law.* Indianapolis, Bobbs-Merrill, 1960.

Howard, C.G., and Summers, R.S.: *Law, Its Nature, Functions, and Limits.* Englewood Cliffs, Prentice-Hall, 1965.

Lorimer, F.: *The Population of the Soviet Union: History and Prospect.* Princeton, Princeton University Press, 1946.

Nice, R.: *Dictionary of Criminology.* New York, Philosophical Library, 1965.

Perkins, R.M.: *Criminal Law and Procedure.* Brooklyn, The Foundation Press, 1966.

Roberts, A.H.: Department of English, Centenary College, Shreveport, Louisiana. (Personal communication, 1956).

Sorokin, P.A.: *Social and Cultural Dynamics.* Boston, Porter Sargent, 1957.

Steinbeck, J.: *The Grapes of Wrath.* New York, Viking Press, 1939.

Sutherland, E.H., and Cressey, D.R.: *Criminology.* Philadelphia, Lippincott, 1970.

Tappan, P.W.: *Crime, Justice, and Correction.* New York, McGraw-Hill 1960.

White, T.H.: *The Making of the President: 1968.* New York, Pocket Books, 1970.

Chapter 2

RESEARCH AND THEORY IN CRIMINOLOGY

RESEARCH AND THEORY IN SCIENCE

ONE COMPONENT OF THE ACTIVITY or behavior of scientists that produces knowledge is *research;* a complementary part of this is *theory construction.* Both areas are fundamental to the systematic study of crime, criminals, crime behavior, and the criminal justice system. Until recently, however, textbook authors dealt rather selectively with criminological theories and generally failed to emphasize the interrelatedness of theory and research. It will help considerably in the following discussion if we bear in mind that most of the impressive terminology and much of the conceptual apparatus of scientific method had their origins in the scientist's efforts to find answers to two rather simple questions: "What do you mean?" and "How do you know?" The former question involves the overwhelmingly important issue of the *meaning* of terms and concepts and establishes the necessity for the laborious lengths to which the scientist must often go to clarify the object, event, or relationship under investigation. The latter question is bound up with specification of the determinants (variables) which are functionally related to the phenomenon in question. To state matters in this fashion is to define the nature of scientific explanation or understanding.

Students in criminology classes are apt to be either consumers or producers of research; and if the class and student are both advanced, the student may well be both producer *and* consumer. As a consumer of research, one reads research reports and articles and sometimes makes use of the information contained in these sources;

as a producer of research, one not only reads about the investigations of others, but may conduct his own study or research project.

Research is essentially a creative enterprise; no one, except in a very restricted way, can tell another how to do it. Such is not our intention in the present discussion. But regardless of whether an individual conducts his own research or makes use of the findings of others, he must possess some understanding of the procedures and purposes of scientific investigation. Lacking such an understanding, he is unable to read critically the research reports in the professional literature or to evaluate the generalizations based on such reports that he encounters in secondary sources. A good deal of the material that passes for research is not genuine because it fails to meet adequate criteria.

In the first section of this chapter, we shall discuss some basic aspects of research in criminology and propose some criteria for the evaluation of such research. A second part of the chapter will be devoted to a discussion of theory construction in criminology. We shall try in this section to emphasize the complementary nature of the relationship between criminological theory and research in a variety of settings and contexts.

Purposes of Research

Generally, the main rationale for research is to find answers to questions through the application of scientific procedures. Implicit to this statement is the assumption that the procedures used in scientific research have proven reliable and valid upon successive occasions. Research has evolved over a period measurable in centuries; at the present time, it appears to be the most reliable means we have at our disposal for advancing our knowledge.

Although a variety of techniques and procedures are used in research, most systematic research is intended to serve one or several of the following functions: (1) to assess the status of given past or present phenomena; (2) to study the properties, characteristics, and constituencies of given phenomena; (3) to examine the growth and development, historical background capacities for change, etc., of given phenomena; and (4) to investigate the cause-and-effect relationships between or among given phenomena.

Types of Research

Research can be categorized in a number of ways. For instance, it can be considered *pure* or *applied,* depending on the extent to which the investigation is focused upon the solution of a specific problem. Pure research marks one end of a hypothetical continuum; the other extreme is characterized by a search for knowledge as an end in itself. This kind of research is motivated entirely by intellectual interest or curiosity; there is no expectation that the findings will ever reach practical application in any form. At the opposite end of the continuum is the kind of research that is directed toward solving a particular problem, despite the fact that a successful solution will not generate any new knowledge.

If a researcher merely wished to discover whether officially adjudicated delinquent boys perform better or more poorly on intelligence tests than nondeliquent boys of comparable age, he could design an appropriate study for this purpose—in which case, he would be doing "pure" research. If, on the other hand, the researcher were interested in testing the efficacy of one type of parole supervision against another, his research would be considered "applied." In the latter case, the problem has a specific and practical aspect: The study is intended to provide an answer that is relevant and significant to the researcher within a pragmatic context.

It is also possible to classify most research in the behavioral sciences as *descriptive, experimental,* and *historical.* While we shall devote limited discussion to historical research, we shall emphasize descriptive and experimental research, which are most representative of the kinds of research conducted in the field of criminology.

Historical Research

The purpose of historical research is to collate and interpret data concerning past situations, circumstances, or events. A study of the events which led to the development of community-based correctional programs is an example of historical research in criminology.

Providing the data collected for purposes of historical research are adequately documented, the investigator is able to draw conclusions which compare favorably in reliability and validity with those based on other kinds of research. However, there is no minimizing the difficulties posed by the systematic study of past events. In some instances, the information which is sought is totally beyond the reach of the investigator; and, at the best of times, the researcher has a difficult task in interpreting the historical data once they have been collected.

An historical researcher makes every effort to secure his data from *primary,* rather than *secondary,* sources. A primary source can be the first-hand account of an actual witness to a particular event, an original document, or a surviving artifact; a secondary source may consist of a report by someone who received the testimony of an eyewitness or the replica of an original document. Sources of historical data in criminology include case reports, manuscripts, institutional records, etc.

Evaluating his sources of data calls for the exercise of critical judgment on the part of the historical researcher. Validation involves two components: *extrinsic* and *intrinsic validity.* The former term refers to the conditions by which the investigator seeks to establish the authenticity of a given document or piece of testimony. The determination of validity of documents, for example, may include exhaustive, detailed, and painstaking analysis of the materials of which such documents are composed.

Once he has managed to establish the authenticity of his data source, the historical investigator must satisfy himself with respect to the internal or intrinsic validity of his information. In the case of documents which purport to be original, inconsistencies in language, discrepancies in dates, and lack of agreement with previously authenticated documents must all be considered when challenging the genuineness and reliability of a given datum.

Descriptive Research

The several types of descriptive research employed in the behavioral sciences—surveys, case analyses, correlational studies, and developmental studies—possess the common characteristic of dealing with current situations. It is worth keeping in mind, as we briefly review these various kinds of descriptive research, that all descriptive studies in a sense are status studies.

SURVEY STUDY. Sometimes it is necessary for an institution to conduct a survey to determine its status with respect to some factor or condition before making a decision concerning certain suggested changes or improvements. For example, the director of a correctional institution for delinquent girls may wish to determine which geographic area or areas in the community accounts for the highest percentage of court referrals among inmates. A social worker in the same institution may wish to follow the progress of girls who have been released from the institution following a particular rehabilitative program. In both instances, the necessary data could be obtained by means of a descriptive survey study.

CASE ANALYSIS. This kind of research is conducted when the researcher is interested in the characteristics or behavior of a single individual. An investigator may employ a wide array of techniques, procedures, and instruments to secure life history, physiological, and psychological information concerning his subjects; and it is possible for an investigator to carry out several case studies simultaneously. In the pursuit of relevant information, the investigator usually is obliged to seek the help of other professional workers—teachers, social workers, clergymen, physicians—who may have had the opportunity to become acquainted with the subject under a variety of circumstances.

CORRELATIONAL STUDIES. Most of the research in criminology is designed to estimate the extent to which different variables are related to one another. With the advent of electronic data processing, we can expect much more of this kind of research in the future. Examples of correlational studies in criminology are numerous. Research on the effectiveness of probation or parole, in which personality variables relating to the probation officer are correlated with similar variables relating to the probationer, has favored this kind of study design. In other correlational studies, test results may be correlated with measures of selected variables to determine whether or not a relationship exists. For instance, an investigator might seek to determine whether the presence of a particular cluster of scores on a test like the MMPI is associated with propensities toward explosive aggression.

DEVELOPMENTAL STUDY. This type of research consists of a study in which the investigator examines the growth and development of a group of subjects over a period of time. In a well-known study by Kagan and Moss (1962), children were examined shortly after birth and periodically thereafter on a number of selected variables. Since this study involved the same subjects over a period of years, it is called a *longitudinal study*. The name distinguishes it from a *cross-sectional study,* which compares (at the same point in time) different subjects representing different developmental stages.

Descriptive research is sometimes, without justification, trivialized as a mere matter of head-counts or tallies. This is quite unfair. Descriptive research is subject to the same canons of rigor in conceptualization and execution that govern research of other types. If a given piece of descriptive research suffers from grievous inadequacies in planning, implementation, and interpretation, the fault is more apt to be found with the researcher than with the method itself.

Experimental and Quasi-Experimental Research

The Controlled Experiment[1]

In a controlled experiment, an investigator manipulates one or more variables (called *independent variable/s*) to determine the effect, if any, produced by this manipulation upon one or more other variables (called *dependent variable/s*). All other aspects of the situation are *controlled,* or held constant, to allow for an assessment of the relationship between the independent variable and the dependent variable.

The term *control* has a second meaning in experimental procedure in addition to the one ascribed to it above. There are occasions when the effect of an independent variable can best be assessed by applying it to one group of subjects—the experimental group—and not to another. The group which is not exposed to the

----

[1]As Mills (1969) has noted, the term *experiment* has occasionally been used to designate *all* research techniques. In this book, the term experiment will be restricted to those procedures in which the researcher maintains some measure of *control* over variables. This usage excludes descriptive studies, surveys based on questionnaires or interviews, correlational studies, or exploratory types of investigation.

independent variable is usually designated the "control group." With all other aspects held constant or controlled, the two groups are compared on some selected dependent variable. If the results noted in the experimental group differ significantly from those obtained in the control group, then the investigator ascribes this difference to the operation of the independent variable.

For example, a criminological research might be interested in testing the effects of a drug that purports to increase retention span within a group of institutionalized mentally retarded delinquents. He might begin by randomly dividing his population into two groups of approximately equal size. Each group would be tested for retention span by means of some standardized device, e.g. the Digit Span subtest on the Wechsler Adult Intelligence Scale. The experimental group is then administered the drug; the control group is administered a placebo, an inert substance, according to an experimental procedure called "double blind." The double blind procedure establishes that neither the subjects nor the person or persons responsible for administering the drug and placebo are aware of what they are receiving/dispensing. All other conditions—the physical setting, physiological status of the subjects, length of time permitted for the test, nature of the instructions, etc.—would be as nearly identical as possible for both groups. The test of retention span is then repeated. If the group that receives the drug performs in a significantly different, i.e. superior, manner than the control group, the investigator might then conclude that the drug did enhance retention span in mental retardates, as represented by his experimental population.

In the example given above, the drug is the independent variable, and the test of retention span is the dependent variable. "Control" is exemplified by random assignment of subjects, identical instructions, common setting, and the like.

Quasi-Experimental Research

Many studies are conducted in prisons, training schools, jails, hospitals, and other types of institutional settings which do not admit of the precise control of variables that is essential to the conduct of a true experiment; these studies we shall refer to as *quasi-*

experimental research. It is necessary to note that this distinction between experimental and quasi-experimental research is not customarily made by the authors of research reports in the professional literature. Many studies of the latter kind, therefore, are treated as though they were actually controlled experiments.

Assets and Limitations of the Controlled Experiment

Controlling all variables but the independent variable is the source of power of the controlled experiment. But while the experimental technique is very powerful, it is not perfect; it has its problems and limitations. Sometimes, experimentation is impossible, for either practical or ethical reasons. Being subjected to experimental procedure may actually modify or distort what is being measured. Experimental conditions may be so pallid, artifical, or contrived that the results bear little relation to the real world. Nevertheless, despite its limitations, the controlled experiment is still the most direct means we have at our disposal for determining causal relationships between variables. As such, it has been widely accepted as the most effective technique for the investigation of basic hypotheses and, consequently, has assumed increasing importance in criminology.

Limitations of Experimental Procedure

To assert that the controlled experiment is the best means available for investigating causal relations between or among variables does not necessarily imply that it is always the best research method to use. What is best is largely determined by the objectives and purposes of the proposed research. On occasion, a correlational or case study might be more appropriate than an experimental approach. Scott and Wertheimer (1962) have cautioned against the *prior* assumption that one research strategy is superior to another: "Choice of design must therefore depend to a large extent on the state of investigation, the resources available, and the specific goals of the research."

A number of behavioral scientists (Bakan, 1967; Deese, 1969; Owens, 1968) have criticized the idea that all problems can be dealt with in terms of the experimental paradigm. Deese (1969), for example, has argued the superiority of observation over experimentation in certain situations. Bakan (1967) is even more outspoken in his condemnation of uncritical attempts to translate all of the problems of behavioral science into a form that is manageable by the controlled experiment. In his discussion of what he considers the crisis of research in psychology, Bakan maintains that an insistence on experimentation at the expense of other methods of inquiry is detrimental to the progress of psychological science:

> Though enormous resources are being expended for psychological research, the yield of new and significant information concerning the nature of the human psyche is relatively small in comparison. We may appreciate why this should be the case by considering the garden variety of experiment "run" by students aspiring to win higher degrees, not to mention the experiments of many of their professors. It characteristically involves converting observational data to numbers, calculating statistics on these numbers, and applying tests of significance to these statistics. *The fact of the matter is that this kind of experimentation, with the abrogations that generally go along with it—characteristically in the very name of science—cannot yield much information, and certainly little that is particularly novel* (italics added).

Requiring that all research be made to conform with the model supplied by the controlled experiment may (1) interfere with the exploration of new phenomena, (2) force the researcher to employ experimental procedures in circumstances where these are inappropriate, and (3) exclude from systematic study many significant areas of behavior by restricting research to only those which can be handled within an experimental paradigm. Owens (1968) believes that the most fruitful approach to research is some combination of descriptive and experimental study.

The Planning and Conduct of Research

Most research is conducted according to an overall design or schema which insures that the problem under consideration will be attacked in an orderly, systematic fashion. The research design or schema generally includes the following stages: (1) defining and delimiting the problem; (2) critically surveying the pertinent literature; (3) formulating testable hypotheses; (4) constructing the study; (5) collecting and analyzing the data; and (6) drawing conclusions from the reesarch findings.

Defining and Delimiting the Problem

The selection of a research topic may come about in a variety of ways. Some research is generated as a result of conflict between two or more theories, each of which may predict a different result. Other studies may be suggested as a consequence of gaps in present knowledge within a given area; still other investigations may be initiated by nothing more tangible than a feeling on the part of a particular individual that a certain kind of research may advance some general body of knowledge. One fact is incontestable: The more one knows about a given subject or topic, the more numerous and specific are the questions he is capable of asking. It is anything but coincidental that the best and most fruitful questions in research are usually raised by those who are totally immersed in a particular subject area and its literature.

The decision to pursue the study of a given problem calls for a judgment on the part of the investigator as to the *feasibility* of conducting research in that area. Some problems are too trivial to repay the time and effort required for their study, and some problems are beyond the reach of current research capabilities. The probable time and expense of the project, the availability of facilities, equipment, subjects, and personnel to carry out the study are among the more obvious factors that play an important role in the decision-making process. The researcher must also decide whether he possesses the necessary skills and experience to conduct the prospective investigation.

Critical Survey of the Literature

Increasingly keen competition for space in the professional journals has truncated the leisurely review of the literature, which used to form the opening section of scholarly and scientific publications, to a few terse sentences or a single paragraph. Nevertheless, a researcher is still obliged to undertake a systematic review of the professional literature that is pertinent to the problem he proposes to study, even though the results of the survey may not appear in the published report. Apart from the obvious and paramount value of discovering whether someone has already performed the contemplated research project, the time-consuming process of culling the literature has other benefits for the investigator. For one thing, bibliographical review aids in sharpening his focus on the prospective problem to be researched. It may also provide fresh ideas, information, and suggestions that find their way into the conceptualization and organization of the study.

The review should be thorough rather than exhaustive. While it is expected that the investigator will make every effort to locate and examine all of the published work that is relevant to his research topic, he is not compelled to track down and read in detail every reference that might be available. Reviews of this sort are subject to a law of diminishing returns: Once the researcher has identified a few of the key studies which bear directly on his particular topic, he generally finds repeated reference to these same studies in earlier publications.

Formulating Testable Hypotheses[2]

There is a natural progression from the definition of the problem and the critical review of the literature to the statement of operating hypotheses. Most researchers consider hypotheses indispensable to their investigatory efforts. An hypothesis can be regarded as *a stated prediction of a research outcome*. Another way to consider an hypothesis is that it represents an informed guess about the probable findings in a research project or study. The following are a few examples of state research hypotheses:

1. There is a systematic relationship between urban residential area and the incidence of cases of homicidal assault.
2. There is a high positive correlation between severity and certainty of punishment of a particular offense and the probability of occurrence of that offense.
3. There is no significant difference in the incidence of alcohol-

---

[2]Lachenmeyer (1970) feels that exploratory research in the behavioral sciences tends to be slighted in favor of specific hypothesis testing. He notes that there is a definite bias toward considering only studies based on prior work or explicitly stated theory as true experimentation: "This limited view of experimentation has a restricting effect on research. The observation-inductive end of the theory construction process is slighted in favor of the deduction-verification end" (p. 621).

ism between high and low scorers on a test of manifest
anxiety.

The last hypothesis is stated in the form of a null *hypothesis,* i.e. as
a prediction that there is no true difference between groups. In the
case of the hypothesis stated above, the implication is that any difference in the incidence of alcoholism between the two groups
(high and low scorers) can be attributed to chance. Research hypotheses are often stated in this form.

Research hypotheses, as we shall note in our later discussion of
scientific theory, may originate in a formal theoretical context or in
less formal empirical contexts. Although many researchers prefer
the rigorous derivation of testable hypotheses from some well-artic-
ulated body of formal theory, other researchers believe that such
procedures impose unacceptable constraints upon the processes of
investigation. They prefer a kind of free inquiry in which a general
statement of objectives or purpose takes the place of specific hypotheses. In their opinion, the statement of specific hypotheses in a
study may lead the investigator to overlook equally plausible and
more fruitful hypotheses or to incur the risk of ignoring important
and valid conclusions from the data he manages to collect.

It seems difficult to be doctrinaire about these matters. Hypotheses have their usefulness in formulating the research problem,
constructing the study design, and selecting appropriate research
techniques. On the other hand, a great deal of valuable information has been gathered under the informal conditions of empirically-based research. Given the kinds of problems which confront
the criminological researcher, both types of investigation can be
seen to possess undeniable advantages.

Constructing the Study

One of the regulative ideals of scientific method is *replicability*
of research. In theory, every study reported in the professional literature ought to be described in sufficient detail to permit exact
replication by another investigator. In practice, this ideal is rarely,
if ever, achieved; nevertheless, the onus is still upon the researcher
to furnish the reader with a clear, detailed, and accurate description
of the procedures employed in his investigation. These are matters

which belong to the province of *research design*.

The varying circumstances of systematic inquiry impose specific and differing requirements with respect to research design. Thus, it is out of the question to specify a model research design which meets the criteria for all types of investigation. But any adequate research design will be formulated with a view to the factors discussed below.

SAMPLE SELECTION. Often when a researcher conducts a study, he intends to generalize, from the findings of his study, to a whole population or to a different situation. For instance, if he assesses some characteristic, e.g. aggressive tendencies, of a representative group of incarcerated delinquents in a correctional institution, he may want the conclusions he draws, from his analysis of the data, to apply to incarcerated delinquents in other correctional institutions, not merely to the group examined in his study. Provided he has followed sound sampling procedures and has obtained valid data, he should be able to make this sort of extrapolation.

A sample constitutes a set of objects, persons, observations, etc. which a researcher has extracted from a larger set—the population. A sample may range in size from a single case to one that is comparable in size to the population. In most research, however, a sample forms only a small part of a total population.

One of the first requirements of research is that the sample studied be representative of the population under consideration. There are several methods for attempting to insure that the sample under study is representative of the total population. From a mathematical standpoint, the simplest method is *random sampling, a* procedure in which each member of the population or *universe* has the same chance of being selected as any other.

An alternative to random sampling is *stratified sampling,* in which the proportions of certain groups are specified in advance. If the exact proportions of each stratum in the sample to the total population are scrupulously observed, the sample may be said to be truly representative of the whole population.

It should be obvious that sampling is a complicated process. One of the more formidable problems the researcher encounters is accurately specifying the characteristics and properties of the population to which he seeks to generalize. Differences in the definition of populations undoubtedly account for at least part of the variance in research findings in similar studies. If psychopathy were defined differently in two comparable studies, for example, researchers might reach quite contradictory conclusions about the relationship between, say, manifest anxiety and psychopathic behavior.

SUBJECTIVE EFFECTS. In all research involving human participants, attitude is a potentially significant factor for which the researcher must make appropriate provisions. Were the subjects cooperative, uncooperative, or indifferent? The answer may have a great deal to do with the outcome of the study. Are volunteers truly representative of a given population or is there a possibility that they differ in some important respects from nonvolunteers?

If people become aware that they are participating as subjects in a research project, they may develop a positive set which leads them to perform certain tasks more effectively than subjects who remain unaware of their participation. This so-called *Hawthorne effect* may, if left uncontrolled, produce the kinds of influence upon the behavior of subjects that completely invalidate the research findings.

There are no facile solutions for the problem of subjects' attitudes in research. As long as people realize that they are taking part in a study or experiment, the possibility exists that they will generate some set, positive or negative, toward the experimenter, the setting, themselves, and other subjects.

Reliability, Validity, and Measurement. Measurement of certain characteristics or variables is the essential feature of most behavioral science research; hence, the investigator must select the most suitable instruments or techniques to accomplish this task. The process of selection is arduous and exacting. The researcher must appraise each technique or device with regard to matters of reliability and validity. Valid and reliable data do not in themselves guarantee good research, but good research cannot exist without them. Unfortunately, many of the constructs that are employed in criminological research—self-concept, antisocial attitude, superego, etc.—are highly inferential in character and exceedingly difficult to measure. Caution should be urged in reading or making use of research which incorporates such constructs.

Comparison of Groups

Many research projects in criminology involve the comparison of two or more groups: "chronic recidivists" versus "first offenders," "adjudicated delinquents" versus "nondelinquents," "much improved," "little improved," and "no improved." Suppose that three *improvement level* groups were compared and their characteristics analyzed; it might prove difficult to determine which differences between groups are responsible for producing "much," "little," and "no improvement." A great many variables or combinations of variables might account for the differences in levels of improvement. To the extent that many factors are allowed to vary, i.e. are not controlled, in this type of group comparison, the findings of such studies are nearly impossible to interpret with any confidence. Sometimes the problem can be resolved, however, through the use of two or more matched groups.

Let us assume that an investigator wished to compare two correctional institutions in terms of the scores obtained by inmates in a given typological classification on a test which purports to measure remission of problem behavior. He might, of course, merely administer the test to a sample of inmates chosen at random from each institution, then compare their average scores to determine whether one group exceeded the other in freedom from problem behavior. However, a more sound approach would be to form two matched groups of inmates, using age, length of incarceration, type of treatment received, etc., as matching variables. Such a procedure would produce groups that are more nearly comparable in constituency; if a difference were found between the groups, the investigator could be much more confident that his results were not due to the operation of sampling error.

Control Groups and Experimental Groups

Variables that may adversely affect the outcome of research are often referred to as *confounding variables*. Although these variables cannot be dealt with in some research efforts, they can be handled effectively in the kind of experimental research design that makes use of control and experimental groups.

In the case of the matched groups of inmates described above, one group might be designated the *experimental group* and the other the *control group*. The researcher might then seek to determine the effect, if any, of a particular treatment program upon test scores in the experimental group; the members of the control group would be given no treatment beyond mere custodial care. Both groups would be administered pretests and post-tests to determine whether any change occurred in the test scores of the experimental group members as a function of the treatment program. Then a statistical test, such as an analysis of covariance, would be used to compare the gains or losses in the two groups. Without the use of a special statistical technique (analysis of covariance) to control for differences in the two groups at the start of the experiment, it would not be sound to conclude that a difference in sources between the two groups was due solely to the treatment given the experimental group.

SYSTEMATIC BIAS. If the groups compared in a study were not formed on the basis of random selection, the assumption can be made that factors over which the investigator has no control might favor one group over the other with respect to the operation of the independent variable. Advantages of this kind reflect the presence of *systematic bias* in research. Even when randomization procedures are followed, there is still the possibility that systematic bias can occur. The researcher must be alert to this possibility.

Systematic bias can be caused by a variety of factors, in addition to the selection process used in the formation of groups. As Rosenthal (1966) has demonstrated so impressively, expectations on the part of the investigator, of which he is unaware, may constitute a potent source of influence upon the outcome of research, particularly in situations of the independent variable.

One method for controlling the influence of variables which cannot be held constant is *balancing*. According to this procedure, factors are allowed to vary in the groups being compared, but they must vary in the same way. If sex, for example, is considered an important factor, there must be the same proportion of males and females in each group. The groups might also be balanced with respect to age, IQ, socioeconomic status, physical health, etc., depending on the nature of the research project.

Another procedure which is used to examine the influence of variables which are not amenable to being held constant is *replication*. If a study were reported in which claims were made regarding the efficacy of a particular psychotherapeutic method, the possibility that the superiority of one method over another was actually a function of the therapist's personality, rather than the difference in technique, could be examined by repeating the study using another therapist. In any event, criminological research in general would stand to profit considerably from replication as a matter of course. The professional literature is filled with "one-shot" studies which have never been repeated and, thus, are difficult or impossible to evaluate.

Collecting the Data

In some kinds of behavioral research, the data-collecting process requires the use of mechanical, electrical, or electronic equipment: Oscilloscopes, sound spectrographs, electroencephalographs, tachistoscopes, and the like. The researcher may have to familiarize himself with the operation of a piece of equipment, or he may have to train someone to operate it for him. When appropriate apparatus is not available, the researcher may be faced with the task of building a piece of equipment himself. In either case, the researcher must be thoroughly familiar with the strengths and weaknesses, the assets and limitations, and the idiosyncrasies of his data-collecting techniques; he must have a detailed appreciation of their claims to reliability and validity.

Pilot Study

On some occasions, a researcher will carry out a pilot study in advance of an actual research project for purposes of testing his data-collecting techniques or sharpening and refining his research design. Whatever additional time this requires is more than compensated for in the conduct of the investigation, for the pilot study can illuminate sources of defect in techniques or procedure which could destroy the work of many months of arduous labor. Moreover, a carefully conducted pilot study serves the inestimable function of appraising the feasibility of a given project. Many a grateful investigator has spared himself untold effort and expense when the results of a pilot study revealed the near impossibility of carrying out a particular piece of research.

Preparation and Analysis of Data

Most research data is unusable in its raw form, especially qualitative types of data such as interview protocols and questionnaire results. Thus, an intermediate step in the analysis of research findings is the conversion of raw data to a quantitative form which lends itself to statistical treatment. If the researcher has access to electronic data-processing facilities, he will transfer data to punchcards which can be read by the computer.

The statistical analysis of the prepared data, the penultimate stage of research, represents the payoff toward which the investigator has been laboring since his original conceptualization of the problem. Statistical analysis is the means by which he is able to ascertain whether his data offer confirmation or rejection of his working hypotheses. Statistics provides the instruments whereby the researcher is enabled to reach a decision regarding the *degree of confidence* he may have in his research findings, i.e. the probability that his results diverge significantly from chance. This information is essential if he is going to be able to draw conclusions or generalizations from his results.

Interpretation and Evaluation of Research Findings

Statistical, i.e. quantitative, analysis of the data is a fundamental part of the interpretative process, but in the case of qualitative data, e.g. historical or individual case information, an appreciable amount of subjective interpretation may be required. Here, the researcher must exercise extreme caution to avoid exceeding the limitations of his data. He must guard against overgeneralizing from his findings. The conclusions drawn in some studies can apply only to the sample used in the study. This is a consequence of the small size of the sample, the method by which the sample was obtained, or other important reasons. In formulating his interpretations, the researcher should be guided by his earlier stated hypotheses; if he wishes to extend his conclusions beyond these limits, he must be able to draw a clear line between objective and subjective interpretation.

The evaluation of research is a matter of crucial importance for both the producer and the consumer of research. The producer of research should critically evaluate his own proposals and completed projects; the consumer of research should be able to critically evaluate the research reports he reads to determine their relevance and value.

Research should be able to withstand detailed and critical scrutiny. If a study fails to fulfill basic criteria with respect to reliability and validity, it is worse than worthless—it is misleading. While the reader has no way of knowing whether or not the study he encounters in a professional journal was conducted exactly as it is reported, he can at least subject the report to a critical review. If the report reveals serious flaws in conceptualization, research design, analysis of the findings, or other aspects of the research, he should be prepared to disregard the investigator's conclusions and interpretations.

THEORY CONSTRUCTION IN CRIMINOLOGY

The preceding description of research dealt largely with the processes by which empirical knowledge is generated by the criminologist. To complete our sketch of the criminologist in the role of behavioral scientist, we must now add a further characterization that depicts the uses to which empirical knowledge is put in the formulation of criminological theory.

The Nature of Scientific Theory

It is of interest to observe that every science is replete with a large number and variety of theories. Since no definition indicates that an area of endeavor, to qualify as a science, must possess theories, we must ask why the theory-building phenomenon pervades all science. The answer may lie in the definition of a theory: *an organized set of constructs designed to mediate prediction and explanation in a particular area of empirical observation.* The fact that, as the definition states, the theory simultaneously serves the functions of organizations and mediation is the basis for the usefulness and, indeed, necessity of theory in a science.

Research and Theory

The relationship between theory and research is exemplified in two types of research. The first, which may be called *theory-based research,* involves studies which are conducted to carry out a test of specific hypotheses derived from a formal theory. This type of research ordinarily involves operations for testing hypotheses concerning a given construct (or its component constructs) as stated and defined by a particular theory. The second type of research, *empirically-based research,* is a more exploratory type of research in which no formal theory provides the hypotheses to be tested. Exploratory research is often done when no extant theory deals adequately with the particular variables of interest to the investigator. It thus does not require that the investigator have a formal definition of the phenomenon under investigation. The definition that he holds need only be implicit and of the most general type. Both types of research have advantages and disadvantages. Theory-based research has the advantage of being generated within a logically consistent framework. This means that a program of related empirical investigations can systematically expand the knowledge of the science while, at the same time, determining the validity of hypotheses and thus of the theory. Empirically-based studies, on the other hand, can be of great value. They may provide the data base upon which a formal theory can be built. The possible contribution of such exploratory research to the science is, however, often diminished by the relative lack of organization and integration of the field of study.

Functions of a Theory

We can view a theory as having two major functions with respect to empirical observation. The theory provides a logical framework for the incorporation and integration of empirical observations previously seen as disparate. As noted above, the scientist often carries out investigations designed not to test a specific hypothesis derived from a theory but rather to "find out" on, a purely empirical level, how the variables of interest operate. This type of investigation is often done because there is no theory which can adequately explain or predict the phenomena of interest. A number of scientists working independently may carry out any number of studies within a general area, each investigation contributing certain specific knowledge. The theorist recognizes that certain general principles appear to underlie the otherwise disparate findings and may, at this point, construct or begin to construct a theory integrating the available empirical observations. The more precisely and comprehensively the theory is able to integrate available relevant empirical observations, the more useful is the theory. While the theorist must, to provide a useful theory, incorporate as much research evidence as possible, he is also constrained to conform to the principle of *parsimony*.

This venerable principle of theory construction states that the theory should explain the phenomena of interest in the simplest possible fashion. Complexities should not be introduced unnecessarily, and, in fact, a concerted effort should be made to avoid unnecessary complexity. We should hasten to point out, however, that in evaluating a theory, adherence to the parsimony principle must be pitted against the adequacy with which the theory explains and predicts the phenomena of interest. The application of the principle of parsimony can be carried too far, to a point where the theory will be simple but relatively useless. Thus, highly complex variables and variable interactions may require a highly complex theory. In the evaluation and comparison of theories, the balancing off of parsimony against adequacy of explanation leads us, then, to a principle of *optimony* by which the theory which achieves the best balance is seen as the best theory. If two theories explain the same empirical observation with equal adequacy, the more parsimonious is selected. If two theories are considered to be equally parsimonious, the more adequate is chosen. Judgments of this sort are, of course, often difficult to make, and scientists may differ as to which of several theories is most optimonious.

The theory provides and generates, within a logically consistent framework, new hypotheses which can lead to systematic empirical research. It is in this second function that the theory makes its greatest contribution to science; it is here that the organizational and mediational functions reach full fruition. The optimonious integration of known empirical data is, of course, important, but a science advances primarily through a process of constantly adding and integrating new observations. The theory provides a logical structure within which scientific knowledge can be expanded *systematically*. The mechanism for such systematic expansion is the derivation from the general theory of testable hypotheses which lead the scientist to carry out research. The resulting empirical observations may then be incorporated into the theory and may, in fact, lead to its modification. At the same time, the knowledge of the science concerning relationships among the variables investigated has been increased. The hypotheses generated by the theory are not, of course, limited to those stated by the theorist in his original formulation. Either the theorist himself or other interested scientists may derive new hypotheses not initially considered. These new formulations may be based logically in either the original version of the theory or in any subsequent modification of aspects of the theory resulting from the incorporation of new empirical findings.

Components of the Theory

Having noted the functions which a theory may serve for science, we must now consider how a theory may be constructed to carry out these functions. What follows is a brief consideration of the terms of a theory and the ways in which they operate to produce a systematic integration and expansion of scientific knowledge.

Primitive Terms: The Data Language

A formal theory contains a number of terms which are defined by reference to other, more basic terms within that theory. At the most basic level, however, the theory must have some terms which are not defined by reference to other terms within the theory. These latter terms, which form the empirical foundation of the theory, are called *primitive terms,* collectively termed the *data language* of the theory. A given primitive term may be defined by the theorist in terms of mathematical symbols, verbal descriptions, observable operations, or it may be left undefined. In the latter case, the theorist is usually relying on current usage of the primitive term in the science to provide an implicit definition.

An important characteristic of the data language is that it is relatively neutral with respect to the theory. It does not reflect the biases of the theorist but rather consists of terms, the definitions of which are generally agreed upon by scientists in the field. The data language is only *relatively* neutral, however, since the particular primitive terms selected by the theorist and the specific ways in which the terms are used are often influenced by the theory. At the same time, the primitive terms are certainly more neutral than the constructs and postulates of the specific theory.

The principal function of the data language is to avoid the ultimate circularity which inheres in any purely formal theoretical system. Some mathematical systems, such as projective geometry, are totally circular; all terms are defined by reference to other terms within the system. The theory, as a result, has no empirical foundation and is thus not testable in the usual sense. While such formal systems are useful to mathematicians, they are of little help to the scientist who wishes to predict and study empirical phenomena. Thus, the more solid and the more neutral the data language of a theory, the more adequate is that theory for predicting the phenomena of interest.

Theoretical Constructs

A construct is an explanatory concept which is not immediately and directly observable. It is usually a label for hypothesized relationships between objects and events. A theoretical construct is used by the theorist, then, as a logical inference to fill in the gaps in the explanation and prediction of empirical data. It should be pointed out that a construct is not the only type of concept. In common usage, the latter refers to a class of objects or events which have common properties. By this definition we have concepts such as "tree," "dog," and "building." Common constructs include such relative abstractions as "democracy," "love," and "patriotism." Theoretical constructs in criminology are exemplified by "self-concept," "prisonization," and "responsibility." It is noteworthy that constructs are more complex if they specify relationships rather than mere descriptions.

To be maximally useful in a theoretical system, a construct must be stated unanimously and employed in such a way that it is possible to define it in terms of observable events. That is, the theorist should provide or readily permit an *operational definition* of each construct in the theory. When a construct is stated in terms of an operational definition, it is measurable, and, to the extent that its constructs are measurable, a theory is testable. Unfortunately, constructs in criminology have not been unambiguously, let alone operationally, defined. We will discuss the problem of operational definition in some detail below.

Propositions and Predictions

It will be recalled that one function of a theory is to predict certain phenomena. We may identify two types of propositions which are utilized to implement the predictive function. The first is the *hypothesis,* which is a relatively specific prediction about some empirical relationship. In its most common form, it is the hypothesis which forms the direct propositional link between theory and data. The second type of proposition, the *postulate,* is a more general statement concerning relationships with which the theory is concerned. There are usually relatively few postulates in a given theory, and it is often possible to derive a number of specific hypotheses from single postulates or combinations of postulates.

We have differentiated between hypotheses and postulates on the basis of relative generality and consequent testability of the two types of proposition. In practice, however, there is a continuum of generality, and whether a given theoretical statement is called a hypothesis or a postulate, often becomes a matter of individual definition or simply the personal preference of the theorist or another scientist interpreting the theory.

The propositions of the theory may be seen as performing three important functions. First, they state, within a logically consistent framework, the functional relationships among variables. Second, it is only through hypotheses that a theory can be tested experimentally. If only very general, non-testable postulates are possible, the theory must exist in scientific limbo; it is not possible to determine whether its postulates are empirically tenable. In general, the more capable a theory is of generating testable hypotheses, the more readily it can be evaluated and, if necessary, modified or extended. A final function of propositions is in mediating the observation of previously unobserved empirical relationships. By functioning in this way, the hypothesis allows the theory to carry out its function in the expansion of scientific knowledge.

Relational Rules

We have thus far viewed a theory as comprising a formal structure and empirical base. The formal structure consists of a number of constructs and propositions, while the empirical base includes the primitive terms of the theory, as well as relevant empirical evidence. To complete the theory, we need two sets of relational rules: one to interrelate the various aspects of the formal theory; the other to relate the theory to its empirical base. The former is called the *syntax* of the theory, the latter the *semantics.*

The syntactical rules formulated by the theorist state how the various constructs and propositions of the theory are related to each other. Together such rules give structure to the theory, where otherwise there would be only a disjointed array of terms. There is wide variation among theories; most criminological theories state relational rules in rather vague, ambiguous terms or even fail to state adequate syntax at all. Others, such as Jeffery (1965), have attempted to provide rigorous and precise statements.

The syntactical interrelationship of theoretical terms is not sufficient. The terms must also be anchored to the empirical data through a separate set of rules, the semantics of the theory. The relationship between theory and data is most importantly expressed in the form of *operational definitions* of the constructs of the theory. Operational definition refers primarily to the specification of measurement operations which will define a given construct. Where operations for the measurement of the construct are clearly specified, the meaning of the construct is relatively unambiguous. More importantly, it is only through the specification of operational definitions that a theory can be subjected to empirical test.

As an example of operational definition, let us consider the theoretical construct, "self-concept" which appears as a major concept in a number of criminological theories (e.g. Reckless, Sykes and Matza). A given theorist may define self-concept verbally as "an organized group of processes which govern behavior and adjustment." But although this definition tells us something about how the theorist views self-concept, it does not permit us to test his hypotheses about self-concept without first tying down the term empirically. If we decide to define self-concept operationally as a specific range of scores on particular subscales of the Minnesota Multiphasic Personality Inventory, we will have provided a definition of the construct in terms of an observable measurement operation, and we can now test the theorist's hypotheses about "self-concept."

A chronic problem incurred in the practical application of operationism is that not all scientists will necessarily agree on a particular operational definition of a given construct. In the example above, the theorist or another scientist may prefer to operationally define self-concept not in terms of the MMPI scores but by reference to the score on a different personality inventory, the behavioral ratings of a clinical psychologist, or a particular set of physiological indicants. The results of tests of self-concept hypotheses might vary considerably as a function of the particularly measurement operation employed. One partial solution to this problem has been to specify that a given operational definition, e.g. of self-concept as MMPI scores, is a *provisional* definition, used on an exploratory basis. The use of a provisional definition recognizes that if the hypotheses are not supported, the fault may lie not in the hypothesis or theory but in the definition employed. A body of research built around a particular construct may lead to fairly general agreement on a specific operational definition of the construct or at least to a better empirical understanding of the construct.

The Theory

With the components of a theory at hand, we can now, by way of summary, describe the theory as a whole. The theory is formally composed of a number of relatively general postulates, each of which is a statement of the functional relationships of certain variables and each of which involves one or more of the constructs of the theory. Each construct, as well as each other major term of the theory, is defined by reference to other terms within the theory. Exceptions are the primitive terms, which are defined, if at all, by reference to terms or observations external to the theory.

The various constructs, terms, and propositions within the formal theory are interrelated by the syntax of the theory. Through the application of syntactical rules, hypotheses concerning relatively specific empirical relationships are deduced from the postulates of the theory. If hypotheses are anchored semantically to the data language, and constructs are operationally defined, various provisional definitions may be provided for use on an exploratory basis. Depending upon results of empirical investigations, the theory may be extended through the formulation of new postulates and/or the deduction of new hypotheses, or the existing postulates, hypotheses, or syntax of the theory may be modified to incorporate the new empirical observations within a logically consistent framework. Through the deduction and testing of hypotheses, the theory may lead to new empirical observations and thus aid in the expansion of scientific knowledge.

Unfortunately, many theories do not conform closely to the structure outlined above. Constructs are often not defined or even readily definable in operational terms. Verbal definitions of constructs and other terms in the theory may be ambiguous, inconsistent, or even nonexistent. Relational rules may be unspecified, weak, or too general to be useful. And the theory as a whole may not, even in its original formulation, be capable of consistently explaining and predicting existing, relevant empirical relationships. We will discuss the evaluation of theories later in this chapter.

What a Theory is Not

A Phenomenon of Nature

We must note first that a theory is not a given or natural phenomenon. It is not a *discovery* but rather a *creation* of the theorist. It is developed out of his *interpretations* of empirical results and is subject to the biases of both the theorist and any scientist who later interprets the theory. Theorist biases, sources of which we will consider later, are based, in general, on the personal and professional experience of the theorist. The prejudices influence the theory in every aspect and at every point in its development. They determine, in part, the area of endeavor in which the theorist chooses to work, his approach to theory construction, the postulates and constructs which he employs, and even, to some extent, the primitive terms which constitute the data language of the theory. Even the theorist's interpretation of empirical results relevant to the theory is influenced by his biases. In addition, the scientist-interpreter, who may wish to apply the theory to an experimental situation to determine its empirical consequences, will be biased in his interpretation and treatment of the theory as a function of his own background and interests.

The Theory as a Law

Theories, or their postulates, may or may not become laws, depending upon the definition of law. If law is defined as a final and irrevocable empirical relationship, a theory can never become a law. If, however, as is more common in science, law is defined as *a well-established empirical relationship which has been repeatedly observed,* a theory or postulate can become a law. In this latter sense, a law is simply a theoretical proposition which has received widespread experimental support. There is no implication that the relationship is absolute or irrefutable, and there is the continuing recognition that the law originated as a theoretical proposition or perhaps simply as an empirical observation. Even when law is used in the second, more conservative sense, there is a danger that some will view a particular law as an established, irrefutable absolute and hence perhaps stifle the pursuit of hypotheses or research not consonant with that law. A classic example of this situation occurred in physics, where some postulates of Newtonian mechanics were quite widely accepted as laws in the absolute sense until the advent of Einstein's relativity theory. Probably as a function of the complexity of the subject matter and the relative youth of the discipline, there are very few laws, in the conservative sense, in psychology and virtually none in criminology.

Why Different Theories

We have noted that the construction of theories is a phenomenon which seems to pervade all science. It is legitimate to ask, then, why this should be so. Why can we not simply perform relevant empirical observations in a systematic fashion, without the necessity for theory, and answer each empirical question factually, rather than theoretically?

EMPIRICAL VARIANCE. Most theories, whether of light, personality, or other phenomena are based on empirical observations. To the extent that these observations vary, the resultant theories may vary. While empirical observations may vary for a variety of reasons, two principal factors in variation are the *control of variables* and the degree of *precision of measurement*. In order for a given experiment to adequately test a hypothesis or demonstrate a relationship, all variables which might affect the outcome of the experiment must be either systematically manipulated, held constant, or measured. Only to the extent that such control is accomplished does the experiment demonstrate a given relationship. The variables requiring control depend upon both the general area of investigation and the particular hypotheses under test. Physicists studying the phenomena of light transmission have found it necessary to control such variables as the temperature and intensity of the light source (which can be manipulated or held constant), and the motion of the earth (which can be measured). Researchers testing criminological theories have found it necessary to control such simple variables as the age, intelligence level, or length of incarceration of subjects. It is often necessary, in addition, to control much more complex variables, such as anxiety level, ego strength, diagnosis, and level of aspiration. Since scientists often differ in the variables they choose to control or in their definitions of such complex variables as anxiety level, and since it is not always possible to control all relevant variables, results of similar experiments may vary.

THEORIST BIAS. A second major reason why we have a variety of personality theories is that each scientist, despite his attempts to interpret data objectively, is influenced by his own pre-theory biases. Perhaps the most important biasing factor is the theorist's background or professional training and experience. This background will include the books and articles which the theorist has read, as well as the course material to which he has been exposed. It will also include his research experience and, in the case of the criminological theorist, his experience with criminal offenders in various segments of the criminal justice system.

The Evaluation and Comparison of Theories

Having discussed some of the characteristics and functions of theories, we are now in a position to evaluate and compare a number of criminological theories. Any given theory may be assessed in terms of its formal or *structural* properties and its *empirical* properties. Any two or more theories may be compared and contrasted according to these two sets of properties and, in addition, in terms of a number of specific *issues,* concerned primarily with the postulated attributes of the criminal offender.

Structural Properties

In our discussion of theory construction, the emphasis was placed on the description of the properties of an *ideal* theory. Since obviously not all theories of personality will attain this ideal, it is useful to consider some specific questions that might be asked when evaluating the formal attributes of a given theory.

1. The Data Language
   a. Does the theory have a data language? That is, are an adequate number of primitive terms specified?
   b. Is the data language neutral, not unduly influenced by the biases of the theorist?
   c. Are the primitive terms clearly and explicitly defined by reference to terms outside the theory?

2. Theoretical Constructs
   a. Are constructs stated and defined unambiguously?
   b. Are definitions operational or merely verbal?
   c. If operational definitions are not supplied, are classes of operations stated or implied in order to make operational definitions readily derivable?

3. Propositions
   a. Are postulates clearly and explicitly stated, or must they be deduced from the general writings of the theorist?
   b. Are hypotheses specifically stated, or must they be derived?
   c. Do the stated postulates and hypotheses provide adequate specification of functional relationships among variables which constitute the theory?
   d. Are hypotheses readily amenable to empirical test?
4. Relational Rules
   a. Is an adequate set of syntactical rules clearly specified?
   b. Are the interrelationships of major theoretical variables made adequately explicit through the application of syntax?
   c. Do the semantics of the theory clearly relate the theoretical variables to empirical data?

While the above outline should suffice for the formal evaluation and comparison of theories, the reader is cautioned that not all writers present precisely the same points for consideration.

Empirical Properties

Far more important than the adequacy of its formal properties is the empirical value of the theory. A theory which closely approximates the structural ideal and contributes little to the expansion of scientific knowledge is of far less value than the poorly constructed theory which nevertheless pushes the frontiers of science a few steps forward.

In evaluating the empirical contribution of a theory, we must consider both the adequacy with which the theory integrates existing empirical evidence and the ability of the theory to generate further research. The scientist who sets out to construct a formal theory ordinarily has available to him a reasonably large body of empirical data. In evaluating a theory, it is essential to determine the extent to which the theory is able to explain or "post dict" existing data. If the theory does not handle available evidence with reasonable adequacy, its value for making further predictions is open to some doubt.

Assuming that available evidence is adequately integrated, the most important single attribute of a theory is its ability to generate scientific research and hence potentially to expand scientific knowledge. The stimulation of research may be accomplished in two ways. First, the theory may generate research *formally* through the statement of postulates and hypotheses. If the hypotheses which are stated or can be readily derived are not testable, the theory will not, of course, generate research. If the hypotheses are amenable to empirical test, the amount of research stimulated will depend largely on the importance placed upon the theory by the scientific community. Thus, if the phenomena with which the theory deals are considered by other scientists to be relatively unimportant or uninteresting, the theory may, despite the testability of its hypotheses, receive little empirical attention.

Aside from its formal hypotheses, a theory may stimulate research quite indirectly. This *heuristic* value of the theory may take any of several forms. The theory may suggest to other scientists particular directions or ideas for research, providing not specific hypotheses but merely an impetus. Secondly, the theory may open a general area of scientific inquiry that has received little previous attention. In this way, the theory may stimulate not only a variety of research efforts, but, eventually, even the development of other theories (for example, the influence of Sutherland's differential association theory on the development of Cloward and Ohlin's theory of differential opportunity). Finally, a theory may generate research, in the process of which new scientific leads concerning phenomena only indirectly relevant to the theory may be obtained.

Summary

This chapter has viewed the criminologist in the role of scientist and has dealt with the two principal components of his information-producing activities in this capacity: research and theory construction. Discussion centered upon the logic of inquiry in criminology; research and theory are both seen as systematic efforts at finding answers to the basic questions: "What do you mean?" (operational specification) and "How do you know?" (scientific explanation). Stress was placed on the interrelatedness of theory and empirical research. In addition to a brief sketch of research procedures, the chapter presented a review of scientific theory construction and concluded with a series of formal and substantive criteria for use in evaluating theoretical formulations in criminology.

REFERENCES

Bakan, D.: *On Method: Toward a Reconstruction of Psychological Investigation*. San Francisco, Jossey-Bass, 1969.

Jeffery, C.R.: Criminal behavior and learning theory. *Journal of Criminal Law, Cirminology and Police Science, 56*:293-300, 1965.

Kagan, J., and Moss, H.A.: *Birth to Maturity: A study in Psychological Development*. New York, Wiley, 1962.

Lachenmeyer, C.: Experimentation—a misunderstood methodology in psychological and social-psychological research. *American Psychologist, 25:* 617-624, 1970.

Mills, J. (Ed.): *Experimental Social Psychology*. New York, Macmillan, 1969.

Owens, W.: Toward one discipline of scientific psychology. *American Psychologist, 23*:782-785, 1968.

Rosenthal, R.: *Experimenter Effects in Behavioral Research*. New York, Appleton-Century-Crofts, 1966.

Scott, W., and Wertheimer, M.: *Introduction to Psychological Research*. New York, Wiley, 1962.

Chapter 3

EPIDEMIOLOGY OF CRIME
IN THE UNITED STATES

SOCIAL EPIDEMIOLOGY may be defined as the study of the distribution and determinants of social pathologies within a given social structure. With regard to the study of crime and criminals, this approach would seek to describe criminal acts as they relate to age, sex, race, and residence; hence, it might be considered an extension of the discipline of *demography* to criminology. Descriptive epidemiology attempts to find answers to such questions as: How many new cases of auto theft occurred annually per 1,000 males in the 15-25 year age category in the United States during the 1960s? Research of this nature leads to the formulation of predictive statements about crime, e.g. the younger a person is when first arrested, the more likely he is to continue in crime (Glaser, 1969).

Epidemiological studies make a distinction between two types of statistical survey. The first, called *incidence rates,* refers to the known number of cases occurring within a specified time interval. A second type, *prevalence rates,* refers to the total number of crimes committed or criminals present in a given population during a specified time interval. This type of survey includes first offenders and recidivists (repeaters).

It ought to be acknowledged at the outset that attempts to arrive at an accurate appraisal of the extent and characteristics of crime and criminals in the United States have proven to be a frustrating venture. Crime by its very nature is not easily measurable, for secrecy is its essential characteristic. To the extent that criminals are successful—that is, able to conceal their actions or identities from discovery—our statistical measures are not accurate. In some categories of crime, especially those "victimless crimes" where the "victim" is a satisfied customer, our measures fall absurdly short of reality. As Geis (1965) points out, there are only about twenty convictions for every sixty million homosexual acts performed. (Homosexuality may or may not be an "illness," but in many states it is a crime.)

We shall begin with a discussion of "crimes known to the police" and the official incidence rates published by the Federal Bureau of Investigation in its annual publication *The Uniform Crime Reports.* The crime Index (seven most serious offenses) will be reviewed in some detail and the characteristics of known offenders will be examined by age, sex, and race. An attempt to achieve some independent assessment of the validity of these official statistics will be made by reviewing prevalence studies, the social behavior of citizens as it relates to crime, and risk insurance rates as an index of property crime. Finally, the limitations of official statistics will be discussed, and we shall suggest some recommendations for improvement.

THE UNIFORM CRIME REPORTS

If the adequacy of criminological theories rests upon a foundation of valid and reliable criminological data, it is immediately apparent to the student of criminal behavior that our principal source of information on crime—the statistics compiled by the Federal Bureau of Investigation—is a focus of controversy and contention. Evaluations of the validity and reliability of the figures reported in the *Uniform Crime Report* issued annually by the FBI range from the certainty of their accuracy voiced by the late J. Edgar Hoover, who said of the UCR, "Today the onslaught continues—with five serious offenses being recorded every minute ... These figures are based on facts—unlike the illogical and inane criticisms which have been voiced by the peculiar clique of sociologists and criminologists who are apparently suffering armchair fatigue" (1965), to the contemptuous dismissal of the same data by Sophia Robinson, when she concluded that "FBI summaries are not worth the paper they're written on" (*Time,* 1966). The truth, as we shall try to show, seems to lie somewhere between these two extremes.

Many crimes go undetected, others are detected but unreported, while others are reported but unrecorded. Thus any attempt to measure the absolute number of crimes committed in a particular locale by such yardsticks as "crimes known to the police," "arrests," "convictions," or "commitments to prison" can only be viewed as a rough approximation at best.

Although these figures represent only a portion, and probably a small portion in some categories, of the total crime rate, police records are closer to the actual crime and are a superior measure of the actual number of crimes committed than are arrest rates, court records, or prison statistics.

Since 1930, the F.B.I. has published "crimes known to the police" in its *Uniform Crime Reports*. This data is voluntarily submitted by law-enforcement agencies from all parts of the United States. Despite its limitations (which will be discussed in detail later), this information is considered the most authoritative summary indicating the extent of criminality in American society.

The *Uniform Crime Report* utilizes seven crime classifications as an index to measure the trend and distribution of crime in the United States. There is no way of determining the total number of crimes which are committed. These seven crimes—murder, forcible rape, robbery, aggravated assault, burglary, larceny over 50 dollars, and auto theft—are selected because, as a group, they represent the most serious offenses and the crimes most consistently reported to the police.

During the calendar year 1970, the *Uniform Crime Reports* received data from law enforcement agencies representing 9,200 jurisdictions (a rise from 400 in 1930) covering 97 percent of the total United States population in other cities, and 71 percent of the rural population. The combined average accounts for 91 percent of the population of the entire nation (*UCR,* 1970). The offenses reported are violations of the criminal law of the separate states; no violations of the federal law are included in the *UCR*.

Since 1958 crimes have been reported by geographical area following as closely as practical the definitions used by the Bureau of the Budget and Census. Standard metropolitan statistical areas (SMSA's) are generally made up of an entire county or counties having at least one core city of 50,000 or more inhabitants. "Other cities" are urban places outside standard metropolitan statistical areas, most of which are incorporated communities of 2,500 or more inhabitants. "Rural areas" are defined as unincorporated portions of counties outside or urban places of SMSA's.

The *Uniform Crime Reports* collect data from law enforcement agencies in all fifty states. Since there are variations in the definition of criminal violations, an arbitrary set of crime classifications has been adopted in an attempt to remove this barrier to uniformity. However, it should be kept in mind that such a system cannot distinguish between "felonies" and "misdemeanors," which vary from state to state. Not only does the definition of what constitutes a felony vary by state statute, it also depends upon the subjective evaluation of the seriousness of the policeman making the arrest. As Wambaugh (1970) puts it: "You know what the detectives say, 'Forty stitches or a gunshot is a felony. Anything less is a misdemeanor'." Brief definitions of the crime classification utilized are as follows:

1. *Criminal homicide—* (a) Murder and non-negligent manslaughter: all willfull felonies, homicides as distinguished from deaths caused by negligence. Excludes attempts to kill, suicides, accidental deaths, or justifiable homicides. Justifiable homicides are limited to: (1) the killing of a person by a peace officer in line of duty; (2) the killing of a person in the act of committing a felony by a private citizen. (b) manslaughter by negligence: any death which the police investigation establishes was primarily attributable to gross negligence of some individual other than the victim.

2. *Forcible rape—*rape by force, assault to rape and attempted rape. Excludes statutory offenses (no force used, victim under age of consent) .

3. *Robbery-stealing* or taking anything of value from the person by force or violence or by the threat of violence: strong-arm robbery, stickups, armed robbery, assault to rob, and attempt to rob.

4. *Aggravated Assault*—assault with intent to kill or for the purpose of inflicting severe bodily injury by shooting, cutting, stabbing, maiming, poisoning, scalding, or by the use of acids, explosives, or other means. Excludes simple assaults, assault and battery, fighting, etc.

5. *Burglary-breaking or entering*—burglary, housebreaking, safe-cracking, or any unlawful entry to commit a felony or a theft, even though no force was used to gain entry and attempts. Burglary followed by larceny is not counted again as larceny.

6. *Larceny-theft* (except auto theft) —fifty dollars and over in value, thefts of bicycles, automobile accessories, shoplifting, pocket-picking, or any stealing of property or article of value which is not taken by force and violence or by fraud; excludes embezzlement, "con" games, forgery, worthless checks, etc.

7. *Auto Theft*—stealing or driving away and abandoning a motor vehicle. Excludes taking for temporary or authorized use by those having lawful access to the vehicle (*UCR,* 1970).

The factors which cause a variation in crime rates are numerous and readers of the *UCR* are cautioned against drawing conclusion from direct comparisons of crime figures between individual communities. Among the conditions which the UCR (1970) lists as affecting the amount and type of crime that occurs in a given locale are:

1. Density and size of community population and the metropolitan area of which it is a part.
2. Composition of the population with reference particularly to age, sex, and race.
3. Economic status and mores of the population.
4. Relative stability of population, including commuters, seasonal, and other transient types.
5. Climate, including seasonal weather conditions.
6. Educational, recreational, and religious characteristics.
7. Effective strength of the police force.

8. Standards governing appointments to the police force.
9. Policies of the prosecuting officials and the courts.
10. Attitude of the public toward law enforcement problems.
11. The administrative and investigative efficiency of the local law enforcement agency, including the degree of adherence to the crime reporting standards.

The Extent of Known Crime

As mentioned earlier, the F.B.I. Crime Index is made up of seven major felonies. These crimes were chosen to comprise the index because they are the types of offenses most likely to be reported to the police. From these statistics a crime "rate" is constructed.

A crime rate can be considered a victim risk rate. According to the 1970 *Uniform Crime Reports*,[1] the Crime Index rate for the United States rose from 2,477 offenses per 100,000 inhabitants in 1969 to 2,740 per 100,000 inhabitants in 1970, an 11 percent increase in the victim rate. The risk of being a victim of one of the seven crimes in the Index has increased 144 percent since 1960, and this increase cannot be explained by population growth alone.

Murder

In 1970, there were an estimated 15,810 murders committed in the United States; this crime comprises slightly more than 2 percent of the crimes of violence and represents less than one-half of 1 percent of all Crime Index offenses. Since 1960 the murder rate has increased 56 percent.

Geographically, the number of murder victims in proportion to population was highest in the Southern states; Georgia possesses the highest murder rate in the nation. Males outnumber females as victims of murder by over three to one, and the ratio of arrests

---

[1] National statistics on juvenile delinquency are gathered by the Children's Bureau of the Department of Health, Education, and Welfare. The Federal Bureau of Prisons reports periodically on the inmate composition of state and federal institutions in its *National Prisoner Statistics*. The National Office of Vital Statistics gathers information on homicide from coroners' reports. Several federal agencies, such as the Treasury Department, publish statistics, and most states compile crime statistics on the violation of state statutes.

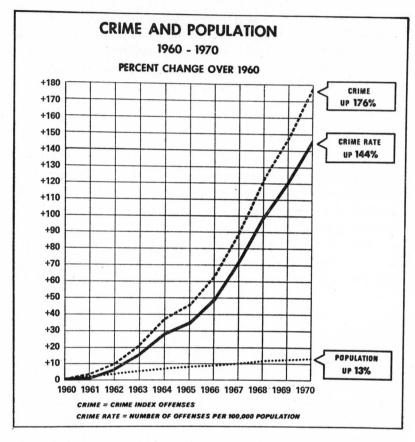

Figure 3-1. Crime and Population. *Uniform Crime Reports.* Washington, U.S. Government Printing Office, 1970. Reproduced by permission of the Department of Justice.

for murder was more than five males to each female in 1970. Forty-four of every 100 victims were white, and fifty-five were Negro.

Firearms continue to be the predominant weapon used in murder (65%). As in prior years, handguns were the principal instrument used, accounting for 52 percent of murders. Since 1964, murder through the use of a firearm has more than doubled. Federal legislation has attempted to restrict the sale of cheap foreign made weapons, the famous "Saturday Night Special," but foreign distributors effectively evade the spirit of the law by shipping to the United States parts which may be readily assembled.[2]

Murders tend to be committed by relatives of the victim or persons acquainted with the victim. Along with our concern for "crime in the streets," we need some focus on "crime in the home." In 1970, killings within the family made up over one-fourth of all murders. Within this figure, over half of these involved spouse killing spouse. (The wife was the victim in 54 percent of the cases and the husband in the remaining 46 percent.) Lover's quarrels were the cause of seven percent of homicides. "Trouble in paradise" resulted in females being the victims in 55 percent of the murders; when a third party entered the scene however, to complicate a romantic setting, a male was the victim in 93 percent of the confrontations. In 1970, 86 percent of the criminal homicides were "solved" (by arrest) —the highest percentage of clearance by arrest of any Crime Index Offense.

Aggravated Assault

In 1970, there was an estimated total of 329,940 aggravated assaults in the United States. This figure represents an increase of 92 percent in the rate per 100,000 inhabitants since 1960. The Southern States had the highest aggravated assault rate in the country. As with murder, this offense tends to increase in the warm summer months.

Most aggravated assaults occur within the family unit or among neighbors or acquaintances. Because of this close relationship the victim is frequently unwilling to testify for the prosecution. Typical of this response was the case observed by one of the authors during a study of sentencing practices in Louisiana. A man was wounded slightly in the head when his "common-law" wife shot him with a .22 caliber rifle. By the time of the trial they had effected a reconciliation and when called upon to testify he

---

[2]Britain, by way of contrast, has much tighter gun control than the United States. Not only is it more difficult for a British citizen to purchase a personal weapon, he also cannot carry his gun except for plausible reasons. Firearms registration must be renewed each year.

reported: "I don't know what happened. I was just sitting there and suddenly got a headache." Because of the *Gemeinschaft*[3] nature of this crime, acquittals run high, almost four out of each ten. This type of disturbance is hazardous to the police as well. From 1961 to 1970, ninety-eight officers lost their lives responding to these type calls.

Forcible Rape

Forcible rape made up less than 1 percent of the Crime Index total and only 5 percent of the crimes of violence in 1970. The rape rate per 100,000 female inhabitants of the United States is up 95 percent since 1960. Women living in large core cities are four times as likely to become the victims of rape than are women living in rural areas. Regionally, females living in the western states, where the male-female ratio is weighted on the male side, were most often the victims of forcible rape. This imbalance, however, does not constitute the sole explanation for the higher rate of forcible rape in this area.

Sixty-four percent of the arrests for forcible rape during the year 1970 were of persons under the age of twenty-five. This offense is probably one of the most under-reported crimes due to the potential public embarrassment. However, as a national average, 18 percent of all forcible rapes reported to the police in 1970 were determined by investigation to be unfounded, i.e. no forcible rape or attempt had occurred.

Robbery

Robbery takes place in the presence of the victim, and the money or other items of value are obtained by use of force or intimidation. In 1970 there were an estimated 348,380 robberies committed in the United States. This represents an increase in the robbery rate of 186 percent since 1960. Cities with a population over 250,000 accounted for nearly three out of every four robberies which occured during 1970. Robbery rates tend to increase in proportion to density of population. Larger cities reported rob-

---

[3]*Gemeinschaft* is a sociological term connoting face-to-face patterns of social relationship in a context of intimacy between or among the persons involved.

bery rates about ten times greater than were reported in the suburban areas. Geographically, this crime tended to occur most frequently in the heavily populated regions of the Northeastern United States. Service station holdups have increased 230 percent since 1960, causing many stations, after dark, to accept only credit cards and to place cash in safes for which the attendant has no key. Six out of every ten robbers were armed, and the preferred weapon was a firearm, 63 percent. Three out of every four persons arrested for robbery were under twenty-five years of age, and 65 percent of those arrested were black. Of the adults prosecuted for robbery in 1970, 47 percent were convicted of the substantive charge.

Burglary

An estimated 2,169,300 burglaries occurred during the year 1970, with the peak month being December. This figure represents an increase of 113 percent in the robbery rate since 1960. Burglary is a crime of stealth and opportunity, and the increase in the number of daytime residential burglaries reflects the increasing number of apartments and houses in the United States which are left unattended with both husband and wife employed. Property owners suffered an economic loss of 672 million dollars to burglars in 1970. Police were able to solve less than one out of every five of these reported burglaries. Arrests tend to be concentrated among young persons; 83 percent of all arrests for burglary in 1970 were persons under the age of twenty-five.

Larceny-theft

Larceny-theft refers to crimes such as shoplifting and purse-snatching—any theft without the use of force or fraud where the value of property stolen is 50 dollars or more. There were 1,756,100 offenses of larceny 50 dollars and over in 1970. This figure may be somewhat unrealistic as an inflationary economy exerts an effect on the value of goods. Thefts which would not have been included in these figures in former years may suddenly become translated into felonies through inflation. Adding further to the tentative character of these figures is the variability of the police estimate of the worth of goods. Further, victims who are insured

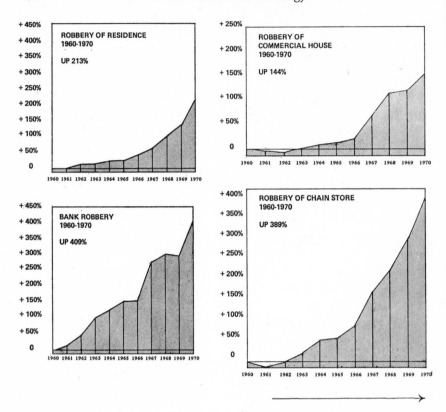

tend to over-estimate their losses. (If this is intentional, it is itself an offense). Larceny is a crime of opportunity. Shoplifting rates are similar in the city and suburban areas, but there is a decided drop in the rural areas. A lack of witnesses and the tremendous volume in these cases make clearancy by the police difficult. Only 18 percent of the larceny offenses brought to police attention in 1970 were solved. Another characteristic of this crime is that females comprised one-fourth of all arrests for larceny-theft; in fact, women were arrested more often for larceny than for any other offense in 1970. In absolute, numbers, twice as many persons were charged for larceny-theft than for any other serious offense, with 71 percent found guilty.

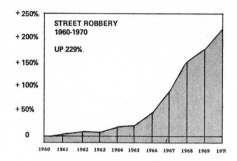

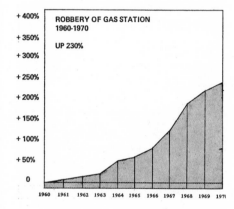

Figure 3-2. The Nature of Robbery. *Uniform Crime Reports.* Washington, U.S. Government Printing Office, 1970. Reproduced by permission of the Department of Justice.

Auto Theft

From 1960 through 1970, the percentage increase in auto theft has been four times greater than the percentage increase in automobile registrations and four times greater than the percentage increase in the young age population, fifteen to twenty-four years. In 1970, 921,400 motor vehicles were reported stolen, an increase of 150 percent since 1960.

Auto theft is primarily a big city problem; five times as many autos are stolen in cities over 250,000 as in the suburbs, and 100 times as many are stolen as in rural areas. Auto theft, like larceny, is a crime of opportunity. Two-thirds of all auto thefts occur at night and over one-half are from private residences, apartments, or

CRIMES CLEARED BY ARREST
1970

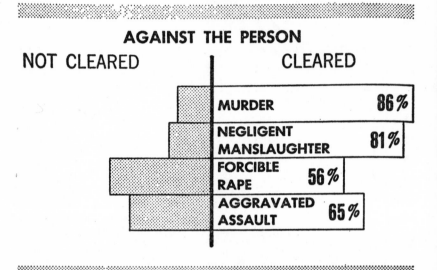

AGAINST THE PERSON

NOT CLEARED | CLEARED

MURDER	86%
NEGLIGENT MANSLAUGHTER	81%
FORCIBLE RAPE	56%
AGGRAVATED ASSAULT	65%

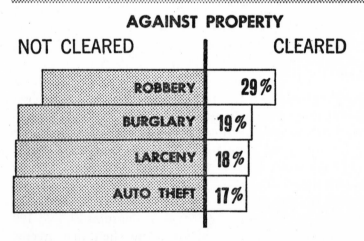

AGAINST PROPERTY

NOT CLEARED | CLEARED

ROBBERY	29%
BURGLARY	19%
LARCENY	18%
AUTO THEFT	17%

Figure 3-3. Crimes Cleared by Arrest. *Uniform Crime Reports.* Washington, U.S. Government Printing Office, 1970. Reproduced by permission of the Department of Justice.

streets in residential districts.

Law-enforcement agencies were successful in solving only 17 percent of these thefts by arrest of the offender. They were, however, successful in recovering 84 percent of the stolen vehicles, but the remaining unrecovered 16 percent represented a loss to owners of 140 million dollars.

Arrests for auto theft comes primarily from the age group under twenty-one, 75 percent. Of all adults prosecuted, 50 percent were found guilty. Sixty-three percent of the persons processed for auto theft were referred to juvenile court jurisdiction.

Characteristics of Known Offenders

Age

Persons under eighteen were arrested for 26 percent of all crimes reported by police agencies in 1970. However, for the seven index offenses, youths under eighteen accounted for 46 percent of these serious offenses. Persons under twenty-five were arrested for 52 percent of all crimes and 76 percent of the seven most serious offenses. The crimes most frequently committed by persons under twenty-five include forcible rape (65 percent of all arrests for that offense), robbery (77 percent), burglary (83 percent), larceny-theft (77 percent), auto theft (86 percent), arson (77 percent), vandalism (88 percent), violation of liquor laws (83 percent). The crimes for which persons over twenty-five are mostly likely to be arrested include criminal homicide, embezzlement, gambling, drunkenness, and drunk driving. The crime with the most dramatic increase in the arrests for young persons is violation of narcotic drug laws. The percentage of persons under eighteen arrested for this offense is four times what it was in 1963. For persons under twenty-one, the increase is two and one-half times the 1963 figure, and for persons under twenty-five arrests for drug law violations has increased 54 percent. Three out of every four persons arrested for violation of narcotic's law are under twenty-five years of age. The increase in the number of arrests for drug violation is due, in part, to the increased sophistication and emphasis of police departments in making drug arrests. (With the lowering of the voting age to 18 in federal elections, it will be interesting to note what effect, if any, this has on legislature and law-enforcement.)

Sex

Analysis of 6,570,473 arrests (from law-enforcement agencies representing over 151,000,000 people in 1970) reveals that 946,897 (14.4 percent) involved females. Females accounted for only nine percent of all arrest for violent crime, but female arrest rate is 18 percent in the area of property crime. The percentage of women arrested for each of the following offenses is higher than their overall arrest average: For forgery and counterfeiting, women accounted for 23 percent of all arrests; for fraud, 27 percent; for embezzlement, 25 percent; prostitution and commercialized vice, 79 percent; narcotics, 15 percent; curfew and loitering law violations, 21 percent. Women are not only arrested much less than men, but are also less likely to be incarcerated.

In 1967 there were a total of 6,235 sentenced female prisoners confined in state and federal institutions (*N.P.S.,* 1967). This represented a decrease in the number of women incarcerated in state institutions by 11 percent from 1966, and a one percent decrease in Federally incarcerated females. At the same time (1967), there were 192,704 males confined in all institutions in the United States. The estimated civilian population of the United States in December 1967 was 196,583,000. Thus, females account for 13 percent of all arrests but comprise only three percent of prisoners in state and federal institutions. In 1967 only one woman in every 32,762 in the United States was incarcerated in a penal institution, while one out of every 1,026 males was behind bars. The state of Vermont had only two women incarcerated; Rhode Island five; North Dakota, three; Idaho, seven; and Nevada sixteen. California had the largest female inmate population, 1,083 (*N.P. S.,* 1967). These figures refer to women incarcerated in state and federal penitentiaries and no not include county jails and lock-ups.

Race

Police statistics gathered from more than 5,000 agencies (population est. 142,000,000) in 1970 revealed that blacks are arrested for 27 percent of all crimes committed in the U.S. and for 36 percent of the seven major offenses (U.C.R., 1970). Blacks accounted for 59 percent of all murder and nonnegligent manslaughter arrests, 48 percent of arrests for rape, 65 percent of arrests for robbery, 46 percent of arrests for aggravated assault, and 36 percent of arrests for auto theft. In the less serious offenses, blacks were arrested for 50 percent of "carrying concealed weapons" charges. Sixty-four percent of the prostitution and commercialized vice arrests involved blacks, and 66 percent of those arrested for gambling were blacks. When an Indian is arrested, two-thirds of the time it is for drunkenness. Interestingly enough, only one Chinese was arrested in the United States in 1970, for manslaughter by negligence.

Blacks are arrested at a disproportionately high rate for "suspicion" (arrests for no specific offense and release without formal charges being filed), but police investigatory practices may result in the underreporting of certain black crimes (Skolnick, 1967). A stabbing by a white woman of her husband would probably be classified as attempted homicide, while a black stabbing or "cutting" is often written off as what Skolnick terms a "North Westfield battery."

The high black arrest rate may be explained in part by the social experiences to which many black people are subjected. According to *Current Population Reports* (1970), blacks are migrating to the inner city in increasing numbers. For the United States as a whole, blacks comprise 11 percent of the population, but in 1969, 21 percent of the central city population was black, an increase of 16 percent in 1960. Within metropolitan areas, most whites reside in suburban rings, while the overwhelming majority of blacks are central city residents. In metropolitan areas of 1,000,000 or more, blacks comprise 26 percent of the central city area. The city is characterized by speed and tension, anonymity, impersonality, regimentation, and heterogeneity. These conditions generate more pressure toward deviance. Blacks accounted for 30 percent of arrests in cities but only 9 percent of all arrests in rural jurisdictions (U.C.R., 1970).

Relating poverty to crime, especially property crimes, would help explain the overrepresentation of blacks in criminal statistics, but this factor fails to explain the relatively low criminality rate among black women who share the same socioeconomic conditions. The role expectations and socialization experiences of women differ from those of men; it would thus not be unreasonable to expect a different response to the same environmental stimuli. Obviously it would be gross error to infer from the high black crime rates that black people have some genetic predisposition toward crime. We must emphasize that black crime rates vary by sex, socioeconomic status, and geographic region. General theories of criminality will be discussed in succeeding chapters; suffice it to say here that race is related to crime only insofar as it affects the nature of social experiences and social interaction.

Prevalence Studies: The Extent of Unreported Crime

Crime Victim Research

In 1965 the National Opinion Research Center took a random sample of 10,000 households, asking people what crimes had been committed against them during the preceding year. (Ennis, 1967). In an attempt to overcome the well-known difficulties in police statistics, the N.O.R.C. decided to survey the individual victims of crime as a means of measuring the crime rate. Realistically, it was assumed that respondents would not easily discuss such illegal activities as abortion, drugs, or gambling; crimes against the person and against property thus became the central focus.

To insure proper classification of crimes, interviewers were instructed to allow the respondents sufficient time to recall all the important facts about the incident, then to probe into the final outcome; was an arrest made? Did it come to trial? The 3400 "crime" interviews were then reviewed by two staff teams, one comprised of lawyers and the other accomplished by two Chicago police department detectives. The teams operated independently. This evaluation reduced the initial 3,400 reported victimizations to 2,100.

Half of the people interviewed were victims of crimes they did not report to the police. The N.O.R.C. sample revealed an estimated rate of crime twice that of the *UCR* index. Nevertheless, in the case of homicide and car theft, there was close agreement between the two sources of crime data. Murder, of course, is the crime most likely to be discovered and reported, and people apparently believe the police can do something toward recovering a stolen car. Other factors include the high value of autos and the fact that cars must be registered and insured. Further 7 to 10 percent of stolen cars recovered are owned by fleet or rental agencies.

Glaser (1970), in analyzing the theoretical implications of crime victims notifying the police, constructed the following hypothesis for property crimes: The proportion of total crimes that are reported by victims to the police varies directly with the proportion of reported crimes on which the police act effectively. In short, people report those crimes they believe the police can or will solve. Improved police work leads to higher reported crime statistics and vice-versa. In the area of assault and rape, these offenses tended not to be reported if the victims perceived these as "personal matters."

Crime by Region

According to the N.O.R.C. data, the myth of the "wild, wild west" was, in fact, a reality. The crime rate, for both property and personal crimes, is higher than that of any other region of the country. The West has almost twice the rates of the Northeast in all three types of communities: central city, suburban environs, or nonmetropolitan area. The South, long considered to lead the nation in violent crimes, did not appear to have so high a rate as anticipated. Assault rates in the South were less than half those of the West, only about three-fourths of those of the North-Central states, and only slightly higher than rates for the Northeastern states.

Glaser (1970) analyzes the impact of this N.O.R.C. data on the previously held conclusion that a subculture of violence distinguishes the South from other regions of the country. Since in all regions except the South, central cities have the highest assault rate, and because southern cities tend to be less segregated, Glaser hypothesized that violence varies directly with the segregation of recent immigrants from high-violence areas or with the size of the ghettos into which they are segregated. As the South still has the highest homicide rates, it may be that the frequency or high rate, of nonlethal violence is characteristic of central cities outside the South. The crime rate declines as one moves from the central city out to the suburb and rural areas, especially for crimes against the person. The violent crime rates for metropolitan centers is five times as high as the smaller city, but surprisingly, the property crime rate is only twice as high. While the city is evidently a more hazardous place to dwell than suburbia, the phrase "crime in the streets" is misleading. About 40 percent of the aggravated assaults and rapes take place within the victim's home, and 45 percent of all the serious crimes against the person are committed by someone familiar to the victim (Ennis, 1967).

Victimology

Blacks in lower income groups (under $6000 per year) are almost twice as likely as whites to be victims of crimes of violence, they are, however, only slightly more likely to be victims of property crimes. For upper income groups the situation is reversed. As a black person moves up in the income hierarchy, his chances of being the victim of a violent crime becomes about the same as his white counterpart, but his chances of losing property is greater than that of a white person in the same income bracket. Burglary is the most frequent property crime against higher income blacks. Unlike whites, poor and well-to-do blacks tend to live near each other. It is more difficult for a black person to move from a ghetto to the suburbs after he becomes affluent than it is for an upwardly-mobile white person. Middle and upper-class persons of either race are victimized most if they live near slums.

Both the N.O.R.C. study (1970) and a more recent government study panel for the National Commission on the Causes and Prevention of Violence conclude that violent crime is predominantly intraracial. Violent crime appears to be markedly higher for blacks than for whites, but blacks also contribute a majority of the victims. The *N.C.C.P.V.* report determined that urban blacks are arrested eight to twenty times more than whites for homicide, rape, aggravated assault, and robbery. Both whites and Negroes tend to commit offenses against members of their own race. The *N.O.R.C.* found that, to the extent that crime is interracial at all, blacks are more likely to be victims of a white offender.

Risk Insurance as an Index of Crime

For crimes against property there is an independent measure of crime; this is the premium rates on the various sublines of burglary insurance. As Price (1966) observes: "Crime rates for crimes against property are highly correlated with premium rates on the most appropriate insurance coverages." There is growing evidence (Falk, 1970) that the urban businessman cannot continue his regular business much longer without burglary and theft insurance at prices he can afford. In January 1968, a Presidential panel studied the areas of Boston, Cleveland, Detroit, Newark, Oakland, and St. Louis affected by riots. They found that 40 percent of the business establishments had severe burglary and theft-insurance problems. Federal Insurance Administrator George Bernstein found in this survey that burglary insurance premiums in Los Angeles have doubled since 1962. Also, in the District of Columbia annual premiums rose to 1028 dollars from 395 dollars for 15,000 dollars burglary coverage on one furniture store. One insurance man conceded in the survey that the only insurance risk he would be willing to take in certain urban areas would be "Pig iron under water."

Social Behavior as an Index of Crime

In 1969 Washington D. C. and its suburbs ranked fourth in national statistics for violent crime *(UCR)*. According to Bryant (1970), a reporter covering the Washington D. C. area, "Crime has become the single most important influence in the way people of the area live and work here in the District of Columbia." As a precaution against crime, Washington households are stocking watchdoys, "peephole" doors, mace, and building fences. Apartment houses take extra security measures. The desk notifies the host of the arrival of visitors and closed circuit TV covers service entrances and exits. Governmental secretaries who must work late at night, park on guarded lots and are escorted to their transportation by guards. Drivers of street buses carry no change to attract thugs. Taxi drivers normally cannot change large bills, and as their cash builds up, they stop off and deposit it with a central office. Social life in Washington has been affected. "Mass parties" are becoming rare because it is difficult to identify uninvited guests. Movement after dark is becoming restricted.

Schumach (1968) after reviewing crime statistics for the New York area and interviewing police and citizens concluded: "Still there is little doubt that the slums of the nineteen-twenties and thirties, for all their poverty and congestion, were much safer for the public than they are today." Schumach noted the changed social behavior of people. Formerly, at night, people often slept on roofs, fire escapes, parks, or beaches in relative safety. Transit policemen were not needed on subway trains late at night, and ice cream shops were not anxious about staying open until midnight to get the business of the late night crowds. "In the slums," writes Schumach, "the poor dig into meager funds to buy iron fences for fire escape windows and reinforced locks and bars for the door." The difference in the crime scene in contemporary New York and during the 1920s Schumach ascribes to the rise of narcotics addiction, racial tensions, and a erosion of the strong community support which the police enjoyed during the 1920s.

Limitations of Official Statistics

The method of reporting utilized by the *Uniform Crime Reports* has been the subject of analysis by a number of sociologists and criminologists since its inception in 1930. (Beattie, 1960; Cressey, 1957; Sellin, 1961; Wolfgang, 1963). The following criticisms will be discussed: (1) use of crime "calendars," (2) defining of a crime as "clearned" when a suspect has been charged regardless of the verdict, (3) failure to base crime rates on a population base reflecting only those persons legally capable of committing a crime, (4) expressing crime rates without some method of weighting their seriousness, and (5) failure to devise a system which would take into consideration "accommodations" which distort present figures.

Although the *UCR* greatly improved the accuracy of its reporting by basing crime rates on annual population estimates, another misrepresentation remains. The *UCR* continues to express changes in volume of crime from one year to another in graphic "crime calendars" and bar graphs without sufficient reference to the importance of population increases. The use of what Wolfgang calls the "tricky alliteration" of summarizing data in the form of "crime clocks" tends, however, to highlight the absolute number of crimes when the crime rate, i.e. the number of crimes per unit of population, is the more important measure.

This "crime clock" is a device which the *UCR* utilizes to "educate the public" on the rising volume of crime. It expresses the number of serious crimes which occur each minute in the United States. For example, in 1970, eleven serious crimes occurred each minute, one forcible rape every fourteen minutes, one murder every thirty-three minutes, one burglary every fifteen seconds, and one larceny every eighteen seconds (*UCR*, 1970).

This "crime clock" presents a distorted view of the crime picture; even if the number of crimes per unit of population remained constant, the "crime clock" would move more rapidly because of increasing population. Conversely, if the population were to decrease and the volume of crime remained constant, the crime rate would actually have increased, yet the "crime clock" would show no change.

Take the presentation of the fact that there were 15,810 murders in the United States in 1970. When portrayed in the "crime clock," it tells us that one murder is committed every thirty-three minutes, a potentially startling figure. Yet, if one divides the number of murders (15,910) by 365 days, the chances of being murdered on a given day in a nation of two hundred million persons is one in 5 million, a considerably less alarming state-of-affairs. And even this figure assumes that all persons in the United States stand the same chance of being the victim of a homicide. When refinements are made with regard to the murder rate in terms of social class, rural-urban residence, etc., the risk of an average citizen falling victim is lessened to the point of near-oblivion. The "crime clock" method of presentation of crime rates does not give us an accurate picture of crime, merely a caricature.

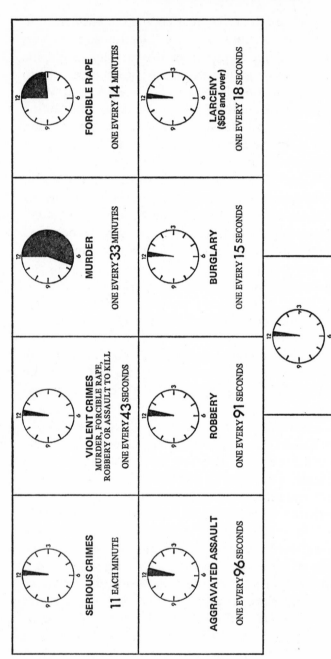

Figure 3-4. Crime Clocks, 1970. *Uniform Crime Reports.* Washington, U.S. Government Printing Office, 1970. Reproduced by permission of the Department of Justice.

Of this method Wolfgang (1963) writes:

> If the purpose of this 'crime clock' is to frighten consumers of the *UCR*, the statements probably succeed, for they are reproduced in scores of newspapers and read by millions, including congressmen, state legislators, and city councilmen who appropriate funds for police budgets. But some other documents should be used for this purpose, not a responsible publication that disseminates official statistics for use by social scientists and other analysts in scholarly research.

The police define a crime as "cleared" when they have enough evidence to take a suspect into custody and charge him with the crime. "Charge," then, to the police statistics serves the same purpose as "guilty" to court records. A crime remains "unsolved" until charges are filed. In effect, the suspect is "innocent" until "charged." The purely juristic view holds that a crime is not validly known to have taken place until a court finds someone guilty of that offense. In England, even today, police statistics are considered less reliable than judicial statistics, reflecting somewhat the lower social prestige of the police than the judiciary (Biderman and Reiss, 1967).

The crime rates presented in the *UCR* are based on the assumption that each person in the United States has the capacity to commit a crime. Legally, there are segments of the population who are not considered capable of forming criminal intent, e.g. children under the age of seven and persons in mental hospitals. Behaviorally, crime is rare in children under the age of twelve and among persons over age fifty. To allow for this, some foreign countries compute crime rates using as a population base "punishable age" or "capable of committing a crime."

Each index offense is assigned the same "weight" in police department reporting. The report of a larceny over fifty dollars is counted as much as a murder. Further, it is not possible to analyze the relationship of "offense" to offenders; the arrest of one person can clear several crimes or several persons may be arrested in the process of clearing one crime.

Superficially, it would seem that the same method utilized in studying changes in mortality would be appropriate for measuring an increase or decrease in criminality. An increase or decrease in the mortality rate is obtained by dividing the number of deaths which occur within the year by the population as it stood at the middle of the year and multiplying the quotient by one thousand. This same method has been used to determine the increase or decrease in criminality. The crime rate is obtained by dividing the total number of crimes of a year by the population and multiplying the result by one thousand. If the result is larger than in the previous year, crime is said to have increased (Robinson, 1969).

The method described above is appropriate for mortality statistics because the variables are identical in their impact on mortality. Whether an individual dies of lung cancer or is run over by a tobacco truck, the result is the same for morality statistics.

With criminal statistics, the situation is different. The only thing that all criminal acts have in common is that they are all labeled crimes. Each fatal disease produces a death, and each death is a phenomenon whose essential characteristics are the same; but even though each criminal act is called a crime, the term crime is used to designate everything from murder to stealing hubcaps. No one would claim that the criminality of a society where one hundred murders occur annually to every one thousand population is the same as the criminality of a society in which the total crime rate consists of one hundred larcenies. The crime rate in an absolute sense is the same in the two societies, but a society which is experiencing an epidemic increase in the murder rate has a much more serious problem than one which is plagued by petty thievery.

In sentencing the prisoner, the judge rates the seriousness of the crime according to its effect on society, and one measure of criminality might be to divide the sum in years of all the sentences imposed during the year by the population as it stood in the middle of the year. Unfortunately, there is too much variation in the sentencing practices of judges for such a system to be an accurate measure of criminality.

The number of reporting agencies has increased from 400 in 1930 to 9200 jurisdictions in 1970. This increased sample size, along with F.B.I. improvements in reporting techniques, has increased the reliability of these statistics. But it should be remembered that the F.B.I. only gathers the statistics. The actual figures are volunteered by local and state law-enforcement agencies. Despite the Bureau's efforts at uniform reporting procedures, the reliability of criminal records varies with the reporting department. The index borrows status from the prestige of the F.B.I. as a crime-fighting agency but, in fact, is only a measure of how many crimes are reported, not an accurate measure of how many crimes are committed. A high total crime index may reflect a "reporting wave" rather than a "crime wave." For example, in 1970 California's "total crime index" (nation's highest) was five times that of Mississippi (nation's lowest), but this is probably due in part to the better reporting system in California.

"Accommodations," the routine and systematic practice on the part of the police, district attorney's office, and judiciary which does not require full implementation of the conviction process in spite of the legal evidence to do so, has an important effect on crime statistics (Newman 1962). The prosecutor has wide discretionary powers in deciding when and what to charge and may even invoke his power of *nolle prosequi,* which means to decline to prosecute. Thus some persons clearly guilty of crimes may never appear in conviction statistics. Further discretionary powers are invested in the judge with respect to sentencing. A judge[4] may accept a "plea bargain," i.e. a plea of guilty in return for a lesser charge and sentence. The judge may even refuse to convict. Newman (1962) refers to the practice of a Detroit judge who routinely acquitted both prostitutes and homosexuals when, in his opinion, members of the vice squad had enticed them into criminal conduct. Offenders turning states evidence, as in the case of some of the Watergate defendants, may be granted immunity and acquittal. The reduction process modifies the label and the sentence of the persons convicted; therefore, any generalizations about the crime problem from conviction statistics is of limited value. While it is necessary to be aware of the two accommodations, acquittal and reduction, and their effect on the validity of crime statistics, the process itself is a necessary and wise one if the law is to func-

---

[4]Legally and technically, a judge is not supposed to be aware of the "plea bargains" negotiated by the district attorney's office.

tion in a flexible and realistic manner.

Difficulty in producing criminal statistics on a national scale is due to the structure of law enforcement in the United States, i.e. it is a function of state and local government, and there is no authority which can compel cooperation in reporting crime data. (Lejins, 1966). Any evaluation of the Reports should take into consideration the magnitude of the task of obtaining the voluntary cooperation of over 9,000 independent reporting units. Only an organization with the level of prestige among law-enforcement personnel such as the F.B.I. could accomplish this. The Bureau of the Census, for example, has been unable to secure the cooperation of the judiciary throughout the U. S. to develop judicial crime statistics. Lejins reminds those who would criticize the Reports that, as a statistical series, they are intended to be a statistical house organ of the police, and he feels it unfair to fault them for failing to be something for which they were never intended.

"House organ" or not, there remains considerable evidence to support the view of Sellin when he remarked that, "The U. S. . . . . has the worst criminal statistics of any major country in the Western world." (*Life,* Sept. 9, 1957). The Reports are the only compilation of crime statistics on a national scale. In the United States there are no national comprehensive judicial criminal statistics, no national probation or parole statistics, no national statistics on the dispositions of grand juries. In short, we have national statistics covering only one step of criminal procedure, the arrest stage.

Finally, the President's task force commission on law enforcement (1967) pointed out that at least four major governmental studies of national criminal statistics were made between the years 1934-1965, and each concluded there was a critical need for a strong, effective Federal statistical program.

The Task Force Report recommended the establishment of a National Criminal Justice Statistics Center either in the Bureau of the Census or as an independent agency. Such an agency would be responsible for bringing about improvements in the gathering, compiling, and interpreting of national crime date. Until such a recommendation becomes a reality, and crime statistics on a national scale can be tabulated with the efficiency and clarity now achieved by the California system, the scientific study of crime will be seriously impaired.

A big step toward the creation of such a national system was taken in June of 1969, when six states, Arizona, California, Maryland, Michigan, Minnesota and New York were selected by the Law Enforcement Assistance Administration as participants in project SEARCH, an accronym for system for electronic analysis and retrieval of criminal histories. Later additions of five states have raised the total participants to fifteen. The project is designed to give criminal justice agencies needed information on offenders in a matter of seconds. Each state participating has its own computer system which included a file of 10,000 representative offender criminal histories. A national central index containing limited criminal history summaries of all state files is maintained by the Michigan State Police, Lansing, Michigan. Long range plans call for the creation of a national system. If this is accomplished, SEARCH would provide a basis for a complete statistical system on every component of the criminal justice system—both within each state and nationally.

Summary

In this chapter we have attempted to locate the frequency, distribution, and characteristics of crime in the United States. Using the incidence rates furnished by the F.B.I.'s *Uniform Crime Reports,* we learned that the crime rate increased 144 percent from 1960-1970. Epidemiologically, crime is associated with young, black males living in urban areas. All seven major Index offenses show an increase (although homicide rates still have not reached depression levels). Independent surveys, risk insurance rates, and social behavior all point to the increased prevalence of criminal acts in American society. Limitations of official statistics, both as to methods of fact gathering and presentation, were discussed and the hope expressed that eventually we may see the creation of a mandatory reporting system to a national research agency. One final caveat must be issued: A rate-producing process is not reducible to the enumeration of criminal acts but reflects the characteristics of the offender, his potential victims, and the attitude of the police—all operating within a community tolerance level.

REFERENCES

Beattie, R.H.: Criminals and statistics in the United States: 1960. *Journal of Criminal Law, Criminology and Police Science, 51*:49-65, 1960.

Bryant, G.: The crime problem overshadows lives in Washington, D.C. *The Daily Reflector* (Greenville, N.C.), August 16, p. 5, 1970.

Cressey, D.R.: The state of criminal statistics. *NPPA Journal, 3*:230-241, 1957.

Ennis, P.H.: Crime, victims, and the police. *Trans-Action, 4*:36-44, 1967.

Falk, Carol H.: Federal pressure is mounting on insurers to make criminal policies available in cities. *The Wall Street Journal,* September 10, p. 30 1970.

Federal Bureau of Investigation: *Uniform Crime Reports: 1970.* Washington, U.S. Government Printing Office, 1970.

Federal Bureau of Prisons. *National Prisoner Statistics, 45:*(August), 1969.

Geis, G.: Statistics concerning race and crime. *Crime and Delinquency, 11:* 142-150, 1965.

Glaser, D.: *The Effectiveness of a Prison and Parole System.* New York, Bobbs-Merrill, 1969.

Glaser, D.: Victim survey research: theoretical implications. In Guenther, A.L. (Ed.), *Criminal Behavior and Social Systems.* New York, Harper and Row, 1970.

Hoover, J.E.: The faith of free men. *Vital Speeches of the Day, 32*:71-74, 1965.

Lejins, P.: The Uniform Crime Reports. *Michigan Law Review, 64*:1011-1030, 1966.

Newman, D.J.: The effects of accommodations in justice administration on criminal statistics. *Sociology and Social Research, 46*:144-155, 1962.

Price, J.E.: A test of the accuracy of crime statistics. *Social Problems, 14*:214-222, 1966.

Robinson, L.N.: *History and Organization of Criminal Statistics in the United States.* Montclair, N.J., Patterson Smith, 1969.

Schumach, M.: Crime statistics often numbers game. *New York Times,* February 4, p. 58, 1968.

Sellin, T.: The significance of records of crime. *The Law Quarterly Review, 67*:489-504, 1961.

The President's Commission on Law Enforcement and the Administration of Justice: *Crime and its Impact—an Assessment.* Washington, U.S. Government Printing Office, 1967.

Violence mostly intra-racial. *The Raleigh News and Observer,* September 9, p. 7, 1970.

Wambaugh, J.: *The New Centurions.* Boston, Little, Brown and Company, 1970.

Wolfgang, M.E.: Uniform Crime Reports: a Critical Appraisal. *University of Pennsylvania Law Review, 3:*408-438, 1963.

Part II

THEORIES OF CRIME CAUSATION

As WE NOTED IN CHAPTER 2 (Research and Theory in Criminology), two of the main purposes of theory are to organize existing information into a coherent, systematic framework and to orient further research by establishing potentially fruitful directions for further exploration. In the case of criminological theories, there is an additional and quite significant objective: to provide some logical basis for programs aimed at controlling, reducing, eliminating, or preventing criminal and delinquent behavior.

But we have already encountered some of the difficulties involved in the formulation of comprehensive and adequate theories of the origins or determinants of criminality, one of which is the problem of defining accurately what constitutes antisocial behavior. Says Shore (1971) :

> Antisocial behavior is not a diagnostic category or unitary phenomenon closely tied to cultural values and often dependent upon the interpretation given a behavior pattern by these agencies responsible for the regulation of social interaction. In certain communities, for example, the tolerance for deviance is lower and certain behavior may be labeled antisocial which, in another context, would not be considered deviant at all.

Nevertheless, Shore points out, there are some people who engage in violent, aggressive behavior despite the advantage of the best social opportunities; others, on the other hand, who are subjected to extremely poor social conditions do not exhibit criminal or delinquent behavior. Thus, Shore concludes, "aside from the

91

need to understand and explain the social and cultural forces that foster criminal behavior, *there is need for a theory of individual behavior that can account for individual differences and the ways in which individuals interpret and respond to social forces"* (italics added). In our view, this is the basic task which confronts criminological theory.

As the material presented in Chapters 4, 5, and 6 demonstrates, research on the causes of criminal behavior has been directed toward three major areas of inquiry: (1) biological factors and genetic predispositions; (2) psychological differences between individuals; and (3) societal influences. The biologist has sought explanations for criminality in the constitutional makeup of the offender; the psychologist and psychiatrist have sought the explanations for criminality in the personality confliguration of the offender; and the sociologist has sought explanations for criminality in the processes which affect the behavior of people living in societal groups. The sociological viewpoint is concerned with attempts to determine how certain acts become defined as crimes, with the manner in which the organizational structures of a society create pressures toward deviance, and with the societal values which dictate acceptable modes of social control and treatment.

At the present time, there is no "grand theory" of criminality which encompasses all approaches to crime and organizes the empirical findings of each discipline into some coherent, integrated schema. For the time being, at least, we must be content with either theories of the "middle range," i.e. those which account for only a limited number of facts about crime, or with "microtheories" that are even further restricted in their range of content and generality than those of the middle range. Some of the biological, psychological, and psychiatric theories we shall examine in Chapters 5 and 6 fall at the extremes of grand theory and microtheory; all of the sociological theories we have discussed in Chapter 4, however, are theories of the middle range.

But criminological theories and theorists do not merely diverge along the clear lines drawn by professional specialization. In recent years deep-seated differences in value orientation and ideology among criminologists have created schismatic tendencies that cut into, as well as across, disciplinary identifications. For the sake of convenience and at the extreme risk of oversimplification, we might identify the respective viewpoints involved as *humanistic* and *scientific-technological*. Once again, we must emphasize that these terms refer to orientations not pigeon holes. The majority of contemporary criminologists, including the authors of the present book, are still gingerly walking a path between the two opposing camps.

The divergence between these orientations is most readily apprehended, perhaps, in their respective outlook on the disposition of criminal offenders. The humanist views the offender as a victim of unfair societal arrangements and conceptualizes the rehabilitative process in terms of reparative resocialization. The scientific-technological criminologist conceives of change in the criminal offender as *behavioral change,* the accomplishment of which is the end result of a behavioral technology based on principles that have been discovered and validated in the experimental laboratory.

Humanism, according to Braden (1971), is broadly defined as a concept of life that puts primary emphasis on the dignity, value, and welfare of individual human beings:

> . . . right now, today, at this moment, on this planet . . . Humanists in this sense would, for example, rather feed the hungry than fly to Jupiter, or at least would feed the hungry before flying to Jupiter; they would also deny that man is some kind of genetic Erector Set for biologists to take apart and put together at their whim; humanists do not consider efficiency an end in itself and therefore will often seek the most satisfying line between two points, not necessarily the shortest; they do not feel challenged to do something simply to prove that the thing can be done, or to climb mountains because they are there; finally, they are not preoccupied with the abstractions of theoretical science ("What is life?") but are more inclined to ask themselves: "What is a good life?"

Humanists insist upon voluntarism and freedom; they charge the scientific-technological group with exploiting conformity and determinism.

As Glock and Stark (1965) have observed, "the basic methodological assumption which has come to inform the social sciences is that man's behavior is determined in the same way that other natural phenomena are determined: that potentially every human act can be understood as a result of antecedent factors which operate to make the act inevitable." B. F. Skinner, in *Beyond Freedom and Dignity* (1971), has drawn the behavioral conclusion from this deterministic assumption that human beings are incapable of regulating their own behavior through the exercise of free will. Only by disposing of the notion of autonomous man, Skinner asserts, can we gain access to the true determinents of behavior.

This focus on behavioral science and the capacity for behavioral control that it has generated through technology leaves a bad taste in the mouth of the humanistically oriented criminologist. To him it implies the loss of freedom at the hands of a bureaucratic elite who possess the power to exercise such control. As David Wexler, a professor of law at the University of Arizona, has pointed out in a recent article in the *California Law Review* (1973), the courts have begun to question the legal implications raised by behavior modification techniques and their employment within institutions.

It is beyond both the scope and the appropriate concerns of this book to examine the controversy between the humanistic and scientific-technological orientations in criminology in greater depth. Our purpose in alerting the reader to the existence of this controversy is twofold. In the first place, it is one important reason, among many, why criminology has been unable to formulate anything approximating an integrative theory of criminality. Fundamentally involved here are differences in philosophical presupposition which lie outside the bounds of empirical verification: questions of free will versus determinism, intuition versus scientific method, etc. Secondly, the presence of this schism in viewpoint among criminologists helps explain, in part, some basic contradictions in approaches to the disposition of the criminal offender.

REFERENCES

Braden, W.: *The Age of Aquarius: Technology and the Cultural Revolution.* New York, Pocket Books, 1971.

Glock, C.Y. and Stark, R.: *Religion and Society in Tension*. Chicago, Rand McNally, 1965.

Shore, M.F.: Psychological theories of the causes of antisocial behavior. *Crime and Delinquency, 17*:456-468, 1971.

Skinner, B.F.: *Beyond Freedom and Dignity*. New York, Alfred Knopf, 1971.

Wexler, D.B.: Token and taboo: behavior modification, token economies, and the law. *California Law Review, 61*:81-109, 1973.

Chapter 4
SOCIOLOGICAL THEORIES
OF CRIMINALITY

CRIME AS INEVITABLE

THE FRENCH SOCIOLOGIST EMILE DURKHEIM (1858-1917) was the first to point out the "normality" of crime (Durkheim, 1950). Human behavior is not intrinsically either "normal" or "pathological," certain forms of conduct simply become labelled so by the host society. Crime is present in all societies; its form changes, but universally men act in such a way as to bring societal repression. It is a normal, regrettable, and inevitable phenomenon of any society characterized by heterogeneity and change.

A society exempt from crime is utterly impossible. The collective sentiments which are protected by penal law have their genesis in reaction to former outrages. For murder to disappear, the horror of bloodshed must become greater in the social strata from which murderers are recruited. The strong states of common consciousness cannot be reinforced without reinforcing feeble states. As the public conscience becomes more sensitive to larger crimes, its toleration of acts once viewed as peccadilloes lessens. Thus, in a society of saints, "singing too loud in church" might be punished as severely as robbery would be punished in a prison grouping.

Since all life experiences are not homogeneous, all societal members do not undergo identical socialization. There must of necessity be some deviants. Nor would a crime-less society necessarily be a desirable situation. Crime, as an avenue of change, can be the harbinger of a new morality, e.g. the death of Socrates for intellectual freedom, and the black freedom riders who engaged

97

in civil disobedience in the interest of greater societal justice. Persons so motivated would justify their actions, saying at times it is necessary to "be illegal in order to not become immoral."

CRIME AND THE SOCIAL STRUCTURE

A second contribution of Durkheim to our understanding of deviant behavior grew out of his attempts to show how suicide is related to an individual's integration or lack of integration into social groups. One cause of suicide, according to Durkheim, results from a condition of "anomie"—a situation in which persons lack integration in stable groups, resulting in a condition of "rootlessness" and "normlessness."

This concept of "anomie" was extended by the contemporary American sociologist Robert K. Merton into a functionalist analysis of the social structure of the United States. Merton's article "Social Structure and Anomie" was first published in 1938 and expresses the theoretical orientation of a functional analyst who considers socially deviant behavior just as much a product of the social structure as conformist behavior. It is in opposition to the Freudian and neo-Freudians who see the structure of society as restraining the free expression of man's nature so that periodically man breaks into open revolt against these restraints toward freedom.

Rather than seeking the explanation for deviant behavior in the pathological personalities of the individual, the functional analyst attempts to determine how the socio-cultural structure exerts pressure toward deviation upon people variously located in that structure. They seek an answer to the question: Why does the frequency of deviant behavior vary with social structure?

The structure of society is composed of a number of elements, but two are of essential importance to Merton's analysis: (1) the culturally defined goals, those objectives defined as legitimate for all to strive toward, and (2) the regulatory norms which define and control the means of achieving the goals. It is the central hypothesis of Merton that aberrant behavior may be regarded sociologically as a symptom of dissociation between culturally prescribed aspirations and socially structured avenues for realizing these aspirations. He uses the example of athletics as an analogy. If "winning" is stressed (goal) to the neglect of emphasis upon winning by the rules, the chances for reaching the goal by deviant means is increased. Athletics as a microcosm of American values is dominated by the philosophy of Coach Vince Lombardi, who said, "Winning is not everything, it is the *only* thing." The admonition of sports writer Grantland Rice—"it doesn't matter if you win or lose but how you play the game"—amounts to athletic heresy.

In American society wealth is a basic symbol of success. Money obtained illegally can be spent just as easily as "hard earned" money and can be translated into the symbols of success. Merton sees American society as placing a heavy emphasis on wealth without an equivalent emphasis upon following legitimate avenues toward reaching this goal. He identifies five types of individual adaptation to this situation. People may shift from one of these adaptations to another as their role and place in the social structure changes. These categories refer to role behavior in specific types of situations and are not an analysis of personality types.

The first adaptation Merton isolates is one of *conformity*. In a stable society, this adaptation is most common and the individual accepts both the cultural goals and the institutionalized means for achieving them. A second adaptation is termed *innovation;* here the individual has assimilated the cultural emphasis upon the goals of society, without also internalizing the institutional norms governing their attainment. When we have an emphasis on monetary success and add to it a social structure which limits the available approved means, there is tension toward innovative practices, resulting in a man like Al Capone.

In the *ritualistic* response, the individual has abandoned the lofty cultural goals of great wealth to a point where his aspirations can be met. Lower aspirations provide an escape from frustration and anxiety, and the individual only goes through the motions of his eight-to-five treadmill of a job. Merton sees lower-middle class Americans as being heavily represented among those making the ritualistic adaptation.

Psychotics, vagrants, drunkards, and drug addicts Merton classifies as making a *retreatist* adaptation to stress. They have given up culturally prescribed goals, and their behavior does not accord with institutional norms. These are society's drop outs. They cannot succeed legitimately and will not resort to illegitimate means. The final adaptation, *rebellion,* is exhibited by persons dissatisfied with both the goals and the norms of the existing state of affairs and who wish to bring in a new social structure, e.g. revolutionaries such as Castro in Cuba.

Masculine Identification Crisis

Talcott Parsons (1954) points out that because the occupational tasks of the typical American father require that they be performed outside the home, female-centered households result. Boys gravitate toward the mother as the central object of identification until they reach adolescence. At this juncture they encounter strong cultural expectations that they behave as males. Immersed in a feminine milieu and unsure of their own identification, they tend to protest against femininity. Aggressive, malicious, irresponsible, and destructive acts may be interpreted as a masculine protest or a compulsive reaction formation.

Cloward and Ohlin (1960) see this approach as inadequate. The theory provides no clear definitions of the types of deviant behavior that are supposedly explained by problems of masculine identification. Of what type delinquent behavior is masculine identification crisis a source? If X (masculine identification crisis) then we can predict . . . .?? An emphasis on toughness, aggressiveness, and hedonism may result in young men playing football and going to dances, rather than gang-fights and illegal drugs. Cloward and Ohlin conclude: "'Proponents of the masculine-identity crisis theory have not as yet been able to show a correspondence between the distribution of values emphasizing masculinity and the distribution of norms prescribing delinquent acts" (1960) .

There is even disagreement as to the distribution of the female-centered family. If the theory is valid, changes in delinquent patterns would be related to changes in problems of masculine identification. Increases in delinquency would be preceded by a greater difficulty on the part of boys to achieve a masculine identity.

Frustrated Access to Adult Status

The passage from childhood to adult status is acknowledged to be especially difficult because of our complex technological occupational structure. Male adolescents must spend a prolonged time in preparation for the occupational roles to which they aspire. During this time they are forced to remain in a state of social, economic, and legal dependency. The frustrations generated by this enforced "delayed gratification" (money, autonomy, legal sexual relations) exert pressure toward deviance. The status needs, denied adolescents by the general society, may be fulfilled by a gang culture (Bloch and Neiderhoffer, 1958). But all gangs are not delinquent gangs. It has not been shown that adolescent status deprivation necessarily leads to delinquent behavior. As Cloward and Ohlin (1960) state: "The theory of adolescent protest may help to explain the emergence of "youth culture," but it does not explain the conditions under which delinquent subcultures develop."

There are a number of questions which must be clarified if proponents of an "adolescent-crisis" theory are to present an adequate picture of the origin and development of delinquent subcultures.

Adult status will come eventually. Does this status deprivation weigh more heavily on the middle-class adolescent because he must delay much longer his expected adult role in a profession? Or, is it more frustrating to the lower-class boy because he has not been socialized to delay gratification to the same degree as his middle-class counterpart? If delinquency rates are increasing, has there been a corresponding increase in the difficulties associated with the transition from adolescence to adulthood? Bloch and Niederhoffer hold that most lower-class delinquency is rational, disciplined, and utilitarian. (They steal money or property rather than vandalize). Why should the frustrations of adolescence yield disciplined behavior rather than the reverse? Finally, Bloch and Niederhoffer attribute the rise in modern delinquency to "pathological states of mind"—a psychological answer unrelated to the original sociological problem, namely the rise of delinquent subcultures.

Delinquent Subculture

The term "delinquent subculture" has been used to denote an antisocial way of life that has somehow become traditional in a society (Cohen, 1955). The impact of membership in a given subculture upon the individual can be better understood if the community is visualized as "defining" or interpreting situations, thereby setting up standards upon the basis of which its members may act. Accordingly, some theorists have hypothesized that if the community is disorganized and weak in its control, it will be easier for the institutions within the community to disintegrate, thus bringing about a breakdown in communication between the generations within one institution (such as the family or the school). As a result, behavior will not be controlled by conventional (middle class) standards. On the other hand, if the community standards are positive, i.e. not disorganized, but not according to accepted codes of the conventional society, the normal learned behavior may be contrary to the standards of the larger society (Glaser, 1965; Shaw et al, 1929). It is thus important to examine the character of the community in which delinquent behavior arises.

Lower Class Culture and Delinquency

A principal advocate of the "culture conflict" approach to delinquency has been Walter B. Miller (1958). He does not go so far as to posit that the lower class in America is a criminal class but sees delinquency as the result of an "intensified response" of some boys to the "focal areas of concern" found in the lower-class culture. The values of the lower-class are seen as distinct from those of the middle-class. The lower-class youth who conform to these values find themselves in inevitable conflict with the prevailing middle-class mores and the law.

Miller uses the concept "focal concern" in preference to the concept "value," reasoning that it is more "readily derivable" from field observation, is descriptively neutral, and facilitates analysis of subcultural differences since it reflects actual behavior uncolored by an official "ideal."

These six "focal areas of concern" are presented in order of the degree accorded each, thus, representing a weighted rank. Concern over "trouble" means avoiding entanglements with official authorities or agencies of middle class society. "Toughness" (bodily tattooing, absence of sentimentality, bravery) is seen as related to being reared in a female-based household (matriarchy). There is almost an obsessive lower-class concern with masculinity and a concern (fear?) over homosexuality expressed in baiting "queers." "Smartness" is defined as the ability to obtain the maximum amount of goods and status with a minimum of physical effort (con-man). Traditionally the deadening routine of lower-class life has led its inhabitants to seek relief in gin or evangelism; Miller's delinquents seek "excitement" in booze, bands, and "broads." Related to the belief among the lower-class that goal-directed efforts are futile is their concept of "fate." Many lower-class persons view their lives as subject to a destiny over which they have no control. (This attitude serves both as an inhibitor to initiative and as a compensation for failure.) Miller sees the lower-class emphasis on "autonomy" as expressing itself in an ambivalent attitude toward authority, i.e. a resentment of external controls while actively seeking out restrictive environments (army enlistments). Their entire life-style is summed-up in the proverb: "Trouble is what life gets you into."

Cloward and Ohlin (1960) criticize the approach of Miller in four areas: (1) Miller's definition of delinquent gangs should differentiate between those who, at best, tolerate delinquency from those who require law-breaking as a criteria for membership. (2) All delinquent acts are not committed by adolescents who are members of the lower-class. Miller's approach does not adequately describe inter-class delinquency, the distribution of delinquency throughout the social structure. (His view that the middle-class adopt lower-class values via the mass media would seem to reverse the expected route of social change.) (3) The conflict between the two classes would presuppose a radical cultural separateness, yet serious felonies violate lower-class values as well as middle-class values. (4) The approach of Miller does not explain the origin of delinquency and regards delinquent norms as "given." While a "culture-conflict" approach might explain a reduction in delinquency as the result of acculturation, it is harder pressed to provide an explanation for an increase in delinquency.

These criticisms should not overshadow the contribution to delinquency theory made by Miller's research. Matza (1964), while regretting the radical cultural determinism of Miller, described his work as a "detailed and perceptive ethnography of slum life"; and Savitz (1967) says of it, "In many ways, Miller's view of lower-class life and the way it relates to delinquency remains the most persuasive model of delinquency currently available."

Delinquency and Social Values

Of particular interest to various social scientists has been the question of how and why unconventional values arise in some groups or subcultures. Among others, Cohen (1955, 1966) has tried to furnish an explanation for this phenomenon. According to him, a collective way of life, a subculture, develops when a number of people with a common problem of adjustment are in effective interaction. The chief common problems around which the delinquent subculture revolves appear to be status problems: Certain children, particularly lower-class children, are denied status in the respectable middle-class society because they cannot meet the criteria of the respectable status system. According to Cohen, the delinquent subculture deals with these problems by providing criteria of status which these children are able to meet. Specifically, the delinquent subculture functions simultaneously to combat internal forces in the individual as represented by a "gnawing sense of inadequacy and low self esteem" and to deal with "the hated agents of the middle class." It does so by erecting a counter-culture which offers "an alternative set of status criteria." The alternative status criteria offered by the delinquent subculture are in direct opposition to those of the middle-class, to the point of rendering a "non-utilitarian, malicious, and negativistic" quality to the subculture. Expanding on the nature of the norms held by the delinquent subculture, Cohen stated:

> The delinquent subculture is not only a set of rules, a design for living which is different from or indifferent to or even in conflict with the norms of the "respectable" adult society. It would appear at least plausible that it is defined by its "negative polarity" to those norms. That is, the delinquent subculture takes its norms from the larger culture but terms them upside down. The delinquent's conduct is right, by the standards of his subculture, precisely *because* it is wrong by the norms of the larger culture (1966).

Although Cohen characterized the norms of the delinquent subculture by their "negative polarity," when compared to the norms of the larger cultural group, it is questionable whether differences between the two sets of values are as clear-cut as his "negative polarity" statement would suggest. As Kobrin (1966) has pointed out, the facts indicate that in high delinquency areas a substantial number of boys who possess police and court records become conventional and law-abiding citizens. Moreover, Kobrin stated, there is evidence that of those who are without juvenile records, many become adult offenders. This apparent reversal of careers is incomprehensible, according to Kobrin, except on the assumption that the individual participates simultaneously in both criminal and conventional value systems. Taking into consideration the constant bombardment which the lower-class boy receives from the educational and news media, representing mainly middle-class values, such a statement appears to be reasonable. Cohen recognized the fact that in such high delinquency areas, the individuals share in both criminal and conventional value systems. As such, he suggested that the individual who finds himself in this conflict-of-values situation may choose among three alternatives: (a) he might accept the middle-class system of values completely; or (b) he might temporize with it; or (c) he might reject it completely. The last alternative would be the one presented by the delinquent subculture.

Complete rejection of the middle-class value system does not solve all of the delinquent's problems; the mere fact that he has internalized these middle-class norms is troublesome to the delinquent. In Cohen's words: ". . . the delinquent boy has internalized the respectable value system, is therefore profoundly ambivalent about his own delinquent behavior, and most contend continuously with the claims of the respectable value system . . ." (Cohen and Short, 1958). Cohen suggested that the delinquent develops reaction-formation mechanisms to deal with this ambivalence. Reaction-formation is then manifested in an "irrational, malicious, unaccountable hostility" towards the norms of the respectable middle-class society (Cohen, 1955).

Cohen summarized his position in the following manner:

> . . . the delinquent subculture . . . (was explained) . . . as a system of beliefs and values generated in a process of communicative interaction among children similarly circumstanced by virtue of their positions in the social structure, and as constituting a solution to problems of adjustment to which the established culture provided no satisfactory solutions. These problems are largely problems of status and self-respect arising among working-class children as a result of socially structured inability to meet the standards of the established culture; the delinquent subculture, with its characteristics of non-utilitarianism, malice, and negativism, provides an alternative status system and justifies, for those who participate in it, hostility and aggression against the sources of their status frustration (Cohen and Short, 1958).

The delinquent subculture theory, as suggested by Cohen, has as its primary concern the explanation of the development of subcultures distinctive of working class male juveniles. It does not purport to explain delinquency in the middle class or female delinquency.

To summarize, it could be stated that, according to certain theoretical positions, some, perhaps the majority of, delinquents may be attributed to differences in the system of values held by other members of society.

The conception of delinquency advanced by the subcultural theory poses a question of the nature of the system of values held by delinquents. Are these values, as maintained by the theory, in reality different from those of the "respectable" society, or are the values held by delinquents basically the same as those of the larger society? If, indeed, delinquents share in a distinctive set of values which are different from those of the middle class, what are its distinctive features?

The Measurement of Values

One procedure which could throw light upon the nature of the values held by delinquents would be to determine the amount of seriousness which samples of delinquents ascribe to different criminal offenses. This is, essentially, a task that involves assessment of the delinquent's value system. Sellin and Wolfgang (1964) have sought to accomplish this objective in a series of research studies which has been described as "the most advanced attempt yet to measure delinquency, an essentially qualitative phenomenon, in quantitative terms" (Rose, 1966). Sellin and his colleagues sought to obtain judgments about the seriousness of crime from carefully selected groups:[1] university students, police line officers, Juvenile Court Division officers, and Juvenile Court judges. The expectation was that consensus within these groups might produce a series of weighted values that would be valid for measuring the extent of delinquency in an area. Although Sellin and Wolfgang's main purpose was the construction of an index of delinquency, the methodology they utilized for determining degrees of seriousness of crimes provides us with a tool with which to quantify the value judgments of both delinquents and non-delinquents. In addition, Sellin and Wolfgang's study provides us with a list of criminal offenses which were thoughtfully chosen and for which a considerable amount of data has been collected, especially on middle-class samples.

The results obtained by Sellin and Wolfgang indicated that groups representative of middle-class standards substantially agree in their judgments. That results suggested by other groups of raters would be substantially different might be determined empirically. Sellin and Wolfgang believe that there would be intrinsic interest in studying not only middle-class groups, but a variety of subcultural groups as well as the judgments of the offenders themselves. In this vein they hypothesized, on the basis of

---

[1]These selections were guided by the idea that the principal cultural themes of legal proscriptions and sanctions come from the middle-class value system. Although the selected groups could be expected to differ in socioeconomic level, it was argued that these groups would be representatives and carriers of middle-class values (Sellin and Wolfgang, 1964).

their data, that the relative offense score values would be pre-served among different groups of raters.

Cross Cultural Studies of Values

Sellin and Wolfgang based their opinion regarding consistency of rating between cultures, partly on cross-cultural studies conducted by Bacon and his colleagues (Bacon, Child, and Barry, 1963) and by Brown (1952). Bacon et al, set out to study correlates of crimes particularly theft and crime, in different preliterate cultures. The results of Bacon's study suggested that even among preliterate societies the most severe prohibitions of Western society could be found. Brown also studied such societies, specifically examining them in terms of the severity of punishment for specific types of sexual behavior on a scale ranging from one (a mild penalty) to four (a severe penalty). It is interesting to note that Sellin and Wolfgang found it possible to compare six offenses for which Brown obtained punishment ratings with mean category scale scores from one of their student groups.

Normandeau (1966) conducted a partial replication of Sellin and Wolfgang's study, utilizing French-Canadian subjects in Montreal. Normandeau considered his study, in part, to be a partial investigation of Sellin and Wolfgang's hypothesis of uniformity of attitude in the judging of criminal offenses over a wide range of subjects. In short, Normandeau found some difference between cultures but explained that concern about the seriousness of crime grows at a faster rate in Montreal than in Philadelphia, at least for the subjects tested.

A study by Akman, Normandeau, and Turner (1967) utilizing a larger number of Canadian subjects than the Normandeau study, and also making comparisons with Philadelphia groups from Sellin and Wolfgang's study, confirmed the findings of the Normandeau study. Although these authors found the same differences between Canadian and Philadelphia subjects as in the Normandeau study, they concluded that "on the whole . . . differences between the judgments of Canadian and Philadelphian subjects are minimum."

Conclusion

To recapitulate, Cohen's theory of delinquent subculture characterized the delinquent as a person who possesses antagonisms against the values of middle-class culture. Such antagonism is a result of status-deprivation or frustration arising mainly in lower-class children. This status deprivation leads to a search for alternate status criteria and the development of reaction-formation against the values of the middle class as a solution to the problem. Such would imply that delinquents reject middle-class values, while non-delinquents either accept these values completely or learn to temporize with them. However, the work of Normandeau et al, along with the work of others, has failed to obtain such value differences between samples of delinquents and non-delinquents. Sellin and Wolfgang were also correct in their assumption that different subcultural groups would rate offenses in a way similar to the ratings made by their Pennsylvania middle-class groups. Such findings and such a hypothesis are definitely in disagreement with Cohen's theory of delinquent subculture as it pertains to cross cultural value ratings.

In defense of Cohen, it is worth noting that similarity in knowledge concerning values does not designate similarity in value acceptance or actual similarity. Consequently, tests of a stricter nature should be offered to measure the degree of internalization of values.

In the absence of sufficient empirical data, the implications of "delinquent subculture" cannot be ascertained. Only the superficial value consciousness of certain individuals can be weighed.

DIFFERENTIAL ASSOCIATION: THE PRINCIPLE OF NORMATIVE CONFLICT

Differential association was an attempt by Professor Edwin H. Sutherland to find the "sufficient and necessary cause" of crime. Dissatisfied with multiple causation theory which admits exceptions in advance, Sutherland sought to abstract from known facts about crime a universal factor applicable to all cases. He sought the single-factor in the application of learning theory to the phenomenon of crime; thus, he stands in the tradition of Gabriel Tarde whose doctrine of imitation stated that men imitate others in proportion to the closeness of their contacts (Tarde, 1912).

The principal thesis of differential association is: "A person becomes delinquent because of an excess of definitions favorable to violation of law over definitions unfavorable to violation of law." With the death of Professor Sutherland the chief proponent and apologist for the theory today is Donald Cressey, his student and colleague. The basic principles are:

1. Criminal behavior is learned. Negatively, this means that criminal behavior, as such, is not inherited; also, the person who is not already trained in crime does not invent criminal behavior, just as a person does not make mechanical inventions unless he has had training in mechanics.

2. Criminal behavior is learned in interaction with other persons in a process of communication. This communication is verbal in many respects but includes all "the communication of gestures."

3. The principal part of the learning of criminal behavior occurs within intimate personal groups. Negatively, this means that the impersonal agencies of communication, such as movies and newspapers, play a relatively unimportant part in the genesis of criminal behavior.

4. When criminal behavior is learned, the learning includes (a) techniques of committing the crime, which are sometimes very complicated, sometimes very simple; (b) the specific direction of motives, drives, rationalizations, and attitudes.

5. The specific direction of motives and drives is learned from definitions of the legal codes as favorable or unfavorable. In some societies an individual is surrounded by persons who invariably define the legal codes as rules to be observed, while in others he is surrounded by persons whose definitions are favorable to the violation of the legal codes. In our American society these definitions are almost always mixed, with the consequence that we have culture conflict in relation to the legal codes.

6. A person becomes delinquent because of an excess of definitions favorable to violation of law over definitions unfavorable to

violation of law. This is the principle of differential association. It refers to both criminal and anti-criminal associations and has to do with counteracting forces. When persons become criminal, they do so because of contacts with criminal patterns and also because of isolation from anticriminal patterns. Any person inevitably assimilates the surrounding culture unless other patterns are in conflict; a Southerner does not pronounce "r" because other Southerners do not pronounce "r". Negatively, this proposition of differential association means that associations which are neutral so far as crime is concerned have little or no effect on the genesis of criminal behavior. Much of the experience of a person is neutral in this sense, e.g. learning to brush one's teeth. This behavior has no negative or positive effect on criminal behavior except as it may relate to associations which are concerned with the legal codes. This neutral behavior is important especially as an occupier of the time of a child so that he is not in contact with criminal behavior during the time he is so engaged in the neutral behavior.

7. Differential associations may vary in frequency, duration, priority, and intensity. This means that associations with criminal behavior and also associations with anti-criminal behavior vary in those respects. "Frequency" and "duration" as modalities of associations are obvious and need no explanation. "Priority" is assumed to be important in the sense that lawful behavior developed in early childhood may persist throughout life, and also that delinquent behavior developed in early childhood may persist throughout life. This tendency however, has not been adequately demonstrated, and priority seems to be important principally through its selective influence. "Intensity" is not precisely defined, but it has to do with such things as the prestige of the source of a criminal or anti-criminal pattern and with emotional reactions related to the associations. In a precise description of the criminal behavior of a person, these modalities would be stated in quantitative form and a mathematical ratio be reached. A formula in this sense has not been developed, and the development of such a formula would be extremely difficult.

8. The process of learning criminal behavior by association

with criminal and anti-criminal patterns involves all of the mechanisms that are involved in any other learning. Negatively, this means that the learning of criminal behavior is not restricted to the process of imitation. A person who is seduced, for instance, learns criminal behavior by association, but this process would not ordinarily be described as imitation.

9. While criminal behavior is an expression of general needs and values, it is not explained by those general needs and values since noncriminal behavior is an expression of the same needs and values. Thieves generally steal to secure money, but likewise honest laborers work to secure money. The attempts by many scholars to explain criminal behavior by general drives and values, such as the happiness principle, striving for social status, the money motive, or frustration, have been and must continue to be futile since they explain lawful behavior as completely as they explain criminal behavior. They are similar to respiration, which is necessary for any behavior but does not differentiate criminal from non-criminal behavior.

Limitations and Criticisms of Differential Association

In terms of the research, discussion, debate, and criticism aroused, differential association stands as perhaps the major theory of criminality in the United States (Sutherland and Cressey, 1966). In 1960, Cressey made a comprehensive review of all the major criticisms made of the theory since its introduction in 1937. He divided the studies into those which he felt were "literary errors," i.e. the readers simply did not always seem to understand what Sutherland was trying to say, and "popular criticisms." Some of these latter criticisms—that the theory does not apply to rural offenders, or to irrational, impulsive offenders—Cressey sees as simply proposals for research and not genuine criticisms.

Some of the more persistent criticisms of the theory are presented as follows with the rejoinder of Cressey.

1. "Not everyone in contact with criminality adopts a criminal behavior pattern." This criticism, Cressey feels, overlooks the words "differential" and "excess" in the theoretical statement. The theory states persons become criminal because of an over-

abundance of such associations.

2. "Some persons exhibit criminal behavior patterns who have not had extensive association with criminals." Cressey sees this criticism as a misreading of the theory. Differential association is concerned with the ratio of associations with patterns of behavior, regardless of the character of the person presenting them. One can learn anti-criminal behavior patterns from confessed drug addicts and criminals. Indeed, this is the assumption upon which inmates are permitted to give speeches to young audiences warning of the dangers of a life of crime.

3. "The theory is defective because it does not explain why persons have the associations they have." This is a desirable, but separate, research problem; differential association is an attempt to account principally for variations in crime rates, not to account for individual associations.

4. "Differential association overlooks the general role of personality traits in determining criminality." Sutherland recognized his theory would probably have to be revised to include personality traits and posed three questions for the proponents of personality traits as supplements to differential association: (a) What are the personality traits to be regarded as significant? (b) Are there personality traits, to be used as supplements to differential association, which are not already included in the concept of differential association? (c) Can differential association, which is essentially a process of learning, be combined with personality traits, which are essentially a product of learning?

5. "The theory does not adequately take into account the differential response pattern of individuals." In answering this objection Cressey states, the reason an unguarded cash register represents an opportunity for crime to one person, and a need to close the register for safe keeping to another, is due to differences in the prior associations with the two types of definition of the situation. Cressey admits the critics are on firm ground when they point out the theory does not identify what constitutes a definition "favorable to" or "unfavorable to" the violation of the law. The theory indicates that associations vary in intensity and the relative prestige of the donor of definitional patterns, but does

not specify how this added prestige affects the receptivity of the person to the presented behavior pattern.

6. "The ratio of learned behavior patterns used to explain criminality cannot be determined with accuracy in specific cases." This is perhaps the most damaging criticism of differential association for it refers to the testability of the theory. Glueck (1956) has asked, "Has anybody actually counted the number of definitions favorable to violation of law and definitions unfavorable to violation of law, and demonstrated that in the predelinquency experience of the vast majority of delinquents and criminals, the former exceed the latter?"

Cressey attempted to elicit from trust violators (embezzlers) the identity of specific persons from whom they learned behavior patterns favorable to trust violation. He found he could not empirically apply the theory to these offenders. Cressey (1952) feels one research method which might enable the testing of differential association would be to analyze the vocabulary of a person to determine where he has been exposed to rationalizations justifying criminal behavior. Prison guards are familiar with underworld argot, yet they do not identify with the prison subculture. Much more cogent criticisms than those reviewed by Cressey have been addressed to fundamental weaknesses and inadequacies in Sutherland's conceptualization of the learning process presumed to underlie differential association. Jeffery (1965) and Burgess and Akers (1966) have both attempted reformations of differential association from a reinforcement theory perspective, but we shall discuss these efforts in detail in a later chapter.

Differential Identification

Through the concept of "differential identification" Glaser (1956) reconceptualizes Sutherland's theory in role-taking imagery (Mead). Sutherland supported the theory of differential association by evidence that a major portion of criminality is learned through participation in criminal groups. Membership groups are, most often though not always, reference groups. Because our identification may be with remote reference groups or highly generalized others, differential association is insufficient to account for all differential identification. Says Glaser: "The theory of differential identification, in essence, is that a person pursues criminal behavior to the extent that he identifies himself with real or imaginary persons from whose perspective his criminal behavior seems acceptable."

During any period prior identifications and present circumstances dictate the selection of the persons with whom we identify. The individual selects a role-model and fashions his behavior after the perspective of this model or ego-ideal. This role-model may be encountered personally, or through books, movies, and television. The background of each individual criminal, his prior frustrations, economic background, group membership, are relevant if they can be shown to have affected the choice of the "significant other" from whose perspective the individual evaluates his own behavior. Differential identification does not account for accidental crimes, it treats crime as a form of voluntary, i.e., anticipatory, behavior.

Delinquency and Drift

Matza, in his book *Delinquency and Drift* (1964) and earlier in an article with Sykes (1957), extended the theory of differential association by pointing out the "techniques of neutralization" which are crucial to an understanding of Sutherland's "definitions favorable to the violation of the law." Sutherland's theory referred to a process of learning criminal techniques and attitudes; Sykes and Matza address themselves to the content of the learning process.

Delinquency occurs on only a comparatively few occasions of the total number of occasions upon which it might occur. During most of the delinquent's life he is constrained by social convention. When he does commit a delinquent act, Matza feels, rather than being an expression of a commitment to a delinquent subculture, or a Freudian compulsion (a "devil in the mind"), the delinquent has found himself in a situation where he drifted into delinquency (Matza assumed a quasi free-will model).[2] This situation of "unregulated choice" tends to be episodic rather than

---

[2]Matza refers to his position as "soft determinism."

constant and is akin to what Durkheim called "anomie." Matza (1964) prefers to define "drift" as "episodic release from moral constraint."

Important to the understanding of Matza's position is the view that the delinquent is at least partially committed to the social order he offends. It is the ancient paradox of puzzling over why men violate laws in which they believe. By contact with the legal system the delinquent learns to extend legitimate legal defenses to his crimes and distort these defenses to his own situation. What is important here is not whether the logic is compelling, but that —in the oft-quoted dictum by W. I. Thomas—"when the situation is defined as real, it is real in its consequences." The function of these rationalizations is to protect the individual from self-blame. These justifications precede deviant behavior and make delinquency possible. Sykes and Matza isolate five principal techniques of neutralization.[3]

DENIAL OF RESPONSIBILITY. Sykes and Matza (1957) quote Justice Holmes who observed that even a dog distinguishes between being stumbled over and being kicked; and society, in turn, takes into consideration the intent of an act. The delinquent includes recklessness in his meaning of the term "accident." The result is to widen the conditions under which he may behave wildly and excuse his behavior as not being intentional but merely the action of a "wild kid." An extension of this denial of personal responsibility is the delinquent's eagerness to "give the problem away" to a slum environment, unloving parents, bad companions. He views himself as the helpless victim of forces outside his control. The law also "excuses" from responsibility those persons adjudged "insane." As in the case of an accident, delinquents may seek refuge from the requirements of the law by pleading extenuating circumstances, e.g. "I was drunk, out-of-my-mind," or "I lost my head." Seeing himself as seized by "momentary insanity" as a consequence of anger, or through the influence of alcohol or drugs, the delinquent excuses himself of responsibility.

---

[3]Matza discusses these techniques in more philosophical thoroughness in his chapter "The Negation of Offense" in his book *Delinquency and Drift*. This summary represents a combination of the article with Sykes and his presentation in book form.

DENIAL OF INJURY. The criminal law has long made a distinction between acts that are wrong in themselves *(mala in se)* and acts that are illegal but not immoral—*mala prohibita*. Similarly, if the delinquent interprets his acts as not clearly hurting anyone, he can neutralize any guilt feelings. A stolen car is simply "borrowed" from someone who was not using it at the time, and a gang-fight is a private quarrel entered into by consenting adolescents. Matza does not argue that these neutralizations represent a systematic ideology but rather a hazy and somewhat Machiavellian set of justifications. In this case the link between the delinquent acts and their consequences is broken by the denial of injury, thus absolving the delinquent of any genuine wrong-doing.

DENIAL OF THE VICTIM. Juvenile delinquents often draw a sharp line between those who can be victimized and those who cannot (much like a street-corner Geneva Convention rules of war). The choice of victims tends to be a function of the social distance between the juvenile delinquent and the target. In this instance the delinquent admits his behavior causes harm. He neutralizes the guilt, however, by asserting the injury is a form of rightful retaliation. Vandalism may be seen as revenge on an unfair teacher, and thefts from a "crooked" store owner are merely an attempt to balance the scales of justice by a ghetto Robin Hood.

CONDEMNATION OF THE CONDEMNERS. The delinquent shifts the focus to the motives of his accusors and denies that they have the right to condemn his actions since they are hypocrites. Police are corrupt, stupid, and brutal; teachers play favorites; and parents use them as scapegoats. The effect is an attempt to shift attention away from the delinquent's own actions and to neutralize the normative sanctioning system which these authority figures represent.

APPEAL TO HIGHER LOYALTIES. In a conflict between the claims of friendship and the claims of the law, the delinquent presents himself as acknowledging the claims of the larger society but can "never squeal on a friend." The law recognizes that self-defense justifies certain actions which might otherwise be deemed criminal. A man attacked in his own home has a legal right, and a moral duty, to stand his ground. Similarly it is the expectation of the delinquent subculture that anyone who would not defend his turf (home) is a coward, thus repelling an aggressor (outsider) is justified. By borrowing this legal defense, the delinquent justifies his allegiance to the gang to which he belongs.

In conclusion, Sykes and Matza have been able to make a significant contribution to delinquency theory by their isolation of specific techniques of neutralization, thus providing us with some content of what is learned in differential association, at least in certain limited urban areas.

Differential Opportunity

Delinquency and Opportunity (1960) by Richard Cloward and Lloyd E. Ohlin, made a threefold contribution to criminology: (1) It synthesized and extended the existing theories of deviance of Durkheim, Merton, Shaw and McKay, and Sutherland; (2) summarized and analyzed the current state of delinquent subculture theory effectively utilizing the analytical principle that "an explanation for the motivational basis for a deviant pattern does not explain the resulting response;"[4] and (3) provided a testable theoretical basis for a treatment plan to attack the problem of delinquency which resulted in the Mobilization for Youth Program.

This book explores two questions: (1) why do delinquent norms, of rules of conduct, develop? (2) what are the social conditions which account for the content of the various delinquent normative systems, e.g. theft, violence, or drug use?

Rather than an emphasis on why particular individuals become delinquent (psychology), their emphasis is upon delinquent norms and "pressures toward deviance" (sociology). Whatever problems of adjustment a person may experience, there are several alternative deviant solutions he might follow. Their book attempts to account for these differing adaptations.

---

[4]In this approach Cloward and Ohlin show the influence of the Durkheimian principle guiding the explanation of social facts: "when . . . the explanation of a social phenomenon is undertaken, we must seek separately the efficient cause which produces it and the function it fulfills" (Catlin, 1964).

Opportunity Structures and Criminality

Cloward and Ohlin ask the question: What pressures lead the young to form or join delinquent subcultures? They find their answer in an extension of the insights of Durkheim and Merton.

Physical needs are regulated by man's organic structure. Once satiated, the boy rejects additional food. But such is not the case with social "needs"—wealth, prestige, and power are insatiable, a bottomless abyss.

An emphasis on achievement and upward striving is characteristic of industrial societies. These widely held cultural values are related to the needs of the industrial world to recruit and train the most talented persons in each generation to perform technical work roles. To motivate persons throughout the social order to compete for these roles, the cultural success-goals are viewed as potentially accessible to all. These unlimited aspirations exert pressure toward disorder for they are a source of "uninterrupted agitation."

The culture structure refers to the goals and norms, the approved ends toward which men orient themselves, and the ways or avenues for reaching them. The social structure is the division of people into social classes according to wealth and/or prestige. Anomie, or a condition whereby social norms no longer control men's actions, develops when there is a breakdown in the relationship between the goals a culture holds out to its members and the legitimate avenues of access to them.

Merton's formulation permits the researcher to make distinctions regarding the severity of pressures toward deviant behavior which originate at different points in the social structure. Merton pointed out that the greatest pressure for deviant behavior was felt by persons occupying positions in the lower-class. Cloward and Ohlin (1960) extend this formulation and see the formation of delinquent subcultures and a result of these pressures and a response to the particular problems facing lower-class youth.

> Adolescents who form delinquent subcultures, we suggest, have internalized an emphasis upon conventional goals. Faced with limitations on legitimate avenues of access to these goals, and unable to revise their aspirations downward, they experience intense frustrations; the exploration of nonconformist alternatives may be the result.

As Thomas (1967) writes in his autobiography of life in Spanish Harlem: "But wasn't it great to work for a living? I calculated how long it would take to make my first million shining shoes. Too long. I would be something like 987 years old. Maybe I could steal it faster."

Social Class and Aspiration Level

The height to which people aspire differs by social class; at whatever their social position, people tend to be dissatisfied with their income. The poor, understandably, are the most dissatisfied. Cloward and Ohlin differ from Cohen, who sees the origin of lower class delinquency as a repudiation of middle-class standards and the creation of a delinquent subculture which provides criteria of status which lower-class children can meet. Delinquency occurs, according to Cohen (1955), where access to middle-class goals is limited. Cloward and Ohlin see the delinquent as wishing to acquire middle-class position but doing so in terms of lower-class values.

The lower-class person tends to rank people in terms of money alone, whereas the middle-class person does so in terms of money and morality, and the upper-class rank people by style of life and ancestry. Participants in delinquent subcultures want higher status within their own cultural milieu, symbols of status being flashy cars and expensive clothes. The orientation of the lower-class youth is not toward middle-class membership, with its emphasis on a morality of conformity, but toward improvement in economic position within the life-style of the lower-class culture. These youngsters become delinquent because they perceive that legitimate channels to the goals they seek will be limited or closed.

Socio-cultural Barriers and Legitimate Opportunity Structure

Why is it a substantial proportion of lower-class males fourteen to twenty do not orient themselves toward acquiring higher education?

CULTURAL VALUES. Their persistence of cultural values—the Jewish regard for intellectual achievement fitted nicely into the role of education and social mobility in the U.S. The middle class minimization of kinship ties to the value of occupational achievement made upward social mobility easier for this class.

Immigrants from Southern Italy tended to regard formal education as a "frill" and encouraged their child to quit school and go to work as soon as possible. Too late they discovered the relationship between school adjustment and upward social mobility. At this point their only recourse to increased income was to turn to illegitimate means, robbery and the like.

SITUATIONAL BARRIERS. Quitting school may not be so much a lack of recognition of the value of education, but a necessary response to the family's need for food and shelter. The lower-class attitude toward education is adaptive, i.e. educational horizons are readjusted to the reality of the situation and the relative probabilities of reaching these educational goals.

ALTERNATIVE AVENUES TO SUCCESS-GOALS. Nature may have provided physical gifts which compensate for social disadvantages —entertainment and sports. But for most there seems no legitimate way out of poverty. Cloward and Ohlin see delinquency, not in terms of inadequate socialization, or conformity to lower-class values, but a specialized adaptation to the problem of adjustment in a society which encourages all its members to hold high aspirations but does not provide equally for the realization of those aspirations. These pressures weigh most heavily on young males since they decide, at this age-juncture, on a career in the occupational marketplace.

THE ILLEGITIMATE OPPORTUNITY STRUCTURE

THE CRIMINAL SUBCULTURE. The criminal subculture, like the legitimate host culture, must provide role models (successful gangsters) and learning opportunities for the transmission of the social heritage (both values and skills). The apprentice criminal passes from one status to another in the illegitimate opportunity structure.

One trait of delinquent behavior is often its aggressive character. In an attempt to overconform to the demands of the criminal subculture, the apprentice delinquent may draw attention to himself by malicious nonutilitarian behavior. Organized crime, however, is bureaucratized, and the impulsive individual is a liability in the orderly functioning of business. The novice must learn that crime and murder is a business, a way of life, to be pursued "naturally" for profit, not for personal revenge or caprice.

THE CONFLICT SUBCULTURE. The emergence of conflict subcultures is facilitated by areas characterized by transiency and social disorganization. The instability of the milieu prevents the establishment of either a stable conventional or criminal opportunity system. Crime in these areas tends to be individualistic and unorganized. Where opportunities are lacking, social controls are likely to be weak as well; the resulting frustration creates the "hoodlum" delinquent who engages in violence for its own sake.

Deprived of cultural guidelines for opportunity and social control the adolescent is thrown back on his personal resources and seeks status, a "rep," by demonstrating his warrior's "heart." As Thomas (1967) describes it: "Moving into a new block is a big jump for a Harlem kid. You're torn up from your hard-won turf and brought into an 'I don't know you' block where every kid is some kind of enemy. Even when the block belongs to your own people you are still an outsider who has to prove himself a down stud with heart."

THE RETREATIST SUBCULTURE. When an individual (Merton) is unable to reach culturally approved goals by legitimate means, and unwilling, because of internalized prohibitions, to resort to illegitimate means, one way of resolving the intense anxiety is to withdraw, retreat, and abandon the struggle.

Cloward and Ohlin do not see Merton's definition of the process giving rise to retreatist behavior as directly applicable to lower-class adolescents because many lower-class children have a history of delinquency prior to becoming addicts. Their lawlessness indicates that they have not internalized conventional norms, thus, their addiction pattern may be seen as a result of "double failure."

Denied, because of their cultural experiences, a realistic entrance into the legitimate opportunity structure, and unable, either because of competition for scare roles, or personal inadequacies, to find a satisfying status in the criminal subculture, the delinquent turns to the retreatist drug subculture as a solution to his status dilemma. A retreatist drug culture becomes a psychic haven for society's "double dropouts."

The Evolution of Delinquent Subcultures

If persons occupying a particular social status in a society experience collective problems of adjustment, they may respond with a collective solution by challenging the validity of the established ruler. Cloward and Ohlin specify several steps if this process is to result in the successful establishment of a delinquent subculture: (1) individuals must question the validity of conventional conduct codes, and (2) seek a collective rather than an individual solution. This is dependent upon (3) finding rationalizations to neutralize guilt feelings over deviance and (4) facing no overwhelming obstacles to the possibility of joint problem solving.

The process of alienation begins when persons either fail or anticipate failing to achieve success-goals by socially approved means and attribute the cause of failure to the social order rather than to a lack of personal qualifications. Failure tends to be externalized when delinquents regard themselves as capable of meeting the formal requirements of the system but feel a sense of injustice from the failure of systems to fulfill their expectations. These feelings of "unjust deprivation" weaken the commitment to official norms.

When the barriers to opportunity are highly visible (racism) it increases the likelihood that persons who fail to achieve their aspirations will attribute failure to the social order rather than to themselves. One task of reform groups is to increase the social visibility of discriminatory practices, but a dysfunctional side effect of this practice can be the corroboration of the unfairness of the established system for those within the lower-class who aspire to material rewards.

Persons who attribute failure to their own shortcomings by definition accept the prevailing ideology of society. The alienation from society's definitions of the situation begins as he seeks peer-group support for justification of his early delinquent career. A lone delinquent would be more likely to feel less secure in his solitary evaluations.

Guilt management is solved in advance of delinquent actions by withdrawal of legitimacy of the controlling norms. Potential guilt feelings are neutralized by rationalizations which project the blame to the social structure, thus producing a definition of the situation which Sutherland describes as "favorable to the violation of the law."

For collective solutions to be conceived, it is necessary for individuals to successfully communicate to each other the extent of their alienation from the established norms. The experience of arrest, juvenile court adjudication, and correctional treatment provide a common experience and basis for interaction and deep communication.

Continuity and Change in Delinquent Subcultures

To remain stable, a subculture must be able to attract new recruits. Functionally, the delinquent subculture serves as an alternate channel of opportunity for those delinquents who either cannot, or will not, participate in the conventional opportunity system.

Delinquent subcultures are differentiated by forms of neighborhood integration. The "criminal subculture" is characterized by the integration of different age levels—a condition necessary for the orderly progression from delinquent to criminal status roles; the "retreatist" subculture is likewise dependent upon a symbolic alliance between a "connection" and the addict, thus a wide range of age levels is typically integrated. As adults generally have no interest in the maintenance of warring gangs, the age range of associates in the "conflict" subculture narrows considerably.

Resistance to change is related to the integration of the subculture with other groups in its immediate milieu. Thus, the criminal subculture is least resistant to change, followed in stability by the retreatist subculture, and leaving the conflict subculture as most socially isolated and therefore most vulnerable to change. The ability of these subcultures to persist is dependent upon a stable lower-class social organization. Forces exerting a stress-strain on this system include: (1) the emigration of the most talented members of the slum areas as they succeed in either the legitimate or illegitimate opportunity structure leaving a society of failures; and (2) the advent of the welfare state (depersonalizing public assistance) and the resulting decline of the neighborhood wardheeler making public housing projects "political deserts." In summary Cloward and Ohlin state that:

> for delinquency is not, in the final analysis, a property of individuals or even of subcultures; it is a property of the social systems in which these individuals and groups are enmeshed . . . . The target for prevention action, then, should be defined, not as the individual or group that exhibits the delinquent pattern, but as the social setting that gives rise to delinquency. It is our view, in other words, that the major effort of those who wish to eliminate delinquency should be directed to the reorganization of slum communities.

Bordua (1961) presents three criticisms of the theoretical position of Cloward and Ohlin. In the first, he was their own favorite analytical tool against them and says they have confused the justificatory function of delinquent subcultures with their causation, i.e. a justification of a response does not explain the motivational basis; for that response, they have equated the end with the beginning. Second, while the delinquents in Thrasher, Cohen, and Miller were once recognizable children, Cloward and Ohlin tend to ignore the life histories of their delinquents which brought them to the point of participation in delinquency. Third, that gang boys are equipped for upward mobility in the legitimate opportunity structure is taken as a given, whereas the experiences in a lower-class milieu are not the most ideal preparation for participation in the disciplined job-world of a middle-class culture.

Group Conflict and Criminality

Vold (1958) applies the principles of Simmel and the formal school of sociology to criminological theory in an attempt to explain the origin of much of crime as an outgrowth of the conflicts of human groups. The content of social conflict may vary in intensity (from individual quarrels to out-right warfare) but, as a social process, social conflict is a universal form of interaction among men.

This view shifts the theoretical focus from a psychological one which would seek the origin of deviant behavior in the personal pathology of the individual, to the assumption that the behavior of man is a product of his group associations. The individual is seen as a pawn in a giant chess match between groups, held together, yet constantly opposing each other in interests and efforts.

Each person in society possesses a status-role within some group. Through collective action in a dynamic society the relative power position of these groups is in constant flux. If the group, be it ethnic, racial, or political, to which one belongs enhances or loses its power position in society, it naturally follows that the individual's status is increased or decreased as well. The entire process of readjustment of societal subgroups in opposition is much of what we mean by the term "social organization."

Individuals form groups when they perceive that they share common needs, interests, and goals which can best be met through collective action. Groups, like individuals, come into conflict with each other when they find themselves in competition for the same unshareable goals. The principal goals of a group is the same as that of a wife faced with competition by a rival for her husband's affections, to keep from being replaced.

In a democratic society, one chief method, conflict-resolution, between groups is through the rule of law. The struggle of groups for dominance and promotion of their special interests is seen most visibly in the competition for legislative majorities and the resulting hold over the police-regulatory powers of the state.

The individual who maintains a minority group orientation and finds himself out-of-step with the required behavior patterns is simply outlawed. Whether it be the conscientious objector who marches to the beat of a different drummer, the rural-bootlegger to whom "moonshining is a way of life," or the college student who prefers marijuana to martinis, each find his behavior "criminalized" by a dominant power group. As Vold writes:

> Members of such a minority group do not accept the definition of themselves, or of their behavior, as criminal. Looking at their own

group of like-thinking associates, they readily persuade themselves that their course of action has been acceptable, and from their point of view, entirely honorable.

Vold isolates four types of criminal behavior which are political in nature and represent the individuals' loyalty to a group struggling to maintain or improve its position for the control of power. The behavior exhibited by these persons is analogous to that of a soldier following orders in a power struggle between nations.

1. Crimes which result from direct political reform type protest movement. How do you "rehabilitate" a conscientious objector?
2. Crimes which result from a clash of interests of company managements and labor unions in that form of industrial conflict that we call strikes or lockouts.
3. Crimes which result as a response to jurisdictional disputes between competing labor unions.
4. Crimes which result from the clashes incidental to change or to upset the caste system of racial segregation in various parts of the world, United States and the Union of South Africa.

The Irishman, weary of the long religious wars between Protestants and Catholics, who signed: "Would that all men were atheists so they could live together like Christians," was simply noting that a common value system, even a non-religious one, would be necessary for peaceful coexistence.

Viewed in the light of an individual responding to a group conflict situation, this type of criminality is a normal, understandable attempt to maintain or enhance a certain way of life. Individual behavior is incidental to, and symptomatic of, societal disorganization. When we ask the counselor's question: "Who's got the problem?", we answer with: society.

Group conflict theory does not, of course, account for irrational and impulsive acts of pathological personalities. Explanations for these acts must come from individual psychology and psychiatry. This fact underscores the argument that criminology is an interdisciplinary science, for no one theoretical system can adequately explain all criminal behavior.

THE IMPACT OF SELF-REPORT DATA
ON CRIMINOLOGICAL THEORIES

Before concluding this brief review of sociological theories of criminality, we must make some mention of a troublesome and perennial issue in criminology—the status of self-report data and its implications for theories of criminality. By employing a definition of crime which states that a criminal act is any illegal act regardless of whether the individual committing the act is apprehended, criminologists face the problem that not all such acts will be reported. Thus any theories of crime will be based on inadequate data. Many criminal acts go undetected and thus unreported by authorities. The problems involved in systematically recording data about detected crimes are great enough to thwart researchers, but the problems involved in finding out what type and how many crimes have gone undetected seem insurmountable. However, instruments which purport to accomplish this objective have been constructed. The development of self-report questionnaire and interview techniques is of recent origin and was begun in the area of juvenile delinquency. In fact, almost all subsequent research on the self-report technique has dealt with juveniles. The two researchers who first developed the self-report method, James Short and Ivan Nye, found that self-report data were much different from official statistics data. If the self-report method can be shown to meet acceptable criteria of reliability and validity, then theories based only on official data will have to be reformulated in light of the more complete self-report data.

The sociological theories we have reviewed, all based on officially reported data, assert that delinquency is a class and, by implication, a race based phenomenon. The majority of adjudicated delinquents are, in fact, from the lower-class. Lower-class juveniles are more likely to have police contacts than middle-class juveniles, they are more likely to be referred to juvenile court, and they are more likely to be sentenced to training school. The official data support the social class theories on delinquency very well.

Self-Report Data

One of the first and most reproduced findings by Short and Nye (as quoted by Gould, 1969) using the self-report method was that "social class . . . is practically unrelated to delinquency measured by self-report indices." They found that delinquency is fairly evenly distributed through every stratum of society. There are differences in type and frequency of offenses but not in the proportion of juveniles in each strata that commit offenses.

Short and Nye also found delinquency to be almost universal. They found that 86 percent of the midwest high school boys had committed at least one offense. The high school boys had not repeated their offenses as frequently as the training school boys but did commit many offenses at least once.

Implications

If delinquency is in fact evenly distributed over all strata of society and is almost universal, there are serious implications for all previous theories. The self-report findings refute the sociological theories that are built on class distinctions. Theories can no longer explain delinquency solely in terms of being a lower-class or race phenomenon. The biological and psychological theories are also on shaky ground. In discovering how universal delinquency is, self-report data refute the theories that claim delinquents are of a particular biological criminal type. Even if delinquents were found to have any common physical characteristic, it would have to be considered normative since such a proportion of the population admits to delinquent behavior. Similarly, psychological theories that approach delinquency as an emotional disorder will have to admit that delinquency is so prevalent that it cannot be considered abnormal. Delinquency cannot be thought of as a pathology of a certain segment of the population.

One self-report study by Gould (1969) found that race is not related to self-perceived (he uses the term self-perceived for self-reported) delinquency, although it is related to official statistics. He maintains that race leads to official delinquency, and for caucasians only, official delinquency leads to self-perceived or self-reported delinquency. He suggests labeling theory offers an explanation. Because arrest is so common for blacks (62% had a delinquency scale score of 3 or higher, and only 8% had no police record) , whether or not an individual has a police record is not the determining factor in whether he calls himself a delinquent. The cultural stereotype of blacks involves a certain amount of delinquency, which has the effect of making the labeling of blacks delinquent almost universal and thus independent on whether or not an individual actually has a police record. However, caucasians are not prey to this delinquent steretoype, so they are individually affected by the label a police record gives them. As Gould says:

> Whether or not official delinquency leads to self-perceived delinquency, then, depends upon the existence of cultural stereotypes. For these divoid of stereotypes regarding their delinquent conduct, official delenquent action plays an important role in determining their delinquent self-conception. For those whom such stereotypes are applied regardless of their official delinquent status, the official status becomes of little consequence in determining self-perceived delinquency.

Summary

A variety of theoretical attempts to account for the origins of criminality on the basis of sociological considerations have been reviewed in this chapter. According to Cloward and Ohlin, the etiology of criminal behavior is to be sought in the dysjunction between the culturally prescribed goals of a society and the socially structured avenues for the achievement of these goals. Further, they isolate the creation of three delinquent subcultures as a response to these pressures. In the view of Sutherland and Cressey, the transmission of criminal norms is accomplished through differential association; individuals learn to be criminals just as they would learn any pattern of normal behavior. A principal ingredient in this learning, according to Glaser, is the "ego ideal" or identifications which one makes, and these identifications can be beyond the immediate membership groups. The content of these transmitted criminal norms are seen by Sykes and Matza as techniques of neutralization of the constraints of the law. Finally, crime is a violation of the law, and Vold points out that, through group conflict, a dominant group may simply outlaw certain normative patterns of a minority group, e.g. prohibition. Each theoretical position has its critics and its limitations, and we await the inclusion of new facts to reformulate, refine, and extend these approaches.

REFERENCES

Akman, D.D., Normandeau, A., and Turner, S.: The measurement of delinquency in Canada. *Journal of Criminal Law, Criminology, and Police Science, 58:*330-337, 1967.

Bacon, M.K., Child, I.L., and Barry, H.: A cross-cultural study of correlates of crime. *Journal of Abnormal and Social Psychology, 66:*291-300, 1963.

Bloch, H.A., and Niederhoffer, A.: *The Gang: A Study in Adolescent Behavior.* New York, Philosophical Library, 1958.

Bordua, D.J.: Delinquent subcultures: sociological interpretations of gang delinquency. *Annals of the American Academy of Political and Social Science, 338:*120-136, 1961.

Brown, J.S.: A comparative study of deviation from sexual mores. *American Sociological Review, 17:*135-146, 1952.

Burgess, R.L., and Akers, R.L.: A differential association-reinforcement theory of criminal behavior. *Social Problems, 14:*128-147, 1966.

Catlin, G.E.G. *The Science and Method of Politics.* Hamden, Archon Books, 1964.

Cloward, R.A., and Ohlin, L.E.: *Delinquency and Opportunity.* Glencoe, The Free Press, 1960.

Cohen, A.K.: *Delinquent Boys.* Glencoe, The Free Press, 1955.

Cohen, A.K.: The delinquency subculture. In Giallombardo, R. (Ed.): *Juvenile Delinquency: A Book of Readings.* New York, Wiley, 1966.

Cohen, A.K., and Short, J.F.: Research in delinquent subcultures. *Journal of Social Issues, 14:*20-37, 1958.

Cressey, D.R.: Application and verification of the differential association theory. *Journal of Criminal Law, Criminology, and Police Science, 43:*43-52, 1952.

Cressey, D.R.: Epidemiology and individual conduct: a case from criminology. *Pacific Review, 3:*47-58, 1960.

Durkheim, E.: *Rules of Sociological Method.* Translated by Sarah Solvay and John H. Mueller. Glencoe, Free Press, 1950.

Glaser, D.: Criminality theories and behavioral images. *American Journal of Sociology, 61:*433-444, 1956.

Glaser, D.: Social disorganization and delinquent subcultures. In Quay, H.C., (Ed.): *Juvenile Delinquency.* Princeton, Van Nostrand, 1965.

Gould, L.C.: Who defines delinquency: a comparison of self-reported and officially reported indices of delinquency for three racial groups. *Social Problems, 16:*325-335, 1969.

Glueck, S.: Theory and fact in criminology. *British Journal of Delinquency,*
    7:92-98, 1956.
Jeffery, C.R.: Criminal behavior and learning theory. *Journal of Criminal
    Law, Criminology, and Police Science, 56:*294-300, 1965.
Kobrin, S.: The conflict of values in delinquency areas. In Giallombardo, R.,
    (Ed.): *Juvenile delinquency: A Book of Readings.* New York, Wiley,
    1966.
Matza, D.: *Delinquency and Drift.* New York, Wiley, 1964.
Merton, R.K.: *Social Theory and Social Structure.* Glencoe, Free Press, 1957.
Miller, W.B.: Lower class culture as a generating milieu of gang delinquency.
    *Journal of Social Issues, 3:*5-19, 1958.
Normandeau, A.: The measurement of delinquency in Montreal. *Journal of
    Criminal Law, Criminology, and Police Science, 57:*172-177, 1966.
Parsons, T.: *Essays in Sociological Theory.* Glencoe, The Free Press, 1954.
Rose, G.N.G. Concerning the measurement of delinquency. *British Journal
    of Criminology, 6:*414-421, 1966.
Savitz, L.: *Dilemmas in Criminology.* New York, McGraw-Hill, 1967.
Sellin, T., and Wolfgang, M.: *The Measurement of Delinquency.* New York,
    Wiley, 1964.
Shaw, C.R., Zorbaugh, P.M., McKay, H.D., and Cottrell, L.S.: *Delinquency
    Areas.* Chicago, University of Chicago Press, 1929.
Sutherland, E.H., and Cressey, D.R.: *Principles of Criminology.* Philadelphia,
    Lippincott, 1966.
Sykes, G., and Matza, D.: Techniques of neutralization: a theory of delin-
    quency. *American Sociological Review, 22:*664-670, 1957.
Tarde, G.: *Penal Philosophy.* Boston, Little, Brown and Company, 1912.
Thomas, P.: *Down These Mean Streets.* New York, Signet Books, 1967.
Vold, G.: *Theoretical Criminology.* New York, Oxford University Press, 1958.

Chapter 5

BIOLOGICAL THEORIES
OF CRIMINALITY

IN PARIS IN 1968, after surrendering himself to the police, a man
named Daniel Hugon was brought to trial for strangling a prostitute to death with one of her stockings. The case, as it was related
in the press, seemed no more than the usual tabloid account of
anomie and violence in a big city. When Hugon attempted suicide,
however, a complete physical examination was ordered. An analysis
of his blood revealed that he was an XYY male, i.e. one of those
presumably rare individuals in whom an extra Y or male chromosome is present in addition to the normal complement of one X
(female) and Y (male) chromosome. Hugon's sentence of seven
years, made after this disclosure, was regarded as lenient.

Since Hugon's trial, evidence of an XYY aberration, coupled
with mental retardation and neurological disorder, brought an acquittal on grounds of insanity to another accused of murder in
Australia and has been presented in several cases in the United
States. The most notorious of these was the case of Richard Speck,
convicted in the slaying of eight student nurses in Chicago in 1966.
Speck, who is the clinical prototype of the XYY anomaly—tall, suffering from acne, with a borderline IQ of eighty-five—was found
not to possess the XYY chromosomal aberration.

Following the brief flurry of interest aroused in the genetics of
abnormal behavior by media coverage of these cases, most of it
poorly informed and provocatively handled, concern over the "born
criminal" appears to have diminished to the vanishing point. Dis-
interest in the potential role of genetic factors in criminality is part
of a larger pattern of antipathy toward biological theorizing among

American criminologists. For reasons which are partly a function of egalitarian social philosophy and partly a reaction to earlier excesses among criminological theorists, American criminological thought has been markedly inhospitable to the notion that organic factors may exert an important influence in the pathogenesis of some forms of criminal behavior. As an example of the latter, Allen (1970) quotes a passage from *The New Criminology* by Schlapp and Smith, published in 1928, in which the authors announce their objectives in the following terms:

> We shall attempt to demonstrate that the vast majority of all criminals, misdemeanants, mental deficients and defectives are products of bodily disorders, that most crimes come about through disturbances of the ductless glands in the criminal or through mental defects caused by endocrine troubles in the criminal's mother. The attempt will also be made to show that criminal actions are in reality reactions caused by the disturbed internal chemistry of the body.

As Lindner, et al. (1970) have put it, the "extravagant claims, meager empirical evidence, naivete, gross inadequacy, and stated or implied concepts of racial and ethnic inferiority" in the work of earlier constitutionalists, morphologists, and endocrinologists constitute a "disreputable history" which thoroughly discredited the few important empirical findings of biological investigations of criminal behavior.

The present chapter focuses upon biological theories of comparatively recent origin and the empirical research generated by those theories. It excludes consideration of constitutionalists like Lombroso and Hooton, morphologists like Kretschmer and Sheldon, and endocrinologists like Schlapp and Smith on the grounds that the work of these individuals belongs more fittingly in a chapter dealing with historical aspects of criminological theorizing than to a discussion of contemporary biological theories of criminality. In the judgment of the present authors, there is no justification for subjecting the reader's attention span to the severity of a test consisting of a catalogue of these dead-end approaches.

We shall devote some attention to theories of criminality which assign potential significance to the operation of cardiovascular and electrocortical factors in criminal behavior. Consideration will also be given to theory and research in the genetics of criminal behavior variation, including studies of the XYY chromosomal anomaly. For purposes of illuminating this rather complex and controversial area of inquiry, it seems appropriate to preface our discussion with a brief review of some basic concepts in genetics.

ELEMENTS OF GENETIC TRANSMISSION

Genes

The fundamental units of heredity are the genes. These structures possess the form of large molecules of desoxyribonucleic acid (DNA) with an extremely complex pattern. The genes are transmitted from one generation to the next without change, unless they become altered by mutation. But mutation is rare; in the absence of biochemical or radiation influences, mutation is thought to occur less than once in every fifty-thousand generations for a particular gene.

The effect of the genes is mediated by their control of biochemical processes, i.e. by accelerating, retarding, or inhibiting biochemical reactions. In this respect they resemble enzymes; they participate in chemical changes without losing their own identity. Variations produced by genetic factors can be observed in the very earliest stages of life, but it is impossible to specify a time in life beyond which all potential influences may be assumed to have occurred.

Genetic differences may be simply demonstrated in *phenyketonuria,* a pathological condition which has been identified with the operation of a single abnormal gene. While the normal gene supports normal biochemical processes, the aberrant gene fails to supply an enzyme which converts phenylalanine, an amino acid, into tyrosine, a food substance which is essential to the brain.

Few genetic-biochemical relationships are of this order of simplicity. Of their complexity, Muller (1956) says: "Whatever be the nature of the primary chemical products of genes within the cell, these products must be of thousands of different kinds . . . Because of the great indirectness of the route connecting the genes with these end results, it is evident that any given characteristic must be a resultant of the action of many genes." Despite the fact that the genes are transmitted as autonomous units, the genetic constitution must be conceived as operating in totality. In fact, the cumulative effects produced by the minor action of a great many genes may equal or exceed the effects produced in other areas by a single abnormal gene.

The influence of the genes is not confined to early development. As Shields and Slater (1960) point out, "Both growth and regression in all stages from the embryonic to senile decay are under genetic control." Some genetically determined conditions, such as baldness in men, do not become manifest until the individual has reached adult years. An understanding of genetic variation, however, must begin with an examination of the process by which the genes are distributed from the parents to the child.

The Chromosomes

Genetic material varies in microscopic appearance with the different life stages of the cell. When the cell is not actively engaged in the process of division, the genetic material resembles a skein of tangled thread lying within the cell nucleus. During cellular division, however, the thread separates into *chromosomes,* rodlike bodies which are presumed to be the locus of the genes.

Nearly every species of living organism possesses its own characteristic number of chromosomes—man normally has 23 pairs—and each cell in the body has its full complement of chromosomes. The only exception to this generalization involves the sex cells, ova and spermatozoa, which contain only half of the normal number, i.e. one from each pair. The genes are situated along the length of the chromosome in a fixed order, so that pairs of genes lie opposite one another in the chromosome pairs. According to Shields and Slater (1960) :

> A particular gene can be shown to be capable of taking, in some instances, one of two or more alternative forms; and each of these forms will be likely to have a slightly different effect in development. Thus one of the genes which determines a man's blood group can take one of three forms, A. B. and O. This gives the possibility of six different types of constitution—AA, AB, AO, BB, BO, and OO. The seriologist can test for the presence or absence of an A or B gene, and so can distinguish some of these blood types from one another; but he has no way of testing for the presence of the O gene, so that some genetic types cannot be absolutely identified by serology alone.

The example quoted above provides an illustration of another fundamental property of genetic transmission. It was pointed out that we are unable to distinguish between AA and OO types because we lack the means for determining the presence of O. Individuals of both AA and AO constitution are both capable of giving reactions typical of A gene-bearers. If the A gene is present, the O gene seems to have not effect, a situation in which A is described as *dominant* and O as *recessive*. If the AA combination produced a stronger reaction than AO, the A gene might be called *intermediate*.

B is also dominant with respect to O; therefore the serologist is also unable to distinguish between BB and BO constitutions. But A and B are not dominant or recessive with respect to one another, and the AB type individual gives both A and B serological reactions. Shields and Slater (1960) observe:

> From knowing what happens in the formation of the sex-cells and at fertilization, we can easily see what the offspring will be when individuals of the various types mate together. O is by far the commonest of the three genes, with A the next, while B is relatively rare. The commonest constitutions are therefore OO and AO. The first, having two genes of the same kind, is said to be homozygous for O, while the second is heterozygous. If an AO man mates with an OO woman, the child will be able to get either an A or an O gene from the father, only an O gene from the mother. The children of such a mating will tend to be AO and OO with an equal frequency.

In the event that the dominant gene were an abnormal gene, instead of the normal A gene, it is quite easy to see how the abnormal pattern of behavior associated with this particular genetic anomaly could be transmitted from parent to offspring in a simple and straightforward way.

Cell Division and Distribution

There are several ways in which cellular reproduction can occur. In the type of division called *mitosis,* the cell nucleus divides into two daughter nuclei which possess identical complements of chromosomes. In *meiosis*—a process unique to bisexual species like our own—two specialized cells, sperm and egg, are produced by the male and female, respectively. The single cell, called a zygote, which results from the fusion of these two specialized cells develops into the new individual.

Mitosis actually occurs as a stage in meiotic division, resulting in a duplication of each chromosome. After cellular division has occurred, one half of every doubled chromosome is apportioned to each daughter cell. Mitotic division thus maintains the constancy of the chromosomal complement of body cells; meiosis, on the other hand, represents a rather effective means of insuring *variation*. Hirsch and Hostetter (1968) have described the sequence of events in meiosis as follows:

> (1) Each chromosome pairs with the corresponding chromosome from the other parent. (2) The chromosome complement is reduced from diploid (a double occurrence of each chromosome) to haploid (a single occurrence of each chromosome) because each gamete /specialized sex cell egg or sperm receives only one member of each pair of chromosomes, and (3) Because the orientation (positioning) of the members of each pair is random. At the first division, each new cell gets a random sample of maternal and paternal chromosomes. (4) Since there are only two divisions in meiosis these divisions yield four cells. In the male, all four cells become mature sperm. But in the female, only one cell becomes an egg; the other three become polar bodies which later disintegrate.

Genetic variability is maintained by the independent meiotic assortment of chromosomes contributed by each parent. Since the number of chromosome pairs in the human being is extremely large, the resulting number of unique chromosomal combinations possible in a gamete is correspondingly large. It has been determined that a mating pair of human beings possesses the capability of producing more than seventy trillion zygotes, each of which is unique. Thus natural selectivity has extremely broad limits within which to operate.

METHODS OF GENETIC INVESTIGATION

Two concepts that are exceedingly important to an understanding of genetic research are the *genotype* and *phenotype*. Phenotype refers to those characteristics or properties of an individual which are accessible to direct observation, by one means or another: hair and eye color, physique, reaction to chemical and pharmacological agents, etc. Among phenotypic aspects, we should also include an individual's behavioral reactions. Genotype, on the other hand, represents the sum total of the individual's genetic endowment. Unlike the phenotype, it can only be derived through inference. This brings us to the first of the two major methods used in human genetic investigation: the family history or pedigree. In human genetics, there is a heavy reliance on the use of family histories, i.e. the phenotypes of an individual's relatives, since the selective breeding procedures which furnish the geneticist with valuable information about animal subjects are obviously out of the question with human subjects.

The family history or pedigree approach to the inheritance of abnormal behavior predispositions was probably the first method used by virtue of its obviousness: If one can look into the genealogy of an individual who exhibits abnormal behavior, it should theoretically be possible to determine how frequently the same or similar abnormalities have been exhibited in previous generations in that individual's family. Certain criticisms are attached to this method of study. In the first place, most clinical descriptions of abnormal behavior syndromes are the fruits of 19th and 20th century psychiatric experience. Thus, if an attempt is made to trace the familial antecedents of a schizophrenic, for example, the necessary records are apt to be difficult or impossible to procure.

A second difficulty is that "mental illness" has been, and still is, regarded by many people as a disgrace to the family in which it occurs. Hence, many families will go to extreme lengths to conceal the present or past occurrence of such conditions among their members.

A final problem has to do with the fact that standards or criteria for the judgment of what is abnormal have varied over time and from one community to another. Labeling, as we have already seen, can be highly misleading; the symptoms designated by a particular nomenclature might be completely different as a function of time and place. At best, then, it is possible to deal only with the histories of certain families in which the abnormality was fairly constant and of such a nature that it could not be concealed from the public.

Another major method of genetic investigation is the *twin study*. Although it is the most demanding in terms of time, effort, and expense, the twin study is also the most reliable approach to genetic research. Inasmuch as monozygotic twins represent the closest approximation to identical heredity that is available to the scientist, they constitute a source of valuable information on the contribution of genetic determinants to behavioral variation. In the extreme rare cases of identical twins reared apart, a further source of information is supplied which could not be obtained through the controlled procedures of laboratory research.

The twin study is not without its drawbacks. Although a given pair of MZ (monozygotic) twins might appear to possess identical genetic endowments, Burt (1966) cautions that one twin may have resulted from the less developed half of the embryo. Therefore, that twin may be smaller and weaker than the other. Monozygoticity, in short, does not guarantee absolutely identical inheritance.

A third method of genetic investigation, *correlational analysis,* makes use of the fact that the genetic correlation between related individuals can be determined by considering their degree of consanguinity. Thus, the genetic correlation between parent and offspring is .5 because one half of the genes are received from each parent. The genetic correlation between siblings, however, varies between .0 and 1.0, with an average of .5 As Hirsch and Hostetter (1968) observe, "Since the degree of meiotic relationship gives us the general genetic correspondence among individuals in a family, we can infer the genetic status of a behavior trait from the relationship of its distribution among the members of a family to the general distribution of known genetic traits in the same family."

As we shall see in the following section, investigators typically make use of more than a single method or approach. A given study may combine the comparison of MZ and DZ (dizygotic) with a correlational analysis of trait variation over three generations of family members. The only method of genetic investigation which is conspicuous by its absence in human behavior genetics is that of selective breeding. And if we can credit our science fiction writers with clairvoyance, controlled mating studies are just over the horizon.

Sex Chromosome Anomalies and Antisocial Behavior

Research in the field of sex chromosomes abnormalities as related to antisocial behavior is a very recent development, having its beginnings in the 1960's. In their survey of the research in this area, Forssman and Hambert (1967) point out that the normal number of chromosomes in humans was not established until 1956 by Tjio and Levan. Since that time, evidence has been reported which presumably demonstrates a relationship between abnormalities in sex chromosomes and a tendency towards criminal behavior; that is, that individuals with certain types of chromosomal anormalies are more likely to be found among antisocial criminal offenders than persons with a normal chromosomal structure. Most of this research has been conducted in Great Britain, (Court Brown, 1962; Casey, Segall, Street, and Blank, 1966a; Hunter, 1967, 1968). As Telfer, Baker, Clark, and Richardson (1968) indicate: "The prevalence of aneuploidy among criminal males who are mentally ill, mentally retarded, or criminally insane, is a phenomenon well appreciated in Great Britain but little recognized in the United States."

According to Montagu (1968), the double Y sex complement is produced during the formation of the sperm between a normal and nondisjunctional gamete. It is during the second meiotic division that nondisjunction occurs as illustrated in Figures 5-1 and 5-2.

The XYY syndrome is reputedly characterized by aggressiveness, mental subnormality, and tallness. Concerning the latter characteristic, the team of Jacobs, Brunton, Melville, Brittain, and McClemont (1965) noted:

> . . .it is already apparent that they are unusually tall. Among the 197 men we studied, the difference between the mean height of the males with one Y chromosome (67.0 inches) and that of those with two Y chromosomes (73.1 inches) is highly significant. In fact in this particular group a man more than 72 inches in height has an approximately one to two chance of having an XYY constitution.

Casey, Blank, Street, Segall, McDougall, McGrath, and Skinner (1966) found that out of every fifty males over six feet tall in the Moss Side and Rampton institutions, twelve had the XYY anomaly. They also found that in the Broadmoor Mental Hospital and Not-

NORMAL MALE MEIOSIS
(Formation of the sperm)

Primary Spermatocyte

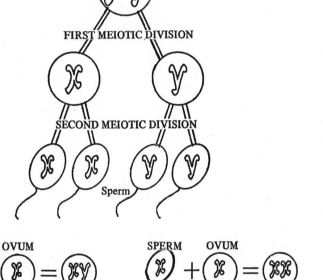

FIRST MEIOTIC DIVISION

SECOND MEIOTIC DIVISION

Sperm

| SPERM | OVUM | | SPERM | OVUM |

NORMAL MALE   NORMAL FEMALE

Figure 5-1. Normal Male Meiosis (Formation of the sperm), Montagu, A.: Chromosomes and crime. *Psychology Today, 2:* 43-49, 1968. Reproduced by permission of the author and publisher.

tingham Prison (sentences range from six months to five years), 8 percent were found to be of XYY chromosome count. Likewise, in a single XYY case of a noncriminal, a twelve year old boy, Sandberg, Ishihara, Crosswhite, and Koepf (1963) reported that the young boy was 180 cm. tall (5'11"). Also, Leff and Scott (1968) found that their forty-four years old patient with the additional Y chromosome to be six and one half feet tall. Richards (1966) also reported his patient to be over six feet tall.

NONDISJUNCTION OF SEX CHROMOSOMES IN MALE MEIOSIS

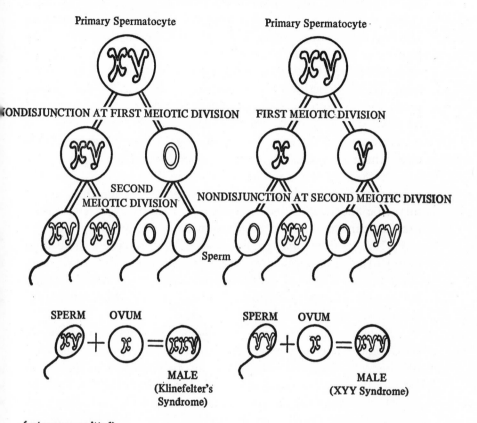

(autosomes omitted)

Figure 5-2. Nondisjunction of Sex Chromosomes in Male Meiosis, Montagu, A.: Chromosomes and crime. *Psychology Today, 2:* 43-49, 1968. Reproduced by permission of the author and publisher.

Sex Development

Although Casey, Segall, Street, and Blank (1966) suggested in their studies of chromosomal abnormalities in two state hospitals (for patients requiring special security) that many physical features of the Klinefelter's syndrome were present in the patients with the XYY chromosomes, only six cases have shown any of the characteristic abnormal sex development. Sandbery, *et al.* (1963) described the twelve year old boy with undescended testes which were, later, successfully treated. In another case, Townes, Zeigler, and Lenhard (1965) reported that their five year old patient (a XYYY mosaic) also had undescended testes. Throughout their discussion, they cite four other cases where patients with the extra Y chromosome had underdeveloped testes. Hauschka, Hasson, Goldstein, Koepf, Sandberg, (1962) described a twenty-three year old XYY male whose penis and scrotum were undeveloped. He had no facial hair, and his auxiliary and pubic hair were sparse.

Nevertheless, there have been many other studies among XYY cases where no remarkable sex abnormalities in sex development has occurred. Hauschka *et al.* (1962) describes his forty-four year old patient with normal sexual development and seven children. (It might be added here that it is considered unlikely that the additional Y chromosome can be transmitted to the offspring.) Of the seven XYY patients that Jacobs, *et al.* (1965) reported, none were found to have abnormal sex development. Richards (1966) similarly reported normal sex development in his patient. Weiner, Sutherland, Bartholomew, and Hudson (1968) found no abnormalities among their four cases.

Although this discrepancy may suggest that sexually abnormal development may not be an important characteristic of the XYY syndrome, Court Brown, Price, and Jacobs (1968), who could find none in their studies, suggest caution. The reason for this warning is that, because of the nature of the groups in which these men are found, they are usually single; rarely is there any information on their fertility. Thus, it is still unclear whether or not there is a definite relationship between the additional chromosome and sex abnormality.

Race

When Welch, Borgoankar, and Herr (1967) surveyed Patuxent Institution in Maryland, they found that despite the fact that over half of the inmates were Negroes, the one individual in whom the XYY syndrome appeared was white. They also noted that no Negro XYY cases had been discovered as of that date (1967). A short time later, however, Telfer, Baker, and Longtin (1968) reported the first Negro case of XYY in an American prison. It seems rather doubtful whether racial factors possess any real relevance for chromosomal aberrations. Reported differences between white and Negro samples are probably attributable, in part, to the fact that the composition of inmate populations in British and American prisons is quite different. Further research in the United States may very well produce something approaching parity in the relative proportions of white and Negro cases.

Mental Subnormality

We have already discussed the consistently high correlations that have been reported between sex chromosomal anomalies and mental subnormality. Forssman and Hambert (1962) have noted the high rate of chromatin-positive males in institutions for hard-to-manage criminals. MacLean, Mitchell, and Harnden (1962) surveyed 4,514 mental defectives and found an unusually disproportionate number of sex chromosome abnormalities among mental hospital patients. Jacobs, *et al.* (1965) suggested that the second Y was likely to be an important factor in the increased frequency of XYY cases in hospitals for the mentally subnormal. They found all XYY's at Carstairs to be below normal in intelligence.

Studies with XYY patients have also offered support for this contention. Of over sixty cases of XYY, all but three have been identified with mentally subnormal individuals. Leff and Scott (1968) found one XYY case with an IQ of 118. According to the report, this individual, although not incarcerated, had been known to embezzle. The remaining two cases were considered of average intelligence.

Abnormal Behavior

It is the hypothesized effect of the Y chromosome on human behavior that has created such a stir among clinical criminologists today. Is it true that the extra Y chromosome predisposes the individual to "super-maleness?" Does the additional Y chromosome exert an extraordinary influence on the individual's social behavior?

Most of the XYY cases discovered thus far have been found in prisons or hospitals for mental defectives, perhaps suggesting that there is some significant relationship between the chromosomal aberration and abnormal behavior. The study of Casey, *et al.* (1966) on the frequency of XYY males in a mentally ill population indicates that an extra Y may have a part to play in abnormal social behavior, even in the absence of mental subnormality. Price, Strong, Whatmore, and McClemont (1966) also reported that severe personality disorders of undetermined cause were found among the XYY'S in a maximum security institution. None were diagnosed in categories of brain damage, epilepsy, or psychosis. Court Brown, *et al.* (1967) pointed out that there were no medical explanations for their presence in the institution.

In 1967, Hope, *et al.* (1967) studied all nine of the XYY patients discovered earlier in Edinburgh's maximum security institution in 1965. Seven were classified as mental defectives and the remaining two as "mentally ill." Using a control group which was matched with the inmate group on a number of selected variables, the researchers administered a series of psychological tests to both groups. Results failed to discriminate the experimental group from the control group. Although the two groups differed little on scores relating to hostility and intelligence, the experimental group appeared to be somewhat more introverted and lower in self-esteem. The greatest difference between the two groups occurred on the "reactive narcissism" scale. The controls received much higher scores, indicating an abhorrence of dirt and strivings toward punctuality, perfection, and orderliness.

Price and Whatmore (1967a) later studied these same patients. They found extremes of instability and irresponsibility in the personality configurations of the XYY cases. As was noted, none seemed to consider any but the most immediate consequences of their actions. They had no constructive aim for the future and what plans they had were unrealistic. The patients were reported to have little depth of affection for others and little capacity to understand. Price and Whatmore pointed out that the subjects' greatest difficulty was in social adjustment arising from emotional instability and an incapacity to tolerate the mildest frustration. Although the experimental groups did not demonstrate greater hostility, they were more capable of violence if frustrated or antagonized.

Moreover, when Price and Whatmore investigated the criminal records of both the control and experimental groups, they found some interesting differences. While none of the controls had ever been convicted of a crime prior to the age of ten, three of nine XYY's showed a history of such convictions. The mean age of the first conviction for the control group was 18.0 years, while 13.1 years was the mean age for the experimental group. At least five of the nine XYY's had records of truancy prior to conviction. There was no evidence of such trouble with the controls. Probably the most striking difference between the two groups was found when their types of offenses were compared. Seventeen out of eighteen controls had records for crimes against persons. Of the nine XYY subjects, only four had been responsible for such crimes. With respect to crime against property, there was little distinction between the two. According to Price and Whatmore (1967), they found that of a total of ninety-two convictions for the XYY group, 8 percent were against person, while 88 percent were against property. In contrast, the control group received 22 percent of their convictions for crimes against person and 61 percent against property.

Again, Price and Whatmore brought forth another interesting factor. When the inmates' records were compared with those of their family, the siblings of the control group had a much higher rate of crime. The control group had a total of sixty-three siblings. Twelve had been convicted a total of 139 times. The XYY group had thirty-one siblings, of which only one had been convicted a single time. These findings seem to suggest a lack of environmental influence in the XYY's background. As Price and Whatmore summarized their study, "There is not predisposing family environment, and their criminal activities often start at an early age before they are seriously influenced by factors outside the home." In short, they found most of the patients showing evidence of immaturity, defective development, or inadequate control. None were considered intellectually capable of control over disordered drives that lead to criminality.

In another survey, Bartlett (1968) found two XYY subjects in prison to be very high in hostility and anxiety. No marked difference in scores was found however, between the two. Both patients were diagnosed as schizoid and homosexual. Both were active in arson and larceny before incarceration. Bartlett noted that cases of arson and larceny were considered by Court Brown to be prevalent among males with the abnormal sex chromosome complement.

Criminological Consequences

The Courts

If the additional Y chromosome should prove to be causally related to "super-maleness," the courts may be required to absolve the defendant of criminal responsibility. As we noted earlier, an accused murderer in Melbourne, Australia was acquitted when he was shown to have the XYY syndrome. In California and Maryland, two men have appealed their guilty verdicts because they are XYY.

Treatment

As in cases of "legal insanity," the XYY offender may be admitted to a state hospital. Thus far, little can be done to treat the syndrome because of the nature of the chromosome anomaly. As Price and Whatmore (1967a) reported, there has been no success at corrective training and treatment despite repeated and prolonged attempts. However, some geneticists claim that if the syndrome is detected at an early age, assistance in the form of psychotherapy, special educational programs, job and family counseling, and medical and surgical care could be provided to control the individual's tendencies toward abnormal behavior.

PATHOLOGICAL HYPOESTHESIA

Clinical descriptions of the antisocial (sociopathic, psychopathic) personality, as Quay (1965) has noted, have emphasized the centrality of certain behavioral features—impulsivity and the lack of tolerance for sameness—as primary and distinctive of this disorder. Says Quay:

> The psychopath is almost universally characterized as highly impulsive, relatively refractory to the effects of experience in modifying his socially troublesome behavior, and lacking in the ability to delay gratification. His penchant for creating excitement for the moment without regard for later consequences seems almost unlimited. He is unable to tolerate routine and boredom. While he may engage in anti-

social, even vicious behavior his outbursts frequently appear to be motivated by little more than a need for thrills and excitement.

In seeking to account for these behavioral characteristics, Quay has advanced an hypothesis which we shall refer to as *pathological hypoesthesia*. According to this hypothesis, the psychopath's "primary abnormality lies in the realm of basic reactivity and/or adaptation to sensory inputs of all types." Thus, pathological hypoesthesia can be understood as *an extreme of stimulation seeking behavior*.

Studies of sensory deprivation and perceptual isolation in both animal and human subjects have affirmed that such experiences are affectively unpleasant and potentially motivating to the extent that the organism will behave in such a way as to increase the level of intensity and variability of available stimulation. If one hypothesizes that the psychopath requires sensory inputs of greater intensity and variability than those of the average person, then much of the psychopathic individual's otherwise inexplicable thrill-seeking behavior and impulsivity becomes comprehensible.

As Quay observes, there are two possible lines of explanation for this apparent pathological hypoesthesia: (1) lessened basal reactivity, and (2) increased adaptation rate. "The first is that basal reactivity to stimulation is lowered so that more sensory input is needed to produce efficient and subjectively pleasurable cortical functioning. A second possibility is that there is a more rapid adaptation to stimulation which causes the need for stimulation variation to occur more rapidly and with greater intensity." Both of these hypotheses have received limited support from empirical investigations.

AUTONOMIC AND CARDIOVASCULAR RESEARCH

In general, increased activity in the sympathetic division of the autonomic nervous system appears to have an excitatory or facilitative effect upon cortical activity in the brain. Lacey (1959), however, has indicated that this apparently does not hold true for increases in heart rate and blood pressure. Evidence is available which suggests that increased heart rate and blood pressure may actually lead to an inhibition of cortical activity.

The autonomic nervous system is not solely an effector system. From most autonomically innervated organs, sensory fibers arise. From these fibers signals are fed back to the central nervous system. Research findings (e.g. Nakao, Ballin, Gellhorn, 1956; Bonvallet and Allen, 1963) indicate that at least one visceral reflex pathway may be of great significance for the control of behavior. The pressure-sensitive receptors in the carotid sinus, long known to participate in cardiovascular homeostasis, have been shown to exercise tonic inhibitory control over cortical electrical activity. The carotid sinus is strategically located to serve as an immediately responsive device for the detection of changes in heart rate and blood pressure; it is joined by pressure-sensitive receptors in the aortic arch and probably also by other pressure-receptors in the walls of the heart itself. If blood pressure goes up, these receptors, under normal conditions, faithfully increase their rate of discharge and reflexly produce a wide variety of adjustments to reduce the blood pressure.

An increase in heart rate or blood pressure, then, is likely to lead to inhibitory effects on cortical activity. Changes in heart rate and blood pressure (autonomic responses) become stimuli to internal receptors, whose activation may well lead reflexly to changes in the relationship of the organism to the environment, in terms of the accessibility of the organism to environmental stimulus inputs. An individual with cardiac lability, i.e. a consistently exaggerated or hyperactive cardiovascular response pattern, might be described as a person who requires a higher level of intensity and broader range of stimuli than the non-labile individual in order to reach some threshold of responding. It is as though he is several "stimulus degrees under par."

In a series of studies beginning with the work of Funkenstein, Greenblatt, and Solomon (1949) and culminating in the Ohio Penitentiary study of Lindner and his associates (1970), the presence of such cardiac lability has been confirmed in a population of psychiatrically identified antisocial offenders. This research, which is discussed later in a chapter dealing specifically with the antisocial personality, is congruent with Quay's (1965) proposal that the psychopath is characterized by pathological stimulation-seeking, and that it is possible" . . . to view much of the impulsivity of the psychopath, his need to create excitement and adventure, his thrill-seeking behavior, and his inability to tolerate routine and boredom as a manifestation of an inordinate need for increases or changes in the pattern of stimulation."

Perceptual Typing

Extensive research by Petrie (1967) on perceptual typing, summarized in a recent book (1967), led her, like Quay (1965), to describe the psychopath in terms of a need for stimulation. This conclusion was based on the study of individuals who evidence different degrees of sensitivity to pain stimulation and different degrees of tolerance of perceptual isolation. Petrie's subjects were categorized into one of three perceptual types:

Augmenters are those individuals who increase the perceived intensity of pain. Apparently because of this automatic tendency to amplify sensory input, they tend to be intolerant of suffering from pain. On the other hand, they tolerate confinement and isolation well. On a kinesthetic figural after-effects procedure they show large overestimations of the size of the test bar after having rubbed an inspection bar for a period of time. This augmenting reaction occurs regardless of whether the inspection bar is larger or smaller than the test bar. *Moderates* are defined as those individuals who do not show extreme reactions to either pain stimulation or to perceptual isolation. Their figural after-effect responses fall between those of the augmenters and those of the third category of individuals, the reducers. *Reducers* are individuals who show a notable tolerance for pain but a relative intolerance for reduced sensory input situations. On the after-effects procedure used by Petrie, they respond by underestimating the test bar after having rubbed an interpolated inspection bar. According to Petrie the psychopathy is a "reducer," one who subjectively reduces the intensity of environmental stimulation and is likely to be in a chronic state of sensory deprivation with a consequently higher drive for sensory input, i.e. in a state similar to Quay's (1965) description.

Petrie, MacCulloch, and Kazdin (1962), moreover, comment that the general conduct of her delinquent subjects was reminiscent of that of some brain-injured patients, the delinquents showed atypical stimulus-governed behavior. The atypical stimulus governed perceptual type had been noted in the first instance in patients in whom there turned out to be clinical indications of brain pathology. This type of subject is characterized by the fact that when a larger object is used for stimulation, he reduces the measured block by the criterion amount or more; when stimulated with a small object, he increases it by more than the criterion amount. The contrast effect of the smaller stimulus tends to encourage augmenting and inhibit reducing. The larger stimulus encourages reducing and inhibits augmenting, hence the stimulus governed persons can be thought of as displaying to an exaggerated degree the normal contrast effect of the juxtaposed sizes. Such a person is least able to escape from the direct and restrictive influence of the relative size of the juxtaposed stimuli.

ELECTROCORTICAL RESEARCH

In terms of the ways in which the brain deals with afferent input, there must be a coding device or process coextensive with units of time. This assumption seems necessary because in intact organisms the sense organs supply the central nervous system (CNS) with a vast, superfluous amount of data. To prevent surplus information from overloading or swamping neural circuits, the CNS must have some method of reducing or coding data. This general assumption would have to be made if changes in afferent stimulation (or reutilization of previously stored input) are to be encoded in proper temporal sequence, as well as for the consequent psychological functions to operate on a common time basis.

The assumption that the brain encodes or reduces sensory data is theoretically dealt with by a general theory alternatively called the "Neuronic Shutter Theory" or the "Cortical Excitability Cycles Theory" (Callaway and Alexander, 1960; Horter, 1967). This theory postulates an ordered temporal sampling, gating or timing device which reduces surplus perceptual data. In essence, there is assumed an intermittent blocking of sensory data into the CNS. This gating is believed to be accomplished by means of cyclic changes in CNS excitability, and EEG alpha rhythm is thought to reflect these cyclic excitability changes. The EEG rhythm, itself, represents the summated effects of changes in the electrical potential of aggregates of neurons. Individual neurons have an excitability cycle which determines their accessibility, probability of being fired, to incoming neural impulses. If neurons in an aggregate are synchronized and have synchronous excitability cycles, the transmission of afferent impulses through them could be gated by their excitability cycle.

This theoretical formulation permits the derivation of a suggestive outline that may account for some aspects of antisocial or psychopathic behavior. It allows us, for example, to consider whether unusual brain wave activity in psychopaths reflects processes involved in central information mechanisms which are functioning differently than in normals. The theory is potentially rich in deductions about the behavior of psychopaths, given the validity of its application to this clinical population. For example, an intriguing notion to be examined is whether psychopaths would perform differently than normals in a task where an overt response is contingent on perceiving two signals occurring in the same "psychological" time interval. The temporal parameters in the experimental literature may be a source of material for examining the notion that psychopaths are hypoesthetic, that is, not properly processing their sensory input. Here we are considering the possibility that psychopaths did not make associations (learn) because the subjects did not temporally experience the task stimuli the way normal subjects did. Assessment of the temporal processes of CNS activity associated with the formation of conditioned responses may be highly illuminating. The perceptual time-set of psychopaths and normals may be different as a function of more basic processes. This deduction allows for looking at aspects of time perception and discrimination. For example, psychopaths and normals may demonstrate interesting differences if they are asked to set the beating of a metronome with the meter of their personal psychological time. Analyzing verb-tense frequency as a measure of latent speech may reflect the psychopath's cultural world-view, or temporal aspects of it. Petrie (1967) says that psychopathic-like juveniles are stimulus-governed. It may be interesting to examine the psychopath within the developmental schedule of Piaget in which the child moves from a spatially-oriented to a temporally perceived world.

Conclusion

It is not our intention in this brief review to criticize exhaustively current biological theories of criminality. To do so would be far beyond the scope of the present discussion and would place entirely unreasonable demands upon the biological knowledge available to the nonspecialist reader. Rather, we hoped to convey some impression of the variety and vitality of biological theorizing in the criminological area. Although our presentation fails to do justice to the theories we have reviewed, the reader cannot help but be favorably impressed by the contrast between earlier and contemporary biological and genetic hypotheses concerning criminality. There is a sophistication and operational specificity to such theoretical formulations as Quay's pathological hypoesthesia, for example, that is notably absent in the crude generalizations of the Schlapp and Smith endocrinological school; and if research on the XYY syndrome is subject to the criticism that findings thus far are more provocative than conclusive, at least the XYY researchers are capable of specifying the relevant variables in their investigations in a way that was not accessible to Lombroso and his contemporaries.

Sociology and psychology spent the first half of the twentieth century divesting man of any functions but those that were acquired through the medium of social learning. The reductionistic period that followed Watson's crude empiricism and behaviorism further contributed to the image of man as an "empty organism." The ethologists were among the first to restore to man some of those lost behavioral functions. Perhaps with a renaissance of interest in biological factors in criminality, the image of the criminal offender as an empty organism—a reinforcement machine—will be replaced by something more realistic and full.

Summary

This chapter explores some of the factors responsible for a resurgence of interest among criminologists in the potential role of biological processes in criminality. Specific attention is devoted to the XYY chromosomal anomaly and some of the implications that such an alleged "super-maleness syndrome" holds for the criminal justice system. As a background for this discussion, a brief review of basic concepts in genetics is presented. Also discussed are theories of criminality which assign potential significance to the operation of cardiovascular and electrocortical structures in criminal behavior. Contemporary research and theory in this area are contrasted with older, less informed views on the biology or genetics of criminal behavior variation.

REFERENCES

Allen, H.E.: A biosocial model of antisocial personality. A paper presented at the Ohio Valley Sociological Society meeting, Akron, Ohio. May 1, 1970.

Bartlett, D.J., et. al.: Chromosomes of male patients in a security prison. *Nature, 220:*120-121, 1968.

Bonvallet, M., and D'Anna, L.: Study of the labile secondary component of the phasic discharge of the reticular system activator. *Journal of Physiology, 5:*116-117, 1963.

Burt, C.: The genetic determination of differences in intelligence: a study of monozygotic twins reared together and apart. *British Journal of Psychology, 57:*137-153, 1966.

Callaway, E. and Alexander, J.D.: The temporal coding of sensory data: an investigation of two theories. *Journal of General Psychology, 62:*293-309, 1960.

Casey, M.D., et. al.: Sex chromosome observations in two state hospitals requiring security. *Nature, 209:*641-642, 1966.

Court Brown, W.M.: Sex chromosomes and the law. *Lancet, 2:*508, 1962.

Court Brown, W.M., et. al.: Males with an XYY sex chromosome complement. *Journal of Medical Genetics, 5:*341-349, 1968.

Funkenstein, D.H., Greenblatt, M., and Solomon, H.C.: Psychophysiological study of mentally ill patients. Part I: The status of the peripheral autonomic nervous system as determined by the reaction to epinephrine and mecholyl. *American Journal of Psychiatry, 106:*16-28, 1949.

Forssman, H.: Epilepsy in an XYY man. *Lancet, 1:*1389, 1967.

Forssman, H. and Hambert, G.: Chromosomes and antisocial behavior. *Excerpta Criminologica, 7:*1-5, 1967.

Hauschka, T.S., et. al.: An XYY man with progeny indicating familial tendency to nondisjunction. *American Journal of Human Genetics, 14:*22-30, 1962.

Hirsch, J. and Hostetter, R.C.: Behavior genetics. In London, P. and Rosenhan, D. (Eds.): *Foundations of Abnormal Psychology.* New York, Holt, Rinehart and Winston, 1968.

Hope, K., et. al.: Psychological characteristics associated with XYY sex chromosome complement in a state mental hospital. *British Journal of Psychiatry, 113*:495-498, 1967.

Jacobs, Patricia A., et. al.: Aggressive behavior, mental subnormality, and the XYY male. *Nature, 208*:1351-1352, 1965.

Lacey, J.P. and Lacey, Beatrice C.: Verification and extension of the principle of autonomic response stereotypy. *American Journal of Psychology, 71*:50-73, 1958.

Leff, J.P. and Scott, P.D.: XYY and intelligence. *Lancet, 1*:645, 1968.

Lindner, L.A., et. al.: An antisocial personality with cardiac lability. *Archives of General Psychiatry, 23*:260-267, 1970.

Maclean, N.J., et. al.: A survey of sex chromatin abnormalities in mental hospitals. *Journal of Medical Genetics, 5*:165-172, 1968.

Montagu, A.: Chromosomes and crime. *Psychology Today, 2*:43-49, 1968.

Muller, H.J.: Genetic principles in human populations. *American Journal of Psychiatry, 113*:481-491, 1956.

Nakao, H. and Koella, W.P.: Influence of nociceptive stimuli on evoked subcortical and cortical potentials in cat. *Journal of Neurophysiology, 19*:187-195, 1956.

Petrie, A.: *Individuality in Pain and Suffering.* Chicago, University of Chicago Press, 1967.

Petrie, A., McCulloch, R., and Kazdin, P.: The perceptual characteristics of juvenile delinquents. *Journal of Nervous and Mental Disease, 134*:415-421, 1962.

Price, W.H. and Whatmore, P.B.: Behavior disorders and pattern of crime among XYY males identified at a maximum security hospital. *British Medical Journal, 1*:533-536, 1967.

Quay, H.C.: Psychopathic personality as pathological stimulation-seeking. *American Journal of Psychiatry, 122*:180-183, 1965.

Richards, B.W. and Stewart, A.: The YY syndrome. *Lancet, 1*:984-985, 1966.

Sandberg, A.A., et. al.: XYY genotype: report of a case in a male. *New England Medical Journal, 268*:585-589, 1963.

Sandberg, A.A., et. al.: An XYY male. *Lancet, 2*:488-489, 1961.

Shields, J. and Slater, E.: Heredity and psychological abnormality. In Eysenck, H.J., (Ed.): *Handbook of Abnormal Psychology.* London, Pitman, 1960.

Telfer, M., et. al.: Incidence of gross chromosomal errors among tall criminal American males. *Science, 159*:1249-1250, 1968.

Townes, P.L., et. al.: A patient with 48 chromosomes (XYYY). *Lancet, 1*: 1041-1043, 1965.

Weiner, S. and Sutherland, G.: A normal XYY man. *Lancet, 2*:1352, 1968.

Welch, J.B., Borgaonkar, D.S., and Herr, H.M.: Psychopathy, mental deficiency, aggressiveness, and the XYY syndrome. *Nature, 214*:500-501, 1967.

Chapter 6

PSYCHIATRIC AND PSYCHOLOGICAL THEORIES OF CRIMINALITY

PROFESSIONAL INTEREST of any appreciable magnitude on the part of psychologists in crime, criminology, and criminal behavior is of comparatively recent origin. This is not to say that psychologists have failed to take a keen interest in crime phenomena or that some psychologists have not made efforts to fashion comprehensive theories of crime causation. But the distribution of professional labor prior to World War II relegated most psychologists to an academic role, where their activities were not of a kind that placed them into regular and frequent contact with criminal offenders.

Psychiatry, on the other hand, as a consequence of the professional responsibilities which the public has invested in its practitioners with respect to the management and control of deviance, has been amply represented at the level of criminological theory. The theoretical orientation of these psychiatric practitioners is supplied in the main by psychoanalysis. Psychiatric thought in the U.S. has been so heavily dominated by psychoanalysis that it would be fair to say the two share the same conceptual, i.e. psychodynamic, approach to the explanation of most behavioral phenomena, including those related to crime. Both the psychoanalyst and the psychiatrist have sought the explanation for criminal behavior in the early life history of the criminal offender; both the psychoanalyst and the psychiatrist have tended to conceptualize criminality in terms of some model of "mental illness" or abnormality. The difficulties and limitations inherent in this approach will be dis-

157

cussed later in this chapter.

All psychiatric theorizing about crime is not Freudian in character even though the influence of the famous Viennese may be present *indirectly,* e.g. as originator of the viewpoint toward criminal behavior against which a particular theorist may be reacting negatively. Glasser (1965) offers an illustrative example of this kind of reaction in his development of "Reality Therapy." At any rate, the ideas of Sigmund Freud provide a convenient place from which to begin our examination of psychological and psychiatric theories of criminality.

PSYCHODYNAMIC MODELS
Architecture of Personality: Sigmund Freud

Freud's basic postulate was that personality is governed by three dynamic systems, to which he gave the names *id, ego,* and *superego.* The *id* consists of instinctual sexual and aggressive drives—the substratum of personality from which all other systems develop. It operates according to the "pleasure principle" by seeking tension reduction through the discharge of impulses. The *ego* develops as a control system which seeks drive satisfaction through contact with reality. The ego functions to control the impulsiveness of the id in order that drive satisfaction can be obtained, but within the limits imposed on the individual by society. The ego has control over all cognitive and intellectual functions. The superego is the moral element of personality: it represents the totality of internalized demands of parents and of society as a whole.

Personality Dynamics

The most basic means by which the ego can control the id impulses is through the defense of repression. Through repression, the ego forces emerging id impulses to remain unconscious and not function in reality. Since the direct expression of primitive impulses is forbidden by social norms, the superego and the id generally operate in opposition to one another. The struggle between the id and superego is often an intense encounter—one of the byproducts of such a struggle is anxiety. Anxiety is a warning signal to the ego to take appropriate steps to control emerging impulses from overthrowing the system. Repression, then, provides the ego with its most direct mechanism for anxiety reduction: The primitive impulse is forced back into the unconscious, and the delicate balance between the id and superego is maintained.

Freud's system is a dynamic one in every sense; consequently the repressed thought is not lost, but makes its presence felt in other ways. One of the avenues through which the repressed thought may emerge is *displacement*. Through displacement, feelings or actions are transferred from their original goal to another object which arouses less anxiety. For example, a son who experiences intense anxiety over his aggressive feelings toward his father, may repress these thoughts; the unconscious aggressive desire, however, is typically displaced via the avenue of *identification* with the father. The displaced hostility may also show itself symbolically through hostile feelings toward other authority figures.

Mechanisms of Defense

Although Freud considered repression to be the most basic defense mechanism, it does not appear to be a very efficient one. Repression rarely, if ever, leads to complete anxiety reduction. Other defense mechanisms were postulated as alternatives which would assist the ego in its effect to reduce tension. These include: (1) projection, (2) reaction formulation, (3) fixation, (4) regression, and (5) denial.

Projection involves attributing one's own unacceptable traits, ideas, or impulses to other people or groups. Anxiety over primitive impulses, for example, may be reduced by attributing those same characteristics to others.

Reaction formation is a mechanism whereby the individual defends against an anxiety-producing impulse or idea by replacing it with its opposite impulse or idea. For example, a mother who unconsciously rejects her child might show smothering control of the child's behavior and overprotection.

Fixation connotes immobilization at a particular stage of personality development because progress to the next stage may be too anxiety-provoking. An example would be the overly dependent child whose efforts toward independence arouse severe anxiety.

Regression implies the return to a previous, more immature, level of development because anxiety or trauma associated with the present stage of development pose intolerable threats. A rather classic illustration here is the man who loses his job and finds solace in drinking.

Denial covers a variety of behaviors which are commonly motivated by the unconscious refusal or inability to face the truth of unacceptable thoughts or evaluations of oneself.

Through the operations of these defense mechanisms, the ego attempts to keep the anxiety caused by emerging id impulses within tolerable limits. If the ego is successful in this task and instinctual energy has been displaced into socially acceptable and creative channels, the personality matures normally. If, however, the ego functions in a faulty manner and the displacement of repressed desires does not keep anxiety within tolerable limits or the displacement is not socially acceptable, the individual is said to have developed abnormally.

Motivational Functionalism and the Unconscious

Behavior, as viewed within the above framework, is *functional* in a twofold sense: (1) it operates to fulfill certain needs or drives, and (2) it has consequences for other aspects of behavior. But the importance that Freud attributed to unconscious factors adds a further element of complexity to the interpretation of behavior, for it requires acceptance of the proposition that much, if not most, of the behavior exhibited by an individual possesses meaning which lies outside the range of awareness. Thus, psychological symptoms in neurosis, for example, are construed as the outward *symbolic manifestation* of dynamic dysfunction. Such behavior represents, for Freud, the unsuccessful attempt of the ego to exercise executive control over id impulses.

The immediate and direct implication of this principle of motivational functionalism for understanding criminal behavior is that a focus upon the criminal action itself (manifest function) defeats any attempt to understand the etiology of the crime. Says Feldman (1969):

> . . . like any other behavior, criminal behavior is a form of self-expression, and what is intended to be expressed in the act of crime

is not only unobservable in the act itself, but also may even be beyond the awareness of the criminal actor himself. So for example, an overt criminal act of stealing may be undertaken for the attainment of purposes which are far removed from, and even contrary to, that of simple illegal aggrandizement; indeed, it may even be, as shall be seen in the sequel, that the criminal, in stealing, seeks not material gain but self-punishment. The etiological basis of a criminal act can, therefore, be understood only in terms of the functions, latent as well as manifest, which the act was intended to accomplish.

Although the specific functions of a given criminal act must be sought in the life history of the individual offender, the general etiological formula for psychoanalytic criminology asserts that criminal behavior is an attempt at maintaining psychic balance or restoring psychic balance which has been disrupted. This is the position represented by Seymour Halleck, a psychodynamically oriented psychiatrist who had written extensively on crime and criminology.

Crime as Adaptation: Halleck

Seymour Halleck, a student of Karl Menninger, views the societal definition of normality as including two major directions of adaptation to oppressive stress. One direction requires a passive acceptance of an oppressive situation and an effort to live within the rules of the society (conformity). The other direction represents an attempt to change an oppressive situation by acting within the rules or by attempting to change the rules through legally approved individual group action (activism). An understanding of relevant norms is, therefore, crucial to the issue of defining criminality.

Mental illness cannot be as succinctly defined as criminality; there exists no unitary model or workable definition which has been unanimously agreed upon among the members of the psychiatric profession. An articulate spokesman for the profession, Halleck (1967) has stated his belief that: "As of this date, the profession of psychiatry has not been able to come up with a consistent definition of mental illness which is acceptable to all of its members."

Definitions of mental illness vary because of cultural biases imposed upon the psychiatrist. Therefore, mental illness, like criminality, is a social definition. It is based upon consistent social needs and purposes but differs because it relies on a somewhat scientific basis for determination.

It is herein that the difficulty arises. Some psychiatrists view mental illness as a process, realizing that mental health and mental illness occupy the same continuum. When an individual acts in such a manner that seems irrational or unreasonable, the individual is viewed as being in a temporary state of disorganization, implying that mental illness is a process which is subject to change or reversibility. The staunch supporter for this viewpoint is Karl Menninger (1963): "Between the individual in his most happy, contented, and constructive moment, and that same individual in the extremity of disorganization, there are an infinite number of points representing states-of-being with varying degrees of adjustment, from something more than zero percent to something less than one hundred percent of satisfactoriness."

Menninger and other psychiatrists, who support such a process model theory of mental illness, are at variance with those of the profession who adhere to static models which they feel supply more definitive answers. The proponents of such mental illness models simply define to what degree unreasonable and maladaptive behavior will be called illness, and then merely determine if the patient has demonstrated such behavior and therefore should be labeled as "mentally ill."

If one adopts Menninger's unitary model of behavior, it would allow one to find some mental illness and some normality in any individual. This view may have some scientific validity, but contains little, if any, social usefulness. Social needs and purposes, then, play a crucial role in determining which view of mental illness the psychiatrist wishes to adhere to.

RELATIONSHIP OF CRIMINALITY TO MENTAL ILLNESS. Keeping in mind the nature and lack of clarity of the definitions of crime and mental illness, we may now proceed to examine the relationship between the two as *adaptations to stress*. Halleck (1967) has developed this view:

> The stresses that lead to mental illness are often the same stresses that lead to crime . . . While both mental illness behaviors and criminal behaviors provide a certain degree of mastery over stress, the adap-

tations themselves often lead to some difficulty with the environment. Mental illness always has a maladaptive quality, and criminality usually has a maladaptive quality. . .

We have previously noted that mental illness is characterized by the communication of personal suffering, by communication of an inability to control one's behavior, and by society's judgment of unreasonableness of behavior.

Examining the first criterion, communication of personal suffering, it must be admitted that the majority of criminals do not communicate evidence of psychological pain except through their overt criminal behavior. It is difficult, however, to determine whether they were present and operative at the time the offense was committed.

The criterion of inability to control one's behavior is much more difficult and complicated to study; concepts of free will and determinism play a crucial role in an examination of an individual's self-control. This inherent difficulty is born out by the following statement by Menninger (1968):

Free will—to a lawyer—is not a philosophical theory, a religious concept, or scientific hypothesis. It is a given, a basic assumption in legal theory and practice. To the psychiatrist, this position is preposterous; he seeks operational definitions of free and will. On the other hand, the psychiatrist's assumption that motivation and mentation can go on unconsciously is preposterous to lawyers, constituting a veritable self-contradiction in terms.

The law assumes that when an individual reaches the magic age of discretion, he should exhibit socially acceptable and approved behavior. Individuals are also equally endowed in the eyes of the law. The psychiatrist, however, sees people as markedly unequal with respect to endowment, discretion, equilibrium, self-control, aspiration, and intelligence; therefore, his views are in direct conflict with those of the legal profession. Again, Menninger (1968) serves as spokesman for this viewpoint:

Basically, the lawyer is interested in formulating correct rules of behavior—through the reasoning of the "reasonable" man, and is not interested in explaining how such reasoning and behavior operate. One might say that one of the greatest dilemmas for the law and the lawyer has been the reasoning of the *unreasonable man:* since the entire system of law, and in some cases, the system of logic supported by the law, is based on the reasonable man and is by definition, pre-scriptive. We find that the premises of the criminal law do not contain such irrationalities. Eluding the descriptive nature of the subject mat-ter of psychiatry and maintaining prescriptive elements the law has complemented this premise with the development of a rule capable of handling, though not describing or understanding the exceptions. We acknowledge the behavioral scientist as one who attempts to put the world of thought and action in some logical system of order. He does so through observation, description, experimentation, and repli-cation. Might then lawyers and psychiatrists use their logic differently?

Criminality then, is viewed as goal oriented manifestations rather than unreasonable or irrational behavior. It is assumed that the criminal is seeking goals which everyone can understand and accept. It is quite different and difficult for society to think of the offender as one whose actions and motives are not directly related to logical, rational goal attainment.

In the final analysis, one can deduce that criminality and mental illness share the same characteristics or similar ones, and one must also admit that if the judgments by which we assign and designate irrational or unreasonable behavior were applied to the law viola-tor, one could readily discern that many criminals behave in the same manner as that of individuals labeled as mentally ill. There is, however, one pitfall inherent in this line of reasoning. The psychi-atrist, no doubt, encounters criminals who seem to him no different from those patients he has come to know and treat as mentally ill. There is, however, the important fact that before the offender can be seen by the psychiatrist, he must first violate the criminal code, as pointed out in the first section of this analysis. As Halleck (1967) observed:

> There is no precise way of knowing whether or not the appre-hended or convicted criminals differ sociologically or psychologically from their more fortunate brethren. If reasonable and self-serving criminal behaviors to occur, they are likely to be seen in that crimi-nal population which eventually comes to prison. The incarcerated offender is by definition an inefficient offender, and just like a person who is inefficient at anything else, he is more likely to be disturbed.

Critique of Psychoanalytic Criminology

Despite a consensus of professional opinion among psycho-analytic criminologists concerning the general etiological ("psychic balance") formula, considerably less unanimity is evident with respect to the specific factors in the socialization of the individual which dispose him toward criminality as an effort toward retaining psychic balance. Feldman (1969) identifies no fewer than five variations on the basic etiological formula:

1. criminality as neurosis.
2. the antisocial character as an instance of defective socialization.
3. criminal behavior as compensation for frustration of conventional psychic needs.
4. criminal behavior as a function of defective superego.
5. criminal behavior as anomie.

As Feldman noted, these variant interpretations range from a concentration on hypothesized internal factors to an emphasis upon external conditions which may exert a deciding influence upon the individual.

The weakness of this etiological formulation is readily apparent. In the case of the first interpretation, "criminality as neurosis," we have already noted that the empirical data simply fail to support the contention that the criminal is typically a neurotic individual compulsively driven toward self-punishment. To the contrary, criminal offenders appear to strain every effort and resource to elude capture. Moreover, the empirical evidence we have been able to gather suggests that neurotic personality characteristics are distributed within the criminal population in approximately the same proportion as that found in the noncriminal population.

Equally dubious is the view of the criminal as an antisocial character who seeks immediate gratification, lives entirely in the present, and is unable to withstand tedium and monotony. It is a criminological commonplace that many kinds of criminal behavior require extensive preparation by way of training in specific skills or in systematic planning. Indeed, as Feldman observes wryly, the areas of professional, organized, and white-collar crime seem to exemplify the operation of Freud's "reality principle."

In failing to assign appropriate emphasis to the fact that patterned criminality is not the spontaneous creation of the individual offender, psychoanalytic criminology minimizes the crucial importance of social learning. According to Feldman (1969) :

> . . . this learning process requires the individual's participation in the formation and maintenance of relationships with others who dispose of the necessary knowledge and put it to use. It is in the context of these relationships that the individual learns his criminality and adopts for himself distinctive criminalistic attitudes and percepts. Presumably, the experiences of such a learning process must have an effect on the personality of the individual undergoing them. Yet, this reciprocating influence of criminal experience on the personality of the criminal appears to have no consideration in psychoanalytic criminology. Indeed, all of the interpretations of the basic etiology formula share this common implicit assumption that the personality differentials to which casual status is attributed are temporally antecedent to the individual's participation in criminal activity. Nevertheless, it is at least a plausible alternative possibility that such personality differentials are consequential precipitants of the individual's induction into criminality. And in failing to take this possibility into account, the entire structure of psychoanalytic criminology becomes vulnerable to the charge that it merely begs the question from the outset.

Finally, in addition to these substantive criticisms, psychoanalytic criminology possesses some serious flaws when judged *as a theory* on formal criteria. Psychodynamic constructs tend to be global and all-inclusive in nature, and little effort is directed toward the specification of variables. Psychodynamic constructs are replete with "surplus meaning," i.e. terms such as ego, defense mechanism, identification, and the like are rarely if every pinned down to explicit empirical operations. Nevertheless, in time such constructs have become the "facts" upon which even more speculative elaborate conceptualizations are based.

Most of the research generated by the theory does not seem to be geared toward the subsequent modification or revision of the theory on the light of newly acquired information but rather to demonstrate the essential validity of the basic postulates and assumptions of the system. Because of the ambiguity of observations and lack of operational specificity of constructs, no hypothesis can ever be clearly confirmed or refuted. For example, the studies by Lazarus and his associates (1953) and by Murray (1959) appear to confirm the operation of the mechanism of repression; yet, had the results been in the opposite direction, they could have been used to confirm the operation of reaction-formation. The critics of psychoanalysis have charged, with justification, that the theory and its proponents do not conform to the widely accepted canons of empirical verfication and refutation in scientific method.

Reality Therapy: Glasser

Reality Therapy is described by its originator, Dr. William Glasser (1965), as a new conceptual approach to psychiatry. Its development stems from Glasser's dissatisfaction with the "futility" of classical psychoanalytic procedures. Glasser, a practicing psychiatrist in Los Angeles, feels that these procedures allow the patient to blame others for his own problems and thus provide a kind of "psychiatric kick" anaolgous to pills or alcohol.

Reality Therapy differs from traditional psychiatric approaches; it views irresponsibility behavior not as an outcome of illness, but rather sees illness as the product of irresponsibility. Problems stem from irresponsibility, not lack of insight. Glasser maintains that everyone who requires psychiatric treatment is suffering from one basic inadequacy. This inadequacy is the inability to fulfill his essential needs as an individual. No matter how foolish one's actions may seem; they are all valid to the individual in his search for adequacy or identity. These actions are overt manifestations of their loss with reality. Reality therapy is concerned with guiding these individuals back to reality and helping them fulfill their basic needs.

To help the individual, it is necessary for the therapist to become involved with the individual. Only when this level of involvement is achieved can the therapist help the patient meet the two basic psychological needs of reality therapy. These needs are the need to love and be loved and the need to feel that we are worthwhile to ourselves and to others. Glasser feels that this need to love and be loved is something that we strive for throughout life. If the person fails to satisfy this need, he will suffer various psychological pains. Glasser states that to feel worthwhile to ourselves and others, we must necessarily conform to the general acceptable behavior patterns. This standard behavior pattern is a rule by which our worth is usually judged. The individuals that are able to meet these basic needs are usually happy and responsible people. Those who are unable to fulfill these basic needs are those who we find in psychiatrists offices or in mental hospitals.

The term responsibility has been used in speaking of the psychological problems faced by individuals. Responsibility is a basic concept of reality and is defined "as the ability to fulfill one's needs, and to do so in a way that does not deprive others of the ability to fulfill their needs" (Glasser, 1965). To help people attain self fulfillment through responsibility, reality therapy teaches that two important things must take place. First, the individual must be taught how to be responsible. This is where Glasser once again stresses the idea of involvement. When the involvement between the therapist and patient is achieved, then the therapist can show the patient that his behavior is irresponsible and totally unworthy of recognition. When the patient realizes that he must alter his behavior to achieve recognition, he will also realize that he alone is responsible for his behavior. Second, reality therapy stresses the fact that the therapist must also be a responsible person. The therapist must be an emotionally strong individual who is able to withstand constant criticism and examination. Glasser believes that unless the therapist genuinely cares about people and becomes involved with them, reality therapy will not work. In this method of therapy, the therapist is not merely a judge for his patient. On the contrary, the therapist is supposed to be a friend who will listen to the present problems an individual is faced with and who will try to offer better suggestions of dealing with reality:

> In summary, then, our basic job as therapists is to become involved with the patient and to get him to face reality. When confronted with reality by the therapist with whom he is involved, he is forced again and again to decide whether or not he wishes to take the responsible path. Reality may be painful, it may be harsh, it may be dangerous, but it changes slowly. All any man can hope to do is to struggle with it in a responsible way by doing right and enjoying the pleasure or suffering the pain that may follow (Glasser, 1965).

Glasser identified six major areas of difference between reality therapy and conventional therapy:

1. Reality therapy does not believe in the term mental illness. Mental illness is felt to be too vague and implies that the entire makeup of the patient is drastically wrong. Reality therapy is con-

cerned with helping people who are able to become responsible.

2. Reality therapy focuses on the present and toward the future. We cannot change the past, nor can we allow past experiences to be used as an excuse for present irresponsible behavior.

3. Reality therapy relies upon the patient becoming involved with the therapist as a therapist and not as a transfer figure. When the patient realizes that the therapist expects him to act in a different manner because he is a concerned friend, then Glasser feels that the patient will realize the necessity of changing his behavior.

4. Reality therapy is not bothered by unconscious problems. Glasser professes that the unconscious is too often an excuse for irresponsible behavior and consequently the therapist forces the patient to understand his present overt behavior.

5. Reality therapy deals with morality. As previously stated, Glasser feels that for people to become worthwhile to themselves and others, they must conform to certain accepted behavior patterns. The reality therapist expounds the idea that to help his patient he must necessarily show him these accepted patterns and help him to follow them.

6. Reality therapy is concerned with the therapist acting in the role of a teacher in showing the patient how to deal with his problems and how to fulfill his needs (Glasser, 1965).

Reality therapy is one of the more controversial psychotherapeutic techniques in current use. Although its creator views it as an answer to many of society's ills, most psychiatrists and psychologists seem to regard reality therapy with a great deal of scepticism. Of course, some of the scepticism must be taken with at least a pinch or two of salt; after all, Glasser created reality therapy as a counterpoise to traditional dynamically oriented psychotherapy. Nevertheless, there are other legitimate grounds for criticism of reality therapy.

O. Hobart Mowrer, who wrote the introduction to Glasser's *Reality Therapy* (1965), claimed that "there is much . . . supporting data of a thoroughly empirical nature and that the premises of RT are rapidly gaining credence in many quarters." Diligent examinations of the professional literature by the present authors failed to disclose any of the empirical evidence to which Mowrer alludes. Although a number of juvenile and adult correctional institutions have experimented with RT, few if any of these experiments thus far appear to have resulted in "supporting data of a thoroughly empirical nature"—the kind that are absolutely required in order to evaluate the effectiveness of RT as an approach to correctional intervention.

PSYCHOLOGICAL CONCEPTIONS OF CRIME
Containment Theory: Reckless

Containment theory is a sociopsychological synthesis which seeks to account for the large middle range of criminality and delinquency that falls between the psychological and character disturbances at one polar extremity and the dominant pursuit of a traditional way of life at the other extremity. It thus provides an explanation of conformity as well as deviance. Containment theory introduces certain concepts relating to the construct of self to explain differential responses to the available models, pressures, and "pulls" in an individual's environment.

The following concepts, propositions, and facts are integral to an understanding of containment theory (Reckless, 1962) :

Concepts
1. self-concept
2. significant other
3. reference groups
4. roles (as perceived by the individual)

Propositions
1. Significant others define our self-concept
2. People act in accordance with their perceptions of approved behavior
3. We refer to our significant others before we act
4. People with good self-concepts will not engage in crime (also an hypothesis)

Facts
1. Incarcerated felons have a poorer self-concept than non-incarcerated felons
2. People with poor self-concepts engage in more criminal and deviant behaviors than people with good self-concepts.

We would therefore predict that people with poor self-concepts are more likely to engage in crime.

Containment theory postulates the existence of two reinforcing aspects which act as insulators against normative deviance, i.e. violation of socio-legal norms of conduct. These consist of an *inner control system* and an *outer control system* .

Outer containment is defined as the ability of society, groups, organizations, and the community to hold the individual within the bounds of accepted norms, rules, regulations, values, and expectations (holding power of the group). It consists of such things as providing the individual with meaningful roles in society and the incorporation or integration of the individual. This latter concept means to offer the person warm, supportive relationships, acceptance, and a sense of belonging and identity. Outer containment is maximized under conditions of isolation and homogenity of class, culture, and population.

Inner containment is defined as the ability of the individual to follow the accepted norms, his ability to steer himself. Inner containment consists of such factors as self-concept, goal orientation, frustration tolerance, and retention of norms.

A predictive model for the two containments can be set up in the following fashion:

1. When the person has a strong inner containment and a strong outer containment, the chance of his being involved in crime or delinquency are almost nil.

2. When the person has a strong inner containment with a weak outer containment, there is not much chance of his being involved in crime or delinquency (although a greater chance than number one).

3. When the person has a weak inner containment and a strong outer containment, the chances of his being involved in crime or delinquency are greater than in numbers one or two.

4. When the person has a weak inner containment and a weak outer containment, this represents the greatest chance of his being involved in delinquency or crime in our modern, urban, mobile world.

Inner and outer containment may be looked upon as acting as buffers against deviance. The following buffer paradigm can be constructed:

1 SOCIAL STRATOSPHERE OF *PRESSURES AND PULLS;* PRESSURES
  ARE ADVERSE LIVING CONDITIONS, PULLS ARE DISTRACTIONS
  THAT DRAW THE INDIVIDUAL AWAY FROM HIS ACCEPTED FORM
  OF LIVING.
2 *OUTER CONTAINMENT* COMPRISES THE INDIVIDUAL'S GROUPS
  AND ORGANIZATIONS.
3 *INNER CONTAINMENT*—THE SELF.
4 ORGANIC AND PSYCHOLOGICAL *PUSHES.*

Figure 6-1. Containment Theory Paradigm.

Pressures or pulls that break through weak outer containment must be handled by the self (inner containment) or the person will succumb to deviance. A strong outer containment may, however, prevent the pressures or pulls from ever reaching the individual. If these containments operate to resist adverse pressures and pulls, they then function as the outer and inner containment buffers against deviance. It is to be remembered that in addition to the pressures and pulls, there are constant organic and psychological pushes that battle the self.

Containment theory is proposed as an operational theory for research, treatment, and prevention, and Reckless proposes several tests of its validity:

1. Containment theory is said to be the theory of best fit for the large middle range of cases of crime and delinquency.

2. The theory explains crimes against the person as well as it explains crimes against property.

3. It is a formulation that psychiatrists, psychologists, and sociologists as well as practitioners can use equally well.

4. It is one of the few theories in which the microcosm (the individual case history) mirrors the ingredients of the macrocosm (general theoretical points).

5. It can be used in the treatment of the offender: restructuring his milieu or strengthening the individual self-concept.

6. It can be used in prevention. Children with poor containment can be spotted early and stronger self-factors can be internalized and their outer containing structures can be rebuilt or reinforced.

Critique. Containment theory has received its full share of criticism—justified and unjustified. It is easy to dismiss the complaint that containment theory does not explain the entire spectrum of delinquency and crime; such was never claimed by Reckless. Of greater importance is the charge that the issue of causality is left unresolved in containment theory; it is impossible to determine whether the poor self-concept emerges before or after the delinquency. Also, it is a demonstratable fact that not all incarcerated felons have a poor self-concept; conversely, not all people with a poor self-concept engage in criminal activity. Containment theory does not explain crimes which result from psychological aberrations, however defined, or strong "inner pushes," nor does it account for criminality which is a part of "normal" and "expected" roles and activities.

Aside from the previously mentioned criticisms of the theory, Reckless does not provide a theoretical definition of self-concept. Tangri and Schwartz (1967) present two additional criticisms:

1. Reckless does not distinguish between an individual's knowledge of other's expectations as matters of fact and those that become part of his self-evaluation.

2. Reckless is missing a theoretical link: Why should a poor self-concept leave one vulnerable to delinquency?

In Reckless's study of the "good boy in a high delinquency area" in 1955 and in his follow-up investigation in 1959, he found that the internalization of a favorable self-concept was as difficult to alter as a delinquent self-image. He concluded that the internalization of a favorable self-concept was the critical variable in the containment" of delinquency.

LEARNING THEORY AND CRIMINALITY[1]

As we noted in the previous chapter, "Sociological Theories of Criminality," Sutherland's attempt to develop a one-factor theory of criminal behavior led to the formulation of *differential association,* a socio-learning theory which seeks to account for the etiology of criminal behavior in the group-based learning experiences of the individual. In its originally stated form, the theory remained untested, primarily as a consequence of difficulties in operationalizing fundamental concepts upon which the theory rests. Despite attempts at expanding the theory (Weinberg, 1954; Glaser, 1956; Sykes and Matza, 1957) and a rigorous axiomatization and deduction of testable hypotheses (DeFleur and Quinney, 1966), criminologists have been unable to resolve the difficulties inherent in handling the mentalistic concepts which differential association contains in abundance.

---

[1]The following discussion draws heavily upon material prepared by Dr. Reed Adams, Director of the Law Enforcement and Management Program, University of North Carolina at Charlotte, and is reproduced here with his kind permission.

New possibilities for eventual resolution of the theory's methodological problems, and possible direct empirical testing of the adequacy of the original Sutherland theory were opened up recently by C. R. Jeffery (1965). His paper was shortly followed by a second paper (Burgess and Akers, 1966a) concerned with the same issues, but differing in several fundamental respects. Despite the suggestions within these two papers for a test of the adequacy of the theory of differential association, the matter rests where Burgess and Akers left it. These two papers represent a fundamentally different approach from that of the voluminous works concerned with the theory over the past thirty years and have attracted considerable attention from sociologists/criminologists, being quoted (Zimberoff, 1968), referenced (Sutherland and Cressey, 1970; Ray and Kilburn, 1970; Karen and Bower, 1968), and reprinted (Cressey and Ward, 1969).

Since Sutherland's death, the individual most closely identified with differential association has been Donald Cressey. Recently he included the Burgess and Akers paper among a group of works identified by him as "the major theories of criminologists" (Cressey and Ward, 1969). Moreover, in the eighth edition (1970) of the Sutherland-Cressey criminology text, Cressey, after discussing past attempts to specify the learning process in differential association, has this to say:

> Even these attempts are, like the differential association statement itself, more in the nature of general indications of the kind of framework or orientation one should use in formulating a theory of criminality than they are statements of theory. Burgess and Akers have recently given the most promising lead in this area by specifying that the conditions and mechanisms through which delinquent and criminal behavior are learned are those indicated in the theory of human learning variously referred to as reinforcement theory. Operant behavior theory and operant conditioning theory (Cressey, 1970).

"Reinforcement theory, operant behavior theory, and operant conditioning theory" (sic) are terms which designate an important body of empirical research and a series of well-tested empirical generalizations that result upon experimental validation. Although the principles of operant conditioning and the experimental analysis of behavior have already made valuable contributions to criminology, the preponderance of empirical reports have appeared outside the traditional criminological literature. Nevertheless, as Burchard (1971) notes, there has been a "remarkable" increase in attempts to apply learning principles within criminology. He identifies as a "critical" problem the "misunderstanding of the basic principles of applied behavior analysis" (Burchard, 1971). It seems imperative, at this early stage in the introduction of criminology students to operant conditioning and the experimental analysis of behavior, to provide a brief statement of the essentials of reinforcement theory before discussing the contributions of Burgess and Akers and of Jeffery to a reinforcement theory reformulation of Sutherland's differential association interpolation of criminal behavior.

Reinforcement Theory

If a hungry dog salivates to the sight or smell of food, this response is unlearned or reflexive in character. When a stimulus such as a bell is made to precede the introduction of the food, however, the resulting salivation in response to the bell must be regarded as conditional, i.e. its occurance depends upon the establishment of a relationship where none had previously existed. In this modest prototypical experiment, the twentieth century Russian physiologist, Ivan P. Pavlov, provided a succinct demonstration of at least one of the ways in which behavior is learned or acquired—through the procedure Pavlov termed *conditioning*.

Pavlov's work aroused a good deal of interest among American psychologists. John B. Watson, in particular, believed that the conditional reflex method offered considerable promise for the objectification of psychology. In his repudiation of mentalism and subjectivism, Watson maintained that the scientific study of another persons private experience is not only a practical but also a logical impossibility. Whereas for Pavlov the conditional reflex was considered a technique for studying higher nervous activity, for Watson and many Americans the conditional reflex seemed important mainly because it provided a source of concepts which could be used in the development of theories to explain behavior other than that represented by the simple reflex. And also in contrast to Pavlov, Watson had few theories beyond the notion that human nature could be completely controlled by the early conditioning of children (Watson, 1925).

In his later writings, Watson continued to elaborate the idea that men are not "born" but rather "built by environment." He continued to regard the conditional reflex as the ontological and methodological solution and the high pragmatic hope of all behavioristic psychology: the basic and ultimate unit of behaviorism's chief operational category, habit; the method destined to successfully replace all introspection; the means of training all phases of personality; and even the philosophy of a better, and balanced, society—in fact, the basis of all that is modifiable in men and animals.

An American contemporary of Pavlov, Edward L. Thorndike, on the basis of extensive work with problem-solving and maze behavior, formulated a series of "provisional laws" of learning. According to the most important of these—the so-called "Law of Effect"—the occurrence of a "satisfying state of affairs" following behavior strengthens the "connection" between that behavior and the stimulus which precedes it; conversely, if the behavior is followed by an "unsatisfying state of affairs," the strength of the connection between the behavior and the immediately preceding stimulus is weakened. Although Thorndike late modified his views concerning the consequences of an "unsatisfying state of affairs," i.e. punishment, for learning or acquisition of behavior, his statements with regard to the influence of reward (a "satisfying state of affairs") upon learning remained the principal basis for an emerging concept of reinforcement. If one accepts the Law of Effect as a theoretical statement of the key element in learning, then the specification of reinforcement, or what constitutes a "satisfying state of affairs" for an organism, becomes a purely empirical matter.

For Pavlov, reinforcement consisted merely of the repeated presentation of the conditioned stimulus, e.g. bell, and the unconditioned stimulus, e.g. food. A later theorist, Clark Hull, enlarged the concept of reinforcement by distinguishing between primary and secondary reinforcement. The distinction rested upon the notion that certain kinds of stimuli—food, water, for example—effected a direct reduction in the tension-states associated with various recurring tissue conditioned, such as hunger and thirst which belong to the class of organically-based needs. Learning, in Hull's view, occur-red whenever behavior took place in conjunction with the process of *drive reduction*. A primary reinforcer, according to this schema, is any stimulus which leads to a diminution in the physiological condition (need) that produces a drive; a secondary reinforcer is any stimulus which, as a consequence of association with a primary reinforcer, acquires reinforcing capacities itself.

Differences he perceived between the prototype experiments of Pavlov and Thorndike led B. F. Skinner (1938) to distinguish be-tween *respondent* and *operant* conditioning or learning. Respond-ent conditioning, which Skinner identified with the "classical" or Pavlovian situation, was conceptualized as a procedure involving the autonomic nervous system and smooth musculature of the body. In this conditioning paradigm, the experimenter has close control over the "elicited" behavior of the subject, i.e. the unconditioned response. Operant conditioning on the other hand, confronts the experimenter with freer and less predictable "emitted" behavior. Once the response has occurred, however, the experimenter can es-tablish stimulus control over the future occurrence of the behavior by controlling the consequences of the behavior. This, in essence, is the defining property of Skinnerian reinforcement—*anything which increases the probability of occurrence of a response is a reinforcer.*

One of the most impressive accomplishments of the operant con-ditioning approach has been its demonstrable capacity to effect be-havioral control over a steadily widening class of responses. At the same time, there had been a consistent growth in the sophistication, versatitity, and usefulness of operant procedures. Repeated syste-matic observations of the ways in which behavior is acquired, main-tained, altered, or eliminated under controlled conditions have led to the formulation of basic principles:

1. The association between a stimulus and a response is strength-ened each time the response is followed by reinforcement. This is *acquisition.*

2. The association is weakened each time the response occurs and is *not* followed by reinforcement. This is *extinction*. Thus, dis-use alone does not lead to extinction.

3. A response to a given stimulus may be seen to recur after complete extinction when the stimulus is re-presented. This phenomenon is known as *spontaneous recovery*.

4. Once a specific stimulus-response habit has been acquired, another stimulus which is similar in some way to the original stimulus can also elicit the learned response. This is *stimulus generalization*.

5. Responses that occurred just prior to the reinforced, learned, response will also be strengthened; those nearest in time being strengthened more than those further away. This is the *gradient of reinforcement*.

6. Responses nearer to the point of occurrence of the reinforcement tend to occur before their original time in the response sequence and crowd out earlier, useless, behaviors. This is the development of *anticipatory responses*.

7. Drives can act as cues and elicit specific learned responses or as responses and become elicited by certain cues, and strengthened by reinforcement. (List adapted from Suinn, 1970).

Although the above list does less than justice to behavioral science and technology, it helps to suggest how far learning theory had progressed from the time Sutherland formulated his theory of differential association to the appearance of the contributions of Jeffery and of Burgess and Akers to a reinforcement theory reformulation of differential association.

Differential Reinforcement: Jeffery

Jeffery (1965) begins by noting the lack of empirical verification or theoretical revision of differential association, and that as originally stated, the theory is untestable. The learning theory concepts relevant to differential association are suggested to be those of operant conditioning (as opposed to classical conditioning) and the various subsidary concepts necessary for the complete exposition of operant conditioning. According to Jeffery (1965): "The theory of differential reinforcement states that a criminal act occurs in an environment in which in the past the actor has been reinforced for behaving in this manner, and the aversive consequences attached to the behavior have been of such a nature that they do not control or prevent the response."

Now these variables vary according to known principles. When these S-R relationships, peculiar to criminal behavior, are considered, we find that:

> The theory assumes that (1) the reinforcing qualities of differential stimuli differ for different actors depending on the past history of each; (2) some individuals have been reinforced for criminal behavior whereas other individuals have not been; (3) some individuals have been punished for criminal behavior whereas other individuals have not been; and (4) an individual will be intermittently reinforced and/or punished for criminal behavior, that is, he will not be reinforced or punished every time he commits a criminal act (Jeffery, 1965).

It follows from this, as Jeffery notes, that those variables distinguishing a situation in which a criminal act is committed from an identical situation in which a criminal act does not occur are:

> . . . (1) the reinforcing quality of the stolen items; (2) past stealing responses which have been reinforced, and (3) past stealing responses which have been punished (Jeffery, 1965).

This is Jeffery's analysis of differential association and criminal behavior generally, according to learning theory. Jeffery does not appear to have intended for this to represent reformulated differential association, as Burgess and Akers (1966, pp. 130-131) suggest. Rather, Jeffery specifies the means of empirically demonstrating the adequacy of the original Sutherland theory.

Jeffery focuses on criminal association, the primary variable in the original theory. He notes that people can reinforce criminal behavior in a number of ways: They may operate as secondary reinforcers, as discriminative stimuli for reinforcers, thereby increasing associating behavior. They can also function as a source of material (nonsocial) reinforcers. In addition, people can be punishers or provide punishment. It is these concrete behaviors that Jeffery identified as Sutherland's attitudes.

He then raises a question which bears directly upon the means for conducting an empirical assessment of the adequacy of Sutherland's original theory. Says Jeffery (1965):

> A research problem presented by the theory of differential associa-

tion is the problem of what environmental consequences maintain criminal behavior. Is it the material gain, or is it the social approval and group membership? Sutherland's theory assumes that the important variable is social reinforcement, and his theory ignores the obvious fact that money, cars, and sex are in themselves powerful reinforcers in our society . . . Criminal behavior can be maintained by money or cars without social approval . . . other individuals are probably as important, if not more important, in the behavioral process as discriminating stimuli rather than reinforcing stimuli . . .

The empirical question to which Jeffery refers is: Which is the greater reinforcer of criminal behavior, social or nonsocial reinforcement?

If it can be demonstrated that just one type of nonsocial reinforcement is as equal or greater reinforcer of criminal behavior than social reinforcement, then the theory is inadequate to explain relevant behavior, and thus an unstable predictor. Furthermore, it would have far reaching implications for the whole of American social science, which has emphasized, across discipline boundaries, the impact of social rather than nonsocial variables in the affairs of men. Such an empirical demonstration would require that an alternation of a sufficient magnitude be made in differential association that the resulting theory will no longer be the theory postulated by Sutherland. In all the past studies, where the issue has been the specification with greater precision of existing, i.e. social, variables, the theory has remained uniquely Sutherland's. This is not the case with the present argument. Jeffery has identified here a critical experiment between two conflicting theoretical issues.

Jeffery considers the possible intricacies of his research question when he suggests how social conditions influence and in some cases determine the contingencies of reinforcement controlling the criminal behaviors; specifically, how they relate to nonsocial reinforcement controlling the criminal behavior. He suggests that "social reinforcement varies directly with the amount of concomitant nonsocial reinforcement."

This then, is a refinement of the empirical question he proposed earlier. If this suggestion is correct, then it would follow that criminals are more generally deprived of social and nonsocial reinforcers than non-criminals. If a measure of diffuse reinforcement deprivation could be devised, and this suggestion is correct, then it should distinguish two groups of individuals alike in all apparent respects case criminality. This, of course, is a matter that has received a substantial amount of empirical and theoretical attention and has been considered from a criminological point of view (Eysenck, 1964) : namely, the issue of the relative conditionability and stimulus hunger of the offender, primarily the psychopath. We shall have more to say about this issue in the next section of this chapter.

Differential Reinforcement: Burgess and Akers

Reed Adams (1973) has conducted a searching analysis of the Burgess and Akers (1966a) reformulation of differential association. In their presentation, Sutherland's proposition one ("Criminal behavior is learned") and proposition eight ("The process of learning criminal behavior by association with criminal and anticriminal patterns involves all of the mechanisms that are involved in any other learning") are fused into a new proposition which asserts that: "Criminal behavior is learned according to the principles of operant conditioning." After presenting evidence that normal social behavior and some noncriminal forms of deviant behavior are acquired on the basis of operant learning principles, they raise the question of whether the acquisition of criminal behavior proceeds according to those same principles. Adams takes them to task on this point: "To ask if behavior which is differentiated from other behavior only by the label we place on it is governed by a separate body of behavioral principles is a pseudo issue."

Sutherland's second proposition ("Criminal behavior is learned in interaction with other persons in a process of communication") is restated to read: "Criminal behavior is learned both in nonsocial situations that are reinforcing or discriminative and through that social interaction in which the behavior of other persons is reinforcing or discriminative for criminal behavior." Thus, the terms "interaction" and "communication" are given a specific meaning within the context of reinforcement and discrimination.

The third of Sutherland's propositions ("The principal part of the learning of criminal behavior occurs within intimate personal groups") is reformulated in this fashion: "The principal part of the learning of criminal behavior occurs in those groups which comprise the individual's major source of reinforcements." Adams notes that this reformulation, which allows for the inclusion of reference groups and the mass media, conflicts with Burgess and Akers' contention that nonsocial variables may affect the acquisition of criminal behavior.

Sutherland's fourth proposition ("When criminal behavior is learned, the learning includes a) techniques of committing the crime . . . b) the specific direction of motives, drives, rationalizations, and attitudes") is changed to read: "The learning of criminal behavior, including specific techniques, attitudes, and avoidance procedures, is a function of the effective and available reinforcers and the existing reinforcement contingencies." As Adams observes, replacing "rationalizations" with "avoidance procedures" is an innovation in the direction of greater clarity, but the retention of the term "attitudes" tends to perpetuate many of the problems posed by mentalistic concepts which have bedevilled differential association ever since its original formulation.

Proposition five by Sutherland ("The specific direction of motives and drives is learned from definitions of the legal codes as favorable or unfavorable") is restated as follows: "The specific class of behaviors which are learned and their frequency of occurrence are a function of the reinforcers which are effective and available, and the rules or norms by which these reinforcers are applied." Adams points out that the use of the term "effective" by Burgess and Akers in revisions of Sutherland's fourth and fifth propositions is superfluous: A reinforcer is effective by definition; when it stops being effective, it no longer functions as a reinforcer. Moreover, Adams suggests that replacing "rules and norms" in propsition five with the term "discriminative stimulus" would permit this proposition to be subsumed under proposition four.

Sutherland's sixth proposition ("A person becomes delinquent because of an excess of definitions favorable to violations of law over definitions unfavorable to violations of law") is rendered by Burgess and Akers in these terms: "Criminal behavior is a function of norms which are discriminative for criminal behavior, the learning of which takes place when such behavior is more highly reinforced than noncriminal behavior." In proposition two, Burgess and Akers broadened Sutherland's formulation to admit the possibility that nonsocial variables might significantly influence the acquisition of criminal behavior. Thus, we find that propositions two and six stand in direct contradiction to one another, and there is no readily apparent resolution for this paradox.

Finally, proposition seven by Sutherland ("Differential associations may vary in frequency, duration, priority, and intensity") is altered to read: "The strength of criminal behavior is a direct function of the amount, frequency, and probability of its reinforcement." A complete specification of the variables required to account for the response strength of criminal behavior must include the level of state variables internal to both the individual and the group, as well as the "nature" of reinforcing and aversive stimuli. Burgess and Akers had included the deprivation level of the organism as a significant variable in their earlier discussion of the learning process and Adams expresses puzzlement as to why they failed to include it in their statement of the causal proposition.

Discussion

Adams contrasts the Burgess and Akers propositions with Sutherland's original statements and emphasizes that the former are not theoretical formulations in the sense with which theory is comprehended in sociology. Rather, these propositions should be regarded as empirical generalizations which have been arrived at through the inductive processes of experimental research. He surveys an extensive and growing body of professional literature which reports the application of learning principles to various problem areas in clinical criminology, with results that are extremely promising. Adams concludes:

> This analysis has suggested that a great deal is to be gained by abandoning biases for types of variables and speculations about intangibles, and simply focusing on the consequences of behavior. It will be found that some consequences are followed by changes, while others are not. It is a simple matter to deal solely with those consequences having an observable impact on

the behavior and disregarding the remainder. By so doing, we increase the likelihood that the relationships we consider are the important ones.

Differential Conditionability: Eysenck

Sutherland anticipated that if his theory were to be complete, the role of the personality would have to be taken into consideration. One potentially fruitful area of inquiry into the relationship of criminal conduct and personality has been the approach of Eysenck.

In his book *Crime and Personality* (1964), Eysenck seeks an answer to the question: Is "honesty" a generalized personality trait, or specific to the situation? Do persons who break the law do so across situations from minor traffic offenses to felonies? To answer these questions, Eysenck reviewed the character studies of two American psychologists in their studies of the development of the moral behavior in children. On the findings of these honesty/dishonesty studies of children, Eysenck (1964) writes:

> Hartshorne and May did, in fact, find a distinct relationship between integration and honest behavior; in other words, honesty was a characteristic which could be predicted from one situation to another: dishonesty, cheating, lying and so on, the whole range of unsocial or antisocial activities, tended to be unintegrated, unstable and unpredictable.

Sutherland had asked: What are the personality traits to be regarded as significant in relating crime to personality? Three traits, according to Eysenck, seem to be conducive to criminal conduct: suggestibility, lack of emotional stability, and a lack of persistence.

Important to Eysenck's theory of "differential conditionability" are the concepts of introversion and extraversion popularized by Jung. When an individual's major orientation is toward the external, objective world, we tend to refer to him as an extravert; if the person's primary focus is inward, toward the subjective, we label him introverted. Both attitudes are present in each personality, and the same person may fluctuate by situation or by mood. As a generalized attitude, however, we refer to a person as being an "extravert" or an "introvert." Eysenck describes these personality types as follows:

The typical extravert is sociable, likes parties, has many friends, needs to have people to talk to, and does not like reading or studying by himself. He craves excitement, takes chances, acts on the spur of the moment, and is generally an impulsive individual . . .

The typical introvert is a quiet, retiring sort of person introspective, fond of books rather than people; he is reserved and reticent except with intimate friends . . . he is reliable, somewhat pessimistic, and places great value on ethical standards.

An important link in the development of Eysenck's theory of differential conditionability is the relationship of extraversion to the so-called psychopathic syndrome. Not all criminals are psychopaths, and not all psychopaths are criminals. Eysenck, however, points to the high degree of extraversion of criminal and psychopathic groups as an important underlying factor in the creation of a criminal.

On the level of stimulation and hedonic tone (pleasantness-unpleasantness), extraverts tend to prefer high levels of stimulation, a stimulus hunger. Introverts, on the other hand, show a preference for low levels of stimulation, when compared with the general population. It follows that we would expect extraverts to smoke more, drink more, eat spicy foods, and take more risks as a result of their need for greater stimulation.

In this view many of the activities of the juvenile delinquent may stem from boredom, a greater need for stimulus excitation, and a greater characteristic of willingness to engage in certain behaviors simply because of the thrill of the risk involved.

According to Eysenck, the basis for a potentially extraverted personality is to be found to some extent in inherited physiological structures. One inherits a predisposition toward extraversion. In the potential criminal the reticular formation, which is part of the brain stem responsible for maintaining a high state of arousal, in the cortex doesn't function properly. This makes it more difficult for him to become conditioned and learn the kind of social habits which constitutes what we call socialization. The result is that he is effectively without a conscience—the end-product of the socialization process.

The criminal behaves criminally largely because he had failed to become properly conditioned and aware of the system of contingency on which society operates: Inappropriate behaviors are punished, and appropriate behaviors are rewarded. Based on this theory, any penitentiary would put these persons who are "undersocialized" through a series of conditioning procedures which emphasize these considerations.

To isolate the role of heredity in criminality, Eysenck reviewed the studies which investigated the criminal careers of pairs of twins (N = 225): ". . . that just about twice as many monozygotic (identical) as dizygotic (fraternal) twins are concordant. In other words, when one twin is a criminal, then among identical twins the other one has twice the chance of also being a criminal that he would have if the twins were fraternal."

Further comparisons of twins in the area of juvenile delinquency, childhood behavior disorders, homosexuality, and alcoholism led Eysenck to the conclusion that" . . . heredity plays an important, and possibly a vital part, in predisposing a given individual to crime." The evidence for this position Eysenck sees as so conclusive and is reproduced by so many different investigators in different cultural settings that he can attribute its lack of acceptance only to the climate of opinion in the United States and Russia, which is tenaciously resistive to all but social explanations of crime. Some theorists tend to oppose hereditary causation for fear it would lead to a "therapeutic nihilism and a abdication of treatment for the offender. Quite the opposite should be the case. By understanding exactly how hereditary works, we can devise treatment methods appropriate to the causative factors.

Legally, we may categorize people as either criminal or noncriminal, but in commission of acts, criminals represent the extreme end of a continuous distribution, just as IQ's range from mental defective to genius. "Criminality," says Eysenck, "is obviously a continuous trait of the same kinds as intelligence, height, or weight."

Summary

While theorizing about criminality has been dominated by sociologists, psychology and psychiatry have not been without their contribution. Psychoanalytic criminology asserts that criminal behavior is an attempt at maintaining psychic balance or restoring a psychic balance which has been disrupted. The foremost modern exponent of this position is Seymour Halleck who sees criminal behavior as an adaptation to stress and, in this light, as a goal-oriented behavior, rather than irrational behavior. In addition to the "psychic balance" model, Feldman has identified five variations on the basic psychoanalytic formula: (1) criminality as neurosis; (2) antisocial character as a result of defective socialization; (3) criminal behavior as compensation for frustration of conventional psychic needs; (4) criminal behavior as a function of a defective superego; and (5) criminal behavior as anomie.

The difficulty with psychoanalytic explanations is that the explanatory concepts have not been operationally defined in such a way as to allow empirical verification or refutation.

Glasser's "reality therapy" is a reaction to the classical psychoanalytic assumptions and sees criminality as the result of "irresponsibility." The offender needs to learn to fulfill his needs in a way that does not deprive others of the ability to fulfill their needs. Thus a youthful car-thief is not exhibiting a "pathology" in traditional psychoanalytic terms; he is acting in a irresponsible manner. His desire to ride forces someone else to walk. Because it deals in the present and eschews the more tortured and esoteric jargon of the Freudians, reality therapy has more "popular" appeal, especially to persons seeing the application of the values of the "Protestant Ethnic" as the solution of the crime problem. As a scientific explanation of criminal behavior, however, it remains an untested and perhaps, untestable hypothesis.

Containment theory (Reckless) is a social-psychological theory built on certain concepts relating to the construction of the "self." Whether this "self" will engage in criminal conduct is dependent upon the interrelation of an "outer containment" system (the holding power of the group) and an "inner containment" system (the individual's ability to steer and control himself). Reckless hypothesized that persons with poor self-concepts engaged in more criminal behavior than did persons with good self-concepts. Critics of this position have pointed out that it is impossible to determine whether a poor self-concept emerges before or after delinquency; not all persons with a poor self-concept engage in criminal activity.

The theory's most crucial unanswered question is: "Why should a poor self-image leave one vulnerable to delinquency?"

Sutherland's "differential association" theory, the subject of much controversy, has been analyzed by Jeffery in terms of modern learning theory and "differential reinforcement," i.e. criminal behavior will be repeated in accordance with the strength of the reinforcing quality of the stolen items (primary reinforcers) if past stealing responses have been reinforced. Further, Jeffery asks the question: "Which is the greater reinforcer of criminal behavior, social or nonsocial reinforcement?" One clue to the nature of criminality suggested by Jeffery is to measure the "reinforcement deprivation level" of individuals.

Sutherland realized that for his theory to be completed it would have to take into full consideration the role of personality. An approach which attempts to do this and is in line with Jeffery's suggestion to locate the "reinforcement deprivation level" of individuals is the "differential conditionability" theory of Eysenck. Eysenck links the biological given—a biological basis for personality—to socialization and psychopathy. For metabolic reasons, some individuals experience a greater "stimulus hunger" (reinforcement deprivation) and are thus more prone to extraversion, more difficult to condition, and more likely to become involved in criminal acts.

Factually, we know that most of the serious crimes reported by the UCR are committed by young black males. Sociologically we can explain the uneven distribution of crimes in this sociological category by the disassociation between the culturally approved goals (materialism) and the socially structured avenues for the attainment of those goals. This pressure for deviance falls most heavily on young black males at the point that they enter the unequal opportunity structure. The clue as to why a particular youth engages in criminal conduct is the task of criminological psychology which at this point says it is related to his intimate associations, his "reinforcement deprivation level," and the biological level of his stimulus hunger.

REFERENCES

Adams, L.R.: Differential association and learning principles revisited. *Social Problems, 20*:458-470, 1973.

Burchard, J.: Behavior modification with delinquents: some unforeseen contingencies. *American Journal of Orthopsychiatry, 41:*306, 1971.

Burgess, R.L. and Akers, R.L.: A differential association-reinforcement theory of criminal behavior. *Social Problems, 14:*128-147, 1966.

Burgess, R.L. and Akers, R.L.: Are operant principles tautological? *Psychological Record, 16:*305-312, 1966.

Cressey, D.R. and Ward, D. (Eds.) : *Delinquency, Crime, and Social Process.* New York, Harper and Row, 1969.

DeFleur, M. and Quinney, R.: A reformulation of Sutherland's differential association theory and a strategy for empirical verification. *Journal of Research in Crime and Delinquency,* 1966,

Eysenck, H.J.: *Crime and Personality.* Boston, Houghton Mifflin, 1964.

Feldman, D.: Psychoanalysis and crime. In Cressey, D.R. and Ward, S., (Eds.): *Delinquency, Crime, and Social Process.* New York, Harper and Row, 1969.

Glaser, D.: Criminality theories and behavior images. *American Journal of Sociology, 61:*440-451, 1956.

Glaser, D.: Differential association and criminological prediction: problems of measurement. A paper presented at the annual meeting of the American Sociological Association, Chicago. September, 1959.

Glasser, W.: *Reality Therapy.* New York, Harper and Row, 1965.

Halleck, S.L.: *Psychiatry and the Dilemmas of Crime.* New York, Hoeber-Harper, 1967.

Jeffery, C.R.: Criminal behavior and learning theory. *Journal of Criminal Law, Criminology, and Police Science, 56:*294-300, 1965.

Karen, R.L. and Bower, R.C.: A behavioral anlaysis of a social control agency: Synanon. *Journal of Research in Crime and Delinquency, 5:*18-34, 1968.

Lazarus, R., Yousem, H., and Arenberg, D.: Hunger and perception. *Journal of Personality, 21:*312-328, 1953.

Menninger, K., Mayman, M., and Pruyser, P.: *The Vital Balance.* New York, Viking Press, 1963.

Menninger, K.: *The Crime of Punishment.* New York, Viking Press, 1968.

Murray, E.: Conflict and repression during sleep deprivation. *Journal of Abnormal and Social Psychology, 59:*95-101, 1959.

Ray, E.T. and Kilburn, K.L.: Behavior modification techniques applied to community problems. *Criminology, 8:*173-184, 1971.

Reckless, W.C.: A non-causal explanation: containment theory. *Excerpta Criminologica, 1:*131-134, 1962.

Skinner, B.F.: *The behavior of organisms.* New York, D. Appleton-Century, 1938.

Sutherland, E.H. and Cressey, D.R.: *Principles of Criminology.* Philadelphia, Lippincott, 1970.

Suinn, R.: *Fundamentals of Behavior Pathology.* New York, Wiley, 1970.

Sykes, G. and Matza, D.: Techniques of neutralization: a theory of delinquency. *American Journal of Sociology, 22:*664-670, 1957.

Tangri, Sandra and Schwartz, M.: Delinquency research and the self-concept variable. *Journal of Criminal Law, Criminology, and Police Science, 5:* 182-190, 1967.

Watson, J.B.: *Behaviorism.* New York, Norton, 1925.

Weinberg, S.K.: Theories of criminality and problems of prediction. *Journal of Criminal Law, Criminology, and Police Science, 45:*412-429, 1954.

Zimberoff, S.J.: Behavior and modification with delinquents. *Correctional Psychologist, 3:*11-25, 1968.

PART III
PATTERNS OF
CRIMINAL BEHAVIOR

THIS SECTION OPENS with a chapter on juvenile delinquency and closes with a chapter on organized crime, white-collar crime, and professional criminals. The range of subject matter spanned by these chapters gives further emphasis to what was said in the preceding section regarding the difficulties of formulating a comprehensive theory of crime causation. It also underlines the crucial importance of social learning factors in the development of "criminal careers."

We have tried to follow a common format in the presentation of these materials. Our major concern was, first, to provide an adequate description of the various configurations of criminal behavior associated with a particular category of criminal offense. Next, we sought to review the relevant and available research findings for each pattern of criminal behavior, together with existing theoretical formulations pertaining to the causes or determinants of such behavior that may have stimulated, guided, or directed research. Finally, wherever possible, we have tried to discuss critically the various means that have been proposed or undertaken by way of intervention in order to control, reduce, eliminate, or prevent the occurrence of such criminal behavior.

Chapter 7
JUVENILE DELINQUENTS AND YOUTHFUL OFFENDERS

CRIMINAL JUSTICE AUTHORITIES have documented a steady increase during recent years in the number and seriousness of crimes committed by young people. The Federal Bureau of Investigation, in its 1967 *Crime Capsule,* noted a 59 percent rise in juvenile arrests for serious crimes during the period from 1960 to 1967 and a 22 percent increase in arrests within the ten to seventeen age group. The picture becomes even darker when we consider that over two-thirds of those arrested went on to commit further offenses.

Lunden (1964) offers twelve major conclusions concerning juvenile delinquency in the past half-century:

1. Delinquency has been increasing during the past fifty years.
2. Delinquent offenses have become more serious in nature.
3. Delinquency is no longer an urban problem because it has been increasing in rural and suburban areas as well as in the cities.
4. Youthful offenses are no longer limited to the poorer or near-poverty level classes of peoples and nations.
5. Those nations which may be classified as more advanced with state welfare programs display as much or more delinquency than the less well developed countries.
6. The current methods of treating delinquent offenders have proven to be unsatisfactory.
7. Almost every approach to the treatment of delinquents has been based on a medico-psychological framework to the neglect of the value systems in society.

195

8. Most juvenile offenders have been considered to be mal-adjusted individuals without due consideration of the total configurations in which they live.
9. Most authorities have approached the problem of delinquency as a minor or temporary factor and fail to relate the problem to the total culture of society.
10. Only a very few individuals have attempted to analyze the problem of delinquency in terms of anomie or the normlessness of contemporary society.
11. Investigators have given little or no attention to how social mobility or mass migration has affected the conduct norms of a population.
12. Unless some other means arise to deal with the increase in delinquency those in positions of authority and the general population will resort to more severe methods of dealing with juvenile offenders to the neglect of certain psychosocial methods.

Lunden acknowledges that the data sources upon which these conclusions are based fail by a considerable margin to meet rigorous standards of completeness, comprehensiveness, and overall adequacy. Nevertheless, his conclusions are of considerable value if we treat them as potential areas of inquiry in our discussion of juvenile and youthful crime.

JUVENILE DELINQUENCY AND LAW

The juvenile in our country is subject to a baffling array of legal codes. As Cohen (1970) points out, the juvenile "must abide not only by all criminal statutes and ordinances governing adult behavior, but also to a second set of clauses applied to him because of his special status as a juvenile." Currently, about 25 percent of the cases which appear before the juvenile courts are youth offenses which have no parallel in adult crime. Says Cohen, a young person may be considered delinquent if he:

1. Is habitually truant.
2. Is incorrigible.
3. Is growing up in idleness or crime.

4. Conducts himself immorally or indecently.
5. Habitually uses vile, obscene, or vulgar language in a public place.
6. Habitually wanders about railroad yards or tracks.
7. Smokes cigarettes or uses tobacco in any form.
8. Makes indecent proposals.
9. Attempts to marry without consent in violation of the law.
10. Is given to sexual irregularities.

Hedged about by such restrictions, it is small wonder that many young people acquire the conviction that they are victims of a legal double-standard. What seems apparent here is that the laws are frequently invoked prematurely or even unnecessarily. It may well be that many of the minor forms of delinquency (those which are not a serious threat to the community or the youngster himself) can best be handled outside the court process through referral or other methods of informal handling, in an effort to keep the youth in the family and community.

THE LABELING PROCESS IN DELINQUENCY

The process by which a juvenile becomes identified and labeled as delinquent involves, among other factors, activities of juveniles and activities of law enforcement agencies and is greatly influenced by the appropriate or inappropriate response to each other. The initial response may be unofficial (informal) or official (formal). Some of the literature in this area suggests that the official response to the behavior in question may often have the effect of pushing misbehaving juveniles toward further delinquent conduct and perhaps make it more difficult for them to reenter the conventional world (Wheeler, Cottrell, and Romasco, 1969).

There seems to be sufficient evidence to suggest that the process of labeling a youngster as delinquent puts him into a separate category and has a definite effect upon how he is viewed by others as well as his perception of himself. Often, those labeled delinquent think of themselves as delinquent, associate with others so labeled, and organize their behavior accordingly. This "deviant amplifying system" then is a form of encouraged alienation from the larger community (Spergel, 1969). The labeling theorist would agree that if the goal is to reduce the probability of repeated delinquent acts, a policy of doing nothing may be more beneficial than active intervention.

While not in total disagreement, Wheeler and his colleagues (1969) offer several counterarguments to the non-intervention approach. First, if the offender is ignored, the delinquency may provide him with some gain, tangible or otherwise, and he will most likely continue the activity, unless apprehended. This approach requires that delinquent behavior be dealt with immediately, before it gets worse. This approach has given support to studies interested in the early identification and treatment of delinquent children (Glueck, 1969).

A second counterargument suggests that the official police handling and court adjudication may have a deterrent effect on the juveniles. Since the juveniles do not want to be treated as delinquents, they will no longer engage in delinquent activity. This argument justifies intervention on different grounds than the first, and it often serves as the standard argument used by those expounding the virtues of the deterrent impact of punishment.

One of the major problems regarding those competing rationales for official actions lies in the difficulty of empirically testing them. Obviously, some youngsters will not cease their delinquent activities following their officially being labeled delinquent. On the other hand, other juveniles may refrain from further delinquent acts once they have been so labeled. The question then remains; What are the factors or conditions which determine these various phenomena? This is definitely an area very much in need of meaningful exploration.

What does appear to be clear is that the effects of the labeling process are undesirable. As Wheeler, et. al. (1969) put it, we are finally beginning to understand that any intervention has the possibility of harm as well as help, and it is conceivable that the actions of even the well-meaning helpers do as much harm as good.

In this same vein, Spergel (1969) using the term "stigmatization" indicates that it may result not only from overzealous and discriminatory law enforcement procedures, but also from those practices of social workers, teachers, and others in the helping professions who are related to the traditional control agencies.

A final comment on the labeling process: It cannot be reversed. Once a youngster has been labeled a delinquent, he will always be a delinquent or a former delinquent.

POLICE-JUVENILE ENCOUNTERS

The initial and key element in the labeling process is the police officer. As the Task Force on Juvenile Delinquency and Youth Crime (1967) has stated, "contacts with the police are the gateway into the system of delinquency and criminal justice." Annually, one million youngsters are estimated to have contact with the police, one-third of whom appear in juvenile court. Since laws regarding juvenile delinquency are much more flexible and the procedures are much less defined than are those used in dealing with adult offenders, law enforcement calls for an unusual amount of discretion in decisions involving the handling of juveniles. What a police officer does or fails to do may have a lasting impact upon a youngster's future and upon his attitudes toward adults and respect for authority in general.

Disposition and Discretion

Many questions might be asked: How many warnings, if any, does a youngster receive before he is taken into custody or arrested? Do age, color of skin, or socio-economic status of parents make a difference? What about his attitude and appearance at the point of encounter? How much emphasis is placed on the seriousness of the offense or previous delinquencies? What effect does the attitude and education of officers have on the disposition of juvenile cases?

Lynn Swanson, a consultant on specialized police services for children with the U.S. Children's Bureau, states that "Dispositions of children coming to the attention of the police should be based upon all the facts of the case, including the seriousness of the offense, the social factors revealed, the protection of the community, the legal requirements of the police, and the previous police experience with the juvenile" (1964).

The external community may exert pressures on the police department which in turn affect the disposition of juvenile cases. Various pressures within the police department such as policy, attitudes of co-workers and supervisors, and personal experiences of the officer himself will certainly influence the decision-making process.

One of the more significant studies in the area of police-juvenile encounters was carried out by Piliavin and Briar (1964) based on nine months' observation of all juvenile officers in a large suburban police department. The officers were observed on duty during this period of time in an effort to determine the factors influencing their dispositional decisions in handling juvenile offenders.

In this study, the officers could select any one of five alternatives: (1) outright release, (2) release and submission of a field interrogation report, (3) official reprimand and release to parents, (4) citation to juvenile court, and (5) arrest and detention confinement. The latter three alternatives were those officially recorded in police files, thus invoking the labeling process.

An analysis of the distribution of police disposition decisions regarding juveniles revealed that the full range of alternatives was utilized primarily because of two factors. First, some officers were reluctant to impose the stigmatization presumed to be associated with official police action, and secondly, the actual use of discretion was sanctioned and encouraged by department policy and the training manual.

Perhaps the most significant finding of this study was that police decisions were more strongly guided by the personal character and demeanor of those juveniles apprehended than by the actual offense committed. Such decisions were based primarily on cues which emerged from the interaction between the officer and the youths, cues from which the officer inferred the character of the youths. These cues included the youths' group affiliations, age, race, grooming, dress, and demeanor. Table 7-I indicates the type and degree of association between the youth's demeanor and police disposition.

Furthermore, certain youths, blacks and boys dressed as

TABLE 7-I.
SEVERITY OF POLICE DISPOSITION BY YOUTH'S DIRECTOR

| | Youth's Demeanor | | |
Severity of Police Disposition	Coop-erative	Uncoop-erative	Total
Arrest (most severe)	2	14	16
Citation or official reprimand	4	5	9
Informal reprimand	15	1	16
Admonish and release (least severe)	24	1	25
Total	45	21	66

Piliavin, I., and Briar, S. Police encounters with juveniles. *American Journal of Sociology,* 1964, 70, 206-214. Reproduced by permission of the editor.

"toughs," were accosted more frequently either because of demeanor or skin color, which the police felt identified them as potential troublemakers. It appears that considerable hostility towards law enforcement personnel would naturally develop if such youngsters were frequently encountered by the police, particularly if they were innocent of wrongdoing. However, regardless of a youth's guilt or innocence, the interactions that constitute recorded delinquency are usually hostile encounters. It is most doubtful that such interactions serve to deter juveniles from further delinquency; rather, it appears that the hostility such encounters create has the opposite effect.

The Piliavin and Briar (1964) study serves to underscore the fact that "the official delinquent, as distinguished from the juvenile who simply commits a delinquent act, is a product of a social judgment, in this case a judgment made by the police. He is a delinquent because someone in authority has defined him as one, often on the basis of the public face he has presented to the officials, rather than the kind of offense he has committed."

Another study, with a slightly different orientation, was by Hohenstein (1969) in Philadelphia. In this well-designed study, Hohenstein found three prominent factors which determined the police disposition decision: (1) the attitude of the victim, (2) the previous record of the offender, and (3) the seriousness of the present offense.

It should be noted that Hohenstein made no attempt to study

the significance of the offender's attitude and demeanor, as influencing factors, although he concluded that such factors may prove relevant. Perhaps the most interesting finding in this study was the fact that regardless of the seriousness of the offense, the victim's attitude was the primary factor influencing the police decision. Also, racial bias was not found to be significant.

Wilson (1968) studied two large police departments, Western City and Eastern City, to compare what difference, if any, a high level of professionalism makes in handling juvenile offenders. It was discovered that in Western City, where the officers were younger and better educated, they tended to investigate, process, and arrest a larger proportion of delinquents than Eastern City. On the other hand, the officers of Eastern City referred three times as many blacks to juvenile courts as whites. This study obviously raises a concern about what kind of training and education police should have to "better" a police department.

Authority, Gangs, and Minorities

Several of the studies mentioned have alluded to a rather latent and sometimes open abuse of authority of police dealing with juveniles. A group of youngsters who were suspiciously congregating could have been arrested for loitering and were warned to move on threat of arrest. They were finally influenced to either leave or behave themselves by the friendly advice of an officer who has previously earned their respect (Terris, 1967). Such situations simply call for a basic understanding of human behavior and an ability and willingness to use authority as an influence rather than a threat of force. Often, such characteristics are not found in policemen because these abilities may not be rewarded in a police department.

Much of the verbal exchange between police and juveniles is seen as a process of validation of power to define, rather than any enforcement procedure (Tauber, 1967). For example, Werthman and Piliavin's (1967) study of gang members and the police provides some beautifully poignant verbatim conversations regarding show of authority:

One time me and a couple of friends, we came down to the corner on Monday night because we was supposed to have our meeting. And we was standing there on the corner bullshitting like we always do, and there was only four of us. Then this cop on a motorcycle pulled over and walked over to us. I seen him before. He rides around the neighborhood a lot. He didn't say nothing. He just zipped down his jacket and there was his big old billy club. And then he started asking questions, identification, what were we doing, and all like that. And he searched us and got our names down on the book and every-things. We wasn't doing anything, except what we usually do on that corner. (What's that?) Stand there bullshitting. They do anything to get our names on that book. You know. They want us to know they in charge.

Perhaps such activity can best be seen as the desire of police to impose their authority over youth and to exhibit the weak control juveniles have over their rights as persons. Such cognitive strain brought about by various methods of degradation and status conflict may frequently result in some negative reaction or attack upon the person or system responsible.

Most confrontations between policemen and gang youths have the potential of conflict—"a conflict over whose conception of proper behavior will prevail, a conflict over whose conception of proper behavior ought to prevail, and therefore a conflict over whose moral identity is to remain publicly intact." (Werthman and Piliavin, 1964).

At any rate, anyone who could conceivably be considered suspicious may frequently be subjected to interrogation by the police, thus increasing his personal sense of injustice and his likelihood of future encounters. One might contend, therefore, that the performance of the police in this manner may be indirectly responsible, in some measure, for the high incidence of delinquency, which seems to pervade lower class ethnic communities. Such groups may feel that the police, in their assessment of themselves, their roles, and their authority, usually serve not to control, but to exacerbate what is already an explosive situation.

Police naturally are concerned about various forms of threat to their authority. Conot (1968) points out that, "Many officers feel that the one sure way to avoid trouble with a suspect is to demonstrate their ability to handle the situation. This may take the form of grabbing on to you, or in general, roughing up the suspect in terms of grabbing him by the arm, pushing him into cars, and so forth." Indeed, such action may occasionally provoke unnecessary trouble.

As mentioned earlier, demeanor and attitude are of considerable importance in police-juvenile encounters. The following comments of a gang member indicates his savvy of the gestural vocabulary necessary when picked up by the police: "If you kiss their ass and say, "Yes Sir, No Sir," and all that jazz, then they'll let you go. If you don't say that, then they gonna take you in. And if you say it funny they gonna take you in. Like, "Yes Sir!, No Sir!" But if you stand up and say it straight, like "Yes Sir" and "No Sir" and all that, you cool (Werthman and Piliavin, 1964)."

This matter of deference often becomes something of a game which juveniles play to irritate an officer. Werthman and Piliavin found that when the policeman is polite with a gang member, he can sometimes mitigate the resentment and the sense of injustice provoked by the situation of suspicion. Such an approach may well serve to erase the insult to moral character that was implicit when the policeman initially decided to interrogate. Thus, the challenge to the authority of a policeman may well hang on whether the initial insult is augmented or diminished during the questioning.

Racial overtones are a frequent source of friction between police and black youth. Tauber and others see the police themselves as products of a society that discriminates, and their job is to deal with minority problems which are a result of that discrimination. The police, in essence, become the focal point of problems which are entirely outside the realm of law enforcement. As a highly regarded civil rights worker expressed it, "I feel sorry for the cop on the beat. He does not recognize that he is a pawn, caught in the middle just as we are" (Yearwood, 1968).

However, there is significant evidence that police all too often verbalize their contempt and racial prejudice, especially in dealing with juveniles.

> Remember that time we was coming home from the show? This cop car pulls up and these two cops jump out quick. The first stud

says, "All right, God damn you! All you black Africans up against the mother-fucking wall!" All that shit. So we got up against the wall over there on Market Street. This long house you know. So then they started. "Where all you ignorant sons of bitches coming from?" We say we coming from the show. "What show?" We say we coming from the Amazon. They say, "Yeah, we got a call there's a whole bunch of shit going on over there! I think I'll call all you mother fuckers in!" So nobody say nothing. So then he starts in again. "What's your name? Let me see your I.D.!" Finally, this cop's buddy say, "You want to run them in Joe? They ain't really done nothing." So then Joe stops. He say, "Now all you black Africans pick up your spears and go home! I don't want you guys walking up the street!" Shit like that man. You know. We wasn't doing nothing. We just coming from the show. That shit happens all the time. There ain't a day we don't get rousted like that (Werthman and Piliavin, 1964).

In defense of the policemen interviewed in the Werthman and Piliavin study, eighteen out of twenty-seven admitted to being prejudiced but argued that they had only become so since their employment with the police department.

The bitterness between police and lower-class minority youth according to Matza (1968) is a pervasive and almost palpable bitterness that arises out of a situation that neither can control: Restless young men are driven by urges they do not understand, but which most of them, somewhat mysteriously, outgrow. The police are also asked to solve problems they cannot solve.

Such bitterness readily develops into conflicts over competing rights, moralities, and tests of manhood to which easy solutions are not readily available.

TYPOLOGIES IN DELINQUENCY

Empirical research has rather consistently yielded several fairly well-delineated categories of delinquent. These groups have been identified with reference to a variety of criteria and dimensions, ranging from the nature of the offense committed to differentiations along some hypothetical psychiatric scale such as "superego development." Although behavioral scientists tend to react suspiciously to anything which smacks of oversimplification or overgeneralization, it is difficult to escape the conclusion that some categorization is essential to a meaningful analysis of delinquency data. As Rodman and Grams (1970) point out: "Any comparison of the findings of the Gluecks (1950) and Nye (1958), for instance, must take into account the fact that the Gluecks studied lower class incarcerated delinquents while Nye studied a sample of schoolchildren who were rated 'most' or 'least' delinquent from their responses to a self-report questionnaire."

The construction of typologies is, in fact, supported by sound scientific reasoning. Typologies are indispensable to the activities of the criminological researcher and theorist. Says McKinney (1966):

> In effect, a type constitutes a reduction from the complex to the simple; hence the careful construction and use of types, as an intermediate procedure, can potentially make many large-scale problems accessible to more refined methodology and technique. The construction of a type or series of types helps us know more precisely what mechanisms or structural relations are being postulated with respect to a problem area, sometimes calling attention to the need for further clarificaton of the operational meaning of relevant definitions and statements. The type assists in the discovery of inconsistencies between the empirical data and the theories used to explain them. It thus lays basis for the further elaboration of theory and frequently suggests further empirical studies in a problem-complex. The type aids in handling complicated, simultaneous inter-relations among a relatively large number of variables in a *preliminary* way, prior to the development of the operational possibility of handling them more rigorously with respect to any particular problem. Indeed, a primary role of the constructed type would seem to be that of a sensitizing device. Its use allows social scientists cognitively to map broad areas of social phenomena through systematic tapping of historical and secondary data. This can quite conceivably result in increased precision of analysis in many areas in the social sciences, particularly in such areas as macrosociology, where the problems are currently often beyond the scope of the more rigorous experimental and qualitative techniques.

Delinquent Types

Rodman and Grams (1970) specify three general types of delinquent which emerge from behavioral descriptions and theoretical formulations in the professional literature.

THE OCCASIONAL DELINQUENT. "Probably the largest subgroup

among delinquents appearing before juvenile court or having police contact is one-time offenders charged with minor violations. Usually these delinquents have participated in acts of vandalism or petty theft, generally in a group." This category includes those casual delinquents elsewhere identified as "prosocial" (Kinch, 1962) or "integrated" (Reiss, 1952) .

THE GANG DELINQUENT. "This is the delinquent who generally commits the most serious infractions, is most often sent to a correctional institution, and most often continues in a pattern of semiprofessional criminal behavior as an adult." Reiss (1952) characterizes this habitual gang delinquent as suffering from "weak superego;" Kinch (1962) has called him "antisocial" and Miller (1958) has described the habitual delinquent as a "lower class gang delinquent." The research finding that the offenses committed by delinquents who fit this general typology divide themselves into two subcategories—crimes against property and crimes against persons—has led a number of theorists (Cloward and Ohlin, 1960; Scott, 1959; Short and Strodbeck, 1965; and Spergel, 1964) to distinguish between conflict-oriented and theft-oriented gangs. Membership in these implies a distinction between conflict-oriented and theft-oriented delinquent subcultures.

THE MALADJUSTED DELINQUENT. This type of delinquent is characterized by tendencies toward criminality which are presumed to be the product of personality disturbance, rather than a function of gang membership or slum residence. Various terms with a heavy loading of psychiatric inference have been applied to this category of delinquent: "weak ego" (Reiss, 1952) ; "neurotic" (Jenkins and Hewitt, 1944) ; "asocial" (Kinch, 1962) ; and some writers (Scott, 1959) have sought to account for the behavior of such delinquents in the process of "abnormal socialization."

Dimensions of Delinquency

Rodman and Grams concluded that the types of delinquents described above are not based upon a single dimension, but rather that three dimensions are involved in the classificatory schema:

Occasional Delinquency——Habitual Delinquency

Gang Delinquency——Lone Delinquency
Maladjusted Delinquency——Adjusted Delinquency

Combining these three dimensions, Rodman and Grams are able to generate eight logical types:

Type 1. Adjusted-Occasional-Gang Delinquent: The gang consists of members showing relatively good personality adjustment, and the major activities of the gang are nondelinquent. Nevertheless, their activities are occasionally delinquent. William F. Whyte (1943) has described a gang of this type.

Type 2. Adjusted-Habitual-Gang Delinquent: The members of the gang show relatively good personality adjustment; their behavior is frequently or habitually delinquent. The accounts by Miller (1958) and Cloward and Ohlin (1960) of gangs manifesting lower class "focal concerns" or oriented to a "criminal subculture" are closely related to this type.

Type 3. Adjusted-Occasional-Lone Delinquent: This type refers to the relatively adjusted adolescent who occasionally engages in delinquency on his own. Many of the delinquents that are turned up on a self-report questionnaire are probably of this type. (Nye, 1958).

Type 4. Adjusted-Habitual-Lone Delinquent: The delinquent is relatively well-adjusted and engages in delinquent behavior largely on his own. The "precocious delinquent" who has taken over a "rational" criminal career would fall into this type.

Type 5. Maladjusted-Occasional-Gang Delinquent: This delinquent, as an individual, may have difficulty remaining a member within a delinquent gang of relatively well-adjusted boys; delinquent behavior therefore takes place only occasionally. His maladjustment would show up in other areas of behavior more than it does in delinquent behavior.

Type 6. Maladjusted-Habitual-Gang Delinquent: The members of the gang show relatively poor personality adjustment; their behavior is habitually delinquent. The "retreatist subculture" described by Cloward and Ohlin (1960) or the gang as a near-group described by Yablonsky (1962) would fit this pattern.

Type 7. Maladjusted-Occasional-Lone Delinquent: The personality disturbance ordinarily manifests itself in nondelinquent ways and occasionally in love delinquent acts.

Type 8. Maladjusted-Habitual-Lone Delinquent: Personality disturbance habitually manifests itself in some type of lone delinquent behavior.

Conclusion

With their rootedness in a kind of cultivatedly dogged empiricism, American criminologists have tended to ignore the value of the hypotheticodeductive approach in their endeavors. This brief exercise in logical analysis by Rodman and Grams offers a commendable example of the potential contribution of such an approach to criminological research. Their eight-fold classification of delinquent types represents what could be the beginnings of a comprehensive program of empirical investigation, which might proceed in several stages to: (1) identify more precisely the behavioral characteristics displayed by the various subgroups; (2) specify the variables which are functionally related to such behavior; (3) postulate the antecedent conditions which affect the operation of these variables; and (4) determine the validity of the typologies in predicting *response to differential treatment* using a variety of correctional intervention techniques. As Gibbons (1965) has argued persuasively, there is a great, and as yet unrealized, potential value in fitting delinquent typologies to the correctional or treatment context, where they become the basis for decision-making with regard to the choice of intervention method.

THE ETIOLOGY OF DELINQENCY

In three chapters dealing with theories of criminality, we dealt extensively with conceptualizations of causality and some of the empirical research that various theoretical approaches to the etiology and/or treatment of criminal and delinquent behavior have generated. Mabel A. Elliott (1967), in her review of trends in delinquency theories and research, summarized these studies under the following areas:

1. middle class delinquency
2. cultural factors and anomie
3. personality traits and delinquency
4. attitudes toward authority
5. emotional factors in delinquency
6. deprivation among Negro delinquents
7. delinquent's self-image
8. street work research

Since we have already discussed these topics in some detail, we shall confine ourselves in this section to some general remarks of a summary kind on the etiology of delinquent behavior.

Theories of Delinquency

Earlier, we noted the unfortunate tendency of most theorists to seek explanations of delinquency as a homogenous phenomenon, without reference to the question of subtypes or differences in the form it takes. Delinquency may consist of a single superficial or incidental act arising from some temporary situation or stress not likely to recur. It may reflect a stage in a youth's development, to be followed by maturation into a socially acceptable adulthood. It may be a fairly normal adjustment to an abnormal environment in which a certain family, neighborhood, or juvenile group standards may differ from and conflict with those of the community as a whole. Some delinquents may be mentally or emotionally maladjusted. Finally, delinquency may be chronic, deeply rooted in the personality of the child and a stage in his development toward more seriously antisocial or criminal behavior.

Bandura and Walters (1959) have offered a theory of antisocial aggression found in delinquents. They believe that such a disorder arises primarily from disruption of the child's dependence upon his parents. Most of the values and standards that will eventually govern his behavior are through imitation of the important adults in his life. A child who lacks close dependent ties to his parents can model himself after them and internalize their standards of behavior. In the absence of such internalized controls, the child's aggression is likely to be expressed in an immediate, direct, and socially unacceptable fashion. Thus an impaired dependency relationship may not only be a source of aggressive feelings, but may also limit a child's capacity to handle such feelings adequately once they are aroused. They felt that aggression is a learned response to frustrating situations, though not the only response to frustration. Aggression behavior is also reinforced insofar as it proves successful in overcoming frustrations that prevent the satisfaction of biological drives or learned motives.

Bandura and Walters also found inconsistency in the way the parents of the aggressive boys' parents handled their son's aggressive behavior. They felt that this may have been an important factor in fostering the boy's antisocial aggressive orientation. Both the mothers and fathers of the aggressive boys encourage their sons' aggression outside the home, while the mothers, through their relative permissiveness of aggression towards themselves, allowed opportunities for aggression to occur and be reinforced in the home. On the other hand, the fathers of the aggressive boys were very non-permissive of aggression towards themselves; both they and their wives had from time to time punished their sons for aggression, particularly for aggression towards adults. The punishment that the aggressive boys received probably served merely to make them more hostile and resentful.

Many researchers have assumed that certain conditions were causally related to delinquency when statistical studies showed them to be present in high incidence in the groups of delinquents studied. Yet, the same apparent causes may affect one child quite differently than another, and frequently the same causes may be shown to exist to a statistically significant degree among nondelinquents. Statistical studies of large groups of delinquents cannot provide the same kind of predictive validity as comparison studies of carefully selected pairs of individuals. The delinquency or nondelinquency of a particular youngster cannot be predicted on the basis of purely normative data.

Theories emphasizing defects in society ask: What is wrong with the neighborhood or other aspects of the face-to-face environment in which the delinquent lives? These viewpoints present conditions which they isolate, ranging from poverty and poor housing to the presence of delinquent subcultures in high delinquency areas. Three general subtypes of such theories can be placed in this general category: theories which maintain that poverty, poor housing, and similar deprivations are causes of delinquency; theories which view delinquency as socially learned behavior rooted in deviant neighborhood traditions and in the function of neighborhood peer groups; theories which hold that delinquency occurs in life situations where legitimate social controls are absent or greatly reduced (Martin, 1964). The most significant principle in these theories is the contention that knowledge of an "inner world" of delinquents is essential to an understanding of their behavior. This world is presumed to be composed of attitudes, values, and beliefs of individual delinquents as these mirror the situational, and especially the cultural, aspects of the individual's face-to-face environment.

The home situation has long been recognized as having special importance in the development of delinquency and in attempts to prevent or control it. Children deprived of one or both parents are, as a group, more prone to delinquency than those living in houses where both parents are present. Lack of positive discipline within the home, conflict between parents or other disturbing interfamilial relationship, and expressions of antisocial or criminal attitudes frequently are cited as contributing to delinquency. Other conditions of stress in the family situation such as poverty, deprivation, or illness, also may have harmful effects.

In Sheldon and Eleanor Glueck's study on *Delinquents and Nondelinquents in Perspective,* (1968) they traced delinquents first to age twenty-five and then to age thirty-one. They found the families of the delinquents' parents were more extensively characterized than those of the nondelinquents' by mental retardation, emotional disturbances, drunkenness, and criminality. Qualitative deficiencies in the immediate families of the delinquents are reflected in a lesser capacity of the fathers to earn an adequate living, in less effective household management, in less refinement of cultural atmosphere, in less self-respect on the part of the parents, in less adequate oversight of the children, and in weaker family ties.

The duration of the educational experience and the proportion of time spent in school are obviously of potential significance for delinquency. Studies have indicated some close relationships between maladjustment in the school on the one hand and the development of delinquency on the other. Shulman (1961) notes that a significantly high percentage of delinquents are found to have been originally chronic truants. Similarly the majority of delinquents are one or more years educationally retarded. They also show a rather high incidence of specific learning disabilities, such as difficulty in learning to read well. The dull-normal slow learners, those with intelligence quotients ranging from seventy-five to ninety, are represented disproportionately among delinquents. Some studies have shown a significantly higher degree of conflict with the school or teacher among delinquents than among non-delinquent character.

The importance of the neighborhood or community in the development of delinquency has been emphasized in many studies. Certain neighborhoods have abnormally high rates of delinquency and crime. Generally of low socioeconomic status, such neighborhoods additionally have developed for various reasons social, cultural, or behavioral standards different from those of the community as a whole. Frequently people living in such neighborhoods feel apart from and oppressed by the larger community. Often within such a setting a juvenile society characterized by gang groups with aggressive or otherwise antisocial standards and patterns of behavior will develop. In such cases the primary loyalty of the child or youth is often to his friends rather than to the alien standards of the school or community. All these causation theories are based on the inter-relationships of the environment surrounding the youth.

Many recent studies of causation theories in juvenile delinquency have turned to a deeper exploration of the personality and inner dynamics of the child himself. These studies have been concerned with the child's feelings of anxiety, frustration, inferiority, deprivation, or rejection as the causes of such neurotic manifestations as unusual aggressiveness, hostility, instability, or egocentricity. Although emphasizing the individual, studies of this kind recognize that faults in the home, school, or community environment may provoke antisocial behavior in already disturbed children. Without a doubt, the most important changes in social patterns affecting delinquency have been those in American family life. An increasing disorganization of the family and the lessening of the feelings of family integration and cohesiveness are apparent in the growing number of divorces and separations. Of great significance too, has been the diminution of the father's status in the family, the loss of his role as the standard-setter and behavior-controlling authority within the family unit.

THE PREVENTION OF DELINQUENCY

Lejins (1967) believes that before we even begin to discuss prevention, we should be sure what kind of prevention we mean. He identifies three types of prevention:

1. *Punitive prevention,* which implies that the threat of a known punishment will effectively forestall the criminal act. But to be truly effective there must be general knowledge of the certainty and severity of punishment;

2. *Corrective punishment,* which is based on the assumption that criminal behavior, like all human behavior, has its causes, is influenced by definite forces, and results from a definite motivation. Here, then, prevention means the elimination of these causes and motivations before crime results. Corrective prevention is much more a product of modern society than is the preventive form and is the kind of prevention commonly accepted today;

3. *Mechanical prevention,* which means that obstacles are placed in the way of the potential offender to make it difficult for him to commit an offense. There is no threat of punishment, nor attempt to eliminate cause and motivation. Burglar alarms and additional police would be examples of mechanical prevention.

The author concludes (1967) by noting that if we differentiate between more immediate and more basic causes of delinquency, then current preventive efforts have turned to the latter. Modern prevention programs are directed toward those groups with excessively high rates of crime and delinquency in an attempt to intervene earlier and more decisively in the causational process.

CONTROLLING DELINQUENCY

As the causes of delinquency are to be found in a combination of conditions in the home, school, community, and personality of the child, efforts to prevent or control delinquency, therefore, must, to be effective, deal with all four areas. The home environment, which probably has the greatest influence in the determination of delinquency, is also the most difficult to remedy. Case work by social workers with the family as a whole, with the parents, or with the children alone has often proved to be of some supporting benefit. The assistance of the church to which the family may belong is sometimes very helpful, as are the contributions of public agencies if poverty, unemployment, or illness is present. When the home situation cannot be much improved by outside assistance, efforts by the school, child-guidance centers, or other interested agencies working directly with the child may help to increase his resistance to the harmful effects of the home environment.

The educational system can do much to prevent or control delinquency not only by cooperating with other interested agencies but by correcting those defects within the school itself which may be helping to create delinquency. Among the contributions which a school can provide directly to the child are an efficient attendance service, designed to search out and to deal with causes of non-attendance, and a well-rounded student-service program, including health examinations, psychological counseling, vocational guidance, and special work with the mentally and physically handicapped. The school can do much by also analyzing and correcting the causes of unnecessary failure and retardation, thereby reducing the harmful effects of such experiences on our youth.

The system of social agenices must work effectively to treat those causes of delinquency which can be traced to the neighborhood or community environment. Public health, housing, sanitation, and recreational facilities may eliminate some of the physical conditions of conducive to delinquency. Public and private social-service agencies, child-guidance programs, vocational counseling and employment services, religious institutions, and recreational groups may deal with different aspects of the human problem. Sheldon Glueck (1959) said, experience has proved the desirability of coordinating the activities of all these varied agencies in dealing with a neighborhood or community, particularly one of the serious problems neighborhoods.

Once a child has been officially adjudged delinquent, his rehabilitation and retraining are generally in the hands of legally constituted authorities. For this aspect of the delinquency-control program, extension of positive juvenile-court practices is necessary. The juvenile court must have close coordination with the other community agenices and the availability of a variety of resources for delinquents who have to be taken out of their homes and neighborhoods for brief or longer periods of time. Such resources include detention homes, study and diagnostic centers, residential treatment centers, specialized private institutions, foster homes, and adequately planned and staffed public institutions.

All the theories of causation and proposals for solution of juvenile delinquency previously explained represent "traditional" attitudes toward juvenile delinquency. They all contend that the juvenile delinquent exhibits a failure of society or socialization to adequately induce proper behavior in the individual. These theories claim that the process of socialization has evidenced a break-down. The solutions to the problem of juvenile delinquency they propose are designed to prevent the break-down in the socialization process: the creation of a better home, school, and community environment. Yet, in spite of all these proposed solutions, delinquency continues to increase within our society. This conclusion seems to indicate that these theories and solutions previously put forth are not completely adequate in explaining and solving the problem of juvenile delinquency.

This apparent flaw in our social theory has been examined and analyzed by Paul Goodman in his recent work, *Growing Up Absurd*. Goodman claims that contemporary theories of causation have failed to consider the alternatives society offers to its youth. Here, he claims, is the source of the present difficulty. The values of our educational and social community fail to present acceptable alternatives to the youth of today. Children are being pushed and forced into life patterns that do not accommodate their nature as free thinking young adults. Society has indirectly "slotted" youth into occupations for which they have no natural desire. Twentieth century America is not providing incentives for its youth; hence, young people rebel, and the rebellion takes the form of juvenile delinquency.

The merits of Goodman's argument are self-evident: Other theories of delinquency and the solutions they have proposed have notably failed to curb the steady increase in delinquency. Thus, Goodman concludes, somewhere along the way alternatives have been excluded; something has been overlooked or under-emphasized. Goodman claims that what has been overlooked is the attitudes of youth toward the world in which they are expected to mature and participate.

Admittedly, Goodman's thesis is rather simplistic and leaves many basic questions unanswered. For instance, that specifically is meant by such arguments as the proposal to allow each individual a chance to develop his "natural creative instincts" instead of forcing him to conform to a particular social pattern? Nevertheless, in an impressionistic and moving series of prose portraits, he has managed to capture some of the malaise and almost visceral antagonism of much of contemporary youth culture.

On a more positive note, Amos and Wellford (1967) maintain that we are finally witnessing a societal commitment to the mobilization of those pertinent social institutions that can be enlisted in the potential prevention of delinquency. Although there has been a token recognition of the need to utilize community resources in the past, now these institutions are involved in the planning of preventive programs.

These authors (1967) also believe that the government must motivate, or at least implement, prevention programs. The federal government must be involved at more than the economic level since some of the agents of prevention are also arms of the government, i.e. police, courts. The federal government, likewise, is much better able to attain the unattainable. As Lohman (1967) states, a delinquent is a person whose spiritual, emotional, educational, and/or social needs are not satisfied. The target of prevention programs is thus not the delinquent act or the delinquent himself, but the framework within which the delinquent career is initiated, nurtured, and confirmed.

Summary

According to the labeling and stigmatization process, which is briefly described in this chapter, at least part of the responsibility for the development of an identity and subsequent career as "juvenile delinquent" appears to rest with the handling of the juvenile offender by the police and the courts. Ambiguity in the laws governing juvenile conduct places a great deal of emphasis upon the exercise of discretionary powers of arrest by the police, and some evidence is reviewed here regarding the kinds of factors which influence police judgments in their encounters with juveniles. Some typologies of delinquent are presented, including the (1) occasional delinquent, (2) gang delinquent, and (3) maladjusted delinquent, along with a discussion of some theoretical approaches to the etiology of delinquent behavior. The chapter ends with a review of efforts toward the control and prevention of juvenile delinquency.

REFERENCES

Amos, W.E. and Wellford, C.E. (Eds.): *Delinquency Prevention: Theory and Practice*. Englewood Cliffs, Prentice-Hall, 1967.

Bandura, A. and Walters, R.H.: *Adolescent Aggression*. New York, Ronald Press, 1959.

Cloward, R.A. and Ohlin, L.E.: *Delinquency and Opportunity*. New York, The Free Press, 1960.

Cohen, B. (Ed.): *Crime in America*. Itasca, F.E. Peacock, 1970.

Conot, R.: *Rivers of Blood, Years of Darkness*. Quoted in Vega, W.: The liberal policeman: a contradiction in terms? *Issues in Criminology, 4*:15-33, 1968.

Elliott, M.: Trends in theories regarding juvenile delinquency and their implication for treatment programs. *Federal Probation, 31*:3-11, 1967.

Gibbons, D.C.: *Changing the Lawbreaker.* Englewood Cliffs, Prentice-Hall, 1965.

Glueck, E.: Efforts to identify delinquents. *Federal Probation, 24,* 45-56, 1960.

Glueck, S.: *The Problem of Delinquency.* Boston, Houghton Mifflin, 1959.

Glueck, S. and Glueck, E.: *Unraveling Juvenile Delinquency.* Cambridge, Harvard University Press, 1950.

Glueck, S. and Glueck, E.: *Delinquents and Nondelinquents in Perspective.* Cambridge, Harvard University Press, 1968.

Goodman, P.: *Growing Up Absurd.* New York, Random House, 1962.

Hohenstein, W.: Factors influencing the police disposition of juvenile offenders. In Sellin, T. and Wolfgang, W. (Eds.): *Delinquency: Collected Studies.* New York, Wiley, 1969.

Jenkins, R.L. and Hewitt, L.: Two types of personality structure encountered in child guidance clinics. *American Journal of Orthopsychiatry, 14*:84-94, 1944.

Kinch, J. W.: Self-conceptions of types of delinquents. *Sociological Inquiry, 32*:228-234, 1962.

Lejins, P.: The field of prevention. In Amos, W.E. and Wellford, C.E. (Eds.): *Delinquency Prevention: Theory and Practice.* Englewood Cliffs, Prentice-Hall, 1967.

Lohman, J.D.: Forward. In Amos, W.E. and Wellford, C.E. (Eds.): *Delinquency Prevention: Theory and Practice.* Englewood Cliffs, Prentice-Hall, 1967.

Lunden, W.: *Satistics on Delinquents and Delinquency.* Springfield, Charles C Thomas, 1964.

Martin, J.: *Delinquent behavior.* New York, Random House, 1964.

Matza, D.: *Delinquency and Drift.* New York, Wiley, 1964.

McKinney, J.: *Constructive Typology and Social Theory.* New York, Appleton-Century-Crofts, 1966.

Miller, W.B.: Lower class culture as a generating milieu of gang delinquency. *Journal of Social Issues, 14*:5-19, 1958.

Nye, I.: *Family Relationships and Delinquent Behavior.* New York, Wiley, 1958.

Piliavin, I. and Briar, S.: Police encounters with juveniles. *American Journal of Sociology, 70*:206-214, 1964.

Reiss, A.J.: Social correlates of psychological types of delinquency. *American Sociological Review, 17*:710-718, 1952.

Rodman, H. and Grams, P.: Types of delinquents. In Telle, J. (Ed.): *Juvenile Delinquency.* Itasca, F.E. Peacock, 1970.

Scott, J.F.: Two dimensions of delinquent behavior. *American Sociological Review, 24*:240-243, 1959.

Short, J.F. and Strodtbeck, F.L.: *Group Process and Gang Delinquency.*

Chicago, University of Chicago Press, 1965.

Spergel, I.: *Racketville, Slumtown, Haulburg.* Chicago, University of Chicago Press, 1964.

Spergel, I.: *Community Problem-Solving: the Delinquency Example.* Chicago, University of Chicago Press, 1969.

Swanson, L.D.: Police and children. In Cavan, R.S. (Ed.): *Readings in Juvenile Delinquency.* Philadelphia, Lippincott, 1964.

Task Force Report on Juvenile Delinquency and Youth Crime. President's Commission on Law Enforcement and Criminal Justice. Washington, U.S. Government Printing Office, 1967.

Terris, B.J.: The role of the police. *The Annals, 374*:58-69, 1967.

Werthman, C. and Piliavin, I.: Gang members and the police. In Bordua, D.J. (Ed.): *The Police: Six Sociological Essays.* New York, Wiley, 1967.

Wheeler, S., Cottrell, L.S., and Romasco, A.: The labeling process. In Cressey, D. and Ward, D. (Eds.): *Delinquency, Crime, and Social Process.* New York, Harper and Row, 1969.

Whyte, W.F.: *Streetcorner Society.* Chicago, University of Chicago Press, 1943.

Wilson, J.Q.: *Varieties of Police Behavior.* Cambridge, Harvard University Press, 1968.

Yearwood, H.: Police-community relations. *Issues in Criminology, 4*:45-57, 1968.

Chapter 8
ADDICTIVE BEHAVIOR: ALCOHOLISM AND DRUG ABUSE

ALCOHOLISM

THE RECENT HISTORY of societal response to alcoholism in this country is dominated by efforts to "decriminalize" alcohol-related offenses by recasting the alcoholic offender in the role of psychiatric patient, i.e. one who is "sick" and therefore, presumably, not responsible for his behavior. The validity of this argument is largely determined by the extent to which the disease or illness model endorsed by psychiatry fits the requirements imposed by the empirical data on alcoholism. As we shall see, behavior pathologists have raised some serious objections to the alcoholism-as-disease model on a variety of grounds.

Obviously, the question of causation is crucially important: Upon the answers to this question depends the success or failure of efforts toward altering the behavior of the alcoholic individual. However, the criminologist and the behavior pathologist do not, and perhaps cannot, view the problems of alcoholism and alcohol-related criminality in the same way. Apart from matters pertaining to the etiology of alcoholism in its various forms is the fact that alcoholic consumption is involved in a wide range of crimes and criminal actions, many of which are related only indirectly or peripherally to some hypothesized clinical condition called *alcoholism*. Criminological consideration of alcohol and its effects must begin by focusing on the *crimes* associated with alcohol.

DRUNKENNESS

Drunkenness is the most severe single law-enforcement problem in the United States. In 1970 there were 1,825,500 arrests for drunkenness. Persons over 25 comprise over 95 percent of all arrests for drunkenness, and males account for 90 percent of all arrests in the same category (Uniform Crime Report, 1970). It should be remembered that one person may be arrested several times for the same offense. Ross (1965) located ten men who had served more than ninety years behind bars for public drunkenness (life-on-the-installment-plan) and had been arrested a total of 1,023 times at a cost to the taxpayer of over 300,000 dollars. The richest and most scientific nation in the history of the recorded world has developed no more creative responses for these alcoholics than to put them in jail. On any given night, alcoholics comprise from one-half to two-thirds of the population of jail inmates, approximately one million per year. It is a case of "revolving door" justice. It is not unusual for a "drunk court" to parcel out "justice" at an average of two minutes per case.

Naive Crimes Associated With Drinking

In addition to the chronic police case inebriate, many crimes are committed by individuals during a sequence of heavy drinking to secure the means to continue their drinking. These crimes, according to Glaser and O'Leary (1968), "are 'naive' in the sense that they are almost certain to result in the offender's apprehension before long." Characteristically, the commission of such crimes requires little or no specialized criminal knowledge or skills. Prominent in this category are naive check forgery and theft or burglary.

Drunken Driving

Annual arrests for drunken driving average one half-million (Uniform Crime Report, 1970). Although the official designation of "driving under the influence" makes no distinction between the effects of alcohol and narcotics, it is alcoholic consumption that accounts for the overwhelming majority of such arrests. Estimates of deaths incurred as an indirect or direct result of alcohol range as high as 25,000 per year, i.e. approximately 50 percent of the nation's annual traffic death toll; if the driver of an automobile involved in a fatality is proven to have been "under the influence" at the same time the accident occurred, he may find himself charged with a much more serious offense than drunken driving.

Drinking and Violence

Wolfgang and Strohm (1956) studied the case files of the Philadelphia Police Department's homicide squad over a period ranging from 1948 to 1952 and tabulated the incidence of homicides in which drinking was implicated. They reported a significant relationship between drinking in the victim and/or the offender and violent homicide in over 60 percent of the cases they examined. If one considers only those cases in which the victim was responsible for initiating the argument that resulted in the homicide, the percentage is even higher, 74 percent.

ALCOHOLISM IN PROBLEM PERSPECTIVE

While other countries may lead the U.S. in terms of *rate* of alcoholism, our country is one of the largest producers of alcoholics in the world. It has been estimated that there are approximately eight million alcoholics of various types in America—a number roughly equal to the population of the state of Texas. This figure includes five million outright alcoholics and another three million "prealcoholics." Alcoholism is now the nation's number three health problem from the standpoint of lives lost and people disabled surpassed only by heart disease and cancer. It is five times more prevalent than cancer and three times more prevalent than tuberculosis. Family relief costs in New York each year, due to alcoholism, were approximately 2,600,000 dollars by 1960.

Each year, industry in the United States loses more than one billion dollars from the absenteeism, accidents, and substandard work of two million problem drinkers. The chronic alcoholic has become a yearly 3,000,000 dollars pain-in the pocketbook to the city of Los Angeles alone. City police arrested 104,000 inebriates in 1960 for public nuisance or disturbing the peace. Each arrest cost an average of thirty-five dollars by the time the drinker was hauled off to jail, sobered up, fed, arraigned, and released (Taylor, 1960).

We get some picture of the magnitude of the problem when we realize that the estimated number of chronic alcoholics alone is ten times the number of persons in mental institutions, jails, and penitentiaries combined.

Historical Background

Almost every nation or tribe since prehistoric times has had experiences with the effects and consequences of alcoholic beverages. Egyptian frescoes reveal that brewing was a thriving industry nearly 5,000 years ago. In Greece and Rome, and among the peoples of the Middle and far East, wine was the chief source of intoxication. The Teutonic tribes had also discovered the principle of fermentation, although their concoctions would doubtless seem strange to a modern palate. Ale was the beverage of the Norse sea-raiders; in the Americas, the Indians made alcohol out of a variety of substances, ranging from cactus juice to palm sap.

When the colonists arrived in the New World, they brought with them deeply ingrained sanctions against excessive drinking. A state of inebriation was considered a grave matter, though alcohol was not regarded as intrinsically evil. Perhaps a 20th century analogy could be sought in the fact that automobile accidents are universally deplored, yet no one would suggest in seriousness that the source of the accidents, the automobile, be eliminated.

Prior to 1700, most drinking in colonial America was done in the home; later, drinking retired to the local tavern, which became a center of community life. The beverages usually consumed there were beer and wine. With the advent of the mercantilism triangle, i.e. West Indian molasses—New England rum—African slaves, distilled spirits became economically attractive to the colonists. Also, the transportation of rum and whisky posed fewer problems than hauling bulky produce like grain or sugar cane to marketing centers. Changes in the colonial population as a consequence of large scale immigration contributed to a significant increase in the consumption of alcoholic beverages.

From earliest times, the use of alcohol has been associated with group gatherings and social affairs; solitary drinking is a relatively rare phenomenon. Since drinking is largely a social and group function, there are numerous sanctions against uncontrolled behavior in the group setting. The individual's behavior reflects the patterns of the group, and variations can be correlated with basic social factors, such as the family, personal associations, religious affiliation, ethnic background, and economic status.

ALCOHOLISM IN THE PUBLIC VIEW

Public attitudes toward alcoholism have been reported by the pollster, Louis Harris. According to Harris (1966), one in every five adults in the United States says someone "close" to him drinks too much alcohol upon occasion. One in fourteen adults says that this person shows the effects of drinking "almost all the time." The principal reasons cited as the causes for alcoholism include: family problems, an inherent craving for alcohol, an emotional need to drink, personal insecurity which can be traced back to childhood, and a desire to escape the realities of life. It is apparent that most people consider alcoholism a psychological disorder. A majority of the public (54%) believes that there is a cure for alcoholism, but that it lies within the individual himself.

Definitions of Alcoholism

One of the leading authorities on alcoholism (Jellinek, 1962) defines alcoholism as "any use of alcoholic beverages that causes damage to the individual or society or both." Hant (1954) states that "when a number of signs, which characterize the drinking pattern as abnormal, present themselves together we can be sure that we are dealing with an alcoholic. Most important among these are loss of control, dependency, and progression."

Fox (1967) also endorses the disease interpretation of alcoholism. She defines alcoholism as "a behavioral disturbance in which the excessive drinking of alcohol interferes with the physical and mental health of the individual." Often there is a disturbance in family and other interpersonal relationships.

Some psychologists maintain that alcoholism is symptomatic of deep inner conflicts and psychological problems. According to this view, one type of alcoholic is the person who is unable to cope with the normal stresses of life and turns to alcohol for help. The psychologist with this orientation may seek to discover why the alcoholic is unable to cope with stress and what, if any, underlying problems exist within the person's personality.

The American Psychiatric Association (1968), on the other hand, recognizes cases in which there is a clear addictive pattern to alcohol without any discernible personality disorder.

The world Health Organization (WHO, 1952) defines alcoholics as "those excessive drinkers whose dependence upon alcohol has attained such a degree that it shows a noticeable mental disturbance or an interference with their bodily and mental health, their interpersonal relations, and their smooth and economic functioning, or who show the prodromal signs of such development." The WHO definition thus agrees more or less with the disease model or conception of alcoholism. Psychological aspects are not emphasized, although the term "dependence" could be construed as being mental and/or physical.

White (1964) feels that alcohol is a narcotic and, therefore, regards alcoholism as similar to drug consumption and addiction. Alcohol produces its first reactions in the areas of the cerebral cortex which mediate inhibitory controls. Reduction of inhibition leads to general relaxation and a feeling of well-being. As ingestion of alcohol continues, the individual loses control of speech and motor behavior, until finally a state of stupor or unconsciousness is reached.

From a social learning point of view, alcoholics are persons who have acquired the habit of alcohol consumption through reinforcement and modeling experiences as widely generalized dominant response to aversive stimulation (Bandura, 1968). Children may learn about drinking from parents who use alcohol extensively for social reasons and for coping with a stressful or frustrating situation. On the other hand, when drinking is limited to specific circumstances such as a ceremony or as a beverage during meals, the child is not apt to learn excessive drinking as a way of life.

To summarize, behavior pathologists have approached the definition of alcoholism as (1) a psychological disorder, (2) symptoms of a psychological disorder, and (3) most recently, as *behavior* which is susceptible to modification by techniques derived from the experimental study of learning and conditioning. (Ullmann and Krasner, 1969)

PHYSIOLOGICAL EFFECTS OF ALCOHOL

Alcohol has some food properties when taken in small quantities, but several differences are apparent. Alcohol is burned rapidly, and food is burned slowly; alcohol is eliminated rather rapidly, food is stored by the body; the use of food stimulates brain and muscular activity, alcohol does not. Alcohol tends to inhibit the subjective aspects of food deprivation without doing anything to relieve hunger.

Alcohol operates as a cortical depressant, and its action increases with intake. This depressant action causes a reduction in speed of reaction time, in ability to discriminate, and in exercise of control over behavior. Sensitivity to light, sound, taste, and odor are also affected. In males, it often has the effect of producing temporary sexual impotence. But the outstanding effect is the reduction in discrimination and the consequent loss of judgement and control. It reduces the muscular and nervous efficiency of the body, which is most important in operating a car. Thus for a time, the individual's total activity is influenced.

Many experiments on the non-emotional effects of alcohol have dealt with attention, reaction time, learning, memory, and reasoning. In auditory and visual experiments, subjects are given a small amount of alcohol (concentration not above .05%). Tests are administered an hour after the dose. With small amounts of alcohol, softer sounds can be heard; there is an increase in acuity but a loss in discrimination. The same results are found in vision experiments (McCarthy, 1959).

Tactile sensation neither increases nor decreases, but the ability to locate points of sensation and pain is diminished. There are no significant changes in muscle strength. Small amounts of alcohol, which may produce relaxation, usually interfere with efficiency. (McCarthy, 1959)

In the area of intellectual functioning, there is an increased flow of ideas, but they are less well organized and integrated. Accumulated evidence shows alcohol to cause impairment of problem-solving behaviors.

A study by Nash (1962) used fifty-six adult volunteers who received a small and a large dose of alcohol, plus a control group which received a placebo. Various tests of psychological and physiological functioning were administered following dosage. One result was that after an individual had consumed three or four highballs on an empty stomach, he was rated incapable of critical judgement. In another test, driving skill under the influence of various amounts of alcohol was systematically evaluated. Functions were shown to be impaired at blood alcohol levels short of 100mg. percent. (Legal standards of intoxication are usually set at 150 mg. percent.)

Results also showed that small amounts of alcohol promote creativity to the extent that they produce a freer flow of ideas. The ideas themselves, however, are apt to be of dubious quality. Large quantities of alcohol are unlikely to produce creative solutions to problems, but moderate amounts may stimulate ideas which differ from one's usual ideas.

Nash also found that intellectual resources were immobilized by alcohol. Detail discrimination, recall of impressions, and making sense out of meaningful visual stimuli were all impaired.

Social Drinking

In certain circles of our present-day society, the standards for social acceptance and approbation have come to rest on an individual's ability to consume alcohol. In the middle and upper classes, where an abundance of leisure time and increased entertaining go hand in hand, a host is judged on how soon he can get a highball into the hand of a newly arrived visitor. And the visitor, in return, is expected to drain and refill his glass as often as possible. The guest with an empty glass and the non-drinker are looked upon as eccentrics or poor sports. The consequences of this increased social drinking, which has become prominent since the end of the second World War and continues to grow in popularity, range from relatively harmless to deeply destructive.

The first result, quite naturally, has been that the total number of alcoholic beverage users in our nation has risen. Another result, also quite natural but much more unfortunate, is that the total number of alcoholics and problem drinkers has also risen. The ratio of alcoholics to total drinkers has appeared to remain constant, but this is small consolation to the families of newly discovered alcoholics who have been initiated into the tragic fraternity as a result of increased social imbibing. It is worth underlining the phrase "has appeared" in the previous sentence; there is growing professional suspicion that an unknown number of "hidden drinkers" exist in our society.

A further result has been observed concerning the caliber of the people affected by this problem. Today the Skid Row derelict is part of an ever diminishing minority. The present army of alcoholics is staffed by highly able executive and professional types, as well as garage mechanics, salespeople, elderly retired individuals, and housewives. Professional people concerned with the problem are becoming quite alarmed at the extent of problem drinking among women. The females involved are not all barflies and prostitutes; they are rather housewives and mothers who do most of their drinking on the sly and in the confines of the home. The majority of them have not taken to inviting in the deliveryman, and it is feared that a high percentage remain "hidden drinkers," undiscovered and unhelped. Coleman (1964) reports that the female rate of alcoholism rose 52 percent from 1940 to 1953, as opposed to a 45 percent rise for males. Since there is no way to compile statistics on the "hidden drinkers," this 52 percent figure is considered by some to be much lower than fact.

The increased incidence of higher class males in the alcoholic ranks is producing its share of problems and worries, too. Alcoholic executives in large companies do not find it difficult to go unrevealed for years; the vast amount of social drinking that is expected of them serves as a cover for the satisfaction of their need, a need that would quickly come to light in a more abstemious culture. Other white collar workers, perhaps not as important but equally as intelligent, realize their position well enough to keep themselves in check during the work week. They drink a moderate amount at lunch and in the evenings to remain somewhat satisfied, but they wait until the weekend before settling down to really serious drinking. Again, the cocktail parties and other social events provide readymade protection from sudden exposure as a problem drinker. If an individual should slip and end up temporally incapacitated, the ease with which he can take sick leave from the job for a day or two is another point in his favor.

SOCIOCULTURAL FACTORS IN ALCOHOLISM

The economic and social structures of society play an important role in establishing the context within which alcoholism must be interpreted. In France, for example, drinking seems to provide an escape from cramped, overcrowded living conditions. Said Jellinek (1962) :

> Beresard (1958), in a study of housing in relation to alcohol consumption, found a definite relation between daily wine intake and the number of rooms occupied by families. In some . . . districts of certain countries, the population is so poor, or there exists such a food shortage, that the inhabitants derive a large proportion of their calories from cheap wine. In the district of Minho, Portugal, a laborer's wages amount to 23 escudos per day; a pound of meat costs 11 escudos and the same price is paid for a pound of the cheapest fish, but a quart of wine costs only 2 escudos . . . The survey mentions daily consumption of wine without stating the amount, and of course, no reference is made to the incidence of alcoholism, but the enormous incidence of death from cirrhosis of the liver indicates the role that alcohol must play in the calories economy.

There is a correlation between the economy of the country and the consumption of alcohol. In such countries as Switzerland, the price of alcoholic beverages was fixed at a much higher rate than that of food. This system was effective until the food prices rose and resulted in an increase in alcoholic consumption. In contrast, such countries as France and Italy have such a low rate for wine that alcoholic consumption is seemingly encouraged. In these countries, the occupational factor must also be considered. As an example, in France ". . . 8 million voters (approximately one-third of the electroate) are partly or entirely dependent upon the production, processing and distribution of alcoholic beverages . . ." (Jellinek). Comparison of the daily intake of alcohol for the average Italian and the average American would differ, as Americans are not as dependent on wine or other forms of alcohol as an Italian. Therefore, based on the differences in economic structure and dependence on alcohol for life, there can be no set rate of daily consumption that would define an alcoholic universally.

In the United States, ". . . drinking is a custom to which society attaches an astonishingly great importance. In a sociological sense, drinking is not an institution, but in some cultures— among them, in America—it comes very near to being one" (Jellinek). What society deems acceptable in regards to drinking habits varies as much as the economic factors. Jellinek states the following hypothesis concerning society and addiction: "In societies which have a low degree of acceptance of large daily amounts of alcohol, mainly those will be exposed to the risk of addiction who on account of high psychological vulnerability have an inducement to go against the social standards. But in societies which have an extremely high degree of acceptance to large daily alcohol consumption, the presence of any small vulnerability, whether psychological or physical, will suffice for exposure to the risk of addiction." (Jellinek).

CLASSIFICATION OF ALCOHOLICS

Jellinek (1960) has devised a classification system for alcoholism which divides alcoholics into non-addictive and addictive types. Although clinical usefulness has been claimed for this system, it must be emphasized that these categories are essentially descriptive generalizations which are subject to constraints in terms of reliability and validity.

Addictive Alcoholic

The addictive alcoholic is characterized by both a psychological and physiological dependence on alcohol. The psychological dependence is the force acting on the individual to cause him to begin drinking again after long periods of abstinence. It is the physiological dependence which causes the alcoholic to continue drinking excessively after beginning again, and upon cessation to encounter a withdrawal syndrome. In the addictive alcoholic there is a loss of control over the use of alcohol, and it is this type that is most prevalent in organizations such as Alcoholics Anonymous.

Non-Addictive Alcoholic

The non-addictive alcoholic shows psychological dependence in alcohol, Littman (1964) describes the alcoholic personality as an individual with a low tolerance for frustration, unreal expectations of himself, and one who suffers from anxiety, insecurity, and inferiority feelings. He is impulsive, fears rejection, feels loneliness and isolation, and is frequently beset with hostility, guilt, and depression.

Many alcoholics, Littman maintains, never had a carefree childhood; they were given too much responsibility too early. Their fathers tended to be aggressive and domineering, consequently their independence was stifled. Therefore, they resorted to alcohol to prove their manliness and maturity.

At least one investigator is skeptical of such quests for the "alcoholic personality." After analyzing thirty-seven studies dealing with alleged characteristics of the alcoholic personality, Sutherland (1960) concluded that an alcoholic could be anxious or relaxed, depressed or euphoric, extroverted or withdrawn, etc. In short, the alcoholic personality defies ready categorization.

This conclusion derives additional support from more recent studies by Bleime and Sheppard (1967), Cheek (1967), Gomberg (1968), Jones (1968), Sanford (1968), and Tahka (1968). In the studies by Jones (1968) and Tahka (1968), for example, systematic comparisons between problem drinkers and non-drinkers, on a wide assortment of personality variables, produced findings which were almost completely contradictory. Even if allowances are made for the difference in cultural backgrounds of the subjects in the two studies (Tahka's study was done with Finnish drinkers), the differences are still too large to reconcile.

Symptoms

Jellinek (1960) gives a comprehensive survey of the syndrome shown by the individual in his progressive development towards addictive alcoholism.

Phase I

Phase I or the pre-alcoholic phase may last from six months to ten years. Here the future alcoholic begins drinking to relax or acquire a general feeling of well-being. Prior to this state the individual may have drunk alcohol only at mealtimes or on social occasions. In this period there is no feeling of social or physical deterioration, but as the stage progresses in time the person starts to drink larger and larger amounts of alcohol to attain his sense of well-being and begins to drink on more frequent occasions.

Phase II

Phase II is referred to as the early alcoholic phase of the stage of nonaddictive alcoholism. With no clear cut-off point, the drinker leaves from Phase I and enters Phase II. This stage is marked by the following characteristics, and the early alcoholic will show most if not all of them:

BLACKOUTS. The early alcoholic begins to experience "blackouts" or "pulls blanks." This symptom may not occur until late in life or, possibly not at all. The blackouts are amnesic periods which occur during or immediately following a drinking session. The individual will appear quite rational and alert while drinking but after sobering up will not remember what took place while he was drinking. The early alcoholic is afraid he has said or done something foolish, and will avoid talking about it.

SNEAKING DRINKS. Another symptom is that of sneaking drinks which may take several forms. The alcoholic may start having a few drinks before a party, drinking it "on the rocks," or possibly have a few extra, or gulp the first few drinks at the party. These forms may later develop into actually hiding a bottle at home and drinking from it when no one is watching.

PREOCCUPATION WITH ALCOHOL. There develops a preoccupation with alcohol. This preoccupation may be observed when the individual asks if there will be liquor served at a party, or if he is afraid there won't be he will take his own bottle.

GUILT FEELINGS. Along with the above symptoms, the early alcoholic has begun to feel guilty about his drinking habits; he realizes they are not normal. These guilt feelings can be seen in the defenses built up by the individual, and by his becoming overly angry when the subject of his drinking habits are brought to his attention.

AVOIDS REFERENCE TO ALCOHOL. Finally, the alcoholic will avoid any reference to alcohol, especially when he is sober. There will be a flat denial that he has a drinking problem, and, since he has no problem, there should be no feelings of guilt about continuing this behavior.

Phase II may last from several months to several years for those who eventually become addictive alcoholics. The early alcoholic is known as a "heavy drinker" to his friends but is not considered as alcoholic; both he and his family know, however, that things are getting out of hand. The early alcoholic's own feelings tell him he is becoming sick and should seek help, but he tends to rationalize these feelings away. Phase II is called the non-addictive alcoholic stage because the individual has become psychologically dependent on alcohol, but not yet physiologically dependent. There is still control of his drinking if he desires to exercise it, but as his drinking becomes heavier, new problems involving his family, friends, job, and health arise. These new problems are dealt with through the defenses or "alibi systems" of the individual. Thus to relieve the anxiety the individual is creating for himself, he will usually use one or more of these defenses:

DENIAL. Denial is the most basic, of the early alcoholic defenses. He will flatly deny any problem, and as his drinking becomes heavier, the denials become stronger. Thus when he says, "I can take it or leave it," it is apparent to everyone but himself that this is merely a cop-out for a sizeable and growing problem.

RATIONALIZATION. When the reality of the situation makes the use of denial impossible, the individual employs the technique of rationalization. This rationalization usually works to bring his drinking behavior into a culturally accepted situation. So, "It was such a hot day and that cold beer looked so inviting," becomes just an elaborate excuse for having a drink.

PROJECTION. Projection is another device used when denial can no longer be used. Here the tendency is to alleviate himself of all guilt and blame someone else for his problem. This person is usually a nagging wife (why is she nagging?) or an overbearing boss (why is he all of a sudden overbearing?).

FRAGMENTATION. This is a defense to blot out periods of reality. When questioned on the amount of drinking he does, an alcoholic may say, "Some days I don't drink at all," to convey the belief to the listener that these periods of sobriety are general living patterns when actually they are small portions of the overall picture.

Phase III

Phase III is called the crucial phase or the stage of addictive alcoholism; it is here that the alcoholic develops a physiological dependence on alcohol. This is also the stage that is easiest to recognize for the outsider because there is complete loss of control by the alcoholic over his drinking. The overt symptoms of this stage are easily seen. The alcoholic exhibits grandiose behavior to cover his guilt feelings and low self-esteem. There is often marked aggressive behavior as he seeks to convince himself that his problems are caused by someone other than himself. There will also be a change in his drinking pattern, possibly to prove to himself that no problem exists. He may change from bourbon to scotch or resolve never to drink before dinner; only alcoholics drink before dinner. Periods of abstinence are a device by which no alcoholic can prove to himself again that "he can take it or leave it." This symptom is important because social drinkers do not need to prove to themselves or anyone else that they do not have drinking problems. In this stage there will be a change of associates and friends. The alcoholic feels the people he knows now are the cause of his problem. Often divorces and severing of old friendships occur here. The most important and also most observable symptom is that, with the cessation of drinking, a withdrawal syndrome occurs due to the physiological dependence. These symptoms may take the form of tremulousness, hallucinocis, or convulsions.

Phase IV

With the occurance of physiological dependence the alcoholic enters Phase IV or the chronic phase. In this stage the individual finds himself engaged in prolonged unplanned drinking sprees, usually referred to as "benders." In the first three phases the alcoholic may have been able to reserve heavy drinking for the weekends. Aside from being condemned by all segments of society and suffering a rapid deterioration in health as the result of an inadequate diet, the alcoholic exhibits other overt symptoms during this final stage.

ETHICAL DETERIORATION. There may be a loss of moral and ethnical restraint, possibly for the first time in his life. He may begin stealing or writing worthless checks. In the case of a female, there may be a turn toward promiscuity and prostitution.

MILD CHRONIC BRAIN SYNDROME. There may develop a condition diagnosed as mild chronic brain syndrome which, even after days or weeks of sobriety, does not allow the alcoholic to assess his deteriorated condition and make plans for rehabilitation.

LOSS OF TOLERANCE. There also develops a loss of tolerance to alcohol, for now much less alcohol is needed to become intoxicated. Along with this loss of tolerance, the alcoholic may begin using any kind of alcohol or alcoholic substitute: shaving lotion, rubbing alcohol, sterno, barbituates, certain tranquilizers, etc.

In addition to the symptoms Jellinek has cited, Weingold, Lackin, Bell and Cox (1968) found that 70 percent of a group of alcoholics they investigated showed signs of mild to deep *depression.*

Some alcoholics with a premorbid history of markedly poor adjustment may exhibit the symptoms *pathological intoxication,* in which they may participate in aggressive or wantonly destructive behavior. Another of the acute alcoholic reactions is *alcoholic hallucinosis,* a relatively rare syndrome marked by the presence of vivid auditory hallucinations. Over a period of time, ranging up to several weeks, the patient experiences hallucinated voices accusing him of sexual misconduct and threatening to punish or torture him. During this time, he usually shows symptoms of fearfulness and depression and may even attempt suicide.

DELIRIUM TREMENS. The so-called "DTs" refers to a markedly disoriented state in which visual and auditory hallucinations may be experienced. One of the chief symptoms of this condition is an uncontrollable coarse tremor—the tremens part of the reaction. In addition, the patient may be almost totally disoriented and out of contact. Fearful and apprehensive, he can be extremely suggestible. An attack of delirium tremens usually lasts about three to four days.

KORSAKOFF'S SYNDROME. This is a symptom complex found in about 1 percent of chronic alcoholics. It is characterized by disorientation for time and place, loss of memory for recent events, and a tendency toward confabulation, i.e. the use of fictitious events and stories to conceal the deficit in memory. As Suinn (1970) notes:

> Current evidence indicates that Korsakoff's psychosis is a result of Vitamin B deficiency and other nutritional inadequacies, rather than directly to alcoholic intoxication. Although the same vitamin deficiency can occur through other circumstances, the chronic alcoholic is particulary prone because of his poor dietary habits and his increased vitamin requirements resulting from the high caloric effect of alcohol.

SOME VIEWS OF ETIOLOGY

Since the physical effects of excessive consumption of alcoholic beverages are plainly visible to all, it is understandable that investigators would turn their quest for the basic answers towards the psychological aspects of the problem. Such possibilities as "cellular craving for alcohol" were proposed and accepted by some (Lemere, 1956). However, the only type of cellular craving suscribed to by the World Health Organization (1959) is "dependence," the physical need of the patient during withdrawal.

It is held that several years of abnormal drinking are required for the alcoholic to build up this dependence, and even then the problem is not as specific as is generally believed; it has been shown that drugs are able to alleviate the withdrawal symptoms.

By and large, most physical aberrations connected with alcohol have been found to be the result of excessive consumption, not the cause. Investigation into the relationship between vitamin deficiency and alcoholism has chiefly demonstrated that the deficiency is due to the alcoholic's habit of drinking his lunch.

The factor of heredity has also undergone close scrutiny, prompted in part by the high incidence of alcoholics who have reported problem drinking by parents. Parental drinking appears to be an important factor in the alcoholic problem. Lisansky (1957) studying a group of patients, who attended the Yale Plan and Connecticut Commission Clinics, found that 35 percent of the males and 44 percent of the females reported excessive use of alcohol by parents. Jellinek (1960) reported an even higher incidence of parental drinking in the alcoholic population he studied. Yet these findings cannot be accepted as *prima facie* evidence for the inheritance of alcoholic predispositions; drinking in such cases might just as easily reflect a pattern of learning.

In the main, the body of chemistry of alcoholics has been found similar to that of normal drinkers. Thus, on any particular occasion, the physical effects of excessive drinking are the same for both groups.

It is no easier to come up with psychological determinants. Many psychologists and psychiatrists have held the view that alcoholism is symptomatic of underlying emotional conflicts. Karpman (1948), for example, has stated that "The chronic alcoholic is invariably the victim of a neurosis first, alcohol second." (p. 7) Alcohol comes to be the chief means by which the individual can cope with his conflicts or perhaps avoid them. Often, by focusing his attention on the procurement of alcohol, a task which comes to be the most important in his existence, the alcoholic manages to relegate to a subordinate position the unconscious problem which is really the more vital.

Freud early in his observations turned to the alcoholic. The strong oral influence of childhood were cited by him as a major cause of excessive drinking. He considered the mood change in the drinker to be a regression, under the impetus of alcohol, to the childhood levels of thinking uncontrolled by logic. Thus, the use of alcohol is an escape from reality (Freud, 1912; 1917).

Later Freud elaborated upon his earlier theory to maintain that unconscious homosexuality, (still related to the strong oral influences of childhood), was the cause of alcoholism (Freud, 1930). It is important to note that Freud thought the drinker gained emotional satisfaction from his male companions in the "public house" of the times. The explanation for today's solitary drinkers, especially the women who make up almost one-sixth of our present alcoholics, would seem much more complex.

Other theories that make use of the concept of regression to the oral stage of development point out that there is a similarity between the megalomania sensed by the infant as he is passively gratified and the alcohol-induced oblivion of the drunken man which inhibits the intrusion of unpleasing external circumstances. Thus there is another flight from reality.

Disagreement crops up when different individuals attempt to define the specific reality from which the alcoholic is fleeing. Some researchers believe it is inferiority. Others think it is insecurity, or homosexuality, or the pressures of modern living, or a hundred other things.

A number of investigators, led by K. A. Menninger, believe that addiction to alcohol is a form of self-destructive behavior derived from inwardly directed aggression. Certainly alcohol is capable of destroying an individual, but it is a long, slow process. Common belief that alcoholic suicides were exceptionally high has done much to foster this concept of alcoholic etiology. But quite recently the theory of self-destructive urges has been challenged by a group of investigators in their longitudinal studies of pre-alcoholics and nonalcoholics. If the theory were correct, they should have been able to observe a higher incidence of suicidal trends among the pre-alcoholics. This prediction confirmed was not in the study (McCord, 1969). In some situations Menninger may be right, but now it should be abundantly clear that it is a mistake to generalize and assert that any single motive or factor plays an exclusive part in all cases.

TREATMENT OF ALCOHOLISM

Modern treatment in clinics, hospitals, and in private practice utilize pharmacological and psychotherapeutic techniques which vary greatly and are used either singly or in combination. Such techniques may include the use of drugs, hallucinogens, individual psychotherapy, group therapy, occupational therapy, and methods related thereto. In the following section we shall examine some of the research that has been addressed to these treatment techniques and the assessment of their efficacy. Catanzaro (1968) has catalogued these approaches as *psychotherapeutic, pharmacologic,* and *experimental.* If there is anything at all which can be singled out as common to the entire group of techniques, it is probably the desirability of instituting intervention procedures with an alcoholic who has sustained motivation to recover and rehabilitate himself.

Psychotherapeutic Techniques

Under psychotherapeutic methods, the two major techniques usually listed are group therapy and conditioned response therapy.

GROUP THERAPY. In group therapy, a single therapist can work with a number of people at the same time, but there are additional advantages to the use of this method. For example many different views of the alcoholic experience can be expressed in the group situation, whereas the counselor can offer only his own. Also, and perhaps more importantly, the group experience offers a spectrum of potential values that range from resocialization to solidarity.

A variety of groups can be employed in group therapy, including the didactic group, interacting group, and non-directive group.

The *didactic groups* operate like a simple classroom. The main purpose here is the education of the alcoholic. The therapist or group of therapists lecture to the alcoholics giving them the information they want to know about their mysterious disease.

Often interaction is invoked among the group by the use of a question and answer session. In the didactic group the size is usually unimportant for this lecture system can be effective with a large number of people. The main factor is that the group must be similar, sharing similar problems.

In the *interacting group,* size becomes an important aspect, because the purpose here is to have the members participate in face-to-face interaction. If the group is too large, all of the members may not participate; if it is too small, the leader tends to assume too much importance. Catanzaro (1968) feels that an optimal size is seven to ten members. The main purpose of this type of group is for the members to simulate real situations within which they must interact outside the group.

Non-directive groups (or client-centered groups) differ from didactic groups in that the patients alone in non-directive groups decide what to talk about or whether to talk at all. The therapist never "confronts" the patients, but assumes a warm, permissive attitude in the interests of giving the patient a sense of dignity in his views. The theoretical assumption that underlies this technique is that the non-directive approach enables the patient to achieve self-actualization and choose the goals he wishes, based on his interests and abilities.

Many of the functions of group therapy are fulfilled by Alcoholics Anonymous. Fox (1967) views AA as "a pragmatic, simplified, spiritual approach to life, a prescription for living." An organization with nearly 12,500 chapters in 90 countries, it probably has reached and helped more alcoholics than has any other method of treatment or organization. If the alcoholic accepts and identifies with the mystique of AA, it may prove the only treatment that he needs. AA gives the person who is alcoholic the feeling that he no longer needs to prove his ability to drink. Unlike any other group settings in everyday life where drinking is the norm and the person who does not drink is under some pressure to drink in order to conform, in AA the norm is not to drink.

Another advantage of AA is that the person can accept the need for outside help and support. All of his fellow members have experienced what he himself has lived through; therefore, he can thoroughly identify with them. The removal of threat may dispel the need for defensiveness; the reduction of anxiety and guilt that comes from sharing problems and helping others supplies an all-important source of strength to maintain the daily vows of abstinence. Merely meeting and talking with alcoholics who have recovered is reassurance that recovery is possible for the newest member. Such groups as the Al-Anon Family Group, a branch of AA, and Alateen, for teenaged children of alcoholics, provide analogous services for the spouse and families of Alcoholics Anonymous members.

CONDITIONED REFLEX THERAPY. Treatment of CR basically consists of an unconditioned stimulus, usually an emeric drug and a conditioned stimulus, the alcoholic beverage. The aim of the treatment is to systematically associate the nausea or vomiting caused by the emetic with the alcohol. To obtain this reaction, the therapist must present the alcohol to the patient just before the nausea or vomiting begins. After several sequential parings, the mere introduction of the alcohol should be sufficient to produce a reaction of nausea or vomiting, and hopefully, this unpleasant learning experience will result in a tendency to avoid alcohol in the future.

The nausea treatment can have adverse side effects, and new techniques of conditioning have been studied. One technique offered by Sanderson, Campbell, and Laverty (1963) uses muscular paralysis rather than vomiting as the conditioned stimulus. This paralysis is brought on by the injection of succinylcholine chloride which is relatively free of side effects.

Hsu (1965) used electrodes attached to the head to condition the patient against the use of alcohol. This procedure has had some success with chronic drinkers who have not responded well to any other types of therapy.

A theory of aversive conditioning that is different from the ones mentioned above is the technique employed by Anant (1967). Anant suggests the use of verbal conditioning as a treatment for alcoholism. Using Wolpe's technique of relaxing the patient, the therapist then asks him to recall scenes of drinking, feeling sick, and vomiting in that order. The therapist by using an appropriate sequence of suggestions to make the patient imagine sickness associated with alcohol can make him desire a soft drink over alcohol. Anant employed this technique on twenty-six patients. One patient left the treatment early, but the other twenty-five have abstained from alcohol to this date.

Anant's contention is that because the treatment requires no drugs or electrical apparatus, the treatment of alcoholism is greatly facilitated.

A common criticism of conditioned reflex therapy is that it only works on the symptoms and does not deal with the underlying cause of the symptom. It helps the patient to obtain abstinence, but for any long range improvement to be shown, psychotherapy must be involved to get at the underlying pathology. However, John Clancy (1968) points out that in his experience just the alleviation of symptoms is sufficient treatment for many of his patients, while others require more uncovering psychotherapy.

Pharmacological Treatment

One pharmacological approach which is based on a counter-conditioning paradigm similar to the one described above consists of dosing the patient with a drug like Antabuse (disulfiram). Taken in tablet form, Antabuse interferes with the normal oxidation of alcohol and causes an increase of acetaldehyde in the body. Should the patient take a drink of alcohol within twenty-four hours after a dose of Antabuse, toxic effects result. The reaction is characterized by palpitations, flushed face, rash, nausea, vomiting, hypertension, and labored breathing. After taking one pill, the effects last for a period of up to four days (Fox, 1967). Because one cannot drink alcohol for several days (at least 72 hours) after ingestion of Antabuse, the decision to remain sober can be made when tempting stimuli are not present. It is considerably easier to interdict the habit of drinking by deciding early in the morning, when the memory of a "hang-over" is present, not to drink, than later that afternoon when a "friend" suggests a drink during "cocktail" hour. One act of the will lasts for several days.

During the 1940s and early 1950s, when Antabuse was widely

administered, many physicians encouraged the patient to be frightened of the reaction they would experience if they did drink. (Antabuse is no trivial drug, and its use should not be undertaken without a physical examination). On occasion the physician would administer antabuse, then have the patient taste his favorite drink so he would experience its aversive effects. This extreme measure has proven to be unnecessary. The dosage also has been reduced. Formerly, patients took as many as five tablets daily, presently, one tablet or a half-tablet proves sufficient. The chief problem with Antabuse therapy had been that the patient switches from his tablets back to the bottle.

Wallerstein (1956) compared the improvement rates of such methods as group psychotherapy, conditioned reflex therapy, and Antabuse and found that Antabuse had the highest improvement rate. Billet (1964) reported that Antabuse was being administered to over six hundred patients at the Alcoholic Rehabilitation Clinic of the District of Columbia Department of Public Health. The difference between this administration and the methods employed in previous decades was that fear was not being used as an overriding force. The fear of Antabuse reaction was played down and the value of its helpfulness was expressed to the patient. Antabuse provided these patients with the concrete reason they needed to stop drinking, and it was found at this rehabilitation center that Antabuse became a very helpful adjunct in their treatment program.

Antabuse Probation

One of the most innovative and effective steps toward eliminating the "revolving door" approach to alcoholics and drunk driving has been the Antabuse probation program experiment in Little Rock, Arkansas. There, when an alcoholic is convicted of drunken driving, if he volunteers to appear in the clerk of court's office Monday through Friday to take an Antabuse tablet, his fine is suspended. The tablet is administered dissolved in water; alcoholics used to slip it under their tongue, leave the office and spit it out. Should a probationer "fall off" the program his sentence is invoked. The court supplies the will power, and for the one-year probationary period, at least, the alcoholic remains "dry," out of jail, his family off welfare.

Experimental Methods

LSD-25 or d-lysergic acid diethylamide, recently a vogue among certain cultures of the United States for its psychedelic or mind-manifesting features, was used quite extensively to cure alcoholism among the American Indians in the nineteenth century. Kenneth E. Godfery (1968) reasoned that since the "cure" rate of most treatment programs is running 10 to 20 per cent, every new treatment that shows promise of working should be attempted. This includes LSD.

Bill W., the co-founder of Alcoholics Anonymous, had obtained the strength to quit drinking through a religious experience while in delirium tremens. LSD also produces a kind of deep religious experience, and it was reasoned that in might prove effective with alcoholics.

Godfrey concluded, from his research on LSD and alcoholism, that LSD is a safe drug, and that its psychedelic reaction seemed very helpful in assisting the alcoholic to sobriety. He further concluded that more research is needed to determine a process of selection of patients that would receive the most benefit from the LSD treatment. He feels that there is a great need for knowledge in the treatment of alcoholics but the efforts to obtain this knowledge must be carried on in a responsible manner.

Ruth Fox (1967), after examining the results of a three-year follow-up study of sixteen LSD-25 treated alcoholics, reported that "LSD, by breaking down the barriers between the conscious and the unconscious mind and by uncovering early traumatic events in their lives, allows the patients to reassess and reevaluate many of their experiences."

Lysergic Acid Diethylamide seems to make the patients feel willing to go through the entire program to recover. However, a patient undergoing LSD treatment must not be left alone for at least eight to ten hours while under the drug and must be given constant support during the treatment.

Sarett, Cheek, and Osmond (1966) conducted an experiment

to see the reactions of wives whose alcoholic husbands were treated with LSD. In giving a questionnaire analysis of the LSD-25 treatment, Sarett, et al. (1966) found that the husbands (one's who were given the treatment) rated their improvement higher than their wives. In the short run, over 60 percent of the wives found their husbands more responsible, talkative and understanding, dependable, less critical, and less erratic. A smaller percentage noticed a broadening of their husband's interests.

An interesting treatment approach has been derived from Eric Berne's "Game" theory (1964). To Berne, a game is an "ongoing series of complementary ulterior transactions progressing to a well-defined, predictable outcome." The transactions which Berne is talking about are certain repetitive patterns of behavior which have a "concealed motivation" and which have an expected result. He states that we all play games in our interactions with others. In his book, *Games People Play* (1964), under "life games," Berne describes the "alcoholic." In this "game there is no such thing as alcoholism or 'an alcoholic,' but there is a role called the Alcoholic in a certain type of game." Game analysis is not concerned with biochemical or physiological factors that cause alcoholism, but it is concerned with the social interactions that are a result of alcoholism.

This theory has been applied in a Veterans Administration Hospital in Topeka, Kansas (Androes, McKenzie, Chotlos, 1967). Berne described five roles in the game: the alcoholic, persecutor, rescuer, patsy, and the connection. In this study, two roles were used, the alcoholic and the patsy or staff member.

It was found that the alcoholic usually blames others for his drinking and is highly skilled at manipulating staff members into positions where they can be blamed for his drinking problems. The alcoholic is aware of this manipulation and when confronted with it, will readily admit to doing it. The staff members were instructed to confront the alcoholic every time he tried to manipulate them.

"The most important therapeutic effects noted with patients was their willingness to become more reflective in assessing their own behavior, both while they were hospitalized and after they left the hospital (Androes, et al., 1967).

Concluding Remarks

On March 31, 1966, the U.S. Court of Appeals reversed a decision which had earlier convicted DeWitt Easter, a chronic alcoholic, of public intoxication. Whether one accepts the alcoholism-as-disease model as valid, any approach which substitutes an attempt at rehabilitation for a senseless repetive pattern of futile jailings is more than welcome. The Easter decision represents a much needed break in this "revolving door" system.

If one accepts the social learning viewpoint of Bandura (1968) toward alcoholism and the acquisition of alcoholic behavior patterns, therapy would have to be directed "toward reducing the level of aversive stimulation experienced by the client and toward eliminating alcoholic stress reactions, preferably by establishing alternate modes of copying behavior." When a person has alternatives equally as effective and rewarding as alcohol, then the person would be less likely to turn to excessive drinking to lessen stress or frustration. These perspectives clearly emphasize the need for preventive action on at least three levels: (1) the prevention of further deterioration in persons already identified as alcoholics; (2) early case finding and special care for the population which is most vulnerable, namely disturbed adolescents and young adults; and (3) changes in the prevailing cultural attitudes toward alcoholism. As Fox (1967) reminds us, prevention has been the most neglected aspect of the alcoholism problem until the present.

DRUG ABUSE

If logic rather than custom dictated the meaning of words, an *addict* would be defined as a person who, for no compelling medical reason, habitually takes inimical substances into his body. This definition would accommodate the misuse of a large variety of substances: alcohol (in excess of moderate quantities), tobacco, pep pills, tonics, analgesics like aspirin, sleeping tablets, and even laxatives. However, the professional view as expressed by the Expert Committee on Drugs Liable to Produce Addiction of the World Health Organization (1957) defines addiction as a state of periodic or chronic intoxication which is detrimental to both the individual and society and which is produced by repeated consumption of a natural or synthetic drug. According to United States federal law: "The term 'addict' means any person who habitually uses any habit-forming narcotic drug . . . so as to endanger public morals, health, safety, or welfare, or who is or has been so far addicted to the use of such habit-forming narcotic drugs as to have lost the power of self-control with reference to his addiction" (Pescor, 1952).

Eddy, Halbach, Isbell, and Seevers (1965) have noted the numerous grounds which can be cited for objecting to the term addiction. They refer to the considerable effort which has been expended in attempts to produce a term less restricted in meaning than addiction, but a term which can be applied to the total range of drug-taking behavior. They acknowledge that they were forced to settle for three terms, instead of a single term, to designate the varieties of problematical drug consumption that have been clinically described:

Drug addiction: a state of periodic or chronic intoxication produced by the repeated consumption of a natural or synthetic drug. Characteristics of addiction include: (a) an overpowering need or compulsion to continue taking the drug, no matter what means may be required to secure a supply of it; (b) a tendency toward increasing the quantity of the dose taken; (c) a psychological and, generally, physiological dependence upon the effects produced by the drug; and (d) deleterious effects on the individual and upon society.

2. *Drug habituation:* a condition (habit) resulting from repeated drug consumption. The characteristics include: (a) a desire, not compulsion, to continue taking the drug to secure the sense of well-being which the drug engenders; (b) little or no tendency to increase the dose; (c) some psychological dependence upon the drug, but without the physiological dependence which leads to withdrawal symptoms; (d) detrimental effects (if any) are primarily restricted to the individual himself.

3. *Drug dependence:* a condition of psychological or physiological dependence which follows the periodic or continuous administration of a drug. Characteristics vary with the particular drug and must be made clear by the designation of the specific

pattern of drug dependence in each case.

In the past, addiction has been rather restrictively identified with physiological dependence upon a given narcotic, as manifested by an increasing tolerance for the drug and the necessity for larger and larger dosages. This pattern, which may be based in part on the capacities of the drug to produce mild euphoria, relieve pain, and remove discomfort, becomes fixed through repetition and ultimately leads to a situation in which the drug must be obtained by any means. But contemporary opinion places an even greater emphasis on psychological dependence, particularly with regard to the potential rehabilitation of the addict. For some time now it has been a firmly established professional fact that regardless of the duration of extent of addiction, physical dependence upon the drug can be terminated within a period of three to five days. Quite the contrary is true for the psychological dependence which the individual develops in relation to the drug. This psychological yearning is seldom completely eliminated. This is the principal reason why many authorities believe that there is not such thing as a cured addict—only one who is temporarily abstinent.

Narcotic drugs can be divided into two types according to physiological effect: *depressants* and *stimulants*. Depressants generally decrease mental and physical activity in varying degrees to the point of a deep sleep coma and finally death, depending on the dosage taken. Stimulants generally produce sustained activity, thwarting sleep, and masking symptoms of fatigue to a point where death may result from exhaustion.

The principal drugs involved in narcotics addiction include the opium derivatives (opiates) and synthetic opiates, cocaine, and marijauna. The opiates are of primary importance, since they constitute the major source of addiction in the world today. In addition to the opiates, natural products of the opium poppy—morphine, heroin, codeine, dilaudid, there is a class of synthetic products called *opioids*. These include compounds such as meperidine (Demerol) and leritime, possessing the same characteristics as the opiates.

Opiates

Opium in its raw state is a milky substance obtained by excising the unripe capsules of a particular species of opium poppy (Papaver Somniferum). It is anything but a recent discovery; the opium poppy has been known and cultivated in Asia, the Middle East, and Europe for over four thousand years. As the present time, the opium poppy is most extensively cultivated in China, India, Yugoslavia, Turkey, Bulgaria, and Iran.

The medical uses of opium were accepted and fairly well understood in Western Europe by the middle of the 16th century. Since that time, as more and more opium derivatives were discovered, the use of pure opium gradually decreased, until it had become practically nonexistent.

The most commonly used and best known of the opium derivatives is morphine, which was first isolated in 1805 by a German pharmacist named Serturner. The principal function of morphine is the relief of pain, and of course, its greatest liability is the danger of addiction. Morphine may be given orally or by injection, and under emergency conditions it is given intravenously. Morphine is not considered a drug of preference by addicts due to the fact that it does not produce the desired euphoric effect.

During the American Civil War, America's lack of knowledge about the opiates became apparent. Patent medicines of the period contained a dangerously high level of opium, yet opiates were never identified as the active agent on the labels of the bottles. Thousands of sick and wounded soldiers became addicted to morphine; physicians of the day held the erroneous belief that morphinism could be avoided by injecting the drug under the skin. The resulting drug dependence was called "the soldier's disease."

In 1898, the search for a curative agent for addiction to opium and morphine led to a discovery which seemed to work. The new drug was hailed as a hero because of its ability to provide the long sought after remedy for a worsening situation. "The Hero" was a tragic discovery: heroin.

Heroin (diacetylmorphine) is an opium derivative which is approximately five times as powerful as morphine. Because of this potency, along with the strong euphoric effect which it produces, heroin is the definite drug of preference to the addict and is the basic item of illicit drug traffic in the world today. Heroin presently sells in Europe for approximately five thousand dollars a kilogram (1 kg. = 2.2 pounds). When it reaches New York, the price increases to eighteen thousand dollars per kilo. Prior to reaching the addict on the street, the heroin is then cut with quinine or milk sugar, with the result that the addict usually is purchasing a composition consisting of never more than 6 percent heroin and sometimes as weak as less than 1 percent. The medical use of heroin is no greater than that of morphine, but the addiction problem is much more severe. The United States now prohibits the importation, manufacture, and sale of heroin.

Heroin addiction is the end product of a complex and ramified pattern of causation. The addict is typically a member of an ethnic minority, comes from an impoverished background, and is lacking in education and readily marketable job skills. He perceives his chances for a decent job, adequate housing, material security, and modest recognition as virtually nil. He is bored, restless, rootless, alienated, and generally embittered; these characterizations he shares with members of his peer group.

Having made these generalizations, we must be alert to their limited utility as explanatory factors in the spread of heroin addiction. As Feldman (1970) has noted, "To observe that emotional pathology is widespread among slum dwellers, or that the general population had a predisposition to addiction, does little to explain how a large minority of slum residents become drug addicts while others, often members of the same family, do not." Feldman's observations on drug experimentation by ghetto youth led him to emphasize sociological and ideological factors rather than presumed intrapsychic processes as the principal locus of causation:

> My observations support neither the usual psychiatric view that drug use emerges from attempts to resolve internal emotional problems nor the Cloward-Ohlin . . . thesis that heroin use is a retreatist adaptation to a youth's double failure in legitimate and illegitimate opportunity structures of the slums. The user turns to drugs, not as a result of anomie, but rather to capitalize on a new mode of enhancing his status and prestige within a social system where the highest

prizes go to persons who demonstrate attributes of toughness, daring, and adventure. Within the life-style of the stand-up cat, movement into heroin use is one route to becoming a "somebody" in the eyes of the important people who comprise the slum social network.

Drugs offer a break in monotony, the prospect of a "kick." But most people do not experience an immediate high the first few times they take heroin; it takes time for them to achieve an euphoric effect, and the results they finally attain are not particularly impressive. Says Lindesmith (1968):

> Contrary to the belief entertained by many if not most, a dose or a series of doses of opium derivatives does not produce a supernormal state. It does not produce the abilities to do things better, to think or reason with greater clearness than would be possible without the drug. It is true that in some conditions of mind or body, and perhaps during the short initial period of addiction, the drug will seemingly lift one up where the perceptibilities are sharpened, where the senses are better able to cope with any given situation that would be the case without drugs. But the careful analysis of the condition of the individual would usually elicit the fact that he was considerably below par, in some respect, before he took the drug. All that it has done is to restore him to normal or a nearly normal state of mind and body.

What begins as a search for kicks ends up as an attempt to maintain the status quo. When the addict injects heroin intravenously, he experiences a brief feeling of well-being, followed by a drowsy state of relaxed euphoria; finally, he starts "coming down." As the effects of the drug wear off (they last up to about four hours), he begins to experience minor sensations of discomfort and mild distress. Depending on the length of time he has been addicted and the number of "bags" of heroin he has been using daily, the severity of the *withdrawal symptoms* that follow abstinence from the drug increases with each passing hour. Restlessness, dysphoria, and irritability are among the immediate behavioral manifestations that may appear; excessive sweating, nausea, severe abdominal cramps, back pains, diarrhea, vomiting, fever alternating with chills, and delirium are some to the physiological reactions that usually occur. The flushing, chills, and sweating are accompanied by excessive pilorection, which leads to familiar "cold turkey" appearance of the skin of the addict.

The compulsive search for the narcotic "high" soon becomes the addict's whole life: His habit, or advanced state of addiction, leaves him functionally disabled. He generally cannot hold a job, continue school, or get enough money by legal means to obtain the heroin and support his family (if he has one).

Periodically, when his habit becomes too large and expensive to maintain, the addict may submit himself voluntarily to the "wringing out" process, using other analgestic drugs to relieve the withdrawal pangs. He may accomplish this at a hospital or, if he can obtain the necessary analgesics, at home. Sometimes he becomes the victim of compulsory withdrawal as the consequence of incarceration. In any event, once he had achieved the withdrawal process and is "clean," he usually resumes the addiction pattern.

Cocaine

Cocaine is probably one of the best examples of a substance upon which no physical dependence develops but one whose use entails the profound risk of crippling psychological dependence. This drug is a prototype of those stimulants which are capable of bringing about hallucinatory experiences when taken in large quantities.

Although the abuse of cocaine takes varied forms, the most common is the chewing of the cocoa plant leaf. This is a centuries-old custom of some Indians of the Andes. The simplest form of abuse of this drug involves attempts to relieve pains or sensation of cold, hunger, and fatigue. Those Americans who fear "drugs" most may be guilty of using coffee or cocoa during cold weather to warm up their bodies; they may drink large amounts of coffee while driving to keep awake; they may take coffee breaks on the job to relieve fatigue and to carry them over until lunch time. With this form of intake of cocaine the quantitative release of the stimulating substance is much too small to induce mental changes which would lead to abnormal behavior.

In addition to leaf-chewing of the cocoa plant, the capacity of the drug for rapid absorption via the mucous membranes led for a period of time during the 1920s and 1930s to the "sniffing" of cocaine. More recently, cocaine has been taken intravenously, producing a pleasurable sensation described by its devotees as similar to a sexual orgasm. This has been cited as the most dangerous use of the drug; it appeals to individuals with psychopathic tendencies which are unmasked by the drug (Eddy, et al., 1965). Such an individual tends to overestimate his mental and physical capabilities and is prone to commit antisocial actions. In fact, newspaper and TV stereotypes of the "hopped-up" criminal may be based, in large measure, upon these behavioral effects of cocaine. Also, cocaine may include hallucinatory and delusional behavior in the user. When these delusions and hallucinations are of a persecutory nature, the cocaine addict may attack friends, acquaintances, family members, or mere bystanders under the demented impression that they are his feared and hated tormentors.

Cocaine has a rapid rate of breakdown in the body, which makes it necessary for frequent administration of the drug. There is no physical dependence, hence it is thought that the body builds up resistance to the drug. A heavy user may discontinue the drug without experiencing the abstinence syndrome, but he may suffer from depression and experience delusions for a period of time following withdrawal. Cocaine has largely been supplanted by preparations such as procaine and is rarely found in quantity these days on the illicit market.

Marijuana

The earliest record of marijuana is contained in a description of the drug in a Chinese compendium of medicines, the herbal of Emperor Shen Nung, dated 2737 B.C. Marijuana was a subject of extravagant social controversy even in ancient times: There were those who thought it led to paradise. Its use as an intoxicant spread from China to India, then to North Africa and from there, about A.D. 1800 to Europe, perhaps introduced by French troops of Napolean's army returning from the Egyptian campaign. In the Western Hemisphere marijuana has been known for centuries in South and Central America, but it did not begin to be used in the U.S. to any significant extent until about 1920. Since the hemp plant *cannabis sativa*, the source of the drug in its various forms, is a common weed growing freely in many climates, there is no way of knowing precisely how extensive the world usage of the drug may be today. A United Nations survey in 1950 estimated that its users then numbered some 200 million people, principally in Asia and Africa.

Cannabis sativa has a long history of use as a drug in tribal religious ceremonies and as medicine, particularly in India. In the 19th Century the drug was widely prescribed in the western world for various ailments and discomforts, such as coughing, fatigue, rheumatism, asthma, delirium tremens, migraine headache, and painful menstruation. Although its use was already declining somewhat because of the introduction of synthetic hypnotics and analgesics, it remained in the U.S. Pharmacopeia until 1937. The difficulties imposed on its use by the Tax Act of 1937 brought about its medical demise.

In any case, the principal interest in the hemp plant throughout history has been in its properties as an agent for achieving euphoria. The name itself, marijuana, is believed to be a corruption of a Portuguese word which means intoxicant. The ubiquity of the drug is evident in the multitude of slang terms by which it is known: weed, grass, pot, hay, stuff, tea, maryjane, etc. In this country it is almost invariably smoked, elsewhere, the drug is often taken in a drink or in sweetmeats.

Marijuana intoxication carries the risk of nausea, vomitting, and diarrhea, particularly if the drug is taken by mouth. Usually, however, the bodily symptoms accompanying the high are slight. There is only very slight, if any, dilation of the pupils accompanied by a sluggish pupillary response to light, slight tremors, and a mild lack of coordination. A consistently observed physiological effect is increase in the pulse rate; in addition there may be a slight rise in the blood pressure. Urination tends to increase in frequency and perhaps in amount. Often the mouth and throat feel dry, causing thirst. One of the most striking results of the intoxication is a sense of hunger. It generates a high appreciation of food, so that a person under the influence may approach an ordinary dish with the anticipation of a gourmet confronting a special treat. This effect suggests that the drug might be useful in the treatment of the pathological loss of appetite known as *anorexia nervosa.*

The prevailing public attitude toward marijuana in the United States is strongly colored by emotional bias. It has been charged that this state of affairs is at least in part the result of an "educational campaign" initiated in the 1930s by the Federal Bureau of Narcotics (now the Bureau of Narcotics and Dangerous Drugs), a campaign that has disseminated much distortion and misinformation about the drug. There are also cultural and social factors that contribute to the public apprehension about marijuana. The still powerful vestige of the Protestant ethic in this country condemns marijuana as an opiate used soley for the pursuit of pleasure—whereas alcohol is accepted because it lubricates the wheels of commerce and catalyzes social intercourse.

It is difficult to avoid the conclusion that social prejudices enter into the public alarm over marijuana: prejudice on the part of the older generation, which identifies marijuana as a symbol of the alienation of youth; and prejudice on the part of white America, which unconsciously perhaps, regards marijuana as an abhorred part of the non-white culture that is rapidly encroaching upon the white preserves. During the period that the most stringent laws were passed against the use of marijuana, it was typically used in the minority enclaves of Negroes, Puerto Ricans, (c. f. *Manchild in the Promised Land; Down these Mean Streets*) and persons of Mexican origin. The use of marijuana is no longer associated exclusively with minority group status. Quite the opposite. According to a 1972 Gallup poll, the proportion of college students who have tried marijuana at least once has grown from 5 percent in Spring 1967, to 51 percent in December 1972. Students whose fathers have had college training are more likely to be users than are students whose fathers have not gone beyond high school. Students majoring in social science are more likely to use marijuana than are students in other areas of study. Nationally, it is estimated that twenty-four million persons have experimented with marijuana. Smoking "pot" is now a part of the collegiate way of life.

There is no substantial body of clinical or scientific evidence

COLLEGE STUDENTS WHO HAVE TRIED MARIJUANA

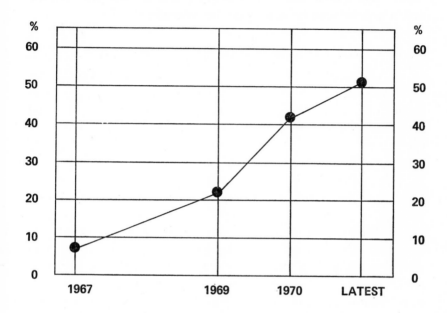

Gallup Poll results published by the New Orleans
Times-Picayune July 7, 1972. Reproduced by the
permission of the publisher.

Figure 8-1. College Students who have Tried Marijuana.

that marijuana is an addictive drug in the same category with the
opiates. Cessation of usage produces no withdrawal syndrome, nor
does the user feel any need to increase the dosage as he becomes
more accustomed to the drug. It would also appear that the widespread and commonly held assumption that marijuana use is the
first step toward opiate addiction is without firm basis in fact
(*Task Force Report: Narcotics and Drug Abuse,* 1967). While
the federal study revealed that about 50 percent of the heroin
addicts had also had experience with marijuana, it was noted that
most of the addicts had been users of alcohol and tobacco. There
is no basis for claiming that marijuana is more likely than alcohol

or tobacco to lead to the use of hard drugs. We obviously need to reduce the emotionalism surrounding this subject and replace myths with facts, so far as they can be determined.

THE TREATMENT OF DRUG ADDICTION

As we noted earlier, a short stay in a penal institution or hospital frees the addict from physical dependence on drugs. Unfortunately, upon release, he immediately returns to the same social environment which originally produced him and is once again surrounded by other active addicts and a readily accessible supply of narcotic drugs.

The American Medical Association and the National Research Council of the National Academy of Sciences recommend a comprehensive program with the following features: (1) after complete withdrawal, follow-up treatment for addicts at rehabilitation centers; (2) measures designed to permit the compulsory civil commitment of drug addicts for treatment on a drug-free environment; (3) the advancement of methods and measures toward rehabilitation of the addict under continuing civil commitment; (4) the development of research designed to gain new knowledge about the prevention of addiction and the treatment of addicted persons; and (5) the dissemination of factual information on addiction (*Joint Statement on Narcotic Addiction*, 1963).

The Therapeutic Enclave

A rather unorthodox approach to the treatment of drug addiction is represented in the development of what might be called the *therapeutic enclave*. Synanon, the prototype of this type of development, is a community composed of former addicts (many of whom have criminal records), living together and encouraging each other to quit and stay off drugs. Synanon has some of the properties of a social movement. It originated with Charles E. Dederich, a former alcoholic, in 1958 in Santa Monica, California. Today there are Synanons in a number of other cities, including Reno, San Francisco, and San Diego.

The word synanon was coined by a newly admitted addict in the early days of the organization. In his attempt to say symposium and seminar in the same breath, he finally managed to blurt out Synanon: "I want to get into another one of those symp . . . sem-synanons" (Yablonsky, 1965) .

People live in Synanon in a pleasant, paternalistic family environment. The members themselves think of Synanon as a family-type club of home—a fraternity of people living together and helping each other to get well. The members are free to leave anytime they wish; they are neither patients nor immates. Therapeutic enclaves such as Synanon and its counterpart, Daytop Village, have arisen as conventional medical treatment has proven ineffective. Despite enormous amounts of money and effort expended in such medical centers and the National Institute of Mental Health at Lexington, Kentucky, attempts to keep the street addict totally abstinent have failed. Physicians,[1] nurses, or the patient who has become addicted through careless medication respond well to conventional treatment, but the "street addict" poses a special problem. It would seem that removal of the physical dependence by gradual withdrawal of drugs followed by psychiatric treatment would work, it hasn't. Relapse rates from these centers run as high as 90 percent, and "many of the addicts treated at these excellent medical facilities do not even show the simple respect for their 50-dollars-a-day treatment by waiting forty-eight hours after release before taking a shot of heroin" (Bassin, 1970) .

Therapeutic enclaves such as DAYTOP deny that the addict has a "medical problem" and see his condition as the result of self-chosen stupidity. Bassin (1970) writes, "At Daytop we know why somebody is a dope fiend—because he chooses to act STUPID! That's the only acceptable explanation for addiction: *stupidity.*"[2]

---

[1]As the cure rate for physicians runs as high as 90 percent, the cause of lifelong addiction must include social factors as well as biological ones.

[2]Such a diagnosis may be functional in "shocking" a heroin addict, but it adds little to a scientific explanation of the etiology of the drug problem. Despite its "common sense" approach, Daytop is based on scientific learning principles paralleling behavior modification techniques: No reinforcement is given for histrionic withdrawal, only those values which aid in rehabilitation (sobriety, etc.) are rewarded. Old sources of reinforcement (family), which may have supported dependency, are severed, creating a new reinforcement milieu to which the addict must respond. The emphasis is placed on present behavior and the belief that attitudes follow actions, leaving psychoanalytic "underlying needs" to those interested in creative literature.

While no hard data is available for the success rate of Daytop, their own figures admit 17 percent dropping out after 90 days. Of those who remain, the directors "estimate" 75 percent will complete the program of around two years. This would mean, if Daytop's own estimate is accurate, a success rate of 63 percent after two years of intensive treatment. But even this figure must be analyzed. Some advocates of Daytop feel that the addict cannot be trusted with the temptations outside his "therapeutic enclave" until he had completed as long as five years of treatment, and others would keep the addict in this semi-cloistered status for the rest of his life.

Daytop's "group-encounter therapy" is superior to jail or any non-directive approach, but the process is lengthy, fraught with logistical problems (host communities are less than enthusiastic about a houseful of "dope fiends" in their midst) , and, finally, the concept is still experimental and unproven.

Methadone Maintenance

Research using Methadone—a dependency inducing morphine-like narcotic analgesic—was begun in 1964 by Dr. Vincent Dole and Dr. Marie Nyswander at Rockefeller University in New York. Methadone has been safely used as a pain-killer for years and has been prescribed for cancer patients or persons who have undergone surgery. This approach treats heroin addiction as a metabolic disease. After six years, more than 5,000 former heroin addicts were being treated in the United States and Canada (Joseph and Dole, 1970) .

A heroin addict is functionally disabled. He lives on a "teeter-totter" or elevator. At one end, he is "high" or euphoric-sedated, tranquiled, absorbed in himself and completely irresponsible. At the other extreme, when he is "strung out" (sick) , he becomes desperate in his need for drugs. His symptoms are nausea, perspiration, tremors, and cramps. His life oscillates between "high" and "strung out," with little time to lead a normal existence.

Methadone works on the same brain centers as heroin and involves a tolerance and cross-tolerance or blockage. During the first six weeks, the patient gets a medical workup, is withdrawn from heroin, and receives methadone in increasing doses until he is "stabilized." After tolerance to the medication has been established, the dose (from 80-120 mg/day) can be held constant, without escalation or euphoria, for years. Joseph and Dole (1970) report "The patient does not experience euphoria, analgesia, or tranquilization from the methadone, and feels little or no euphoric reaction if he takes a shot of heroin." The methadone blocks out the effects of heroin. An addict "shooting" heroin while maintained on methadone would get little more "kick" than if he was shooting water in his veins.

The second phase of the program lasts about a year. The patient comes to the clinic to drink his methadone (given in a glass of Tang to preclude injection) and leaves a urine specimen which is checked against the injection of other drugs. In the final phase, the patient becomes a functioning, self-supporting member of the community and may pick up his supply of methadone one week at a time. Extreme caution should attend this level of trust as addicts are extremely manipulative with treatment personnel.

Joseph and Dole (1970) see Methadone as a normalizer rather than a narcotic and compare its use to insulin for the diabetic, digitalis for the cardiac patient, or cortisone for the arthritic. Female patients have undergone normal pregnancies without reducing their stabilized doses. The babies born to patients were not affected adversely by the methadone.

Methadone is not a "cure" for addiction but a stabilizing agent. During the past six years, Joseph and Dole report that 350 patients have been withdrawn. In every case, upon the completion of withdrawal, the patient experienced a craving for heroin, regardless of social or psychological adjustment. After withdrawal, the patient felt no craving for methadone, but rather a recurrence of the desire for heroin.

The "acid" test of the methadone program is its impact upon crime. Joseph and Dole (1970,) write:

Analysis of the records of 912 patients admitted to the program over a 4½ year period showed a 90% drop in criminal convictions. Prior to admission the group amassed 4,500 convictions—a rate of 52 convictions per 100 man-years of addiction—felonies, misdemeanors, and petty offenses. After admission only 12 percent were arrested, and these were mostly for misdemeanors and lesser offenses. Approximately half of the charges were dropped; there were 51 convictions on a rate of 5.8 convictions per 100 man treatment years.

A statistic cannot stand alone. To have meaning, the methadone program must show that it can surpass a base rate comparison of addicts under legal constraint without methadone treatment. The civil commitment program of California reported that five out of six patients on outpatient parole status over a three-year period reverted to drug use or crime or were removed from the program for other violations of probation (Joseph and Dole, 1970). Any program which reduces the crime rate is useful, in that sense, even if the patient does not become drug-free.

Critics of the methadone program compare the switching from heroin to methadone to the switching of an alcoholic from scotch to bourbon (Yablonsky, 1966). This is a false analogy, for if you give an alcoholic a shot of whiskey of any variety you disable him. Methadone stabilized the patient.

Methadone is not a panacea for the ills of the drug problem. No drug can give a person values or instill within him habits of industry and honesty where none existed before. What methadone does accomplish is to stabilize the addict from his not-so-merry-go-round of being sick, high, or in jail so that genuine rehabilitation can take place. Methadone, combined with an efficient program of social services and counseling, offers a realistic hope for adjustment to society for the "street" addict.

Summary

Crimes related to the consumption of alcohol or drugs range from the criminal negligence of the drunken driver or the nuisance created by the public inebriate to the commission of armed robbery as a means of obtaining funds to buy heroin. This chapter notes that the criminal justice system and the helping professions tend to approach alcohol and drug-related behavior in different ways, neither of which has proven effectual in reducing the magnitude of the problem. Repeated rearrest and sentencing merely lead to a kind of "revolving door" management of the drunk; harsh punitive measures toward the drug consumer have aggravated rather than lessened the problems associated with drug abuse.

Alcoholism and drug abuse are both viewed as addictive behavior in this chapter. Although the problems of causation tend to become obscured as a consequence of excessive consumption of alcohol or habitual use of potentially dangerous drugs, the results of extensive clinical and experimental investigation seem to support the contention that both alcoholism and drug addiction are the result of social learning. In both cases, the treatment problem involves the planned use of a variety of aids to help the individual relinquish the pattern of substance abuse he has acquired and to replace it with a pattern of behavior that is personally and socially more acceptable.

REFERENCES

American Medical Association and National Research Council: Joint statement on narcotic addiction in the U.S. *Journal of the Indiana Medical Association, 55*:1056-1057, 1963.

American Psychiatric Association: *Diagnostic and Statistical Manual of Mental Disorders.* Washington, American Psychiatric Association, 1968.

Anant, S.: A note on the treatment of alcoholics by a verbal aversion technique. *Canadian Psychologist, 11*:1921, 1967.

Androes, L., McKenzie, L., and Chotlos, J.: The 'game' and alcoholic patients. *American Journal of Nursing, 67*:1672-1674, 1967.

"Anon:" *Alcoholics Anonymous.* New York Alcoholics Anonymous Publishing Company, 1955.

Bandura, A.: A social learning interpretation of psychological dysfunctions. In London, P. and Rosenhan, D. (Eds.): *Foundations of Abnormal Psychology.* New York, Holt, Rinehart and Winston, 1968.

Bassin, A.: Daytop Village. *Addictions,* Summer: 42-48, 1970.

Bell, K.G.: Blood-alcohol levels and toxic drinking. *University of Toronto Medical Journal, 30*:133-139, 1953.

Berne, E.: *Games People Play.* New York, Grove Press, 1964.

Billet, S.L.: The use of deterrent drugs at the District of Columbia Alcohol Rehabilitation Clinic. In Catanzaro, R.J. (Ed.): *Alcoholism.* Springfield, Charles C Thomas, 1968.

Blume, Shelia B. and Sheppard, C.: The changing effects of drinking on the changing personalities of alcoholics. *Quarterly Journal of Studies on Alcoholism, 28*:436-443, 1967.

Catanzaro, R.J. (Ed.): *Alcoholism.* Springfield, Charles C Thomas, 1968.

Chafetz, M.E.: Addictions. III: Alcoholism. In Freedman, A.M. and Kaplan, H.I. (Eds.): *Comprehensive Textbook of Psychiatry*. Baltimore, Williams and Wilkins, 1967.

Cheek, F.E. et al., Sarrett, Mary, Newell, J., and Osmond, H.: A survey of the experience of tension on alcoholics and other diagnostic groups. *International Journal of Neuropsychiatry, 3:*477-488, 1967.

Clancy, J.: Conditioned reflex therapy. In Catanzaro, R.J. (Ed).: *Alcoholism*. Springfield, Charles C Thomas, 1968.

Clinebell, H.J.: *Understanding and Counseling the Alcoholic*. Nashville, Abingdon, 1960.

Cohen, B.J. (Ed.): *Crime in America*. Itasca, Peacock, 1970.

Eddy, N.B.: Methadone maintenance for the management of persons with drug dependence of the morphine type. *Drug Dependence, 3:*17-26, 1970.

Eddy, N.B., et. al.: Drug dependence: its significance and characteristics. *Bulletin of the World Health Organization, 32:*721-732, 1965.

Feldman, H.W.: Ideological supports to becoming and remaining a heroin addict. *Drug Dependence, 3:*3-11, 1970.

Fox, R.: A multidisciplinary approach to the treatment of alcoholism. *American Journal of Psychology, 65:*57-58, 1967.

Freud, S.: *Civilization and Its Discontents*. London, Hogarth Press, 1930.

Glaser, D. and O'Leary, V.: *The Alcoholic Offender*. Washington, U.S. Government Printing Office, 1968.

Godfrey, K.E. LSD therapy. Catanzaro, R.J. (Ed.): *Alcoholism*. Springfield, Charles C Thomas, 1968.

Gomberg, E.L.: Etiology of alcoholism. *Journal of Consulting and Clinical Psychology, 32:*18-20, 1968.

Grant, M. and Tatham, R.: The District of Columbia's experiences with the alcoholic. *Journal of the American Medical Association, 202:*107-110, 1967.

Harris, L.: One in every five reveals drinking problem. *Washington Post*, May 2, 1966.

Hsu, J.J.: Electroding therapy of alcoholics. *Quarterly Journal of Studies on Alcohol, 24:*449-459, 1965.

Jellinek, E.M.: *Disease Concept of Alcoholism*. New Haven, United Printing Services, 1960.

Jones, M.C.: Personality correlates and antecedents of drinking patterns in adult males. *Journal of Consulting and Clinical Psychology, 32:*2-12, 1968.

Joseph, H., and Dole, V.D.: Methadone patients on probation and parole. *Federal Probation, June:*42-48, 1970.

Kant, F.: *The Treatment of the Alcoholic*. Springfield, Charles C Thomas, 1954.

Karpman, B.: *The Alcoholic Woman*. Washington, The Linacre Press, 1948.

Lemere, F.: What causes alcoholism? *Journal of Clinical and Experimental Psychopathology, 17:*202-206, 1956.

Lindesmith, A.R.: *Addiction and Opiates.* Chicago, Aldine, 1968.

Lisansky, E.S.: Alcoholism in women: social and psychological concomitants: I. Social history data. *Quarterly Journal of Studies on Alcohol, 18:*588-623, 1957.

Littman, G.: Bright light on the alcoholic. *New York Times Magazine,* Section *6:* April 5, 1964.

Mann, M.: *New Primer on Alcoholism.* New York, Rinehart, 1958.

McCarthy, R.G.: *Drinking and Intoxication.* New Haven, Yale Center of Alcohol Studies, 1959.

McCord, W., McCord, J., and Sudeman, J.: Some current theories of alcoholism—a longitudinal evaluation. *Quarterly Journal of Studies on Alcohol, 20:*727-749, 1959.

Menninger, K.A.: *Man Against Himself.* New York, Harcourt, Brace, 1938.

Nash, H.: *Alcohol and Caffeine.* Springfield, Charles C Thomas, 1962.

Pescor, M.J.: The problem of narcotic drug addiction. *Journal of Criminal Law, Criminology, and Police Science, 43:*471-481, 1952.

Rosen, A.C.: A comparative study of alcoholic and psychiatric patients with the MMPI. *Quarterly Journal of Studies on Alcohol, 21:*253-266, 1960.

Samuels, G.: Methadone—fighting fire with fire. *New York Times Magazine, October 15:* 44-63, 1967.

Sanford, N.: Personality and patterns of alcoholic consumption. *Journal of Consulting and Clinical Psychology, 32:*13-17, 1968.

Sarrett, M., Cheek, F.E., and Osmond, H.: Reports of wives of alcoholics of effects of LSD-25 treatment of their husbands. *Archives of General Psychiatry, 14:*171-178, 1966.

Sinclair, U.: *The Cup of Fury.* Great Neck, Channel Press, 1956.

Skolnick, J.H.: Religious affiliation and drinking behavior. *Quarterly Journal of Studies on Alcohol, 19:*452-470, 1958.

Suinn, R.: *Fundamentals of Behavior Pathology.* New York, Wiley, 1970.

Sutherland, E.H., Schroeder, H.G., and Tordella, C.L.: Personality traits and the alcoholic. *Quarterly Journal of Studies on Alcohol, 11:*544-561, 1950.

Tahka, V.: *The Alcoholic Personality: a Clinical Study.* Helsinki, Maalaishuntien Luiton Kirjapaino, 1966.

Task Force Report: Narcotics and Drug Abuse. Washington, U.S. Government Printing Office, 1967.

Wallerstein, R.S.: Comparative study of treatment methods for chronic alcoholism. In Catanzaro, R.J. (Ed.), *Alcoholism.* Springfield, Charles C Thomas, 1968.

White, R.W.: *The Abnormal Personality.* New York, Ronald Press, 1964.

Weingold, H.P., et al.: Depression as a symptom of alcoholism: search for a phenomenon. *Journal of Abnormal Psychology, 73:*195-197, 1968.

Wolfgang, M., and Strohm, R.B.: The relationship between alcohol and criminal homicide. *Quarterly Journal of Studies on Alcohol, 17:*411-426, 1956.

Yablonsky, L.: Stoned on methadone. *The New Republic, August 13:*14-16, 1966.

Yablonsky, L.: *Synanon: the Tunnel Back.* Baltimore, Penguin Books, 1968.

Chapter 9

THE SEX OFFENDER

IT IS DOUBTFUL WHETHER the divergence between codified legal norms and actual human behavior is anywhere as wide as it is between sex offense laws and sexual behavior. Long before Kinsey and his research associates conducted their empirical surveys of sexual behavior in the American population (1948, 1953), it was a commonplace observation that laws seeking to regulate sexual activities were totally unrealistic and generally ignored. The anomalous character of these legal statutes was merely accentuated by the selective manner in which they were enforced. After listing a series of so-called aberrant sex practices defined by statute as illegal, Kinsey (1948) had this to say:

> All of these and still other types of sexual behavior are illicit activities, each performance of which is punishable as a crime under the law. The persons involved in these activities, taken as a whole, constitute more than 95 percent of the total male population. Only a relatively small proportion of the males who are sent to penal institutions for sex offenses have been involved in behavior which is materially different from the behavior of most of the males in the population. But it is the total 95 percent of the male population for which the judge or board of public safety, or church, or civic group demands apprehension, arrest, and conviction, when they call for a clean-up of the sex offenders in a community. It is, in fine, a proposal that 5 percent of the population should support the other 95 percent in penal institutions.

As Ploscowe (1970) observes, the severity of Kinsey's conclusions is partially mitigated by several circumstances. In the first place, Kinsey seems to assume that all sexual activities excepting solitary masturbation and normal marital intercourse are universally prohibited and that jail or prison sentences are prescribed by the law for their violation. Such, however, is not the case. Second, Kinsey's statements assume a uniformity of sexual statutes throughout the country. Ploscowe notes that, "One of the most remarkable features of American sex offense laws is their wide disparity in types of sexual behavior and their extraordinary variation in penalties imposed for similar offenses" (1970).

As we have already pointed out with regard to criminal behavior in general, the legal proscription of a given action presupposes the existence of some social norm from which the behavior in question is presumed to represent deviation. If one uses heterosexual genital intercourse as the norm, the potential range of "deviation" is nearly inexhaustible; London (1968) observes that there are "about as many varieties of sexual activity as there are erogenous parts, orifices, and means of manipulation of the human body." Says Karpman (1962):

> English and American codes consider all pre-marital, extra-marital and post-marital intercourse, mouth-genital and anal contacts with animals, and the public exhibition of any kind of sexual activity, as sexual offenses punishable by penalties. Normal sexuality is regarded as heterosexual relations voluntarily practiced in a normal manner by responsible adults not too closely related and married to each other or (possibly) not married at all. All else is taboo.

The circumstances which led to the present situation are part of our cultural history and are outside the scope of this discussion. Ploscowe (1970) suggests a plasible explanation for the sequence of events that began with the founding of the original colonies in the New World:

> Only a small part of the sexual behavior legally proscribed here today was prohibited by the criminal law of Tudor England. Forcible rape, sexual intercourse with a female under ten, the sexual corruption of children, lewd and indecent acts in public, bestiality, buggery, the maintenance of houses of prostitution, too, might be punishable under the old English criminal law, but large areas of sexual behavior —for example, fornication, adultery, incest, fellatio, cunnilingus, mutual masturbation—were beyond the reach of the law and were punishable only as sins or ecclesiastical offenses by the Church of England. Since the ecclesiastical courts were not received in this country, our laws, therefore, initally provided no institutionalized means for dealing with sexual behavior that had been ignored by the common law.

But the lacunae did not long remain, for legislators, prodded by moralistic constituents, rushed to fill these gaps.

LEGALLY PROSCRIBED SEXUAL BEHAVIOR

Expressions such as "crime against nature," "unnatural practices," "lascivious acts," etc. are typically found in the laws of many states. The following quotation is taken from the *current* statutes of the state of Florida: "800.01. Crime against nature: punishment.—Whoever commits the abominable and detestible crime against nature, either with mankind or with beast, shall be punished by imprisonment in the state prison not exceeding twenty years." The definition of "crime against nature" is presumably left to the discretion of local magistrates.

The categories of sexual behavior which are commonly prohibited and penalized include: (1) forcible sexual assault (without coitus), (2) forcible rape, (3) statutory rape (coitus with a female under the "legal age of consent," usually 16 or 18 years, regardless of consent), (4) incest, (5) noncoital sex relations with a minor, (6) exhibitory sexual behavior, (7) obscenity (defined as making indecent or offensive proposals to a member of the opposite sex, use of improper language in public, and disseminating "obscene" materials), (8) homosexual behavior, (9) transvestism, (10) voyeurism, (11) murder involving sexual context or circumstances, (12) bestiality, (13) sodomy, (14) adultery, (15) fornication, (16) prostitution, (17) pimping or pandering, and (18) managing a house of prostitution (Ellis and Abarbanel, 1967).

Gebhard, Gagnon, Pomeroy, and Christenson (1965) conducted a massive study of 1500 incarcerated sex offenders under the auspices of the Institute for Sex Research, founded by Kinsey. Their project represents the largest and most comprehensive empirical study of sex offenders ever conducted, and we shall make frequent reference to their findings in attempting to sketch an accurate picture of sexual criminals. They interpret their vast array of data to show two broad classes of sex offenses:

1. Offenses consisting of behavior which is statistically normal motivated by desires which most laymen and clinicians would consider within our cultural norms. One might sum-

marize these offenses as "normal" but for various reasons inappropriate and punishable. Such offenses would include sexual activity with willing postpubescent unrelated females and occasional opportunistic peeping. These offenses do not seriously threaten social organization, and psychological damage to the individual is generally absent or minimal. Consequently our social sanctions should be tempered accordingly and society should expend a minimum of time and money with such cases.

2. Offenses consisting of behavior which is statistically uncommon and motivated by desires which most laymen and clinicians would consider definitely outside our cultural norms and/or pathological. Such offenses would include those involving force or serious duress, those involving prepubescent children, most incest offenses, exhibition, and compulsive peeping. These offenses tend to disrupt social organization, if only by the furor they cause; the possibility of individual psychological damage is greater; and the offense may constitute a public nuisance. It is on these offenders that society should focus attention and be prepared to spend money for detention, treatment, and research.

Sexual Psychopath and "Sexually Dangerous Persons" Laws

Half of the states and the District of Columbia have enacted statutes which deal with the commitment of so-called psychopathic sexual offenders. In general, there does not seem to be any consensus as to what "psychopathic" sex offender means, and in recent statutes the term is replaced by "sexually dangerous person." But usually, he is defined as one lacking the power to control his sexual impulses or having criminal propensities toward the commission of sex offenses. Some of the statutes set up civil proceedings, some criminal. The civil statutes permit a state's attorney to initiate proceedings to determine whether a person charged with a crime or suspected of having propensities toward dangerous sexual behavior is a sexual psychopath within the meaning of the statute. If, after examination by court-appointed psychiatrists and a hearing, a condition of sexual psychopathy is found, the criminal proceedings may be suspended and the defendant civilly committed to a mental hospital or other state institution for an *indefinite period,* release depending upon recovery.

In some states, the civil proceedings may be commenced without any crime being proved. According to Burick (1968), however, recent statutes usually authorize proceedings only after a conviction of a crime. Upon conviction of a crime, a hearing is held on the question of sexual abnormality, and if the finding is affirmative, special provisions for commitment and release are invoked.

Half of the statutes do not provide for a jury hearing. In some states, the examining physician need not be a psychiatrist. In several states, the psychiatrist is not subject to cross-examination and the defendant may not introduce expert witnesses. Where the commitment is for sexual psychopathy and not a criminal case, Swanson (1960) adds that the commitment is not a bar to a later prosecution for the crime. Under many statutes, the prisoner-patient may be discharged only upon complete recovery, generally meaning that he is believed to be unlikely to commit any more sexual offenses. In some jurisdictions, the commitment is for life, although subject to parole.

Origins of SP Legislation

How did these laws come about? Probably the best historical analysis is the study of sexual psychopath laws by Sutherland (1950). Sutherland points out that in general, the sexual psychopath laws did not stem from either an increase of a noticeable extent in sex crimes or a sudden advance in knowledge of how to deal with sexual offenders. They are the outcome of community panic based on a few serious sexual crimes given wide publicity, with committees of inquiry turning to procedures for supposed control. The rationale underlying the passage of such laws has been summarized by Sutherland (1950) :

> Implicit in these laws is a series of propositions which have been made explicit in an extensive popular literature, namely: that the present danger to woman and children from serious sex crimes is very great, for the number of sex crimes is large and is increasing more rapidly than any other crime; that most sex crimes are committed by "sexual degenerates," "sex fiends," or "sexual psychopaths" and that these persons persist in their sexual crimes throughout life; that they always give warning that they are dangerous by first committing minor

offenses; that any psychiatrist can diagnose them with a high degree of precision at an early age, before they have committed serious sex crimes; and that sexual psychopaths who are identified and diagnosed should be confined as irresponsible persons until they are pronounced by psychiatrists to be completely and permanently cured of their malady.

Certainly the newspapers did their share in whipping up hysteria, which may be typical of this field as Bloch and Geis (1962) have stated:

The inability to counteract inaccuracies and exaggerated stereotypes concerning crime and criminals may be attributed largely to firmly established methods of news coverage. The press does not necessarily make sinister, deliberate attempts to distort the news. Rather, the coverage of crime stories reflects the highly competitive nature of the news industry and news syndication, and the intimate relationship between high circulation and advertising appeal.

When this agitated public sentiment was communicated to the legislature, it usually established investigative commissions, and the law was well on its way. Psychiatrists were usually brought into the studies as experts. It takes an unusually independent and well-informed commission to reject the established statutory pattern and expose the fallacies on which it is based. It would appear, from both older and more recent examples, that few commissions rejected the pattern.

There are numerous examples of how the public fear produced the incentive for these sexual psychopath laws. According to Sutherland (1950), Indiana passed its sexual psychopath law after three or four sexual attacks in Indianapolis, with murder in two cases. As implied before, fear is seldom or never related to statistical trends in sex crimes. New York City's terror of 1937, resulting from four sex murders of girls, was at its height in August, although that was not the month when sex crimes reached their peak. The number of sex crimes known to police in New York City was 175 in April, 211 in May, and only 159 in August! Sutherland adds that the result of this community panic was a committee which after two years of investigating the sexual patterns for a ten year period, declined to recommend legislation along the lines of a sexual psychopath law.

Sometimes, the legislature enacts the sexual psychopath law before the committee recommends pro or con. This situation occurred in Massachusetts. Before the committee appointed by the Massachusetts legislature had had time for even a superficial investigation, the impatient legislature enacted a sexual psychopath law. The commission reported several months later that it did not recommend such a law which had just been enacted. Massachusetts is one of the states that has the heading of its law "sexually dangerous person."

As previously stated the passing of these laws is a combined effort of psychiatrist and legislators. A committee of psychiatrists and neurologists in Chicago enacted the bill which became the sexual psychopath law of Illinois. The bill was sponsored by the Chicago Bar Association and by the state's attorney of Cook County and met with little opposition. Another example is Minnesota, where all the members of the governor's committee except one were psychiatrists; and in Wisconsin, the Milwaukee Neuro-psychiatric Society shared in pressing the Milwaukee Crime Commission for enactment of the law.

We can see then, how psychiatry contributed to the pattern of the statutes with approval and support. The statutes usually came into being after a study by a specially-appointed committee. In effect, the psychiatrists made themselves partners of the legislators and in effect were influenced by public pressure and politics.

Defining the SP Offender

Overholser (1963) writes of the sexual psychopath group as dealt with in the legislature:

> Although the group is not all well-defined psychiatrically, the demand for such legislation arose as a result of public recognition of the fact that many persistent sexual offenders show themselves to be entirely unamenable to routine correctional treatment, that although they are not "insane" in the eyes of the law, they are, by reason of mental deviation, not readily deterrable. Some of these offenders are sociopaths, more of them in my opinion are neurotic, but in any event the principle has been established that there is a group of something other than frankly insane persons who should be dealt with by an indeterminate period of detention and where possible, treatment; actually a fair proportion of these offenders are amenable to psychiatric treatment.

According to Stanton and Wheeler (1960), the most aggressive sex offenders are not psychiatrically disturbed and are more likely to be judged normal by psychiatric diagnosis. They are less inhibited sexually and tend to give fewer indications of severe emotional disturbance. A surprising find is that their prior arrest histories show few sexual offenses, but many non-sexual offenses.

The sexual psychopath statutes also ascribe treatment methods to cure deviated sex offenders, but Guttmacher (1961) notes:

> The trend that runs through popular thinking concerning the sex offenders is this; sexual psychopathy is an illness, not a crime; the offender needs treatment not punishment. Most psychiatrists promptly say "amen" to that noble sentiment. The difficulty is that we have no way of successfully treating the sexual psychopath. Cures, if any, must be extremely rare. . . . It looks like we talked ourselves into holding the bear by the tail. . . . Today we have nothing to offer but custody —a field in which penal authorities are far more efficient than we are. . . . It is of course, a good thing that popular legal thinking about the sex offender is veering away from the purely punitive. But it is not yet at the point where the psychiatrist can appear before the public as the man who has the answer.

To further emphasize the negative aspects of the sexual psychopath laws, Guttmacher states that it is his opinion that new measures to regulate sexual behavior are ill-conceived and fail in their highly commendable purpose for the following reasons: Since most of the aggressive sex offenders have no prior sexual offense records, these measures are similar to locking the stable after the horse runs away. It is based on the premise that serious criminal behavior evolves progressively from less serious sexual offenses. Guttmacher feels this is a faulty premise. In fact he believes that burglary might be far more likely to be a forerunner of rape than lesser sexual offenses like voyeurism or exhibitionism. One impressive point Guttmacher makes is: The exhibitionist, voyeur, transvestite, and homosexual . . . are pathetic instances of individuals with maladjustments; but from society's point of view they are seldom harmful. Surely we do not need this specially drastic legislation merely to curb these activities.

Critique

Statutory and administrative control of sex offender behavior is something in the nature of forensic folklore. In the first place, the current statutes fail to provide protection for the public because, at least in part, they neglect the defendants who are *potentially* dangerous sex offenders but whose previous or current offense(s) do not represent violations of existing sex laws. It can be argued that the existence of such statutes is a barrier to progressive legislation and does harm to any efforts to better acquaint the public with the truth concerning the sex offender.

In the second place, the overwhelming mass of informed psychiatric opinion regarding the sex offender who more accurately fits the definitional criteria of "sexually dangerous person" is that he is notoriously refractory to present methods of treatment. If the rationale for the kind of statute which assigns indeterminate sentences to the sex offender is to insure that such a person will receive effective treatment, rather than mere custodial sequestration, then there are serious reasons for questioning the validity of this rationale.

The question of whether the combination of indeterminate sentence and psychiatric treatment of the sex offender leads to a significant reduction in recidivism—or more specifically, to the deterrence of later and more serious offenses by the psychiatrically treated offender—is, in the final analysis, one which requires an empirical answer. Charges and countercharges of ineffectiveness can only be dealt with in terms of actual data.

PUBLIC VIEWS OF THE SEX OFFENDER

Public misconceptions concerning the sexual offender are numerous. Coleman (1964) has summarized the more common of these:

1. Sexual offenders are typically homicidal sex fiends.
2. Sexual offenders progress to more serious types of sex crimes.
3. Sexual offenders are "oversexed."
4. Sexual offenders suffer from glandular imbalance.
5. Sexual offenders are usually repeaters.

To the extent that the views of many people are shaped by beliefs such as these, it is not difficult to understand why the sexual offender can come to be regarded as a depraved beast who will attack with violent intent. A compilation of some basic factual information about sex offenders (Abrahamsen, 1950; Ellis and Brancale,

1956; Karpman, 1962) helps to place these common myths in proper and reasonable perspective:

1. The majority of convicted offenders are found to be rather harmless, "minor" deviates rather than dangerous "sex fiends."

2. Only a relatively small number (about 20 percent) use force or duress upon their victims.

3. When they are not psychologically treated, convicted offenders are found to be frequent repeaters of both sexual and nonsexual offenses, even though their rates of recidivism may be lower than those of nonsex offenders.

4. Very few offenders may be designated as true "sexual psychopaths" since most of them, when intensively examined with modern psychological and psychiatric techniques or investigation, are found to be severely neurotic, borderline psychotic, psychotic, or to have organic brain impairment . . . .

5. Aside from those convicted of statutory rape and incestuous relations, most offenders tend to be sexually inhibited and constricted rather than overimpulsive and oversexed. The great majority of them are distinctly immature emotionally.

6. Convicted offenders tend to show subnormal intelligence in a higher percentage of the cases and bright normal or superior intelligence in a smaller percentage of the cases than does the general population. Subnormal intelligence is more likely to be found among offenders convicted of statutory rape, incestuous relations, and bestiality and less frequently found among offenders convicted of forcible rape, exhibitory acts, and disseminating "obscene" material.

7. The majority of offenders are quite young, being in their teens and early twenties. From 50 to 60 percent of the convicted offenders are unmarried. Most of the offenders come from relatively poor educational and socioeconomic backgrounds (Ellis and Abarbanel, 1967).

These facts depict the typical sex offender as an individual who differs strikingly from the stereotypes portrayed in fiction and the mass media. Overreaction to these distorted images has created much of the misguided public policy with respect to nonviolent sexual behavior. Thus, an individual may be a sex offender, e.g. statutory rapist, and exhibit conventional (genital) sexual behavior; or he may show considerable deviation in sexual behavior, e.g. compulsive masochism, and never commit a statutory sex offense, *unless that particular category of behavior has been specifically prohibited in that particular jurisdiction.*

VARIETIES OF SEXUAL OFFENSE AND SEX OFFENDER

Forcible Rape

During the year 1970, there were 130,450 arrests for sex crimes in the United States according to the *Uniform Crime Report* (1971). These arrests break down into the following categories:

Forcible rape:	19,050
Prostitution and commercialized vice:	51,700
All other sex crimes:	59,700

The last category above includes *statutory rape,* defined as sexual intercourse by a male with a female who is under the specified legal age, regardless of consent.

The total number of *reported* cases of forcible rape for this same period was 37,270—an increase of 800 over the year 1969. For reasons which involve fear of embarrassment or potential retaliation, there is some reason to believe that an official figure of this kind is an inaccurate gauge of the actual incidence of forcible rape. On the other hand, it is noteworthy that 18 percent of the cases reported in 1970, upon subsequent investigation by law enforcement agencies, turned out to be without foundation.

Guttmacher (1951) has proposed a threefold classification of forcible rapists into:

1. *explosive* rapists, those in whom the assault is an outbreak of pentup sexual impulses;
2. *sadistic* rapists, those in whom aggressive cruelty is an inseparable feature of sexual gratification;
3. *aggressive* criminals, those in whom rape occurs as merely "another act of plunder."

Guttmacher considers the second and third categories as questionable in terms of their relationship to "true rape," which he identifies exclusively with the explosive rapist. This classificatory schema has thus far received relatively little attention from researchers and, as a consequence, suffers from a lack of empirical documentation.

Some Misconceptions About Rape

Amir (1967) reports a study of 1,292 offenders involved in single and multiple rape and 646 rape victims in Philadelphia,

Pennsylvania during two one-year periods (1958 and 1960). His findings led Amir to identify the following misconceptions concerning rape:

1. *Negroes are more likely to attack white women than Negro women.* Rape, we found, is an intraracial act, especially between Negro men and women.

2. *Rape reflects a demographic strain due to sex-marital status imbalance in the community.* This theory was refuted, along with the derivative assumption about age-sex imbalance which might exist within the general populations.

3. *Rape is predominantly a hot-season crime.* The "thermic law of delinquency" was not confirmed by the present study.

4. *Rape usually occurs between total strangers.* This assumption was challenged by the analysis of several variables.

5. *Rape is associated with drinking.* In two thirds of our cases alcohol was absent from the rape situation.

6. *Rape victims are innocent persons.* One fifth of the victims had a police record, especially for sexual misconduct. Another 20 percent had "bad" reputations.

7. *Rape is predominantly an explosive act.* In almost three-quarters of the cases rape was found to be a planned event.

8. *Rape is mainly a dead-end street or dark alley event.* Rape was found to occur in places where the victim and offender initially met each other (especially when the meeting was in the residence of one of the participants).

9. *Rape is a violent crime in which brutality is inflicted upon the victim.* In a large number of cases (87 percent) only temptation and verbal coercion were used initially to subdue the victim.

10. *Victims generally do not resist their attackers.* As it is commonly believed that almost no woman wants to be deprived of her sexual self-determination, it was surprising to find that over 50 percent of the victims failed to resist their attackers in any way.

11. *Victims are responsible for their victimization either consciously or by default.* The proportion of rape precipitated by the victim and the characteristics of such acts refute this claim.

Amir's findings challenge Guttmacher's conception of the explosive rapist as the "true rapist." They are also in clear contradiction of his categorical statements that "the Negro criminal is not primarily a sexual criminal" and that "the native white American male is predominant among sex offenders" (Guttmacher, 1951). According to Amir (1967): "Negroes exceed whites both among victims and offenders in absolute numbers as well as in terms of their propor-

tion in the general population. Negroes have four times their expected number of victims, and the proportion of Negro offenders
was four times greater than their proportion in the general population of Philadelphia."

Voyeurism[1]

In dealing with voyeurism as a sexual phenomenon, we must
begin by noting the importance of the visual element inherent in
most forms of sexual behavior. This element functions to make the
situation, object, or action more pertinent and more arousing to the
individuals involved. Visual appreciation often seems necessary for
complete participation in sexual behavior. The visual element can,
for some individuals, take on such additional importance and significance that all other aspects of sex or sex-related activity are de-
emphasized or even replaced by the overpowering urge to "see."
Thus in voyeurism, as in many other forms of atypical sexual behavior, some act which, in normal individuals, is part of the pre-
liminaries or foreplay acquires greater importance than genital
union itself.

For the male, the sight of the nude or nearly nude female body
is generally, though not always, a titillating experience. According
to Ullerstam (1966), women rarely derive any pleasure from looking at the nude male body.[1] On the other hand, it has been reported
(Ellis, 1938) that obscure sexual excitement engendered by the
sight of animals copulating occurs more frequently in girls than in
boys. For the purposes of the present discussion, voyeurism will refer to deviate sexual activity involving men looking at women
under clandestine circumstances, since homosexual or female voyeurs are extremely rare.

An important factor in distinguishing the voyeur is not merely
the seeking of visual sexual stimuli, but the willingness to incur

---

[1]Also known as scopophilia, scotophilia, mixoscopia, etc. The onomastic syndrome is even more pronounced among sexologists than among other specialists
in behavior pathology.

[1]Ronald Akers (*Deviant Behavior: A Social Learning Approach*. Belmont, California, Wadsworth Publishing Company, 1973) notes that recent research findings
raise questions about this widely held belief. Akers observes that social and cultural inhibitions may prevent women from reporting arousal to sexually provocative stimuli.

risks in securing access to the stimuli (Gebhard, Gagnon, Pomeroy, and Christenson, 1965). The voyeur, for example, does not merely avail himself of unexpected opportunities to view sexual stimuli, but actively seeks out such opportunities, in spite of the attendant risk to himself that arises from his actions.

Another complicating, but necessary, distinction must be made between those socially harmless individuals, "who spend their lives unmolesting and unmolested in the world of the burlesque theatre, pornographic literature, stag films, and even beauty contests," and the so-called "offensive voyeurs" from whom the common notion of "the night prowler who takes considerable risk peeping through bedroom windows" was developed (Yalom, 1961). Here again there is some question as whether individuals in the former group are truly voyeurs. Some behavior pathologists would hesitate to classify them as such; their definition of voyeurism includes elements which are displayed only by the latter group. One of the most important of these is the feature *by stealth*. These individuals cannot derive satisfaction from attending burlesque theatres, stag films, beauty contests, or looking at pornographic material. The key element for them—the lure of the forbidden—is missing in these activities. Moreover, this entire approach (to their way of thinking) is far too contrived and artificial to prove erotically arousing. The offensive voyeur (peeper) must observe, without being seen, someone who has given him no permission to do so (Yalom, 1961). By limiting himself in this way, he is by necessity forced to commit illegal actions which, aside from providing a thrill, also place him in danger of legal sanctions.

According to Gebhard, et al. (1965) the majority of peepers try to avoid detection, although some few deliberately attract attention to themselves. In the latter case, this is usually done with the intention of frightening or humiliating the victim, or even eliciting, some reciprocal interest, characteristics usually associated with the exhibitionist. In reference to this latter group, evidence has been acquired to show that "peepers who enter homes or other buildings in order to peep, the peepers who deliberately attract the female's attention, are more likely to become rapists than the others" (Gebhard, et al., 1965). As for the others, they spend their lives on the outside looking in.

In recalling the features common to offensive voyeurs, we see that the "exaggerated desire" is a serious hindrance to treatment, and that the voyeur is not well motivated to change his behavior "because of the intense pleasure achieved by his voyeuristic activities—a pleasure he is unwilling to give up." (Yalom, 1961). On the other hand, the voyeur is usually uneasy about his actions and often finds that his compulsion bothers him to the point that he seeks a resolution for his difficulties in marriage. This almost never works out, however, because his desire for peeping remains unabated. The thrill of illicit peeping provides more satisfaction for the voyeur than normal intercourse, and most peepers tend to avoid intercourse, which, in any event, they usually find unsatisfying.

This statement becomes additionally pertinent in light of the fact that for most voyeurs, the victim must be a stranger. "This is not a precaution against being recognized; he simply does not find in known females the satisfaction he seeks" (Gebhard, et. al., 1965).

With regard to their choice of victims, peepers often have specific criteria. Most prefer at least moderately attractive adult women preferably engaged in some sort of sexual activity; some, however, have specific goals or scenes in mind, e.g. breasts, buttocks, fellatio, masturbation, or lovemaking between lesbians. The peeper is very optimistic about each escapade and perseveres, hoping that something more erotically provoking will be just around the next corner.

With regard to etiology, both dynamic and extrapsychic theories tend to view the source of voyeurism as social learning within the family context. In many cases, the behavior seems to have been elicited and reinforced by provocative behavior of the mother. London and Rosenhan (1968) describe a case in which a thirteen year old boy's mother "actively conditioned voyeuristic behavior toward herself by sleeping with the boy and by being physically and verbally seductive while appearing nude before him . . . the boy's strongly established voyeuristic behavior generalized to the maid and other persons . . ."

Exhibitionism

Exhibitionism, along with voyeurism and transvestism, is regarded as a "public nuisance offense" as distinguished from some of the more dangerous sexually deviant behaviors. In one of the first extensive studies of the sex offender, East (1924) found that 107 of 209 individuals admitted to Brixton Prison in England were cases of indecent exposure, but that only 49 of these had used the exposure of their genitals as a means in itself. East categorized the majority of the offenders as "depraved" and included in this group psychotics, alcoholics, and "visionaries." In a later investigation, East (1946) studied 449 males and 81 females guilty of indecent exposure. Although his study was inconclusive, it did point out the inability of the law to differentiate between exhibitionists and other offenders; clinically the term exhibitionist applies only to males.

Kraft-Ebbing (1912) defined the exhibitionist as a male who derives sexual titillation and/or gratification from exposing his genitals to a member or members of the opposite sex. Sometimes the exposure involves actual pursuit of the victim, although Kraft-Ebbing believed such incidents were relatively infrequent. However, he recognized that a wide range of variation can be found among exhibitionists with respect to this factor. He divided exhibitionists into four categories, which Mohr, Turner, and Jerry (1964) have collapsed into two major classes. In the first category, exposure is construed as symptomatic of a general deterioration in moral and ethical restraint or social behavior as an accompaniment to organic brain damage, epilepsy, senile dementia, or some type of functional psychosis. In the second group, exposure is presumed to arise from an impulsive/compulsive drive.

The Nature of the Act

The great majority of exposures occur in public and semipublic places—the street, in parks, within buildings, in parked vehicles. The act itself is quite variable, ranging from exposure of the flaccid penis without sexual satisfaction to exposure of the erect penis, often accompanied by masturbation and intense sexual satisfaction. The nature of the act can differ with the same individual according to circumstances and intensity of the sexual urge.

Hirning (1947) and Guttman (1953) have both described the exhibitionist's exposure as compulsive neurotic behavior. In some cases, the act is described as an "uncontrollable urge" which overcomes the individual, even though the act was often carefully premeditated. Compulsive tendencies and lowered abilities to tolerate stress also show up in other aspects of the offender's behavior.

Mohr and his associates (Mohr, Turner, and Ball, 1962; Mohr, Turner, and Jerry, 1964) have stated that the intent of the exhibitionistic act is to evoke an emotional response from the victim. Ellis (1956) suggests that the offender receives the most satisfaction when the victim laughs or smiles upon exposure of his penis. Other investigators agree that an emotional reaction is sought, but that a pleasure response is not the goal of the exhibitionist. Rather, the exhibitionist seems more intent on evoking fear or shock. In many cases the offender is attempting to get his victim to acknowledge the fact of his masculinity by eliciting a reaction of shock, fear, or embarrassment. It is also generally agreed that the exhibitionist does not usually seek further contact with his victim and may, in fact, even fear it.

The Victim of Exposure

The exhibitionist is usually rather unspecific in his choice of victims. This is reflected in the fact that: (1) In almost all cases the victim is a stranger, (2) and the exhibitionist will often choose multiple victims, as in the case of exposures on playgrounds, crowded streets, and public parks. In a study made by Taylor (1947), it was found that in sixty-seven exposures to adults, thirty-four victims were alone. There were two victims in fourteen cases, and in nineteen cases the victims were in groups larger than two. In exposures to children, nine cases of thirty-one were exposures to single victims; eight cases involved two victims, and fourteen cases involved exposure to more than two victims.

The proportion of children as victims of exposures varies between 20 percent and 50 percent of the total number. Mohr, et. al. (1964) note, however, that the proportion of child victims may be higher among those charged as offenders because exposure to children is regarded more seriously and is more likely to be prosecuted.

It has been frequently stated that in the majority of cases the victim is determined more by impulse and situational factors than by anything else.

Relationship Between Victim and Offender

As has been previously stated, the victim and offender are usually strangers, and the exhibitionist does not generally seek any further contact or relations with the victim. Specific areas of the victim's body (breasts, legs, hair, etc.,) rather than the entire person may serve as stimuli to elicit exhibitionistic behavior. The author recalls a case in which a man whose wife did not want to have children exposed himself once to a pregnant woman and once to a woman pushing a baby carriage. Thus, it appears that the man was reacting to a particular stimulus rather than to the women as individuals.

Effects of the Act on the Victim

Since pursuance of further contact is not one of the goals of most exhibitionists, they are generally regarded as a nuisance rather than a danger to their victims. The effects of this nuisance, however, can vary according to the emotional stability, intellectual adequacy, and social maturity of the victim.

Pedophilia

Pedophilia means literally "love of children." According to Karpman (1962), pedophilia is defined as "erotic craving for children; sexual attraction to children, or gratification from sexual intimacies with children." This may be expanded to include the exposure of genitals, manipulation of the child, penetration—partial or complete, and any indecent or immoral practice utilizing the sexual parts or organs of a child so as to bring the offender in contact with the child's body in any directly sexual manner.

The pedophile requires some exceptional or unique experience to stimulate and satisfy his sexual drive. He has a preference for young children and knows a variety of ways to attract and maintain their interest in him. Clinical literature describes the pedophile as psychosexually immature and prey to feelings of inferiority and personal inadequacy.

Age Factors

Data concerning the pedophile reveals that most pedophilic behavior is distributed among three distinct age groups, with peaks in puberty (adolescent group), the mid-to-late thirties (middle-age group), and the mid-to-late fifties (senescent group). According to Mohr, Turner, and Ball (1962), studies of offenders, especially those who have been institutionalized, have shown consistently that the middle-age group is the largest. The adolescent pedophile is frequently passive, immature, and insecure about his capacity to have normal sexual relations with a heterosexual partner of his own age group. He is often shy and uneasy while in the company of adults yet perfectly at ease among children or young adolescents. Reinhardt (1957) suggests that "Some pedophiles have turned to children after repeated failure to achieve a satisfactory sexual relation with older people." This, in part, explains the motivating force behind the attraction to children for the adolescent and middle-age group; a different set of factors, however, is necessary to account for such behavior in the senescent group. Men in this group usually have had no previous history of pedophilic behavior prior to the onset of old-age. Karpmen (1962) discovered these men to be incapable of erection and aware of a definite decline in their erotic reaction as well as reduction in their emotional lives; this diminishing them to scarcely more than children in the eyes of their immediate contemporaries. For the majority of pedophilic offenders, acts of pedophilia are more or less incidental occurrences. It is only for a very small group of offenders that the behavior becomes chronic and is often repeated.

Personal and Social Characteristics

INTELLIGENCE. In early studies of the pedophile, the majority were believed to be suffering from retardation or senile dementia. According to Mohr, Turner, and Jerry (1964), however, recent studies have demonstrated that their intelligence levels are comparable to those of the general population, with a tendency toward the lower end of the scale.

EDUCATION. In general, the educational level of pedophiles has conformed to that of the normal population.

OCCUPATIONS. Studies show pedophiles as members of all occupational groupings, but heterosexual pedophiles (offenders interested in children of the opposite sex) tend to be found in the trades and the semi-skilled occupations. Homosexual pedophiles (offenders interested in children of the same sex) are generally found among the business and service occupations.

SOCIAL INTERESTS. One factor which seems to emerge as common to both heterosexual and homosexual pedophiles is their relative isolation from adult social contacts. Most of their social contacts are with children in youth work or church activities.

RELIGION. Their choice of religion seems to conform with that of the general population.

COUNTRY OF BIRTH AND RESIDENCE. There does not appear to be any consistent relationship between country of origin and place of residence and pedophilic tendencies.

FAMILY BACKGROUND. According to Mohr, et. al. (1964), "Relationships with parents and to a lesser degree with siblings, have been seen as primary factors in the genesis of sexual deviation." Both kinds of pedophilia—and even bisexual pedophilia, where the object or victim may be of either sex—originate from a family situation in which the mother tended to be the stronger parent. The heterosexual pedophile lacked identification with his father, resulting in a retarded emotional maturation and perception of his relationship with his father. He was deprived by his mother because she failed to meet his emotional needs and as a result sought gratification from immature individuals of the opposite sex. The homosexual pedophile indicates a greater awareness of the lack of closeness to his father and the need for a closer relationship with him. Through the years, his relationship with his mother had become idealized and deepened. For both groups, siblings do not play an important part, except in either adding to or detracting from the individual attention able to be given by a particular parent to the developing pedophile.

MARITAL STATUS. The majority of heterosexual pedophiles either are, or have been, married. This is true for only one-third to one-half of the homosexual pedophilic cases (Mohr, et. al., 1962).

The Object

The object of pedophilic behavior is a child, either male (homosexual pedophilia), female (heterosexual pedophilia), or both (bisexual or undifferentiated pedophilia).

AGE OF VICTIM. Since the deviation is related to the sexual maturity of the object, the natural break-off point is the onset of puberty, determined by the presence or absence of secondary sex characteristics. According to Mohr, Turner, and Jerry (1964), the majority of the victims of heterosexual pedophilia fall between the ages of six and twelve, peaking between the ages of eight and eleven. Homosexual pedophilia victims increase in numbers into puberty resulting in a statistical overlap with adult homosexuality victims; this peaks between the ages of twelve and fifteen.

AGE DIFFERENCE BETWEEN VICTIM AND OFFENDER. One can only label certain behavior pedophilic if there is a significant age difference between the offender and his object. Generally, a five-year difference is considered the absolute minimum, taking into consideration the pre-puberty, post-puberty line, but in most cases the difference is better than seven to ten years.

Relationship of the victim to the offender. Mohr, Turner, and Jerry (1964) report that, "Contrary to common public conception, . . . the victim is seldom a total stranger to the offender." Rather, the object or victim is the pedophile's own child or stepchild. Other likely victims are the pedophile's nephew or niece, his friend's child, or his neighbor's child. All these victims are caught quite unaware and uninformed; Uncle Charley is never pictured by mother as the "beware of stranger" type, and the child is quite unprepared for his advances. Homosexual pedophiles are more likely to engage in acts with strangers as their victims.

The Act

In assessing the nature of the sexual act, two things have to be considered—the act itself and the direction or intentionality of the act. There are basically two kinds of deviant acts open to the pedophile, heterosexual and homosexual acts.

HETEROSEXUAL ACTS. Acts which engage a child of the opposite sex seem to be more frequent than those that demand a child of the same sex as the offender.

COITUS. Among the heterosexual pedophiles only a small minority engage in penetration and intravaginal coitus with their victims, and this is mainly with the age group over fourteen and with their permission. Usually the act is not the intention of the offender and is, in most cases, anatomically unfeasible.

DEVIANTLY DIRECTED ACTS. Deviations like exhibitionism, sadomasochism, and fetishism may be directed toward children. In milder forms, such acts as spanking may be engaged in expressly for the purpose of sexual gratification, and therefore deemed deviant even though never prosecuted.

IMMATURE GRATIFICATION. The majority of sexual acts in heterosexual pedophilia consist of the sex-play type. This may include such things as looking, showing, fondling, or being fondled. According to Mohr, Turner, and Jerry (1964) :

> The predominant intentionality of the pedophilic act is therefore one of immature gratification. The pedophilic act represents an arrested development in which the offender has never grown psychosexually beyond the immature pre-pubertal stage, or a regression or return to this stage due to certain stresses in adult life, or a modification of the sexual drive in old age.

HOMOSEXUAL ACTS. The homosexual pedophilic offenses occur less frequently than the heterosexual. The acts are substantially the same as those which occur in adult homosexuality with adult partners, with the possible exception of anal and intercrural intercourse. According to Mohr, Turner, and Jerry (1964), homosexual pedophilic offenses account for only about 30 to 45 percent of all sexual offenses against children under fourteen. Among sexual offenses against children, those resulting in violence or death are extremely rare.

Psychosexual Inversion

Psychosexual inversion can be conceptualized as a spectrum of atypical behavior patterns, ranging from mild effeminacy, transvestism, homosexuality, through transsexualism—a condition characterized by intense and emotionally disruptive desires toward change of gender. Transsexualism is not well covered in the professional literature of behavior pathology. Its principal symptoms have occasionally been described by psychiatrists and psychologists but only recently has much attention been paid to the feasibility of behavior modification or therapeutic intervention in this condition.

At a time when spokesmen for the "erotic minorities" are demanding the decriminalization of sexual statutes, and propaganda of the Gay Liberation Front has become standard reading fare on college and university campuses across the country, it is difficult to avoid the conclusion that transvestism, transsexualism, and homosexuality are topics more appropriate for study by the behavior pathologist than the criminologist. The cases in which the invert is likely to come into contact with the criminal justice system involves instances where the solicitation or activity is so openly flagrant as to constitute a public nuisance. But this stipulation applies equally to those heterosexual individuals arrested during 1970 for prostitution or commercialized vice. The present authors find themselves in agreement with Gebhard, et. al. (1965) in their contention that sexual offenses should be restricted to the following categories of behavior:

> (1) cases where force or threat was employed, (2) cases involving sexual activity between an adult and a child, or (3) cases of sexual activity or solicitation so open as to constitute a public nuisance. The same philosophy stated in another form is this: what two or more consenting adults do sexually in private should not be governed by statute law.

MODIFICATION OF DEVIANT SEXUAL BEHAVIOR

The notable lack of success of psychotherapeutic and psychoanalytic methods in the treatment of sexual deviations has led to an increasing hospitality on the part of psychiatric and criminal justice authorities to treatment methods based on experimentally validated learning techniques. The practitioners of these methods reject the treatment concept of the medical/psychodynamic model along with its approaches; they prefer to speak of their methods in terms of behavior modification. The fundamental principle of this approach, as Raymond (1967) contends, "is that a sexual deviation is a learned or acquired pattern of behavior." No matter how complex or elaborate this behavior is, it is founded on a conditioned response established early in life. It is believed that a chance sexual response to some abnormal stimulus in childhood was subsequently reinforced by deliberate phantasizing during masturbation and probably by similar processes during dreaming.

The methods used by behavior therapists in the modification of deviant sexual behavior fall (and somewhat overlap) into five basic categories: classical aversive conditioning with drugs, classical aversive conditioning with shock, instrumental escape and avoidance conditioning with shock, aversion-relief therapy, and aversive imagery.

Classical Aversive Conditioning with Drugs

Nausea-inducing drugs, mainly apomorphine and/or emetine, received considerable use in early studies. These drugs were usually given by injection to induce vomiting while the patient carried out his pattern of deviant behavior. This procedure was designed to condition the patient to feel nausea whenever he subsequently tried to carry out the deviant behavior. The general technique (unpleasant and often traumatic) has been explained by Barker (1965):

> The patient was treated in bed in a darkened room. A projector was mounted behind the head of his bed and a 48 inch screen was repeatedly checked and liveral fluids and daily injections of parentrovite were administered . . . . Aversion therapy was continued 2-hourly for 6 days and 6 nights, the principal agent being apomorphine. As soon as the injection took effect—the patient usually reporting a headache followed by nausea—a slide was projected on to the screen and the tape recording switched on. Both were continued until he either vomited or became intensely nauseated . . . he received a total of 66 emetic trials, one every 2 hours, which consisted of: 53 intramuscular injections of apomorphine, one intramuscular injection of emetine hydrochloride, 5 oral doses of emetine hydrochloride in a glass of warm water, one dose of two dessertspoonfuls of mustard in a tumbler of warm water, 3 doses of two tablespoonfuls of salt in a tumbler of warm water, and 3 intramuscular injections of sterile water . . . the dose of apomorphine ranged between gr. 1/40 and gr. 1/8. Copious emesis lasting for 95 minutes followed the first injection of gr. 1/10 . . . vomiting invariably occurred in the earlier trials, but owing to drug tolerance it was either absent or replaced by headaches, nausea and giddiness in the later ones . . . . The stimulus was terminated as soon as the patient vomited or reported relief . . . the patient's physical condition remained excellent during the greater part of the treatment.

According to Raymond (1967), the drowsy state that envelops the patient after nausea is most profitable. The patient is encouraged to speak of his earliest deviant sexual behavior and will then often recall factors in its development which he had forgotten. "I do not believe that the mere retelling of these early facts or phantasies will benefit the patient much . . . the value of these recalled early details depends on the extent to which they can be incorporated in the deviant stimulus during subsequent sessions."

This technique has encountered considerable criticism: The method is time consuming; the patient must be hospitalized and in optimal physical condition; a close vigil must be kept on the patient by a team of workers; the drugs used are variable in their action and tolerance to them rapidly develops; the treatment is especially unpleasant for the patient; and the important timing relationships between the unconditioned and conditioned stimuli are difficult, if not impossible, to achieve and maintain. Due to the abundance of disadvantages of this technique, alternative techniques have been sought.

Classical Aversive Conditioning with Shock

Excepting Raymond and O'Keefe (1965) who have continued to use the drug-aversion technique, the difficulties mentioned previously have led to the abandonment of this method, and efforts have been concentrated on the use of aversive shock conditioning. Barker again provides a vivid description of the technique (1965) :

The electric grid was made from a 4 feet by 3 feet rubber mat with a corrugated upper aspect. Tinned copper wire, one-tenth of an inch thick, was stapled lengthwise in the grooves of this mate at approximately half-inch intervals . . . a manually operated G.P.O. type generator . . . produced a current of approximately 100 volts a.c. when resistance of 10,000 ohms and upwards were introduced on to the grid surface. Two rapid turns of the generator handle were sufficient to give a sharp and unpleasant electric shock to the feet and ankles of persons standing on the grid . . . . Treatment sessions were administered every half hour, each session consisting of 5 trials with one minute's rest between each trial. A total of 400 trials was given over 6 days (average 65 to 75 per day) . . . . The patient utilized his own clothing, which was not interfered with in any way, except that slits were cut into the feet of his nylon hose to enable a metal conductor to be inserted into the soles of his black court shoes. He commenced dressing up at the beginning of each trial and continued until he received a signal to undress irrespective of the number of garments he was wearing at the time. This signal was either a shock from the electric grid or the sound of the buzzer which was introduced

at random into half the 400 trials. The shock or buzzer recurred at
regular intervals until he had completely undressed.

The unconditioned stimulus was shock to the soles of the feet; the
conditioned stimulus was dressing up and undressing; and unconditioned response was aversion to the shock; and the conditioned
response was aversion to wearing the clothes or perhaps the sight of
them. Here, also, the patient had no control over the shock and
could not escape or avoid it.

Although this method appears superior to drug aversion treatment, it, too, is not without disadvantages. These include monotony
and tolerance to shock (satiation), as well as anxiety occasioned by
the use of shock. In dealing with masochistic individuals, it was
initially thought that this technique would be pleasurable rather
than aversive as such. However, Marks et. al. (1965) have found
that "the pleasure experienced in masochism was restricted to a
certain range of stimuli and the shock, for example, was perceived
as equally aversive by these patients as by normal subjects" Yates,
1970). They point out, however, that it is possible for shock, in certain patients, to become itself a discriminative stimulus. In this
case, alternative techniques might have to be used, or shock itself
will turn into an aversive stimulus first.

McGuire and Vallance (1964) have since shown that a simpler
method of providing the shock stimulus—to the arm or leg, rather
than the soles of the feet—is equally effective. There is also good evidence now that the dressing and undressing procedure is unnecessary; The shock may be associated with fantasy of the sexual deviation by the patient with equally good results (Barker, 1964; Mees,
1966).

Instrumental Escape and Avoidance Conditioning with Shock as the Aversive Stimulus

The use of an instrumental avoidance paradigm for aversive
conditioning with shock has been described by Feldman and Mac-
Culloch (1965). In their study, psychophysical procedures were
used initially to identify homosexual pictures attractive to the individual patient and to establish a level of shock which he regarded as
unpleasant. The procedure consisted of, firstly, presenting homo-

sexual pictures tachistoscopically, sometimes being followed by shock and sometimes not (partial reinforcement). The patient could either escape or avoid the shock altogether depending on whether he turned the picture off and how quickly he did so. In the second stage, which was carried out simultaneously with the first, a positive stimulus was presented (a slide of a female figure) as the shock ceased. In this way cessation of shock was associated with relief from shock, and the relief from shock in turn was associated with heterosexual stimuli. This method overlaps aversion-relief and positive conditioning techniques which shall be discussed shortly.

The Aversion-Relief Technique

This method, introduced by Thorpe, Schmidt, Brown, and Castell in 1964 is a simple, standard technique which can be readily adapted for any patient, regardless of the precise nature of his sexual deviation. A series of words associated with the sexual deviation are presented accompanied by strong shock; this is followed by cessation of shock accompanied by presentation of an incompatible word associated with the desired change. To illustrate, a series of "homosexual" words with shock would be followed immediately on cessation of shock by a "heterosexual" word.

A variant of the aversive-relief technique was devised in 1965 by Solyom and Miller in which the patient terminates a strong shock voluntarily and is immediately presented with a female slide. Clark also devised a variant procedure where the patient is required to perceive and discriminate two types of stimuli, i.e. heterosexual and homosexual verbal and visual material, presented simultaneously before terminating or not terminating the shock.

The Aversive Imagery Technique

Relatively little work has been reported on this technique, sometimes referred to as verbal aversion therapy. Pioneers in this area are Rachman, Anant, Cautela, Kolvin, Gold, and Neufeld. In this procedure, descriptions of extremely noxious scenes are paired with scenes of the undesired behavior, or the individual may be asked to imagine scenes based on aversive situations and to practice the imagination of these scenes for a certain length of time (until a particular fright level has been achieved).

To illustrate, the therapist might address a homosexual in the following quite vivid, manner:

> As you get closer to the door you notice a queasy feeling in the pit of your stomach. You open the door and see Bill lying on the bed naked and you can sense that puke is filling up your stomach and forcing its way up to your throat. You walk over to Bill and you can see him clearly, as you reach out for him you can taste the puke, bitter and sticky and acidy on your tongue, you start gagging and retching and chunks of vomit are coming out of your mouth and nose, dropping on your shirt and all over Bill's skin, (Barlow, Leitenberg, and Agras, 1969).

Kolvin in 1967 treated a fetishist be requiring him to imagine vividly a story relating to his fetishism. When the imagined story reached its climax, an aversive image was introduced.

In another study Anant (1968) successfully treated a promiscuous girl by having her imagine aversive scenes based on three situations and practicing them until her fright was close to 100 level. She was asked to imagine scenes in which her indiscriminate sexual behavior would "lead to pregnancy (with strong emphasis on the embarrassment to her, as she was asked to imagine that she was living in a respectable neighborhood), a veneral disease, and a strong possibility of being murdered by a sex-criminal."

Research has thus shown that intensely imagined noxious scenes can act as an effective aversive stimulus. There seem to be a few advantages to using a noxious scene in clinical situations: "First, the patient is less likely to refuse treatment because of the pain involved, and, second, it can be widely employed by many therapists, since it does not require drugs or apparatus." (Barlow, Leitenberg and Agras, 1969).

Conclusions

Behavior therapy has the advantage at present over other methods of treatment that are specifically based on some particular view or interpretation of sexually deviant behavior. It seems improbable that, until much more is known about the determinants of atypical sexual behavior, the application of methods which depend essentially on delving into the past are likely to be of much use in modifying such deviant behavior.

The criticism has been fairly made that since treatment for sexual deviation has shown that patients tend to relapse, it would be desirable to incorporate into the training situation those variables which increase resistance to extinction. Feldman and MacCulloch (1965) suggest several steps: (1) learning trials should be distributed, not massed, (2) contiguity of stimulus and response should be maintained throughout, (3) shock should be introduced at whatever level is unpleasant rather than gradually increased, and (4) partial reinforcement should be used in conjunction with instrumental techniques. (5) In general, the greater the variation in the conditions of training the more this will approximate the real life situation. Progress can be noted in the replacement of classical conditioning procedures by instrumental or operant conditioning, and in the preference of electrical treatment over drugs. Recent developments in correlating the changes that occur at various response levels also represent a notable advance over the earlier inadequate assessment of the results of treatment. The criticism still remains, however, that generally the length of follow-up treatment has been quite inadequate. Behavior therapists working in this field are now also well aware of the fact that deviant sexual behavior involves a great deal more than its purely sexual aspects and that, consequently, techniques will need to be devised for coping with the more complex behavior in the deviant individual's social relations.

Summary

Public policy and attitudes toward the sex offender are strongly conditioned by a leak of information and misinformation concerning atypical sexual behavior. Although sexual deviation covers an exceedingly broad spectrum of behavior, most sterotypes which affect legislation are drawn from a comparatively narrow band of sexual misconduct in which actual or threatened force is involved. It is noted that the majority of sexual offenses or sex-related crimes are of the nuisance variety, such as peeping or exhibitionism, where the victim of the offense is not confronted with the prospect of violence.

Some representative types of sexual deviation were examined, along with various views on the origins of atypical sexual behavior and its amenability to modification or elimination. Research and clinical findings support the contention that there is no simple relationship between a pattern of deviant sexual behavior and the presence (or absence) of other kinds of deviation, e.g. neurosis or psychosis.

REFERENCES

Abrahamsen, D.: *The Psychology of Crime.* New York, Columbia University Press, 1960.

Amir, M.: Forcible rape. *Federal Probation, 31:*51-58, 1967.

Anant, S.S.: Verbal aversion therapy with a promiscuous girl: case report. *Psychological Reports, 22:*795-796, 1968.

Barker, J.C.: Behavior therapy for transvestism: a comparison of pharmacological and electrical aversion techniques. *British Journal of Psychiatry, 111:*268-276, 1965.

Barlow, D.H., Leitenberg, H., and Agras, S.: Experimental control of sexual deviation through manipulation of the noxious scene in covert sensitization. *Journal of Abnormal Psychology,* 74:597-607, 1969.

Bloch, H. and Geis, G.: *Man, Crime and Society.* New York, Random House, 1964.

Burick, L.T.: An analysis of the Illinois sexually dangerous persons acts. *Journal of Criminal Law, Criminology, and Police Science, 59:*254-266, 1968.

Clark, D.F.: Fetishism treated by negative conditioning. *British Journal of Psychiatry, 109:*404-407, 1963.

Coleman, J.C.: *Abnormal Psychology and Modern Life.* Glenview, Scott Foresman, 1964.

East, W.N.: *Forensic Psychiatry.* London, J. and A. Churchill, 1927.

East, W.N.: Sexual offenders. *Journal of Nervous and Mental Diseases, 103:* 626-666, 1946.

Ellis, A. and Abarbanel, A.: *The Encyclopedia of Sexual Behavior,* New Charles C Thomas, 1956.

Ellis, A. and Abarbanel, A.: *The Encyclopedia of Sexaul Behavior.* New York, Hawthorne Books, 1967.

Feldman, M.P., and McCulloch, M.J.: The application of anticipatory avoidance learning to the treatment of homosexuality, I.: Theory, technique, and preliminary results. *Behavior Research and Therapy,* 2:165-183, 1965.

Gebhard, P.H., Gagnon, J.H., Pomeroy, W.B., and Christenson, Cornelia V.: *Sex Offenders.* New York, Harper and Row, 1965.

Guttmacher, M.: *Sex Offenses: the Problem, Causes, and Prevention.* New York, Norton, 1961.

Hirning, L.C.: Genital exhibitionism, and interpretive study. *Journal of Clinical Psychopathology, 8:*557-564, 1947.

Karpman, B.: *The Sexual Offender and his Offenses.* New York, Julian Press, 1962.

Kinsey, A.C., Pomeroy, W.B., and Martin, C.E.: *Sexual Behavior in the Human Male.* Philadelphia, Saunders, 1948.

Kinsey, A.C., Pomeroy, W.B., Martin, C.E., and Gebhard, P.H.: *Sexual Behavior in the Human Female.* Philadelphia, Saunders, 1953.

Kolvin, I.: Aversive imagery treatment in adolescents. *Behavior Research and Therapy, 5:*245-248, 1967.

London, L.: Nymphomania. In Eidelberg, L. (Ed.): *Encyclopedia of Psychoanalysis.* New York, Free Press, 1968.

London, P.: The major psychological disorders. In London, P. and Rosenhan, D. (Eds.): *Foundations of Abnormal Psychology.* New York, Holt, Rinehart, and Winston, 1968.

Marks, I.M. and Gelder, M.G.: Behavior therapy. *British Journal of Psychiatry, 111:*561-573, 1965.

McGuire, R.J., and Vallence, M.: Aversion therapy by electric shock: a simple technique. *British Medical Journal, 1:*151-153, 1965.

Mees, H.L.: Sadistic fantasies modified by aversive conditioning and substitution: a case study. *Behaviour Research and Therapy, 4:*317-320, 1966.

Mohr, J., Turner, E.R., and Ball, R.B.: Exhibitionism and pedophilia. *Corrective Psychiatric Journal of Social Therapy, 8:*172-186, 1962.

Mohr, J., Turner, E.R., and Jerry, M.: *Pedophilia and Exhibitionism.* Toronto, University of Toronto Press, 1964.

Overholzer, W.: Criminal responsibility: a psychiatrist's viewpoint. *American Bar Association Journal, 48:*527-530, 1963.

Ploscowe, M.: Sex offenses: the American legal context. In Cohen, B. (Ed.): *Crime In America.* Itasca, F.E. Peacock, 1970.

Raymond, M.J.: Treatment by revulsion. *Mental Health, 26:*24-25, 1967.

Raymond, M.J., and O'Keefe, K.: A case of pin-up fetishism treated by aversion conditioning. *British Journal of Psychiatry, 111:*579-581, 1965.

Reinhardt, J.M.: *Sex Perversions and Sex Crimes.* Springfield, Charles C Thomas, 1957.

Solyom, L., and Miller, S.: A differential conditioning procedure as the initial phase of the behavior therapy of homosexuality. *Behavior Research and Therapy, 3:*147-160, 1965.

Stanton, C. and Wheeler, W.: Sex offenders: a sociological critique. *Law and Contemporary Problems, 25:*272, 1960.

Sutherland, E.: The diffusion of sexual psychopath laws. *American Journal of Psychiatry, 106:*142-148, 1950.

Swanson, C.: Sexual psychopaths statutes: summary and analysis. *Journal of Criminal Law, Criminology, and Police Science, 51:*215-227, 1960.

Taylor, F.H.: Homosexual offenses and their relation to psychotherapy. *British Medical Journal, 2:*525-529, 1947.

Thorpe, J.G., Scmidt, E., Brown, P.T., and Castell, D.: Aversion-relief therapy: a new method for general application. *Behavior Research and Therapy, 2:*71-82, 1964.

Uniform Crime Reports for the United States. Washington, U.S. Government Printing Office, 1970.

Yalom, I.: Group therapy of incarcerated sexual deviants. *Journal of Nervous and Mental Diseases, 132:*158-170, 1961.

Yates, A.J.: *Behavior Therapy.* New York, Wiley, 1970.

Chapter 10
THE
ANTISOCIAL (PSYCHOPATHIC)
PERSONALITY

THE TERM *psychopathic personality* is a designation for a group of behavior disorders in which the identifying characteristics are impulsiveness, antisocial tendencies, immorality, and a seemingly self-destructive failure to modify this pattern of behavior in spite of repeated painful consequences. Some authorities (Karpman, 1961: Cleckley, 1964) feel that it is this inability to profit from experience and training which is the outstanding defect of the psychopath. Psychopathic persons are described as being prone to seek immediate gratification of the sudden impulse, without concern for the consequences of the act. Defective in self-control, they are preyed upon by impulse, and when challenged for the ill-fated consequences of their actions, they become experts in the projection of blame upon members of the social environment. The clinical literature has generally described the psychopath as hedonistic, callous, and immature.

During the years that have elapsed since 1835, when the psychopathic personality was first described, a variety of other terms (mania without delirium, moral insanity, psychopathy, constitutional psychopathic inferiority, semantic dementia, moral mania, moral imbecility, egopathy, anthopathy, anomia, tropopathy) have been employed as labels for this abnormality. The semantic carousel was brought to a halt in 1952 by the American Psychiatric Association with the terminology "sociopathic personality disturbance, antisocial reaction." This action did nothing to change the nature of the disorder or to discourage the continuing debate about the nature or causes of the syndrome. It did, however, establish the condition as a diagnostic category which most mental health professionals popularly referred to as "psychopathy" or "psychopathic personality." In its most recent edition of the diagnostic manual (1969), the American Psychiatric Association has once again altered its nomenclature for this disorder and currently employs the label "antisocial personality." According to the manual, this term:

> . . . is reserved for individuals who are basically unsocialized and whose behavior pattern brings them repeatedly into conflict with society. They are incapable of significant loyalty to individuals, groups, or social values. They are grossly selfish, callous, irresponsible, impulsive, and unable to feel guilt or learn from experience and punishment. Frustration tolerance is very low. They tend to blame others or offer plausible rationalizations for their behavior.

Despite the official change in nomenclature, one doubts whether the popular reference will be readily abandoned; the term "psychopath" seems to possess a certain utility and specificity.

Psychopathy is one of the least understood of the personality disorders. The concept, like its label, has been plagued by controversy since its inception, probably for the same reasons. Perhaps the most basic of these is the fact that both the terms and their various meanings have been used so imprecisely by so many people that they have become hopelessly connotative in character. Many authorities consider the term psychopath a useless semantic repository.

An attempt was made by Albert, Brigante, and Chase (1959) to identify specific areas of agreement or disagreement in the definition of the psychopathic personality. The authors did a content analysis of a sample of ten articles selected from journals and books listed in the *Psychological Abstracts* from 1947 to 1953 under the headings "psychopathic personality," "behavior problems," and "psychopath." This analysis yielded a list of 165 statements descriptive of adult psychopathic personality and 45 descriptive of children diagnostically classified within this nosological condition. Further analysis produced a final list of seventy-five items. The three investigators analyzed and independently coded

the ten attributes mentioned as always characteristic, not characteristic, or occurring as often in the general population as among
psychopaths. These researchers concluded that there was large
agreement shown with respect to the concept of psychopathic personality. There was decided agreement regarding the psychopath's
antisocial and aggressive behavior, lack of ability to delay gratification, lack of insight, inadequacy of superego functioning, deficiency in planning ability, hyperactivity, and callousness. There
was agreement with reference to such characteristics as inability
to identify with others and disturbed early parent-child relationships. Disagreements were found among writers with respect to
the presence of conflict and anxiety in the psychopath and his
capacity to alter his behavior.

Included in the difficulties considered specific to the concept of
psychopathy is the fact that legal definitions vary so widely
throughout the United States that psychopaths are often jailed
with no referral for psychiatric evaluation or treatment. It is on
this assumption that most researchers working in the area of
psychopathy consider prisons the best source of subjects: Possibly
as many as 10 to 15 percent of prison inmates are psychopaths.
Another factor contributing to the impossibility of measuring the
incidence of psychopathy is the refusal, generally, of psychopaths
to seek any kind of treatment. They go through life acting upon
impulse, and when held accountable for their actions, they rationalize their behavior or attribute the blame to someone else.

The disruptive effects of psychopathy have been felt severely
within the armed forces as a consequence of the tendency on the
part of the psychopath to reject constituted authority and to behave as though social regulations did not apply to him. This finding had been well-documented by the U.S. Navy, where character
and behavior disorders account for 90 percent of punitive discharges, rank first in invalidations from service, produce the
second largest number of sick days, and rank fourth as the cause
of new admissions in medical facilities (Accord, 1967). The general classification "character and behavior disorder" is understood
to include a large percentage of psychopaths. These results can
probably be considered indicative of the incidence of psycho-

pathy in other branches of the service, as well.

The psychopath is responsible for another thorn in the side of society: He is an immeasurable monetary burden in the form of police services and lost manhours of work, not to mention treatment costs, and in instances where psychopathic lawbreakers are referred for therapy, the costs of incarceration.

While there may be general agreement among clinical observers regarding the distinctive characteristics of gross behavior in the psychopath, there is considerable disagreement concerning the variables which are presumed to control this behavior. Indeed, the literature provides a variety of viewpoints relative to the determinants and characteristics of psychopathy. Extensive discussions of these positions are available elsewhere (e.g. Cleckley, 1964; Harpman, 1961) and, therefore, only a brief overview of the various perspectives on the etiology of psychopathy will be presented in this chapter.

One major position stresses the role of the constitution and, thus, heredity (Stott, 1962). Because a large percentage (in some studies, as high as 60 percent) of those studied appear to come from "neuropathic" family backgrounds, it is felt that the constitutional factor is significant. Although it is possible that certain variables, e.g. emotional-temperamental, physical, and environmental, seem to be associated with psychopathy, it does not necessarily follow that field studies, which tally the number of "odd" relatives, are capable of providing the kind of evidence needed to establish the role of constitution or of heredity.

Use of the word inherited implies that the phenomenon appears as the fulfillment of a process of development prescribed by the genetic constitution of the individual, as determined at the fertilization of the ovum. On the other hand, the term *congenital* merely implies that the antecedents of the condition date from birth or before, possibly including factors that might operate during gestation or delivery. However, it does not exclude hereditary factors.

The evidence concerning genetic factors in delinquency, particularly that form of aggressive male psychopathy attributed to individuals with an XYY karyotype, is interesting but inconclusive. Apart from methodological issues, such as sampling and research design, there are some unresolved problems of an even more fundamental nature having to do with the complex linkage in mediating mechanisms assumed to account for inherited propensities toward criminal behavior of a highly specific type. A great deal more needs to be done along these lines before investigators can begin to ask research questions which are sufficiently specific to yield information of any clinical or social value.

A second major theoretical position is represented by writers like Karpman and Cleckley who interpret the poor judgment and need for immediate gratification of the psychopath as manifestations of an inadequate internalization of the norms of society. Thus, the probability of behavior that violates legal and moral codes is higher because this behavior is not followed by feelings of anxiety or guilt. Here the implicit assumption is made that guilt and anxiety in the normal individual are socially conditioned responses, consequent to the violation of societal mores.

Karpman (1961) holds that the label psychopath has been misapplied in 80 to 85 percent of cases involving antisocial personalities who, after complete study, have been called psychopaths. These *secondary psychopaths,* as he terms them, actually belong to other nosological groups for whom treatment may be available. Thus, the schizoid, the cycloid, the antisocial neurotic, the psychotic who acts out, and the brain-damaged individual are excluded—they merely act like psychopaths. The remaining 15 to 20 percent are considered true, idiopathic, pure, or primary. In the secondary group, Karpman claims to have always found psychogenic forces (i.e. personality dynamics) operative; in the primary group, he claims to have found none. For the latter group, he has suggested the term *anethopathy* as a means of avoiding the differences connoted by the term psychopathy for various researchers and practitioners. This approach, Karpman claims, removes from consideration many individual who do not belong to the category of psychopath.

Cleckley assumes that the basic difficulty is a disorder in semantics. He stresses the operation of unspecified psychogenic factors resulting in a semantic defect which, in turn, he labels a regressive adjustment technique. This implies that the psychopath at some previous time has not been psychopathic; an unspecified series of events has occurred, with the result that thoughts, feelings, and actions—though maintaining a mask-like resemblance to normality—are isolated, thereby requiring the individual to come to terms societally by the development of a decremental adjustment process designated as *semantic dementia*. This concept suggests that psychopaths fail to react to words which bring about emotional reactions in normal people.[1] However, there is nothing in the way of direct evidence in the professional literature that psychopaths exhibit normative behavior with regard to the connotative meaning of lexical unit prior to the onset of some regressive process or development. What the literature *does* suggest is that the psychopath has been atypical in many aspects of behavior, including verbal behavior from the earliest years (Stott, 1962).

In a study dealing with both the process and content characteristics of the free verbal productions of psychopaths, Eichler (1966) noted that psychopaths differed from normal controls on the following dimensions:

1. *Negation:* use of negatives such as "not," "no," "never," "nothing," etc.
2. *Qualification:* (a) evidence in a clause, phrase, or word which would indicate uncertainty; (b) the use of any modifier which serves to detract from the forcefulness of a statement; (c) the use of a phrase or word which introduces an element of vagueness or looseness.
3. *Retraction:* the use of any word, phrase, or clause which partially or totally detracts from the statement which has immediately preceded it.
4. *Evaluation:* verbal expressions of value judgment divided into the following areas: (a) goodness and badness, (b) usefulness and uselessness, (c) right and wrong (in the sense of correct and incorrect), (d) propriety and impropriety, (e) pleasantness and unpleasantness.

---

[1] As Johns and Quay (1962) have put it, the psychopath may be characterized as one "who knows the words but not the music."

Although the nature of the Eichler study is such that it does not support any strong conclusions with respect to Cleckley's concept of semantic dementia, the data seem to suggest that psychopaths possess some conventional affective appreciation of the meaning of words. However, the issues of acquiescent set, e.g. the psychopath as an excellent con man, and demand characteristics of human experimentation are too inextricably bound up in Eichler's work to go beyond casual observation in the present context. On the matter of the presumed inability of the psychopath to respond to words produced by a second person, e.g. as a species of social reinforcement, Bernard and Eisenman (1967) found that psychopaths reacted to this class of verbal stimuli more effectively than did the normal controls. We shall deal with the Bernard and Eisenman study at greater length when we take up the more general topic of learning in a later section.

A third viewpoint toward the psychopath hypothesizes a physiological basis for a certain range and type of antisocial behaviors (Allen, 1969; Allen, 1970; Lindner, Goldman, Dinitz, and Allen, 1970). Based upon the results of research conducted with inmates at Ohio Penitentiary, the investigators distinguished between "hostile" and "simple" psychopaths. According to Allen (1970), a psychopath, due to improper functioning of his nervous system, vacillates between two states—being "turned off" or "turned on." In the "turned off" state:

> . . . the sociopath is relatively unaffected by ordinary external stimuli, including those that would be mildly or even moderately anxiety and/or fear producing in "normal" individuals. Thus, punishment, reward, discipline, affection, and other cognitive and affective stimuli which profoundly influence the actions of "normal" individuals seem to have no greater impact on the conduct of the sociopath than the most minor or inconsequential stimuli.

In the "turned on" state; the sociopath:

> . . . reacts maximally to all stimuli, however important or unimportant, exhibiting the type of impulsive, hedonistic, trivial, explosive, and irrational conduct which every clinician has observed and many have described. Thus, such "impaired" individuals can make only "on-off," but not graded, emotional responses. . .

Allen points out that this approach only describes the manner in which the psychopath makes widely different responses to stimuli, but makes no attempt to explain the cause of the disorder.

Still another viewpoint is expressed by McCord and McCord (1964) who state that "although inconsistent and purposeless behavior is a product of impulsivity, it may also be due to a deficiency of the psychopath's ego . . . the normal person's self-concept arises through emotional interaction with other people. The child records the evaluations of those around him and gradually absorbs these into his feeling toward himself. If these early evaluations are missing or are inconsistent, the child is unable to develop a coherent attitude toward himself. Absence of long-range goals and static impulsivity may be due to the psychopath's *underdeveloped attitude toward his 'self'.*"

Investigations in this area indicate that the psychopath displays a high degree of egocentrism, a marked tendency toward criticism of others, and low self-criticism. The egocentrism is described by Cleckley (1964) who considers his "self-centeredness" apparently unmodifiable. Foulds (1958, 1960) and his associates (Foulds, et. al., 1960) found that "alcoholic psychopaths" displayed significantly higher critical tendencies toward others than did neurotics on the Foulds Superiority-Inferiority Index.

Foulds, Caine, and Creasy (1960) employed scales derived from MMPI items and the Superiority-Inferiority Index with psychopaths, neurotics, and normals. They found, as expected, evidence of significantly more acting-out hostility and criticism of others among psychopaths than either of the two groups. However, psychopaths scored significantly higher in self-criticism than normals and were not different on the Superiority-Inferiority Index, although they did score higher than neurotics. In addition, the psychopathic group was significantly higher than normals on a delusion guilt scale. The authors suggested that these latter findings were due perhaps to a possible difference in view taken of the rests by the psychopaths. Nevertheless, the fact that the diagnostic classification criteria did not exclude secondary psychopaths would lead one to believe that the group might be expected to show at least some degree of self-criticism and guilt.

The bulk of the experimental and clinical evidence indicates that the psychopath entertains a high opinion of himself. These findings are clearly inconsistent with the statement by the Mc-Cords that self-concept is inadequately developed in the psychopath. It appears that not only does the psychopath have an adequate self-concept, but that his self-concept is stronger than that of normal individuals. This contention is made in full recognition of the difficulties presented by attempts to operationalize all of the preceding constructs: self-concept, "adequate," "strong," etc. While the objective reality and validity of such a personality attribute in the psychopath are certainly questionable, the potential importance of self-concept as a major theoretical construct and the desirability of rigorous empirical research relating to self-concept are matters beyond dispute.

RESEARCH ON PSYCHOPATHIC BEHAVIOR

The studies which will be cited here are generally directed toward two major aspects of the clinical literature on psychopathy: (1) the nature of learning in the psychopath or the effects of experience on subsequent behavior, (2) and the role of affect (anxiety and feelings presumably elicited by the use of positive social reinforcement) as a generic variable relevant to psychopathic behavior.

These two major classes of investigation employ three types of experimental design: instrumental avoidance learning, probability learning, and verbal operant conditioning. In the first subdivision of this section, we shall review experimental studies which make use of verbal operant conditioning methods; in the second subdivision, we shall review studies which make use of instrumental avoidance learning and probability learning.

Verbal Operant Conditioning

The use of verbal operant conditioning as a research tactic in the study of psychopathy is of theoretical relevance to Cleckley's (1964) postulate that the basic characteristic of the psychopathic personality is a lack of the normal affective accompaniments of experience. Cleckley emphasizes the failure of the psychopath to react appropriately to words and phrases which evoke emotional responses in normal individuals.

Johns and Quay (1962), in a verbal conditioning study with neurotic and psychopathic criminals, found that psychopaths were less sensitive to social conditioning than were neurotic offenders. They interpreted these findings as support for Cleckley's semantic dementia hypothesis.

Persons and Persons (1965) have pointed out that the Johns and Quay study contains numerous methodological flaws. They note that Johns and Quay selected their subjects from a military population on the basis of scores on the neurotic and psychopathic subscales of the Delinquency Scale (Peterson, Quay, and Cameron, 1959; Peterson, Quay, and Tiffany, 1961). Persons and Persons cite unpublished graduate research which failed to substantiate the separate subscales of neurotic and psychopathic delinquency as measured by the Delinquency Scale. The subscales were positively correlated, and both were in the same direction as the variables under investigation.

In the Johns and Quay study, the psychopaths and neurotics were subdivided into experimental and control subjects. During the first twenty operant trials on the Taffel procedure[2] there was a significant difference between groups, with the experimental psychopaths receiving significantly higher mean scores. The investigators then measured the amount of improvement once conditioning had begun; they concluded that the initially low-scoring neurotics showed greater improvement than did the initially high-scoring psychopaths. As mentioned above, they considered their results as confirmation for the semantic dementia hypothesis. However, Johns and Quay did not take fully into account the

---

[2]According to the Taffel (1955) procedure, a series of 3" x 5" index cards is presented to the subject. Typed on each card are personal pronouns and a sentence fragment. The subject is instructed to use any of the pronouns and to combine his choice with the sentence fragment to form a complete sentence. Reinforcement is contingent upon the use of a predetermined pronoun. This procedure derived from Skinner's (1957) concept of verbal behavior as "behavior reinforced through the mediation of others" has contributed to the development of the experimental area of verbal conditioning. Greenspoon's (1955) work has given us the other of the two principal methodologies now in use in verbal conditioning. By using "uh-huh" as a reinforcing stimulus, Greenspoon was able to increase the frequency of a vocal response class (plural nouns). This was accomplished in a free responding situation where the subject was instructed to speak single words and was reinforced for using the contingent response class.

fact that the psychopath group demonstrated superior performance within each block of twenty trials and was never surpassed by the neurotic group. It is conceivable that the psychopaths were operating at an initial effective ceiling rate. Moreover, the Johns and Quay data may actually represent refutation of the semantic dementia concept, inasmuch as Cleckley maintains that psychopaths reject or are indifferent to social approval. If this notion were correct, one might predict a decline in performance by the experimental psychopaths during the social reward trials. Not only did the psychopaths in the Johns and Quay study not decline, they made more conditioned responses than any other group.

Quay and Hunt (1965), also using the Taffel procedure, found that their psychopathic subjects (once again selected by means of the non-orthogonal Delinquency Scale) gave fewer conditioned responses than did neurotic subjects.

Bryan and Kapche (1967) concerned themselves with the hypothesis that the purported failure to obtain verbal conditioning to the word "good" in the studies by Johns and Quay and by Quay was caused by the use of individuals outside the psychopath's reference groups as dispensers of social reinforcement. Employing Quay's Delinquency Scale to discriminate between psychopathic and "normal" incarcerated naval personnel, Bryan and Kapche compared the effects of social reinforcement dispensed by graduate students and by exconvicts. Although they failed to obtain significant differences in experimenter and role-playing effects, they did note that psychopaths were influenced by positive social approval, a result which contradicted findings of previous studies.

While the Bryan and Kapche study was essentially an attempt to replicate the methodology of the two studies by Quay and his co-workers, they did manipulate the affective properties of the social relationship between subject and experimenter. There were other differences, as well: Bryan and Kapche used volunteers, Quay and Hunt did not; in the Bryan and Kapche study, psychopaths and normals did not differ significantly in baseline means, whereas significant differences between psychopaths and normals were noted in the Johns and Quay investigation.

If psychopaths are deficient in social learning because of an hypothesized inability to respond affectively to verbal symbols, it is possible that psychopaths might learn more effectively when some kind of tangible reward is used instead of a social reinforcer like "good" or "m-hmm." Using the Taffel procedure, Bernard and Eisenman (1967) compared the effects of a monetary reward (nickles) and the social reinforcer "good" to determine whether psychopaths could be conditioned.

The psychopathic group consisted of forty female prisoners selected on the basis of MMPI (Minnesota Multi-phasic Personality Inventory) profiles, while the normal subjects were thirty-nine student nurses, who obtained T-scores on the Pd scale of the MMPI between thirty-five and sixty-five and who did not exhibit psychopathic tendencies. A variant of the Taffel procedure was employed under four conditions to study the effects of shifting from one kind of reinforcement to another. Psychopaths showed a significantly higher emission rate for the reinforced pronoun in the task, than normals. Social reinforcement was more effective than monetary rewards for both groups, but the difference was even greater in the psychopathic group. In their discussion of this study, the authors point out that situational or subject variables must be taken into account when considering the effect of social or monetary rewards upon psychopaths. The effect of either or both is dependent upon the situational value system in effect at the time of testing. Inasmuch as the psychopathic subjects in this study were females who had been confined with little contact with males, the fact that the social reinforcement was praise from a male investigator might have produced a significant effect upon the results.

Spielberger, Patliff, and Bernstein (1966) investigated the effects of monetary and verbal reinforcers on the verbal conditioning of forty-four college women. These investigators were primarily concerned with the possible influence of the respective types of reinforcer on post-awareness performance of subjects who could verbalize a correct response-reinforcement contingency, i.e. who were able to state correctly the nature of the response for which they were rewarded during the experiment. Spielberger and his associates reported that introduction of the monetary reinforcers did not increase attempts by the subjects to receive reinforcement. Reports by the subjects in the study, however, tend to indicate that appropriate use of monetary rewards might constitute an important determinant of the behavior of a psychopath used as a subject in a verbal conditioning experiment.

Accord (1967) took account of all of the above findings in a study of the learning performance of psychopaths as compared with non-psychopaths on a simple verbal learning task under each of four different reinforcement conditions. The subjects were male, enlisted Navy personnel and were selected as psychopathic or non-psychopathic on the basis of MMPI profiles. The conditioning situation consisted of the typical Taffel task, with first-person pronouns selected as critical; reward or punishment depending on the experimental condition. Verbal reward was the word "good" spoken aloud by the experimenter; verbal punishment was the phrase "not so good" spoken by the experimenter; material reward was twenty-five cents; physical punishment was electric shock. An extensive interview was conducted to assess the subject's awareness of the correct response-reinforcement contingency.

Results supported the hypothesis that: (1) there are no significant differences between psychopaths and non-psychopaths in the amount of learning which takes place under any of the four reinforcement conditions, and (2) there are no significant differences between psychopaths and non-psychopaths in verbalizing the correct response reinforcement contingency.

Accord concluded that psychopaths are at least as capable as non-psychopaths of learning in a verbal conditioning task. This finding, together with the lack of any major difference between non-psychopaths and psychopaths in awareness of the reinforcement contingency, led the author to suggest that psychopaths may be amenable to behavior modification, particularly if rewards rather than punishments are used.

The implications of these findings shed some light on the problems encountered in the verbal conditioning of psychopaths. Some of the incongruent and inconsistent results in the studies we have reviewed appear to be a function of inconsistencies in the selection of psychopathic subjects from one study to another. Once again we are confronted by the need for more adequate, objective, and precise criteria for defining psychopathy.

Speilberger and his co-workers have emphasized the importance of the subject's awareness of the response-reinforcement contingency in the verbal conditioning process. In supporting this contention, Vetter (1969) observes that, "once the subject discovers which responses produce reinforcement, his performance depends upon his motive state and the appropriateness of the reinforcement." This observation has relevance, in particular, for the Johns and Quay study, in which the psychopaths did not condition a situation which may have been due to either the subject's unawareness of the response-reinforcement contingency or his indifference to the reinforcement. This criticism can, in fact, be applied to many verbal conditioning studies. The word "good" spoken in a flat voice hardly seems to be a potential motivator for verbal conditioning, especially with incarcerated felons. More valid and effective results might be obtained with verbal conditioning of psychopaths if the reinforcement were made more appropriate to the experimental situation. In the case of institutionalized psychopaths, reinforcement in the form of tangibles— money, cigarettes, candy, food—or an experimenter of the opposite sex might serve to retain the subject's attention and provide additional motivation for the performance of the conditioning task. This also reopens to consideration and reevaluation the Bryan and Kapche study and the idea that interpersonal relations between subject and experimenter are significant in verbal conditioning.

A further implication of apparent importance is the attitude of the subject toward participation in the study. This factor may have seen a source of difference in results among the studies we have reviewed, since some of the investigators used volunteers while others selected subjects on the basis of criterion measures. Consideration should also be given to the importance of obtaining baseline measures between experimental and control subjects prior to conditioning. Disregard for this factor may have caused the difference between results obtained in the Johns and Quay study and those reported by Bryan and Kapche.

Accord's (1967) study did much to eliminate the shortcomings of previous investigations. It seems to be the most definitive study of verbal conditioning with psychopaths that has been conducted to date. If Accord's findings are substantiated by further research, then subsequent investigation will have to be directed toward resolving the discrepancies in the research that preceded it. Once this is done, systematic study can be devoted to other aspects of psychopathic behavior.

INSTRUMENTAL AVOIDANCE AND PROBABILITY LEARNING

A comprehensive theory of classification founded on factor analytic studies by Eysenck (1957, 1961) sees the psychopath as an individual who ranks high in the factors of neuroticism and extroversion; the study predicts that he would experience more difficulty in learning than would less extroverted individuals, who cannot learn as readily as others can due to a particular type of cortical organization. In other words, as summarized by Franks (1961), psychopaths ". . . would not respond to any form of learning or treatment and would be constitutionally largely unable to acquire the rules of the society in which they lived."

In effect, therefore, the theories of both Cleckley (1955) and Eysenck (1957) postulate that the psychopath does not learn the social rules of the society of which he is a member, and this to a great extent explains his behavior.

The question which must of necessity be answered before more effective methodology can be devised for treating psychopaths is whether or not psychopaths can learn and, if so, under what conditions. It is common knowledge that psychopaths can learn some things. Cleckley (1955) cites numerous case studies of psychopaths who were capable of learning to the extent of reaching above-average levels of professional attainment. McCord and McCord (1964) describe the psychopath as basically associal, motivated by primitive desires, and possessing an exaggerated craving for excitement. They view him as exhibiting actions that are usually unplanned and guided by whim, and although he had learned some socially acceptable ways of dealing with frustration, he seems incapable of profiting from experience.

In the preceding section, it was seen that psychopaths can acquire responses to verbal conditioning stimuli at a rate equal or superior to normals (Bernard and Eisenman, 1967). From meager results using highly restricted and artificial environments, it seems that a dichotomous perspective on the effects of social reinforcement, as a means of eliciting affective responses in the psychopath, may be inappropriate. Further aspects and features of psychopathic learning are investigated under a variety of circumstances in the next series of studies we shall review.

Fairweather (1953), working with a criminal population, required each subject to learn in twenty-five trials under one of three conditions (no reward, certain reward, and uncertain reward) a list of ten nonsense syllables. The reward was two packages of cigarettes at the end of the experimental session. The group working under uncertain reward conditions was told at the start of a session that they would receive the cigarettes "if they did as well as the others did yesterday." The data indicated that the psychopath learned best when reward was uncertain. The psychopath reached the performance level achieved by the normal prisoner with incentive. The often stated belief that the psychopath does not learn from experience may require qualification couched in terms of motivating conditions or to an enhanced arousal due to the variability of stimulation induced by the uncertainty.

Owing to some specific set of circumstances, an impulse to some antisocial act may be generated. Whether or not an antisocial impulse will be inhibited or will result in a crime depends on a multitude of factors, some situational and some psychological. For example, Hymes and Blackman (1965) found that group membership and type of military training are significant determinants of the frequency of antisocial deviant offenses. They also found that the offense rates of trainees are significantly related to those of their immediate superiors, indicating the importance of the social models in a training (learning) environment.

Of the battery of restraints which can inhibit an antisocial impulse, one is fear or anxiety. Other things being constant, the greater the fear or anxiety, the less likelihood that an antisocial impulse will be acted on. Lykken (1957) conducted research based upon the premise that among individuals diagnosed as psychopathic personality, i.e. those who resemble Cleckley's picture of having a lack of normal affective accomplishments of experience, are people clearly defective, as compared to normals in their ability to develop anxiety in the sense of an anticipatory emotional response to warning signal previously associated with nociceptive stimulation.

Lykken (1957) selected three groups (primary psychopaths, neurotics psychopaths, normals) using psychometric scales to measure anxiety and psychopathy. The measures included the Taylor Manifest Anxiety Scale, the Welsh Anxiety Index, the Lykken Anxiety Scales (measuring the extent to which anxiety behavior choices within the range of life situations sampled by the test), and the MMPI Pd scale.

The chief problem involved in testing the relationship of anxiety to avoidance learning is that of restricting the effects of motivations other than anxiety. The demonstration that subjects can differentially learn to avoid painful stimuli is of little consequence if such learning can be explained by higher order need satisfactions, such as social approval or self-administered ego rewards. In Lykken's research, this problem was overcome by making the avoidance task "incidental" to another simultaneous "mainfest" task to which the subject could direct all his ego-serving needs. The subjects were placed in an experimental situation where, at one and the same time, measures were taken of his ability to learn a reinforced task on which his attention was concentrated and an avoidance task which was structured so as to seem completely incidental to the learning of the reinforced task (verbal social reinforcement was used).

The manifest task consisted of performance on a complicated mental maze with twenty choice points. At each choice point the subject could advance to the next choice point only by pressing an arbitrarily correct switch (one of four). When the subject pressed the correct switch a green light flashed, and with the sound of relays (from the interior of the mechanism), the machine moved to the next choice point. If the subject pressed one of the three incorrect switches, the machine didn't advance and an error accumulated on a counter that the subject could see. The subject was told to get through the maze with the fewest errors and was given twenty-one runs through the maze. The sequence of switches defined as correct was the same for each of these runs. At the end of each run the machine was reset to the starting point, and the number of errors was recorded as the score on the manifest task.

The avoidance task was superimposed upon the manifest task by punishing certain errors with an electric shock. Anxiety reduction from avoiding a strong electric shock served as positive reinforcement. At each choice point, one of the three incorrect switches was arbitrarily programmed to deliver a moderately painful shock through a pair of electrodes attached to the fingers of the subject's left hand. A post-experimental questionnaire was given to ascertain how painful the shocks were. There was no significant difference in the degree of pain experienced by the two groups of psychopaths and normals.

By attending to his errors, a subject could avoid the shock. No indication was given in the instructions that this was desirable or even possible; the subject was given a set to attend to the manifest task.

Lykken (1957) found that primary psychopaths, as compared with normals, showed significantly less anxiety on questionnaire devices, less GRS reactivity to a conditioned stimulus associated with shock, and less avoidance of punished responses on a test of avoidance learning.

Painting (1962), like Lykken (1957), used negative as well as positive reinforcement to determine whether the behavior of psychopathic subjects was differentially affected by a correct response's being followed by the attainment of a reinforcing stimulus of the avoidance of an aversive one. A two choice partial reinforcement procedure was used. This type of procedure seems to have similarity to naturally occurring reinforcement schedules. It also seems to be a worthwhile kind of procedure because of the comment by many writers concerning the abnormal risk taking behavior of psychopathic individuals.

Three probability learning sequences, in which a correct response on trial (n) was determined by a preceding stimulus of successively greater distance from trial (n), were employed. This served as a test of the contention that the psychopath is less capable of perceiving the relationships between past events and the consequences of present action.

The three probability learning sequences were: (1) where the correct alternative an trial (n) was independent of all preceding trials; (2) where an alternative repeated itself with p. = .25 and changed to the other alternative, p. = .75; (3) where trial (n) was independent of trial (n-1) but dependent on trial (n-2). Performance under (1) served as a baseline against which (2) and (3) might be compared and as an index of behavior under conditions which precluded a strategy insuring greater than 50 percent reinforced. The number of instances in which the subject selected a response opposite the responses which were correct on the preceding trial served as the dependent variable.

On the basis of the internalization ratio (IR), which Welsh derived from the MMPI, two experimental groups of subjects were selected from among Negro male, post-narcotic drug addicts. The IR was designed to indicate the direction in which anxiety is expressed, either toward the self or toward the environment. One group of experimental subjects were primary psychopaths (according to Cleckley and Karpman) and one group consisted of neurotic psychopaths. Both groups had Pd scores greater than seventy. A third group consisted of control Negro college students.

The three groups were portioned into three equal subgroups, each of which received one of the sequence treatments; for one-half of each subgroup, five correct responses resulted in a reward of two cigarettes; for the other half, five incorrect responses resulted in the loss of two cigarettes from an original eighty given to the subject at the beginning of the experiment. All subjects, after having been told the manner in which cigarettes could be won or lost, were given 200 trials on the appropriate sequence.

No differences were found between groups under positive reinforcement sequence on (1). However, where a correct response seemed to avoid the loss of a cigarette, significant differences between groups emerged; primary psychopaths made fewer alternatives than neurotic psychopaths, but neurotic psychopaths and controls weren't significantly different.

Under sequence (2), optimum performance required that the subject learn to choose that response which was incorrect on the preceding trial. Under avoidance conditions, all groups approximated the proportion of actual alteration in the last 100 trials. Under reward conditions, primary psychopaths alterated in excess of the actual conditional probability, a strategy superior to that adopted by either of the other groups.

Under sequence (3), adequate performance required the subject to alter his responses on trial (n) in accordance with the correct response on trial (n-2). Primary psychopaths deteriorated generally under conditions necessitating a temporally remote determination of response.

Painting's data demonstrate that psychopathy, when defined solely on terms of a deviant Pd score, is not a homogeneous behavioral entity. Rather, a subdivision of his subjects (all scoring over 70 on the Pd scale), on the basis of the Welsh IR, led to the formation of two subgroups, neurotic psychopaths (IR 1.00) whose response in the partial reinforcement situation were quite different. With manipulation of sequence and reinforcement conditions, the performance of the neurotic psychopath was indistinguishable from that of the normal, whereas the behavior of the primary psychopath was significantly affected by both treatment variables.

The frequency with which the primary psychopath alternated his responses under the various conditions provides an interesting parallel to clinical observation. Where the reinforcement schedule disallowed any regularity in S-R contingency (as in sequence 1), the primary psychopath tended to repeat that response which had been correct on the preceding trial. To the extent that the alteration measure reflects on attempt to secure an appropriate strategy, the behavior of the primary psychopath became stereotyped and rigid in displaying a strong positive recency effect.

With a schedule permitting the control of reinforcement by

response (as in sequence 2), all groups approximated the dependency with the primary psychopath tending to maximize his gains in the reward condition. Performance in sequence 2 isn't compatible with the position that the primary psychopath is incapable of profiting from experience. If anything, when the stimulus and response are in close temporal proximity, the level of primary psychopathic performance is superior to that of normals.

Under a more remote S-R correlation (as in sequence 3), the performance of the primary psychopaths deteriorates, however. This deterioration tends to be general and not restricted to a particular reinforcement operation. It would appear that with remote determination of the correct response, the most common naturally occurring relationship, the primary psychopath is less proficient than the normal.

It is well known clinically that the psychopath tends to avoid immediate discomfort and that he appears to be relatively unconcerned about the long term consequences of his behavior. On the basis of these considerations, Hare (1966) hypothesized that when faced with a choice between immediate and delayed shock, psychopaths would show less preference for immediate shock than would nonpsychopathic subjects. Psychopathic and nonpsychopathic criminals and noncriminals were presented with six trials in which they were required to choose between an immediate shock and one delayed ten seconds. The results confirmed hypothesis. The psychopaths chose immediate shock significantly less frequently than nonpsychopaths. The preference for immediate shock increased over trials for the nonpsychopathic subjects but not for the psychopathic ones.

In Hare's (1965a) study, the subjects indicated to the experimenter the level of shock which they felt to be their maximum. A limitation of this study is that it is not known to what extent nonsensory variables affected the subject's reported pain threshold. It is possible, for example, that some subjects, in an attempt to avoid strong shock, reported that their maximum had been reached where in fact it had not. Also, tolerance for pain and pain threshold are mistakenly identified. The pain threshold is the intensity at which the subject says, "This is pain." The total time for which a subject can stand the stream of sensory bombardment accompanying electrical shock may be a factor more important in tolerance for pain than is the pain threshold.

In another study concerned with the time dimension in the behavior of psychopaths, Hare (1965b) used the MMPI Pd scale to separate subjects (summer college students, males and females) into high and low psychopathic groups. A self-report inventory measure of psychopathy was used on the assumption that the diagnosed psychopaths represent only the extreme of a dimension of emotional reactivity and fear conditionability. Skin resistance was recorded while the numbers one to twelve were consecutively presented on a memory drum, with the subjects having been previously informed that an electric shock would be received when eight appeared. The results indicated that as shock became imminent, the increase on conductance was greater, more rapid, and began earlier for the low Pd subjects than for the high Pd ones. The clinical observation that the psychopathic person is relatively unaffected by the threat of punishment receives laboratory support from this research.

Schachter and Latane (1964) have proposed, based on earlier work of Schachter's (Schachter and Singer, 1962), that an emotion be considered a function of a state of psysiological arousal and of cognitions appropriate to this state of arousal. Given specified conditions, an individual will react emotionally or describe his feelings as emotional only to the extent that he experiences a state of physiological arousal. The implication of this is that given a criminal impulse, given the existence of restraining fear-inducing conditions, the likelihood that a crime will occur can be manipulated by the manipulation of sympathetic activation. If this reasoning is correct, it should be possible experimentally to encourage crime by the use of sympatholytic drugs and to discourage it with sympathomimetic agents. This led Schachter and Latane to replicate Lykken's work, but, with the additional feature of introducing the sympathomimetic agent epinephrine.

After a fairly elaborate screening method employing Cleckley's signs of emotional flatness and incorrigibility, Lykken's scale, in addition to two objective aspects of the dimension of chronic misbehavior (number of criminal offenses and the proportion of a subject's life since age 9 spent in jail), Schachter and Latane divided their hard core chronic convicts into three groups, psychopaths, mixed (psydhopathic like), and "normals." Half of each group were given a placebo, and half were given epinephrine, an agent whose effects mimic the action of the sympathetic nervous system. Measures were taken to check on the effects of the drug, included pulse rate changes, EKG changes, and reports by the subjects about their subjective feelings (compared to normative reports of palpitation, tremor, and sometimes a feeling of flushing and accelerated breathing).

Their data indicated that normal and mixed subjects who received placebos decreased their proportion of shocked errors steadily during the replication of Lykken's experiment; the placebo psychopaths, however, only gave a slight indication of learning. This last point confirms Lykken's conclusion that on an avoidance learning task, presumably mediated by anxiety, psychopaths learn not at all. However, Schachter and Latane discovered that psychopaths who seem virtually incapable of learning to avoid pain when under placebo, learn dramatically well under the influence of adrenalin; normals, however, are adversely affected under adrenalin and learn not at all. A marked interaction between degree of psychopathy and the effects of sympathetic arousal on avoidance learning ability existed. All groups were equally capable of positively reinforced learning.

The occurrance in the psychopath, for whatever the cause (endocrinological, neurological, or learning history), of low autonomic responsiveness should lead to emotional flatness and low anxiety, according to Schachter's formulation. However, Schachter and Latane (1964) found, in part, greater autonomic reactivity on the part of the psychopaths. Their data indicated that for heart rate nonemotional subjects are more reactive autonomically (i.e. have accelerated heart rates) than are emotional subjects. This result lies in direct opposition to much of the work on the relationship of high anxiety states to autonomic arousal (Duffy, 1962).

A NEW PERSPECTIVE ON PSYCHOPATHIC BEHAVIOR

For reasons which are partly a function of egalitarian social philosophy and partly a reaction to earlier excesses among theorists, American criminological thought has been markedly inhospitable to the notion that organic factors may play an important role in the pathogenesis of some forms of antisocial behavior. As an example of the latter, Allen (1970) quotes a passage from *The New Criminology* by Schlapp and Smith, published in 1928, in which the authors announce their objectives in the following terms:

> We shall attempt to demonstrate that the vast majority of all criminals, misdemeanants, mental deficients and defectives are products of bodily disorders, that most crimes come about through disturbances of the ductless glands in the criminal or through mental defects caused by endocrine troubles in the criminal's mother. The attempt will also be made to show that criminal actions are in reality reactions caused by the disturbed internal chemistry of the body.

As Lindner, et. al. (1970) has put it, the "extravagant claims, meagre empirical evidence, naivete, gross inadequacy, and stated or implied concepts of racial and ethnic inferiority" in the work of earlier constitutionalists, morphologists, and endocrinologists constitute a "disreputable history" which thoroughly discredited the few important empirical findings of biological investigations of criminal behavior.

The position endorsed by the Ohio State researchers in urging a reconsideration of organic factors in psychopathic behavior is not a repudiation of social, cultural, and interactional viewpoints toward criminal and delinquent behavior. Says Allen (1970):

> The enormous and readily observable variability of human social institutions, interpersonal relationships and normative standards, including cross-cultural differences in the definition and content of deviancy, certainly compels extreme caution in raising the issue of organicity. Still, embracing a socio-cultural perspective does not preclude the potential fruitfulness of including other models as explanations on the micro, individual, or clinical level. There is nothing in differential association, differential identification, subcultural, limited opportunity neutralization or labeling theory which suggests that biological concomitants, such as an XYY chromosomal pattern, can play no role at all in criminality and other anti-social conduct.

The research which led to the formulation of the so-called "juice model" began with the work of Funkenstein, Greenblatt, and Solomon (1949) who reported a significant increase in systolic blood pressure in male and female antisocial individuals following an intravenous injection of epinephrine, as compared with mentally ill and normal controls. Lykken (1955) reported diminished galvanic skin responses to forced lying and impaired avoidance conditioning in institutionalized felons as compared with reactive antisocial prisoners and non-institutionalized controls. In 1964, Schachter and Latane confirmed the increased cardiovascular activity to epinephrine in fifteen imprisoned male psychopaths as compared with fifteen inmate control subjects. Lippert (1965) compared 21 psychopathic delinquents with 21 non-psychotpathic delinquents and found that their GSR patterns were characterized by lower resting levels, lesser increase during experimental manipulation, and increased adaption to repeated stimuli.

Hare (1968), like Lippert, confirmed the presence of higher skin resistance and lowered variability in twenty-one *primary* psychopathic prisoners as compared with *secondary* psychopaths and non-psychopathic controls. He also noted that orienting responses to mild stimuli were impaired in the experimental subjects.

The multidisciplinary project conducted by Lindner, et. al. (1970) at Ohio Penitentiary was conceived as an attempt to replicate and extend the provacative research reported by Schachter and Latane. Forty-three inmates, comprising nineteen primary psychopaths, ten mixed, and fourteen non-psychopathic controls, were selected from 1375 consecutive admissions and were carefully screened to meet all of the criteria (age, IQ, physical status, MMPI profile, Cleckley Checklist, Lykken Scale scores, offense, and incarceration) for inclusion as subjects. They were subjected to a double-blind experimental procedure in which they were randomly assigned either epihephrine or saline injections prior to work on Lykken's avoidance learning task. As Allen (1970) reports:

> Two major findings emerged from our experimental work. First,

unlike previous investigators, we found two obvious and distinct types of so-called *primary* sociopaths which we have designated as *hostile* and *simple* forms. These groups were found to differ from one another on almost every parameter, including cardiovascular responsibility, criminal history (i.e., number of arrests, types of offenses, number of incarcerations, length of time incarcerated, parole violations) military history (i.e., number accepted into armed forces, length of time in service, types of termination), familial characteristics (i.e., from intact families, present marital status, number of times wed), and psychological profiles (on various MMPI profiles, especially the Ma and Pt, and on the Taylor Manifest Anxiety Scale). Secondly, as a group, the *simple* sociopaths differed from the non-sociopaths as well as the *hostile* sociopaths in cardiovascular reactivity (i.e., heart rate) to epinephrine.

This work has been extended to inmates at the Ohio Penitentiary for Women and is currently planned for extension to Florida State Prison at Raiford.

Although these investigators are becoming modest in the appraisal of their findings, the value and significance of this research and of the "juice model" on which it is based are beyond dispute. It is from such carefully-wrought interdisciplinary studies, which employ the approaches, procedures, and instrumentation of the life sciences, that investigations of deviance at the micro-level of analysis offer realistic prospects for finding some solutions to the baffling and perplexing problems of treating the antisocial personality.

Treating the Antisocial Personality

One of the very few points on which consensus can be found among professionals with regard to the psychopath is his poor prospects for treatment or behavior change. A Psychiatrist was once lecturing to a class in which the present author was enrolled, and he described the psychopath as "the kind of person who convinces you that you have helped him to see the light." He vows that he is going to be different, said the psychiatrist, "then you go downstairs and find that he has stolen your car." A great deal of psychiatric lore is communicated to mental health students in this fashion during their training, with the result that they have thoroughly assimilated the doctrine of the untreatability of the psychopath long before they ever have their first contact with one in the flesh. To the present writer, this smacks of the self-fulfilling prophecy: The conviction that the psychopath cannot be treated successfully leads to failure in the treatment of the psychopath. Most correctional authorities seem all too ready to join the physician in Shakespeare's *Macbeth* in saying, "this disease is beyond my practice."

The assessment of therapeutic results with psychopaths is subject to all of the many problems that bedevil the assessment of psychotherapy in general, not the least of which is the ambiguity and unreliability of psychiatric diagnosis. Wallinga (1956), for example, claims that the designation *psychopathic personality* is given to any individual seen clinically or within the correctional setting who exhibits unusually hostile, defiant, or aggressive behavior. Reporting success in his own efforts with offenders, Wallinga maintains that "either psychopaths are treatable, contrary to the popular definition of the concept, or far too many individuals are erroneously receiving this label." We ought to be openminded to the possibility that *both* alternatives possess some intrinsic validity.

Most psychiatrists assign the principal difficulty in treating the psychopath to his inability to establish a positive relationship with the therapist as a consequence of his suspicious and hostile attitudes, particularly in the traditional one-to-one relationship. Bromberg (1954) states that the psychopath reacts to psychotherapy "with defiance, acting as society unconsciously wishes him to—as an irretrievably rebellious person." According to Bromberg, the psychopath often acts defiant to preserve a defensive weapon which serves a "double-edged purpose." Specifically, the psychopath preserves an unconscious masochistic desire which can be traced to childhood when he was rejected or denied adequate emotional care. As an adult, he still has need for affection, although these needs operate outside the range of his awareness. Therefore, the psychopath strives for masochistic gratification by placing himself in a position where he is despised and rejected by society. To maintain his protective structure, he finds that he must struggle against unconscious motivations. He thus becomes a "rebel with a cause."

Bromberg remarks that "control of the psychopath, incarceration rather than hospitalization, restriction rather than treatment, have become officially accepted, even lauded, attitudes." Such attitudes, in Bromberg's view, defend the members of society against the recognition of hostile, aggressive, or defiant impulses within themselves by projecting these impulses upon the criminal psychopath. Bromberg feels that it is the duty of psychiatrists to demonstrate the same sympathy and therapeutic skill that have been employed in the treatment of neurotic and psychotic patients. Says Bromberg: "One wonders, in relation to this complex problem, whether psychiatry has not been frightened by the sardonic, smiling mask of the psychopath, behind which lies the frightened, lonesome face of neurotic character."

The foregoing discussion (including the dubious terminal metaphor), with its heavy emphasis upon psychodynamic inference and intrapsychic constructs, is fairly typical of most of the literature on treatment of the psychopath. If society opts for "control of the psychopath" and "incarceration, rather than hospitalization," the reasons for such a choice are not hard to find: Given the exceedingly poor record of dynamic psychiatry in dealing with the neuroses and psychoses, further application of psychiatric "sympathy and therapeutic skill" to the psychopathic offender is scarcely calculated to arouse enthusiasm or optimism.

It is against this background that Bromberg's treatment recommendations must be considered. Bromberg maintains that the psychopath can be best treated in the group situation, where he has an opportunity to express aggressive impulses with his peers rather than with a therapist who may appear threatening to him. (Bromberg reasons that the psychopath's hostile feelings for people in positions of authority can be traced to a basic unconscious dependence upon the very authority figures against whom he rebels. He fails to add, however, that the therapist may find the psychopathic patient equally as threatening, or more so.) Once the psychopath begins to identify with the group, according to Bromberg, the therapist will have an opportunity to establish a positive relationship with its members if he can remain firm but permissive. In addition, he cautions against the development of negative counter-transferences. He sees the group setting as a mechanism by which the ego filters off and satisfies threatening instinctual impulses: "it is an oblique approach to an instinctive urgency, satisfying simultaneously the wish to experience a dangerous emotion and the mastering of affective tensions connected therewith." Thus, the psychopath may act "as if" society accepts his hostilities and aggression without actually having to give up his protective structure.

The emotional environment of the group setting serves a very important function, namely, to "unfreeze" the psychopath's defensive character structure. This is accomplished by presenting him with a comfortable emotional atmosphere in which he can experience his feelings of aggression, dependence, and hostility in a controlled manner. As the offender expresses some of his repressed feelings (catharsis) to the group, emotionally traumatic situations within his own life (and those of his peers) are re-enacted. However, the defensive impulse to escape now decreases and, hopefully, a degree of transference will develop to other group members as well as the group therapist. (It is often advisable for the therapist to use the language of the group to promote a positive relationship with the members.) For the psychopath, group therapy is essentially a method of mastering "anxiety-provoking situations" by re-enacting them.

The notion that therapy for the psychopath is best defined as an attempt to create a permissive atmosphere within which the offender can express his aggressive impulses is basic to the approach described by Fox (1969). He states that the psychopath responds best to a father figure who can "structure the relationship with authority and social standards." When the psychopath benefits from an authoritarian relationship, the improvement is mostly in the area of intellectual control and ego strength. If the offender improves in the emotional area, it is most likely to be the result to his relationship with a permissive but firm therapist whom he can look to for security and support. In the words of Fox: "These are children in the shells of men, calling to their fathers almost frantically for authoritarian but accepting guidance. The therapist absorbs in the process the tensions the psychopath needs to dissipate, thereby reducing the need for acting out."

As a consequence of the difficulties posed by the hostility of the psychopath, Fox feels that the therapist must attempt something "unusual, unorthodox, and unexpected" to reach this type of offender. Such techniques as "telling the prisoner the best way to escape and then evaluating it with him, discussing methods of killing his mother, accepting a rather extreme homosexual rather than incarcerating him in solitary, displaying of legal knowledge that structures his situation for him, and engaging in a boxing bout with the psychopathic prisoner" have all been used with some degree of success, according to Fox.

Although many psychopathic offenders can be found within penal institutions in the United States and Europe, those who have written most extensively on the aggressive, impulsive, acting-out type of offender rarely describe their procedures and approaches as psychopathis treatment programs. An exception is Boslow (1966), who describes the organization and treatment program for the rehabilitation of the psychopathic offender at Patuxent Institution in Maryland.

Through the use of a graded tier system, which provides rewards for socially acceptable behavior, the inmate is encouraged to work his problems through in group therapy. Since all inmates at the Patuxent Institution are committed with indeterminate sentences, they realize that parole is dependent upon their efforts to gain insight into their own behavior. Or to put it another way, the inmates eventually realize that the way to get out of Patuxent is to give serious consideration to their own personal problems.[1] The group therapist focuses attention on their "distorted perceptions, feelings, and attitudes, and the part these distortions play in developing their anti-social behavior patterns. Manipulative, self-destructive behavior and unconscious motivations are also attacked in group therapy." According to Boslow, most in-

---

[1] One undesirable side-effect is to give the staff virtually unchallenged control over inmates. For a sharply critical journalistic view of patuxent, see Jessica Mitford's *Kind and Usual Punishment,* New York, Alfred A. Knopf, 1973.

mates realize that mere conformity to institutional rules does not necessarily mean that they have gained insight and maturity. The indeterminate sentence is the "wedge" or stimulus which motivates the inmate to conform and understand his own behavior and that of his fellow inmates.

As the inmate advances vertically in the tier system, he acquires additional privileges. However, these privileges are accompanied by more obligations and responsibilities. The aim of the institution is to motivate (through reinforcement of and rewards for socially acceptable behavior) the inmate to "function more maturely as well as to delay gratification of his impulses. The rewards reinforce the positive aspects of his behavior; additional reinforcement occurs through the Patuxent milieu and the therapeutic endeavors of the staff."

Dr. Boslow points out that the staff at the Patuxent Institution limits its treatment goals with the psychopathic offender since many failures in individual treatment occurred when the therapist attempted to "restructure the entire personality into an approximately normal one." The aim at Patuxent is merely to effect a change in personality that will enable the offender to return to society as a productive member. Treatment is considered successful if a paroled inmate can return to society without repeating the same type of violation that brought him to the institution in the first place. As a matter of fact, treatment would also be considered successful if the inmate developed neurotic defenses in place of psychopathic traits provided that these defenses allowed the released offender to remain in society without breaking the law and provided that they did not severely handicap the person as to be self-destructive.

Once the inmate is able to recognize some of his unconscious motivations (as a result of consistent, continuous and supportative treatment—group therapy) for self destructive behavior and is able to delay gratification of his impulses, he is usually granted leave status by the Patuxent Board of Review (the institution's parole board). The inmate begins with holiday leaves and, as his stability increases, he is advanced to monthly leaves. Eventually, the inmate is granted parole from the institution; however, his treatment program continues. The social worker who treats the inmate while on parole is the same one who treated him while in the institution. As a result, he has someone to assist him in making the transition from the institution to the community. The parole worker is not only interested and familiar with him, but he is an individual whom the inmate has learned to trust. In short, he is applying the learning and behavior that brought him rewards in the institution to an environment that will test his recently acquired social skills. This new learning, however, is supported by his parole worker and other members of the staff at Patuxent.

Britain: The Special Hospital System

Until 1959, there were no special legal provisions for the treatment of the psychopathic offender in England (Craft, 1966). If such an individual were convicted of a criminal offense, he was committed to a penal institution. He could be hospitalized only if the court were able to squeeze him into one of the mental defect classifications.

As a result of the 1959 Mental Health Act, special treatment provisions were made for the rehabilitation of the psychopathic offender. (Provisions were also made for the treatment of three additional classes of "mental disorder," but these are not germane to the present discussion.) These provisions included special hospitals for treating this type of offender as well as compulsory detention laws which authorize the courts to commit the individual for a period of up to one year. The 1959 Mental Health Act did not, however, eliminate the use of the British Prison System as a resource for the psychopathic offender. Instead, the offenders who were not seriously disturbed, although psychopathic in nature, continued to be placed within the prison setting. The psychopath, who after examination was deemed to be seriously disturbed, could be committed to any number of hospitals that had been authorized to treat this type of offender under the new law. For the seriously disturbed offender who had committed a heinous crime, the 1959 Mental Health Act created a "Special Hospital System" which included facilities for the treatment of the dangerous and violent criminal (psychopath).

As of 1966, there were three special hospitals for the treatment of the psychopathic offender (Broadmoor in Berkshire, Rampton in Nottinghamshire, and Moss Side in Liverpool). Since all three hospitals are administered by the Ministry of Health, they are identified with the medical rather than the penal system of the country. The inmates, in turn, are committed and protected under the provisions of mental health, rather than penal legislation. They tend to be, however, the most extreme of the aggressive and sexually deviant psychopaths.

Analytically oriented group therapy and individual psychotherapy have been used within the "Special Hospital System" to a limited extent. However, less structured forms of group therapy are used to an even greater extent since they appear to be more suitable and less costly than the analytical methods. In addition, committees, elected by the inmates, are formed so that these individuals have an opportunity to interact with one another without the supervision of the therapist. The biggest advantage of the committee system is that it helps the inmate to become emotionally involved with the staff and other inmates. Craft remarks that the patients "tend to show a real concern not only for the rights, but the clinical interests of their fellows."

The philosophy of treatment in the "Special Hospital System" is quite similar to the treatment philosophy of the Patuxent Institution for Adult Offenders in Jessup, Maryland. Craft relates that all methods of treatment are "based on careful, patient training towards social conformity, with a complex system of rewards, both social and monetary, and as equivalent range of disincentives to unacceptable behavior, by loss of privilege and amenities, and a return to a more strictly structured and closely observed stratum of the hospital society." Inmates refer to this system as a "system of rewards and punishments."

The "Special Hospital System" in England has not been in operation long enough to evaluate the results of treatment with any degree of accuracy. However, since the program was initiated in 1960, figures point to a fairly good achievement record (approximately 10 percent of the entire hospital population had been discharged each year as "improved"). In addition, all three hospitals maintained a low re-admission rate, less than 3 percent.

Summary

The term "antisocial personality" has replaced older terms such as "psychopath" and "sociopath" as the official psychiatric label for individuals who show a characteristic pattern of behavior which often brings them into continual and repeated conflict with legal authorities. While the clinical literature has tended to emphasize social forces as the key determinants of antisocial behavior, recent evidence has suggested that physiological factors may account for the deviant behavior of at least some of those who are labeled antisocial personalities. The chapter concludes with a discussion of therapeutic intervention techniques with the antisocial personality and reviews evidence which challenges the stereotype of the antisocial individual as intractable to all forms of therapy.

Conclusion

The evidence we have examined suggests that the psychopath is not only amenable to treatment, but can be treated with reasonable prospects for success. Although relatively unstructured forms of group therapy appear to be more widely used than any other forms of therapeutic intervention, it would appear that the psychopath can be "reached" in a variety of ways, some of them more effective than others. Unfortunately, most treatment programs which are designed to rehabilitate the psychopathic offender have not been in existance long enough to accurately appraise the results, despite promising recent accomplishments. In England, where a national program of mental health has been in operation since 1959, the results are quite encouraging. Glover (1960) refers to a study of 2079 cases in which the results of treatment of psychopathic offenders compared favorably with those obtained in neurotic offenders. Says Glover, "Although there may be many sources of error, particularly diagnostic error in such surveys, the results are sufficiently striking to offset the standard pessimistic view."

REFERENCES

Accord, L.D.: Psychopathy and conditioning. (Unpublished Ph.D. dissertation, Case Western Reserve University, 1967).

Albert, R.S., Brigante, T.R., and Chase, M.: The psychopathic personality: a content analysis of the concept. *Journal of Abnormal and Social Psychology, 60:*17-28, 1959.

Allen, H.E.: Biosocial correlates of two types of anti-social sociopaths. (Unpublished Ph.D. dissertation, Ohio State University, 1969).

Allen, H.E.: A biosocial model of antisocial personality. (A paper prepared for presentation at the Ohio Valley Sociological Society meeting, Akron, Ohio, 1970).

American Psychiatric Association: *Diagnostic and Style Manual of Mental Disorders.* Washington, American Psychiatric Association, 1968.

Bernard, J.L. and Eisenman, R.: Verbal conditioning in psychopaths with social and monetary reinforcement. *Journal of Personality and Social Psychology, 6:*203-206, 1967.

Boslow, H.M. and Kandel, A.: Administrative structure and therapeutic climate. *Prison Journal, 46:*23-31, 1966.

Bromberg, W.: The treatment of the psychopath. *American Journal of Psychiatry, 110:*604-608, 1954.

Bryan, J.H. and Kapche, R.: Psychopathy and verbal conditioning, *Journal Abnormal Psychology, 72:*71-73, 1967.

Cleckley, H.: *The Mask of Sanity.* St. Louis, Mosby, 1964.

Craft, M.: *Psychopathic Disorders and Their Assessment.* London, Pergamon Press, 1966.

Duffy, E.: *Activation and Behavior.* New York, Wiley, 1962.

Eichler, M.: The application of verbal behavior analysis to the study of psychological defense mechanisms: speech patterns associated with sociopathic behavior. *Journal of Nervous and Mental Disease, 141:*658-663, 1965.

Eysenck, H.J.: *The Dynamics of Anxiety and Hysteria.* New York, Praeger, 1957.

Eysenck, H.J.: Classification and the problem of diagnosis. In Eysenck, H.J. (Ed.): *Handbook of Abnormal Psychology.* New York, Basic Books, 1961.

Fairweather, G.W.: The effect of selected incentive conditions on the performance of psychopathic, neurotic, and normal criminals in a social role learning situation. *Dissertation Abstracts, 14:*394-395, 1954.

Foulds, G.A., Caine, T.M., and Craesy, M.: Aspects of extra- and intropunitions. *Journal of Clinical Psychology, 14:*163-166, 1958.

Foulds, G.A.: Attitudes toward self and others of psychopaths. *Journal of Individual Psychology, 16:*81-83, 1960.

Foulds, G.A., Caine, T.M., and Creasy, M.: Aspects of extra- and intropunitive expressions in mental illness. *Journal of Mental Science, 106:*187-192, 1960.

Fox, V.B.: Psychopathy as viewed by a clinical psychologist. *Archives of Criminal Psychodynamics, 4:*472-479, 1961.

Franks, C.M.: Conditioning and abnormal behavior. In Eysenck, H.J. (Ed.): *Handbook of Abnormal Psychology.* New York, Basic Books, 1961.

Funkenstein, D.H., Greenblatt, M., and Solomon, H.C.: Psychophysiological study of mentally ill patients. Part I: the status of the peripheral automonic nervous system as determined by the reaction to epinephrine and mecholyl. *American Journal of Psychiatry, 106:*16-28, 1949.

Glover, E.: *The Roots of Crime.* New York, International Universities Press, 1960.

Greenspoon, J.: The reinforcing effect of two spoken sounds on the frequency of two responses. *American Journal of Psychology, 68:*409-416, 1955.

Hare, R.D.: Psychopathy, autonomic functioning, and the orienting response. psychopathic and non-psychopathic criminals. *Journal of Psychology, 59:*367-370, 1965.

Hare, R.D.: A conflict and learning theory analysis of psychopathic behavior. *Journal of Research in Crime and Delinquency, 2:*12-19 (b), 1965.

Hare, R.D.: Detection threshold for electric shock in psychopaths. *Journal of Abnormal Psychology, 73:*268-272 (a), 1968.

Hare, R.D.: Psychopathy, autonomic functioning, and the orienting response, *Journal of Abnormal Psychology, 73:*1-24, (b), 1968.

Hymes, J.P. and Blackman, S.: Situational variables in socially deviant behavior. *Journal of Social Psychology, 63:*149-153, 1965.

Johns, J.H. and Quay, H.C.: The effects of social reward on behavior conditioning in psychopathic and neurotic military offenders. *Journal of Consulting Psychology, 26:*217-220, 1962.

Karpman, B.: The structure of neurosis: with special differentials between neurosis, psychosis, homosexuality, alcoholism, psychopathy, and criminality. *Archives of Criminal Psychodynamics, 4:*599-646, 1961.

Kohlmeyer, W.A.: Changing concepts of psychopathy and their therapeutic implications. *Excerpta Criminologica, 7:*274-275, 1967.

Lindner, L.A., Goldman, H., Dinitz, S. and Allen, H.E.: An antisocial personality with cardiac lability. *Archives of General Psychiatry,* (in press).

Lippert, W.W.: The electrodermal system of the psychopath. (Unpublished Ph.D. dissertation, University of Cincinnati, 1965.)

Lykken, D.T.: A study of anxiety in the sociopathic personality. *Journal of Abnormal and Social Psychology, 55:*6-10, 1957.

McCord, W. and McCord, J.: *The Psychopath.* New York, Van Nostrand, 1964.

Painting, D.H.: The performance of psychopathic individuals under conditions of partial positive and negative reinforcement. *Journal of Abnormal and Social Psychology, 62:*353-358, 1961.

Persons, R.W. and Persons, C.D.: Some experimental support of psychopathic theory: a critique. *Psychological Reports, 16:*745-749, 1965.

Peterson, D.R., Quay, H.C., and Tiffany, T.L.: Personality factors related to juvenile delinquency. *Child Development, 32:*355-372, 1961.

Peterson, D.R., Quay, H.C., and Cameron, G.R.: Personality and background factors in juvenile delinquency as inferred from questionnaire responses. *Journal of Consulting Psychology, 23:*395-399, 1959.

Quay, H.C. and Hunt, W.A.: Psychopathy, neuroticism, and verbal conditioning: a replication and extension. *Journal of Consulting Psychology, 29:*283, 1965.

Schachter, S. and Singer, J.E.: Cognitive, social, and physiological determinants of emotional state. *Psychological Review, 69:*379-399, 1962.

Schachter, S. and Latane, B.: Crime, cognition, and the autonomic nervous system. In Levine, D. (Ed.): *Nebraska Symposium on Motivation.* Lincoln, University of Nebraska Press, 1964.

Schlapp, M.G. and Smith, E.: *The New Criminology.* New York, Boni and Liveright, 1928.

Spielberger, C.D., Ratliff, R.G., and Bernstein, I.H.: Verbal conditioning with social and monetary reinforcers. *Psychological Reports, 19:*275-283, 1966.

Stott, D.H.: Delinquency and cultural stress. *British Journal of Social and Clinical Psychology, 1:*182-191, 1962.

Taffel, C.: Anxiety and the conditioning of verbal behavior. *Journal of Abnormal and Social Psychology, 51:*496-501, 1955.

Vetter, H.J.: *Language Behavior and Psychopathology.* Chicago, Rand McNally, 1969.

Wallinga, J.V.: The psychopath: a confused concept. *Federal Probation, 20:* 51-54, 1956.

Chapter 11
CRIMES OF VIOLENCE

EXPRESSIONS OF CONCERN over mounting levels of violence in contemporary American life encompass events as disparate as criminal homicide and student seizures of university buildings, forcible rape and the assassination of public figures like Martin Luther King and Robert F. Kennedy, warfare in southeast Asia and convict insurrections in the prisons, violence in the entertainment media and urban riots and looting. Much of this writing reflects the assumptions that these variegated acts or events (1) are different aspects of the same phenomenon, (2) are linked by common causes, and (3) can be comprehended in terms of the operation of the same variables.

There is no denying the scope and significance of the existential and theoretical problems posed by these assumptions. Without questioning the philosophical importance of a viewpoint toward violence that includes moral, social, and political perspectives, we are compelled to place the greater portion of this literature outside the limits of the present discussion. Our focus of conecrn here is not violence in general, but violent crimes and violent criminals in particular. We are committed to dealing with such phenomena as civil disturbances and violence in the mass media within the narrower context of violent crime.

A disproportionate amount of the ensuing discussion is devoted to criminal homicide and aggravated assault. Four of the seven categories of "serious crime" on which the *Uniform Crime Report* is based—criminal homicide, aggravated assault, forcible rape, and robbery—are classified as violent crimes because they involve the threatened or actual infliction of criminal homicide and aggravated assault. Although four of the seven categories of "serious crime" on which the *Uniform Crime Report* is based—criminal homicide, aggravated assault, forcible rape, and robbery—are classified as violent crimes because they involve the threatened or actual infliction of bodily injury, we have excluded the latter two types of offenses because they have been dealt with elsewhere in this book. In addition, criminal homicide and aggravated assault have been studied in sufficient breadth and depth in the professional literature to afford a characterization which possesses some generality.

THE VIOLENT OFFENDER: AN OVERVIEW

Before embarking upon a discussion of specific characteristics of the perpetrator of murder and assault, we might gain some orientation for our subject by referring to the following summary statement on the violent offender which appeared in an official publication of the National Parole Institutes:

> Despite the complexities and inconsistencies in legal labels for violent offenses and despite the incompleteness of statistical reporting for some of these offenses, a few trends in crimes of violence are apparent. First, homicide has clearly declined in the past few decades. Secondly, aggravated assault statistics have clearly climbed, although this may reflect primarily an increase in police intervention and recording in these offenses, rather than an increase in violent behavior by the public. This change in police involvement may also account for the slight rise in rates of recorded rape.
>
> Homicide and assault are disproportionately frequent in the South Atlantic States and low in New England. Rape, like property offenses, is most frequent in rural as in urban areas.
>
> Crime of violence are most frequently among the most impoverished and poorly educated segments of the population. Homicide is especially more frequent among Negroes than among whites in the United States, but much of this discrepancy is accounted for by their poverty and their recent migration from the States where homicide rates, for both Negroes and whites, were highest.
>
> Both the statistical concentration of violent offenses and case data suggest that the cause of these crimes may rest largely in attributes of groups, rather than in purely individual traits: homicide and assault are most frequently in social circles where violence is the expected reaction to a rebuff or insult. Nevertheless, the concept of psychopathy, frustration, aggression, and displacement seem to account for many distinctively individual violence patterns. (Glaser, Kenefick, and O'leary, 1968)

It shall be our task in the following pages to examine the evidence on which these generalizations are based.

Some Definitions

Homicide

Homicide, a general term for referring to the killing of one human being by another, may be classified as lawful or criminal. Lawful homicide includes *justifiable homicide* and *excusable homicide*. Justifiable homicide, according to Wolfgang (1958), "is an intentional killing sanctioned by law, such as the execution of a felon who cannot otherwise be taken." Excusable homicide is "an unintentional killing where no blame attaches to the killer. It may have resulted from negligence on the part of the victim, but if negligence appears in the actions of the perpetrator, it is involuntary manslaughter" (Wolfgang, 1958). Excusable homicide generally includes killing in self-defense and accidental killing during the commission of lawful acts.

Criminal homicide, the crime with which we are concerned in this chapter, includes murder and manslaughter. Says Wolfgang (1958): "Murder, as defined by the common law, consists of the unlawful killing of a human being with malice aforethought, express or implied." The meaning of "malace aforethought" requires some explanation. The "malice" may actually imply nothing malicious and need not be "aforethought," except in the sense that desire or intention must necessarily precede the act which is desired or intended, if only by an instant. As MacDonald (1961) puts it:

> Express malice refers to the actual intent to kill. It matters not if the actual victim was not the intended victim. Malace is usually implied if there was intent to inflict great bodily harm; if the act or its omission was likely to cause great bodily harm; and if the killing occurred during resistance to lawful arrest or commission of certain felonies.

The last provision constitutes a rather controversial point of criminal law: the so-called *felony-murder* doctrine which was briefly discussed in chapter one. By the terms of this provision, if a death occurs during the commission of a felony, the individual who commits the felony may be charged with first-degree murder. According to Bloch and Geis (1962):

A person setting fire to a barn, for instance—thereby committing the felony of arson—might burn to death a tramp who, unbeknown to the arsonist, was sleeping in the barn. If so, the arsonist can be charged with murder, though his act lacked both malice aforethought and premeditation in regard to the death.

The authors cite the application of the felon-murder doctrine to a case in which a first-degree murder charge was brought against the surviving member of a pair of robbers, one of whom was shot and killed by the police during the commission of the robbery. The charge held that the second robber would not have been slain if he had not been engaged in a felony; therefore, his partner was held legally responsible for his death! Although some states, e.g. New York, will invoke the felony-murder doctrine in all felonies, many states have restricted the doctrine to a limited range of serious crimes, such as rape, robbery, and arson.

Murder is divided into two degrees according to the intent, premeditation, or deliberation of the offender. *Murder in the first degree* is "the wilful, deliberate and premeditated killing of a human being, feloniously and maliciously" (Wolfgang, 1958). A first-degree murder verdict is usually mandatory if the murder occurred during the commission or attempted commission of such crimes as arson, rape, or robbery. *Murder in the second degree* constitutes the killing of a human being, feloniously and maliciously but without specific intent to take life.

Manslaughter differs from murder in that there is no malice aforethought, either express or implied. *Voluntary manslaughter* is "the unlawful killing of another in a sudden heat of anger, without premeditation, malice or depravity of heart" (Wolfgang, 1958). *Involuntary manslaughter* consists of the killing of another "without malice and unintentionally, but in so doing some unlawful act not amounting to a felony nor naturally intending to cause death or great bodily harm" is committed. Involuntary manslaughter also includes "the negligent omission to perform a legal duty" (Wolfgang, 1958). This would include illegal abortion operations, reckless driving, and similar violations.

Aggravated Assault

Aggravated assault is defined by the *Uniform Crime Report* (1970) as "an unlawful attack by one person upon another for the purpose of inflicting severe bodily injury usually accompanied by the use of a weapon or other means likely to produce death or serious bodily harm." Included in this category are *attempts at assault*. The rationale is that serious personal injury could, and probably would, result if an attempt, involving the use of a gun, knife, or other weapon, were successfully completed.

Robbery

Robbery, according to the *Uniform Crime Report* (1970) is "a vicious type of crime which takes place in the presence of the victim to obtain property or a thing of value from a person by use of force or threat of force." As the *Uniform Crime Report* notes, data on *armed robbery* are reported in instances where any weapon is used; other robberies, such as muggings, are reported as *strong-arm robberies*.

Forcible Rape

The *Uniform Crime Report* (1970) defines forcible rape as "the carnal knowledge of a female through the use of force or the threat of force." Separate counts are kept of attempted forcible rapes and actual forcible rapes, although the two categories are summated in the total reported figure. Statutory rape (not involving force) is not included in this category.

Frequency and Distribution of Violent Crimes in the U.S.

The year 1970 is credited with attaining a new national high in the total number of violent crimes for a single year: 731,400. These crimes were tallied as follows:

Murder and non-negligent manslaughter	15,810
Aggravated assault	329,940
Forcible rape	37,270
Robbery	348,380
TOTAL	731,400

As Figure 11-1 shows, the period from 1960 to 1970 witnessed an increase in the incidence of all four categories of criminal offense designated as violent. In 1967, the President's Commission on Law Enforcement and the Administration of Justice estimated that the true rate of total major violent crimes was roughly *twice* the reported rate. Other estimates, as we shall note later, place the total for unreported violent crimes even higher.

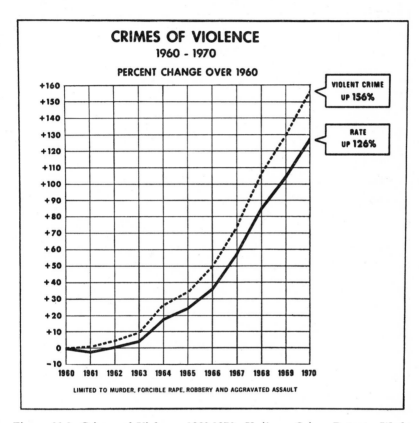

Figure 11-1. Crimes of Violence 1960-1970. *Uniform Crime Reports.* Washington, U.S. Government Printing Office, 1970. Reproduced by permission of the Department of Justice.

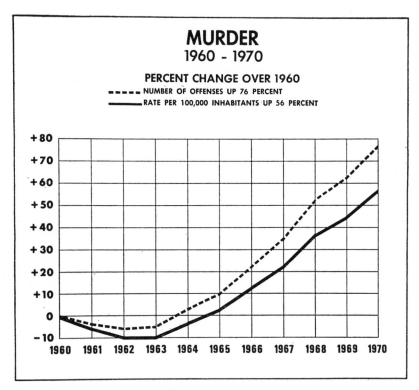

Figure 11-2. Murder 1960-1970. *Uniform Crime Reports.* Washington, U.S. Government Printing Office, 1970. Reproduced by permission of the Department of Justice.

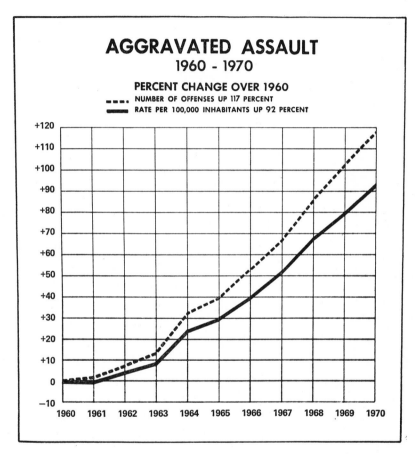

Figure 11-3. Aggravated Assault 1960-1970. *Uniform Crime Reports.* Washington, U.S. Government Printing Office, 1970. Reproduced by permission of the Department of Justice.

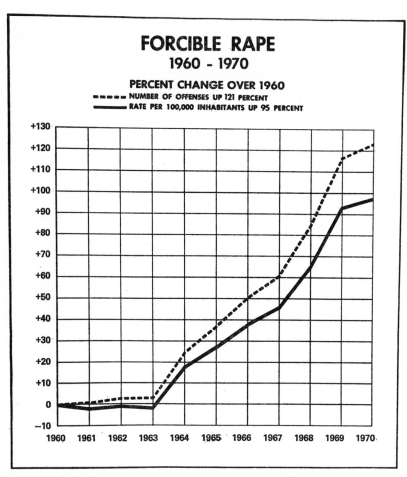

Figure 11-4. Forcible Rape 1960-1970. *Uniform Crime Reports.* Washington, U.S. Government Printing Office, 1970. Reproduced by permission of the Department of Justice.

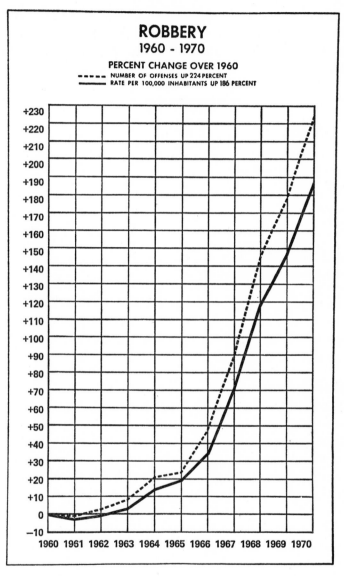

Figure 11-5. Robbery 1960-1970. *Uniform Crime Reports.* Washington, U.S. Government Printing Office, 1970. Reproduced by permission of the Department of Justice.

With regard to geographic area, the South led the nation in 1970 in three of the four categories of violent crime reported. The figures cited below in Table 11-I are percentages of the total number of reported violent crimes for the nation as a whole.

TABLE 11-1.

Crime	North Eastern States	North Central States	Western States	Southern States
Murder and Nonnegligent Manslaughter	18%	23%	14%	45%
Aggravated Assault	20%	22%	20%	38%
Forcible Rape	17%	26%	27%	30%
Robbery	33%	28%	16%	23%

Uniform Crime Reports. Washington, D.C.: U.S. Government Printing Office, 1970. The above table was prepared from information presented in pages 5-15 of the *Uniform Crime Reports* for 1970.

Before any interpretations can be made of the possible meaning and significance of these and the preceding statistics, we must take a closer look at the nature of the offenses themselves and of the offenders who perpetrate them.

Criminal Homicide

Most studies of homicide have dealt with small numbers of cases and few have concerned themselves specifically with the relationship between the offender and the victim. Typically, such studies have sought to investigate background circumstances which appear to culminate in murder. Unfortunately, most of these investigations have been psychodynamically oriented, speculative, hypothetical, and intuitive in nature, presenting serious difficulties in trying to separate fact from inference.

Black, Weiss, and Lambert (1963) conducted an analysis of forty-three sudden murderers. "Characteristically," they say, "the sudden murderer was a young man from a close-knit family in which the mother was a domineering, over-protective figure who emphasized conformity."

They found that such a person had never been involved in any previous serious aggressive antisocial acts or attempts to kill another human being. "When he seemed to be getting along quite well, when society apparently expected him to be even more conforming and mature, and when he had no one to blame, he would become more and more tense and angry."

Typically, there was a period of approximately a month preceding the murder when the murderer seemed to make an adequate social adjustment. However, the very effort to maintain a facade of competence and independence weakened some of the defenses with which the killer warded off his more basic feelings of insecurity and inadequacy. It was during this period that the murderer became more and more preoccupied with his feelings of helplessness and the necessity to terminate his ever-increasing inner disequilibrium. Of the forty-three sudden murderers studied, twenty-nine demonstrated this behavior pattern.

Occasionally sudden murders occur for which no motives can readily be identified. Stearns (1957) studied four such murderers and found that they displayed certain common elements:

> The perpetrators have all been adolescent males, their reputations have all been uniformly good, the victims have all been females—two scantily clad, and the crimes have been wanton and ferocious. No motive has ever been established. When such a murder case occurs, I think it fair to assure that the same pattern will be present.
>
> It has been assumed quite largely that there has been gross mental disease to account for such crime. It has further been assumed that these persons should be confined for life, that there is indication of some morbid quality which would make it dangerous to ever release them.

While this type of person seems identical to the "sudden murderer," he can attribute no motive such as anger, jealously, or humiliation for the killing.

The Wolfgang Study

Marvin Wolfgang conducted one of the most comprehensive and detailed sociological studies of criminal homicide ever reported and one from which a great many conclusions have been drawn by criminologists and other criminal justice specialists. His research covered 588 cases of criminal homicide which occurred during a five-year period from 1948-1952 in Philadelphia. The study is note-worthy for the close attention it devoted to the characteristics of the victim as well as those of the offender.

Although it has been demonstrated that criminal homicide is largely an unplanned event, Wolfgang found that the act is characterized by a number of discernible uniformities. The following associations were revealed by his study:

(1) . . . there is a significant association between criminal homicide and the race and sex of both victims and offenders. Negroes and males involved in homicide far exceed their proportions in the general population, and have rates in homicide many times greater than whites and females. The race-sex specific rate per 100,000 for both victims and offenders reveals the following rank order of magnitude: Negro males, Negro females, white males, white females. Although Negroes of either sex, and males of either race are positively related to criminal slayings, the association between race and homicide is statistically more *significant* than that between sex and homicide (1958).

(2) A *significant* association exists between age and criminal homicide, with the age group 20-24 years having the highest rate among offenders, and the age groups 25-29 and 30-34 having the highest rate among victims. Offenders, in general, are younger than victims.

(3) *Significant* associations exist between methods of inflicting death and the race and sex of both victims and offenders.

. . . We have seen that 39 percent of all 588 criminal homicides were due to stabbings, 33 percent to shootings, 22 percent to beatings, and 6 percent to other and miscellaneous methods.

. . . Males, if Negro, usually stab and are stabbed to death; and if white, beat and are beaten to death. Females generally stab their victims with a kitchen knife, but are very often beaten to death.

. . . We have also noted a general and crude relationship between age of the offender and predilection for certain types of weapons, with the incident use of firearms highest among offenders under 20 and those over 50 years of age.

(4) Although criminal homicides tend to increase during the hot summer months, there is no significant association either by seasons or by months of the year.

. . . But homicide is *significantly* related to days of the week and hours of the day. The weekend in general, and Saturday night in particular, are *significantly* associated with criminal homicide, as are the hours between 8.00 P.M. and 2:00 A.M.

(5) There is a *significant* association between place where the crime occurred and the race and sex of both victims and offenders. In terms of total cases, the most dangerous single place is the highway (pub-

lic street, alley, or field) , although more slayings occur in the home than outside the home. Men kill and are killed most frequently in the street, while women kill most often in the kitchen but are killed in the bedroom.

. . . Most cases of Negro males who kill Negro males involve a stabbing in a public street; most cases of white males who kill white males involve a beating in a public street.

. . . In general, there is a slight tendency for homicides to occur outside the home more frequently during the summer months when collective life is more frequently outdoors than during the winter months, but no association is found between the home/not home dichotomy and days of the week or hours of the day.

(6) Either or both the victim and the offender had been drinking immediately prior to the slaying in nearly two-thirds of the cases. The presence of alcohol in the homicide situation appears to be *significantly* associated with Negroes—either as victims or offenders—and, separately, with Negro male and female victims.

. . . Alcohol is a factor also strongly related to the violence with which an offender kills his victim. Homicides committed by men are *significantly* more violent than those committed by women; but there is no association of violence with race or age of the offender.

. . . slayings with excessive degrees of violence predominate in the home, and are most likely to involve a husband-wife realtionship in which the wife is the victim of her husband's brutal beating.

(7) . . . analysis of offenders in criminal homicide reveals a relatively high proportion who have a previous police or arrest record.

. . . Having a previous record is *significantly* associated with males both among victims and offenders . . .

. . . a greater proportion of Negro male and female victims have a previous arrest record than white male and female offenders, respectively.

. . . A *significant* relationship is noted also between presence of alcohol in the offender and the offender with a previous arrest record.

(8) Criminal homicide usually results from a vaguely defined altercation, domestic quarrel, jealousy, argument over money, and robbery . . . Homicide appears, however to be more personalized when directed against or by women. There are few important differences according to motive and the race or either victim or offender.

(9) Most of the 550 identified victim-offender relationships may be classified as primary group relations. Close friends and relatives accounted for over half of the contacts.

(10) . . . In 94 percent of the cases, the victim and the offender were members of the same race, but in only 64 percent were they of the same sex.

(11) In 32 cases of criminal homicide involving 57 offenders and 6 victims, a felony, in addition to the killing, was perpetrated at the time of the slaying. In most cases, the other felony was robbery, and white males accounted for a larger proportion of these felony-homicides than they did among all homicides in general.

Wolfgang's study is of inestimable value for the factual information it provides concerning what might be termed the *modal* or typical homicide, i.e. the kind of criminal homicide which is almost a feature of daily routine in metropolitan police departments. He does not, as Bloch and Geis (1962) remark, "provide information on the dynamics of the relationship between offender and victim, both of whom represent carriers of a culture that has not been able to totally inhibit murderous behaviors." Despite these and other limitations, the Wolfgang study marks a clear advance toward understanding criminal homicide.

Juvenile Homicide

One of the most disturbing features of the latest (1970) reported figures on homicide in the disparately large increase noted in the incidence of criminal homicides committed by youthful or juvenile offenders. Ten percent of those arrested for murder during 1970 were under eighteen years of age, and 43 percent were under twenty-five. As compared with a 94 percent increase in murder arrests among adults over twenty-five during the ten year period of 1960-1970, there was a 203 percent increase in under-eighteen age group.

Crowdon (1954), research director of the Ohio State Bureau of Juvenile Research, studied fifty-four cases of juvenile homicide referred to the bureau during the period 1921 to 1947. The group studied was composed of forty-eight boys and six girls, ranging in age from nine to nineteen years; forty-two were white, and twelve were black. The 1940 census reports and a group of unclassified delinquents, similarly studied by the bureau, provided comparative data. The outstanding observation of the study was the great similarity between children involved in homicide and those involved in other types of delinquency. It was difficult to establish that the homicide group was materially more inferior, or more unusual, or more abnormal than juvenile delinquents involved in other offenses. But victims of juveniles were found to include, in comparison with those of adults, more blood relatives and fewer of those types slain in connection with other crimes. Revenge (12 cases) led the list of motives most clearly established in the fifty-four cases. The pistol was the weapon most frequently used, and murder was seldom premeditated over a long period of time.

During a period of nearly twenty-five years, the psychiatrist Lauretta Bender (1960) examined thirty-one boys and two girls who had killed or were accused of killing another person before reaching the age of sixteen years. Twenty of these boys were between eleven and fifteen years of age. Of the total, two were severely retarded, five were borderline defectives, twenty were found in the range of recorder IQ's from eighty to one hundred and ten, and six had higher IQ's. Eight of the thirty-three were nonreaders, and nine were retarded readers. Four were superior, and the others had average reading ability. The methods involved in these deaths included fire-setting, drowning, stabbing with sharp instruments, blows with a heavy object, and shooting. Six boys (11-14) had fatally shot their victims. Except for one case which seemed to be accidental, the shooting involved some planning and preparation or defective judgment. The final diagnostic classification of these thirty-three subjects included three familial defectives, twelve schizophrenics, three epileptics, seven chronic brain syndromes without epilepsy but impulse disorders, and ten psychoneurotic depressions relative to the situation. Bender felt that these studies pointed out certain significant factors which are dangerous symptoms of a psychiatric nature, especially when they occur in combinations. These were organic brain damage with an impulse disorder, childhood schizophrenic with preoccupations with death and killing, compulsive fire-setting, reading disability, extremely unfavorable home conditions and life experiences, and a personal experience with violent death. In speaking of "death wishes," while such wishes rarely find menacing expression, Bender felt they become dangerously exaggerated in five situations: (1) the family rivalry situation becomes intensively severe due to some external factors; (2) foster home situations fail to give positive experiences of love and security to a child who has already suffered deprivation and rejection from his own parents; (3) conditions of organic inferiority make the child feel helpless and in need of greater love than he receives; (4) educational difficulties such as a reading disability present insurmountable problems to a child who has insufficient help or support from the significant adults, such as parents and teachers; and (5) the child identifies with aggressive adults and a family pattern of violent behavior.

Banany (1947), in an attempt to study young persons who have been involved in homicide, gathered data concerning the personality formation, environmental influences, and subsequent development of twenty such persons; he traced their life course and reactions for at least five years following their offenses. In each of these cases the individual himself performed the act; none was merely technically involved by reason of having participated in an act committed by another. Sixteen white males, two black males, and one white and one black female were involved.

The composite statistical picture of these offenders portrayed a preponderance of unfavorable factors in home life and in personal and family relationships, although the data are also notable for the presence of many favorable factors. According to Banay (1947) :

> In 12 of the cases the father-mother relationship was unsatisfactory. In only 4 cases was the father's relationship to the son good. The mother-son (daughter) relationship was disturbed and harmful in 10 cases; the son (daughter)-mother factor inadequate and conflicting in 8 cases, ambivalent in 5, and affectionate in 6. Eight of the mothers and 7 of the fathers were pictured as righteous, industrious and emotionally stable. Eleven of the families were in comfortable circumstances; 5 were impoverished.
>
> There had been delinquency in the family in only 5 of the 20 cases; but in 12 cases there had been prior delinquencies in the subject's own records.

Also of note:

> Eight of the 20 perpetrated the homicides by stabbing, 7 by shooting. In 6 cases the victim was a member of the family circle. Sixteen fled from the scene of the crime, either fearful, relieved, nervous, or amnesic. Six of the crimes were committed during quarrels and 6 had sexual connotations.
>
> Twelve of the offenders were of average intelligence, 4 were superior, and 4 boderline. Fourteen had attended high school, 2 had gone

to college, and 4 had not gone beyond sixth grade. The physical condition of 9 was good. Six were classified as products of demoralized homelife, 3 as psychotic, 4 with borderline or defective intellect, 2 as emotionally starved, neglected and abused, and 5 as 'model children.'

MacDonald (1961) examined three children between the ages
of eleven and thirteen who had committed homicide. All three
had experienced an unhappy childhood due to harsh discipline, a
strict father, and an over-protective mother, Sibling rivalry was
also a contributing fact. The victims represented parental figures
as well as siblings.

In conjunction with the unhappy, unfavorable homelife, Sargent (1962) attempted to investigate the hypothesis that "sometimes the child who kills is acting as the unwitting lethal agent of
an adult (usually a parent) who unconsciously prompts the child
to kill so that he can vicariously enjoy the benefits of the act." This
hypothesis has also been supported by Easson and Steinhilber
(1965) who state that, "Murder and murderous violence committed
by children occur when there is parental fostering—albeit unconscious."

Sargent presented five cases demonstrating, with varying degrees
of clarity, the relationship between a child's homicide and an
adult's (unconscious) desire for the results of that crime. In this
study none of the children were aware that their acts were anything but their own doing, and all of them were willing to take
full responsibility for their acts. There was no tendency to project
the blame onto anyone else, nor were they able to see any connection between the behavior of the surviving provocative parent and
their own action.

While the surviving parents were questioned closely, none of
them were able to admit that they had consciously wished that the
victims were "somehow out of the way." They all felt guilty that
their children had become involved in their marital problems. Of
interest, most of them reacted to the killings with sufficient guilt to
suggest that in some indirect way they felt responsible for the
deaths of the victims. "In all the 'fatal' cases the surviving parents
—despite feelings of guilt—acted as though the deaths of their
spouses had relieved them of a burden" (Sargent). (While this is

interesting, it is entirely speculative.)

None of the children in this study had a prior history of disobedient or delinquent behavior. "It can be assumed, then," says Sargent, "that they were tractable and obedient to their parents' wishes. Might this also include obedience to the parents unconscious command to kill?"

"Unconscious motivation" is a favorite explanatory construct with psychodynamically oriented psychiatrists seeking to interpret adult as well as juvenile homicide. Satten et al. (1960), for example, accounts for several murders "without apparent motive" on the basis of alleged unconscious drives which caused the murderers to perceive innocuous and relatively unknown victims as provocative and thereby suitable targets for aggression." The authors allow for some range of individual differences when suggesting that some murderers can be provoked by almost any person who triggers their unconscious homicidal impulses, whereas others require a highly specific kind of stimulus person to release their murderous unconscious drives.

The Prediction of Homicide

Wertham, a forensic psychiatrist, advanced the theory of *catathymic crisis* as a potential paradigm for the typically explosive or impulsive homicide. Wertham refers to the "aberration of reasoning under the impact of emotional complexes (technically called catathymic) resulting in the outbreak of violence, directed towards oneself or others as a condition of 'catathymic crisis' " (1949). This condition consists of five stages: (1) the stage of initial thinking disorders which follows the original precipitating circumstances; (2) the stage of the crystallization of a plan, when the idea of a violent act emerges into consciousness; (3) the stage of extreme tension culminating in the violent crisis in which a violent act against oneself or others is attempted or carried out; (4) the stage of superficial normality beginning with a period of lifting or tension and calmness immediately after the violent act; and (5) the stage of insight and recovery, with the reestablishment of an inner equilibrium. If the last stage is not reached, the person may return to the second stage and think again of a violent act which has a symbolic psychological connection with the first violent act.

Central to this conception is the proposition that suicide and homicide, at a particular stage in the development of catathymic crisis, are equally possible occurrences. If this is true, Wertham has presented something very close to one of the rare empirically testable hypothesis in criminological theory. One would expect to find a potentially significant difference in the incidence of suicidal attempts between homicidal and nonhomicidal individuals.

Although he did not conceptualize his study as an empirical list of the catathymic crisis hypothesis, MacDonald's (1967) investigation of homicidal threat provides some evidence which is relevant to Wertham's theory. MacDonald examined the incidence of potential predictors of homicide among three groups—hospital patients who have made threats to kill, convicted homicide offenders, and a control group of hospital patients who have no history of homicidal behavior.

Suggested prognostic factors contributed by psychiatrists include: assaultive behavior, alcoholism, paranoid delusions, latent homosexuality, sadism, and desire for attention. MacDonald, however, had the clinical impression that parental brutality, maternal seduction, childhood firesetting, and cruelty to animals were also unfavorable prognistic factors in those who threaten homicide.

The incidence of eight potential prognostic factors was studied in three groups: the first group numbered 80 consecutive Colorado Psychopathic Hospital admissions who made verbal homicidal threats; the second group consisted of 192 convicted criminal offenders in the Colorado State Penitentiary; and the third group was composed of psychiatric patients admitted to a Veterans Administration hospital for reasons other than suicidal or homicidal ideas, threats, or attempts.

Twenty homicide threat and homicide offender pairs were matched according to race, sex, age within a decade of the time of the homicide, freedom from psychosis, and social class of the parents. The V.A. patients were also matched according to these criteria. The mean age in the threat-to-kill group was thirty-one years, six months, in the homicide group thirty-two years, and in the V.A. group thirty-seven years, nine months. Included in each group were three Spanish-Americans, one Negro, and one female.

Character disorders and alcoholism were prominent in all three groups, but the V.A. group included more patients diagnosed as neurotic. The factors studied included the following:

(1) *Parental brutality,* which not only generates aggression in the child but also provides a model for future behavior. . . . Parental brutality was recorded when whippings caused bruises, welts, or blood loss or when the child was struck with a closed fist.

(2) *Parental seduction,* which may arouse in the child of the opposite sex great anxiety and hostility that may find later expression in murderous attacks on the parent or substitute victim. Parental behavior may have a seductive effect even though it is not intended. Parental seduction was recorded when the parent of the opposite sex slept in the same room or bed with a child to the age of five or beyond, exposed breasts or genitals, had sexual relations with marital partner or lovers in the presence of the child, discussed sex in a pathological manner, or sexually assaulted the child.

(3) *Firesetting.* Fenichel has commented on the sadistic drives and vindictive impulses of firesetters. Bender (to be discussed later) noted compulsive firesetting as a feature of children and adolescents who have killed. Firesetting was recorded whenever there was destruction of property whether or not this was attributed to an accident while playing with matches. Pleasure in lighting matches and burning weeds were not classified as firesetting.

(4) *Cruelty to animals.* In childhood, sadism often shows itself in cruelty to animals. This factor was recorded when a child caused deliberate injury or death to animals or birds in a sadistic manner. Thus shooting rabbits and birds was not included but setting a cat on fire with gasoline and disembowelling a pet rabbit were included.

(5) *Police arrest record.* The general impression that persons who commit criminal homicide are usually first offenders has been questioned by Wolfgang, who found that 53

percent of his 154 white homicide offenders had a previous arrest record. The arrest rate in all three groups in this study was higher than 53 percent.

(6) *Arrests for assault.* Poorly controlled anger with assaultive behavior may well be an unfavorable factor in those who threaten to kill.

(7) *Alcoholism.* Alcohol impairs self-control, and homicide is commonly associated with drinking.

(8) *Attempted suicide.* Freud stated that no neurotic has thoughts of suicide who has not turned back towards himself murderous impulses against others. The intimate relationship between murder and suicide is illustrated by the finding that in England between 1952 and 1960 one-third of all murderers committed suicide. In the United States, Dublin and Bunzel found that in 611 cases of homicide nine percent of the slayers committed suicide. (four percent of the initial threat-to-kill group later committed suicide). (MacDonald, 1967).

Statistically significant differences for attempted suicides and for firesetting were reported among the three groups. There were not significant differences among the three groups with respect to parental brutality, parental seduction, cruelty to animals, alcoholism, a police arrest record, and arrest for assault.

The incidence of any of four factors was higher in the homicide threat group than in the control group. However, the presence of any one factor did not affect the likelihood of another factor being present.

The McNemar test was then applied to localize the differences among the three groups with regard to attempted suicide and firesetting. While firesetting was more frequent in the homicide-threat group than in the other two. Differences did not attain the level of statistical significance. The test did show a significantly higher incidence of attempted suicide in the homicide-threat group than in the homicide-offender group and in the control group. (Twelve of the homicide-threat group, compared to four in the homicide-offender group, had attempted suicide.) "These data suggest the following conclusions regarding persons who threaten homicide: Absence of suicide attempts indicates a higher risk of homicide. Prior suicide attempts indicate that the person is more likely to kill himself than to kill others (MacDonald)."

Aggravated Assault

In the introduction of their descriptive study of aggravated assault, Pittman and Handy (1970) note that, by popular definition, "the crime of aggravated assault is known as 'attempted murder,' 'assault with intent to kill,' 'assault with intent to do great bodily harm,' or just 'assault.'" Whether or not these distinctions constitute the basis for a meaningful subclassification of assaultive crimes, they do tend to offer support for the contention of many criminologists that aggravated assault and criminal homicide share many characteristics in common. Indeed, as Pittman and Handy themselves point out, "often the line dividing aggravated assault from homicide is so thin that a factor such as the speed of an ambulance carrying the victim to the hospital will determine whether the crime will be aggravated assault or homicide."

Pittman and Handy studied a random 25 percent sample of 965 aggravated assault cases seen in 1961 by the St. Louis police. They analyzed their sample in terms of such variables as time and place of occurrence, relationship and kinship status of the offender and the victim, the type of force employed, disposition of the offender, etc. The emergent pattern which characterized the model or "typical" case is described by the authors:

> An act of aggravated assault is more likely to occur on a weekend than during the week, specifically between 6:00 p.m. Friday and 6:00 a.m. Monday, with peak frequency on Saturday, between 10:00 p.m. and 11:00 p.m. While the event shows little likelihood of being more frequent in the four summer months considered together than in the winter, this type of assault peaks in the months of July and August.
>
> The crime will occur on a public street, or, secondly, in a residence. If a female is the offender, the act will occur indoors, if a male, outdoors. When offender and victims are related, the act will more likely occur in a residence than elsewhere. The general neighborhood context is one populated by lower socioeconomic groups—especially Negroes of this class.
>
> The weapon used by both men and women will in most cases be a knife, with a gun the second choice. In acts involving white offenders,

personal force will be used more often than in those involving Negro offenders.

Generally, the act will be reported to the police by the victim. The victim will be wounded seriously enough to require hospitalization, but the offender will not. More than 75 percent of the aggravated assault cases will be cleared by arrest within one hour after the crime occurs. A Negro is no more likely to be arrested for his crime than is a white.

These records indicate that neither the offender nor the victim will be under the influence of alcohol, nor will they have been drinking together, and neither will be a user of drugs.

The aggravated assault will be preceded by a verbal argument, most likely centering around a domestic quarrel.

The offender and victim will be of the same race and the same sex; there will be only one offender and one victim, and both will have been born outside of the city in which the crime occurs. Both will be of the same age group, usually between the ages of 20 and 35, with the offender being older. The victim will more often be married than the offender, but both will be blue collar workers. A female is more likely to be related to her male victim than is the male offender to his female victim. Females assault males with whom they have had a previously close relationship (such as dating, sexual intimacy, or common-law marriage) ; but this is not the case with males assaulting females.

Negro offenders are no more likely than their white counterparts to have a prior arrest record. Offenders in the age bracket 20-34 will in the majority of cases have a prior arrest record (Pittman and Handy, 1970).

A further component of the Pittman and Handy study was a comparison of their findings on aggravated assault with those reported previously by Wolfgang (1958). Despite dissimilarities in time periods, cities, and police departments, the comparison reveals more similarities than differences:

1. *Time.* For both aggravated assault and homicide, occurrences were higher on Saturday, with the time of day being most frequently late evening and early morning hours; for homicide, between 8:00 p.m. and 2:00 a.m., and for aggravated assault, between 4:00 p.m. and 3:00 a.m. The next highest time for both acts were the hours immediately following the highest period.

2. *Location.* Both crimes occurred more often on a public street than in any other location, with residences second. Summer months accounted for a higher percentage of crime in both cases, but to a greater extent for homicides. In winter these crimes occurred indoors. Females

committed both acts more often indoors than outdoors. If the victim and offender were related, the crime most likely occurred in a residence. Both types of acts usually took place in a lower class, Negro neighborhood.

3. *Weapon.* The weapon most often used differed between homicide and aggravated assault; a pistol or revolver was most common in homicides, while a knife was common in assaults. White females used a revolver or pistol most often in homicide, while they used a knife most often in assault.

4. *Police Processing.* No other Index Crime was involved in the majority of both crimes, and there was a high cleanup rate for both, although it was higher for homicides. The offender in both crimes was arrested within a short time of committing the act, and he was known to either witnesses or police. Clearance was higher for females and Negroes than for males and whites, in both homicide and assault.

5. *Alcohol Involvement.* The ingestion of alcohol was more common in homicide than in assault, as was a drinking episode between offender and victim prior to the crime.

6. *Situational Context.* Verbal arguments preceded both crimes, but alcohol was involved in the arguments in homicide situations more often than in aggravated assault cases.

7. *Offender-Victim Relationship.* For both crimes, the victim and offender were typically of the same age, sex, and race. There were most often only one victim and one offender. Negro males were disproportionately involved in both types of crime. The participants in both acts were usually married, blue collar workers, and the victims of interracial assaults were white more often than Negroes. In acts of homicide, a wife attacked her husband more often than a husband attacked his wife, while the reverse was the case in aggravated assaults.

8. *Prior Arrest Records.* For both homicide and aggravated assault, the majority of the victims had no prior record, while the majority of the offenders did. For homicide offenders, two-thirds had a prior record of a crime against the person, while for aggravated assault the number of offenders having this type of record, if one expects peace disturbance, was negligible.

Further support of the Pittman and Handy findings were reported by Pokorny (1970), who compared homicide, aggravated assault, suicide, and attempted sucide. Pokorny, concluded that homicide and aggravated assault "were similar in all aspects studied, which suggest that these are basically the same category of behavior."

VIOLENT CRIME AND THE CULTURAL CONTEXT

At the conclusion of their study, Pittman and Handy (1970) suggest that the chief factor in the underlying similarity of patterns in criminal homicide and aggravated assault is the social or cultural milieu in which both crimes originate: "Both acts, of course, are reflections of population sub-groupings which tend to externalize their aggression when confronted with conflict situations." The contribution of what Glaser et. al. (1968) have termed the "subculture of violence" to the causal background of violent crime has been stated in both general and specific terms. The 1967 crime commission report calls the linkage between slum conditions and violent crime "one of the most fully documented facts about crime" in our possession.

The general features of the urban areas that exhibit the highest rates of violent crime are depressingly familiar. As the terminal report of the *National Commission on the Causes and Prevention of Violence* (1970) observes, both the perpetrators and victims of violent crime live in sections of the city characterized by:

    low income
    physical deterioration
    dependency
    racial and ethnic concentrations
    broken homes
    working mothers
    low levels of education and vocational skills
    high unemployment
    high proportions of single males
    overcrowded and substandard housing
    low rates of home ownership or single-family dwellings
    mixed land use
    high population density

The review of the evidence on violent crime and the violent offender led the Commission to summarize their conclusions in the following "profile":

1. Violent crime in the U.S. is primarily a phenomenon of large cities.

2. Violent crime in the city is overwhelmingly committed by males.
3. Violent crime in the city is concentrated especially among youths between the ages of fifteen and twenty-four.
4. Violent crime in the city is committed primarily by individuals at the lower end of the occupational scale.
5. Violent crime in the city stems disproportionately from the ghetto slum where most Negroes live.
6. The victims of assaultive violence in the cities generally have the same characteristics as the offenders; victimization rates are generally highest for males, youths, poor persons, and blacks. Robbery victims, however, are very often older whites.
7. Unlike robbery, the violent crimes of homicides, assault, and rape tend to be acts of passion among intimates and acquaintances.
8. By far the greatest proportion of all serious violence is committed by repeaters.
9. Americans generally are no strangers to violent crime. The homicide rate for the United States is more than twice that of our nearest competitor, Finland.

We shall return to some of these points for further discussion, particularly the last two in the list.

Subculture of Violence

Glaser and his colleagues (1968) suggest that one possibly important basis for violent crime in the urban ghetto "may be simply that in some groups, more than in others, the socially expected behavior in certain common situations is an act of violence." They refer to the presence of "a shared belief that an affront, rebuff, or insult obliges the recipient to react with physical violence."

Earlier, we noted that the southeastern states (Georgia, Florida, Alabama, Mississipi, South Carolina) have a disproportionately higher rate for criminal homicide, aggravated assault, and robbery[2]

---

[2]Interestingly enough, the geographical distribution of forcible rape resembles that of property offenses more than that of homicide or aggravated assault. The same subculture that inculcates a lack of consideration for someone else's property rights apparently instills an exploitative attitude toward women.

than other geographical areas of the country. Glaser and his associates suggest that: (1) the cultural values of what Wolfgang and Ferracuti (1967) have called a "subculture of violence" are more intense in the southeast than in other parts of the U.S.; (2) this subculture is shared by both whites and blacks in this region; and (3) the cultural values of this subculture are transferred largely intact to the urban north by black and white migrants alike.

Pettigrew and Spier (1962) have provided some corroboration for these interpretations. They have shown empirically that the geographical variation of *black homicide rates in the U.S. can be accounted for by the white homicide rate of the state in which the blacks were reared.* The persistence of the cultural pattern which socially sanctions violent behavior may be equally strong among white migrants from the southeast; unfortunately, separate data are not available for these different groups within the white urban population.

Further evidence of a somewhat indirect nature is available from the study conducted by Bensing and Schroeder (1960). An analysis of homicide rates in the city of Cleveland disclosed that homicide rates were highest in those neighborhoods where median income level was lowest, regardless of the racial character of the neighborhood.

Violence in American Culture

While there seems to be substantial evidence for existence of subcultural norms and values within the ghetto which foster violent behavior, we must relate this subculture to the larger context of American majority cultural and social values. Americans—black and white—as the Commission report reminds us are no strangers to violence. A sampling of advertising appeals by Wolfgang (1969) yielded the following specimens:

Glamour and thrills in the cars are meant to be associated with speed and power through such verbs as *roars, growls;* adjectives like *dynamic, powerful, exciting, wild, ferocious, swinging;* nouns like *missile, rocket, tiger, stinger.* Phrases of advertising include: just pull the trigger, start billing yourself as the human cannon ball; want action?; fire the second stage, aim it at the road. Longer excerpts make clear the intended associations: (a) For stab-and-steer men, there is a new 3-speed automatic you can lock in any gear . . . make small noises in your throat. Atta boy, tiger; (b) Bring on the Mustangs, Wildcats, Impalas . . . We'll even squash a few Spyders while we're at it. Dodge has made it a little harder to survive in the asphalt jungle. They just uncaged the Coronet; (c) This year let yourself go for power; (d) All new! All muscle! . . . With advanced thrust engineering . . . and an almost neurotic urge to get going. Drive it like you hate it—it's cheaper than psychiatry!

Movie fare, if anything, presents an even more lurid situation, with unrestrained sadism and gratuitous violence.[2]

Perhaps the real issue, as Wolfgang suggests, is not that certain features of American mass culture may "promote acceptability of male violence or make violence so banal that large segments of the population are no longer sensitive to expressions of violence" (1969). Whether or not a steady diet of movie and TV violence is causally linked in some direct way to propensities toward the commission of violent crimes is a question for which no scientific research can presently supply an answer. On the other hand, Wolfgang notes:

> The sheer frequency of screened violence, its intensity as well as context, and the myriad forms it takes, cannot be claimed to instill firm notions of non-violence in the children who are witnesses. Unless the logic of the assertion that violence in mass media encourages violent behavior is destroyed by scientifically acceptable evidence, we play dangerous games with the socialization process and its adult products (1969).

Theories of Aggression

The fundamentally atheoretical orientation of American criminology is nowhere more strikingly highlighted than in the almost

---

[2]Television and movies have reached the "zenith" or "nadir" depending on your values, in their capacity to portray violence. *Newsweek* movie critic Joseph Morgenstern describes the level of violence offered movie patrons in 1972:

"In the highly praised 'A Clockwork Orange,' roving bands of dehumanized hoodlums deal out a cool, affectless violence that includes kicking, stomping, gang rape and beating a woman's brains out with a big phallic sculpture. 'Straw Dogs' dispenses with the cool and comes to a devastatingly powerful climax of rape, knifing, mutilation, acidtossing, shooting, beating and burning. Santa Claus tries to crush a fallen kid's rib cage in the 'French Connection.' A maniac 'hippie' in 'Dirty Harry' does unspeakable violence to his victims; what the detective hero does to the maniac hippie is not more speakable and equally visible" *(Newsweek,* February 14, 1972). As any psychologist with a passing knowledge of the role of "modeling behavior" in learning theory can attest, persons feasting on such fare do not typically leave the theater and become pacifists.

complete absence in the professional literature of any serious efforts to relate the empirical facts on violent crime to some theoretical framework, within which the facts might assume some real generality. Despite the existence of an impressively large body of theory and experimentation in psychology with regard to aggression and aggressive behavior, the criminologist seems to have ignored any potential contributions from this source—with the possible exception of the psychodynamic interpretations of the psychoanalyst and psychiatrist. In referring briefly in the following section to recent and current theoretical and experimental studies of aggressive behavior, we hope to encourage our readers to end this professional hiatus.

Attempts to understand and interpret human violence in its myriad forms have led to a variety of theoretical formulation; some of them vague and speculative, others tied fairly closely to empirical evidence. Among the former, we should have to place those theories which postulate the existence of an instinct of aggression in the human species. According to this type of theory, aggressive behavior is a human characteristic that may admit of some modification through learning, but which is fundamentally ineradicable to the species. Some of these formulations postulate a continuous distribution of the aggressive instinct in infra-human species; some contend that aggression is specific to primates. We can only acknowledge that ethological evidence on nearly every point of contention is much too sketchy and inconclusive to justify a detailed examination of instinct theory.

Similarly, we must exclude Freud's postulate of a *death instinct* (Thanatos), the counterpoise to the so called *life instinct* (Eros). In fairness to Freud, we must note that while the concept of death instinct has been attacked as speculative and metaphysical, even by some Freudians, it was Freud's formulation of an aggressive instinct as one of the primary motivational constructs of human behavior which aroused professional interest among psychologists in the problem of aggression.

In this section, we shall examine briefly three theoretical formulations concerning the antecedents and dynamics of aggressive behavior which have all been subjected to experimental investigation. They are: (1) the frustration-aggression hypothesis; (2) aggression as instrumental response; and (3) aggression as a socially learned (modeled) response. These theories are of incalculable importance for the criminologist because they have structured most criminological thought on both the genesis and the control or modification of aggressive behavior.

The Frustration-Aggression Hypothesis

The first extended systematic research program on the antecedents of aggressive behavior came in the 1930's with the Yale school, including Dollard Miller, Doob, Mowrer and Sears. Their formulation, the frustration-aggressive hypothesis, became the first scientific attempt to explain the occurrence of aggressive behavior and the conditions that could modify it.

The original hypothesis can be roughly phrased in the following manner: Aggression is always a consequence of frustration, and frustration always results in some aggression (Dollard et al., 1939). Frustration is most succinctly identified when one can specify two things: (1) that the organism could have been expected to perform certain acts, and (2) that these acts have been prevented from occurring. Any sequence of behavior which has as its goal response, i.e. injury to the person to whom it is directed, is called "aggression," and this aggression is considered the primary and characteristic reaction to frustration. The independent definition of aggression then, is an act whose goal response is to injure an organism or a surrogate organism. The dependent definition of aggression (embedded in their theoretical system) is that response which follows frustration, reducing only the secondary frustration-produced instigation and leaving the strength of the original instigation unaffected.

Putting the hypotheses into quantifiable form, the authors phrased it in the following way: The strength of instigation to aggression varies directly with the amount of frustration. Phrased in these terms there are three factors that account for the amount of frustration and consequently the strength of instigation to aggression: (1) the strength of the instigation of the frustrated response (was the dog hungry or satiated when it was prevented from eating); (2) the degree of interference with the frustrated response (slight vs. great distraction) ; and (3) the number of frustrated response-sequences. Also, essential to this formulation are the effects of punishment anticipated to be a consequence of that action.

In summary, the original theoretical formulation of the frustration-aggression hypothesis posits that though there are other consequences of frustration (substitute responses and rational problem solving) some instigation to aggression is an inevitable result of the organism being frustrated. The aggression need not always be overt. It may be expressed in fantasy, dreams, or well-thought out plans of revenge. Furthermore, the aggression may be displaced to some altogether innocent source (not the frustrating agent) or towards oneself. The strongest instigation aroused by frustration is to acts of aggression directed against the agent perceived to be the source; progressively weaker instigations are aroused to progressively less direct acts of aggression.

The frustration-aggression hypothesis is crammed with postulates that have never been adequately tested. Quantification of postulates relating to the strength of the instigation to aggress has never been fully developed, and research along where dimensions has not yielded much concrete verification. Assumptions about the role of the expression of aggression in fantasy and dreams conspicuously indicate Dollard's basic allegiance to Freud's system and his effort to elaborate Freudian hypotheses within the framework of objective, behavioral science. This orientation alone has caused some critics to severely question the underlying rationale of his system, but the overwhelming bulk of criticism has been directed toward the basic hypothesis that frustration always leads to aggression.

Though popularity of the approach in its early years was great, there was enough immediate criticism of the primitive frustration-aggression link, that Miller (1941) saw fit to change the hypothesis, putting it into a more reasonable, less dogmatic form. He amended the basic hypothesis to read that frustration produces instigations to a number of different types of response, one of which is an instigation to aggression. This reformulation meant that if other responses were stronger than the instigation to aggress, they will occur first and prevent, at least temporarily, the occurrence of aggression. Though this theoretical modification, by one of the authors of the original hypothesis, recognized the over-simplification of the first effort, Buss (1961) reports that many psychologists still accept the original form of the frustration-aggression hypothesis that denies any antecedents of aggression other than frustration.

Aggression as an Instrumental Response

Many of the attacks on the frustration-aggression hypothesis have concentrated on demonstrating that aggression in not the only possible reaction to frustration, and that it may not even be the primary one. Anthropologists, such as Bateson (1941), pointed out that in some cultures, such as that of the Balineses, aggression was by no means a typical response to frustration. Baker, Dembo, and Lewin (1941) demonstrated that nursery-school children may regress when frustrated. Scott (1958) claims that the proposition that aggression always follows frustration, fails to account for many animals observations. For instance, with the stickleback, frustration habitually results in nest-building activity, definitely a non-aggressive behavior. He feels that there are more than enough animal observations to prove that though frustration is "highly likely" to produce aggression, the result may very well be other kinds of behavior. There are many instances where frustration actually seems to interfere with aggressive behavior, and he concludes that frustration leads to aggression only in a situation where the organism has a habit of being aggressive.

However, as Yates (1962) points out, this kind of attack is primarily meaningless because of Miller's (1941) early recognition of the inadequacy of the provisional frustration-aggression hypothesis. This resulted in an acknowledgement that frustration produces instigations to several different types of response, one of which is aggression. It seems that many critics choose only to attack the earliest form of the hypothesis, which was so obviously oversimplified that one of the authors changed it himself.

The kind of criticism that seems most meaningful is the type provided by Buss (1961); one that questions not only the inevitability of aggression following frustration, but also of frustration necessarily preceding aggression. Epstein and Taylor (1967) note that conceiving of the frustration-aggression link as reflex-like fails to consider that social learning establishes how a person reacts; circumstances that arouse a person to anger, no less than those that determine whether he will act on his anger, are culturally determined. Neither, they feel, bears an invariant relationship to frustration.

Buss (1961) conceives of aggression as an instrumental response that administers punishment. The term "aggression" includes as large number of responses, differing in topography, energy expenditure, and consequences. However, all consist of: (1) the delivery of noxious stimuli, and (2) an interpersonal context. The two major classes of reinforcement occurring as a consequence of aggressive behavior are someone suffering injury or being in pain, and extrinsic rewards.

Buss feels that Dollard's approach deals only with "angry aggression," which is reinforced by the victim's pain. Almost completely neglected is the class of instrumentally aggressive responses, where the attainment of some extrinsic reinforcment or the cessation of aversive stimuli are the main consequences. He feels that "anger" (a response with facial-skeletal and autonomic components) need not be present in aggression. His approach is a nondrive approach to aggression; no assumption is made that aggression must be preceded by a drive state of any kind.

Berkowitz (1962) gives the example of a person stepping on someone's toes as being capable of arousing anger if this action interrupted the person's internal response oriented toward the preservation of attainment of security and comfort. Buss (1966) feels that using this kind of definition makes it difficult to conceive of a behavior sequence where "some drive" is not being interfered with, especially when things such as "security and comfort" are included as drives. With Berkowitz's contextual framework, "frustration" is bound to be everpresent and would therefore be an antecedent of not only aggressive behavior, but just about all behavior. Buss' definition of "frustration" is much more restricted: the blocking of ongoing instrumental behavior that had led to reinforcement in the past history of the organism.

Buss (1961) recognizes that when a person is engaged in instrumental behavior that has led to reinforcement in the past, and this behavior is blocked, aggression may be successful in overcoming this interference. Also, when a person is confronted with noxious stimuli, one way of eliminating these stimuli is to attack the delivery source. So, there are at least two classes of situations that serve as antecedents of aggression: frustration and noxious stimuli.

The emphasis that Dollard, Maier, and others have put on frustration has led to the neglect of other types of antecedents, such as noxious stimuli as well as the entire concept of aggression as an instrumental response. Frustration is only *one* antecedent and probably not the most potent one, as indicated by the experimenter's dependence on using insults (a form of noxious stimulation) to elicit aggression in the lab.

Briefly, Buss', position is that the strength of aggressive responses is determined by four variables. First, the frequency and intensity of the antecedents of aggression (attack, frustration, and annoyers) constitute one determinant of aggressiveness. Second, and the factor generally neglected by frustration-aggression theorists, is the reinforcement history of the response. Aggression owes its habit strength to the consequences that follow. The reinforcement may be internal, such as a sharp drop in physiological "anger" level or external, such as the elimination of a noxious stimulus, or the attainment of some external reward. A study by Davitz (1952) demonstrates both the inadequacy of the frustration-aggression hypothesis and the importance of direct training in the development of aggression modes of response. In this study, half the subjects were rewarded with praise and approval for making aggressive and competitive responses during training. The other half were similarly rewarded for cooperative and constructive responses. Then all the children were frustrated by exposure to a film that was interrupted just as it approached the climax. At this point, the children were returned to a free-play situation. Children who had been reinforced for constructive play responded more constructively in the free-play situation and vice-versa. Bandura and Walters (1963) interpret this study as demonstrating that "frustration" should be viewed simply as stressful stimuli that will elicit, according to the stimuli that are present, the response pattern that is currently dominant in the organism's response hierarchy.

The third factor that will affect aggressiveness is social facilitation: i.e. group tendencies and attitudes toward aggression. The fourth factor is temperament, which refers to characteristics of behavior that appear early in life and remain relatively unchanged. Included here is the organism's impulsiveness (ability to delay gratification), activity level, intensity of reaction, and independence of group pressures. Most of Buss' experimental and theoretical work has concentrated on the reinforcement history of aggressive responses.

Aggression as a Socially Learned (Modeled) Response

The frustration-aggression position has argued that aggression is a response to frustration. The instrumental learning approach (Buss) emphasizes the consequences (reinforcement) of aggressive behavior as most important in the development and maintenance aggression. Still another approach, the "social learning" or "modeling" of Bandura, Walters, and others, stresses the importance of observational learning in the acquisition of aggressive behavior. This orientation emphasizes the strong influence on the learning of aggression that occurs from seeing another person (a model) perform a similar aggressive response.

Bandura and Walters (1962), in reviewing the frustration-aggression hypothesis, point out that the crucial problems of how aggressive responses are originally learned, what form the aggressive responses initially take, and the role of factors, other than interference with an ongoing response-sequence, involved in the shaping and maintaining of aggressive behavior are largely ignored. They feel that it has most importantly inhibited the search for antecedents of aggression other than ones that have been called "frustrating."

They feel that the same learning principles that account for the development of other social responses can account for the learning of aggressive responses. Extensive experimental work by Bandura and his co-workers has demonstrated that one important way in which novel responses can be elicited is through learning by exposure to cues produced by the behavior of others; i.e. through imitation. Once these responses are elicited, they can be reinforced and become relatively dominant in the habit hierarchies which are elicited by cues similar to those present during acquisition.

Influential adults (parents and experimenters) can provide aggressive role-models and sometimes reinforce aggressive behavior when it occurs. Studies by Bandura and Hutson (1961), and Bandura, Ross, and Ross (1961, 1962) have shown that the mere observation of aggressive models, regardless of the nature of the relationship between the model and the child, is sufficient to produce imitative aggression; these imitative responses generalize to settings where the model is absent, and even film-mediated aggressive models are effective in producing the effect. If the model is shown being reinforced for his aggressiveness, the children will show greater aggressiveness in later tasks. The authors believe that children learn the aggressiveness, even if the model is punished, but fail to perform it, unless it is reinforced. (Bandura, Ross, and Ross, 1963).

In summarizing the relationship between frustration and aggression, Bandura and Walters (1963) conclude that frustration may produce a temporary increase in drive and lead to more vigorous responding. Interference with the ongoing response-sequence may serve as a stimulus for eliciting response-hierarchies in which, because of past learning, pain-producing responses tend to be dominant. Past experience, in the form of prior reinforcement of aggressive behavior and exposure to aggressive models, make the occurrence of aggressive responses to frustration more probable. Responses of high magnitude, such as kicking an object, are usually learned in non-frustrating situations. But, once these responses are learned they can be elicited under frustrating conditions.

Walters and Brown (1963) elucidate this point clearly in an experiment where they trained boys to hit a Bobo doll. Two of the groups were reinforced with marbles, one on a continuous reinforcement schedule and one on a fixed ratio. The third group received no reinforcement. Then half of each group was frustrated in a task. In the test period, each child was paired with another child who had been trained to hit the doll and the two competed in physical contact games, with aggressive responses being tallied. The results indicated that there were no difference in aggression between the frustrated and non-frustrated groups, but the subjects trained on the FR schedule exhibited significantly non-aggressive responses than the other groups. The authors conclude that the relationship between frustration and aggression is by no means a necessary one. Physically aggressive responses may be learned under non-frustrative conditions (direct reinforcement during play) and then transferred to interpersonal situations. Frustration, in the form of delay or withholding rewards, appears to increase the intensity of children's responses and thus may transform a harmless response into one that is capable of inflicting pain. Also, the occurrence of frustration inevitable produces stimulus changes, both internal and external, and consequently may elicit response hierarchies in which, because of past learning, pain-producing responses are dominant.

THE CONTROL AND PREVENTION OF VIOLENT CRIMES

We have referred to an imposing array of empirical studies and findings during the course of this discussion on homicide and aggravated assault. How reliable and valid are these findings and the generalizations based upon them? What can we say with confidence about crimes of violence in the U.S. and those who commit such crimes?

1. *Has the rate of violent crime increased or decreased in recent years?*

The Report of the National Commission on the Causes and Prevention of Violence (1970) states that, "between 1960 and 1968, the national rate of criminal homicide per 100,000 population increased 36 percent."

The National Parole Institute publication (Glaser, Kenefick, and O'Leary, 1968), to which we have previously alluded, states a seemingly contradictory interpretation concerning the incidence of homicide:

> Despite the complexities and inconsistencies in legal labels for violent offenders and despite the incompleteness of statistical reporting for some of these offenses, a few trends in crimes of violence are apparent. First, *homicide has clearly declined in the past few decades* (emphasis added).

What apparently has happened is that the homicide rate has risen dramatically in the past decade but has not reached the level of depression years.

2. *Are violent crimes committed primarily by first-offenders or repeaters?*

According to the National Commission report (1970), "By far the greatest proportion of all serious violence is committed by repeaters."

Glaser et al. (1968), on the other hand, has this to say about the recidivist:

> A previous National Parole Institute publication *(Personal Characteristics and Parole Outcome*. Washington, D.C.: U.S. Government Printing Office, 1955). showed that crimes of violence are associated with lower parole violation rates than are other offenses. Data from Pennsylvania, easily checked in other states, also indicate that *these violent offenders are less likely than any other type of criminal to repeat the same offense, should they fail on parole (emphasis added).*

3. *Does drinking play a significant role in violent crimes?*

According to the National Commission (1970), "The victim, the offender, or both are likely to have been drinking prior to homicide, assault, and rape."

In analyzing their data on aggravated assault, Pittman and Handy (1970) concluded that "neither the offender nor the victim will be under the influence of alcohol, nor will they have been drinking together."

The points of disparity at issue in the above passages do not involve complex and controversial positions on causation or remediation of violence; they are simple matters of factual interpretation and reporting. If it is possible to find such glaring discrepancies at this level of analysis, one despaires of finding professional consensus with regard to more involved and potentially inflammatory controversial issues such as those named above.

Violent crimes may represent in the first instance, as Daniel P. Moynihan (1969) has stated, "noting more complex than the failure of law enforcement." But, it is difficult to see the validity of his argument with respect to criminal homicide and aggravated assault. Increased day-and-night foot patrols and a massive increase in police-community relations programs may produce some impact upon the incidence of crimes such as forcible rape and robbery. Homicide and assault, as we have seen, are predominantly passionate crimes among intimates or acquaintances. In other words, they are inherently outside the potential reach of law enforcement agencies. There seems little doubt that the passage of adequate, and long-delayed, legislation on gun sales and distribution, particularly hand guns, might represent a more realistic approach to the reduction of criminal homicide in the U.S. than an increase in metropolitan police personnel.

As Moynihan (1969) notes, "when authority systems collapse they are replaced by power systems, which are coercive." The poverty and social isolation of minority groups in the American city is inseparable from the feeble and ineffectual efforts of obsolescent and archaic urban governments to cope with urban problems. Says Moynihan:

> Black rage and white resistance, Third World separatism, and restricted covenants all may define a collapse in the integuments of the social contract; but, again, in the first instance, they represent, for the most part, simply the failure of urban arrangements to meet the expectations of the urban population in the area of jobs, schools, housing, transportation, public health, administrative responsiveness, and political flexibility.

In the long view, the factors which are primarily responsible for violent crime—the dismal list compiled by the National Commission on the Causes and Prevention of Violence—will only yield to persistent efforts at thorough social and humanitarian reform. In the short view, however, no means can be ignored that might increase the effectiveness of control.

Summary

The historical interest that researchers have in studying aggression centers around the intuitive feeling that "aggression" is a particular kind of response, with unique characteristics and antecedents. Freud considered aggression a manifestation of one of the two basic drives in the human being, and though more recent personality theorists and researchers have altered this conception considerably, some still conceive of aggression as a more or less unique response tendency.

Dollard and Miller, the first experimentalists to systematically study aggression, were heavily influenced by Freudian concepts and conceived of aggression as a peculiar response. After all, it was considered by them to be a response that inevitably followed certain stimuli that occurred in a social situation. How many other complex social responses have ever been considered to occur in such a reflex-like manner?

Recent theoretical positions (Buss, Bandurs, etc.) have moved away from the conception of aggression as a unique response. Instead, modern approaches have tended to view aggression as a more conventional, learned response, not much different than any other human response. Buss has consistently advocated that aggression hasn't the unique property of being an unconditioned reaction to frustration. Rather, it is conceptualized primary as an instrumental response, established and maintained by environmental contingencies. Aggressive behavior, like other behavior, continues to the extent that is effective in manipulating the environment (producing positive consequences from the environment) and ceases to the extent that it fails to elicit positive consequences (through extinction and/or punishment).

Bandura's social learning position similarly views aggressive behavior as just another response, determined by environmental circumstances. Aggressive behavior can be learned through imitation of a model exhibiting such behavior. Though this view of aggression is somewhat different from a strict operant approach, the difference is in the basic learning paradigm that it proposes, and not in its conception of aggression as a unique response. Here, too, aggression is learned just as any other response class. The major difference between Bandura's and Buss' positions on aggression is in terms of their different models of learning.

Both approaches have received a great deal of experimental support. It has been quite thoroughly demonstrated that aggressive behavior can be learned through imitation, and that it can be maintained through positive reinforcement. One is tempted to ride along with the times and accept the non-uniqueness of aggressive behavior (or any other behavior) and leave the study of aggression to be incoporated into the larger framework of an operant-social learning position. This would treat it as a response possessing important social implications, but lacking any other unique characteristics.

In looking to the future several directions can be clearly seen. In relation to extinction-induced aggression, this research should be extended to humans to see if the phenomenon holds up. If the discontinuance or irregularity of positive reinforcement can lead to aggressive tendencies, it seems logical that, while extinguishing certain deviant behaviors, we may "create" or elicit a degree of aggressive behavior. If this is demonstrated, it means that we should probably always teach someone alternative, constructive behavior, while extinguishing other behavior. This has been recognized (for different reasons) in regard to punishment techniques, but the importance of it in all conditioning procedures may have to be considered.

Besides the possibility of rediscovering some frustration-aggression link in humans, there are even wider issues to be dealt with in the study of human aggression. For example, one important question is whether these different theoretical approaches toward aggression contradict or complement one another. Does Bandura's social learning theory contradict the frustration-aggression hypothesis? Is it that the frustration-aggression hypothesis explains certain phenomena of aggression and modeling explains others?

A parallel situation exists in the more general area of basic learning theory. Though for years some psychologists have tried to prove that all learning eventually boils down to classical conditioning *or* instrumental conditioning, it seems quite apparent that neither system seems adequate to explain all behavioral phenomena. There are many cognitive theorists who claim that *both* of these theories together can't account for all learning. We seem to accept this ambiguity, and learning theorists, for the most part, are now attempting to map out just what situations and which responses lend themselves most naturally to which type of learning.

The same type of approach must be followed in the study of aggression. It seems clear, if one can believe the literature, that aggressive behavior can be acquired in several different ways. Some evidence cited re-opens the possibility that some aggressive behavior is not accounted for through instrumental or classical conditioning. Through experiments that allow more than one kind of response to a stimulus situation, we may start to be able to map out aggression more finely. If we expose a person to a model who is engaged in constructive behavior, and then put him into a frustrating situation where he may express aggressive or constructive behavior, which will he exhibit? The prediction can not be a straightforward, absolute one. Instead, it will most surely depend on the stimulus factors in the situation. Some of these stimulus parameters have been touched upon, others hardly looked at. Pitting theoretical predictions against each other, while varying the relevant parameters of the situation may begin to yield precise, less theory-bound predictions of when aggression will occur and to what degree of intensity.

Meanwhile, we must be able to accept the fact that each theory will predict in certain situations, and that each theoretical account of aggression holds up under some conditions. The task ahead for researchers is to ascertain which stimulus factors must be taken into account to yield more consistent, demarcated predictions.

REFERENCES

Banay, R. S.: Homicide among children. *Federal Probation, 11*:13-19, 1947.

Bandura, A., Ross, D., and Ross, S. A.: Transmission of aggression through imitation of aggressive models. *Journal of Abnormal and Social Psychology, 43*:575-582, 1961.

Bandura, A., Ross, D., and Ross, S. A.: Imitation of film-mediated aggressive models. *Journal of Abnormal and Social Psychology, 44*:213-218, 1962.

Bandura, A., Ross, D., and Ross, S. A.: "Vicarious" reinforcement and imitation. *Journal of Abnormal and Social Psychology, 45*:163-174, 1963.

Bandura, A., and Walters, R. H.: Aggression. In Stevenson, H. W. (Ed.): *Child Psychology.* Chicago, University of Chicago Press, 1963.

Barker, R. G., Dembo, T., and Lewin, K.: Frustration and aggression: an experiment with young children. *University of Iowa's Studies in Child Welfare, 18*:1-314, 1941.

Bateson, G.: The frustration and reduction of hostility. *Psychological Review, 43*:350-355, 1941.

Bender, L.: Children and adolescents who have killed. *American Journal of Psychiatry, 116*:510-513, 1961.

Bensing, R. C., and Schroeder, O.: *Homicide in an Urban Community.* Springfield, Charles C Thomas, 1960.

Berkowitz, L.: *Aggression: a Social-Psychological Analysis.* New York, McGraw-Hill, 1962.

Blackman, N., Weiss, J., and Lamberti, J. W.: The sudden murderer. *Archives of General Psychiatry, 8*:289-294, 1963.

Bloch, H. A., and Geis, G.: *Man, Crime, and Society.* New York, Random House, 1962.

Buss, A. H.: *The Psychology of Aggression.* New York, Wiley, 1961.

Buss, A. H.: Instrumentality of aggression, feedback, and frustration as determinants of physical aggression. *Journal of Personality and Social Psychology, 3:*153-162, 1966.

Davitz, J.: The effects of previous training on post-frustration behavior. *Journal of Abnormal and Social Psychology, 47:*309-315, 1952.

Dollard, J., Miller, N.E., Doob, L. W., Mowrer, O. H., and Sears, R. E.: *Frustration and Aggression.* New Haven, Yale University Press, 1939.

Epstein, S., and Taylor, S. P.: Instigation to aggression as a function of degree of defeat and perceived aggressive intent of the opponent. *Journal of Personality. 35:*265-289, 1967.

Glaser, D., Kenefick, D., and O'Leary, V.: *The Violent Offender.* Washington, U. S. Government Printing Office, 1968.

MacDonald, J. M.: *The Murderer and his Victim.* Springfield, Charles C Thomas, 1961.

MacDonald, J. M.: Homicidal threats. *American Journal of Psychiatry, 124:* 61-68, 1967.

Miller, N. E.: The frustration-aggression hypothesis. *Psychological Review, 48:*337-342, 1941.

Moynihan, D. P.: Introduction. *Violent Crime: Homicide, Assault, Rape, the Causes and Prevention of Violence.* New York, George Braziller, 1969.

Moynihan, D. P.: Introduction. *Violent Crime: Homicide, Assault, Aape, Robbery,* New York, George Braziller, 1969.

National Commission on the Causes and Prevention of Violence: Final Report. New York, Praeger, 1970.

Pettigrew, T. F., and Spier, Rosalind, B.: The ecological structure of Negro homicide. *American Journal of Sociology, 67:*621-629, 1962.

Pittman, D. J., and Handy, W. J.: Patterns in criminal aggravated assault. In Cohen, B. (Ed.): *Crime in America: Perspectives on Criminal and Delinquent Behavior.* Itasca, Peacock, 1970.

Pokorny, A. D.: Human violence: a comparison of homicide, aggravated assault, suicide, and attempted suicide. In Cohen, B. (Ed.): *Crime in America: Perspectives on Criminal and Delinquent Behavior.* Itasca, Peacock, 1970.

Sargent, D.: Children who kill—a family conspiracy? *Social Work, 7:*35-42, 1962.

Satten, J., Menninger, K., Rosen, I., and Mayman, M.: Murder without apparent motive. *American Journal of Psychiatry, 117:*48-53, 1960.

Scott, J. P.: *Aggression.* Chicago, University of Chicago Press, 1958.

Stearns, A. W.: Murder by adolescents with obscure motivation. *American Journal of Psychiatry, 114:*303-305, 1957.

Uniform Crime Report for 1970. Washington, U. S. Government Printing Office, 1971.

Walters, R. H., Brown, M.: Studies of reinforcement to aggression: transfer of responses to an interpersonal situation. *Child Development, 34*:543-551, 1963.

Wertham, F.: *The Show of Violence*. New York, Doubleday, 1949.

Wolfgang, M. E.: *Patterns in Criminal Homicide*. Philadelphia, University of Pennsylvania Press, 1958.

Wolfgang, M. E.: Violent Behavior. Cambridge, W. Heffer and Sons, 1969.

Chapter 12

ORGANIZED CRIME, WHITE-COLLAR CRIME, PROFESSIONAL CRIMINALS

THE AMERICAN AMBIVALENCE toward gambling is illustrated by a leading Catholic Bishop who told a Boston protestant minister: "Gambling in moderation is not a sin." "Yes," replied the Protestant minister, "but in this state, it is a crime." As Daniel Bell (1953) put it, "Americans have an extraordinary talent for compromise in politics and extremism in morality." The political crimes committed in the Watergate fiasco provide an extreme illustration of this principle. Nothing mirrors quite so well the inconsistency of American society and the gap between the espoused "ideal" culture and the facts of the "real" culture as our attitudes and practices in the areas controlled by organized crime. Sociologists attempting to draw generalizations about the phenomenon of organized crime in America are faced with the dilemma of studying a secret society that provides some desired services, albeit illegal ones. Most of what is known about organized crime, and the Mafia, has come from law enforcement, Congressional hearings, and reporters with "connections." General "popular" periodicals, contain more information about the details and operations of organized crime than do the professional journals.

There has been a continuing debate among criminologists whether the Mafia was a "myth" or reality (Gibbons, 1968). Thus, when Cressey was appointed to the President's task force to study organized crime, he listed the four possible conclusions which he might reach about the data he was to study (1967) :

1. An organization of "organized criminals" does not exist[1]
2. An organization of "organized criminals" exists, but it is so secret that we cannot learn anything about it that law enforcement personnel do not already know.
3. Any organization of "organized criminals" that exists must not be much of a social problem or we would know more about it.
4. An organization of "organized criminals" exists, but it must be studied by methods not ordinarily utilized by social scientists.

Choosing the first alternative one must then "explain away" a whole host of observations made by local, state, and Federal law enforcement agencies, Congressional investigating committees, and the President of the United States. The second alternative invests law enforcement agencies with a level of infallibility that they do not claim for themselves. The third alternative contains the fallacy in logic known as a *non sequitur*. It does not necessarily follow that if organized crime existed, we then would be fully informed of its operations. Fourth, since there is a two-step flow of information, with an "informer" screening the original data, or a law enforcement officer "decoding" a peculiarly worded wire-tap, any conclusions drawn from such data must of necessity be suspect and open to question. It should be noted, however, that wire-taps are used only to gather evidence of a specific crime or criminal conspiracy that can be clearly shown to be operating and to be using a specific phone. The "decoding" is not difficult for anyone experienced with the terms used in a given criminal activity, e.g. "juice" is the interest paid on an extortion loan and "line" is the point spread between two teams in sport betting. Code words are used, and used successfully, to conceal the identities of the individuals involved. For example, a gambling organization will often give its members numbers rather than use names.

Cressey listed at least three other methodological problems to

---

[1]Even as sophisticated an interpreter of the American scene as Daniel Bell was agnostical about the existence of the Mafia and wrote in 1953 "Why did the Senate Crime Committee plump so hard for its theory of the Mafia and a national crime syndicate? In part, they may have been misled by their own hearsay." Bell saw Italians as rising to positions of importance in politics, gambling, and in the mobs but referred to references to the Mafia as a "legend" and the writings of Jack Lait and Lee Mortimer *(Chicago Confidential)* on the subject of the Mafia as "vicious sensationalism."

be faced by the researcher who would study organized crime:[2] (1) information on organized crime is generally presented to the public in a sensational manner: Nicknames of racketeers are often used, e.g. "Jake the Plumber"; references are made in underworld argot—usury is called "the juice racket" and murder is referred to as a "hit" or a "gangland slaying." These terms create the impression that these activities are taking place in some unreal, remote world or have been taken from the plot of a late-night television "B" movie about prohibition days.

(2) Layman and many behavioral scientists have tended to view crime in individualistic terms. Typically, when a crime is committed we wonder what is pathological about the offender's personality and feel if we could but divine the responses to ink blots we would find the malignancy within his personality. Rarely do we ask: "How is this criminal behavior the result of the individual's participation in social systems?" As a reflection of this common view, our law enforcement process has been designed, principally, for the control of individuals, not organizations.

(3) The confidential nature of police intelligence work prevents full disclosure of important data. It is one thing to "know" a bank is controlled by hoodlums, quite another to prove it in a court. The situation is analogous to the historian who aspires to write a full and accurate account of our involvement in the Vietnam War. Much of the data which would be indispensable to an accurate account is classified by the government for security reasons and unavailable. Similarly, law enforcement agencies may be in possession of valuable data[3] which would aid a researcher in the understanding of organized crime, but the release of this information might jeopardize an intelligence system of informants.

---

[2]Personal Communication, David Holt, Attorney; Organized Crime section, Criminal Division, Department of Justice.

[3]For an interesting account of the frustrations experienced by Peter Maas in gaining permission to publish the most complete account to date of organized crime in America—*The Valachi Papers*—see the introduction to that work. Although the Bureau of Prisons had a regulation barring federal inmates from publishing anything about their crimes, the Justice department first authorized the publication of the manuscript as being of benefit to law enforcement. They revised their stand after a vigorous protest by the American-Italian Anti-Defamation Council, whose executive board contains relatives of Cosa Nostra mobsters.

The Extent of Organized Crime in America

Sellin (1963) points out that while a team of jewel thieves may need organization, we generally reserve the term "organized crime" to refer to "economic enterprises organized for the purpose of conducting illegal activities and which, when they operate legitimate ventures, do so by illegal methods." Organized crime pursues the same goals as organized legitimate business: financial profit and power. Like any other business enterprise, organized crime has an elaborate hierarchy of command, voluminous records, a system of recruitment for new personnel, and problems of competition. Organized crime has the additional problem of neutralizing the threat of police interference on the local level, and more important, the threat of prosecution by Federal authorities.[4]

In Merton's catagories, these men have internalized the goals of American culture, but have pursued an "innovative" (illegal) route to the attainment of these goals. As a latent function of their operation, they have created an "illegitimate opportunity structure" (Cloward and Ohlin) which parallels the legitimate opportunity system of lawful society.

Organized crime makes its profits from gambling, narcotics, loansharking, labor racketeering, extortion, kickbacks, "skimming" (not paying taxes on gambling profits—an estimate of $280,000 per month in Nevada alone), vending machines, and other legitimate businesses. The annual income produced by organized crime is twice that compiled by all other criminal activities combined (Ruth, 1967). Schulz (1971) reports that organized crime grosses six billion dollars in the state of New Jersey alone. While it is impossible to measure accurately the total gross "business" of organized crime, it has been estimated that the Cosa Nostra ("This thing of ours") takes in as high as forty billion dollars per year, of which ten billion is profit *(Challenge of Crime in a Free Society,* 1967). Some concept of the magnitude of organized crime can be grasped from this selection from Salerno and Thompkins (1969):

---

[4]Despite the magnitude of the problem of organized crime only about 2 percent of the money available to the President's Crime Commission was spent on the organized crime study.

"If the profits from one division alone (gambling) had been invested for the past seventeen years (since the Kefauver investigation) so as to earn only 5 percent on the principle, the sum today would be sufficient to purchase every share of common stock in the ten largest corporate complexes in the United States . . . and the small change left over would buy up American Telephone and Telegraph."

The Types of Organized Criminal Activity

Crime has a functional role in society. It caters to public demands and provides goods and services that, although illegal, are desired by millions of Americans.

GAMBLING. Gambling is a basic institution in American life, and law enforcement officials feel that it is the greatest source of revenue for organized crime. Senator McClellan (1969) estimated that the net "take" annually in syndicated gambling is seven billion dollars. When asked by the Kefauver crime commission why people gamble, James J. Carroll, who admitted to having been in the betting business for fifty years replied (Bell, 1953): "I think gambling is a biological necessity for certain types. I think it is the quality that gives substance to their daydreams." Whatever morality Americans may publicly profess, it is a social fact that we are a nation of gamblers. Legally, we may salve our conscience by outlawing gambling, but behaviorally we supply the underworld with an enormous income by denying in practice what we profess in principle. As Bloch (1962) observed, "Much of this dilemma arises from the peculiarly American ambivalent penchant for moral disapproval of a variety of publicly enjoyed practices." Bloch sees the motivation to gamble as being related to the element of chance which is involved in our competitive economic system. Stock market speculation and getting rich "quick" by skillful manipulation of the market is part of the American dream. Similarly, more Americans play poker than any other card game; La Franchi and Martinez (1969) see this as the recreational expression of living in a competitive culture. They reject the Freudian theory that gambling is an unconscious substitute for masturbation and conclude: "If poker playing is a substitute for other things in life, they are likely to be social and not necessarily sexual satisfactions that are substituted for." Kefauver estimated some fifty million adult Americans participated in some form of syndicated gambling, involving thirty billion dollars a year with a profit to the gamblers of six billion. And Mower (1950) documented that gambling tends to increase during war, postwar, and inflationary periods. Salerno (1969) notes a crime commission in conservative Massachusetts which reported that more money is wagered on illegal gambling in that state than is spent for food.

Inner city areas are inhabited by persons in the lower socioeconomic class who feel they are trapped in a closed opportunity structure and are strong believers in "luck" or "fate" (Walter Miller) . They are psychologically susceptible to a form of a lottery known as numbers. Bets are placed on any three-digit number from 1 to 1,000. The mathematical odds of winning are 10,000 to 1. Yet the gambler seldom gambles. The payoff is seldom over 500 to one. On the more frequently played numbers, called "cut numbers," which are played for superstituous reasons, the payoff is even less. Each week enormous sums of money are drained from the ghettos—money which could have been spent for badly needed food, clothing, shelter, and medical services.

NARCOTICS. Senator McClellan (1969) ranks narcotics as second only to professional gambling as a source of income (estimated at $350 million annually) for organized crime. Heroin is the principal drug sought illegally, and more than one-half of the known heroin users in the United States reside in New York City. The death toll from overdoses of narcotics in New York has risen to several hundred annually. A single addict must obtain more than 35,000 dollars worth of "crime in the streets" each year to support his habit. This is more than the government of the United States allowed for the President's Crime Commission to spend for studying organized crime.

LOAN SHARKING. Usury or the "juice racket" gets its initial capital from gambling profits and ranks alongside narcotics as a source of revenue for organized crime. Its estimated take is 350 million dollars (McClellan, 1969) . A top level boss loans money to lieutenants at one percent per week, these men, in turn, pass it on to street level loan sharks who loan this money at five percent per week (260 percent per year) .

Persons who have a pressing need for cash and no regular credit channel become victims to these men. Gamblers, who must repay gambling losses or need a "stake," narcotic addicts, "sick" and in need of a "fix," and small businessmen on the verge of bankruptcy turn to the loan shark to bail them out of trouble only to find they now have "double trouble." A justice department lawyer told this writer of a man who had borrowed 2,000 dollars from loan sharks, had repaid 22,000 dollars over a period of eighteen months, and was still in debt to them. Although the classic loan is "6-for-5" (soldiers are familiar with this practice the weekend before payday), the interest rates vary from 1 to 150 percent a week, according to the size of the loan and repayment risk. The loan shark's term for usurious interest is "vigorish." The loan shark is more interested in perpetuating interest rates than in collecting the principal; thus the borrower is placed into perpetual servitude. It is reminiscent of the old share-cropper system in the South where the small farmer could never leave the land because he could never make enough to pay his bill at the inflated prices at the company store. Repayment is compelled by force, and "your body is your collateral." There is a lien on your life.

Cook (1968) calls the "juice racket" ". . . the safest and most remunerative racket in the underworld." With no fixed headquarters, no elaborate telephone setup, and no army of runners, the loan shark may "work his precinct" often with from 7,000 to 15,000 dollars cash upon his person. Cook illustrates the profits in loan-sharking by describing one mob boss who pyramided $500,-000 into $7.5 million in five years.

LEGITIMATE BUSINESS. The extensive profits which organized crime obtains from gambling, narcotics, and loan-sharking may be invested in a variety of legitimate businesses. In many cities, organized crime dominates jukebox and vending machine distribution. Liquor, laundry services, nightclubs, record manufacturing, the garment industry, real estate, and even securities firms and the stock exchange itself have been the targets of organized crime. These types of businesses can provide a cash-flow through which the "dirty money" made from criminal activities can be "washed." They are also types of businesses that are difficult from a tax point of view in terms of determining what they owe the government.

Typically, organized crime simply buys a legitimate business, but on occasion a legitimate business may be taken over by organized crime through the use of extortion or payment of a gambling debt or loan shark debts. Professional arsonists may then burn the business or the business debts may be liquidated through a bankruptcy fraud. Through the use of fear and intimidation the organization will secure a monopoly in the services or product and then, unchecked by competition, charge exorbitant prices.

On November 14, 1957, seventy-five leaders of organized crime met at the upstate New York home of Joseph Barbara. When apprehended, investigators were shocked to learn that (McClellan):

> Of the 75 or so racket leaders who met at Apalachin, N.Y., in 1957, we found . . . that at least nine were in the coin operated machine industry, 16 were in the garment industry, 10 owned grocery stores, 17 owned bars or restaurants, 11 were in olive oil and cheese business, and 9 were in the construction business. Others were involved in automobiles, coal companies, entertainment, funeral homes, ownership of horses and race tracks, linen and laundry enterprises, trucking, waterfront activities, and bakeries.

In 1969 the Internal Revenue Service revealed it had investigated 113 major underworld figures. The findings: 98 of the 113 operated a total of 159 "legitimate" businesses, including everything from nightclubs to funeral parlors.

LABOR UNIONS. Called the "second government" by Mafia defector Joseph Valachi, the "mob" has more than two dozen unions in New Jersey under its influence   (Schulz, 1971) . The business agents of these Mafia dominated labor unions negotiate "sweetheart contracts" with employers, i.e. they guarantee no strikes or problems in return for a "kickback." Under the regime of Newark Mayor Hugh Addonizio (1962-1970) contractors would not be awarded city business without a "kickback" of ten percent to city officials.

Control of labor unions means control of the labor supply and places the mob in a position to either prevent the unionization of some industries on the one hand or guarantee "sweetheart" contracts on the other. Other side benefits to the mob include: theft and manipulation of union welfare-pension funds and extortion of management in return for labor peace.

PROSTITUTION AND BOOTLEGGING. With the repeal of prohibition, organized crime began to look for other areas in which to make a profit. "Stills" are expensive to establish, and there is a heavy investment loss when they are destroyed by revenue agents. Prostitution jars on a sensitive nerve in the American conscience, and the publicity is "bad" for more profitable illegitimate business ventures. Except for the case of Lucky Luciano, major criminal executives have been cautious about investing in prostitution. Any place of prostitution operated by organized crime is protected by police "pay-offs." It is impossible to hide any large operation in prostitution from the police, and its continued operation depends upon political corruption. It is not unusual to find entire sections of a police department, e.g. the "vice-squad" being "paid-off" on a regular basis.

Internal Structure of the Mafia

According to the President's Crime Commission (1967), there are twenty-four core Mafia "families" in the United States containing 5,000 members cemented together by a common ethnic bond. Each "family" contains a membership varying from 20 to 700. The organization is bureaucratized so that no one member is indispensable—not even top leaders. When "Lucky" Luciano was deported, the leadership of his New York family was simply passed to Vito Genovese.

Each family is headed by a "boss" whose authority is absolute and who in turn answers to a national "advisory" group. Each boss has an "under-boss," or vice-president, in charge of relaying instructions. On the same hierarchical level, but operating in a staff capacity, is the *consigliere,* usually an elder member of the family who functions as an advisor.

On the next level are the *caporegime.* Leaders of the Mafia avoid direct contact with the workers to make their connection with the rackets harder to detect and prove. A *caporegima* serves as a buffer between the hierarchy and lower echilon personnel and is analogous to a plant supervisor.

The actual direction of mob activities—loan sharking, dice game, smuggling—is carried out by *soldati* (soldiers) who report to the *caporegime*. The soldiers employ persons who are not members of the family and may not be of Italian descent. A lottery in a Negro neighborhood will typically be run by a Mafia-backed black. These "little folk" have no insulation from law enforcement other than the "pay-off". They make the least profits, take the greatest risks, and are the most vulnerable to arrests.

Two positions in the organizations of the Mafia make it a unique form of criminal activity. The first is the "enforcer" whose duty is to maintain organizational discipline by the beating or killing of wayward members. The holder of the second position, "the corruptor," is expected to neutralize law enforcement and to act as a public relations lobbyist with public officials to insure the Mafia influence in government.

The Distribution of Organized Crime in America

Every section of our country has organized crime groups working in its area, but the most influential core groups according to the President's Crime Commission Report operate in New York, New Jersey, Illinois, Florida, Louisiana, Nevada, Michigan, and Rhode Island. In response to a Commission survey of seventy-one cities, organized crime groups were found to be operating in cities with populations ranging from 100,000 to cities with over a million residents.

The persistence of the Mafia in the face of repeated investigations is illustrated by the case of Louisiana. The first Mafia family in the western hemisphere was founded in Louisiana in 1875 by a group of Sicilian Mafiosi and survives today under the leadership of Carlos Marcello, described by Chandler (1970) as "controlling the state."[5] Chandler and a special investigating team found that Marcello had not only avoided paying state taxes on his operations, but has managed through his deep involvement in state government to turn his one million dollar investment in a Louisiana swamp into a "real estate bonanza" valued at sixty

---

[5]While Mafia influence in Louisiana government is well-documented, it is doubtful that in an absolute sense the mob "controls the state".

million dollars.[6] Louisiana's Governor McKeithen admitted the accuracy of the Chandler report on Mafia influence in the state government, but two years following the report no substantial convictions had been obtained. A justice department "strike-force" lawyer described Louisiana, to this writer, as an "impacted area," which meant in his opinion, nothing would be done about organized crime in Louisiana unless the Federal government did it.

Origin of the Mafia

According to Anderson (1965) "Mafias" arose in Sicily as a pre-industrial peasant institution. Their function was to correct abuses via feud and vendetta when a disinterested official government failed to keep order. Although originally an intimate organization functioning in face-to-face communities, it now operates in the highly urbanized and industrialized milieu of the United States. Result: The Mafia has become bureaucratized.

The traditional Mafia, according to Anderson, around the turn of the century operated as a vigilante group protecting the community in return for regularized tribute. Although not necessarily predatory, the absolute power placed in the hands of the Mafia chieftain tended to support Lord Acton's observation that "power corrupts, and absolute power tends to corrupt absolutely." The lines between tax assessment and outright robbery, peace enforcement and murder became difficult to distinguish. Anderson (1965) concluded:

> An overall inventory of Mafia activities leaves no doubt that it is a criminal institution, serving the interests of its membership at the expense of the larger population.

The origin of the Mafia is connected with the Sicilian concept of family. The most significant social bond in Sicily is that of family; it is the basic social group thus facilitating social action. But as a functioning group it has the drawback of a relatively inflexible membership. The European concept of the artificial ex-

---

[6]For a scholarly account of the working of Louisiana politics see T. Harry Williams *Huey Long,* a journalistic and entertaining account of this same family can be found in A.J. Liebling's *The Longs of Louisiana.*

tention of kinship ties through ritual kinship has been important in providing flexible recruiting patterns for the modern Mafia. In Europe, Godparenthood, child adoption, and blood brotherhood are taken very seriously and are equated or even superior to true kinship.

This ancient "ritual kinship" custom has survived until today. Joe Valachi describes his initiation into the Cosa Nostra (Maas, 1968) :

> Now Mr. Maranzano said to everybody around the table, "This is Joe Cago," which I must explain is what most of the guys know me by. Then he tells me to sit down in an empty chair on his right. When I sit down, so does the whole table. Someone put a gun and a knife on the table in front of me. I remember the gun was a .38, and the knife was what you would call a dagger. After that, Maranzano motions us up again, and we all hold hands and he says some words in Italian. Then we sit down, and he turns to me, still in Italian, and talks about the gun and the knife. "This represents that you live by the gun and the knife," he says, "and you die by the gun and the knife." Next he asked me, "Which finger do you shoot with?" I said, "This one," and I hold up my right forefinger. I was still wondering what he meant by this when he told me to make a cup out of my hands. Then he put a piece of paper in them and lit it with a match, and told me to say after him, as I was moving the paper back and forth, "This is the way I will burn if I betray the secret of this Cosa Nostra." All of this was in Italian. In English Cosa Nostra would mean "This thing of ours." It comes before everything—our blood family, our religion, our country.

In America, the traditional Mafia has evolved into a complex organization which has perpetuated those selected features of the older peasant organization necessary for survival of the group in an urban society. Its goal in American society is best expressed by Anderson when he refers to the mob as a "predatory satrapy."

Controlling Organized Crime

The number of principal operators in organized crime (not counting employees, runners, etc.) is about 10,000. To fight this at all levels of government, in the entire United States, there are about 500 men working full time against the mob (Salerno, 1969). The following approaches have been initiated with some hope of reversing the gains by Mafia gangsters:

Strike Force

The strike force, a team of lawyers and investigators from different government agencies "blitz" an area thought to be under Mafia influence. By 1971, strike forces had been set up in sixteen cities. Over 320 indictments had been filed and 60 convictions obtained. Each strike force is headed by an attorney from the Department of Justice and includes other attorneys and senior investigators from the Federal Bureau of Investigation, Bureau of Narcotics and Dangerous Drugs, Labor, Post Office, Bureau of Customs, Internal Revenue Service, and other branches of the Federal Government.

The Grand Jury and the Immunity Squeeze

"As an instrument of discovery against organized crime," writes Senator McClellan (1969), "the grand jury has no counterpart." The modern grand jury is a "proto-type" of its ancient English counterpart. Under Federal law the grand jury is empowered under *Hale v. Henkel* (1905) to inquire into and return indictments for all crimes committed within its jurisdiction. The power of the grand jury rests on the subpoena. Through this legal device, witnesses can be compelled to appear and produce records. As subpoenas are issued only out of court, the grand jury functions as an arm of the court and is subject to the courts supervision. The court impanels it, charges it, chooses its foreman, protects against abuses of its authority, and ultimately discharges it.

A grand jury can compel the attendance of a witness and the production of books and records, but the grand jury has no power to compel the witness to testify or turn over the books and records when the witness invokes the privilege against self-incrimination.

But as the Supreme Court notes in *Piedmont v. United States* (1961), the "public has a right to everyman's evidence." The duty to testify is not absolute; it qualified by the privilege against self-incrimination. The modern privilege against self-incrimination applies to any question the answer to which would furnish a link in a chain of evidence which would incriminate the witness. The privilege is personal; it may not be claimed to protect another.

Further, it protects only natural persons—not corporations or unions.

The privilege against self-incrimination is not as absolute. Should a witness refuse to testify before a grand jury, it is possible to displace the privilege with a grant of immunity. With the threat of prosecution removed, a witness who refuses to testify may be jailed for the life of the grand jury, in some cases eighteen months.

Antitrust Actions

In civil cases the measure of proof is proponderance of the evidence, not beyond a reasonable doubt as in criminal actions. A Mafia family found to have control of all the juke boxes in a city may have the juke boxes, warehouses, and delivery trucks seized as a result of an anti-trust action.

Disabling Sentences

"Sentencing a Mafia chieftain for purposes of rehabilitation is nonsense," writes Edwards (1963). Higher ups in the rackets rarely come before a sentencing judge. Existing statutes too often are aimed at the symptoms—the operation of crime—rather than the underlying cause—the organization of organized crime. Sentencing the minor employees, the runner, the strong arm extortionist, or the addict/peddler, simply causes organized crime a nuisance replacement problem but does nothing to destroy the organization *per se*. As Senator McClellan pointed out, the killing of Jesse virtually ended the James gang: When Luciano was deported, the leadership of his New York family was simply passed to Vito Genovese.

Senator McClellan (1970), whose committee investigates labor racketeering and organized crime, quotes President Nixon as saying that, despite the government's attempt to eliminate organized crime in America, not one of the twenty-four Cosa Nostra "families" has been destroyed—rather, their hold on American society remains more entrenched than ever. One reason for this, according to McClellan, is that the investigative work of the F.B.I. and other law enforcement agencies has been nullified by the lenient sentences meted out the syndicate criminals. A study by McClellan's Senate Subcommittee on Criminal Laws and Procedure revealed that of 129 Cosa Nostra members convicted by the Justice Department since 1960, most received only half the maximum sentence. Fifteen received no jail term at all, only fines or probation, and eighty got less than the maximum jail terms for the crimes for which they were convicted. McClellan cites the case of John Lombardozzi, who pleaded guilty and was convicted of bankruptcy fraud, conspiracy to smuggle funds into federal jail, assaulting an F.B.I. agent, and of the theft of more than a million dollars worth of securities from Wall Street brokers. For these four separate felony convictions, Lombardozzi was sentenced to just over five years (he faced a possible 28 years) .

Members of La Cosa Nostra have obtained dismissals or acquittals on the charges against them more than twice as often, for their numbers, as ordinary defendants (69.7 percent as compared to 34.8 percent) . In their ability to obtain dismissals or acquittals five or more times, Cosa Nostra members have proven themselves to be five times as successful as their unaffiliated criminal counterparts. The average criminal career of organized crime members is estimated as twice as long as that of other offenders (Wilson, 1970) .

McClellan cites an F.B.I. study of 386 *mafiosi* which showed them at an average age of forty-seven to have also averaged eight arrests over the preceeding twenty years of their criminal careers. In the case of such hardened criminals "rehabilitation" is a joke, and only long prison terms which incapacitate the mobster can protect society.

The National Council on Crime and Delinquency's advisory council of judges has prepared a model sentencing act which recognizes that criminal activities committed within organized crime require separate sentencing statutes. Model sentencing act number five provides:

> The court may sentence a defendant convicted of a felony to a term of commitment of thirty years, or to a lesser term, if it finds that because of the dangerousness of the defendant, such a period of confined correctional treatment of custody is required for the protection of the public, and if it further finds . . . the defendant is being sen-

tenced for the crime of extortion, compulsory prostitution, selling or knowingly and unlawfully transporting narcotics, or other felony, committed as a part of a continuing criminal activity in concert with one or more persons.

DECRIMINALIZATION OF MORALISTIC CRIMES. Organized crime exists because it has expanded into the vacuum created by the criminalization of certain goods and services demanded by a significant portion of the American public. One method which would deprive the mob of a major portion of its revenue would be to make a number of these activities legal. Bell (1953) quotes the venerable Bernard Baruch philosophizing: "You can't stop people from gambling on horses. And why should you prohibit a man from backing his own judgment? It's another form of personal initiative."

Certainly all out movement against organized crime must concentrate upon reducing the number of dollars available to the mob for financing its operations either legitimate or illegitimate. As Woetzel writes (1963):

> The removal of criminal sanctions against certain activities like gambling, prostitution under supervision of state police and health authorities, homosexual relations between consenting adults in private, and the use of drugs under medical care, as well as lowering of the tax on liquor, would undoubtedly diminish the income achieved by organized criminals.

VIGOROUS LAW ENFORCEMENT. The reaction of state and federal law enforcement agencies and allocation of men and resources should be in proportion to the danger that a particular crime poses to society. There are less man hours spent, by far, fighting organized crime—America's number one crime problem—than in sobering up drunks. As Senator McClellan put it: "When Bob Kennedy left the Department of Justice the organized crime program seemed to leave with him; it just seemed to fall apart." By (1971), however, there were 140 attorneys in the organized crime section of the criminal division of the Justice Department; in 1970 there were only forty-nine.

Few areas in law enforcement present problems in the gathering of evidence as difficult as does organized crime. "Victims" of gambling do not report their losses to the local police station, and informants are reluctant to testify in court as the mob occasionally enforces "capital punishment." Because of the resulting publicity, the "mob" would prefer less visible methods. Documentary evidence is hard to obtain. If kept at all, records of gambling operations are usually kept on highly combustible "flash paper" which is immediately ignited with the touch of a cigarette.

Denied live testimony and facing the alarming power of organized crime, it appears essential that law enforcement should utilize every weapon at its disposal including electronic surveillance. In the opinion of Justice Department attorneys in the organized crime division, the power of organized crime is less now (in 1974) than it was five years ago and will be weakened as more "middle management" persons are convicted.

Technology has presented law enforcement with some Orwellian-like tools for surveillance. Fly (1969) describes some of these:

A remote controlled amplifier and microphone no larger than the period at the end of this sentence can capture a conversation and transmit it by wire for 25 miles. A parabolic mike, without wires or radio transmitter, can catch the conversation of a couple in a canoe in mid-lake and record it on shore. A battery-powered transmitter, running for 100 hours, can be concealed in the heel of a victim's shoe, sending his words a block away. By switching a single wire, an intruder can convert any telephone in the United States into a live microphone.

The use of "wire taps" is one of the more controversial methods utilized by law enforcement. In July 1965, President Lyndon Johnson issued an executive order banning all electronic surveillance. Congress later enacted legislation authorizing court approved wire taps in the fight against organized crime, but Attorney General Ramsey Clark refused to use them. Not until 1969 did the government renew its "bugging." Technically, court approved wire taps are not used against "organized crime" but are for specific offenses listed in Title III, Sect. 2516. These offenses are the types of criminal activity usually associated with organized crime. Also, Title III authorizes states to enact wire tap statutes for any crime punishable by one year in prison.

Civil liberatarians have expressed concern over the wire tap and the use of the "immunity squeeze" as an assault on a citizen's constitutional rights. The issue becomes: How much latitude are we willing to give law enforcement in its fight on organized crime? Which is the greater threat, organized crime or . . . the possibility of an Orwellian 1984 police state?

PUBLIC OPINION. Organized crime can exist only so long as the American public will tolerate its activities. The mob thrives in America because there is demand for the illicit goods and services it has for sale. As Cressey (1967) observes, the effect on the socio-economic system of the complete reformation of all burglars would be slight, felt principally by burglar insurance companies and lock manufacturers. If, however, La Cosa Nostra were abolished, a large minority of the American public would miss its services. Efforts against the Mafia will only be "piecemeal" until an aroused American public realizes the price for its illicit services is too high.

WHITE COLLAR CRIME

The chief commodity margin clerk of a prestigious Wall Street security house, described as a trusted employee, traded in an account, supposedly for a customer, but used the firm's finances to do so, resulting in a company loss of 2.5 million dollars. The firm did not press criminal charges for fear of creating "market instability" (*Newsweek*, 1969).

This case would be classified as a "white collar crime" by Sutherland, (1949) who defined this as "a crime committed by a person of respectability and high social status in the course of his occupation." Had the same clerk committed a crime which was not in connection with his occupation, such as murder, rape, or drunken driving, it would not be included under the classification "white collar crime." Among those crimes Sutherland lists as white collar crimes are: misrepresentation in advertising, violations of antitrust laws, infringement of patents, trademarks, and copyrights; violations of labor laws, frauds, and violations of trusts of various types.

The concept of white collar crime was first introduced in 1939 by Professor Sutherland in his presidential address to the American Sociological Society. It was a landmark address in the history of criminology for it enlarged the scope of inquiry to include crimes of the "upper-world"—to use the phrase of Albert Morris —as well as the conventional crimes of the lower-classes.

Sutherland introduced the concept to reformulate existing theories of criminality to include persons of high social status and to challenge the view that criminal behavior can be explained only by pathological factors, e.g. social pathologies such as poverty, or personal pathologies such as emotional instability. Sutherland felt that the statistics which placed the center of crime in the lower-class were biased for two reasons: (1) Wealthier persons escaped conviction because of their influence, and (2) persons in the business class who violate such laws as pure food and drug acts are not tried in criminal courts. The principle difference between crimes of the upper-classes and those of the lower-classes, argued Sutherland, was in the administrative procedures which are used in dealing with the offenders.

Newman (1958) has suggested that the scope of these type crimes be extended to cover blue-collar as well as white-collar crimes, e.g. a farmer who "waters" his milk, or an automobile mechanic who makes unnecessary repairs: all crime which occurs in the course of an occupational activity without regard to the social status of the offender. The essence of the criterion for selection of criminal behavior to be included in the concept "occupational crime" is that the offense must be directly related to occupations that are regarded as legitimate by the general society. Thus (Quinney, 1963), occupational crime can be defined as violation of legal codes during the course of activity in a legitimate occupation.

A further refinement of the concept of occupational crime is suggested by Bloch (1962). They separate occupational crimes into three types, divided on the basis of the nature of employment and the direction of the crime: (1) by individuals as individuals, such as lawyers or doctors, (2) by employees against the corporation for which they work, such as embezzlers, and (3) by policy-making officials on behalf of the firm, such as price fixing.*

If the concept "white-collar crime" is to be rescued from

ambiguity, then it must refer to criminal acts which are of the same nature, i.e. essentially alike. Mannheim (1965) cuts to the heart of the matter when he points out that Sutherland's definition of white-collar crime has five elements: (1) It was a crime (2) committed by a person of respectability, and (3) of high social status, (4) in the course of his occupation and (5) is usually a violation of trust. It is essential, of course, that a crime has been committed, and Sutherland has been accused of extending the concept to include violations of all administrative regulations (Caldwell, 1959), but Sutherland sought to isolate the essential ingredients in the statutory definitions of crime and keep the concept within the scope of criminal law.

Ambiguities in Sutherland's definition arise in the use of the term "respectable." Does he mean by this an absence of a criminal record? The third element "high social status" is less ambiguous. However, social class position is one thing, and the respect accorded the holder of that position is quite another. It is entirely possible to be highly respectable and illiterate on the one hand, or a member of the upper-class, yet held in contempt by the general society on the other. Sutherland committed two definitional errors which made the concept even more vunerable to attack: limiting the concept to crimes of corporations and utilizing illustrative case material not associated with corporate crimes, e.g. bank clerks and typewriter repairmen.

Mannheim sees two alternatives open to give the term greater definitional integrity. One is to either use the term to include the whole of the middle-class (bank clerks, etc.) or restrict its use to crimes of persons with high social standing and deal with the crimes of middle and lower class occupations separately. Social class is one of the most, if not the most, powerful analytical tool of the sociological schema. Religious affiliation, voting patterns, and mate selection all tend to follow class lines. Separation of occupational offenses along class lines would help to "homogenize" the concept.

Mannheim entitles his chapter on white-collar crime "White-Collar and Other Non-Working Class Crimes." Both an automobile mechanic and a bank president may commit crimes in the course of their occupations. But at this superficial level the similarity ends. Because of the social class differential, the potential danger to society and the possibility of incarceration varies greatly between these two occupations. Paradoxically, white-collar crimes cause much greater harm to society, with a lesser chance of the criminal law being involved, than do blue-collar or no-collar crimes. Practically the only significant similarity between the mechanic and the bank president is that they were both employed. Research into the nature of crime causation and an understanding of differential societal response will be more productive if it is carried out along class lines than if pursued with occupation alone as the key variable.

Political Crimes

Political crimes are those crimes committed by elected or appointed public officials in the course of the execution of the responsibilities of their office which involve a violation of the public trust. Political crimes are differentiated from occupational crimes, or white-collar crimes, in that public officials violate the *public* trust while private citizens offend only a segment of the citizenry. Examples of political crimes would be a Governor who required a "kick-back" of $50,000 in order to approve the charter for a new bank; or, a legislator who accepted a bribe to vote for laws favoring special interests over the public good.

The most famous political crimes in American history are those lumped under the rubric "The Watergate Affair." Mankiewicz (1973) identified over sixty criminal statutes which, at this writing, appear to have been violated by members of the Nixon White House staff, or officials of the Nixon campaign. These crimes range from bribery of public officials to influence an official act to delay of mail by Postal Services employees.

Is White-Collar Crime a Crime?

Sutherland (1949) analyzed the decisions of courts and administrative commissions against seventy of the largest manufacturing, mining, and mercantile corporations in the United States. Of 980 decisions rendered against the corporations, only 158, or

16 percent, were made by criminal courts. Since not all unlawful behavior is criminal behavior, may the word crime be applied to the other 822 white-collar infractions as well?

Sutherland argues that the essence of the word crime is to be found operationally when two conditions exist: (1) a legal description of an act as socially injurious, and (2) a legal provision of a penalty for commission of the act. Using this criterion, Sutherland concluded that in 779 of the 980 decisions against the corporations a crime had been committed.

Tappan (1947) objects to Sutherland's definition of white-collar crime, any violation of any law—civil or criminal—when it is "socially injurious," as being too vague to form the basis for scientific research and is, thus, likely to open a Pandora's box for mischief-making by over-zealous governmental administrators. Would we then criminalize businessmen who overprice their products, or who are guilty of unfair labor practices? Terms like "unfair," "infringement," and "injurious to society," argues Tappan, are merely epithets which allow the criminologist to attach the status "criminal" to any group which violates his subjective sense of what is socially correct.

Tappan feels that, despite its limitations, the law has defined conduct, which is to be deemed criminal, with greater clarity and precision than the nebulous alternatives proposed by "antilegal criminologists" and thus remains a safer guide for determining when a crime has been committed. He advocates the "juristic" view:

> We consider that the "white-collar criminal," the violator of conduct norms, and the antisocial personality are not criminal in any sense meaningful to the social scientist unless he has violated a criminal statute. We cannot know him as such unless he has been properly convicted. He may be a boor, a sinner, a moral leper, or the devil incarnate, but he does not become a criminal through sociological name calling unless politically constituted authority says he is.

Sutherland rejoins that the limitation of calling an act criminal only if a criminal court has officially determined that the person accused of the act has committed a crime is proper if the subject under consideration is an administrative one. He writes (1949): "The warden of a prison would not be justified in receiving an offender in the penal institution unless the offender had been officially convicted and sentenced to a term of years in the institution. . . . In contrast, the criminologist who is interested in a theory of criminal behavior needs to know only that a certain class of acts is legally defined as crimes and that a particular person had committed an act of this class.

Another objection to the position taken by Sutherland is that administrative procedures do not follow the rules of proof and evidence demanded in criminal courts and thus do not provide adequate safeguards for the defendant (Tappan, 1947). Sutherland replied that rules of criminal intent and presumption of innocence are not required in all prosecutions of criminal courts and administrative agencies are significantly different and sees the differences which do exist as an attempt to spare upper-class businessmen from the stigma of criminal prosecution. "The important consideration here," writes Sutherland (1949), "is that the criteria which have been used in defining white-collar crimes are not categorically different from the criteria used in defining some other crimes."

The Debate Illustrated: The Case of O.P.A. Violations

Hartung (1950) conducted a study of white-collar offenses in the wholesale meat industry in Detroit. Specifically, he dealt with violations of Office of Price Administration regulations between 1942 and 1946. His study revealed 122 cases of price violations and other violations of statutes which were processed by regulatory agencies in Detroit.

Hartung argued that his data supported four conclusions:

1. Violations of OPA regulations in the pre-retail meat industry are criminal acts; they meet the criteria of formally defined proscribed and prescribed acts and of punishability. In this view he follows the criteria set down by Sutherland: (1) a proscribed act with (2) sanctions specified. The Emergency Price Control Act of 1942 isolated eight areas of external social harm ranging from an attempt to prevent abnormal increases in prices, to the aim of protecting persons with fixed incomes. Violation of these agency provisions could incur fines, imprisonment, and/or the suspension of the right to do business.

TABLE 12-1.

SUMMARY OF VIOLATIONS AND SANCTIONS IN THE DETROIT
WHOLESALE MEAT INDUSTRY
DECEMBER, 1942, THROUGH JUNE 30, 1946.

No. of cases	122
No. of concerns	83
No. of personal defendants	132
Persons having previous criminal records*	2

VIOLATIONS:

a) Open overceiling	65
b) Evasive overceiling	58
c) Record-keeping	72
Total**	195

Damages paid: total	$132,811.71
Range of damages***	$40.00 - $6,000.00
Fines paid: total	$97,500.00
Range of fines***	$100.00 - $15,000.00

SANCTIONS IMPOSED:

a) License Warning Notice	45
b) Injunction	63
c) Damages	58
d) Prison only	3
e) Prison and fine	12
f) Fine only	22
g) Suspended sentence	6
h) Probation	8
i) Suspension orders****	16
Total	233

Prison terms: total months	105-77
Range of prison terms***	3 mo. - 1 yr.

*As indicated by a check of Detroit Police Department and Federal Bureau of Investigation records.

**Not the actual number of offenses but the total of the three types of violations, tallying one complaint for an injunction of one criminal in as one case, regardless of the number of counts alleged.

***Exact limits not given, so as to avoid possible identification.

****Estimated total days of partial or total suspension of business: 2,129.

Source: Frank Hartung. White-collar offenses in the wholesale meat industry in Detroit. *The American Journal of Sociology*, LVI, (July, 1960).

2. The distinction between civil and criminal sanctions is not held to distinguish between two different types of sanctions. Hartung argues: "The distinctions between civil and criminal sanctions seems to be less meaningful, at least in the case of the laws here considered, than that between misdemeanor and felony." His third point is intended to make this lack of distinction more evident.

3. Willfulness or deliberate intent to violate is not essential to making a white-collar offense a criminal act. To support his ideas that willful intent is not a universal criterion for a criminal act, Hartung illustrates with the following "strict liability" cases: statutory rape, bigamy, adultery, uttering and publishing, the sale of mortgaged property, and negligent homicide.

4. At least in the industry considered in this study, the commission of an offense almost always necessarily involved the commission of another similar offense by a different party. If the violation was by a secondary wholesaler, all the stages after him were involved. No wholesaler could commit a violation alone. The chain of violations was completed by their overcharges to their customers. The "buck" stopped at the cash register in the grocery store.

Table 12-II reveals at least three interesting facts. First, these white-collar crimes tend to resemble the usual criminal offenses; they range from systematic to technical violations and are both single and repeated offenses. Second, the penalties were generally lenient in light of the seriousness of the offenses. Third, only 2 of the 132 personal refendants had a previous criminal record. This fact leads to the conclusion that the established businessman or firm was the blackmarketeer. On the basis of these facts Hartung calls for a recasting of criminological theory. He argues:

> There is no available information on white-collar offenses as far as the usual "factors" are concerned: broken home, childhood experiences, race nativity or nationality background, amount of formal education, occupational training and experience, physical characteristics a la Hooten and Sheldon, and the like. Imagine what a cry of outraged ego would have electrified Congress, if, upon establishing an evasive overcharge, the OPA had inquired into the businessman's love

TABLE 12-2.
WHERE THE FAST-BUCK BOYS OPERATE

In its survey Sales Management *magazine also compiled a list of the businesses that in recent years have been most frequently invaded by gypsters. The list, plus a summary of the shady tactics used in each, is reprinted by permission.*

Insurance. Major offenses: falsely stating that policies are "guaranteed renewable"; using terms like "seal of approval" without explaining their meaning; alleging that policies are sponsored or underwritten by government agencies. Also: selling high-risk insurance at inflated rates, then disappearing before claims are paid out.

Publishing. Major offenses: understating the true cost of magazine subscriptions; selling ad space in bogus business directories designed to resemble well-known reputable publications; approaching encyclopedia sales prospects under the pretext that they've won a contest or have been selected for "test marketing."

Mail-order land sales. Major offenses: misrepresenting tracts as "improved" when they aren't; failing to tell new owners that they must pay for future improvements; staging bogus contests whereby "winners" of free tracts must pay "closing costs" that exceed the true value of their property.

Home-improvement contractors. Major offenses: "bait-and-switch" advertising; requiring customers (mainly low-incomers) to sign high-interest payment plans that turn out to be second mortgages, making their entire home subject to confiscation in event of default.

Automotive repairs. Major offenses: advertising ultra-low specialty repair prices (examples: transmission, brakes), then stripping down a customer's car and suddenly "discovering" a major malfunction that requires more money to fix than the stipulated price. Also prominent: warranties that aren't honored.

Home freezer plans. Major offenses: falsely claiming that the price of a freezer can quickly be "made up" through food cost savings; welching on promises of regular deliveries; substituting inferior products when filling orders; turning sales contracts over to finance companies without notifying the customer.

Correspondence schools. Major offenses: offering courses falsely promising employment after graduation; offering courses of little or no value.

Vending machines. Overestimating potential sales and profits; falsely guaranteeing to secure top locations for prospective franchises; supplying franchises with merchandise inferior to the quality promised.

Dance instruction. Major offenses: preying upon lonely people with matchmaking promises; offering instruction to persons too infirm or otherwise unfit to profit by it; signing up elderly persons for future lessons that stretch far beyond their remaining life expectancy.

Medical devices. Common offenses: inflated therapeutic claims for cosmetics and curative gadgets with little or no therapeutic value.

Changing Times, The Kiplinger Magazine, March 1969, p. 12. Reproduced by permission of the publisher.

An Organized Crime Family

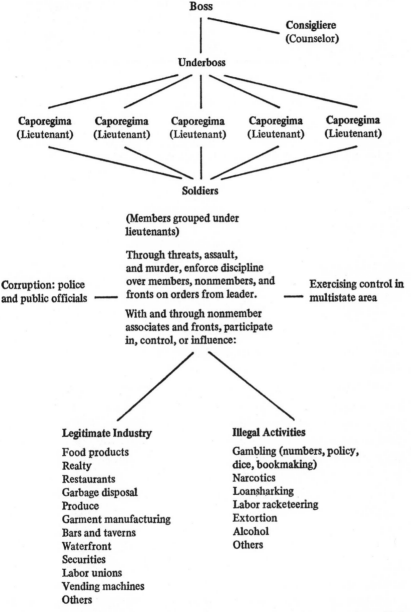

Figure 12-1. An Organized Crime Family. *Task Force Report: Organized Crime.* Washington, U.S. Government Printing Office, 1967. Reproduced by permission of the Department of Justice.

life to ascertain if he were frustrated; or had investigated at what grade he had quit school; or had measured his cephalic index and his mesomorphy; or had tried to obtain any of the usual items that compromise that subject matter of current empirical studies of offenders. To restate Sutherland, the study of white-collar crime will not so much reform the criminal as it will the criminologist.

Burgess (1950), when commenting on the article by Hartung, criticized his approach as a "legalistic and not a sociological position." In Burgess's view the differences between the OPA violator and the burglar are too great to consider them as a homogeneous group. To Burgess, what separates the two is of more importance than what unites them. Legally, they are the same; they violated the law; but sociologically, they are different. Burgess points out five outstanding differences:

1. There is no evidence presented that OPA violators conceived themselves as criminals or were so considered by the public. In fact, for only 2 out of 122 has a previous criminal record reported.

2. The Emergency Price Control Act and the Second Wars Powers Act were suddenly imposed upon businessmen, defining many business transactions as offenses which had previously been legal.

3. No concerted, organized, effective attempt was made by civic leaders, churches, schools, the press, and governmental agencies to apply social condemnation to violations by businessmen and to purchases by consumers. Consequently, these acts were not stigmatized by the public as falling in the same category as murder, burglary, robbery, forgery, and rape.

4. Large sections of the population, comprising perhaps over half the adults, participated in black-market purchases during the war.

5. Few cases of violation, only 6.4 percent, drew prison sentences, and these were very light when compared with nonwhite-collar "crimes," averaging only from three months to one year.

Hartung, in his rejoinder, observes dryly that Tappan is opposed to the concept because he says its proponents are sociological and not legalistic. Burgess, however, objects because it is a legalistic and not a sociological position. To Burgess's assertion that the OPA violators were only "technically criminal," Hartung (1950) asks the rhetorical question: "On what other but a technical, legal basis should one be adjudged criminal?" Professor Burgess's concluding comment that a person is a criminal only if he so regards himself and is so perceived by society, if implemented, would reduce the study of criminology from an objective science to the capricious world of self-images. Mannheim writes that: "while the "image" which the offender has of himself is of very considerable, often even crucial significance psychologically for such matters as crime causation and the prevention of recidivism, it cannot be the decisive factor for our judgement whether or not he should be legally or sociologically classified as an offender."

The Nature and Extent of White-Collar Crime

The classic example of white-collar crime in which policymaking officials place company interest above the public good is "The Incredible Electrical Conspiracy" (Smith, 1961). The largest criminal case in the history of the Sherman Act involved twenty-nine corporations and their top management. Forty-five defendants were convicted of conspiring to fix prices, rig bids, and divide markets on electrical equipment valued at 1,750,000,000 dollars annually. Fines were levied against the corporations totalling 1,787,000 dollars; General Electric and Westinghouse payed the greatest amounts. More dramatic, however, were the thirty day jail terms meted out upon seven of the defendants: four vice-presidents, two division managers, and one sales manager.

The *modus operandi* of these upper-world business leaders would do justice to the methods used by leaders of underworld organized crime. They invented fictitious names, used public pay phones when discussing illicit business, were careful to use plain manila envelopes if mailing material, and were cautious in what went into wastepaper baskets at the close of a meeting.

The penalties incurred by these businesses may seem high to the average man, but the fines must be viewed in perspective. As Geis (1967) put it: "The original fines were, of course, negligible: for General Electric, a half-million dollar loss was no more unsettling than a 3 dollar parking fine would be to a man with an income of 175,000 dollars a year." As for serving a thirty day jail sentence for attempting to hold-up the American public in a billion dollar fraud, it is something less than the traditional city-court measure of "ten dollars or ten days." Perhaps the best commentary on the reaction of society to this type of crime was made by the Pullman porter who observed, "Steal ten dollars and you go to jail, steal the railroad and you go to the Senate."

It is impossible to measure with any accuracy the full extent to which the American public is victimized by price-fixing and collusion on the part of corporations in the United States. Sutherland's investigations (1949) [7] are perhaps the most comprehensive attempt to ascertain the extent to which corporations abide by the laws and regulations controlling them. Sutherland found that the seventy largest manufacturing and mercantile corporations in the United States had, over a forty-five year period, been involved in 980 "infringement" proceedings, ranging from a high of fifty decisions for one firm to a low of a single decision for the least implicated incorporation. What is at stake in the regulation of American business practices is not quibbling over the gray-area of where sharp business practices end and criminality begins, but the survival of the free-enterprise system.

The dictum *Caveat emptor* (let the buyer beware) is wise counsel for the American consumer. Recent frauds are listed in Table 12-2.

Interpretation

"A complete explanation of white collar crime," wrote Sutherland (1949), "cannot be derived from the available data" (1949). Sutherland hypothesized that white collar crime had its origin in the same general process as other criminal behavior, i.e. differential association. Unfortunately, the personal documents which he used to trace the manner in which criminal behavior becomes defined favorably were biographical documents of the career of a

---

[7]Sutherland wrote prior to the rise of prominence of Ralph Nader. What Sutherland hypothesized in a general manner about business practices, Nader has documented.

used-car salesman, a graduate student who worked part-time as a shoe salesman, a detail man for a book publishing company, and a certified public accountant. It is puzzling why a scholar of Sutherland's stature would attempt documentation on the basis of four case histories for which no claim of representativeness is made and, in each instance, illustrated theft in "penny-ante" operations.

A second type of evidence Sutherland presents to support his theory of differential association is the diffusion of illegal practices, e.g. one firm devises a method (legal or illegal) of increasing profits; and, other firms, guided only by the "profit motive" (the ancients called it 'greed') , adopt it to remain competitive.

This practice of diffusion through imitation is facilitated if the firms are competitors. They keep up with each other more closely by the trend toward centralization of the control of industry by investment banks and by the conferences of business concerns in trade associations. Sutherland felt that businessmen were isolated from definitions unfavorable to white collar crime. As large corporations supply the mass media with their principle source of income via advertising, any media which vigorously attacked the shady practices of these corporations would do so at the risk of losing a large portion of their advertising income. Government agencies, the only other major regulating source for business, have a less critical attitude toward businessmen and generally select equity procedures for businessmen accused of restraint of trade and criminal procedures for trade unionists accused of the same crime. Sutherland explains this attitude on the basis that persons in government and business are recruited from the same social class and are culturally homogeneous. Thus isolated from criticism from a mass media neutralized by advertising fees, and from governmental employees conscious of their own kind, the businessman learns criminal attitudes in a milieu relatively free of competing definitions of the situation.

Sutherland employs differential association to explain individual crime, and the concept of social disorganization to explain the type and extent of crime on a societal level. Social disorganization may refer to anomie or the lack of standards to guide the behavior of individual members of society or to a conflict of standards of behavior between competing groups in society. The individual does not know what to do, the groups cannot agree. Because society is complex, technical and changing fairly rapidly, old standards break down before new ones are adopted. For example: The movement from a *laissez-faire* economy, i.e. the idea that supply and demand will create a self-regulating economy (Adam Smith's "Invisible Hand"), toward an economy with government's quite visible hand, regulating and promoting sections of the economy, required a new set of business standards. This period, which Sutherland locates roughly three to six decades after the Civil War, created an uncertainty with both business and the consumer, which is not fully resolved. However, Sutherland himself was not satisfied with the concept of social disorganization, feeling it was imprecisely defined, had ethical implications which were non-scientific, and could not be tested for validity.

The concept is best seen as a point of departure. It points to the problem and describes the conflict of standards; it does not, however, explain the origin or content for this conflict of standards. This does not mean that the concept is without use, only that it is incomplete in its present form.

Quinney (1963), in his study of prescription violation by retail pharmacists, found that violation is related to the structure of the occupation. Pharmacy incorporates two different roles, professional and business. Structural strain is built into the occupation. The pharmacist must orient himself either toward the businessman role, whose function is to make a profit at merchandising, or toward the role of the professional man, whose duty it is to render a medical service. Prescription violation occurred with greatest frequency among "business pharmacists" and least among "professional pharmacists." Professional-business pharmacists and indifferent pharmacists were intermediate in the frequency of prescription violation. Quinney concluded that prescription violation is related to the structure of the occupation and the differential orientation of retail pharmacist. The implications for the study of "white collar" crime is that the structure of the occupation itself must become the focus of study if the criminal behavior is to be clearly understood.

Cressey (1950) interviewed all prisoners at the Illinois State Penitentiaries at Joliet who could be classified as "trust violators." When told by a prisoner that embezzlement would not occur if the trusted person always told his wife and family about his financial problems,[8] Cressey began a line of revision of his initial hypothesis which resulted in his explanation of trust violations in terms of three conditions necessary for violation: (1) psychological isolation, (2) technical skills necessary for such violation, and (3) an adequate rationalization for his conduct, e.g. he is "borrowing" the money as a businessman and not stealing it as a thief. In final form the statement read:

> Trusted persons become trust violators when they conceive of themselves as having a financial problem which is nonsharable, have a knowledge or awareness that this problem can be secretly resolved by violation of the position of financial trust, and are able to apply to their conceptions of themselves as trusted persons with their conceptions of themselves as users of the entrusted funds or property.

PROFESSIONAL CRIMINALS

Crime has its professionals, just as any other occupation or activity. We separate professional criminals from other offenders on two bases: (1) his skill and competence as an expert; and (2) his self-concept that crime is his career, and the degree of his committment to the criminal subculture.

Typically, the professional criminal engages in nonviolent crimes which require shrewdness rather than force. The classic work in the field is Sutherland's analysis of *The Professional Thief* (1937).

Professional criminals (Clinard and Quinney, 1967) are highly skilled, both in the techniques of fraud and in their ability to have charges dropped when they come under the scrutiny of the

---

[8]"As for Cressey's 'The Criminal Violation of Financial Trust,' I have known, personally and professionally, many violators of financial trust in and out of prison who, self admittedly, had no nonsharable financial problem. Most of them faced no problem of adjusting their conceptions of themselves as trusted persons to their misuse of entrusted funds or property. They didn't go to the sociological trouble! What is a nonsharable problem?" (p. 92) .

law. Because of their shrewdness, professional criminals are accorded the highest prestige by their fellow criminals (child-molesters are at the bottom of the criminal status-hierarchy). Professional criminals tend to come from a slightly higher socio-economic background, enter their criminal career patterns relatively late in life, and due to their skill in avoiding arrest, remain actively engaged in crime longer than other offenders. Essential to the successful pursuit of any criminal activity is a supporting justification or ideology. The professional criminal views himself as a businessman, dismissing the honesty of other men as simply a lack of opportunity to make money illicity.

Con "Games"

Schur (1957) states that "con" games of whatever type follow a pattern. The first step is the selection of a "mark" or victim. The con man then establishes rapport with the intended victim, and when he feels the mark has sufficient "confidence" in him, he "shares" with the victim a scheme by which they can make some fast money. Too late, the mark realizes that he has been the betrayed victim—the "pigeon"—rather than the clever participant in a swindle.

Victims of criminal fraud rarely report their loses, either due to their own involvement in a questionable enterprise, reluctance to "get involved," or embarrassment at being "taken." In 1970, according to the *Uniform Crime Reports,* there were 104,600 arrests for fraud. On the thirty offenses listed, fraud ranked sixteenth in the total number of arrests. There were 10,000 arrests for embezzlement. It is important to remember that the same person may be arrested several times during one year for the same offense. As with all criminal statistics, arrest data is primarily a measure of police activity; it may, however, be used, with caution, as an index of criminal activity. Conviction in a confidence charge is difficult to obtain; when sentence is imposed, it tends to be light.

Schur reminds us that a con game is just that, a type of game. The mark is compared to an actor in a carefully rehearsed play in which every other member of the cast except the victim has memorized his lines perfectly.

As in prostitution and drug-sales, the character of the victim is a necessary ingredient for the successful completion of the crime. A confidence man must find a mark with a little larceny in his heart before he is in business. Honest men do not knowingly become involved in swindles, which raises some interesting questions concerning prosecution. Is a confidence game a "victimless" crime? Often, the victim gets the criminal he deserves.

Psychoanalytically oriented psychiatrists have seen the victim of a swindle as having a "need" to be punished and attribute his acts to an unconscious desire to be punished for his participation in a wrongful act. Such masochistic behavior or unconscious "death wish" motivations are best left to those who feel they can read the unconscious.

Structurally, Schur relates fraud to a society which fosters salesmanship and risk-taking to achieve success. Confidence games are based on salesmanship and the ability to "sell" one's personality. (Students who wish a practical application of this phenomena are invited to visit a new or used car dealer) .

The implication for the sociology of crime, according to Schur, is to view confidence swindling from a structural-functional prospective. According to this view, the deviance in question must be seen as serving both manifest and latent functions. Since our fraud laws are ineffective, Schur hypothesizes fraud may be serving some durable function in the social structure. Schur does not identify that function nor is he certain what sort of adjustment should be made in the social system to legitimize whatever function is served by this crime. He does suggest the solution as beginning by viewing deviance structurally on a social-system level.

Roebuck (1971) has isolated a number of the more common frauds utilized by professional con artists. Con games are separated into the category of "big con" or "long con," involving numerous accomplises and elaborate props, and the "short con" games with fewer actors, which demand less skill and finesse. The following four frauds are considered "short con" games.

HIGH DICE. This bunko game is based on the mark's desire to be recognized as an important person in his community. The operation requires two confederates. The stage is usually a railway station. Operator 1 will select a well-dressed man or woman who appears to have resources. While he is establishing rapport with the mark, Operator 2 will disembark from an incoming train and stand around "yokel-like" in seeming bewilderment. Operator goes over to him in the guise of offering some aid. He returns to the victim with the story that this simple farm boy has come to the city with substantial savings and is concerned that he will be duped of his funds unless he can find some honest person to help him handle his money.

Operator 1 confies to the victim that it would be an easy mark to relieve this yokel of his money. The yokel, he explains, is too dumb to call the police. The "plot" thickens as the yokel expresses a fear of banks but is willing to part with his money if the victim will withdraw some of his own money and place it with his. Under this condition the yokel will allow the victim to deposit both lots of money in any safe place that he choses. The victim goes to the bank, withdraws his money, and is persuaded by the seemingly naive yokel to place both lots of money in a large brown envelope. As the yokel (Operator 2) diverts the victim with animated conversation, Operator 1 cleverly makes a switch, placing the envelope with the two rolls of money in his breast pocket and hands the victim a similar envelope containing folded paper. The yokel, satisfied that his money is safe, obtains the victims address and promises to come to his house within the hour. Each operator departs in separate directions while the victim hurries home to count his "easy" money.

PIGEON DROP. An ancient con game reported introduced into this country by Chinese immigrants, it is based on the victim's own greed. The plot has three acts. In the first act, the "catch man" approaches a victim with a tale designed to win sympathy and develop trust. In the second act, the "hit partner" enters the play with the news that he has found some money, usually bookie receipts. In order to partake of this "windfall," the victim is asked to produce his own "earnest money," and in a "switch," the money which the victim is asked to put-up in "good faith" comes into possession of the players. In the third act, the "blowoff," the victim is given some final bogus instructions which allow the confederates to leave his presence before he realizes he has been victimized.

SPANISH PRISONER GAME. This con game would warm a novelist's heart. The "mark" is approached with an impressive looking "smuggled" letter from a prisoner (ordinary Latin American). The prisoner's letter promises the mark a sizeable portion of his estate, and his daughter's hand in marriage, if he will effect his daughter's escape from this terrible country by sending a large sum of money to a certain courier. (A picture of a beautiful girl is attached). Thus avarice, sex, romance, intrigue—all combine to make a Walter Mitty fantacy a realistic con game.)

THE GREASY PIG OR THE OLD SHELL GAME. One of the oldest of con games is the old shell game of State Fair fame. Three nut shells are used, and a pea-shaped object is shifted from one cover to another by a nimble fingered operator. On most occasions, the pea is held under the operator's fingernails instead of under the shell. The victim is allowed to win just enough to whet his appetite, and this "variable reinforcement" maintains the victim's futile attempt to gain some fast money.

Other small time con games are the "Badger Game" and the "Murphy Game." In the former, a prostitute brings the mark to her room and during their activities a confederate breaks in upon them and feigns the role of the shocked and outraged husband. The mark pays off the "aggrieved" husband and slinks away embarrassed and poorer. A "spinoff" to this game is the "Murphy Game"; the con man poses as a pimp, accepts the money from a mark to procure a prostitute and then simply disappears.

Summary

Organized crime, as this chapter attempts to show, depends for its continued existence on public complicity or, at least, upon public apathy toward its activities. Gambling, loan sharking, prostitution, narcotics, and the infiltration of labor unions and legitimate business constitute the principal revenue sources of the Mafia, whose organizational structure and functions are briefly described. To a lesser extent, public acquiescence ("the mark") is essential to the successful operation of con games like "the pigeon drop," "greasy pig," and "the Spanish prisoner," all of which call for a willingness on the part of the potential victim to engage in quasi-legal or actually illegal behavior. The chapter also explores in some detail the category of so-called "white collar crimes," those offenses committed "by a person of respectability and high social status in the course of his occupation," as criminologist Sutherland originally defined them. Attention is given to problems of detection, enforcement, and prevention of all three major categories of criminal action.

REFERENCES

Anderson, R. T.: From Mafia to Cosa Nostra. *American Journal of Sociology, 71:*302-310, 1965.

Bell, D.: Crime, an American way of life. *Antioch Review, 13:*131-154, 1953.

Bloch, H. A.: The gambling business: an American paradox. *Crime and Delinquency, 8:*371-378, 1962.

Caldwell, R. G.: Book review. *Journal of Criminal Law, Criminology, and Police Science, 50:*610, 1959.

The Challenge of Crime in a Free Society. New York, Avon Books, 1968.

Chandler, D.: Louisiana's unshaken mobster boss. *Life, 68:*30, 1970.

Cook, F. J.: Just call 'the doctor' for a loan. *New York Times Magazine, 19:* Jan, 28, 1968.

Clinard, M. B. and Quinney, R.: *Criminal Behavior Systems: a Typology.* New York, Holt, Rinehart, and Wilson, Inc., 1967.

Cressey, D. R.: The criminal violation of financial trust. *American Sociological Review, 15:*738-743, 1950.

Cressey, D. R.: Methodological problems in the study of organized crime as a social problem. *The Annals, 374:*101-112, 1967.

Edwards, G.: Sentencing the raketeer. *Crime and Delinquency, 9:*391-397, 1963.

Fly, Sally: New taps on freedom. *The Nation, 208:*697-699, 1969.

Geis, G.: White collar crime: the heavy electrical equipment antitrust cases of 1961. In Clinard and Quinney: *Criminal Behavior Systems: A Typology,* New York, Holt, Rinehart and Winston, Inc., 1967.

Gibbons, D. C.: *Society, Crime and Criminal Careers.* Englewood Cliffs, Prentice-Hall, 1968.

Hartung, F. E.: White collar offenses in the wholesale meat industry in Detroit. *The American Journal of Sociology, 50:*25-34, 1950.

Holt, D.: Attorney, Organized Crime Section, Criminal Division, Department of Justice. (Personal communication.)

LaFranchi, R. and Martinez, T. M.: Why people play poker. *Trans-Action*, *6*:30-35, 1969.

Maas, P.: *The Valachi Papers*. New York, Putnam, 1968.

Mankiewicz, F.: *Perfectly Clear: Nixon From Whittier To Watergate*. New York, Quadrangle Books, 1973.

Mannheim, H.: *Comparative Criminology*. New York, Houghton Mifflin, 1965.

McClellan, J. L.: Weak link in our war on the Mafia. *Reader's Digest, 96*:56-61, 1970.

McClellan, J. L.: Organized crime in the United States. *Vital Speeches of the Day, 35*:388-400, 1969.

Mower, E. R.: Social crises and social disorganization. *American Sociological Review, 15*:64, 1950.

Newman, D. J.: White collar crime. *Law and Contemporary Problems, 23*: 735-753, 1958.

Quinney, R.: Occupational structure and criminal behavior: prescription violation by retail pharmacists. *Social Problems, 10*:179-185, 1963.

Roebuck, J. B.: *Criminal Typology*. Springfield, Charles C Thomas, 1971.

Ruth, H. S.: Why organized crime thrives. *The Annals, 374*:113-122, 1967.

Salerno, R.: Organized crime: an unmet challenge to criminal justice. *Crime and Delinquency, 15*:333-340, 1969.

Schulz, W.: The mob's grip on New Jersey. *Reader's Digest, 98*:111-115, 1971.

Schur, E. M.: Sociological analysis of confidence swindling. *Journal of Criminal Law, Criminology and Police Science, 48*:296-304, 1957.

Second Interim Report of the Kefauver Committee. Washington, U. S. Government Printing Office, 1951.

Sellin, T.: Organized crime: a business enterprise. *The Annals of the American Academy of Political and Social Science, 247*:69-71, 1963.

Smith, R. A.: The incredible electrical conspiracy. *Fortune, 63*:132-180, April, 1961; *63*:161-224, May 1961.

Sutherland, E. H.: *White Collar Crime*. New York, The Dryden Press, 1949.

Tappan, P. W.: Who is the criminal? *American Sociological Review, 12*:96-102, 1947.

The clerk's wild ride. *Newsweek, 73*:82, 1969.

Uniform Crime Report for 1970. Washington, U. S. Government Printing Office, 1971.

Williams, T.H.: *Huey Long*. New York, Knopf, 1969.

Woetzel, R. K.: An overview of organized crime: mores versus morality. *The Annals of the American Academy of Political and Social Science, 347*:1-11, 1963.

Wilson, W.: The threat of organized crime: highlighting the challenging new frontiers on criminal law. *Notre Dame Lawyer*, 46, 41-54, 1970.

Part IV

LAW ENFORCEMENT AND CRIMINAL JUSTICE

Aᴌᴛʜᴏᴜɢʜ ᴛʜᴇ ᴘᴏʟɪᴄᴇ do not bear the primary responsibility for most of the social problems that originate within the community, there is an inevitable tendency on the part of the public to look to the police for their solution—or at least for their control. Thus, when the rising incidence of crime became a public issue in the middle of the 1960s, most Americans considered "the crime problem" essentially a matter for the police. Now, nearly a decade later, the public is still largely ignorant of the complexities concealed by such a facile phrase as "the crime problem," particularly with regard to causation and prevention. As Wilson (1968) has noted: "The police can do relatively little about preventing most common crimes. . . . A community concerned about lowering its crime rates would be well advised to devote its attention and resources to those parts of the criminal justice system, especially the courts and correctional agencies, which, unlike the police, spend most of their time processing—often in the most perfunctory and ineffective manner—persons who repeatedly perpetrate these crimes." Nevertheless, most private citizens remain completely unfamiliar with the workings of the criminal justice system, only one portion of which, the police, is visible in its daily operations.

Although the nature of their work places them in full view of the public, the police are one of the least understood occupational groups in American society. Chapter 13 (The Police) attempts to examine some of the reasons why law enforcement personnel are subject to social isolation and a tendency to regard

421

themselves as members of a minority group. An antidote to isolation has been sought in the development of police-community relations programs, but this goal must be seen as part of a more comprehensive and long-range effort toward the upgrading of law enforcement to meet the increasingly rigorous standards of police professionalization.

Chapter 14 deals with the apparatus of criminal justice administration and its functioning. Our objective here was not to present a detailed description of the American court system—one of the most complicated and ramified judicial structures in contemporary society—or the manifold tasks and duties of the prosecutor, defense counsel, and the judge. Rather, our purpose was to convey a general impression of the overall operation of the administration of criminal justice, beginning with arrest and concluding with trial and sentencing.

The final chapter in this section focuses on the issue of criminal responsibility and the variety of ways the court has devised for handling its diminution or impairment through conditions affecting "defect or deficiency in reason." As the chapter attempts to show, these efforts have largely involved the reconciliation of the fact-finding processes of the medical and psychiatric approach with those of the adversary trial. The result has been a continuing controversy that has been freshly fueled by behavioral scientists who are equally critical of both the legal and the psychiatric approaches to the issue of criminal responsibility.

REFERENCE

Wilson, J.Q.: *Varieties of Police Behavior.* Cambridge, Massachusetts, Harvard University Press, 1968.

Chapter 13

THE POLICE

IN THE BEST SELLING NOVEL *The New Centurions,* written by a veteran Los Angeles policeman, the rookie patrolman Serge Duran is lectured by an experienced officer about the vantage point held by police in the criminal justice system (Wambaugh, 1970) : "You're going to find out before too long that we're the only ones that see the victims," said Galloway. "The judges and probation officers and social workers and everybody else think mainly about the suspect and how they can help him stop whatever he specializes in doing to his victims—but you and me are the only one who sees what he does to his victims—right after it's done. And this is only a little burglary."

The police represent some 420,000 people, working for approximately 40,000 separate agencies that spend more than $2\frac{1}{2}$ billion dollars a year. They are the part of the criminal justice system that is in direct daily contact with both crime and the public. Thus, the responsibilities of the police are more distinctive than those of other service agencies. The police are charged with performing their function where all eyes can see, where the going is toughest—on the street. Since this is a time of rising crime, increasing social unrest, and growing public sensitivity, it is also a time when police work is particularly important, complicated, conspicuous, and delicate.

POLICE TASKS: THE OPERATIVE LEVEL

What kind of jobs are the police expected to perform? According to the *Task Force Report: The Police* (1967) , "It is generally assumed by the public that the police enforce the criminal laws and preserve peace mechanically, simply by arresting anyone who has deviated from legislative norms of acceptable behavior." On the contrary, police work is highly discretionary. First of all, the police do not possess the resources to enforce all criminal laws equally. Second, the other agencies of the criminal justice system are unable to cope with all violators. Corroboration for this contention can be found in crowded and backlogged court calendars, large probation and parole caseloads, and overcrowded prisons. Further, the police are faced with the necessity for enforcing many laws which seek to regulate social conduct—laws which are often unpopular, ambiguous, unenforceable, or which can apply to the common activities of law abiding citizens, even though they were intended to apply only to the activities of certain kinds of criminals. Gambling is an example of just such an activity.

Finally, the police are responsible for considering the foreseeable consequences of an arrest. As the Task Force Report states, "In light of these inherent limitations, individual police officers must, of necessity, be given considerable latitude in exercising their arrest power. As a result, no task committed to individual judgment is more complex or delicate. A mistake in judgment can precipitate a riot on one hand or, culminate in subsequent criminal activity by a person who was erroneously released by an officer on the other hand." An unjustified arrest can seriously, perhaps permanently, affect the future course of a man's life. The importance of the arrest power and the need for rational exercise of this power cannot be overstated.

Police are called upon to make legally correct decisions instantly, under stress and often without advice, that will hold up under hours of scrutiny and legal research by a defense lawyer. Further, police are often required to settle domestic family fights, deliver babies, and a vast variety of other tasks which do not involve criminal conduct directly. They are also called upon to prevent crime, which requires above all an intuitive sense for suspicious conduct and an understanding of human behavior; in short, they must be "streetwise." As Dr. Ruth Levy (Task Force Report, 1967) has stated:

> Reviewing the tasks we expect of our law enforcement officers, it

is my impression that their complexity is perhaps greater than that of any other profession. On the other hand, we expect our law enforcement officer to possess the nurturing, caretaking, sympathetic, empathizing, gentle characteristics of a physician, nurse, social worker, etc., as he deals with school traffic, acute illness and injury, suicidal threats, missing persons, etc. On the other hand, we expect him to command respect, demonstrate courage, control hostile impulses, and meet great physical hazards . . . He is to control crowds, prevent riots, apprehend criminals, and chase after speeding vehicles. I can think of no other profession which constantly demands such seemingly opposite characteristics.

The police mission or task is basically to protect life and property and preserve the peace. To accomplish this goal, the police officer's job will include (but not be limited to) the following categories of function:

1. preventive patrol
2. investigation of criminal law violations, detection and apprehension of offenders
3. prosecution-court witness
4. traffic accident investigation and traffic enforcement
5. juvenile work
6. routine calls—disturbing the peace complaints, advice, some drunk calls, etc.
7. service calls
8. family beefs (domestic quarrels)
9. public relations
10. first aid

A criminologist (Fox, 1964) claims that only about 10 percent of the policeman's time and energy are taken up by law enforcement per se; the rest is occupied by what might be called "social welfare functions." There seems to be a contest among some police departments today to see who can undertake the largest number and the most unusual non-law enforcement type projects. There are "Junior Mounted Posses," "Police Athletic Leagues," and the like springing up faster than youngsters can be found to put in them. A juvenile officer is many times judged by how many ball clubs he has formed and is actively involved in. One police administrator (Clark, 1968) recently recommended that from "delinquency prevention" and "family prevention" police departments move on to various forms of offender treatment such as detoxification units, work furloughs, "week-enders," and halfway house programs.

Much of the confusion about the role of the police officer, both from the viewpoint of the public and from the viewpoint of the officer himself, stems from confusion of the terms "law enforcement" and "crime prevention." Both are the designated duties of today's policeman, but they are not one and the same. The concept of the policeman evolved from the necessity for an agency of government to enforce the law. As a matter of administrative convenience, in this country he has also been charged with the prevention of crime. His existence, of course, serves as a deterrent to some crimes. What he does beyond that is left up to him.

Police Discretionary Powers

Basic to the performance of law enforcement duties is the discretionary arrest powers of the police officer. It is almost impossible to conceive of a criminal justice system without built-in discretionary provisions at every level of operation. As La Fave (1965) puts it, "If every policeman, every prosecutor, every court, and every post-sentence agency performed his or its responsibility in strict accordance with rules of law, precisely and narrowly laid down, the criminal law would be ordered but intolerable." The power of decision to invoke or not to invoke the law is one of the few areas of autonomy remaining to the police. One spokesman from the field of law (Goldstein, 1969) has called the police discretion, with regard to the invocation or non-invocation of the criminal process, the "outer limits of law enforcement." Skolnick (1967) mentions that "Whether it is a question of writing out a traffic citation, arresting a spouse on a charge of assault with a deadly weapon, or apprehending an addict informer, the policeman has enormous power . . ." What are some of the things that govern the courses of action he will take?

This process comes to light at a much greater frequency in the so-called lesser crimes or in areas where no arrests may be involved at all. Aaron (1967) emphasizes this when he states "The critical problem in the control of police discretion, however, is not the discretion employed by the police in criminal investigations, rather it is the area of day to day police routine involving non-arrest and prosecution citizen contact which is the bulk of police activity in the United States today."

By their very nature and importance, decisions involving occurrances of felonies and some more serious misdemeanors are the subject of specific approaches; rules and procedures for handling them are carefully laid out and adhered to by most law enforcement agencies. It is the minor infractions or stopping of people in the streets that call for exercise of descretion. Says Niederhoffer (1967) :

> It is the individual policeman's responsibility to decide if and how the law should be applied, and he searches for the proper combination of clues on which to base his decision. These are derived from the typical sociological variables: class, education, clarity of role prescriptions, reference groups, self conception, and visability. Because the application of the law depends to a large degree on the definition of the situation and the decision reached by the patrolman, he, in effect, makes the law. It is his decision that establishes the boundry between legal and illegal.

THE STRUCTURE OF AMERICAN LAW ENFORCEMENT

There are at least five strata of police services in the United States: (1) police agencies of the Federal government, (2) state police, (3) sheriffs and their deputies, (4) metropolitan police departments, and (5) town or village police departments. With few exceptions, each local government, regardless of how small or weak it may be, insists upon its own police department and thus the most striking characteristics of American police patterns are decentralization and fragmentation.

During the 18th and 19th Centuries, when communications were poor, transportation inadequate and slow, and towns and cities were widely dispersed, local autonomy on the part of each township was a sound approach to the problem of controlling crime. Presently, criminals do not "stay home," organized crime is international in scope, and criminals commit offenses in more than one state. By comparison, the police system in this country is antiquated and inefficient.

The President's Commission on Law Enforcement and Administration of Justice has stated, "The machinery of law enforcement in this country is fragmented, complicated, and frequently overlapping" (Task Force Report, 1967). It goes on to say that the ineffectiveness of the state and local administration of criminal justice is largely the consequence of inadequate organization of their agencies.

There is no centralized supervision, but instead, many small police forces each having its own jurisdictions. The Kefauver investigation stated that this has created islands of lawlessness where law officers seem unable to enforce the statutes. A criminal does not recognize the police's territorial boundaries; in fact, he often exploits this weakness to his advantage.

The agencies have inadequate systems of information and control, lack of departmental boundaries, and wasteful duplication in office services. Most agencies have not publicly admitted that this departmentalism and failure in coordination has led to failures and wastes in their own cases. The various departments display tension, mutual distrust, jealousy, and confusion: all of which prevents mutual cooperation and coordination. To increase their credits, each police department withholds information which might lead another department to make the arrest.

The local autonomy has encouraged decentralization and, in some jurisdictions, corruption. Local politics often gets in the way of police departments, inasmuch as the politicians want to be able to control the police. There are also other instances of defective internal organization, e.g. too many uncoordinated administrative units reporting directly to the head of police.

Not only do the agencies waste money through the individual purchase of special equipment, they often seem indifferent to the potential savings involved in the consolidation of training programs, laboratories, information about criminals, and communications facilities. Because the police system is ineffective in many ways, the public opinion of police officers tends to be rather poor; this is a possible factor in the difficulty of recruiting able men. The career of police officers is not a job with sufficient prestige or honor to attract enough top-flight men to fill all positions.

The Police and the Public

Traditionally, the American policeman has been characterized as stupid, corrupt, brutal, and abusive. It is easy to see how the policeman acquired this stereotype. As the Task Force Report (1967) has indicated:

> In years gone by it was the attitude among police and public that any man of general ability could learn to police by doing it. Consequently, the then prevailing philosophy was one of providing the recruit with a uniform and badge; arming him with a baton, revolver, and handcuffs; assuring his geographical orientation by issuing him a local street map; and instructing him to "hit the street" and enforce the ten commandments.

With background and entrance requirements such as these, it is not surprising that, by 1939, the field had attracted enough maladjusted individuals to warrant the findings by sociologist Read Bain (Niederhoffer, 1969) that "three-quarters of the policemen in the United States were mentally unfit for their work." Kates (Niederhoffer, 1969), after studying the results of Rorschach tests given to New York policemen, concluded that "the more maladjusted policemen tended to be more satisfied with their work than the less maladjusted." In 1944, in his book *An American Dilemma*, Gunnar Myrdral commented: "Almost anyone on the outside of a penitentiary who weighs enough and is not blind or crippled can be considered as a police candidate."

As recently as 1965, an Albany, New York veteran police officer made the following disclosure when asked about education and training for police: "You can't apply book training out in the street. You have to rely on men with experience. The training is all right, but you can't take it too seriously" (Wilson, 1968). Another senior police officer in Newburgh, New York, when asked about college level courses for police, said, "Police science courses are not necessary. You can't teach a man to be a good policeman: he must have the aptitude naturally" (Wilson, 1968). Attitudes of this kind among police find a ready counterpart among public attitudes toward the police, as evidenced by the prevalence of abusive terms like "pig," "fuzz," and "the heat"— the verbal component of negative stereotypes of the police.

What Policing Does to the Police

Skolnick (1966) has addressed himself to the analysis of how the features in the policeman's environment interact with the paramilitary police organization to generate what he calls a "working personality."

The danger present in the policeman's environment makes of him a "suspicious" person. He must respond to reported assaults against person and property. Because of his preoccupation with violence, he develops a stereotyping perceptual shorthand to identify "symbolic assailants," e.g. "black equals danger." The individual policeman's "suspiciousness" does not necessarily derive from a personal experience but may be achieved by a vicarious identification with fellow policemen who may have been the victims of violence in the line of duty. Socially isolated from a community which perceives them as occupying soldiers in an occupied country (especially in ghetto sections) the police band together with a solidarity surpassing most occupational groupings.

The authority invested in the policeman's role further isolates him from a public which resents his direction of their activities (traffic, sports events) and resents his regulation of public morality. The policeman is further charged with hypocrisy for he has probably engaged in some of the activities he forbids (drunkenness).

The law is conservative. It reinforces the status quo. It should not be surprising that the men who enforce these laws are conventional persons, political and social conservatives. Attitudes follow actions, and the drive toward consistent cognitions (cognitive dissonance) makes the policeman's role an unattractive one for political radicals.

According to Banton (1964), the British policeman is more impersonal in his approach to offenders than his American counterpart because the role of the policeman in British society is more clearly defined and confers authority in a wider range of situations. The American police officer cannot rely solely upon the authority of his badge and must develop effective public relations skills for handling such "sticky" situations as domestic disputes and the arrest of a public drunk.

The typical Britisher is less likely than his American cousin to challenge the authority of the police. Secure in his role, the Bobbie-on-the-beat is much more likely to behave in a deferential manner to a wider range of persons. (No one likes to be given a ticket, however, and even in rigid Russia, citizens grumble over traffic tickets.) The American policeman who behaved in an overly respectful manner would almost certainly be misinterpreted by a skeptical public.

Banton was impressed that the role of the policeman in Britain was filled with a wide variety of personality types, ranging from the "clown" to the "mandarin." He quotes the conclusion of a team of management consultants who appraised senior members of the Chicago police department and found them to be, not a bundle of psycho-sadistic neurotics, but resembling more the Gary Cooper image of "High Noon"—rather decent, kindly men "with a job to do."[1]

After comparing the relative respect ascribed to the policeman's role in Britain and America, Banton concluded that the police were a "sacred" (less open to satire and ridicule) sort of institution in Britain. He explains this is a reflection, in part, of the values of the British social system which is more integrated, less pluralistic, and more traditionally oriented than the social system of America. Police symbolize the social order of Britain to a greater extent than is true of the United States.

Police Brutality

To find some (Reiss, 1968) answers to the questions: How widespread in police brutality? Do the police mistreat blacks more than whites? Thirty-six people working for the Center of Research on Social Organization observed police-citizen encounters in the cities of Boston, Chicago, and Washington, D.C. for seven weeks. In only 37 of 3826 encounters did the police use undue force. Other findings were:

1. The rate of excessive force for all white citizens in encounters with the police is twice that for black citizens.

---

[1]When we showed this statement to a student who had been nightsticked by a Washington, D.C. cop during a peace demonstration, her reaction—to put it as delicately as possible—was vigorous disagreement with this image.

2. There is little difference between the rate of force used by white and black policemen.
3. About one in every ten policemen in high crime rate areas of cities sometimes uses force unnecessarily.
4. The most likely victim of excessive force is a lower-class man of either race.
5. Police are likely to use force in settings they control (they select their own turf).
6. Policemen do not restrain their fellow policemen.

The answer to incidents of police brutality appears to lie in either greater supervision of professionalization, but it should be kept in mind that even established professions, e.g. law and medicine, experience malpractice.

The Policeman as Minority Group Member

The policeman's role in society tends to alienate him from society as a whole. Lipset (1969) indicates that "the policeman's role is particularly subject to fostering feelings of resentment against society, which flow from a typical source of radical politics, 'status discrepancies'." This refers to the ranking of individuals who are high on one status attribute and low on another. The policeman is given much authority by society to protect life, property, and to keep public order and is expected to risk his life if necessary. However, the policeman feels that he receives little prestige for his actions. He gets paid much less than other occupational groups who are given comparatively less authority. He is ranked high, in that he is given the authority to act, but is given very little reward once he has acted, which shows a low ranking.

This isolation and rejection of the police from society, James Q. Wilson (as quoted by Lipset, 1969) argues, "results in a sense of alienation from society, which presses the police to develop their own "sub-culture" with norms which can provide them with 'a basis for self-respect independent to some degree of civilian attitudes'." As Lipset (1969) points out, "many police have consciously come to look upon themselves as an oppressed minority, subject to the same kind of prejudice as other minorities."

Wagley and Harris (1966) have distinguished five features of minority groups:

1. Minority is a social group whose members experience at the hands of another social group various disabilities in the form of prejudice, discrimination, segregation, or persecution (or any combination of these).

2. The disabilities experienced by minorities are related to special characteristics that its members share, either physical or cultural or both, which the dominant group holds in low esteem.

3. Minorities are self-conscious social units; they are characterized by a consciousness of kind.

4. Generally a person does not become a member of a minority voluntarily; he or she is born into it.

5. Members of a minority group, by choice or necessity, tend to marry within their own group (endogamy).

The first three of the above criteria are applicable and help in comprehending the process by which the police image has changed from that of the good, honest Irish cop to that of the faceless, anonymous "pig".

Evaluation of Criteria

A minority is a social group whose members' experiences at the hands of another social group various disabilities in the form of prejudice, discrimination, segregation, or persecution (or any combination of these).

Because of their occupation and responsibilities, people tend to isolate police from their circle of friends. Such social discrimination is depicted in the following quotation:

> Several months after I joined the force, my wife and I used to be socially active with a crowd of young people, mostly married, who gave a lot of parties where there was drinking and dancing, and we enjoyed it. I've never forgotten, though, an incident that happened on one Fourth of July party. Everybody had been drinking, there was a lot of talking, people were feeling boisterous, and some kid there—he must have been twenty or twenty-two—threw a firecracker that hit my wife in the leg and burned her. I didn't know exactly what to do—punch the guy in the nose, bawl him out, just forget it. Anyway, I couldn't let it pass, so I walked over to him and told him he ought to be care-

ful. He began to rise up at me, and when he did, somebody yelled, "Better watch out, he's a cop!" I saw everybody standing there, and I could feel they were all against me and for the kid, even though he had thrown the firecracker at my wife. I went over to the host and said it was probably better if my wife and I left because a fight would put a damper on the party. Actually, I'd hoped he would ask the kid to leave, since the kid had thrown the firecracker, But he didn't so we left. After that incident, my wife and I stopped going around with that crowd, and decided that if we were going to go to parties where there was to be drinking and boisterousness, we weren't going to be the only police people there (Skolnick, 1966).

Police are also apt to isolate themselves as well as be isolated by others. Neighbors and friends never divorce the man from the badge. At parties and social gatherings when guests discover there is a policeman present, they typically tell about the crooked cops they knew or how unfairly a friend of theirs was handled by a cop. Most veteran officers grow weary of defending the police and withdraw into close associations with other officers. Given a choice they would prefer to relax in the company of their associates at gatherings sponsored by the Fraternal Order of Police. Further, the irregular hours created by shift work makes it difficult for policemen to mesh their off-hours with those of neighbors engaged in "normal" occupations. A police officer is never "off-duty." Most departments require an officer to carry a gun when not working and make arrests in outstanding cases.

Not only does the discrimination affect the policeman, but also his wife and children. The following concerns the difficulties encountered by the wife of a policeman:

Whenever I go downtown shopping I feel like I'm wearing Bill's uniform. When people do special things for you, you're not sure if it's because they like you, or because you're a policeman's wife. It works the other way too. If I park in the wrong place some people will talk about it. You live in a goldfish bowl" (Preiss and Ehrlich, 1966) .

Even more vitriolic attacks have been made upon the police. Jerry Rubin (1970) in *Do It* vividly describes the reaction against the police by youthful protesters:

Some were reluctant at first to call cops "pigs". "Pigs" was a Berkeley-San Francisco thing, inspired by Black Panthers. Also it was an insult to Pigasus. But we took one look at Chicago's big blue-and-white porkers: "Man, those fat fuckers really do look like pigs'."

Sunday night a police car drove through Lincoln Park . . . Creatures from the Smoky Lagoon, grotesque, massive machines like tanks lit with powerful lights, entered the park and shot tear gas that made you vomit . . . Pigs with masks—looking like sinister spacemen—led the way, ghouls in hell, turning the park into a swimming pool of gas.

The disabilities experienced by minorities are related to special characteristics that its members share, either physical or cultural or both, which the dominant group holds in low esteem.

To begin with, a policeman is highly visible. His uniform, gun, badge, stick, and marked car set him apart. This visability can add danger or prestige to his position, usually danger. Margaret Mead (1969) states, "On millions of television screens, the policeman appears not as an identifiable individual but as one of an impersonal mass of men, helmeted and armed, charging a mass of demonstrators who are yelling derisive obscenities." As Bayley and Mendelsohn (1969) put it: "Policemen are anonymous persons. Their uniform, badge, gun and nightstick distract and hold the eye, obscuring the face and personal characteristics of an officer. In this respect policemen are like members of a minority group, to nongroup people they all look alike."

Minorities are self-conscious social units; they are characterized by a consciousness of kind. Policemen are quite aware of their minority status. Bordua (1967) refers to a study in which 171 police recruits were asked to express agreement or disagreement with the statement: "The respect that citizens have for a patrolman and his position has been steadily increasing over the years." Twelve percent of the recruits agreed with the statement; seventy-two percent of them disagreed. In another study reported by Skolnick (1966), only 2 percent of 282 policemen rated the prestige of police work as excellent; nineteen percent ranked it as good; and 70 percent ranked it as only fair or poor.

Nowhere is the minority status of the policeman more painfully apparent than in his pay envelope. As Marden and Meyer (1968) point out, "Discrimination operates to create unequal rewards for work that is done in wage differentials or in access to promotion in a minority group." Says Taylor (1969) : "Police salaries are generally at an inadequate level to attract and retain in sufficient numbers the best qualified people. In many places, the pay of experienced police officers is less than $7,000 a year." "For a 40 hour week, salaries run from $4,600-$5,500 a year" (The President's Commission on Law Enforcement and Administration of Justice, 1967). Considering the job of a policeman, this wage is far from adequate. Promotion is also a discouraging device in that, regardless of his qualifications, an officer must normally wait several years before he can be considered for promotion to the rank immediately above his own.

The Police Dilemma

What Bloch and Geis (1962) have called the "police dilemma" refers to the:

> . . . inadequate and conflicting definitions of the role that the police are expected to play in our society. Members of society want to be secure against annoyances and depredation brought about by criminal activity and they expect the police to provide such security. At the same time, police are expected to operate within the confines of restrictive laws. Thus, police are charged with doing a job, but are handicapped to some extent from doing it well. This dilemma is clearly seen in many day-to-day areas of operation. For example: the search and seizure rules often frustrate a policeman who "knows" that illegal activity is occurring almost under his nose. Equally illustrative are laws regarding police interrogation.

To further emphasize this dilemma that the police face, it is stated: "Society has confidence in the local police despite perennial and justifiable criticism as to their philosophy and methods" (Barnes and Teeters, 1959). So, policemen are expected to act effectively, and do, in fact, live up to such expectations, yet their methods of action are severely criticized. This creates frustration and discourages the police in their job performance. A poor job performance has a negative effect upon society, which in turn reflects its disapproval. The police sense this disapproval and, consequently, their negative attitudes are reinforced, and they act accordingly.

Police Professionalization

Apart from the rather obvious tendency to seek improvement in the relations between law enforcement agencies and the communities within which they serve, increasing concern is given to the matter of police professionalization. Wilson (1967) states that "a thoroughly professional police department—one that is honest, competent, impartial, and ably led—will command the respect and cooperation of citizens and will thus produce in the members of such a department pride and a confidence that they have the support and understanding of the citizens whom they are required to protect."

Origin and Growth of Police Professionalism

The widely recognized founding father of police professionalism is August Vollmer. Vollmer laid the foundations of the present trend toward police professionaliam in 1908. As Police Marshall of Berkeley, California, he introduced a number of startling innovations which continue to influence law enforcement all over the world. Indeed under Vollmer's leadership American law enforcement has been brought to what many consider to be the brink of full professionalization.

Vollmer began in 1908 by revolutionizing the first police training school. In addition, he was instrumental in establishing the School of Criminology at Berkeley. He is also credited with being the father of scientific police investigation. His was the first fully mechanized police patrol system, and he pioneered two-way radio for the police. Lastly, Vollmer wrote many widely read books on methods of improving police service.

Between Vollmer and the 1930's not much of importance transpired with respect to police professionalization. The 1920's were lean years for police professionalization, especially in the Eastern United States. In addition to the social upheaval known euphemistically as the "Roaring Twenties" with their attendant police problems, recruiting encountered qualitative problems. The security conferred by civil service benefits attracted many immigrants of inferior educational attainment. The 1930's saw a reversal in this trend. The Volstead Act was repealed, and Prohibition came to an end. Gangsterism, initiated during Prohibition, become a real threat. The Depression, while it imposed great hardships on the whole country, proved to be a blessing in disguise for the cause of police professionalization. There was now great competition for civil service jobs, and the better educated held an edge in the qualifying examination. Thus, notes Niederhoffer (1967), by 1940 more than half of the New York City policemen being hired held college degrees. The same situation held, to a much lesser extent, in other American cities. In this same period, promotion became much easier for those with higher educational attainments. According to Niederhoffer, within fifteen years the top ranks of the police service in America were held by the better educated.

World War II also acted as a stimulus toward increasing police professionalism. The war brought many technological advantages, e.g. radar. However, the war was not without its drawbacks. Many college educated young men who might otherwise would have entered the police service were drawn into the armed services as officers—a process which the end of the war did not reverse. The less educated, fearful of mass post-war unemployment, joined the police. Many of the better educated went into industry. Thus, cliams Niederhoffer (1967), only 5 percent of men being recruited at this period by the New York Police Department were college educated.

In the post-war years police science received a strong impetus from a better educated recruits of the 1930's, who now occupied the top ranks in the police service. A new and stronger emphasis was at this time placed on education and training. A new college-based discipline of "police science" was created. College programs especially designed for law enforcement officers, often in junior colleges but sometimes within the police department itself, were thus implemented. College degrees came to be urged as a requirement for supervisory ranks and eventually for all ranks.

Men who joined the police service in the 1930's began to consolidate their gains in the post-war years. Since few men with professional potential were joining the police at this time, much was being done to transform the likely prospects that did join up into men of a professional caliber. Entrance standards were tightened and pay increases were obtained. There was wide encouragement for the application of science and technology. Thus the better class recruit of the 1930's, now occupying top ranks in police service generally succeeded in raising police prestige in the middle and late forties.

Despite these advances, the gap between the need for policemen with advanced degrees in education and its realization remains large. In a survey conducted of 6,200 officers in 1964, only 30.3 percent had taken one or more college courses and only 7.3 percent possessed a college degree. A 1966 survey of 5,700 police officers employed by police agencies in the metropolitan area of Detroit revealed that over 75 percent of these officers had not attended college. In many departments, particularly in the Southern States, and New England States, a majority of the officers are not high school graduates (*Task Force Report—The Police,* 1967).

Defining Professionalism

Many of the studies on professions list the characteristics that set a profession apart from an occupation. One such study by Niederhoffer (1967) lists the criteria for professionalism:

1. High standards of admission.
2. A special body of knowledge and theory.
3. Altruism and dedication to the service ideal.
4. A lengthy period of training for candidates.
5. A code of ethics.
6. Licensing of members.
7. Autonomous control.
8. Pride of the members in their profession.
9. Publicly recognized status and prestige.

These foregoing characteristics, as Niederhoffer points out, are closely and complexly interrelated.

Some observers of the professional scene find it useful to view the characteristics of professionals in the context of historical development. Wilensky (1964) , for example, views the professional process as going through the following stages:

1. The job becomes a full-time occupation or specialty.
2. A school to train new recruits is established.
3. In time the training school becomes part of a university.
4. First local, then national, professional associations are established. At this stage, admission standards are set up, functions are carefully defined.
5. Legal sanction is sought by means of licensing laws.
6. A formal code of ethics is drawn up.

Other studies, such as that of Vollmer and Mills (1969), categorize occupations from the most to the least professional, thus:

1. Old fashioned professions, fully accepted by the public, e.g. religion, law, and medicine.
2. New professions which have mostly created their own branch of learning, e.g. engineers, social scientists.
3. Semi-professions which are more concerned with technical than with theoretical activities, e.g. nurses, teachers.
4. Would-be professions, which are often concerned with business and government, e.g. police officers, funeral directors.
5. Marginal professions. These are long-established groups providing largely technical services, e.g. draftsmen, laboratory technicians.

A number of other characteristics are common among professionals. One of these is career orientation. The high entrance standards usually insure that those who enter remain in the profession until retirement or death. However, few professionals actually retire completely. Those who are insufficiently interested or devoted, together with the incompetents, either drop out or are eliminated by the licensing process.

The setting in which professionals work is the basis for still another characteristic of this class of occupation. Historically, professionals have been relatively independent of bureaucratic institutions, especially of bureaucratic institutions under the supervision of non-professionals. Vollmer and Mills (1966) outline the possible areas of conflict between professionals and bureaucratic institutions. Basically it amounts to this, the professional sees himself as a member of an autonomous profession, with a fully developed set of standards, interested primarily in his client, not in the institutional setting in which he receives his clients. Thus the professional in the service of the government may find himself torn between his own standards of autonomy, competency, and ethical norms, and the restraints of bureaucratic discipline.

Application to Law Enforcement

In the report he submitted to the President's Commission, Germann (1967) proposed the following criteria for professions, in general, and law enforcement as a professional task, in particular:

1. Its members are service oriented, rather than product oriented.
2. Its representatives have achieved a high level of competence based on a mastery of considerable intellectual content.
3. Its representatives are given extensive autonomy and authority in exercising their special competence.
4. There exists in the profession a utilization of scientific knowledge and specialized technique.
5. Its representatives have strong committments to a career based on a mastery of considerable intellectual content.
6. Its representatives are committed to the spirit of free inquiry, and their loyalties relate more to the profession then to an employing organization. Their values relative to personal accomplishments relate more to esteem of professional peers than to hierarchical supervisors.
7. They have representatives who are determined to influence change by taking action to eliminate or ostracize all incompetent and immoral members of the organization.

Germann (1967), while considering the police to be a profession insofar as they satisfy these criteria, is careful to note: "It would seem, to this Commission, that there are many policemen of professional competence and character in the American police service, but that the police service does not meet the standards of a profession to the degree that it should, even though it be a professional activity." Germann (1967) then makes an important distinction on this very basis, i.e. professional police as determined by character and competence: ". . . because there are today several varieties of police who are highly visible, some commentators have suggested that one variety of policemen can be considered professional and then another cannot." Thus Germann notes the suggestions made to the President's Commission for several levels of service in recognition of the fact that true professional recognition may need to be reserved for a highly qualified group within law enforcement.

While some argue that the label "professional" be attached to all sworn personnel, so that morale may be maintained and that higher salaries may be justified for all personnel, this does not seem to be consistent with the consensus opinion of the President's Commission. For Germann further notes that as long as rigid assignments prevail, as long as the situation exists wherein an officer may devote his entire time to issuing bicycle licenses or directing traffic, it would be difficult to justify extension of the term "professional" to every member of the vocation. As long as low educational standards prevail, as long as high school diplomas are accepted without regard to the quality of high school work, it will be difficult to justify the extension of the term to all members of the vocation.

Barriers to Professionalism

There has been an increase in private watchmen and industrial security forces that duplicate the public policeman's task of protection of property. These services often wear uniforms and in the public view may be perceived as police officers. Their presence presumes that anyone can handle the job and implies the industrial concern, employing these extra men, has feelings of insecurity regarding the ability of the police to adequately discharge their protective responsibilities.

The practice of using civilians as auxiliary and reserve policemen is viewed by many policemen as a barrier to professionalization (Barker, 1971). If the word "professional" implies a body of knowledge unshared by laymen, then by definition police work cannot be a task dischargable by persons untrained in those skills. One of the signs of a genuine professional police force will be the arrival of standards which prevent the use of any but qualified professional police on assignments.

Professionals and Cynics

Niederhoffer (1967) suggests that there are two polar types of police officers: the professional and the cynic. The professionals are dedicated to law enforcement as to a true profession and some already display the characteristics of professionals. On the other hand the cynic stands firmly "on an ideological plank deeply entrenched in the ethos of the police world, and it serves equally well for attack or defense. When officers succumb they lose faith in people, society, and eventually in themselves. In their Hobbesian view the world becomes a jungle in which crime, corruption and brutality are normal features of the terrain. Such a philosophy, softened by a touch of compassion or a sense of humor, converts men into tolerant observers of the human comedy. Without these saving graces, it leads to misanthropy, pessimism and resentment—a dangerous combination." Niederhoffer then notes, however, that a great many officers fall into a middle-of-the-road position, somewhere between professionalism and cynicism.

LAW ENFORCEMENT ASSISTANCE ADMINISTRATION

Perhaps the most important event in recent years with respect to the upgrading of law enforcement was the passage by Congress in June of 1968 of the Omnibus Crime Control and Safe Streets Act. Although a modest law enforcement grant program had been in existence since 1965, the Crime Control and Safe Streets Act marked the first massive infusion of federal funds into the improvement of the criminal justice system. This landmark legislation resulted mainly from the work of the President's Crime Commission which, in its 1967 report, *The Challenge of Crime in a Free Society,* declared that financial resources at the local level were totally inadequate to deal with the necessity for innovation and change in approaches to crime:

> [Most] local communities today are hardpressed just to improve their agencies of justice and other facilities at a rate that will meet increases in population and in crime. They cannot spare funds for experimental or innovative programs or plan beyond the emergencies of the day. Federal collaboration can give State and local agencies an opportunity to gain on crime rather than barely stay abreast of it, by making funds, research, and technical assistance available and thereby encouraging changes that in time may make criminal administration more effective and more fair. (p. 284)

This legislation authorized the Department of Justice to create an administrative instrumentality, the Law Enforcement Assistance Administration, to provide criminal justice planning and program grants to state and local governments. It also authorized the establishment of the National Institute of Law Enforcement and Criminal Justice, in order to stimulate, promote, and encourage basic research in the areas of crime, criminal behavior, and the criminal justice system.

Since 1969, there has been a steady and significant annual increase in the total appropriation to LEAA. According to an LEAA study referred to by Lewis (1972), *Expenditure and Employment Data for the Criminal Justice System: 1969-1970,* the total bill for criminal justice operations at the federal, state, and local levels in the 12-month period ending June 30, 1970, was more than $8,500,-000,000. It was determined that nearly three-fifths of that total figure, approximately $5 billion, went to law enforcement. In the three years that have elapsed since the completion of this study, the figures have continued to grow larger.

The sudden accession of relative prosperity has had at least one of the effects for which it was intended: the encouragement of novel and innovative approaches toward crime control. Although as one might have expected, the bulk of LEAA funds has been put into block grants for action programs, there have been sufficient resources to experiment with new concepts and techniques in policing. The results are extremely encouraging: Lewis (1972) was able to report on a series of projects that included the use of policewomen for street patrol in Washington, D.C.; the Community Sector Team Policing experiment developed by Chief Carl Goodin of the Cincinnati Police Division; Chief Frank Dyson's "Project Pride" in Dallas; and the Proactive-Reactive Patrol Deployment Project originated by Chief Clarence Kelley of Kansas City, who has recently become the new director of the Federal Bureau of Investigation. Evaluating the outcomes and effects of experiments in policing like these, as Lewis points out, is a formidable task: "The rules of rigorous experimental design are almost impossible to follow fully in social experiments in real life" (p. 19) and chances cannot be taken with peoples' safety. Nevertheless, from the standpoint of professionalization of law enforcement, the willingness to experiment is a fundamental necessity.

This point needs reiteration and emphasis, principally because the importance of basic research is often not readily apparent. It was certainly not apparent to at least one Congressman in the debate which preceded the vote to increase the budget of the National Institute for Law Enforcement and Criminal Justice, the research wing of the LEAA. In 1970, LEAA was requesting that, within the total appropriation for fiscal 1971 of $480 million, the National Institute budget be raised from $7.5 million to $19 million. The following exchange, as quoted by Krantz and Kramer (1970), took place during the debate:

Mr. Scheuer. Is it not true that the administration requested $19 million for the National Institute of Law Enforcement and Criminal Justice in effect to apply science and technology to improve our criminal justice system? Is it not also true that in the committee report (House Committee on Appropriations) it was mandated that additional funds requested for research and development should be used for increases in the action grant programs, which in effect denies these funds to the National Institute of Justice?

Mr. Rooney of New York—The committee felt that the action grant programs are far more important. We need policemen to keep law and order—and not professors writing books and creating expensive nonproductive studies . . .

Mr. McClory. However, the Federal Government should encourage the best talents to devote time and study to the solution of problems connected with criminal justice and then disseminate the results of the studies among state and local law enforcement officials. Also, we must recognize that law enforcement and criminal justice are, in the words of the Attorney General, an uncharted field. If we did not have the great research facilities we have with regard to health, science, and defense, we would not have the capability that we have in those fields. Yet in the field of criminal justice we are operating, for the most part, in the dark . . . (p. 358)

Research capibility is an essential requirement for any field which aspires to professional status. If "police science" is to be truly scientific, it simply must develop a research orientation toward its methods and subject matter.

Current State of Police Professionalism

At present, and on the basis of professionalism, American police might be divided into "law officers" or "specialists" and "peace officers" or generalists. Vollmer and Mills (1966) note much the same thing. They point out that technological change is a major stimulant to professionalization. Within law enforcement, specialization and technological change have produced some groups that seem very close to professionalization, while the generalist remains far from it. F.B.I. agents command much of the prestige of professionals, as do police laboratory experts, some high ranking police officers, professors of police science and certain other specialty groups. However, it is important to note that all these latter have relatively little contact with the clients of the police, and the general public.

In spite of many obstacles, professionalization of law enforcement has been widely accepted as a goal. Work has already begun on many of the changes that are regarded as necessary in this process. It is encouraging to note that much progress has been made in many areas, as noted in the following:

1. *Police Science:* The theoretical and technical bases for the profession of law enforcement has now been established as "police science." As subject matter, police science treats the following: applications of public administration to police work, criminal law, sociology, psychology, psychoanalysis, human relations. To this general framework have been added marksmanship and physical education.

2. *Higher Education.* Specialized law enforcement programs are now offered by hundreds of educational institutions in the United States, most of which are junior colleges or community colleges. The most promising sign in this context is the increasing number of graduates who had not previously been law enforcement officers. However, little information is as yet available to us with respect to the benefits of college-educated patrolmen, although such a requirement is widely regarded as desirable. There is even some evidence to the contrary i.e., that college education may actually hinder the performance of certain police tasks, such as certain rather routine affairs like issuing parking tickets.

College training can actually create personnel problems for local police forces. Many officers, when they have completed college, quit local police forces for better paying positions as federal marshalls, F.B.I. agents or secret service agents. Others may dropout of law enforcement altogether to pursue graduate studies. Those who remain may find that their merit increases are resented by other non-degree officers who are working at identical tasks.

3. *Training.* Almost everywhere in the United States the training of police recruits is being upgraded. Yet it is worth noting that, as of 1967, the *task force report; the police* reported that only 23 states had laws making such training mandatory.

4. *Professional Organizations.* Although there are many organizations of police officers in the United States, most of them bear more resemblance to labor unions than to professional associations. Perhaps the most professional of these is the International Association of Chiefs of Police, founded in 1894.

5. *Code of Ethics.* A statement of the canons of the International Association of Chiefs of Police was issued in 1957. How-

ever, the statement included no provision for the enforcement of these canons.

6. *Publications.* There are eight national periodicals published for and by police officers. Only one—that which has the smallest circulation—may be considered truly scholarly, *The Journal of Criminal Law, Criminology and Police Science.*

7. *Optimism Warranted.* Law enforcement appears to have fulfilled to some degree many of the qualifications for professionalization. Some specialists within the occupation seem to have already achieved something akin to professionalism. Recent improvements in standards indicate that the whole occupation may be on the verge of becoming a profession.

In conclusion, it might be well to point out a certain obvious advantage of police professionalization that, unfortunately, tends to be overlooked. Professionalization is a stimulating tonic for the police occupation. It brings to an institution the enthusiasm, pride, and ideals which it needs to grow and develop. Changes in the name of professionalism are long overdue in law enforcement. The movement toward professionalization is a valuable and dynamic force in a critically important but beleaguered sector of our society.

Summary

Despite the fact that the nature of their work tends to place them in the full glare of public scrutiny, the police comprise one of the least understood occupational groups in our society. Some of the reasons for the social isolation of the police and the consequent development among law enforcement groups of a minority group identity are examined in this chapter. Efforts on the part of the police to improve communication with other sectors of society have been directed toward police-community relations programs and, in a more general way, toward self-improvement through police professionalization. The developmental trend toward police professionalism, which originated with August Vollmer, is reviewed and an attempt is made to gauge the current status of professionalization in American law enforcement.

REFERENCES

Aaron, T.J.: *The Control of Police Discretion*. New York, John Wiley and Sons, 1967.

Banton, M.: *The Policeman in the Community*. London, Tavistock, 1964.

Barker, T.: Police officer, Birmingham, Alabama. Personal communication, 1971.

Barnes, H.E. and Teeters, N.K.: *New Horizons in Criminology*. Englewood Cliffs, New Jersey, Prentice-Hall, 1959.

Bayley, D.H. and Mendelsohn, H.: *Minorities and the Police*. New York, The Free Press, 1969.

Bloch, H.A. and Geis, G.: *Man, Crime, and Society*. New York, Random House, 1962.

Bordua, D. (Ed) : *The Police: Six Sociological Essays*. New York, John Wiley and Sons, 1967.

Clark, B.: Is law enforcement headed in the right direction? *Police, 12*:31-34, 1968.

Fox, V.B.: Dilemmas in law enforcement. *Police, 9*:28-31, 1964.

Germann, A.C.: Recruitment, selection, promotion, and civil services. Paper presented to the President's Commission on Law Enforcement and the Administration of Justice. *The Challenge of Crime in a Free Society*. Washington, D.C., U.S. Government Printing Office, 1967.

Goldstein, J.: Police discretion not to invoke the criminal process. Yale Law Review Journal, 69.

Krantz, S. and Kramer, W.D.: The urban crisis and crime. *Boston University Law Review, 50*:343-359, 1960.

La Fave, W.R.: *Arrest: The Decision to Take a Person Into Custody*. Boston, Little, Brown and Company, 1965.

Lewis, J.H.: *Evaluation of Experiments in Policing: How Do You Begin?* Washington, D.C., Police Foundation, 1972.

Lipset, S.M.: Why cops hate liberals and vice versa. *The Atlantic, 223*:76-83, 1969.

Marden, C. and Meyer, G.: *Minorities in American Society*. New York, Reinhold, 1968.

Mead, Margaret: The police and the community. *Redbook, 113*:46-50, 1969.

Niederhoffer, A.: *Behind the Shield: The Police in Urban Society*. Garden City, New York, Doubleday, 1967.

Niederhoffer, A.: On the job. In R. Quinney (Ed.), *Crime and Justice in Society*. Boston, Little, Brown and Company, 1969.

Rubin, J.: *Do It!* New York, Simon and Schuster, 1970.

Skolnick, J.: *Justice Without Trial*. New York, John Wiley and Sons, 1966.

Task Force Report: The Police. President's Commission on Law Enforcement and the Administration of Justice. Washington, D.C., U.S. Government Printing Office, 1967.

Vollmer, H.J. and Mills, D.L.: *Professionalization.* Englewood Cliffs, New Jersey, Prentice-Hall, 1966.

Wilensky, H.L.: The professionalization of everyone. *American Journal of Sociology, 70:*139-158, 1964.

Wilson, J.Q.: Police morale, reform, and citizen respect: the Chicago case. In D. Bordua (Ed.), *The Police: Six Sociological Essays.* New York, John Wiley and Sons, 1967.

Wilson, J.Q.: *Varieties of Police Behavior.* Cambridge, Massachusetts, Harvard University Press, 1968.

Chapter 14

THE ADMINISTRATION
OF JUSTICE

THE ADMINISTRATION OF JUSTICE in the United States, as in all
modern nations, has become a task of epic proportions. As
the role and structures of government increase in response to the
needs of a scientific and technological society, so also the criminal
justice system expands in size and scope. The image of a King
Solomon meting out justice to his subjects with intuitive wisdom
has been replaced by the reality of a huge bureaucratic structure
of judicial administration reaching into many aspects of human
life. The manner in which this system exercises its responsibilities
influences considerably the functioning and direction of the
society it serves.

The police officer, whom we have identified as the cutting edge
of social control, is the most visible representative of this system.
His visibility, however, is analogous to that of the iceberg tip; by
far the larger portion of the criminal justice system, like the mass
of the iceberg, is submerged and concealed from view. We are
referring to the criminal and juvenile courts, judges, the clerks,
bailiffs, and other officials who handle the innumerable details of
court administration, the prosecuting and defense attorneys, and
those who are charged with the responsibilities of detention, corrections, probation, and parole. Taken in the aggregate, these
individuals, the offices they hold, and the jobs they perform comprise the remainder of criminal justice system.

The expression "criminal justice system," by the strictest rules
of semantics, is a convenient fiction—an abstraction with no
specific counterpart in reality. What we have referred to above

451

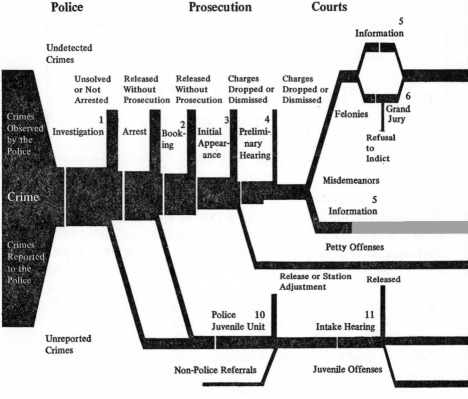

Figure 14-1. A General View of the Criminal Justice System. *The Challenge of Crime in a Free Society*. Washington, U.S. Government Printing Office, 1967. Reproduced by permission of the Department of Justice.

Corrections

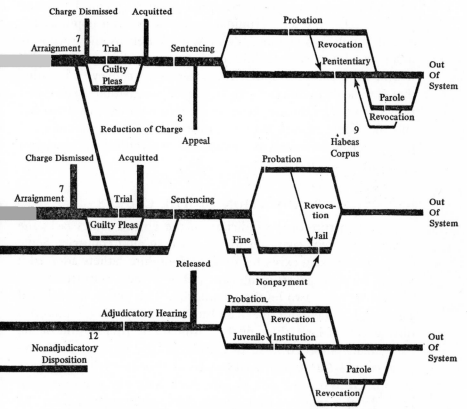

7 Appearance for plea; defendant elects trial by judge or jury (if available); counsel for indigent usually appointed here in felonies. Often not at all in other cases.

8 Charge may be reduced at any time prior to trial in return for plea of guilty or for other reasons.

9 Challenge on constitutional grounds to legality of detention. May be sought at any point in process.

10 Police often hold informal hearings, dismiss or adjust many cases without further processing.

11 Probation officer decides desirability of further court action.

12 Welfare agency, social services, counselling, medical care, etc., for cases where adjudicatory handling not needed.

collectively as the criminal justice system is a system in the same sense that government is considered a political system. Unfortunately, perhaps, the term criminal justice system is a popular one; and although it is employed loosely, and often by those who are unaware of the complexities or even contradictions concealed within its apparent simplicity, it nevertheless conveys a meaning that is difficult to capture with any other designation. Figure 14-1 provides a diagrammatic sketch of the system in both its structural and functional aspects. We shall treat the various components of the system in succession as we examine the process of bringing a case from arrest to trial.[1]

ORGANIZATION OF THE COURTS

The structure of the judiciary in the United States lacks the relative simplicity characteristic of courts in most countries. Some of this complexity exists because the founding fathers adopted a federal form of government with public powers constitutionally divided between two levels of authority. This action necessitated some arrangement for the handling of cases arising under two distinct sets of laws, those of the national government and of the individual states. To solve this problem, two separate and complete court systems, with trial as well as appellate tribunals, were established to operate side by side. Each state was free to fashion it's judicial machinery as it saw fit. As a result we now have 100 district and appellate courts which comprise the federal judiciary as well as the individual judicial systems of the fifty states, each with its own organization, personnel, and rules of procedure. Constitutionally, both parallel structures, national and state, are independent and equal in their respective spheres of jurisdiction.

The federal court system is arranged in hierarchical fashion, with the district courts at the base, the courts of appeals at the intermediate level, and the Supreme Court at the apex. The ninety-one district courts are the tribunals of original jurisdiction

---

[1]While there may be variations in details from one country or state to another, the major features of the criminal justice system depicted in Figure 14-1, and discussed in this chapter, are generally representative for the country as a whole.

or first instance. It is here that the vast majority of suits arising under national law are instituted and terminated. Each state contains no less than one district court (some with multiple divisions); sixteen states have two tribunals, eight contain three, and New York and Texas have four. Every district has at least one judge, depending on the work load; there are as many as twenty-four in the Southern District of New York. A single judge conducts the trials in these lower tribunals except in cases involving the constitutionality of national and state statutes. Three judges must preside in trials of the latter type.

Immediately above the lower tier of tribunals are the eleven United States Courts of Appeals (including one for the District of Columbia), each with jurisdiction over a geographical section of the country. These intermediate tribunals were established by Congress in 1891, to relieve the growing burden on the Supreme Court. The number of judges in each court of appeals ranges from three to nine. Normally decisions are made by a panel of three. The composition of these subgroups varies from case to case, with the presiding judge in each court making the assignment. On occasions, when disagreement arises among the members over an important issue of law, the matter may be decided by the full court in what is called an *en banc* decision (all the judges of the tribunal sitting).

Technically, the Supreme Court has both original and appellate jurisdiction. As specified in Article III of the Constitution, it is the Court of first instance in cases involving diplomatic representatives of foreign powers and in controversies in which a state is a party. Virtually all cases which are heard under the Court's original jurisdictional powers relate to disputes between two states, usually over water rights, or between the federal government and a state.

The appellate jurisdiction of the Supreme Court makes up the overwhelming bulk of its business. It reviews cases coming from lower federal courts and from state tribunals when issues pertaining to the Constitution or laws of the United States are involved. The Court has almost absolute power to control its agenda, and this enables it to be highly selective and to assume jurisdiction only in those cases which raise the issue it currently wishes to consider. Over half of the requests come from the losing parties in the United States Courts of Appeals, and most of the remainder are from disappointed litigants in the state tribunals of the last resort.

Only at the level of the Supreme Court is there a bridge between the federal and state judicial structures. Few paths of appeal exist from a state court to any federal tribunal at lower levels in the hierarchy. If the Supreme Court accepts jurisdiction, it will scrutinize the constitutional issue at stake and either sustain the state tribunal's finding or reverse the decision, returning the appellant who is fortunate enough to have his appeal accepted; the Supreme Court reverses its state counterparts in a substantial number of the cases it hears.

In the parallel structures of state courts, the general organizational pattern, despite considerable variation among the individual systems, is basically similar. There also exists a close resemblance between this pattern and the organizational framework of the national judiciary. Like the latter, the court system of each state is arranged in hierarchical fashion. At the bottom of the scale are numerous minor tribunals of purely local character. These bodies, known as justice of the peace, magistrate, municipal, police, and small claims courts, have various duties and various degrees of inferior jurisdiction. They are not, in legal terms, courts of record; no official transcript of their proceedings is made. Consequently, appeals from this level are usually for a completely new trial before the next tier in the judicial pyramid.

The jurisdiction of justices of the peace and the other lesser court functionaries is confined to minor infractions of the law, such as disorderly conduct, vagrancy, traffic violations, and civil suits involving small sums of money. In some states, justices of the peace and magistrates also conduct preliminary hearings in criminal matters to determine whether accused individuals should be bound over for trial in a higher tribunal. Historically, American experience with these lesser organs of the system has not been very edifying. They have been widely regarded as the weakest link in the administration of justice, although in recent years various reforms have been accomplished under pressure from bar associations and civic groups. It was common practice in the past, and still is in some areas, for these courts to be presided over by laymen without formal legal training and with little judicial aptitude. Considering this background, the comment of one justice of the peace on defendants brought before him is hardly surprising: "I don't ever remember having one who wasn't guilty. If the sheriff picks up a man for violating the law, he's guilty or he wouldn't bring him in here. Anyway, I don't get anything out of it if they aren't guilty" (Banks, 1961).

At the next tier above the minor tribunals are the courts of general jurisdiction, known as district, circuit, or superior courts. Numerous structural differentiations exist from state to state. Some systems provide for separate criminal and civil divisions; a few retain equity or chancery tribunals; and others have special probate and domestic relations courts. Regardless of how constituted, the judicial bodies on this level handle the bulk of major litigation under state law. All important civil litigation originates here, and persons accused of offenses, other than petty, are tried. These tribunals also serve as appellate units for cases instituted in the courts of limited jurisdiction. However, because they try such cases *de novo,* as though they had nor previously been heard, further appeal normally lies with a higher court.

Similar to the federal system, about one-third of the states, those most heavily populated, have two levels of appellate tribunals: a supreme court and intermediate units corresponding to the United States Circuit Courts of Appeals. As in the national judiciary, these intermediate bodies provide relief for overburdened state supreme courts and serve as tribunals of last resort for the majority of appeals taken from the courts of original jurisdiction. New York was the first state to create a subtier of appellate courts, shortly before the turn of the present century; Michigan has recently taken similar action.

Each state has a supreme court (in New York and Maryland it is called the Court of Appeals) which stands at the top rung of the judicial ladder. Presided over by three to nine judges, although usually there are seven, these tribunals relate to the lesser state courts in much the same way that the Supreme Court of the United States does to the lower national judiciary. As the highest judicial organ of the "sovereign" states, these tribunals are the final authority on all questions of law originating within their territorial boundaries, except those issues which involve the Constitution or laws of the United States.

The Initiation of Prosecution: Misdemeanors

While the public imagination and interest are captured by trials involving bizarre crimes or show business celebrities, the vast majority of criminal justice transactions occur within the lower courts and typically consist of misdemeanor offenses carrying sentences of less than one year in the county jail or relatively small fines. Despite their petty nature, one legal authority (Puttkammer, 1953) considers them "conceivable of more social significance than the major crimes."

In these misdemeanor cases, prosecution is usually initiated upon the complaint of a victim of, or witness to, the crime. Often it is the arresting officer who is the complaining witness. After a suspect has been arrested by the police, he is brought to some place of detention, e.g. a police station, where he is interrogated. Following interrogation, he may be released for lack of evidence of wrongdoing, or, based on the available evidence and results of the interrogation, he may be "booked," i.e. have formal charges entered against him. Then, he may be released on bail, placed in the jail, or locked up to await trial.

In theory, a suspect should be brought before a magistrate's court or justice of the peace to have bond set within a "short time" after he is arrested. In fact, as a study by the American Civil Liberties Union (1959) has shown, individuals are sometimes illegally detained for more than several weeks and sometimes months without formal booking or appearance before an inferior court.

The Magistrate

The setting within which misdemeanor justice is administered is not apt to inspire much respect for law or confidence in the impartiality of justice. As Bloch and Geis (1962) have remarked:

> Misdemeanor justice in its usual form is meted out by magistrates or justices of the peace who as often as not appear to have secured their positions because of their political coloration and activity rather than because of their legal acumen, human compassion, or social insight. Misdemeanor justice usually takes place in rather sordid surroundings and involves in many instances defendants who through considerable exposure to its operation have become as familiar as the bailiff with its routine. Guilty pleas are the rule.

The magistrate has "summary jurisdiction," i.e. he is empowered to determine guilt or innocence and can impose minor sentences for petty offenses. In many states the accused can request a jury trial. In the case of more serious crimes, the magistrate holds a preliminary hearing to determine whether sufficient evidence has been presented to justify holding the suspect for further action.

The Initiation of Prosecution: Felonies

Some felony offenses are settled by dismissal or the entrance of a guilty plea at some early stage in the criminal justice system. Those which are not settled in this manner progress through a series of stages that begin with a preliminary hearing.

Preliminary Hearing

Following arrest, an individual who is accused of a felony offense is brought before a lower court justice for a preliminary hearing. At this point, he is "arraigned", i.e. the prosecutor reads the formal charges, and the defendant enters a plea. Following the Gideon decision, the defendant is informed by the judge that if he is indigent (poor), an attorney will be appointed to defend him.

The prosecuting attorney, who is legally empowered to negotiate with the accused and his counsel, may accept a plea of guilty to the charges at this stage in return for a plea of guilty to some lesser charge. Many misdemeanors begin as felony offenses: Drunken driving may be reduced to "reckless driving," or statutory rape may be reduced to "contributing to the delinquency of a minor." Guilty pleas are the mainstay of the criminal justice system, and experienced offenders soon become adept in the techniques of plea bargaining or "copping a plea." If no agreement for a plea to a lesser charge is reached and the defendant pleads "not guilty," the state is constrained to show "probable cause" to hold the accused for trial. The expression "probable cause" has the distinct flavor of legal cant; it is highly *improbable* that a prosecutor would initiate judicial proceedings unless he believed in the strength of his case. Nevertheless, the legal view persists that the preliminary hearing is of benefit to the accused.

The state seeks to reveal only enough of its evidence against the accused to support its contention that further prosecution is warranted. If the defendant is fortunate enough to be represented by an alert and experienced counsel, he may be able to extract some definite advantages from the preliminary hearing, particularly in discovery of the strength of the case to be presented by the state. Some jurisdictions still fail to provide free counsel for indigent defendants at this early stage of the judicial process; most unrepresented defendants are not equipped to take full advantage of the preliminary hearing. Thus the preliminary hearing tends to be weighted heavily on the side of the prosecution. For these and other reasons, the preliminary hearing has been fairly criticized as a moribund proceeding that is little more than a dress rehearsal for the prosecution's case.

Bail or Jail?

An additional function of the lower court magistrate, once it had been determined that there is probable cause to bind over the defendant to the grand jury, is the settling of bail. Bail (Weston and Wells, 1967) is a legal procedure for securing temporary liberty following arrest through a written promise to appear in court as required. In support of this promise, it may be necessary to provide cash bail, post a surety bond, or supply evidence of an equity in real property, together with the written assurance of another person or persons.

The basic purpose of bail is to furnish a means for the release of a detailed individual while his case is pending, subject to the proviso that the accused is ready to give reasonable and sufficient assurance of his willingness to appear in court at the appropriate time. In providing for release on bail, the presumption of innocence goes beyond its well-known place in trial proceedings, i.e. the necessity for proof of guilt beyond a reasonable doubt, and emphasizes the fact that, in American criminal jurisprudence, guilt is the decision of the court and is not inherent in accusatory pleadings. At the federal level, release on bail in noncapital cases is a constitutional right.

Types of Bail

Release on bail may require the posting of a formal bond for the amount of the bail, along with sureties as "guarantors," the deposit of cash bail without sureties, or release upon the personal recognizance of the defendant. These forms of bail have been with us since colonial times. The so-called schedule of bail contains a list of misdemeanors and the amount of bail required for release. It may also specify a particular amount as standard bail for all misdemeanor offenses not listed in the schedule.

Conditions of Bail

During the post arrest period of detention, the amount of bail (Weston and Wells, 1967) depends upon the severity of the offense, whether the arrest is with or without a warrant, and whether or not the defendant has been arraigned upon the charge. When the arrest is made on a warrant alleging a public offense, bail should be in the amount specified in the endorsement upon the warrant by the magistrate who issued it. When the arrest is for a misdemeanor, the amount of bail should be fixed by the magistrate at the time of arraignment. If prior to arraignment, bail should be as fixed in the warrant of arrest; and if arrested without a warrant, then the amount of bail should coincide with the countrywide schedule of bail for misdemeanants. When the arrest is for a felony, the bail should be fixed by the judge before whom the prisoner is arraigned upon the formal complaint, and if prior to the arraignment, the amount of bail is to be as stated upon the arrest warrant. If, without sufficient excuse, a defendant neglects to appear as required in his bail agreement, or upon any other occasion when his presence in court is required by law, the court will direct the fact to be entered in its minutes and the under-taking of bail, or the cash bail deposited, will be declared for-feited. If the amount of the bail or deposit exceeds fifty dollars, the bondsman or depositor must be notified.

Forfeiture of Bail

After the date of forfeiture and notice, the bondsman or de-positor is allowed one hundred and eighty days in which to adjust the forfeiture. The three possible procedures are: (1) defendant and bondsman or depositor appear in court and provide an ac-ceptable explanation or justification for the defendant's neglect or satisfactorily indicate to the court that his absence was not with the connivance of the bondsman or depositor; (2) the bonds-man may appear in court and certify that the defendant is dead or physically unable to appear during the time period (one hundred eighty days) allowed; and (3) the defendant may be surrendered.

Bail System Inequities and Defects

When the accused lacks financial resources, the bail system adds a discriminatory element to the administration of criminal justice. In Johnson's (1964) review of major findings in studies of the bail system of New York and Philadelphia, he noted that many defendants were unable to furnish bail, even of a nominal amount, but especially when bail was set above one thousand dollars. The bail usually was set so high for serious offenses that few defendants in such cases obtained pretrial release. From 10 to 20 percent of those incarcerated pending trial were not convicted. For similar crimes, jailed offenders were more likely to be con-victed and receive longer sentences than those who were released on bail. The indigent defendant is unable to hire a lawyer, locate witnesses, and pay for the investigation necessary to present his case adequately, especially when incarceration pending trial inter-rupts his normal earnings. The appearance of the defendant in court under guard may have an adverse effect on the jury. Even when convicted, the bailed defendant has the advantage of show-ing evidence of steady employment and good conduct while awaiting trial. These support his plea for probation.

Bail System Encourages Criminality

The bail system also has the consequences of encouraging criminality (Chambliss, 1969) by creating a situation in which bondsmen are willing to set bail for thieves. The thief is, then, put in the position of having to acquire a large sum of money very shortly after he has been arrested for a crime to repay the bail bondsman.

For short-term bail bonds, a bondsman will usually be legally permitted to charge an interest rate of from ten to twenty percent. This means that if a known thief is arrested and bond is set at twenty-five thousand dollars, he must pay a bondsman between 2,500 and 5,000 dollars for the "loan" (surety) of 25,000 dollars for a period of several weeks. This money must also be raised, resulting in another probable crime.

Kickbacks to Authorities

There is still another way (Chambliss, 1969) in which the bail system encourages crime. A person under arrest, even the professional thief, does not always know from whom to get bond. Jailers, sheriffs, and police officers are in a position to recommend a bondsman, and the makings of a system of gifts and payoffs for recommending one bondsman rather than another is thus set in motion.

Suggestions for Bail Reform

The Manhattan Bail Project, which began operation in New York City in late 1961, was administered by the Vera Foundation in cooperation with the Institute of Judicial Administration student assistents from the New York University Law School. The Vera Foundation had originally planned to provide a revolving bail fund available to indigent defendants but rejected this solution on the grounds that it merely perpetuated reliance upon money as the criterion for release.

The project lasted for three years (1961-1964). It was the Vera Foundation's hypothesis that, with appropriate controls and careful screening techniques, release on recognizance could be safely expanded. With financial aid from Ford Foundation and a go-ahead from the lower court system of New York, the project got underway.

The process went as follows. When a prisoner was brought in for booking and detention prior to his first court appearance, a staff member checked his previous record and current charge with the arresting officer to see if he was bailable in the initial arraignment court. The first criterion was to see if his crime was bailable or not. The crimes considered not bailable included homicide, most narcotic offenses, and certain sex offenses (Sturz, 1965). If his offense was bailable, the defendant was then interviewed to ascertain whether he was working, how long he had held the job, whether he supported his family, whether he had contacts with relatives in the city, how long he had lived in the city, and how long he had lived at his present address.

Based on the above, the accused was scored according to a point-weighting system. If the prisoner appeared to be a good release on recognizance (ROR), risk and summary of the information was provided to the bench at initial arraignment. Thus R.O.R. rested finally with the judge.

When a defendant was released, a project staff member would notify him in writing of the date and location of subsequent court appearances. If the defendant was illiterate, a factor found in the initial questioning, he was telephoned as well as notified in writing.

During the first year of the project, half of the recommendable cases were set aside as a control group and were not recommended to the court. This was to determine how accused persons who met R.O.R. standards fared without R.O.R. recommendations. The court granted R.O.R. in 60 percent of the cases in which an actual recommendation was made but in only 14 percent of the parallel cases with no recommendation.

During the next two years of operation, the number of persons released increased due to two factors: (1) greater proficiency in screening with a more subjective set of standards; (2) a greater reliance by the court upon Vera's recommendations (Sturz, 1965).

As of August 31, 1964, 3505 accused persons were released on recognizance of the Vera Staff. Of these, 98.4 percent returned to court when required. Only 56 persons, 1.6 percent, willfully failed to appear. In contrast, the forfeiture rate on bail bonds during the same period was 3 percent *(Interim Report,* 1966).

Due to the preliminary success of the Manhattan Bail Project, its operation has now been taken over by the Office of Probation of the City of New York. The City operation has been in effect for less than a year, and over 3,000 persons have been R.O.R.'d with about the same results as the pilot project *(Interim Report,* 1966).

By 1965, there were eighty projects in operation or on the drawing board in thirty-three states. Most of these are patterned primarily after the Manhattan Project. One of the major drawbacks, other than public resistance, is funding. Very few government agencies are willing to expend funds for R.O.R. projects. Private foundations such as Ford, Sarah Mellon, William Penn Center, and local Bar Associations are the primary sources. In some areas, the Chamber of Commerce, Junior Chambers of Commerce, and other such civic clubs have lent financial and physical assistance.

Grand Jury

The function of the grand jury[2] is the investigation of criminal charges to determine whether the defendant should be brought to trial. The Fifth Amendment states that "no person shall be held to answer for a capital or otherwise infamous charge unless on a presentment or indictment of a grand jury." According to Bloch and Geis (1962), "Grand juries were intended to allow the defendant to avoid a public accusation and the trouble and expense of a public trial before establishing the likelihood of his having committed the crime. They were also intended to prevent hasty, oppressive, and malicious prosecutions." The grand jury does not seek to determine guilt or innocence; rather, the grand jury duplicated in many respects the function of the preliminary hearing, the major difference being that the defendant has not

---

[2]The term *grand jury* originated in England; "grand" (large) designated a jury of 23 members, as distinct from the "petit" (regular or "small") jury of 12 members. In the United States, the grand jury can range from 5 to 23 members (Mayers, 1964).

legal right to be present at the grand jury deliberations. Therefore, the decision on whether or not to indict is made solely on the
evidence presented by the prosecuting attorney.

If the grand jury is convinced by the prosecutor's evidence that
a *prima facie* case has been made, a "true bill" of indictment will
be returned, indicating probable cause to proceed to trial. If, on
the other hand, the grand jury has not been persuaded by the
prosecution's evidence, it can "ignore" the charges by returning
a "no bill" finding. In the overwhelming majority of indictment
presentations, the grand jury tends to follow the inclinations of
the prosecutor.

Prosecuting Attorney

Under present circumstances, the most important and powerful figure in the criminal justice system is the prosecutor or
district attorney. He is armed with broad and plenary powers. He
may decide whether or not to prosecute a particular case; he has
discretionary authority to grant immunity to an individual who
wishes to turn state's evidence; he can make the choice of submit-
ting a case to the grand jury for indictment, or he can bypass the
grand jury altogether by using a bill of information; he is empowered to bargain with the defense of the nature of the final
plea, which generally means accepting a guilty plea to a lesser
charge in exchange for a recommendation of leniency; he is responsible for organizing and presenting evidence in court and is
influential with regard to the disposition of cases by suggesting
appropriate penalties to the judge and jury. In summary, as
Puttkammer (1953) phrases it, "there are not important limitations on the prosecuting attorney's power to terminate a case."

Nevertheless, as we noted earlier, the prosecutor is generally
an elected official and, as such, is susceptible to both political pressures and the distractions from official business that are the inevitable accompaniment to office-seeking. Perhaps the most important consequence of his political status, as Sutherland and
Cressey (1970) point out, is the fact that his reaction to crime
must be *selectively punitive*. If he is to continue in office or seek
a higher position in the political structure, he is compelled to

develop partisan attitudes toward criminal offenders. The following acid-etched portrait by John Mason Brown (1956) of the
prosecutor, cast as a villain, may be a distorted exaggeration of
the prosecutor's role, but it is a faithful relection of the feelings
such a perceived role is capable of engendering:

> The prosecutor's by obligation is a special mind, mongoose quickly,
> bullying, devious, unrelenting, forever baited to ensnare. It is almost
> duty bound to mislead, and by instinct dotes on confusing and flourishes
> on weakness. Its search is for blemishes it was present as scars, its
> obligation to raise doubts or sour with suspicion. It asks questions not
> to learn but to convict, and can read guilt into the most innocent
> answers. Its hope, its aim, its triumph is to addle a witness into con-
> fession by trickling, exhausting, or irritating him into a verbal indiscre-
> tion which sounds like a damaging admission. To natural lapses of
> memory it gives the appearance either of strategems for hiding mis-
> deeds or, worse still, of lies, dark and deliberate. Feigned and wheed-
> ling politeness, sarcasm, intimidation, supprise and besmirchment by
> innuendo, association, or suggestion, at the same time that any in-
> tention to besmirch is denied—all these as methods and devices are
> such staples in the prosecutor's repertory that his mind turns to them
> by tote.

Bloch and Geis (1962), who quote the above passage, suggest that
some support for Brown's description can be found in the instructions for attorneys in "How to Humiliate and Subdue a
Recalcitrant Witness" in a book by Lake (1954) entitled *How to
Win Lawsuits Before Juries:*

> When you have forced the witness into giving you a direct answer
> to your question you really have him under control; he is off-balance,
> and usually rather scared. This advantage should be followed up with
> a few simple questions such as, "You did not want to answer that
> question, did you?" If the witness says that he wanted to answer it, ask
> him in a resounding voice, "Well, why did you not answer it when I
> first asked you?" Whatever his answer is you then ask him, "Did you
> think that you were smart enough to evade answering the question?"
> Again, whatever the answer is you ask him, "Well, I would like for the
> jurors to know what you have behind all this dodging and ducking you
> have done!" . . . This battering and legal-style "kicking the witness
> around" not only humiliates but subdues him.

It has been suggested that some of the ills endemic to the
office of prosecutor could be speedily cured by the adoption of the

British system, in which prosecutors and defense counsels are drawn from the same group of barristers. Under this arrangement, the same attorney may be called upon to defend or prosecute a case on various occasions, thus averting the development of special interest in the potential advantages of either position. Despite the superiority claimed for this system, it seems doubtful whether its adoption would be feasible in the United States, given the rather substantial differences between the British and American criminal justice systems. A more realistic, albeit less satisfactory, solution might be an attempt to free the prosecutor from the demands of election, somewhat in the manner by which justices of the Supreme Court are installed at the present time.

Defense Counsel

The Sixth Amendment to the Constitution states: "In all criminal prosecutions, the accused shall enjoy the right . . . to have the Assistance of Counsel for his defense." The framers of the amendment did not envision the problem of a man too poor to hire a lawyer. It was a long road from the constitutional provision and the final determination of the issue: Does an indigent defendant have an absolute right to a lawyer in a criminal trial?

In the celebrated Scottsboro Case, *Powell v. Alabama* (1932), a group of young, illiterate Negro youths were accused of raping two white women who were riding a freight car. The boys were sentenced to death, but the Supreme Court found that the failure of the trial court to appoint counsel was a denial of due process "within the meaning of the Fourteenth Amendment." *Powell v. Alabama* was the first occasion on which the Supreme Court had reversed a state criminal conviction because of a violation of due process at trial. The law to this point was interpreted to mean a defendant in a *capital* case had a right to counsel only under "special circumstances": illiteracy, or feeblemindedness.

The second landmark case was *Johnson v. Zerbst*—a federal counterfeiting case. In this ruling, Justice Black stated that now there must be appointed counsel for all who could not afford it in federal criminal cases. But this ruling did not apply to the states. In *Betts v. Brady* (1942) , a farm hand, Smith Betts, was charged with robbery and requested a lawyer be appointed for him as he was too poor. The Judge refused as this was a non-capital case. The high court had again refused to extend the right-to-counsel to the states.

Here the question lay dormant until 1962 when the court received a petition from Clarence Earl Gideon (proceeding *in forma pauperis*) who was an inmate of the Florida State Prison. Unable to satisfactorily explain his presence at 5:30 a.m. outside the burglarized Bay Harbor Poolroom in Panama City, Florida, Gideon had been arrested by the police and charged with breaking and entering with intent to commit a misdemeanor. (This is a felony offense under Florida state law). Without the means to provide a lawyer at his own expense, Gideon asked the court to appoint one for him. The judge refused; Florida state law provided an indigent defendant a court-appointed lawyer only in capital cases. Gideon was left to defend himself and attempted to do a professional job. He presented witnesses in his own behalf, cross-examined the states witnesses, declined to testify himself, and made opening and closing statements to the jury. It was a clumsy job at best. Pitted against a trained state attorney, it was hopeless from the start. He was sentenced to five years in the state prison at Raiford. Gideon was not one to give up easily, and he filed a habeas corpus petition with the Florida Supreme Court on the grounds that his conviction was illegal; he had been denied the right to counsel provided for in the Sixth Amendment, and he had not received due process of law embodied in the Fifth and Fourteenth Amendments. The state supreme court declined to review his case. His next move was to apply to the United States Supreme Court. The high court granted him *certiorari* and appointed Mr. Abe Fortas to represent Gideon. The primary question to be considered by the Supreme Court was: "Should this court's holding in Betts vs. Brady, 316 U.S. 455, be reconsidered?"

In a brief largely prepared by John Hart Ely, a third-year student at Yale Law School, Fortas argued: (Anthony, 1964)

> The Fourteenth Amendment requires that counsel be appointed to represent an indigent defendant in every criminal case involving a serious offense.

First, "the aid of counsel is indispensible to a fair hearing." Even a trained criminal lawyer will not undertake his own defense. Many constitutional rights, such as the new protestion against the use of illegally seized evidence, are meaningless in the absence of counsel. *Second,* the absolute requirement of counsel in federal prosecutions confirms the need. *Third,* requirement of the trial judge to assert the defendants right is misplaced because a man cannot be both judge and counsel. *Fourth,* the distinction between capital and non-capital cases is invalid as a basis for determining the constitutional right to counsel. The due process clause protects one's 'liberty' and 'property' as well as one's 'life.' Moreover, the need for counsel is greater in some non-capital crimes.

The high court reversed its rulling in *Betts v. Brady* and found for Gideon. Gideon then confounded everyone by refusing his newly appointed counsel and demanded to defend himself. He reluctantly accepted his hard fought rights and was acquitted in the new trial. His court appointed counsel was able to seriously question the reliability of the state's witnesses, and it was proven that Gideon was allowed, on occasion, to operate the Bay Harbor Poolroom. Because of the Gideon decision all states must now furnish counsel to a defendant if he is financially destitute and cannot afford one at his own expense. No plea or indictment may be entered by a defendant (even a guilty plea) until the judge has offered counsel to a defendant if he cannot afford one.

The ruling in Gideon further opened the door to more and greater judicial reform decisions by the high court. *Massiah v. United States* (1964) held that placing a radio transmitter in the car of Massiah's accomplice, who was a police informer, constituted a violation of the Sixth Amendment because it resulted in a clandestine interrogation of the defendant when he did not have adequate counsel. In *Escobedo v. Illinois* (1964), the court ruled that the suspect could not be denied counsel during a police interrogation even if no formal charges had been filed against him. The mere suspicion of the suspect's guilt is sufficient to warrant the protection of counsel. The decision of Escobedo soon was carried even further by the ruling in *Miranda v. Arizona* in 1966: the suspect must be advised of his right to remain silent during questioning by the police; any statement he makes may be held against him in a court of law, and he has the right to have an attorney, either his own or court-appointed, during any and all questioning by the police, if he so desires.

The Public Defender

The alternative to nonrepresentation by counsel as a consequence of indigence is the appointment by the court of counsel for the defense. The indifferent quality of attorneys appointed in this manner—recent law school graduates and superannuated or incompetent lawyers with little or no trial skill—has tended to inspire comments which sound like a paraphrase of the remark of the famous general who, after ruefully surveying his seedy troops, said, "I don't know whether they'll frighten the enemy, but—God —they certainly frighten me!" As an antidote to this sort of situation, there has been a noticeable growth in the use of the public defender.

Begun in Los Angeles County in 1913,[3] the public defender system has been adopted by at least half of the states. The advantages claimed for the public defender over assigned counsel are manifold: There is a reduction of delays and motions made on technical grounds; the use of specialists with more adequate financial resources strengthens protection for the accused; there tends to be greater respect on the part of prosecutors, judges, and juries for both the person and position of public defenders; and it is claimed that the office of public defender is more influential in molding public opinion in support of judicial reform than that of the court-appointed defense counsel.

On the negative side, anyone conversant with constitutional law would be prey to misgivings about the propriety of the assumption by the state of the power of defense over those it has charged with crimes. Moreover, being on the public payroll is scarcely a guarantee of objectivity and lack of self-interest. To the contrary, a distinguished record of brilliantly argued acquittals seems hardly calculated to win a public defender reappointment or reelection. Finally, it is fallacious to argue on behalf of special considerations for those whom the public defender represents over

---

[3]This must be reckoned a very late start, for the concept of the public defender has been traced back at least as far as Rome in the days of the Republic.

those who secure the services of private counsel. Any system of criminal justice which accords such preferential treatment would be categorically, and by definition, unjust in its operations.

The Judge

The symbolism and ritual which surround the judicial process are best summarized, perhaps, in the figure of Themis, which conveys the concept of the judge as a passionless vehicle for applying the law to the facts of a case. According to this image, the judge "finds the law, he does not make it." Cohen (1933) has dubbed this interpretation the "phonographic" theory of the judicial function, implying that the judge is a mere instrument for playing back the words of the law as they have been recorded into him.

The notion of an Olympian judiciary that impartially arbitrates the wars of conflicting interests is an idealized, unrealistic image. Courts are integral parts of the political system and perform policymaking functions not unlike those of legislative bodies and executive agencies (Peltason, 1955). As such they often become the subject of furious controversy as their decisions create both praise and damnation. A great difference exists between the image created by the dignity of the Supreme Court chamber and that evoked by the billboards reading **IMPEACH EARL WARREN** or by the outpouring of indignant comments which greeted the school prayer case: "An outrageous edict that spits in the face of our history, our traditions, and our heritage as a religious people." and a decision that "tampers with America's soul, striking a blow to the faith of every believer in a Supreme Being" (Barker and Barker, 1965).

It was legal realists such as Benjamin Cardoza, Jerome Frank, and Thurman Arnold who helped dispel the myth of judges as judicial automations and the law as a system of definite, consistent rules readily discoverable by the exercise of pure reason. When a man becomes a judge, he is not suddenly cleansed of all his prejudices or given immunity against social pressures. How he will act depends on his personality, background, attitudes and beliefs, and value preferences. In a statistical analysis of the split decisions of the 1960 term of the United States Supreme Court, Schubert (1962) found almost all votes could be explained as representing the justices' attitudes or preferences: "A justice reacts in his voting behavior to the stimuli presented by cases before the Court, in accordance with his attitudes toward the issues raised for decisions."

Other scholars believe judges make decisions according to conflicting principles and inconsistent interests, affected by what they think will be the decision's impact on society and what they perceive will be society's advantages. Believers in this thesis deny jurists decide questions according to personal preferences. They point out that, as trained lawyers, judges are influenced by the doctrine of *stare decisis* (stand by the things decided) and wish to achieve as much stability in the law as possible (Miller, 1965). The result of reconciling societal considerations with *stare decisis* often produces judicial decisions that are in effect compromises.

Selection of Judges

In the selection of judges, it is necessary to distinguish between the formal procedures and requirements (those specified by constitutional or statutory law) and the actual practices employed. The former provide the legal specifications to be followed in choosing judicial personnel, but they necessarily leave an undefined area in which informal practices develop. State law may call for the popular election of judges, but who runs may be determined by the political parties. The law may provide for gubernatorial appointments, but the decision may actually be dictated by political leaders or bar associations.

In the judicial system of France and other European continental countries, the office of judge is treated as a distinct profession, separate from that of the lawyer. Those who aspire to a judgeship must meet rigid qualifications and undergo specialized training. They usually begin their service as apprentices and are promoted within the judicial hierarchy. This procedure is alien to the United States where judges are drawn from the membership of the bar and where few formal requirements other than age, residency, and citizenship are prescribed. Candidates with prior experience have no better chance to achieve judicial posts than those without such qualifications. Since its establishment, 40 percent of the nominees to the Supreme Court have had previous judicial careers; the percentage is no higher for the appellate tribunals of most states. Only in the case of the United States Courts of Appeals does experience appear to give a candidate a decided advantage. More than 60 percent of the nominees to these bodies, in recent decades, had extensive experience on the bench before their appointments.

There are various methods of formal selection, and each has its advocates and its supporting arguments. The procedures employed in the United States may be grouped into three general categories: elective, appointive, and appointive with modifications. The first prevails in thirty-three states, with an almost equal division between partisan and nonpartisan elections. The second is the procedure employed for the federal judiciary and for somewhat less than one-fourth of the states. The third, referred to as the Missouri Plan or the Nonpartisan Court Plan, is utilized in five states: Alaska, Iowa, Kansas, Missouri, and Nebraska. Its major features apply also to judicial selection in several other states, including California and Illinois.

Popular election of judicial personnel did not appear in the United States until the rise of Jacksonian democracy shortly before the middle of the nineteenth century. According to supporters of this practice, occupants of the bench should be politically responsible to the people for the conduct of their offices. Proponents of the appointive system decry the necessity for judicial candidates to compete with each other for popular favor in partisan or even nonpartisan campaigns. They maintain that the average voter is ill-equipped to assess the technical fitness and judicial apptitude of the individuals who seek judgeships. They contend that a judge who is dependent upon popular support for his office incurs political obligations which may affect his independence and impartiality.

Popular election of state court judges is actually not as predominant as the formal provisions suggest. Numerous vacancies on the bench occur through death, resignation, or retirement of incumbents before the expiration of their term of office. When this occurs, the governor usually has the power to fill the position for the remainder of the term or at least until the next election. In other words, the governor makes the original selection of a substantial percentage of judges in states with elective systems. Since individuals who receive such appointments have the distinct advantage of later running for "re-election" as incumbents rather than new aspirants for the office, the significance of the gubernatorial power to fill judicial vacancies needs not elucidation.

The modified appointment plan was developed by the American Bar Association and The American Judicature Society and was first adopted in Missouri in 1940. It seeks to combine restricted executive selection with popular approval. As it operates in Missouri, the governor fills judicial vacancies on the circuit courts of Jackson County (Kansas City) and St. Louis City, the intermediate appellate tribunals, and the supreme court from lists submitted by nonpartisan nominating commissions. The latter are composed of gubernatorial appointees, lawyers, selected by the bar, and the presiding judge of one of the appellate courts. The commission in Jackson County, for example, consists of two laymen from the area, two lawyers elected by members of the local bar, and the presiding judge of the Kansas City Court of Appeals. After the newly appointed judge has served on the bench for one year, his name is placed on the ballot for the voters of the area to determine whether he shall be retained in office. A similar referendum is held every six years thereafter in the cases of circuit court judges and every twelve years for appellate justice.

An examination of the selection process in the federal court system should dispel any illusions about the apolitical character of judicial appointments. When a vacancy occurs on the federal bench, a set pattern of procedure is followed. Names of suggested nominees are submitted to (senatorial patronage) the attorney General's office which serves as a clearing house or screening agency for all appointments to the national judiciary. Informal discussions then take place between members of the Justice Department, White House staff, senators, and other party leaders from the state where the vacancy exists. When the choice has been narrowed, the committee of Federal Judiciary of the American Bar Association is invited to comment on the candidates. This practice was inaugurated during Eisenhower's administration and has been followed since by every Attorney General.

The bar association committees do not initiate or suggest prospective nominees; it simply takes recommendations on those names submitted by the Attorney General. In this latter capacity, however, it has exerted influence in deterring the nomination of individuals it deems unqualified. Simultaneously with the committee's consideration, a full field investigation of the potential nominees is made by the Federal Bureau of Investigation. Following these activities, the Attorney General makes his recommendation to the President. By this time the acceptability of the candidate to the senator or senators (of the Chief Executive's party) from the relevant state has been established. Only in rare instances would the President submit the name of a judicial nominee over the objection of these officials.

The difficulty in excluding "politics" from the selection process, even under a restrictive appointment method, has been demonstrated by experience under the nonpartisan court plan in Missouri during the plan's first twenty-five years. Of the sixty judges appointed during this period, over 70 percent have belonged to the same party as the governor. Charges have been made that the governors attempt to influence the choice of the nominee lists through their appointees on the nominating commissions. These allegations have led to proposals to take the appointment of the lay members of such commissions from the governor (Roberts, 1965). To what degree can the selection process be removed from politics? To deny the governor any voice in the composition of the nominating panel further strengthens the role of the organized bar in the choice of judicial appointees. Over one-half the members of the Missouri bar, as a recent poll (Hearnes, 1965) revealed, feel that the court plan has already substituted bar politics and gubernatorial politics for the traditional politics of party leaders and political organizations. Few of them, however, look upon this result with disfavor, and some would eliminate the element of gubernatorial politics altogether by removing the governor's power to appoint a portion of the nominating panel. Should this happen, only bar politics would remain. In the final analysis any selection method, no matter how designed, presupposes a political decision at some point in the procedure.

The relationship between the formal methods of selection and the caliber of the judges who staff the courts remains more a matter of impression than a systematic study. Does the appointive process produce better judges than the popular election or is the Missouri-type plan superior to either appointment or election? The subject has been debated for some time. Proponents of executive selection point to the experience of the federal bench, which has traditionally enjoyed a higher reputation for competency than its counterparts in the states. How much of this relative superiority can be attributed to the mode of selection is not known. The greater benefits of federal judgeships-lifetime tenure, better pay, and higher prestige are probably much more important factors. It can be assumed that the more attractive a position is because of money, security, and prestige, the more it will appeal to those of ability and talent.

When we inquire into the relationship between background characteristics and the decision propensities of judges, we again find the data fragmentary. From the few studies pertaining to this question, findings like these emerge: Judges from families of lower socio-economic status are more likely to abandon precedent than those coming from upper status families; judges with prior judicial experience tend to deviate from precedent more frequently than those without such experience (Schmidhauser, 1963). Democrats, rather than Republicans, are more likely to vote for the defense in criminal cases and for the injured in motor vehicle accidents; and former public prosecutors are less likely to support the defendant in criminal cases than their colleagues who have not served in such a capacity (Grossman, 1966). Statistical relations of this kind may, of course, be reflections of other factors. The greater sympathy exhibited by Democratic judges toward the "underdog," for example, is probably due less to party affiliation than to the fact that more liberally inclined individuals belong to the Democratic party. At this point, the scattered empirical findings do little more than support the common sense assumption that judges' values are shaped by their background and environment and manifested in their decisions.

Arraignment and Plea Bargaining

Following the return of a true-bill, the defendant is brought before the trial court for formal arraignment. At this stage, the prosecutor formally reads in open court the bill-of-indictment which specifies the charges brought against the accused by the state. He is again informed of his constitutional right-to-counsel. Then, with or without counsel, he enters a formal plea of guilty or not guilty.

The reader will recall that at the preliminary hearing the accused could "plea-bargain" for a reduction in *charge* (felony/ misdemeanor). At the formal arraignment the accused can attempt to plea-bargain in hopes of a reduction of *sentence*.

The advantages to the defendant in plea bargaining are rather obvious; they include such considerations as a lighter sentence or having prosecution waived for additional charges. On the other hand, there are advantages for the prosecutor who feels that his case against the accused is weak and wishes to be cetrain of a conviction. Prosecutors may defend the practice of plea-bargaining on more altruistic grounds, claiming that the state is spared the expense of conducting costly trials or that justice is expedited by clearing jammed court calendars. Apart from altruism, it is well to remember that most prosecutors are elected officials with a personal stake in acquiring an impressive record of "convictions," which they can display to their constituents for political profit. Close scrutiny of such a record would undoubtedly reveal that a substantial majority of these "convictions" were obtained by plea-bargaining.

In noting the disproportionate amount of attention given in higher court decisions to such matters as improper trial procedure, illegal search and seizure, and confessions obtained under duress —matters which they consider of secondary importance from the standpoint of sheer numbers involved—Bloch and Geis (1962) deplore the dearth of systematic research on guilty pleas. They suggest the likelihood that justice is more apt to miscarry in guilty pleas than in situations such as those mentioned above:

> Many offenders plead guilty to charges out of fear of conviction for greater offenses, when in fact no charges could be sustained. Others assume that a lesser sentence, which might be probation, is more ac-assure that a lesser sentence, which might be probation, is more acceptable than the risk of a prison term ensuing from a prolonged jury trial. Others may plead guilty from a misunderstanding of the nature of the proceedings, and still others to avoid the publicity and expense of a more elaborate trial.

CRIMINAL TRIALS

However essential the criminal jury trial may be to the purposes of the novelist or dramist, it occupies a relatively minor role in the administration of criminal justice in the United States. The preponderance of cases that proceed to indictment are settled by guilty pleas. For example, 90.1 percent of those convicted in U.S. District Courts in calendar year 1964 were convicted on guilty pleas/and nearly comparable figures have been reported for the state of California during the same period (Sutherland and Cressey, 1970). It should be added that not all of the cases which did go to trial were tried before a jury.

The adversary nature of American criminal jurisprudence reaches its apotheosis in the jury trial, which one critic (Dressler, 1962) has called "trial by combat"; another (Frank, 1949) has christened it "a sublimated brawl." While it cannot be denied that drama is inherent in this conflict model of fact-seeking, on prosaic grounds the trial is defended because it has proven itself capable, over the centuries of evolution into its present form, of getting at the truth. The means whereby it does this—the central mechanism in the trial procedure—is formally elaborated set of rules for the presentation of evidence which conscientiously seeks to deny advantage to either party, the prosecution or the defense. Much of what the layman is apt to regard with impatience as a fussy, pedantic preoccupation with nitpicking procedural details or interpretations of legal precedent is, in fact, the expression of painstaking efforts to eliminate bias from the trial. These procedural safeguards are subsumed under the general rubric *due pro-*

cess. This includes the presumption of innocence until proven guilty beyond a reasonable doubt, the right against self-incrimination, and the right to be present at every session of the trial.

The Jury

In theory, jurymen are chosen at random from a panel of qualified prospects for jury duty. In practice, the prosecutor exercises his peremptory challenges during the *voir dire* to exclude as many prospective jurors as possible whom he perceives as potentially sympathetic to the defense; and the defense counsel similarly seeks to exclude people who might for reasons ranging from race to sex to age and occupation, be hostile to his client. When a capital offense is involved, such as the recent case of Manson and his "family" in California, the time required to empanel a jury may stretch into months, and the number of prospective jurors examined may reach a total of hundreds or even thousands.

The sacrosanct nature of the trial process has posed insurmountable obstacles to the systematic study of actual jury deliberations. Studies based on mock juries suffer from the obvious limitation that the crucially important variable of personal responsibility for deciding an individual's fate is missing is such sham trials. About the only source of evidence we have on the complex processes of social interaction and decision-making are anecdotal accounts from former jurors, and this kind of evidence is inherently subject to serious problems of reliability and validity.

Evidence and Testimony

The principal substance of a criminal trial is evidence given in court by witnesses. This evidence may be of a physical nature, much of it given by specialists in the employ of, or under consultant contract to, the state: ballistics data, information on fingerprints, chemical and toxicological analyses, polygraph findings, coroner's reports, and the like. Other evidence is introduced via direct testimony or cross-examination. All evidence—physical factual, or circumstantial—is, at least in theory, subject to honest error or deliberate falsification, i.e. perjury.

With regard to the former, the kinds of distortion to which

the testimony of an honest but inexpert, witness may be prone is depicted in Frankfurter's (1927) analysis of the testimony given by one of the key prosecution witnesses, Mary E. Splaine, in the traggic Sacco-Vanzetti trial:

> Splaine, viewing the scene from a distance of from 60 to 80 feet, saw a man previously unknown to her, in a car traveling at a rate of from 15 to 18 miles per hour; she saw him only from a distance of about 30 feet, that is to say for one and a half to three seconds; and yet she testified (more than a year later):
>
> *The man that appeared between the back of the front seat and the back seat was a man slightly taller than the witness. He weighed possibly from 140-145 pounds. He was muscular, and active-looking man. His left hand was a good-sized hand, a hand that denoted strength.*
>
> Q. The hand you saw where?
>
> A. *The left hand that was placed on the back of the front seat. He had a gray, what I thought was a shirt, had a grayish, like navy color —and the face was what we would call clear-out, clean-cut face. Through here (indicating) was a narrow, just a little narrow. . . . The forehead was high. The hair brushed back and it was between, I should think, two inches and two and one-half inches in length and had dark eyebrows, but the complexion was white, peculiar white, that looked greenish.*
>
> The startling acuity of Miss Splaine's version was, in fact, the product of a year's recollection . . . Let Dr. Morton Prince, professor of abnormal and dynamic psychology at Harvard University comment on this testimony:
>
> "I do not hesitate to say that the star witness of the government testified, honestly enough, no doubt, to what was psychologically impossible. Miss Splaine testified that she had seen Sacco at the time of the shooting from the distance of about 60 feet for from $1\frac{1}{4}$ to 3 seconds in a motor car going at an increasing speed at about 15 to 18 miles an hour; that she saw and at the end of the year she remembered and described 16 different details of his person, even to the size of his hand, the length of his hair as being between 2 and $2\frac{1}{2}$ inches long and the shade of his eyebrows! Such perception and memory under such conditions can be easily proven to be psychologically impossible."

In the matter of perjury, practically the only official safeguards against dishonest testimony are the oath and the threat of prosecution. Whatever the deterrent value of the latter, it seems doubtful that the moral and ethical constraints imposed by the oath would constitute an effective bar to perjury, especially in cases where large sums of money or life and death issues are involved. The use of the polygraph ("lie detector") or methods such as hypnosis and "truth serum" has likewise failed to provide a tamperproof means for detecting guilty knowledge. We can only conclude that the true extent of perjury is unknown, but we can speculate that it is appreciably greater in magnitude than the number of successfully prosecuted cases of perjury in a given year would suggest.

Verdict, Sentence, and Appeal

We now reach the end stage of the process by which twelve adult strangers, undistinguished by special aptitude, training, or experience, must find their way to a unanimous verdict on the guilt or innocence of the accused through a welter of conflicting evidence and testimony. That juries can arrive at such a verdict in a substantial number of cases may be marveled at by some as one of the glorious mysteries of criminal justice system, but more probably results from the operation of group pressures toward conformity which have been the target of intense study by social psychologists for several decades. However, until or unless jury deliberations become the legitimate focus of behavioral research, the processes by which consensus is reached on verdicts must remain a matter of conjecture and hypothesis.

Savitz (1967) claims that there are some features of law and its administration which place limits on the irrationality of jury decisions: "If the presiding judge decides that the prosecution has not made a prima-facie case, he will instruct the jury to return an acquittal verdict. Additionally, his charge to the jury specifically mentions the only possible verdicts the jury can return." Apart from these considerations, we are faced by the fact that little if any systematic research has been devoted to the impact of judicial instructions on jury decisions. Lacking empirical evidence, we can only assume that the instructions issued by the trial judge do, in fact, produce some effect on juries.

If the jury finds the defendant guilty, the judge has discretionary powers, within statutory limits, to impose what he considers an appropriate sentence. In earlier times, the imposition of sentences was regarded as a fairly cut-and-dried procedure. Inasmuch as specific punishments for specific offenses were laid down by the law, once a verdict of guilty was returned, the judge merely ordered the appropriate sentence to be carried out. The focus of attention was the offense, not the offender. This situation has changed in recent years as the nature of society's reactions to crimes and criminals has changed. Judges today thus have a broader range of alternatives available to them for dealing with offenders. Many of these alternative methods involve the assistance of professionals from disciplines like psychology, sociology, social welfare, and education. We shall devote some attention to these in the chapters which follow.

A considerable number of convictions are appealed to a review or appellate court, which may overrule the conviction for any of a variety of reasons, most of them involving substantive or procedural errors of law, e.g. misconduct by the prosecutor or jurors, errors in the drawing up of the bill of indictment, erroneous rulings by the trial judge, or contamination of evidence by either the defense or the prosecution. Contrary to popular belief, the appellate court does not overrule most convictions because it disputes the verdict, but rather because it finds flaws in the administration of justice.

Summary

The structure of the American court system is among the most complex found in modern society. A rather simplified overview of this judicial structure is presented in this chapter, together with a brief description of some of its major components, including the prosecutor, defense counsel, jury, and judge. The functioning of the criminal justice system is depicted with reference to its operations at various stages, beginning with the initiation of prosecution and proceeding through the preliminary hearing, arraignment, and trial. The practice of plea bargaining is discussed and some observations are made on the inequities of the bail bond system. The concluding portion of the chapter is devoted to a discussion of sentencing and appeal.

REFERENCES

American Civil Liberties Union: *Secret detention of the Chicago police.* New York, The Free Press, 1959.

Banks, L.: The crisis in the courts. *Fortune, 64*:186-189, 1961.

Barker, L.J. and Barker, T.W.: *Freedom, Courts, Politics: Studies in Civil Liberties.* Englewood Cliffs, Prentice-Hall, 1965.

Brown, J.M.: *Through These Men.* New York, Harper, 1956.

Chambliss, W.J.: *Crime and the Legal Process.* New York, McGraw-Hill, 1969.

Cohen, M.R.: *The Law and the Social Order.* New York, Harcourt, Brace, 1933.

Dressler, D.: Trial by combat in the American courts. *Harper's, 222*:31-36, 1961.

Frank, J.: *Courts on Trial.* Princeton, Princeton University Press, 1949.

Frankfurter, F.: The Case of Sacco and Vanzetti: A Critical Analysis for Lawyers and Laymen. Boston, Little Brown and Company, 1927.

Grossman, J.B.: *Lawyers and Judges: the ABA and the Politics of Judicial Selection.* New York, Wiley, 1965.

Hearnes, W.E.: Twenty-five years under the Missouri plan. *Journal of the American Judicature Society, 49*:100-104, 1965.

Interim report of the national conference on bail and criminal justice. Washington, U.S. Government Printing Office, 1966.

Johnson, E.H.: *Crime, Correction and Society.* Homewood, Dorsey, 1964.

Lake, L.W.: *How to Win Lawsuits Before Juries.* Englewood Cliffs, Prentice-Hall, 1954.

Lewis, Anthony.: *Gideon's Trumpet.* New York, Random House, 1964.

Mayers, L.: *The American Legal System.* New York, Harper and Row, 1964.

Miller, A.G.: On the need for "impact analysis" of Supreme Court decisions. *Georgetown Law Review, 53*:365-401, 1965.

Peltason, J.W.: *Federal Courts in the Political Process.* New York, Random House, 1955.

Puttkammer, E.W.: *The Administration of Criminal Law.* Chicago, University of Chicago Press, 1953.

Roberts, L.E.: Twenty-five years under the Missouri plan. *Journal of the American Judicature Society, 49*:92-97, 1965.

Savitz, L.: *Dilemmas in Criminology.* New York, McGraw-Hill, 1967.

Schmidhauser, J.: *Constitutional Law in the Political Process. Chicago,* Rand McNally, 1963.

Schubert, G.: The 1960 term of the Supreme Court: a psychological analysis. *American Political Science Review, 56*:90-107, 1962.

Schubert, G.: *Judicial Policy-Making.* Chicago, Scott Foresman, 1965.

Sturz, H.J.: *National Conference on Bail and Criminal Justice.* Washington, U.S. Government Printing Office, 1965.

Sutherland, E.H., and Cressey, D.R.: *Principles of Criminology.* Philadelphia, Lippincott, 1970.

Weston, P.B. and Wells, K.M.: *The Administration of Justice.* Englewood Cliffs, Prentice-Hall, 1967.

Chapter 15

CRIMINAL RESPONSIBILITY

L AW, LIKE BEHAVIORAL SCIENCE, is concerned to a large extent
with attempts to understand the actions of individuals and
their relationships with others. However, law operates on the basis
of various concepts and assumptions regarding human behavior
which are quite far removed from the present state of knowledge
in the behavioral sciences, a situation that often elicits strong criticism of the entire system of jurisprudence from behavioral scientists. While psychologists refer to behavior in terms of drives, motives, and stimulus control, the legal system tends to conceptualize
man as a rational agent who (except in specified instances) freely
chooses his modes of behavior. Thus, the legal lexicon is filled with
terms such as *intent, responsibility,* and *premeditation.*

The concept of criminal responsibility implies the fact of moral
knowledge. It presumes an acknowledgement that the individual
is required not to act in ways contrary to those sanctioned by social
custom or traditional and embodied in the law. Further, the concept of criminal responsibility presupposes that the accused is capable of making functional distinctions between what is "right" and
"wrong," as these terms are defined in codes of social conduct, and,
apart from the adverse effects of mental aberration or mental deficiency, is "able to do what is right." The fundamental link between moral knowledge and free choice is indicated by the legal
principles which allow for the diminution or elimination of responsibility under certain conditions which lessen or destroy the individual's capacity for discriminating between "right" and "wrong"
and acting in accordance with such discriminations.

The general and consistent view within the law has been that
wrong doing must be conscious to be criminal. With the aim of

making the above determination, a variety of tests or formulae, which of course have no claim to be scientific, have been developed over the years for the instruction of juries.

Basically what the various rules and tests seek to accomplish is to provide some relative gauge of criteria, based on numerous cases and upon moral, social, and philosophical orientations of the community, to decide how society should deal with the particular offender. The issues raised and tried before a judicial tribunal are never simple; definitions which are both precise and inclusive are difficult to arrive at. Therefore, considerable confusion exists as to the questions being raised for expert testimony.

Early Antecedents

Abnormal mental conditions in primitive man were regarded as the result of the influence or possession of good or evil spirits (Biggs, 1955). The principle of "mens rea" or guilty mind was recognized in the Hebrew Talmud, which specified that minors, the deaf and dumb, and the mentally disordered were not to be held culpable because ". . . with them only the act is the consequence, while the intention is of no consequence" (Guttmacher, 1963). Another early provision that an unintentional killing or a murder by a minor or lunatic was considered involuntary homicide was found in Mohammedan Law. The accused in these cases was subject only to compensation for which there was a fixed tariff, together with religious expiation. The Greek Draconian Code, though very harsh and punitive, also embodied the "mens rea" concept in its clear distinction between involuntary homocide and murder (Biggs, 1955).

Biggs suggested that the first open conflict between law and psychiatry occurred during the sixteenth century; Johann Weyer, a physician, insisted that the confessions of witches were an indication of severe mental disease. Interestingly, a lawyer and contemporary of Weyer's, Jean Bodin, defended the prosecution of witches in terms, as Biggs pointed out, that sound remarkably like modern reasoning: "If Weyer's sophisms and those of his wonderful doctors held good, the thieves and robbers might always appeal for mercy by blaming the devils we might as well cancel all those divine and human laws which deal with the punishment of crimes. Throughout most of the Renaissance and Reformation, however, the treatment of insane persons was determined by witchcraft and astrology.

In English law, which is acknowledged as the model for our own, the origin of the defense of insanity has been traced to the reign of Henry III (1216-1272) (Simon, 1967). The writings of Bracton during the thirteenth century clearly reveal the influence of Roman law. Bracton's famous maxim that "A madman knows not what he does and lacks mind and reason, and is not much removed from a brute," was believed to foreshadow the influential "wild beast" test. The "wild beast" pronouncement was actually made in 1723 by Justice Tracy, who, in the murder trial of Edward Arnold, stated that to avail himself of the defense of insanity" . . . a man must be totally deprived of his understanding and memory, so as not to know what he is doing, no more than an infant, a brute, or a wild beast." Since Arnold had some semblance of sanity, in that he could write and had purchased a gun and ammunition, he was found guilty and sentenced to death (Biggs, 1955).

Platt and Diamond (1965), in an interesting commentary on the subtle meaning of the "wild beast" concept of mental illness, observed that the tendency to displace insanity on to beasts or animals seems to reveal the threatening, non-personal characteristics attributed to the insane. Traces of this same attitude persists even today, they contend, as exemplified by the exemption from punishment of children and the insane and the treatment of these groups as "non-persons" by the law. The paternalistic approach of the mental hospital towards its patients and of society in general toward the mentally ill may stem from the coupling of these two groups in the eyes of the law.

Perhaps the most serious implication of the reduction of these two groups to non-person status, however, is the abdication of rights which ensues. Goldstein and Katz (1963), for instance, stated that while a successful defense against a criminal charge through due process of law usually results in the criminal being freed, the successful use of the insanity defense may result in the defendant's being restrained. Thus, they contend, the insanity defense is not a "defense" but a device for authorizing indeterminate restraint.[1]

It may seem then that there is a long history of men, with what would seem to be a deeply ingrained sense of justice, grappling with the *mens rea*, or "guilty mind" concept. Perhaps the most liberal application of this principle was made in Germany, where the Bavarian Code of 1813 provided for the exemption from punishment of many categories of persons: the deaf and dumb, the senile, and those who had committed a crime "while in a confused state of mind or senses for which they were not answerable" (Biggs, 1955).

M'Naghten

The M'Naghten ruling, which still prevails in England and thirty states in the United States, was pronounced in 1843 in a case which takes on added contemporary interest in view of some of the striking parallels with the case of Lee Harvey Oswald, or more recently, Sirhan Sirhan. (That the insanity defense would have been invoked in Oswald's defense had he lived to stand trial seems to be a foregone conclusion.)

Though it is commonly believed that this period in England was characterized by orderliness and complacency, Biggs (1955) observed that liberal ideals were beginning to penetrate the Victorian indifference to the suffering and poverty of the masses. It was against this backdrop that Daniel M'Naghten, a native of Scotland and political fanatic, was found not guilty on grounds of insanity for the murder of Sir Robert Peel's secretary. M'Naghten had mistaken the secretary for Peel, himself, who as Prime Minister was said to have been a highly conservative upholder of the status quo

---

[1] In a cogent commentary on the treatment by the courts of the other "nonperson" category, children, Green has observed, "It is an incongruous and contentious mixture of social work procedure with criminal-law decision which . . . results in neither impartial justice nor protective care. Most often, child and parents are not represented by counsel. To maintain privacy there is no jury; but neither is there any regard for the child's reputation, no record is kept; but if he is not guilty there is no way to announce that fact publicly, and his schoolmates and his neighbors more often than not are aware that he has been charged and brought to court . . . Again, he has granted neither the formal justice of law nor the protective care of social work."

(Biggs, 1955).

Though the form of M'Naghten's "insanity" was not designated at the time, contemporary psychiatrists would probably have labeled him paranoid (Glueck, 1962). He seemed to have been entangled in an elaborate system of delusions, including the belief that he was being pursued by spies and that the Tories and the Prime Minister were after him because he had voted against them in the previous election (Robitscher, 1966).

Many segments of Victorian society and, in fact, Queen Victoria[2] herself were indignant at M'Naghten's acquittal. The House of Lords, as a result of this, asked the judges of England for an authoritative statement of existing law. Their answer to the key question was:

> To establish a defense on the grounds of insanity, it must be clearly proven that, at the time of committing the act . . . the party accused was labouring under such a defect of reason from disease of the mind, as not to know the nature and quality of the act he was doing, or if he did know it . . . he did not know he was doing what was wrong (Glueck, 1962).

Since its pronouncement, the M'Naghten ruling has been a focal point of legal and psychiatric controversy. The following is an attempt to present the substance of this controversy.

First, it has been charged that the ruling does not make clear whether it is legal or moral "wrong" that is being referred to. Robitscher (1966) illustrated this ambiguity with a hypothetical case quoted from Sir James Stephen, English legal commentator: "A kills B with knowledge of his act and its illegality, but under the insane delusion that the murder of B was directed by God and would result in the salvation of the human race. If the word "wrong" means illegal, A's act is a crime. If the word "wrong" means immoral, A would not be criminally responsible for the act." Robitscher pointed out in this regard that, since in Texas legal wrong is the criterion for the right-wrong test, Jack Ruby could not have invoked the plea that he knew his act was legally wrong, but felt it was morally justified.

The most frequently recurring criticism of the M'Naghten rul-

---

[2]Glueck (1962) recounted, "In a delightful blend of wit, wisdom, and royal concern . . ." Victoria commented that she did not believe that anyone who wanted to murder a conservative Prime Minister could be insane.

ing emanating from psychiatric circles has been of its cognitive-moral emphasis. The thrust of this argument, Goldstein (1967) stated, is that M'Naghten is a restrictive rule which reflects an outmoded faulty psychology. It sees thought processes as separated into cognitive, emotional, and control components and classes a man insane only if he suffers from serious cognitive or intellectual impairment. It thereby limits the definition of insanity to the most deteriorated psychotics. "As a result," Goldstein continued, ". . . the elimination of M'Naghten and willingness to adopt one of the newer rules had been treated as a liberal test of faith."

Perhaps the most compelling objection to the M'Naghten ruling, particularly from the point of view of the testifying psychopathologist, has been stated by Roche (1958), who views the tests of responsibility as expressed in the M'Naghten ruling when applied to cases other than that of "disturbed consciousness" or "profound mental deficit," as "untenable propositions within the discipline of scientific medical psychology." Leifer (1964), voicing essentially the same objection, elaborates further when he argues that inferences pertaining to the verb "to know" can only be made from behavior criteria. "It is not possible to infer behind that behavior," he continues, "to a private sphere of events, the mind. . .The psychiatrist has no special skills or tools which enable him to penetrate the mind much as the toxicologist has skills and tools for examining the blood."

Plus "Irresistible Impulse"

Dissatisfactions with the M'Naghten ruling, particularly with its emphasis upon the rational, has led to a series of attempts to add to, amend, or replace it. A supplement to the M'Naghten ruling exists in eighteen states, starting with Alabama in 1896 and in the federal system is the "irrestible impulse" ruling. In English law this doctrine antedated the M'Naghten ruling which later overshadowed it. In more recent times it has been applied to defendants who may know the quality of their acts and be aware that they are wrong but, nevertheless, be driven to commit them by an overpowering impulse resulting from a mental condition (Robitscher, 1966).

One of the assumptions upon which the "irrestible impulse"

ruling rests is that there are, in fact, mental diseases which impair volition or selfcontrol, even when cognition is relatively unimpaired (Goldstein, 1967) or, stated differently, that there is such a thing as an irrestible impulse, as distinct from an unresisted impulse.

Davidson (1958) has challenged this assumption with the following argument. Using current psychiatric nosologies, he suggests that the irrestible impulse label might be applied to three categories of behavior: first, explosive reactions in psychotic persons; second, obsessive-compulsive neurotics; and third, rage reactions in persons with no psychosis or neurosis.

As first contemplated by the law, Davidson pointed out, "irrestible impulse" was intended to refer to the first of these categories. There is general agreement, he feels, that persons in this category should not be treated as guilty. He contends however, that this group already receives adequate protection under the M'Naghten ruling since such a person would not appreciate the wrongfulness of the act. He therefore needs no special doctrine to protect him.

The nub of the problem, Davidson contends, is the second category—the neurotic compulsion, most frequently kleptomania or pyromania. "It is technically incorrect," he asserted," . . . to say that such a person is in the helpless grip of an irresistible impulse . . . "since the neurotic" . . . can and usually does control it in the presence of a third party." True compulsions, he maintains, are always related to insignificant and harmless rituals: counting the cracks in the sidewalk or washing the hands. No one, he stated, "has to" commit a criminal act.

Cressey (1958) who upholds essentially the same point of view, stated:

> In most cases now labeled kleptomania, pyromania, etc., however, the actors appear to be motivated in the same way other criminals are motivated. Consequently they are, in the terminology of the criminal law, responsible. They select secluded places in which to perpetrate their acts, plan their activities in advance, realize that they will be arrested if detected, and do many other things indicative that there is a conscious normative referent in their behavior.

Cressey further questioned the assumption that larcenous behavior, i.e. shoplifting, is compulsive: "The economic status of the observer, is of great importance in determining whether he thinks a person is not in economic need and is consequently compulsive . . . If all psychiatrists were poverty-stricken the proportion of shoplifters called 'kleptomaniacs' would probably be higher than it is" (1958). With regard to the neurotic compulsive, Davidson summarized his position by stating that, though his abstinence may cause discomfort or anxiety, he can refrain from the act, and it is "socially hazardous" to exempt this group from accountability (1958).

Insofar as the third category is concerned, i.e. an otherwise normal person who commits a crime because of a rage reaction or acute alcoholism, Davidson argued that if such acts were not considered crimes then ". . . no one would ever be responsible for anything."

Implicit in the reluctance of the English and most American courts to adopt an "irresistible impulse" clause seems to be the sum of the logic presented by Cressey and Davidson: i.e. a doubt that any truly irresistible impulse exists: the belief that if it does exist it is too difficult to prove or disprove as a defense; and the belief that such a defense is dangerous to society (Guttmacker and Weihofen, 1952).

The New Hampshire Doctrine

New Hampshire was the only state which did not adopt the M'Naghten ruling. Influenced by the ideas of the influential forensic psychiatrist, Issac Ray and by its own Judge Doe, New Hampshire courts have been governed by a far more "liberal" provision: if the criminal action were the "offspring or product of mental disease," then the accused may plead not guilty by reason of insanity (Robitscher, 1966). Perhaps the most important implication of this ruling is that the question of responsibility is left to the discretion of the jury (Guttmacher and Weihofen, 1952).

Durham Ruling

The New Hampshire test had little influence outside that state until 1954 when the United States Court of appeals for the District of Columbia discarded M'Naghten and introduced the Durham ruling, apparently modeled after the liberal New Hampshire doctrine.

Monte Durham's crime, unlike that in most insanity defense trials, was not murder, but housebreaking. Durham, who was diagnosed as a psychopathic personality with psychosis, had a long history of mental disorder, had been hospitalized, and had attempted suicide several times. When the testifying psychiatrists were asked, however, if, in their opinion, the defendant could distinguish right from wrong, they could not answer categorically. The jury was instructed along the lines of M'Naghten, and Durham was found guilty. He was granted an appeal, however, and it was at this time that Judge Bazelon abrogated the M'Naghten ruling for the new formula, which, like the New Hampshire doctrine, stated that a defendant must be held not guilty if the jury finds that his act was the product of mental disease or defect (Simon, 1967).

The Durham decision was widely hailed in most psychiatric and some legal circles as a more liberal ruling, one which was more in keeping with the "new psychology"—permitting, thus, a full range of psychiatric testimony to be presented to the courts.

Most lawyers, however, take a dim view of the Durham ruling. Their chief criticism, as expressed by Goldstein (1967), is that it is a "non-rule"; it doesn't give the jury any standard by which to judge the evidence, and it leaves to a group of laymen the additional burden of passing judgment on highly technical psychiatric testimony.

Leifer (1964), viewing it somewhat differently, pointed out that the jury is rendered unable to make its own decision; it must agree with one of two teams of psychiatrists, each of which presents technical language which it cannot understand.

Simon (1967) conducted an empirical study of the impact of the Durham ruling. She first presented descriptive statistics indicating that there has been a fifteenfold increase in the proportion of defendants who were acquitted on grounds of insanity in the District of Columbia since the adoption of Durham. In a skillfully constructed experimental study in which "juries" listened to tape recorded trials, she then attempted to determine the effects of this ruling on their deliberations. The high degree of congruence in verdicts between a Durham instructed jury and an uninstructed jury led her to conclude that the Durham ruling is ". . . closer to the jury's natural sense of equity" which is desired. However, one may raise the question of the need for any rule at all. Judging by the fact that juries instructed under Durham deliberated significantly longer than those instructed under M'Naghten, she further concluded that the Durham rule ". . . serves to enhance the juror's responsibility." This writer would further question the extent to which the longer deliberations under Durham were a function of the ambiguity of its wording. When the juries were asked what ruling they would recommend for future use they were divided thirty-six percent for M'Naghten, thirty-one percent for Durham, and thirty-one percent indicating no preference. Her results, therefore, insofar as jury preferences are concerned, were inconclusive.

The courts have been almost unanimous in their failure to follow the lead of the District of Columbia in the adoption of Durham. The courts have moreover used the occasion, as Goldstein (1967) pointed out, to . . . "reaffirm its faith in "free will" and deterrence, its hostility to psychiatry and the "deterministic" view of human behavior, its skepticism about psychiatry's status as a science, its fear that the concept of mental disease was so broad that it might encompass all or most serious crime, and especially the psychopath."

The Durham ruling has recently received its share of criticism from psychiatric, as well as legal circles. Gaylin (1965) pointed out that carrying the holistic stress theory of behavior to its logical conclusion can lead to such absurdities as acquitting persons with psychosomatic ills, such as asthma, for crimes which they might commit. He further points out that society could not afford to exempt from criminal responsibility all actions resulting from mental disease, such as alcoholism, drug addiction, and sexual deviation. "Would we," he asks rhetorically, "grant immunity to the addict who steals to fed his habit, while we hold liable the pauper who steals to feed his hunger?"

Leifer (1964) contends that there are what are perhaps more basic logical fallacies in the Durham ruling. "The ascription of responsibility on the basis of mental health," he states, "is no more scientific than the ascription of responsibility on the basis of personal wealth." Any ascriptions, he contends, are not facts nor scientific principles, but are "human actions." He further pointed out the paradox of the formulation of the Durham ruling on the grounds that it was based upon a more "scientifically valid" concept of mental illness, while at the same time the validity of the concept of mental illness itself is being challenged by critics like Szasz. Thus the Durham ruling, which met with immediate criticism from judicial circles, is now being questioned by psychiatrists as well.

Model Penal Code (ALI Rule)

The Durham ruling had hardly been in existence a year when the American Law Institute, in an attempt to clarify the ambiguity of the "product of mental disease or defect" clause, made its recommendations on insanity for its Model Penal Code (1962). Rejecting the advice of its psychiatric advisory committee which endorsed Durham, the A.L.I. proposed the following formulation:

1. A person is not responsible for criminal conduct if at the time of such conduct as a result of mental disease or defect he lacks substantial capacity either to appreciate the criminality of his conduct or to conform his conduct to the requirements of law.
2. As used in this Article, the terms "mental disease or defect" do not include an abnormality manifested only by repeated criminal or otherwise antisocial conduct.

The second provision here is noteworthy in its obvious exclusion from consideration of the "psychopathic personality" category, psychopathology's "bete noire." Glueck (1962) suggested that some of the complexities involved in the courts' dealing with the psychopathic personality are first, whether in view of their resistance to treatment, acquittal on grounds of insanity would serve any purpose and second, the high rate of recidivism among these individuals.

In spite of their initial opposition, psychiatrists came to view the new ruling as an improvement over previous ones in its substitution of "appreciate" for "know," a seeming recognition of emotional as well as intellectual awareness of conduct. The substitution of "conform" for "control" was also deemed an improvement. The wide acceptance which the A. L. I. ruling has received in some circles was demonstrated empirically by Sadoff, Collins, and Keeler (1966), who asked military attorneys and psychiatrists to rank order their preferences among the five most used tests of criminal responsibility. Psychiatrists ranked the Model Penal Code first. The attorneys chose M'Naghten plus irresistible impulse first.

The ruling was hardly on the books, however, when criticism was voiced concerning the vagueness of the terms, "appreciate" and "substantial." The question of the extent to which a lay jury could grasp the significance of the expression "to conform his conduct to the requirements of the law" was also raised.

"Currens"

Another recent major attempt to define insanity was pronounced by Chief Justice John Biggs, speaking for the majority of the United States Court of Appeals in the Currens Case (1961). The Currens test states that the jury may find the defendant not guilty on grounds of insanity if he ". . . as a result of mental disease or defect, lacked substantial capacity to conform his conduct to the requirements of the law which he is alleged to have violated." Though the "substantial capacity to conform" clause is like the A. L. I. formula, Currens omits what has been regarded as a cognitive criterion, "appreciate the criminality of his conduct" (Glueck, 1962).

It has been criticized, however, on the grounds that it would deny to jurors a ground for finding insanity when the capacity for self-control is unimpaired, but when the defendant, nevertheless, did not "appreciate" the criminality of his conduct (Goldstein, 1967).

"Diminished" Responsibility

The legal concept of "diminished" or "partial" responsibility perhaps deserves brief consideration, particularly in light of the attempts to invoke it on behalf of Sirhan Sirhan.

The origins of this plea may be traced to seventeenth century English law when Sir Matthew Hale, Lord Chief Justice of the

Court of the King's Bench, differentiated two forms of insanity, "partial insanity of mind," and "a total insanity." Partial insanity, Hale prophetically observed, could excuse but would be a matter of great difficulty (Biggs, 1955).

The Homocide Act of 1957 made the doctrine of diminished responsibility a part of the Law of England (Robitscher, 1966). The plea has since become so popular in England that, in Goldstein's (1967) view, it threatens to replace the insanity defense entirely. In the United States the doctrine of "partial responsibility" was first invoked in cases in which evidence of intoxication was admitted as a defense against murder in the first degree. Unlike the situation in England, however, the extension to other types of mitigating evidence has been slow (Goldstein, 1967). Only about a dozen states recognize this doctrine.

Partial responsibility assumes partial importance, as the case of Sirhan demonstrated, when the question of capital punishment is involved; it offers the defense an alternative to the insanity defense which frequently brings with it indeterminate commitment. Guttmacher (1963) expressed the reservation that many of the critics of the "diminished responsibility" concept seem to hold when he warned: "Let me protest against the maudlin and much too frequent error, that the partially responsible merit shorter sentences. In many instances their abnormality calls for more prolonged incarceration than that of other offenders for the protection of society, but it should be in a benign and therapeutic environment."

The foregoing, then, has been an attempt to chronicle the highlights of man's struggle through the centuries with the "free-will vs. determinism" question as it relates to criminal responsibility. The search for casual explanations for criminal behavior, it was seen, began not with the determinism of Darwin or Freud, but was deeply rooted in Judeo-Christian belief. Thus, as Leifer (1964) somewhat sardonically observed: "Eve was influenced by the Devil, Adam was influenced by Eve, and, their descendants have been influenced by a succession of malevolent factors from demons to instincts, to twisted molecules to mental disease." Aberrant chromosomes can now be added to Leifer's list.

Recent efforts, it was seen, have centered around the search for the right "test" for criminal responsibility by legal experts, who have been aided, abetted, or in the view of some, impeded by behavioral scientists.

WHERE DO WE GO FROM HERE: SOME CONTEMPORARY POINTS OF VIEW

If the period from M'Naghten to Durham was characterized by a "liberalizing" of the legal definition of insanity, the pendulum now seems to be swinging in the direction of a desire for greater restriction in this regard. The following are some representative contemporary points of view.

A Sociological Theory

An interesting sociological view of "motivation" as applied to criminal responsibility has been presented by Cressey (1958) in the context of the differential association theory. The essence of this theory is that criminality is learned in interaction with others in a process of communication, and that there are differences in the degree to which acts are controlled by the linguistic constructs which the actor has learned from his social groups. Motives are not, therefore, "inner biological mainsprings of action but linguistic constructs which organize acts in particular situations." By this definition, criminal behavior would be considered "motivated" if a person defines a situation as one in which there are alternatives, if there is evidence of planning, etc. It is pointed out that if this were used as the criterion for criminal responsibility it would render those accused of what have traditionally been considered "compulsive crimes" legally responsible.

A Return to M'Naghten

The desire for a more restrictive interpretation of insanity has been expressed, particularly in some legal circles, as a desire for a return to or a tenacious clinging to M'Naghten; this is in spite of efforts to liberalize the ruling. Representative of this viewpoint is Goldstein (1967), who contends that this ruling most clearly identifies the "insane"; the terms "know," "nature and quality of the act," and "'wrong" need not have a narrow and constrictive meaning if the jury is instructed by the judge to interpret them broadly.

The wide contemporary support of the M'Naghten ruling among certain legal circles was given empirical support by the survey study conducted by Sadoff, Collins, and Keeler (1966). When asked to rank order the five most used tests of criminal responsibility, military attorneys ranked M'Naghten plus the irresistible impulse first and M'Naghten alone second.[3]

Abandonment of the Defense

Finally, recognition must be given to the growing body of articulate spokesmen from both law and psychiatry, who, when asked who shall be excluded from criminal responsibility, reply, in effect, no one. The position of this group is, in general, that reappraisal of the situation must be made not in terms of more up-to-date concepts of mental illness, but in terms of what the procedure of a criminal trial is all about. Wiseman (1961), a lecturer in Law at Boston University, skillfully used the recorded proceedings of a murder case[4] in which the defense of insanity was invoked to illustrate several problems in the use of psychiatric "expert" testimony in the courts. Essentially these problems were that such testimony is usually too complex for a judge or jury to understand and utilize in the interest of a just disposition of a case,[5] and that the courtroom confrontation of psychiatrists with different theoretical orientation can lead to confusion and can impede the due process of law. After providing documentation for each of these claims, he concluded that the function of a jury in a murder trial should be limited to a finding of guilty or not guilty for the defense charge. A more appropriate function for the psychiatrist would be, he suggested, to serve on a "sentencing authority" with other professionals to determine what

---

[3]Military psychiatrists, when asked the same question, ranked the Law Institute Model Penal Code First, Both groups ranked Durham last by a considerable margin.

[4]Case of Jim Cooker, airplane mechanic, convicted of murder and tried in Roxbury, Massachusetts.

[5]One judge was reported to have literally thrown down a deck of projective cards in anger and to have refused to admit the evidence presented (Jeffery, 1964) .

combination of treatment and/or punishment is appropriate.

Goldstein and Katz (1963) based their argument for the abolition of the insanity defense upon the grounds that the legal concepts of "voluntariness" (free-will) and *mens rea* (evil intent) already adequately serve all defendants, including those now classified as "insane." The requisite material elements of a crime have traditionally been a voluntary act purposely causing a result. They further contend that abolition of the insanity defense would force a more needed focus upon the adequacy of criteria for civil commitment and the discharge of the mentally ill.

An estimate of the prevalence of this view among psychiatrists was made by Guttmacher (1958) when he stated that more than 10 percent of all psychiatrists refuse all courtroom employment and another 20 percent refuse employment as partisan experts.[6] One can only speculate about the percentages of psychopathologists who hold this view today. Some more recent evidence related to this question was found, however, in the 1965 questionnaire study of Sadoff, Collins and Keeler (1966). When asked, which nosological categories of individual they would consider not mentally responsible for criminal acts, the fifty military psychiatrists, who responded, ranked psychotics first; interestingly, "no one" was the second most frequent response. The following are representative views from those who would fall into the two groups which Guttmacher has designated.

Among psychiatrists, perhaps the most outspoken critic of the insanity defense is Szasz (1963), who during the pre-trial speculation about the mental state of Jack Ruby, called the defense "a hoax"—"A legal tactic for beating the murder rap."

In a more "scholarly" formulation of his viewpoint, Szasz (1957) points out the logical fallacy of the casual relationship between "mental illness" and criminal behavior. This fallacy has arisen, he believes, as a result of the use of the medical disease model.

---

[6]Guttmacher added, "One can smugly assert that that still leaves seventy percent of the nation's psychiatrists to draw upon and that that is more than enough. The truth of the matter is that in this dissenting third are to be found most of the leaders of American psychiatry" (p. 118).

Psychiatrists, moreover, have attained great social power, which he contends is, at least in part, because of the "mysteriousness of psychiatric operations." The public, he feels, has vested in them magical powers. Szasz (1957) stated, therefore, that

> When it comes to matters of responsibility and of who should or should not be punished, psychiatry should, it seems to me, disavow the aggrandizements which have been foisted on it and disclaim any special competence in these areas. The legal profession and society at large makes the law and should take responsibility for their handiwork.

Szasz has, furthermore, characterized the frequency stated view that psychiatry and law should work toward mutual understanding as "a sentimental prejudice" and feels that the best interest of both would better be served if each made its unique contribution to the field of criminology. Leifer (1964), though essentially in agreement with Szazs' position, has somewhat pessimistically warned: "Any challenge to the psychiatrist's status as an expert is not likely to be well-received by either psychiatry or the law—for psychiatrists would have to abdicate from a favored function and law would be forced into the painful search for its own formulae and justifications for the ascription of criminal responsibility."

Taking a somewhat more moderate position are those who, though in agreement with Szasz that they should not serve as "expert" witnesses, believe that psychopathologists can serve other useful and appropriate functions in work with the courts. Dr. Karl Menninger's comment after being invited to examine Jack Rudy would seem to place him in this camp. He was reported to have replied that he would be glad to do so after the verdict was in. (Gaylin, 1965).

Guttmacher (1963) suggested that the psychopathologists might serve a legitimate function in conducting a pre-trial examination of the accused and rendering a professional determination as a neutral expert.

Gaylin (1956) based his opposition to psychiatrists' playing a role in determining guilt and innocence upon the premise that, since psychiatry is inherently deterministic, guilt and innocence are not functional concepts within this context. To the typical psychiatrist, he stated, "Guilt is an emotion and innocence—an age." He maintains, however, that the psychiatrist can play an appropriate role in criminology in the determination of such matters as which kind of punishment will be most effective, whether punishment discourages recidivism, and whether one man's punishment will deter another man's attempt. All of these questions, he believes, are amenable to investigation by methods which are compatible with the psychiatrist's discipline.

Halleck (1969) takes what seems to be an even more moderate position. Acknowledging that a complete abolishment of the insanity defense would not now be acceptable to many segments of our society, he maintains that the psychiatrist should only be required to present a judgement as to the extent of the defendant's psychological impairment without being required to make such determinations as whether he could distinguish right from wrong.

PROPOSALS FOR FUTURE STANDARDS

The Subcommittee on Criminal Laws and Procedures of the Committee on the Judiciary of the United States Senate is considering a revision of the criminal code of the Federal government. The Commission recommended, among many other things, that the "insanity" defense to criminal responsibility be codified because "present federal law as to the defense of insanity is not uniform." They accepted and proposed as Section 503 of the new Code a somewhat modified version of the so-called A. L. I. formulation: "A person is not responsible for criminal conduct if at the time of such conduct as a result of mental disease or defect he lacks substantial capacity to appreciate the criminality of his conduct or to conform his conduct to the requirements of law. 'Mental disease or defect' does not include an abnormality manifested only by repeated criminal or otherwise antisocial conduct. Lack of criminal responsibility under this section is a defense."

Among the many alternative suggestions heard by the Subcommittee were the following:

(1) Retain the present law under which each Circuit Court of Appeals by case law sets the defense for the Federal courts in that circuit;

(2) Enact a defense, but ask the question directly and make it

a ground for acquittal if the defendant's capacity to appreciate the criminality of his conduct or to conform his conduct to the requirements of law "is so substantially impaired that he cannot justly be held responsible";

(3) Enact a defense, but limit the defense to the mental or culpability element of the crime, to wit:

Mental disease or mental defect is a defense to a criminal charge only if it negates the culpability required as an element of the offense charged. In any prosecution for an offense, evidence of mental disease or mental defect of the defendant may be admitted whenever it is relevant to negate the culpability required as an element of the offense;

(4) Abolish the insanity defense, but make it mandatory in the case of conviction that the defendant be treated or hospitalized and not sent to prison, to wit:

For a crime which someone has committed under the influence of insanity, feeble-mindedness or other abnormality of such profound nature that it must be considered equivalent to insanity, no other sanction may be applied than surrender for special care or, in cases specified in the second paragraph, fine or probation; cf. Swedish Penal Code, Chapter 33.

(5) Enact the so-called M'Naghten and irresistible impulse tests. The present confused state should be aided as prominent law schools turn to a law-science model for training our future lawyers and jurists.

Summary

This chapter explores some aspects of the interaction between the law and psychiatry within the context of the determination by the court of the criminal responsibility of the defendant. The antecedents of the insanity plea are sketched in English law, culminating in the M'Naghten ruling of 1843 which established criteria for assessing the mental status of the defendant at the time the offense occurred. These criteria, together with the concept of "irresistible impulse," have been the focus of controversy for more than a century. More recently, behavioral scientists have been equally critical of both the legal and the psychiatric approaches to the question of criminal responsibility.

REFERENCES

American Psychological Association: *Ethical Standards for Psychologists.* Washington, APA, 1953.

Arbitt, J.: The psychologist as expert witness: a case report and analysis of personal experiences previously reported in the *American Psychologist. Amer. Psychol., 15:*721-727, 1960.

Biggs, J. Jr.: *The Guilty Mind.* New York, Harcourt Brace and Company, 1955.

Burtt, H. E.: *Legal Psychology.* New York, Prentice-Hall, 1931.

Centor, A.: Services of the psychiatrist. *Amer. Psychol., 23:*133, 1968.

Cressey, D. R.: The differential association theory and compulsive crimes. In Nice, R. (Ed.): *Crime and Insanity.* New York, Philosophical Library, 1958.

Davidson, H. A.: Irresistible impulse and criminal responsibility. In Nice, R. (Ed.): *Crime and Insanity.* New York, Philosophical Library, 1958.

Diamond, B. L.: Law and psychiatry. In Deutsch, A. and Fishman, H. (Eds.): *The Encyclopedia of Mental Health.* New York, Franklin Watts, 1963.

Dreikurs, E.: Issues of legal process. *Amer. Psychol., 21:*928-983, 1966.

Franck, I. H.: Psychological testimony in the courtroom. *Amer. Psychol., 11:*50-51, 1956.

Gaylin, W. M.: Psychiatry and the law: partners in crime. *Columbia University Forum, 8:*23-27, 1965.

Geiser, R. L., and Newman, R. N.: Psychology and the legal process: opinion pools as evidence? *Amer. Psychol., 16:*685-690, 1961.

Glueck, S.: *Mental Disorder and the Criminal Law.* Boston, Little, Brown and Company, 1927.

Goldstein, A. S.: *The Insanity Defense.* New Haven, Yale University Press, 1967.

Goldstein, J., and J. Katz: Why an insanity defense? *Daedalus, 92:*549-563, 1963.

Green, A. W.: *Sociology—an Analysis of Life in Modern Society.* New York, McGraw—Hill, 1964.

Guttmacher, M. S.: *The Mind of the Murderer.* New York, Grove Press, Inc., 1960.

Guttmacher, M. S.: What can the psychiatrist contribute to the issue of criminal responsibility? *Journal of Nervous and Mental Disorders, 136:*103-117, 1963.

Guttmacher, M. S., and H. Weihofen: *Psychiatry and the Law.* New York, W. W. Norton & Co., Inc., 1952.

Halleck, S. L.: The psychiatrist and the legal process. *Psychology Today,* February: 25-28, 1969.

Hoch, E. L., and Darley, J. G.: A case at law. *Amer. Psychol., 17:*623-654, 1962.

Jeffery, R.: The psychologist as an expert witness on the issue of insanity. *Amer. Psychol., 19:*838-843, 1964.

Karson, S.: Reply to Jeffery. *Amer. Psychol., 21:*244-245, 1966.

Kendler, Tracy S.: Contributions of the psychologist to constitutional law. *Amer. Psychol., 5:*505-510, 1950.

Leifer, R.: The psychiatrist and tests of criminal responsibility, *American Psychologist, 19:*825-830, 1964.

Lerner, J.: The role of the psychologist in the disability evaluation of emotional and intellectual impairments under the social security act. *Amer. Psychol., 18:*252-256, 1963.

Liebenson, H. A., and Wepman, J. M.: *The Psychologist as a Witness.* Mundelein, Callaghan and Company, 1964.

Loevinger, L.: Foreword. In Marshall, James: *Law and Psychologist in Conflict.* Indianapolis, The Bobbs-Merrill Company, Inc., 1966.

MacDonald, J. M.: *Psychiatry and the Criminal.* Springfield, Charles C Thomas, 1958.

McCary, J. L.: The psychologist as an expert witness in court. *Amer. Psychol., 11:*8-13, 1956.

McCary, J. L.: A psychologist testifies in court. *Amer. Psychol., 15:*53-57, 1960.

Mariner, A. S.: A critical look at professional education in the mental health field. *Amer. Psychol., 22:*271-281, 1967.

Marshall, J.: *Law and Psychology in Conflict.* Indianapolis, The Bobbs-Merrill Company, Inc., 1966.

Munsterberg, H.: *On the Witness Stand.* New York, Clark, Boardman, 1925.

Newman, E. B.: A psychologist in court: the special master. *Amer. Psychol., 18:*262-264, 1963.

Overholser, W.: *The Psychiatrist and the Law.* New York, Harcourt Brace and Company, 1953.

Platt, A. M., and B. Diamond.: The origins and development of the wild beast concept of mental illness and its relation to theories of criminal responsibility. *Journal of the History of the Behavioral Sciences, 1:*4, 1965.

Polier, J.: *The Rule of Iaw and the Role of Psychiatry.* Baltimore, The John Hopkins Press, 1962.

Rice, G. P.: The psychologist as expert witness. *Amer. Psychol., 16:*691-692, 1961.

Robitscher, J. B.: *Pursuit of Agreement—Psychiatry and the Law.* Philadelphia, J. B. Lippincott Company, 1966.

Roche, R. Q.: *The Criminal Mind.* New York, Farrar, Straus, and Cuday, 1958.

Rodnick, E. H., and Hoch, E. L.: . . . and justice for all. *Amer. Psychol., 16:*718-719, 1961.

Sadoff, R. L., D. Collins, and W. J. Keeler: Psychiatric testimony in military courts. *American Journal of Psychiatry,* June: 1344-1348, 1966.

Schofield, W.: Psychology, law and the expert witness. *Amer. Psychol.*, *11*:1-7, 1956.

Schwarz, W.: When the psychologist testifies. *Amer. Psychol.*, *15*:555, 1960.

Schwarz, W.: Psychological testimony. *Amer. Psychol.*, *21*:914, 1966.

Shearn, C. R.: Testimony of an expert witness. *Amer. Psychol.*, *21*:376, 1966.

Shoben, E. J.: Psychologists and legality: a case report. *Amer. Psychol.*, *5*:496-498, 1950.

Simon, R. J.: *The Jury and the Defense of Insanity*. Boston, Little, Brown and Company, 1967.

Spector, J. A.: Ethical and legal aspects of survey research. *Amer. Psychol.*, *18*:204-208, 1963.

Szasz, T. S.: Psychiatric expert testimony—its covert meaning and social functions. *Psychiatry, 20*:313-316, 1957.

Szasz, T. S.: The myth of mental illness. *Amer. Psychol.*, *15*:113-118, 1960.

Szasz, T. S.: *Law, Liberty, and Psychiatry*. New York, Macmillan, 1963.

Szasz, T. S.: *Psychiatric Justice*. New York, Macmillan, 1965.

Teahan, J. E.: Clinical training and expert testimony. *Amer. Psychol.*, *21*: 244, 1966.

Wigmore, J. H.: *The Science of Judicial Proof*. Boston, Little, Brown and Co., 1937.

Wiseman, F.: Psychiatry and the law: use and abuse of psychiatry in a murder case. *American Journal of Psychiatry, 118*: 1961.

Woodward, J. L.: A scientific attempt to provide evidence for a decision on change of venue. *Amer. Soc. Rev., 17*:447-452, 1952.

Zilboog, G.: The reciprocal responsibilities of law and psychiatry. *Shingle, 12*: 79-96, 1949.

Part V
TREATING THE CRIMINAL OFFENDER

THIS BOOK CONCLUDES, appropriately enough, with a brief discussion of society's disposition of some of its criminal offenders. Chapter 16 describes penal incarceration and the impact of institutionalization upon both inmates and custodial personnel; Chapter 17 deals with probation and parole as alternatives to institutionalization. This discussion is a supplement to our earlier consideration of various intervention techniques with various specific categories of criminal behavior covered in Chapters 7 through 12; it is necessarily suggestive rather than conclusive, since the subject of corrections is broad and complex enough to require coverage in a separate volume.

Prison riots like those which occurred at Attica and in New Jersey have dramatized for the public what criminologists have been saying in scholarly terms for years: Whatever one chooses to call the prison, "correctional institution" is possibly the least accurate designation one could find. In our own experience, they are best regarded as human dumping grounds for society's losers. Most of these men and women have failed at everything they have tried, including crime. Ironically enough, their incarceration is a testimonial to their inability to become even moderately successful as criminals. The following are two speeches given by inmates at the Louisiana State Penitentiary at Angola. They provide some interesting insights into the backgrounds of the convicts who gave them. The first inmate was asked to talk about some incident in his childhood; the second was asked to describe an interesting experience in his life or job.

509

Inmate #1:

Good evening, class. The incident which happened to me in my child-hood life was when I was at the age of five. In the first grade of school my teachers had a certain dislike for me. They never would assist me in any of my problems. They would always push me to the back of the class, but yet still I was promoted in grades for something that I know I did not deserve. It continued to the eighth grade where it became a task I could not cope with. It was so embarrassing until I dropped out of school and accepted life on my own as a man. I ended up in jail-houses and institutions. Now I stand before you here at Angola. Some people say that education only comes once in a life time, but I believe it is a second time and I am not going to wait for the third or the fourth. I am going to grab the second so I may be able to walk with a better understanding in life and forget things that happened to me in the past. I thank you.

Inmate #2:

Good evening, class. The experience that I had in my life was when I got shot in the mouth playing Russian roulette. That was the first time I got shot. The second time was when I got shot in the stomach by a police officer. I am sure that each of you can see the marks on my face and arms which is the result of cuts and stabs. I considered all of this as just being luck—the reason that I was still living. Until it came the fourth time I was shot, which was by a thirty-thirty carbine rifle. The third time was by a twelve-gauge shotgun which hit me in the right hip. Then I realized that it was not just luck, but rather it was the good Lord above that wanted me to live. Maybe if I had not had to suffer the hardships that I did, coming up through the years, maybe I would not have been as good a man as I am now. I thank you.

These two men are part of a prison population which is heavily drawn from urban areas like New Orleans. Men, whose background is entirely urban, are sent to this 22,000 acre sugar plantation, serve their time, and are then returned to the city. Since there is no particular demand for cane-cutters in the city, their time has been spent in useless drudgery—a point which is reiterated each year to the legislature by the Louisiana Division of Corrections. But there is only one budget, and prison reform is normally a low priority item. It is not that life in prison is so brutal, but rather that it is so pointless. Until we provide inmates with meaningful work, we can scarcely expect our "correctional institutions" to do more than keep their occupants out of circulation. Inevitably, when they are released, they return to society coarsened, rather than improved, by their prison experience.

Chapter 16

INSTITUTIONALIZATION: SOCIETY REACTS TO THE CRIMINAL

BECAUSE PUBLIC INTERESTS in crime centers on the offender, national magazines focus their articles on the criminal and, in so doing, confer instant notoriety upon the felon. The killer of Dr. Martin Luther King not only saw his name in print in every magazine, but was paid 25,000 dollars for exclusive rights to the story of how he planned and committed the murder.[1]

Criminologists, on the other hand, are just as interested in the societal reaction to the criminal as in the personality of the offender. For, as Winston Churchill said in 1910, "The mood and temper of the public with regard to the treatment of crime and criminals is one of the most unfailing tests of the civilization of any country" (Size, 1957).

Truman Capote, in his book *In Cold Blood,* told the story of two sociopathic killers who slaughtered the Cutter family in the village of Holcombe, Kansas. The reader or movie viewer might think that the only purpose of the book was to give us insight into the "criminal minds" of the killers. This it does. Perry Smith, an undersized, half-breed aspirin addict (his legs ached from a motorcycle accident) could read of the funeral of his victims with no feelings of remorse and only wonder how much money such a large funeral would cost. Such a personality response was the reaction of a man who, as a child, watched his mother and father

---

[1]Of such magnitude in the American fascination with crime and criminals. *Time* (February 21, 1972) magazine replaced the President of the United States on its cover with Clifford Irving, an almost unknown novelist, granting him the title "Con Man of the Year."

fight each other with horsewhips, scalding water, and kerosene lamps. (His mother died in a drunken stupor by strangling in her own vomit); He had been beaten in a orphanage for bed-wetting by nuns he remembered as Black Widows; and he had been held under in a tub of ice-water for the same infraction by a sadistic employee of a Salvation Army shelter. His partner, Dick Hick-cock, was a child molester who suffered from migraine headaches and ran over dogs for sport. The book shows us how a combination of experiences produced the personalities capable of commiting their demented acts. Their acts, then, can be understood, though not forgiven. But the case study of these two offenders is not the central point of the book or its title. For, systematically, without passion, and for no personal profit other than salary, the officials at the Kansas State Penitentiary carry out the dictates of the society they serve and hang these men in the same way the criminals dispatched their victims: *In Cold Blood.*

Punishment as a Societal Reaction

Corrections is defined as that branch of criminology which deals with the treatment of the offender. It has largely replaced the older term *penology,* the generic term for the organized body of concepts, theories, and approaches centered upon the prison and the institutional experiences. Although the nomenclature has changed, there are reasonable grounds for questioning the extent to which the underlying mystique and ideology of prison confinement have also changed. Most prison systems in the United States reflect a punitive societal response orientation rather than a treatment-oriented philosophy. The term penology derives from the Greek *poena,* meaning punishment; thus penology might be defined as the scientific study of the application of pain.

The punitive reaction looks backward to the past and treats the criminals in terms of what he did, rather than to the future and his capacity for improvement. Courts sentence an offender to serve time at "hard labor," although enforced idleness is more often the case. State penitentiaries are generally under no legal obligation to do anything but keep an offender in custody at some unpleasant task.

Reflecting this philosophy, an associate warden, with whom the authors once worked, was accustomed to telling prisoners upon their arrival: "Prisons were not meant to be nice places. If they were, you might want to come back." This man, a fundamentalist minister, was in charge of treatment.

Prisons become systems of "organized pain" for the inmate. The offender is sentenced to hard labor, but his punishment is greater than the loss of liberty alone. Deprived of normal social and sexual relations, cut off from any opportunities to accumulate savings of property, he is sentenced to live in the company of frustrated misfits, sociopaths, and homosexuals; he will soon learn that his greatest danger lies in potential violence from other inmates, rather than punishment from his captors. The convict's greatest enemy is another convict. Many prisoners prefer the term *convict* over that of *inmate;* the latter term cannotes cooperation with the system and smacks of a mental institution. The authors once asked a prisoner if he would prefer to be called an "inmate" or a "convict." His reply: "I've been called both and treated the same."

How is this punishment justified? Is punishment inherently just, or must it be rationalized pragmatically in terms of the results it brings?

Justifications for the punitive response range from the belief that punishment is the necessary response to a societal wrong—evil deserves evil—to the assumption that it serves the purposes of reform and deterrence.

Society anticipates that if the offender is incarcerated, nice things will happen to society. First, society will be protected from dangerous criminals. There is no doubt that this is true. Vicious men abound in prison. As the old convict aphorism states, "These men are not sent here for singing too loud in church."

This goal—to deter the offender from the commission of further crimes—is only partially served by incarceration. Society receives protection, but crimes are still committed by prisoners upon their fellow inmates. One of the authors recalls an inmate who had come to prison on a five-year sentence. Before he had served his time, he murdered two other prisoners and had two life sentences added to his original term. One of the men he killed was slain in an argument over a pillow.

A second argument for the punitive reaction is that it will serve as a deterrent to further crimes, both for the individual punished and for others who may be influenced by his example. The recidivism rate varies for American prisons, but a fairly reliable figure would be a return rate of roughly 50 percent. This does not mean that we are succeeding with the other 50 percent. These may have learned only to be more clever criminals and escape apprehension; or if they were apprehended, were not convicted. Even if this remaining 50 percent are leading lawabiding lives, we cannot assume it was the punitive prison experience that caused this change. Many penologists feel that men probably go straight in spite of prison experiences, not because of them. From the standpoint of crime reduction, there are no good prisons, only varying degrees of bad ones.

Inasmuch as the normal individual tends to avoid pain, one might reason that the problem with the punitive reaction is that not enough pain has been applied to the offender. This position assumes that the more you punish a person, the more he will be deterred from repeating the act. If there is one theory that has been applied by man to his fellows with almost unbridled fury, it has been the attempt to punish him into conformity. From the Romans, who used to rake the faces of young Christian girls with a tiger's claws, to contemporary prisons, where men are confined naked in complete darkness on a reduced, monotonous diet (called "skinny rats" by the Marines) , the result has been to create frustration, resentment, psychosis—but not genuine conformity or rehabilitation.

Punishment may produce results which are the exact opposite of those intended and make of the victim a hero in the eyes of fellow convicts.

One of the authors asked a highly literate convict which book best captured the spirit of imprisonment. His answer was *Cool Hand Luke*. (Some of our colleagues in the university were somewhat piqued when informed of this choice; they felt that the book was "not very academic.") The book tells the story of the hero,

Cool Hand Luke, who endured solitary confinement and finally escaped. The fortitude he displayed during punishment elicited the hero-worship of his fellow convicts, to whom Luke became an ego-ideal. Donn Pearce (1965) describes their admiration for the graduates of their crime school:

> We argued as to how he was making a living. When he first drove by he wasn't a professional thief but a year of living with the Family had taught him the tricks of many trades. So we wondered, inventing all sorts of fantastic exploits for the greater glory of his name. We imagined that he was slyly engaged in Dipping, Boosting, Pushing, Creeping, Heisting, or Hanging Paper. Since it represented the very acme of his own ambitions, Dragline firmly believed that Luke was now a Hollywood pimp. But Kokp, for the same reasons, was convinced that he had gone to Paris and had become an International Jewel Thief. Others insisted he was a Gigolo, a Con Artist, a Gun Runner, a member of the Syndicate. Some of us, to be sure, thought that he had simply found himself a job. But this was sacrilege. That Luke should become a Square John was too much. Not Luke. Not our very own Cool Hand.

If punishment has been such a failure as a deterrent to crime, why do men have the urge to punish other men? One theory is the "Scapegoat hypothesis." The term is borrowed from the ancient Hebrew practice on the day of Atonement; the high priest placed his hands on the head of a goat and confessed over it the sins of the people. The sins (and crimes) of the people were laid on its head. It was made the sin-bearer of the community and was sent away into the wilderness laden with the collective guilt of the community. Similarly, people find vicarious relief from their own guilt feelings in the suffering of the modern scapegoat—the criminal in prison.

Cesare Beccaria, the 19th century criminologist, observed that the certainty and promptness of punishment are the most important factors in the deterrence of crime. The principle may be stated thus: The smaller the interval of time between the punishment and the crime, the stronger and more lasting will be the association of "crime and punishment" in the minds of men.

In reality, many crimes are not even reported to the police, e.g. possibly as high as 90 percent of confidence games; of each 100 offenses known to the police, only about 13 result in the perpetrators being found guilty. No normal person deliberately puts his hand on a hot stove; the certainty and promptness of "punishment" deters him. But no such certainty exists in the world of crime and punishment.

Not all persons respond alike to punishment. One of the latest findings about individuals response to pain is that all healthy individuals have approximately the same capacity for perceiving pain. There are variations from one part of the body to another, but under normal circumstances the pain perception threshold is not believed to vary significantly from one individual to another or in the same individual from one time of the day or year to another.

Unlike the pain perception threshold, the pain reaction threshold varies markedly from one individual to another and in one individual as he finds himself in different circumstances. How an individual reacts to pain and punishment is determined by what the painful situation means to him, psychologically and physically. Thus, even though two men receive the exact sentence for the same crime, e.g. two years for burglary, they probably have not been "punished" equally. The "pain" that our society has selected for offenders is typically institutionalization.

INSTITUTIONALIZATION AND ITS IMPACT

"These half million or so people in prison are not yellow dogs," writes Clemmer (1958), "they are not the public rats they have been called. They were born into this world, utterly innocent . . . What then makes them thirty years later, the double-crossing, dishonest, unfaithful, unaffectionate people they so frequently turn out to be? *Is it not true that they have learned to be that way?*" (Emphasis of present authors).

There is no finer school for crime than a state or federal penitentiary. Youthful offenders who have been incarcerated for "sticking up" a service station learn to hold up banks (that's where the money is). Illiterate "B & E" men (breaking and entering) who are taught by prison educators to read and write are similarly encouraged by fellow inmates to use their new found skills to become a "paper-hanger" (hot check artist). Association, Durkheim reminded us, is not an infertile phenomenon. Attitudes and ambitions are the result of associations. They are the products of group living. There is no more convincing test of Sutherland's theory of differential association than the recidivism rates of American prisons. Sutherland concluded that when persons become criminal, they do so because of contacts with criminal patterns and also because of isolation from anti-criminal patterns. It is with very little tongue in cheek that the present authors suggest that the American prison system should be called a "Sutherland Box"—similar to the encapsuled device for training children, developed by the psychologist Skinner. Isolated geographically and socially from normal society, an inmate spends most of his sentence in intimate association with other convicted felons. As personality is the subjective side of culture, it should not be surprising that the result of this participation in a convict culture is a personality even more dedicated to a life of crime.

In 1940, Clemmer published his classic study *The Prison Community,* in which he introduced the term "prisonization." By this term he meant the taking on, in greater or lesser degree, of folkways and the general culture of the penitentiary. By participation in the infraculture of the prison world, the inmate becomes acculturated and assimilated into the prison mores. He internalizes a set of norms based on the prisoner's codes. It is no linguistic accident that new inmates are referred to by the host inmate population as "fresh fish."

Changes in the philosophy and treatment of offenders in the United States has been painfully slow in a society generally characterized by rapid advance in other areas. Correctional reform has moved with the speed of a "cautious glacier" (to use Norval Morris' phrase). A student graduating from medical school in 1940 who had not kept current could not understand the medical books written today. But a student of penology, or a prison worker, who took a twenty year furlough from the field could return today and face many of the same problems and some of the same ineffective responses to those problems. The data for the Prison

Community were collected in the Depression Years of the 1930's, yet Clemmer wrote in the preface to the 1958 reissue that "Some 40 percent of American prisons appear little different today in basic organization, institutional program . . . than they were twenty years ago." Of 187 fortress type prisons in the United States, 61 of them were built before 1900 (Time, January 18, 1971).

Clemmer estimates that 60 percent of the penal institutions in the United States have shown some progress since the Depression days, e.g. television, group counseling, work release, etc. These improvements he attributes to increasing social concern in the general society the influx of dedicated professionals choosing careers in corrections, and scientific advances. But despite these hopeful signs, prisons in America remain monotonous, stupefying warehouses of forgotten men. Homosexuality and virtually meaningless work assignments are still the hallmark of prison life. As a symptom of the frustrations created in men by these conditions, Clemmer points to the 105 riots and serious disturbances which occurred in the American prison community during the relatively brief period 1950-1957.

The Prison Community

The prison community, as described by McCorkle and Korn (1954), is a social group made up of "custodial and professional employees, habitual petty thieves, one-time offenders, gangsters, professional racketeers, psychotics, pre-psychotics, neurotics and psychopaths living under extreme conditions of physical and psychological compression." The restrictions placed on prisoners represent more than simply acculturation or assimilation. A prolonged sentence can produce "disculturation"—an untraining of the knack of handling certain situations in outside daily life (Sommer, 1959). Yet all of these contacts are, to a remarkable degree, controlled and censored, and life within the walls of the prison acquires a unique character. Because the atmosphere of the prison is strictly authoritarian, there is a great deal of conflict between the administration and the inmates. In most prison systems, a wide gulf of fear and distrust separates the authorities and the inmates. This chasm is bridged in many ways; otherwise the system could not function at all. Many institutions have sought ways to relieve the tension generated by the separation of prison administration and convicts, through the use of experiments designed to create a greater degree of cooperation. The development of inmate self-governing bodies, inmate advisory councils, and the honor farm system can be seen as attempts on the part of prison administration to cope with the problems of separation. To these efforts must be added group therapy, discussion group methods, and guided group interaction approaches.

The inmate spends the major part of his time in close contact with his fellow convicts. From identification with fellow prisoners and with certain groups, the prisoner derives much of the additional strength required to bear the adversity and hardship of confinement. This situation places a premium upon getting along with the other inmates. To understand fully the functioning of the social system, one must understand the informal system of organization that exists among the prisoners. According to Reckless and Walter (1961), "This informal organization, together with the informal relationships which are maintained with the guards and the professional staff, mediates and controls the functioning of the formal system." In the majority of prisons, the leaders among the inmates are those who verbalize antiadministration and contraconventional values. Inmate cliques tend to form about such men, who serve as models of opposition to the administration.

Prisoner Types

Schrag (1944) originally classified prisoners into four role alternatives, which, in prison argot, are called: "square John," "right guy," "con-politician," and "outlaw." "Square Johns" perceive norms according to the official social system of the prison; "right guys" adhere to the norms of prisoner society; "con-politicians" shift in their adherence; and "outlaws" rebel against both normative systems.

Prisonization should have the greatest effect on the "right guy," fewer effects on the "politician" because of his shifting tendencies, still less effect on the "square John" (he would be prisonized just enough to take care of necessities), and next to no effect on the "outlaw" (since he is an isolate).

In a latter study (1961) Schrag selected a more neutral terminology and labeled these as *prosocial, anti-social, pseudosocial* and *asocial.* Prosocial inmates are most often convicted of violent crimes against person or naive property offenses. Their offenses are situational, and few have earlier arrests. Prosocial inmates retain strong ties with their families and friends, show strong guilt for their crimes, and expect to begin again with a clean slate.

Antisocial inmates are highly recidivistic, committing unsophisticated crimes such as robbery, assault, and burglary. They rebel against conventional norms in their careers, continue rebellion in prison, and accept slogans such as "all politicians are crooks" to ease their own guilt. They do, however, remain close to their families.

Pseudosocial inmates are accused of mostly subtle, sophistocated, profit-motivated offenses: fraud, embezzlement, forgery; they are often middle class and have learned to play different roles at an early age. Educationally and occupationally superior to antisocial offenders, they are ingratiating, pragmatic, shifting in their allegiances, and often become mediators in staff-inmate conflicts.

Asocial inmates vary in offenses against persons and property, often using bizarre methods without clear motive. Recidivism is high; early evidence of severe behavior disorders are seen (they are frequently reared in institutions and shifted around to various foster homes). They are related to social abilities and skills in the use of social symbols, and are highly egocentric.

In general, prosocial offenders, though geared to legitimate standards, are not able to cope with intense social pressures or personal problems; antisocial offenders grow up in an environment oriented toward illegitimate social norms; pseusosocial offenders grew up under patterns of inconsistent discipline; and asocial offenders grew up rejected.

Whereas prosocial offenders tend to evaluate problems with reference to legitimate norms (and have access to them), antisocial offenders have access to and employ deviant norms as standards of reference. Pseudosocial offenders shift their frames of reference to facilitate personal achievements, rather than collective goals; asocial offenders are detached from social conventions and moral commitments, do not know their role requirements, are incapable of sharing affection with prisoners or officials, and are impulsive in their behavior.

At the time of admission to the prison, antisocial offenders know the lingo the best. Pseudosocial offenders learn faster and sometimes gain a higher degree of proficiency than the antisocial offender. Asocial inmates have a less adequate vocabulary, even less than the prosocial offenders.

Inmates seek friends among those with like beliefs and values. Prosocial offenders however, tend to prefer pseudosocial friends. Interestingly enough, the asocial prisoners are most often identified as leaders, because they believe that they won't make deals with anybody. Actually most prisoners do not admit to identifying with any one of the types.

The prosocial inmate sees the correctional institution and the broader community as supportive agencies, while the antisocial criminal sees these as restrictive and antagonistic. The prosocial inmates are the cultural conservators, preferring stability and even oppression over social experimentation. Pseudosocial inmates, on the other hand, are the great innovators. The antisocial prisoners represent the rebels with a cause, which is to subvert the established authority. The asocial inmates are the nihilists, often appointed leaders in riots and escapes (Cressey, 1961).

The Initial Phase

What is a neophyte inmate's first impressions and experiences when he arrives at the prison? He most likely enters an Auburn-style structure, consisting of a high stone wall and a large square building—five stories high, narrow windows, an inner building which contains the cell-block four stories high. In it are identical cells about the size of a large grave, which contain no windows; the cell is not made to receive the sun (Tannenbaum, 1922). A more current description of prisons in England (Wolff, 1967) sounds like this: "The security of closed institutions is based on a combination of wall, lock and key, bars and counting of heads." All prisons built before 1955 are surrounded by a wall, and almost all prisons have an outer wall—twenty to thirty feet in height along the perimeter of the grounds. It does not sound like a great improvement. Tannenbaum (1920) mentioned a new "improved" structure, the Panopticon (suggested by Jeremy Bentham in 1792), which allows the guard to watch the entire population of 500 cells. In other words, privacy for the men would be an impossibility. Tannenbaum (1922), in fact, suggested that the prison structure be done away with and replaced by a farm, school or factory, hospital, playground—any structure but a prison.

So, the convicted man enters the structure. Procedures then call for a thorough shakedown, handling of his cash or property, fingerprinting, photographing, bathing, searching, medical examination, issuance of jail clothing (for the sake of controlling vermin and preventing the entrance of contraband), and explanation of regulations (Alexander, 1957). In British prisons, the first night is spent in the Reception Hall rather than in a cell (Wolff, 1967).

As the inmate is separated from the outside world he undergoes role dispossession, a clean break with the past in a short span of time; he receives a uniform on the first day and may not speak of his family background or wealth. He may not receive money from home, will money, write checks, contest divorce, or vote (temporarily or permanently). In short, he experiences a "civil death" (Cressey, 1961).

In addition to the minimum amount of procedures, he may be asked to tell his life history, have a haircut, and be given a number. His first moments of socialization involve an obedience test and even a will-breaking contest. His property and former importance is lost; so is his name, in some cases. What he receives in place, belongs to the institution. He faces personal defacement; he may be deprived of his general appearance, and the tools and services by which he maintains it, i.e. combs, cosmetics, and clothes are taken from him. Permanent disfigurement may occur through brands, beatings, or shock therapy. Even threats of disfigurement are enough to cause incipient anxiety. He may be subjected to verbal or gestural profanity, i.e. called obscene names, cursed, or pointed out. He may have to beg for little things like a cigarette or the use of a telephone, and he will begin the deference routine of "sir-ing", shuffling, and looking down in the presence of an officer.

The new prisoner is made to adhere to a type of life alien to him. Lack of heterosexual activity may produce fear of becoming unmasculine. He is exposed to contamination—common use of bathrooms, clothes, towels, blankets, even underwear. The food may be unclean, and he may be forced to eat. Privacy is minimal or non-existent (even during visits). All this takes place within the realm of the "mortification process" (Cressey, 1961).

The prisoner then goes through a process of social exclusion and status reduction. His uniform is a symbol of his slave status. He has no choice of housing, neighbors, or food. He is limited in visits with family and friends and is subjected to an authoritarian structure which is filled with fear and suspicion. He is afraid of official power on one side and of the inmate "kangaroo court" on the other side. He is resentful and hostile to the society that got him into this mess (Vedder and Kay, 1964).

Prison Culture

The inmate quickly transfers his loyalty from the larger society to the prisoner community where he knows he will be accepted. He is willing to pay for this acceptance by devotion to the inmate community. A great deal of rationalization is involved with this transfer of loyalties (Vedder and Kay, 1964). Out of the feeling of personal failure of which he is constantly reminded, the prisoner will develop a story, a sad tale, a line which he and other prisoners will constantly expound to each other.

Although the prison authorities have formal control over most of the inmate's overt behavior, their control is limited in comparison with that of the prisoner's themselves. In a system of friendships, mutual obligations, loyalties, and intimidations, the inmate learns that conformity to prisoner expectations is just as important to his welfare as conformity to the formal controls exercised by prison officials. Inmates must be orthodox in word and action.

Orthodoxy is more important in prison life than in conventional circumstances because in normal life the individual has a freedom of mobility which is denied him within the prison. Orthodoxy in prisoner conduct is promoted by a system of rewards and punishments, the latter emphasizing gossip, laughter, and ridicule, but not excluding corporal punishment and even, on occassion, execution.

The prison may be viewed as a social system that is closed and self-contained. However, the prison community is constantly in touch with developments and changes taking place in the outside world and receives fresh ideas of what is going on through reports from the continuous stream of newly admitted prisoners. Prisoners also keep in touch with the outside world through newspapers, magazines, and visits from friends and relatives.

The Prisoner's Code

The existence of informal categories like those mentioned above within the prison community indicates that inmate solidarity is never complete or certain. The cliques of "right guys" are continually under pressure to extend their control over other inmates to improve their position of relative power within the prison community. The control system by which they seek to enforce their influence is mostly informal. Pressures are exerted against those who are not in the "right" group by means of gossip, laughter, ridicule, and isolation. This informal control may readily be seen in the persistence of the fundamental principles of the prisoner organization called "the code" (Sutherland and Cressey, 1970).

The basic tenet of the code is that prisoners must be loyal to other prisoners in all prisoner-official contacts; prisoners are not permitted to have cordial or friendly relations with officialdom in any capacity. This code is a set of values for the prisoner which is defined, sanctioned, and controlled by the informal groups in the prisoner community. It represents a codification of criminal values in opposition to the values of conventional society, particularly as these are seen as embodied by prison officaldom. It seeks to confer status and prestige upon those who stand in opposition to the administration. The code places high premiums on physical violence and strength, on the exploitation of sexual relations, and upon predatory attitudes toward money and property (Ohlin, 1965). There is also a strong emphasis upon in-group loyalty and solidarity. This code, in short, reflects an adaptation of the criminal value system to the conditions and circumstances of prison life.

The newly admitted prisoner absorbs criminal values, beliefs, and attitudes along with the terminology or "lingo" which will enable him to communicate successfully with his fellow inmates. (We shall devote more detailed attention to prison language or argot a bit latter in this chapter.) The code is learned by word of mouth, and to a certain degree, inmates are guided by the code in their relationships both within the prison and in the free community following release. The code is, naturally, not immune from violation. Men who violate the code by becoming finks, however, do so secretly, not only because secrecy is essential to their activities, but also because they know they risk reprisals from their fellow convicts if discovered (Tappan, 1960). If the code is not actively promoted in all prisons, it is at least confirmed and respected by the vast majority of prisoners. This code can be seen as aiding the newly admitted prisoner in adjusting to the prison world. The new inmate faces many personal conflicts, and the prisoner's code helps to make his adjustment within the prison community somewhat easier.

The following list from Galtung (1956) is given in the form of commands and is a fairly comprehensive compilation of elements basic to the prisoners code:

P1: You shall not ask another person why he is here.

P2: You shall never openly say that you are guilty.

P3: You shall never moralize.

P4: You shall never claim that you are morally superior to other prisoners.

P5: You shall never openly say that the sentence was correct.

P6: You may say that your status as a criminal is undesirable, but not that the prison is a means to resocialization.

P7: You shall say that the prison has no effect on you or harmful effects only.

P8: You shall express as your opinion that the guards and partly the officials are inferior beings.

P9: You shall be on the prisoner side in all conflicts.

P10: You shall exploit the prison to your own advantage.

P11. You shall not be an informer.

P12: You shall never contradict another prisoner in his interpretation of his own situation if he likes his own interpretation.

P13: You shall tolerate deviance from usual social norms but never deviance from these norms. (Refers to deviation from sex norms.)

P14: You shall talk about the outside world in such a way as not to increase the frustration for other prisoners.

P15: You shall not be different from other prisoners.

The prisoner's code is generally accepted as the basis for the norms of the subculture, but the reasons for this are a matter for dispute.

The Task Force Report: Organized Crime gives the Mafia and the Old World criminal code as the prototype for the prisoner's code. The American version of this code for criminals is briefly as follows:

1. Be loyal to members of the organization. Do not be an informer.
2. Be rational. Be a member of the team. Don't engage in battle if you can't win.
3. Be a man of honor. Respect womanhood and your elders.
4. Be a stand-up guy. Keep your eyes and ears open and your mouth shut. Don't sell out.
5. Have class. Be independent. Know your way around the world.

The fact that the Task Force reporters selected this idea from Irwin and Cressey (1962) over others suggests that official opinion believes that the Mafia is the source of the prisoner's code. However, Irwin and Cressey argue that "the orgin of these values is situational: the value system arises out of the condition of imprisonment." The Task Force was evidently selective: They quote from Sutherland and Cressey (1966) for the list of five code norms; they then quote from Irwin and Cressey (1962) to reinforce the concept of an inmate code evolved as part of a larger criminal code. The substance of this view can, in fact, be found in Sutherland and Cressey (1966) : "The code, like other behavior patterns among inmates, arises in part out of the conditions of deprivation in the prison. However, it also consists in part of a more general *criminal* code, brought into prison and utilized there by career criminals and other sophisticated criminals."

Wellford (1967) believes that the prisoner's code is the natural result of administrative norms. The officials in any given correctional institution generally expect the inmates to supply information concerning escapes, smuggling, and deviant behavior; to support the treatment program (presumably on the basis of enlightened self-interest and the motivation to better himself) ; to be diligent in all work assignments; and to be careful in his choice of friends. The prisoner's code calls for the precise opposite of these official goals and desires. A prisoner's code, according to this line of thought, would arise spontaneously to aid the prisoner in doing "easy time," to achieve the means for sexual gratification, and to facilitate the process of apparent rehabilitation in order to favorably impress the staff.

Rubenfeld and Stafford (1963) give an example of an inmate system they feel evolved by default. In the juvenile correctional facility which they selected for study, no program existed in the cottages. The inmate social system of norms originated, therefore, as a vehicle for the transmission of illegitimate norms.

Ohlin and Lawrence (1959) view the development of criminal norms as a means of protection against guilt feelings. The legal process labels the individual as deviant and socially inferior. When he arrives at the correctional facility, the labels are confirmed by the treatment he receives. Under these circumstances, a good defense is to reject the official norms and standards. The norms that replace those which are rejected offer an opportunity for status that is denied in other areas. This conception very much resembles the Cloward and Ohlin model of Differential Opportunities: neutralization of norms and rejection of the rejectors.

Berk (1966) sees the development of inmate subcultures as based on three factors: (1) inmates are cut off from the rest of society and isolated within a society of their own; (2) "institutionalization generates common problems of adjustment which require cooperation for their solution while simultaneously providing a situation with opportunities for effective interaction with others similarly situated"; and (3) the formal organization in which all inmates are members is incomplete and needs the informal structure to fill in the gaps.

There seems to be general agreement in the professional literature that, at least in part, the subculture comes into existence to meet some of the unexpected and unforeseen events and factors involved in being incarcerated. Even though the federal government may wish to place official blame for prisonization on the Mafia, there is really very little solid basis for this contention except the obvious similarities between the prisoner's code and the criminal code.

Prison Argot and Its Function

The prison culture is supported by a distinctive argot which is continually reinforced with new terms and meanings by recently admitted convicts. This language is distinctive and important; it represents a means for shaping and supporting the basic criminal value orientations. This argot is saturated with words whose meanings express attitutes, beliefs, opinions, and orientations which run counter to those of prison officialdom.

Argot develops as a special language for a special group which is organized within the framework of a larger society (Lewis, 1943). Argot may mean different things to various criminal groups outside prison, but its importance for the prison setting lies in the fact that it provides a map of the inmates' social and behavioral systems.

Some writers have claimed that argot functions in the prison situation to maintain secrecy—a device for keeping the law abiding members of society and custodians in ignorance. This claim seems to be of rather dubious validity; the guards in the typical penitentiary usually know the meanings of argot terms at least as well as the prisoners and sometimes even better.

Other writers, noting the identifying function of criminal argot, state that, far from being a means of maintaining secrecy, argot has its greatest importance as a distinguishing symbol. A "solid con" or "real man" is not a mere slang term; it is a title of respect that implies allegiance to the inmate culture. Conversely, a "rat" is viewed as a betrayer of his peers to the custodians. Yet, in argument against this interpretation, it is necessary to note that the prison officials use argot as much as, if not more than, the convicts themselves.

The most critical function of argot appears to be its utility in ordering and classifying experience within the prison walls in terms which deal specifically with the problems imposed by prison life (Strong, 1943). Students of language and psycholinguistics will recognize that this conception of argot is essentially a statement of the principle of *linguistic relativity,* according to which language is viewed as more than the mere passive vehicle for the expression of culture; it is seen as an active influence in shaping an individual's perceptions of the world in which he lives (Brown, 1958). In terms of the prison argot, activities of group members are analyzed, classified, and labeled. These labels supply an evaluation and an interpretation of experience in the culture by means of a set of convenient names or verbal designations, i.e. argot. New words are coined, and old words are applied in a new way. In brief, different experiences require a different language code, and the result, in prison, is argot (Sykes, 1958).

In an article concerning social roles in prison, Garabedian (1963) notes that these roles are recognized by staff and inmates alike and are frequently identified in terms of prison argot. These roles seem to be allocated on the basis of formal observation on the part of prisoners of the behavior and verbalizations of an individual to a variety of real and contrived situations. The role that is defined in this fashion tends to become a major component of the personality structure of the inmate.

The Influence of Argot

As we noted above, social roles within the prison community are identified in terms of argot, which orders and classified prisoner experiences within these role specifications. We might raise some questions concerning the extent to which the argot system influences other aspects of the system. For example, what are the consequences for the individual of being labeled a "fag" by his peers? How strongly does argot cement him into his social role?

In the autobiography *My Shadow Ran Fast* by Bill Sands, the author's account of his experiences as a convict in San Quentin emphasizes the importance of argot to prisoners in their values and responses to their imprisonment. He maintains that argot and the labeling of experiences were prime considerations to the man in prison. No one wanted to look bad in the eyes of his fellow prisoners, yet the system of checks and balances within the prison prevented everyone from being a "real con."

In *Society of Captives,* Sykes (1958) expresses the belief that an understanding of argot roles is the key to understanding the social structure of the prison. He insists that these patterns of behavior, defined by argot, are social roles and not personality traits.

Argot roles, therefore, appear to play a significant part in the social structure of the prison. Argot maintains the equilibrium of the prison, groups the men into different behavioral categories, and gives them a common ground to face their custodians.

Clemmer (1968) lists 1200 words and phrases commonly used by inmates to evaluate the actions and experiences of other prisoners. Of these, more than 600 refer to roles and types of inmates in the prison system. For purposes of illustration, we shall examine four categories of argot role: those which relate to sexual behavior, food seeking, toughness, and betrayal or treason (Garabedian, 1963).

TRAITORS. Perhaps the lowest rung on the ladder in the prison social system is occupied by the "rat." To be labeled thus represents the most serious accusation that the prison community can make against an inmate, for it charges a betrayal of confidence which is directed against the very structure of prison society. The rat is concerned only with selfish ends and lacks consideration for the consequences of his actions.

Another example of a traitor to the prison system is the "center man." This is a person who shares the viewpoint of his captors and is even more hated than the rat, for he had not only betrayed his peers, he had joined forces with the hated custodians.

FOOD SEEKING. Under this category, two types of argot roles can be distinguished. One is the "gorilla," who takes what he wants from other inmates by force (Sykes, 1958). He uses violence when necessary, but the mere threat of brute force is usually sufficient to secure compliance. He is scorned by fellow inmates because the food he coerces other men into giving up is food that ought to be shared.

The "merchant," however, is even more contemptible. He exploits the needs of others and demands a price for food stolen from the prison. He treats his fellow prisoners as objects rather than people, and he rejects the solidarity of prison company. In turn, he is scorned and hated by the prison community. Like the rat, he is a threat to the order of the prison and is therefore assigned an appropriate argot role (Fisher, 1965).

SEXUAL BEHAVIOR. The unnatural strain of confinement applies additional pressure with regard to sexual behavior. Deprived of heterosexual relationships, the social structure of the prison adjusts to fulfill the sexual and emotional needs of the inmates. The prison system distinguishes, in its employment of argot roles, between the true homosexual and the normal individual driven to homosexuality as a consequence of sexual and emotional deprivation. The roles are first divided according to whether the individual is aggressive ("wolf," "hog") or passive ("queen," "gal boy"); in addition, the true homosexual ("fag") is distinguished from the individual ("punk") whose homosexuality is situational, transient, and role-related.

TOUGHNESS. The last general category involves some characteristic modes of inmates response to their environment: the social structure of the prison employs various labels to distinguish the "solid con" from the dangerous convict.

"Tough" is a term used to characterize an inmate who is always spoiling for a fight in a community where violence runs like a bright thread through the fabric of interaction (Sykes, 1958). He is viewed as dangerous because he is ready to fight at the least provocation. He upsets the social balance of the prison community and his argot role is assigned out of fear rather than scorn.

The "real con" or "real man" hold the position of highest prestige in the prison. He is a man who "pulls his own time" (Sykes, 1958). He is an example to the other prisoners because he endures with fortitude which cannot be avoided. His argot role is won by inner strength and stamina. His actions defy his captors to strip him of his ability to control at least some aspects of his life. He "keeps his cool," retains his autonomy; he is a hero to his fellow convicts.

The Process of Prisonization

There is a good deal of dispute in professional circles concerning the method or methods by which an individual is assimilated into the intraculture, the norms of which are embodied in the prisoner's code. Disagreement centers around the basic issue of whether or not inmates are coerced into noncompliance with official rules by pressures originating within the prison subculture, or whether the official rules are defined by the inmate subculture as illegitimate and therefore not binding.

Jones (1964) found that the coercion was not evident as a factor in conformity to deviant norms in the two juvenile correctional institutions he studied. He speculated that, instead of endorsing coercion, the inmate system merely defined staff directives as illegitimate.

Clemmer (1950), in his classic study, indicates that association with criminals, coupled with isolation from the outside world, causes about 60 percent of inmates to become prisonized: "The manner and way in which the prison culture is absorbed by some of its people can be thought of as a process of prisonization." Association, from the outside and on the inside, affects prisonization.

Clemmer lists five factors that are claimed to influence prisonization:

> (1) . . . his susceptibility to a culture . . . depends . . . primarily on the type of relationships he had before imprisonment . . . (2) . . . the kinds and extent of relationships which an inmate has outside . . . (3) . . . whether or not a man becomes affiliated in prison primary and secondary groups . . . (4) . . . chance, a chance placement in work

gang, cellhouse, and with cellmate . . . (5) whether or not a man accepts the dogmas or codes of the prison culture.

The following seven points are offered by Clemmer as factors which are related to a low degree of prisonalization:

Influencing Factors in Prisonization

1. A short sentence, thus a brief subjection to the universal factors of prisonization.
2. A fairly stable personality made stable by an adequacy of positive and "socialized" relationships during pre-penal life.
3. The continuance of positive relationships with persons outside the walls.
4. Refusal or inability to integrate into a prison primary group or semi-primary group, while yet maintaining a symbiotic balance in relations with other men.
5. Refusal to accept blindly the dogmas and codes of the population, and a willingness, under situation situations, to aid officials, thus making for identification with the free community.
6. A chance placement with a cellmate and workmates who do not possess leadership qualities and who are also not completely integrated into the prison culture.
7. Refraining from abnormal sex behavior, from excessive gambling, and a ready willingness to engage seriously in work and recreative activities.

Clemmer counters this series with a list of seven items which effect a *high* degree of prisonization:

1. A sentence of many years, thus a long subjection to the universal factors of prisonization.
2. A somewhat unstable personality made unstable by an inadequacy of "socialized" relations before commitment, but possessing, nonetheless, a capacity for strong convictions and a particular kind of loyalty.
3. A dearth of positive relations with persons outside the walls.
4. A readiness and a capacity for integration into a prison primary group.

5. A blind, or almost blind, acceptance of the dogmas and mores of the primary group and the general population.
6. A chance placement with other persons of a similar orientation.
7. A readiness to participate in gambling and abnormal sex behavior.

The individual, by association, comes to share the memories, traditions, and eventually the sentiments of the prison community. This process begins as soon as the prisoner arrives. Whatever status he may have held in the outside world is suddenly gone. He receives a number to replace his name, he obtains regulation clothing, and he goes through the cold, impersonal administrative process—which give him something in common with all of the other prisoners. Thus the prison has taken the initial step in confirming the individual's acceptance of the unofficial system he finds on the "inside."

After a while, the newly admitted inmate falls into the same patterns as those which characterize the other prisoners. He learns from others new ways to dress, eat, work, and use leisure time. His outward changes in behavior reflect a process of attitude change, and he begins to think and verbalize about the guards and administration in terms supplied by the argot. Clemmer is careful to note that not all inmates undergo a thorough change of attitude, but all do experience some changes based on the universal experiences of sexual deprivation, regimentation, and general exposure to the conflict between official and unofficial norms. In brief, "American prisons contribute in some degree to the criminality of those they hold" (Clemmer, 1950).

Some writers feel that assimilation into the inmate subculture is coerced, and they see the official and unofficial systems as highly competitive. Caldwell states that ". . . a state of covert conflict, 'psychological warfare,' or open hostilities may develop between . . . the two systems. If the conflict becomes too severe, the informal group may go 'underground.' "

The new inmate must choose between one of the two systems. Most often the choice is made in favor of the inmate subculture. To have any status and to make the best out of the situation in which he finds himself, the new inmate, at least in the traditional custodial setting, is practically forced to accept the norms of the inmate subculture. Lerman (1968) suggests that the swiftness and degree with which it is accepted will depend to some extent on the type of involvement experienced on the "outside".

Tittle and Tittle (1964) suggest that outward behavior does not necessarily reflect the degree of socialization into the inmate subculture: for some, adherence to the prison code is merely a device for approval, and had little effect on participation in the rehabilitation program. There authors see the inmate subculture, in part, as a means to overcome the deprivations experienced in prisons.

Ohlin and Lawrence (1959) in their application of the concept of prisonization to juvenile correctional facilitates, see prisonization as one of three choices presented to the incarcerated juvenile. These three choices present themselves as adaptation to the conflicting demands of the officials and inmate systems:

(1) complete rejection of the official system of values;
(2) direct opposition to the inmate system of values;
(3) an attempt to meet the minimum expectations of both groups.

The authors believe that choice one is most frequently utilized. "This adaptation . . . renders the inmate, under existing forms of clinical organization, virtually inaccessible to effective treatment experience." The first choice is also the easiest to make because the inmate then does not have to fear rejection by his peers or any other of the punitive sanctions that would follow the other choices. Completely rejecting the inmate system and having to live in the middle of it would be very difficult. Probably for this reason few make the choice in favor of the first alternative. The third choice, being the most subtle is the most difficult to identify. By seeming to be acceptable to both groups, the inmate is able to function without any great conflicts with either system but can have little status among inmates.

Ohlin and Lawrence offer a suggestion at the end of their presentation which is being increasingly followed, "It would seem profitable to restructure the institutional situation so treatment interaction is focused directly on the group."

Foreman (1953) contends that an inmate's socialization into the inmate subculture depends on how other prisoners perceive him. This system assumes that all inmates are prisonized to some degree and, in the process, are placed somewhere in the hierarchy. The process of being evaluated occurs primarily in work groups and secondarily in associations outside the work group. The inmate sizes up and is sized up; a group consensus is eventually reached. When this consensus is reached, the new inmate is placed in one of four categories:

1. Rejection appears to be invited wherever another's evidenced acts or perceived attitudes sharply violate an observer's own personal tenets on any one of these systems of value, this reaction perhaps being subject to compensation by assessments in terms of correlate values. Further, it appears to be invited, even when a person is not well known, if he commonly associates with individuals whom the observer rejects.

2. A more or less neutral aloofness appears to be invited wherever another's acts or attitudes are insufficiently known either through observation or gossip, for judgment.

3. Acceptance appears to be invited wherever another's attitudes or acts conform to an observer's principal tenets, or when he is not well known, if he commonly associates with individuals who so conform.

4. Once ingroup bounds are established, interpersonal allegiance seems to depend upon mutual perceptions of being 'right'—i.e., upon harmony in perceived dominant personal or social values.

Prisonization and the Time Factor

Clemmer made the first comparison of prisonization versus time incarcerated. He stated that an individual who was in prison for a comparatively short time, a year or so, would be able to leave prison and adjust to life in an open community with relatively little trouble. This is possible because the short term inmate has not fully been prisonized. The inmate who has spent many years in prison will find it next to impossible to adjust on the "outside," he has thoroughly internalized the inmate subculture. In other words, the longer one is exposed to the prison subculture, the greater the degree of prisonization, carried to a point when resocialization into legal norm system is not possible.

Wheeler (1960) reports that Clemmer was mistaken about the prisonization-time relationship. Wheeler divided the inmates into three groups according to their phase of life in prison: phase one were those who had spent less than six months; phase two were those that had spent more than six months in prison and had more than six months left to serve; phase three included those that had six months or less to serve. Wheeler used a study designed to measure the degree of conformity to the inmate code during each of the three phases. The drop on prisonization at the end of a prisoner sentence is seen as being based on the inmate's increased interest in the "outside," his increased contact with the "outside" including prospective employers, relatives, and friends. (The study was not longitudinal and has been criticized on that basis.) Wheeler's U curve contrasts sharply to Clemmer's continual rise in prisonization.

Atchley and McCabe (1968), in an attempt to bring some sort of unity on the prisonization—time problem, sought the opposite conclusion. After conclusion of the study, they could confirm none of either Clemmer's or Wheeler's postulations. The high regard that Atchley and McCabe hold for their study can be seen in the following: " . . . results of our research leave existing theories concerning the social psycho-dynamics of prison life in shambles."

Content of the Subculture

There is general agreement in the field that the major function of the subculture is to serve as an agent for problem solving. The contents of the subculture can be explained on this basis.

Wheeler sees the subculture as offering solutions to the problems of adjustments to prison life, sexual deprivation, the frustration of confinement, and the general pall of prison life. The official system offers no solution to those problems, thereby offering the inmate subculture a strong point on which to demand inmate loyalty.

McCorkle and Korn (1954) offer a very interesting point of view. They consider the central problem, which the subculture was designed to meet, to be one of social rejection. The inmate subculture gives an individual an opportunity to reject his rejectors, rather than himself. The concept that seems to influence all other aspects of prison life is that there is no escape from the influence of the inmate subculture. "The offender is not only incarcerated in a physical prison without exit; he is enmeshed in a human environment and a pattern of usages from which the only escape is psychological withdrawal."

McCorkle and Korn see a rigid hierarchy as another characteristic of the subculture. There is a tremendous amount of group pressure which helps sustain the subcultural norms and limit vertical movement in status. The inmate has little choice in his status position. From the time he arrives at the prison or correctional facility he undergoes a series of experiences which define his position in the inmate subculture. The experience will involve other inmates to the extent to which they perceive the new inmate as a threat to their status. An extremely tough and powerful new inmate will pose no threat to the weaker inmates who will readily acquiesce, recognizing that his challenge will be to the leadership clique. The new man will be a threat to the recognized "tough guys." The leader of the clique into whose sphere of influence the new inmate will move is expected by all the inmates, no matter their status, to challenge the new arrival. The outcome of the challenge, or lack of challenge serves to redefine the leader's position and give the new inmate a place in the status hierarchy.

Another characteristic of inmate subculture is extreme authoritarianism. McCorkle and Korn suggest that " . . . the victims of power tend to regard its possession as the highest personal value."

The last characteristic offered by McCorkle and Korn to be discussed here is the use of coercive power to enforce inmate norms. They suggest that a good measure of the degree of internalization of the subcultural norms is the degree to which coercion is used to enforce norms. The higher the degree of internalization the less interpersonal coercion. It is interesting to note that the subculture that provides means by which to disobey official directives also provides means to disobey its own directives. The most highly emphasized restriction is against informing, yet it is practiced. This contradictory factor in the inmate subculture renders it especially weak when compared to the official system. This weakness, however, is never exploited.

POSSIBILITIES FOR TREATMENT AND CHANGE

Before treatment can become a reality the power of the inmate subculture must be lessened considerably. Elias (1968) explains: ". . . before innovations can have a serious impact on the training school, whether it is based on a model of custody, treatment, or human care, or a combination of these models, it will be necessary to find ways to crack the allegedly impregnable inmate system.

When Ohlin and Lawrence applied the concept of prisonization to juveniles they offered what they felt to be the preconditions necessary for any program that aimed at the change of values. First, the individual must publicly declare to peers that he will benefit from the changes he intends to make. Secondly, he must be allowed the freedom, both of action and deed, to go about realistically achieving his goals. Third, the program must be so structured that his positive changes are rewarded and that he receives support from peers, adults, and cultural norms.

The Provo experiment conducted by Empey and Rabow (1961) incorporated the general ideas of Ohlin and Lawrence. The Provo study may not be altogether relevant because the boys were not incarcerated. However, since the basic experiment was continued by Empey at Silver Lake, it is significant that the content of the program was designed to alter and use the subculture in a treatment oriented manner.

The new approach was followed because the traditional approach had proven unsuccessful. Under the traditional program the official and unofficial systems were incompatible, and constant conflict was the result. Empey and Rabow point out that the actual functioning and workings of the inmate system is rather nebulous and uncertain. The old system stressed behavior that could be observed—manners, cooperation, conforming to rules—and ignored the decision making process outside the institution which would be the real test of treatment. This allowed the delinquents to "do time" with a minimum of change if they outwardly conformed with the program. The purpose of the Provo experiment was to put the delinquents in a situation where their true behavior patterns would be assimilated into a positive subculture in a manner resembling the process of prisonization without the implied degradation and coercion.

The program differs from what boys expect on the basis of past institutional experiences or stories. The boys receive no orientation, are given only a few rules, are not told to refrain from obscene language, and are able to obtain no answers to stock questions. As the authors point out, all newly incarcerated boys have questions about release requirements and length of stay. Since the boys are able to obtain no answers from staff, they are forced to turn to the peer group.

The lack of rules gives versatility to the program, and situations can be dealt with as they arise on the basis of what is best for those involved. Guided Group Interaction (G.G.I.) is the heart of the change program. G.G.I. has three primary goals:

(1) . . . to question the utility of a life devoted to delinquency; (2) to suggest alternative ways for behavior; and (3) to provide recognition for a boy's personal reformation and his willingness to reform others. In G.G.I. the group has tremendous power to the extent of deciding when various members are ready for release.

G.G.I. has built around it a norm system which stresses work, becoming involved in the group process, discussing one's past delinquency with peers, the future of delinquency (prison), and caring what happens to other boys. Work is stressed because it is difficult for sophisticated delinquents to deceive peers in this area. According to Empey and Rabow, sophisticated delinquents can "con" their way through most situations and might be able to convince others that they are ready for release. A good work program prevents this; it is difficult for sophistocated delinquents, who have internalized the concept that only suckers work ("skim it off the top"), to work consistently.

Peer involvement in the G.G.I. is supported by the norm system, and there are numerous sanctions for one against those who resist, including weekends in jail if the group decides it is necessary. The result of this program is that the delinquents has to consciously make a choice between two alternatives:

(1) They can continue to be delinquent and expect, in most cases, to end up in prison; or (2) they can learn to live a rather marginal life in which they will be able to operate sufficiently within the law to avoid being locked up.

It is interesting to note that the Provo experiment came under attack by W.H. Gordon (1962) because of similarities between the experiment and Communist technique used in Korea. "In many ways . . . the techniques used at Pinehills are reminiscent of those employed by the Communists in Korea on selected groups of American prisoners of war." Under consideration was a comparison between delinquents discussing their past and the Communist interest in public conferences and demands for candor. The reluctance of staff to supply answers was compared with " . . . the infinite patience and inscrutability of authority." Gordon contended that not enough was known about what might result from such programs. He did not state that the Provo experiment was unethical, he asked if it were ethical and hinted at a negative answer.

In their reply, Empey and Rabow (1962) point out that numerous parallels exist between Communist and non-Communist nations in the fields of medicine, politics, and science. These do not, however, signify any relationship or parallel between ideological systems. They admit that there are some similarities but call for Gordon (and others that would criticize on the same basis) to examine the alternatives to the type program Provo exemplified.

At Silver Lake, Empey, Newland, and Lubeck (1965) constructed a program for incarcerated youth very similar to the Provo program. Cartwright (1951) offers eight principles necessary for programs desiring to alter behavior and value systems:

Principle No. 1. If the group is to be used effectively as a medium of change, those people who are to be changed and those who are to exert influence for change must have a strong sense of belonging to the same group.

Principle No. 2. The more attractive the group is to its members, the greater is the influence that the group can exert on its members.

Principle No. 3. In attempts to change attitudes, values, or behavior, the more relevant they are to the basis of attraction to the group, the greater will be the influence that the group can exert upon them.

Principle No. 4. The greater the prestige of a group member in the eyes of the other members, the greater the influence he can exert.

Principle No. 5. Efforts to change individuals or subparts or the group which, if successfully, would have the result of making them deviate from the norms if the group will encounter strong resistance.

Principle No. 6. Strong pressure for change in the group can be established by creating a shared perception by members of the need for change, thus making the source of pressure for change be within the group.

Principle No. 7. Information relating to the need for change, plans for change, and consequences of change must be shared by all relevant people in the group.

Principle No. 8. Changes in one part of a group produce strain in other related parts which can be reduced only by eliminating the change or by bringing about readjustments in the related parts.

Cressey (1955) used Cartwright's eight principles combined with some of the concepts of differential association to produce an applicable form of differential association. The result is a set of six guides for the practical application of differential association to correction.

1. If criminals are to be changed, they must be assimilated into groups which emphasize values conducive to law-abiding behavior and concurrently, alienated from groups emphasizing values conducive to criminality. Since our experience has been that the majority of criminals experience great difficulty in securing inmate contacts in ordinary groups, special groups whose major common goal is the reformation of criminals must be created. . .

2. The more relevant the common purpose of the group to the reformation of criminals, the greater will be its influence on the criminal member's attitudes and values.

3. The more cohesive the group, the greater the members' readiness to influence others and the more relevant the problem of conformity to group norm. The criminals who are to be reformed and the powers expected to effect the change must, then, have a strong sense of belonging to one group: between them there must be a genuine "we" feeling.
4. Both reformer and those to be reformed must achieve status within the group by exhibition of 'proneform' or anticriminal values and behavior patterns.
5. The most effective mechanism for exerting group pressure on members will be found in groups so organized that criminals are induced to join noncriminals for the purpose of changing other criminals.
6. When an entire group is the target of change, as in a prison of among delinquent gangs, strong pressure for change can be achieved by convincing the members of the need for a change, thus making the group itself the source of pressure for change.

Both Street (1965) and Berk (1966) conclude from their studies that custodial type institutions tend to produce inmate subcultures at odds to treatment programs. They found that treatment oriented institutions tend to produce positively oriented subcultures following fairly close to the aims of treatment and reflecting conventional norms.

Summary

In the professional literature on institutionalization and its impact, among those areas that lack consensus is the relationship of time to prisonization. A longitudinal study has not yet been reported on this problem; such a study would probably give more accurate results than preceding studies. The origin of prisonization is another topic of debate. Whether it evolved naturally or was an offspring of the Mafia does not seem to affect its control. What is more significant for consideration is why the subculture exists and exactly how it maintains itself.

There is general agreement on several points. No one disputes the existence of inmate subcultures or prisonization. There is general agreement that the subcultures are powerful and can effectively block attempts at treatment. There also seems to be a trend toward Guided Group Interaction (G.G.I.) as the method of treatment which is effective in changing individuals and the structure of the subculture itself. This is vitally necessary for it seems that we have a vicious circle operating: prisonization into a criminal subculture, which supports and is supported by illegitimate norms, which in turn governs the process of prisonization.

REFERENCES

Alexander, M.E.: *Jail Administration*. Charles C. Thomas, 1957.

Atchley, R.C. and McCabe, M.P.: Socialization in correctional communities: a replication. *American Sociological Review, 33:*774-485, 1968.

Berk, B.B.: Organizational goals and inmate organization. *American Journal of Sociology, 71:*522-534, 1966.

Brown, R.: *Words and Things*. New York, the Free Press, 1958.

Caldwell, R.G.: *Criminology*. New York, Ronald Press, 1956a.

Caldwell, R.G.: Group dynamics in the prison community. *Journal of Criminal Law, Criminology, and Police Science, 46:*648, 657, 1956b.

Cartwright, D.: Achieving change in people: some applications of group dynamics theory. *Human Relations, 4:*381-392, 1951.

Clemmer, D.: *The Prison Community*. New York, Holt, Rinehart, and Winston, 1968.

Clemmer, D.: Observations on imprisonment as a source of criminality. *Journal of Criminal Law Criminology, and Police Science, 41:*311-319, 1950.

Cloward, R.S.: Social control and anomie: a study of a prison community. Columbia University, unpublished Ph.D. dissertation, 1959.

Cressey, D.R.: Changing criminals: the application of differential association. *American Journal of Sociology, 59:*116-120, 1955.

Cressey, D.R.: *The Prison: Studies in Institutional Organization*. New York, Holt, Rinehart and Winston, 1961.

Elias, A.: Innovations in correctional programs for juvenile delinquency. *Federal Probation, 12:*38-45, 1968.

Empey, L. and Rabow, J.: The Provo experiment in delinquency rehabilitation. *American Sociological Review, 26:*679-696, 1961.

Fisher, S.: Informal organization in the correctional setting. *Social Problems, 11:*214-223, 1965.

Foreman, P.B.: Guide theory for the study of informal inmate relations. *Southwestern Social Science Quarterly, :*34-46, 1953.

Garabedian, P.C.: Social roles and process of socialization in the prison community. *Social Problems, 2:*139-152, 1963.

Gordon, W.H.: Communist rectification programs and delinquency rehabilitation programs: a parallel? *American Sociological Review, 27:*256, 1962.

Irwin, J. and Cressey, D.: Thieves, convicts, and the inmate culture. *Social Problems, 10:*142-155, 1962.

Lerman, P.: Argot, symbolic deviance, and subcultural delinquency. *American Sociological Review, 32:*209-244, 1967.

Lerman, P.: Individual values, peer values, and subcultural delinquency, *American Sociological Review, 33:*219-225, 1968.

Lewis, M.M.: *Language in Society.* New York, Social Science Publishers, 1948.

McCorkle, L.W. and Korn, R.: Resocialization within walls, *The Annals,* May:88-93, 1954.

Ohlin, L.: *Sociology and the Field of Corrections.* New York, Basic Books, 1956.

Ohlin, L. and Lawrence, E.: Social interaction among clients as a treatment problem. *Social Work, 4:*3-14, 1959.

Reckless, W. and Walters, J.: *The Crime Problem.* New York, Appleton-Century-Crofts, 1961.

Sands, B.: *My Shadow Ran Fast.* New York, The New American Library, 1964.

Street, D.: Inmates in custodial and treatment settings. *American Sociological Review, 30:*40-55, 1965.

Shame of prisons, the, *Time, 99:*50-55, 1971.

Size, Mary: *Prisons I Have Known,* London, Allen and Unwin, 1957.

Schrag, C.: *Social Types in a Prison Community,* M.A. Thesis, University of Washington, 1944.

Schrag, C.: A preliminary criminal typology, *The Pacific Sociological Review, 4:*11-16, 1961.

Strong, S.A.: Social types in a minority group. *American Journal of Sociology, 43:*563-573, 1943.

Sutherland, E.H. and Cressey, D.R.: *Principles of Criminology.* Philadelphia, Lippincott, 1966.

Tannebaum, F.: *Wall Shadows: a Study in American Prisons.* New York, Putnam, 1922.

Tappan, P.: *Crime, Justice, and Correction.* New York, McGraw-Hill, 1960.

Task Force Report: Organized Crime. Washington, U.S. Government Printing Office, 1967.

Tittle, C.R. and Tittle, D.P.: Social organization of prisoners: an empirical test. *Social Forces, 43:*216-221, 1964.

Vedder, C.B. and Kay, B: *Penology: a Realistic Approach.* Springfield, Charles C Thomas, 1964.

Wellford, C.: Factors associated with adoption of the criminal code. A study of normative socialization. *Journal of Criminal Law, Criminology and Police Science, 58:*197-203, 1967.

Wheeler, S.: Socialization in correctional communities. *American Sociological Review, 26:*697-712, 1961.

Chapter 17

TREATMENT IN FREEDOM: PROBATION, PARDON, AND PAROLE

W HILE THE LAW CONTAINS specific penalties for its violation, it also provides for the mitigation of severe sentences. A person convicted of a crime may be: (1) placed on probation instead of incarcerated, (2) paroled prior to the maximum expiration of his prison sentence and released from prison under supervision, (3) have his sentence and/or fines commuted to a lesser term of years, or (4) receive a full or conditional pardon, which usually carries with it the restoration of civil rights. A fifth method of avoiding the full force of legal sanctions deals with groups rather than individuals and is called amnesty—a group pardon.

Historical Background of Probation

To avoid a mechanical and mindless application of the punitive criminal law, there have evolved a number of legal practices which lend flexibility to its requirements. The thread which runs through all of these is the idea of a conditional suspension of punishment dependent upon good behavior.

These legal devices assume that the individual offender is capable of social rehabilitation and reflect the broader cultural trend, initiated during the Enlightenment, away from a punitive response and toward the humanitarian treatment of offenders.

One of the first methods used for this purpose began in the thirteenth century (Sutherland and Cressey, 1970).[1] A criminal could

---

[1]Actually, one can trace mitigation procedures back to ancient Rome. If a condemned man encountered a Vestal Virgin en route to the gallows, his life was spared (Czajkoski, 1972).

"secure sanctuary" by seeking refuge in a church for forty days, after which time he was forced to leave the area by a designated road or port. By the sixteenth century, the practice had been altered so that a criminal, who secured sanctuary, might be compelled to spend the rest of his life in an assigned region with the name of the locality branded on his thumb. In the later part of the fifteenth century, certain offenses, such as murder, rape, burglary, and arson, no longer carried the right of sanctuary. The entire sanctuary concept disappeared with the breakup of the monasteries.

A second early system for mitigation of penalities grew out of the ecclesiastical courts and reflected the influence of religion upon law in the Middle Ages. The church demanded a "right of clergy" by which it sought to try its own officers. In practice, this was primarily a device to avoid capital punishment; church courts were not permitted to impose the death penalty and, except in cases of heresy and witchcraft, generally imposed less severe penalities than did secular courts. Those persons who qualified as "clergy" evolved from a strict definition of the term finally to include all persons who could read—literacy being defined as the ability to comprehend the first verse of the fifty-first Psalm: "Have mercy upon me God, according to thy loving kindness: according unto the multitude of thy tender mercies blot out my transgressions." Finally, this right was extended to the peers of those who could read. Thus, those persons who shared cultural similarities to the lawmakers were made exempt from the more stringent penalities. Although the absolute number of persons who could claim the right of clergy increased, the number of times a person could claim his right and the number of offenses for which the right could be claimed were reduced. The application of the law gradually came to be little different for those under the protective right of clergy than for those in the general society. By the eighteenth century and the general decline of religious influence, the right of clergy meant nothing.

A "reprieve" may temporarily suspend either the imposition or execution of a sentence. Such a stay of sentence may be issued by a trial judge to permit the convicted person to apply for a pardon or if the presiding judge is dissatisfied with the verdict. In cases of execution, public opinion may be aroused in favor of the condemned.[2] The present practice of American courts on the indefinite suspension of sentence has its precedence in the early practice of reprieve in English courts.

Release on one's personal recognizance is a device used to avoid both the demoralizing and possibly contaminating influence of short terms of imprisonment, and to ensure the appearance of an offender before the court. English courts for centuries released minor offenders on their recognizance. This procedure, with or without the device of sureties (or bail), has been of major historical importance in the evolution of probation; it adhered to the fundamental principles of probation: (1) suspension of penalty, (2) conditions, and (3) supervision.

Origin of Probation in the U.S.

Massachusetts was the first state in the union to initiate probation (Newman, 1968). When offenders received suspended sentences or were released on their own recognizance, volunteers began to assist them during the time of their suspended sentences. The most famous of these volunteers was a Boston cobbler, John Augustus, who was in attendance at police court and decided to stand bail for a chronic drunkard. When the defendant reappeared after three weeks, the judge was so impressed with the signs of sobriety and rehabilitation, he imposed only a nominal fine of one cent and costs ($3.75). The man escaped the House of Correction. For the next seventeen years, Augustus acted as surety for over 2,000 men and women with a high proportion of successes. He is generally considered to have been the first probation officer.

The first legal provision for probation officers employed by the state was the Massachusetts law of 1878. The act authorized the Mayor of Boston to hire a probation officer and allowed the municipal court to place offenders on probation. The legislature in 1880, extended this authority to all mayors of the state. It became manda-

---

[2]Hollywood prison movies used to capitalize on the drama of a warden waiting anxiously for a phone call from the "Governor's Mansion." Caryl Chessman was sentenced to die on June 25, 1948. He subsequently survived eight execution dates with reprieves ordered by lower courts, the United States Supreme Court, and California's Governor Pat Brown (at the request of the U.S. State Department). He was finally executed on May 2, 1960, leaving the epitaph, "This is my ninth life. Not even I have more lives than a cat" (Machlin and Woodfield, 1961).

tory, by 1891, for lower court judges to appoint probation officers.

By 1957 all states had juvenile probation laws,[3] Mississippi being the last state to pass an adult probation law. Probation had existed in Mississippi prior to 1957, during which period offenders were placed under the care of the welfare department. The picture is not so bright as it may seem at first glance. Many states have provisions for probation, but insufficent funds are provided to hire trained professional probation officers. And probation is not provided carte blanche for all offenders; in only fifteen states can probation be granted regardless of the type of crime. In areas where probation is considered judicial leniency, there are a greater number of legal restrictions upon the type of offended who may receive this disposition. In thirty-five states certain factors, such as prior convictions or whether the offender was armed at the time of the offense can determine whether or not an offender can be a candidate for probation. Offenders guilty of rape and murder are the most widely excluded from probation consideration *(Task Force Report: Correction,* 1967) .

PROBATION: TREATMENT OR PUNISHMENT?

Probation is a combination of both treatment and punishment. It is a legal disposition: An offender is sentenced to serve time on probation. At the same time, it is a process of treatment in the context of community-based corrections. Ideally, the offender receives guidance and counseling in an attempt to ensure his adjustment to free-society. Probation is punitive because restrictions are placed on the probationer. (Many authorities would deny the punitive aspects and would say their policies are rehabilitative.)

Three methods of implementing probation are used: The law may allow the trial judge to suspend the execution of sentence and place the offender on conditional probation; a state statute may on the other hand, require sentencing but permit the suspension of

---

[3]No word in the correctional vocabulary is thrown around with less precision than the term "rehabilitate." It is almost invariably used in a sarcastic manner by the benefactors of the "rehabilitation" process, e.g. "I got four years rehabilitation." Perhaps we could take a cue from the Vocational Rehabilitation department of Florida State University who finally renamed their venture "habilitation," arguing that they were not restoring anything but were starting from scratch.

imposition; a third method leaves both alternatives to the discretion of the trial judge. In the case of an offender, upon whom sentence has been imposed but not executed, violation of conditions of probation results in the judge ordering the execution of the original sentence. When the judge has suspended the imposition of sentencing, violation of probation might result in a stiffer prison sentence than would originally have been imposed. By definition, probation implies that the offender has not served time in a penitentiary (at least on this offense) ; the courts thus have no jurisdiction over parole, except in matters of procedural due process. They cannot order a man to serve time in the state penitentiary and then set the date of his release on parole. Some states do allow judges to utilize "split-sentencing" or "shock-sentencing." Offenders are placed on probation with the stipulation that they spend a portion of their probationary period in the county jail, the assumption is that a "taste of confinement" or the "shock" (as might be utilized by a psychologist in therapy) might lead to the modification of behavior. "It gets their attention," a judge told one of the authors. His court utilized this method principally with college students convicted of marijuana possession.

To send all persons convicted in our courts to prison would be both unnecessary and uneconomical. A suspended sentence without supervision would appear to be tantamount to being found "not guilty," but there still may be the loss of civil rights; the resulting "stigma" is also punishing. Probation serves the twin objectives of protecting the public and affording guidance for those who give evidence of potential rehabilitation.

To determine whether probation, in practice, was in accordance to the high ideals it holds in theory, the American Bar Association conducted a nationwide survey. The report (Bates, 1960) listed the following criticisms:

1. Probation was granted without sufficient knowledge of the defendant and his background.

2. Presentation reports often may contain a bias either for or against the offender.

3. Sentencing sometimes becomes a public spectacle.

4. Probation is often used to clear the docket, to induce the de-

fendant to plead guilty, and to alleviate crowded prison conditions.

5. Probation is often used as a collection agency to induce payment of fines, restitution, and alimony.

6. Cost of probation are sometime borne by the probationer—in effect a "probation tax." The offender pays for the "privilege."

7. Probation officer's recommendations were ignored, neglected, or overruled in many jurisdictions.

8. There was inadequate supervision of probationers on the part of probation officers due to heavy caseloads or apathy.

9. There was an over-identification on the part of the probation officer with the social-work expectations of his role to the neglect of law-enforcement responsibilities.

10. There was inadequate and unreliable statistical research making it nearly impossible to discover the success or failure of the system.

Despite these shortcomings, probation remains a superior method of dealing with many offenders than a dehumanizing institutionalization. Whenever possible men and women should be treated in relative freedom. It is axiomatic that to function as a "normal" person, one must live in a relatively "normal" environment. Institutionalization should be utilized only when the offender is a danger to himself and/or the community. To determine which offenders will make good candidates for probation, the sentencing judge needs a well prepared presentence report.

The Presentence Report

Information secured in a presentence investigation can be utilized at every stage of the criminal justice system: (1) by the courts in determining the appropriate sentence, (2) by the prison classification team in assigning custody and treatment, (3) by the parole board in deciding when the offender is ready to return to the community, (4) by the probation and parole officers as they aid the man in his adjustment to the community, (5) by the correctional researchers as they try to locate these characteristics that are associated with success on probation (Carter and Wilkins, 1970).

552 *Introduction to Criminology*

The primary purpose of the presentence investigation is not to determine the guilt or innocence of the defendant, but to give those persons who will be working with him insights into his personality and some understanding of the social milieu which produced him.

Some type of a presentence investigation should be made in every case, which is to the criminal justice system what diagnosis is to medicine. Objectivity is a must in the preparation of this document; the probation officer must see things as they are and not as he would wish them to be. Under our adversary system of justice, the district attorney and the defense counsel are committed to particular points of view, but the preparer of the presentence investigation is free to include all facts pertinent to the case. Included in the report should be: description of the offense, including statements of co-defendants; the defendant's own version and his prior record; family and marital history; description of neighborhood in which the defendant was reared; and facts regarding his education, religion, interests, and mental and physical health records, employment history, and military service record. All of these items are essential if the probation officer is to present a complete picture of the defendant. He may choose to include other optional data, such as "attitude of defendant toward arresting officers," "amount of bond," and "attitude of arresting officers," if he feels that this information adds substantially to the report. The evaluative summary is the most difficult and significant aspect of the presentence report. It is here that professional probation officers are separated from merely fact-gathering clerks. It requires considerable analytic skill and understanding of human behavior to interpret the cold facts in a presentence report and on the basis of them make a meaningful recommendation to the court. A presentence report can be no better than the skills of the investigation officer. Many judges ask for recommendations for sentencing alternatives, or if the defendant be placed on probation, recommendations regarding what treatment plan should be inaugurated.

The Presentence Investigation: Confidential Information or Public Document?

The issue of the confidentiality of the presentence investigation illustrates once again the conflict between law and social work in the disposition of the offender. With the increased concern for the protection of the defendant's rights, there has been a trend toward furnishing the defense counsel with a copy of the presentence investigation. Some probation officers resist this trend, feeling that should the investigation become a public record, it could become a source of embarrassment to the probationer. The investigatory process itself might thus be inhibited since informants would be reluctant to speak "on the record." In the federal courts, the amount of disclosure is left to the discretion of each district court. Some districts require that the report be read aloud in court; others allow no one but the sentencing judge to read it. However, the general trend of the courts has been to liberalize disclosure practices for presentence reports *(U.S. v. Fischer)*.

The court of Appeals for the Fourth Circuit, while acknowledging the general rule of law that disclosure of information in presentence reports is in the discretion of the trial court, did, however, hold matters of record prejudicial to the defendant must be disclosed *(Baker v. U.S.)*. The court further stated that no conviction of criminal charge should be included in the report of consideration unless referable to an official record. The Ninth Circuit Court of Appeals *(Verdugo v. U.S.)* held that the inclusion of information in the presentence report based upon illegally-seized evidence is tantamount to a denial of the right to effective counsel and is in violation of the defendant's Fourth Amendment rights. If an attorney is powerless to correct errors in a presentence report because he is unaware of them, it follows that nondisclosure effectively denies the defendant of his right to counsel and due process of law.

The probation officer serves as the "eyes and ears" of the court. In 1944, an advisory committee of the Supreme Court recommended full disclosure of the presentence reports. As now stated, the court generally has full discretion to disclose information when the court believes that it is necessary or desirable to do so. In preparing the presentence investigation, the probation officer must depend on sources of information such as the welfare department, juvenile court files, and mental hospitals—agencies which assume confidentiality of information. Even though the officer does not reveal the source of his information, it would be a dull defendant indeed who could not deduce from the facts presented where they originated. If agencies working with the defendant know that such highly sensitive information as infidelity, homosexuality, and insanity will be read aloud in open court, they will be reluctant to open their files. Thus, in an effort to treat the defendant fairly, the court inhibits the sources of its knowledge about the defendant and must then make a disposition of the case with inadequate information.

Judge James B. Parsons (1964), in arguing for the confidentiality of the report, wrote:

> The development of the presentence report signaled a major breakthrough in the fight for individualized justice. The report has become to be the foundation stone on which modern probation practice rests. A key ingredient of the presentence process is the assurance it affords the defendant, the court, and the community that this inquiry will be thorough and objective and that the report will accurately mirror the defendant and his life. Mandatory disclosure of portions of this document is a retrogressive action which cuts away at the heart of this notable criminological advance. The presentence report must be preserved as a meaningful, professional, dispassionate, confidential document. The efforts of our courts should be directed at preserving confidentiality and not destroying it; for confidentiality offers the best insurance of fairness and wisdom in the best interests of both the defendant and society.

Probation and Parole Conditions

Even though probation usually is managed by the courts, and parole by an executive department of government, the general and special conditions are similar. The conditions of probation and parole are generally fixed jointly by the legislature, the court, and the probation and parole department. Some of these regulations are fixed by statute and affect all persons. These laws are usually general in nature and require such reasonable conditions as admonishing the probationer to live a law-abiding life, not to leave the state without the court's consent, report periodically to his probation or parole officer, and, perhaps, to pay the costs of court. These general conditions are fixed by law and with no allowances for discretion by the trial court or the parole board. Unique conditions may be applied according to the individual case. For example, the man may be required to either stay or leave home, support his mother and father, join the Navy, "not to cuss the Sheriff," make restitution to the victim of his crime, or attend church regularly.

Some conditions of probation and parole have been unfair and unrealistic. When this occurs, the probation officer may choose to enforce them judiciously, thereby muting their effect in the interest of common-sense justice.

In the application of these conditions, the concerned probation officer will ask: Are these rules reasonable? Are they effective? Do they serve the best interests of the individual and the community?

Revocation of Probation

Similar to the disparities in sentencing are the disparities of the revocation of probation. There are no uniform criteria for revoking probation throughout the country, not even among judges in the same district court.

Conditions of probation should be realistic, and they should be applied flexibly. Unrealistic conditions of probation only further frustrate the offender and inevitably lead to violations. It is pointless to place an excessive fine or restitution on an individual when financial problems were the genesis of his difficulty. Compulsory church attendance may create resentment on the part of the probationer as well as any attempt to turn him into a strict teetotaler. Conditions of probation should be guidelines to assist the probationer in leading a law-abiding life, not rigid vows of chastity and obediance which only the most disciplined cloistered monk could endure.

When a probationer violates the conditions of his probation, care should be taken to determine if his violation was the result of unrealistic probation rules or an arrogant and indifferent attitude on the part of the probationer (Dicerbo, 1966). The probation officer should ask: To what extent is this violation reflective of deeper hostile attitudes? And to what extent is it just symptomatic of an individual floundering, trying to "find himself"? Revocation is justified only when the probationer defies the courts or when he becomes a threat to the community. In cases involving restitution, when the probationer is sentenced to imprisonment, the victim of his crime suffers the entire loss. No violation should result in an automatic revocation. One guideline question to ask is: How would we have responded to his act had the man not been on probation? For example, we do not sentence people to jail for losing or quiting their jobs. All violations should be judged in the light of the probationer's total adjustment to society.

Legal Rights of Probationers

What is acceptable evidence upon which probation can be revoked? A federal probationer who is arrested on a charge of violation of probation is granted, by law, a hearing before the court having jurisdiction over him and given an opportunity to explain the accusation. Should the court revoke probation, it may require the probationer to serve the sentence imposed, or any lesser sentence. If imposition of sentence were suspended, the court may impose any sentence which might have originally have been imposed. Further, a probationer or parolee who is revoked has no right to "street time" but may be imprisoned for the remainder of his unserved sentence.

The Court of Appeals for the Second Circuit in the *U.S. v. Nagleberg* ruled that the sentence imposed upon probation revocation must comply with minimum mandatory requirements. Thus, the judge at probation revocation is limited in the same way as was the judge at the time of original sentencing. The law does not require a jury trial at revocation, nor must violation be proven beyond a reasonable doubt; the standard of review is whether the district court abused its discretionary powers.

Revocation hearings then are not trials in the technical sense. A revocation hearing is not an adversary proceeding, and the rules of evidence do not apply. Nor is it required that an inquiry be fitted to the needs of the occasion to justify the conclusion that there was no abuse of discretion in revoking probation. The defendant must be given an opportunity to make a statement or offer evidence if he desires to do so. The degree of proof justifying revocation need not convince the court beyond a reasonable doubt as it must in a criminal trial. It is sufficient if the court be reasonably satisfied that it is in the best interests of the community that probation be revoked.

The legislation in this area varies tremendously from jurisdiction to jurisdiction. Some states do not require a hearing prior to revocation. Others do not elaborate on what rights the accused may expect. In general, however, probation revocations are more formal procedures than parole revocations, probably because they are conducted by the courts rather than parole boards.

Success Rates on Probation

It is generally estimated by probation authorities that placing a man in prison costs the "state" ten times more than probation. Success rates published by probation and parole commissions serve two purposes: to justify probation and to extract financial support from the legislature. The Florida Probation and Parole Commission's annual report for 1968 boasted that from the beginning of its operation in 1941, 88 out of every 100 persons placed on probation had successfully completed their probations and were "rehabilitated." Translating this success rate into savings for the taxpayer, the commission estimates that for every five inmates released on probation or parole, the savings of 9,855 dollars (computed on a yearly cost of $2,200 for confinement per man) would finance one supervisor who in turn could supervise fifty additional probationers and parolees at a total savings of 98,550 dollars per year, per supervisor. As persons on probation and parole pay taxes, make restitution to victims, pay fines, and support dependants who might otherwise be "on welfare," the savings is even greater than this figure would indicate. In Florida during 1968, persons under supervision paid over 6,000,000 dollars in taxes, and made restitution to victims involved in their offenses in the amount of 155,000 dollars. There is considerable justification then, for the claim by probation and parole departments that their services "represent one of the greatest bargains purchased by society's tax dollar" (28th Annual Report, Florida Probation and Parole Commission, 1968).

Of course, we would save even more money if we placed even fewer persons on probation. Many probation case-loads contain a lot of "dead wood," i.e. offenders who need little or no supervision and who would have better been dealt with by a suspended sentence or a fine.

Probation is more economical than incarceration as a method of responding to offenders. It is, however, successful in "rehabilitating" the offender? And how is "success" of probation measured? Vasoli (1967) lists the several criteria used for evaluating probation outcome. Probation may be considered a "failure" if: (1) the probation officer petitions for revocation, (2) if a revocation hearing is held (regardless of the outcome), or (3) if the probationer commits a misdemeanor or felony.

It would seem that any probationer committing a felony would have his probation automatically revoked. Vasoli discovered, however, in a study of 814 federal offenders placed on probation between the years 1946 and 1960, that 155 of 622 probationers officially listed as successes had committed at least one felony during their probationary period. This failure to revoke did not occur as a result of laxity on the part of the federal probation officer, but was a result of a federal probationer being imprisoned for a state offense. Rather than filing a detainer against him, the probation officer would terminate probation, surrendering jurisdiction to the state. District officers, in their monthly statistical report, would fail to indicate why probation had been terminated, and the case was counted as a success. This errant system has been rectified somewhat by F.B.I. "flash notices." It is still possible, however, for offenses committed by probationers to go unrecorded in national statistics.

Whether probation can realistically be termed a success depends upon several factors. The criteria for judging success may range from something as subjective as "adjustment to society" to a more objective measurement such as revocation statistics.

Since measures of probation departments are typically limited to the probation period itself, we need to take into consideration crimes committed in the post-probation period to adequately assess the success or failure of this method of handling offenders. During the period 1963 through 1969 the Uniform Crime Reporting Program processed data on 240,000 offenders in order to document the extent to which criminal recidivism contributes to the crime rate. The basis of selection in this study was a federal offense. Therefore, the offenders under consideration differ slightly from a profile of state offenders. Of 16,332 offenders released to the community, by all methods in 1965, 63 percent had been rearrested by the end of the fourth calendar year after release.

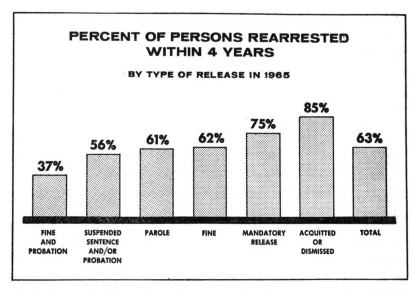

Figure 17-1. Percent of Persons Rearrested within Four Years. *Uniform Crime Reports.* Washington, U.S. Government Printing Office, 1970. Reproduced by permission of the Department of Justice.

Offenders who received a sentence of fine and probation in 1965 had the lowest recidivism rate of the six categories, 37 percent rearrested. Probation and fine is generally the response of the courts to such federal violations as income tax, fraud, and embezzlement.

Diana (1955) analyzed the records of 280 delinquents placed on probation and found: Eighty-four percent had not been *convicted* again during a ten-year period; their contact with their officers during this period was minimal; and they had received little attention that could be classified as "casework." Diana concluded his study by questioning the assumption that casework is a significant factor in probation outcome.

England's (1957) findings supported the conclusion of Diana. England studied the post-probation recidivism (6 year period) rates of 490 offenders who successfully completed probation terms between 1939 and 1944. By 1951 only 17.7 percent of the 490 persons had again been convicted of felonies or misdemeanors. Of the rehabilitative efforts which were made on behalf of the 490 clients,

England wrote that ". . . most of the aids and services given were not of a type requiring extensive social work training, but could have been performed by anyone possessing intelligence, tact, and a good knowledge of the institution and agency facilities in his probationers' communities." England concluded that recidivism rates are not significantly associated with the quality of the probation to which offenders are subjected. The relative uniformity of probation outcomes, lies not so much in the social work skills of the probation officers, but in the nature of probation. The basic approach to probation (a suspended sentence plus supervision) has remained virtually unchanged since the 1840's and John Augustus.

Augustus and his Boston disciples achieved an impressive success rate in the reformation of the men placed under their supervision. This was done without the benefits of degrees in social work. What Augustus and his colleagues did share with the modern college trained probation officer is that his "case load" was comprised of first offenders charged with relatively minor crimes. And it is in this similarity that the explanation for the uniformity in probation success-failure rates may be found.

Selection for probation is from the pool of offenders who are least likely to recidivate or slide back into crime—the "cream." Using Scragg's typology, a "Square John" would be the best candidate for probation. One dysfunctional aspect of the increased use of probation is that prison populations now characterized by a greater percent of "hard-core" types: outlaws, con-politicians, and right-guys (solid cons).[4]

When we compare the F.B.I. rearrest rates with the figures of probation departments of re-conviction rates, it appears that former probationers do not avoid re-arrest so much as they avoid reconvictions.

The central issue in this discussion remains: What type of offenders succeed on probation and under what conditions? As a generalization, with an increase in age, there is a corresponding decrease in the probability of being arrested. Aging is still the most effective "rehabilitating" factor in corrections—crime takes energy. There is also a relationship between the type of offense and prob-

---

[4]As Governor Lester Maddox of Georgia observed, the problem with prisons is that we need a "better class of inmates."

ability of a re-arrest; embezzlers (older men) make good probation risks, while auto thieves (youths) do not. See Figures 17-2 and 17-3.

METHODS OF RELEASE FROM PRISON

Repeated studies have shown that 95 percent of all men sent to prison will eventually be returned to free society. The question then, is not will we release offenders from prison? It is, rather, under what circumstances will we release them? Release may occur through expiration of sentence (serving "day-for-day"), commutation of sentence, reduction of time by earning "good time," parole, pardon, or successful appeal of conviction.

Sentences may be either determinate (fixed), indeterminate (one day to life), or mixed (not less than five, nor more than ten years). Older penologists felt that a strict indeterminate sentence was preferable for all offenders. Historically, they were responding to a

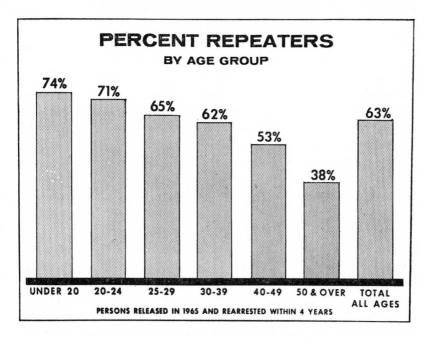

Figure 17-2. Percent of Repeaters by Age Group. *Uniform Crime Reports.* Washington, U.S. Government Printing Office, 1970. Reproduced by permission of the Department of Justice.

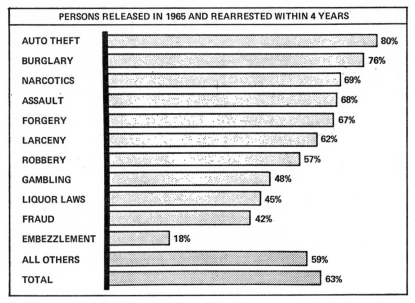

Figure 17-3. Percent of Repeaters by Type of Crime in 1965. *Uniform Crime Reports*. Washington, U.S. Government Printing Office, 1970. Reproduced by permission of the Department of Justice.

determinist-positivist model and attempting to individualize treatment. The sentence, then, bore no relationship to the offense. Just as you do not "sentence" an individual to a hospital for a term of months per disease (a strict two years for cancer, regardless of your progress toward health), so an offender was to be sentenced to prison until he was "rehabilitated." It was similar to medical reasoning, was logical on its face, and has created a multitude of frustrations and inequities.

In practice, the indeterminate sentence can be oppressive. The inmate is punished for behavior in prison, rather than for his crime. The sentence can be constantly reset if the inmate does not conform to what the board of corrections or parole board feels is appropriate progress. The system of indeterminate sentences is unpopular with inmates because of the uncertainty of their release date. The student may be able to gain some rapport with the situation of an inmate serving an indeterminate sentence if he imagines he had to take courses until a faculty board decided he "knew enough" for a college degree, instead of completing a specifically outlined number of required courses. The present writers feel a better system would be to diagnose what social skills were lacking in the repertoires of social responses available to the offender, sentence the inmate to an institution until he had completed specific requirements, e.g. finish high school, serve at least six months with no disciplinary write-ups, attend group counseling for a specified period, then relesae the inmate under supervision. There is no guarantee that institutional adjustments will mean the released man will "go straight," but it is the principle criteria for release we have at our disposal.

Juvenile "commitments" are quasi-indeterminate; it is possible to keep the delinquent in an institution until he reaches his majority, normally at age twenty-one. Release of the criminally insane and defective delinquents is usually dependent upon the judgement of the medical profession and not strictly a matter regulated as criminal law.

Pre-Release Centers

If a deep sea diver or scuba diver surfaces immediately from a great depth, he experiences severe cramps known as the "bends." Similarly, after being immersed in the confining atmosphere of a "total institution" (Army, religious order, prison) an individual suddenly released to autonomy of the "free world" may experience what might be termed "psychological bends."

To ease the reentry of the inmates into society a number of modern prison systems have adopted the concept of the "pre-release" center. These centers are typically located within, or near, the institutional walls. Here the inmate spends his last month prior to release preparing for a society which may have changed dramatically during his time in prison. Some of the courses provided are:

1. A driver's education course in which the inmate obtains his license.

2. A clothier may discuss how dress styles have changed so that the inmate has some concept of contemporary fashion.

3. Individual and group counseling sessions address themselves

to such potentially incendiary topics as: "How will you react if you discover your wife/husband has been unfaithful?"

4. Representatives from groups such as Alcoholics Anonymous, welfare, insurance agents, banks, schools and religious organizations speak to the inmates on their particular area of expertise.

5. If the center is funded federally through vocational rehabilitation, the inmate receives aid in obtaining a job, "maintenance money,"[5] and transportation to his new home.

Parole

Parole[6] is the conditional release, under supervision, of an offender from a correctional institute after he has served a portion of his sentence. The word is taken from the French and is used in the sense of *parole d' honneur*—word of honor. The concept has its roots in military history, referring to the practice of releasing a captured soldier on his "parole," i.e. on his word of honor that he would not again take up arms against his captors. Similarly, the inmate is released to free society on his parole, or his word of honor, that he will not again become an enemy of society. Parole differs from probation because it implies that the offender has "served time." Administratively, parole is a function of the executive branch of government, while probation is a judicial act of the court.[7] Selection, supervision, regulations, revocation, and release procedures are similar, and the two kinds of conditional release often become confusing to the public.

History of Parole

Prisoners have always been released upon the arrival of their

---

[5]"Maintenance money" is a broader concept than the traditional "gate money" ($10 and a suit of clothes) and a response to the total needs of the newly freed man. The benefits of a pre-release center are obvious. However, in many instances, only inmates granted parole (the best "risks") go through the pre-release center. "Flat timers" (men who have served their whole sentence) leave the institution with nominal gate money and a hand shake.

[6]"Bench parole" is granted by judges during adjournments or interim periods between court appearances, hearings, or trials. This status is really nothing like regular parole; there is no supervision or conditions of behavior and it is not managed by the executive branch of government.

[7]There are some strange variations here, such as the "split sentence" and the ability of a Federal judge to fix various parole eligibility dates.

"mandatory release date." That is, sentences normally have a termination date. In inmate jargon, this is referred to as serving "flat time" or "day-for-day." Parole is a conditional release. Inmates who appear to be making genuine progress toward rehabilitation are selected to serve a final portion of their sentence, under some form of supervision, in the community.

Historical precedent for the modern practice of conditional release under supervision, may be found in at least four areas: (1) the system of indenture and "transportation" in the 18th and 19th centuries, (2) Alexander Maconochie's "ticket-of-leave" system, (3) the Irish system which had incorporated the marks system, and (4) the role of "Prisoner Aid Societies" in their philanthropic work with ex-convicts in the United States.

The practice of indentured children being bound over to their employers date back to 1562 and originally had no relation to persons convicted of crime. The contract of indenture is similar to modern parole conditions. Newman (1970) quotes Van Doren's biography of Benjamin Franklin and the conditions imposed upon Franklin when he was indentured to his brother:

> . . . During which term the said apprentice his master faithfully shall or will serve, his secrets keep, his lawful demands everywhere gladly do . . . At cards or dice tables or any other unlawful game he shall not play. Matrimony he shall not contract nor from the services of his master day or night absent himself but in all things as an honest faithful apprentice shall and will demean and behave himself toward said master all during said term.

Through this method, children could earn their discharge from indenture. Failure to satisfy the demands of the employer could however, result in return to an institution.

Dressler (1959) relates the British practice of deportation of felons to the colonies to what was later translated into parole. The decision, on the part of the British government, to grant stays of execution to convicted felons was a response to a need in the colonies for cheap labor. Deportation then, contained the elements of mitigation of prison sentence and placement of the offender in the free community under supervision. By 1775, England was transplanting approximately two thousand felons annually in the colonies. The practice ended abruptly with the advent of the American revolution.

Alexander Maconochie, a captain in the Royal Navy and prison reformer, is credited by Dressler as being, more than any other one man, the "father" of parole. Maconochie's contribution to parole was the mark (point) system. Prisoners in his Norfolk Island (Australia) prison earned their freedom by acquiring a required number of marks. In cases of a poor work record, or insubordination, the convict was fined marks—rather than lashed.

As Dressler (1959) explains:

> Maconochie had struck on an idea that gave prisoners hope. They, and they alone, could reduce their sentences. They could hasten the day when they would be on ticket of leave. And when that time came, it was now understood, they might return to England. Declare Maconochie: 'When a man keeps the key of his own prison, he is soon persuaded to fit it to the lock.' The prisoners responded.

Under Maconochie's plan an offender moved through degrees of freedom, from strict custody to liberty. He was finally released on a "ticket-of-leave." The program ended in 1867 when free settlers, competing with "ticket-of-leave" holders for the discovery of gold in Australia, demanded that they be deported.

Walter Crofton, head of the Irish prison system, added refinements to the ticket-of-leave Maconochie had devised. He agreed with Maconochie that the purpose of prison was to rehabilitate, and his prisoners moved through his system from solitary confinement to conditional release under supervision. Crofton had devised a more careful program of supervision than had existed heretofore. He created the position of "Inspecor of Released Prisoners" whose function it was to protect the community by checking on his charges and further to assist the offender in his readjustment to society.

Ex-convicts have never had an easy time re-entering the society which rejected them. The stigmatization of the prison experience makes them immediately suspect. In the 19th century ticket-of-leave men were blamed for most of the crimes committed. The public complained (in England especially) that the ticket-of-leave system was simply a leniency which endangered the public safety. Victor Hugo graphically describes the plight of the 19th century French ex-convict, Jean Val-Jean, with his "yellow passport," in a moving scene in *Les Miserables* (1862).

"See here! My name is Jean Val-jean. I am a convict; I have been nineteen years in the galleys. Four days ago I was set free, and started for Pontarlier, which is my destination; during those four days I have walked from Toulon. To-day I have walked twelve leagues. When I reached this place this evening I went to an inn, and they sent me away on account of my yellow passport, which I had shown at the mayor's office, as was necessary. I went to another inn; they said: "Get out!" It was the same with one as with another; nobody would have me. I went to the prison, and the turnkey would not let me in. There in the square I lay down upon a stone; a good woman showed me your house, and said: 'Knock there!' I have knocked. What is this place? Are you an inn? I have money; my savings, one hundred and nine francs and fifteen sous which I have earned in the galleys by my work for nineteen years. I will pay. What do I care? I have money. I am very tired—twelve leagues on foot, and I am so hungry. Can I stay?"

"Madame Magloire," said the bishop, "put on another plate."

The man took three steps, and came near the lamp which stood on the table. "Stop," he exclaimed; as if he had not been understood, "not that, did you understand me? I am a galley-slave—a convict—I am just from the galleys." He drew from his pocket a large sheet of yellow paper, which he unfolded. "There is my passport, yellow as you see. That is enough to have me kicked out wherever I go. Will you read it? I know how to read, I do. I learned in the galleys. There is a school there for those who care for it. See, here is what they have put in the passport: 'Jean Val-jean, a liberated convict, native of _____,' you don't care for that, 'has been nineteen years in the galleys; five years for burglary; fourteen years for having attempted four times to escape. This man is very dangerous. There you have it! Everybody has thrust me out; Will you receive me? Is this an inn? Can you give me something to eat, and a place to sleep? Have you a stable?"

"Madame Magloire," said the bishop, "put some sheets on the bed in the alcove."

Madame Magloire went out to fulfill her orders.[8]

Prisoner Aid Societies arose with the idea of providing aftercare for discharged prisoners. The services they provided were similar to those furnished by contemporary parole departments: secure employment, housing, clothing, and other needs of the newly released men. Each prisoner given assistance by one of these societies was expected to report his progress toward readjustment to society.

Parole in its modern form was adopted first by New York State

---

[8]In 1964, a priest in San Antonio Texas shot an ex-convict for stealing money out of the "poor box." Apparently he was trained by a different religous order than that which produced the kindly bishop of Hugo's *Les Miserables*.

when the 1869 law authorized the building of Elmira Reformatory. To be eligible for parole, prisoners at Elmira must have established a good record of conduct for twelve months and must have been able to present a suitable plan for employment. The men were given a new suit of clothes (symbolizing a new beginning) and transportation expenses. The parolee was to report to his "guardian" once a month. The parole period was limited to six months; a longer period was felt to discourage the prisoner.

The first National Parole Conference was convened in Washington, D.C. in 1939 by President Roosevelt. At that time, parole was little more than an ideal. Over half the nation's parole officers were in five states, and the individual case load in one state was 2,500![9] According to Wright (1939), "after-care" in those days was little more than "after-thought." By 1941 parole as a concept had fallen into such public disfavor that in a survey of 25,000 policy holders of the Northwestern National Life Insurance Company, 83 percent of the men and 88 percent of the women asked felt that pardon and parole should be abolished; persons convicted of crimes should serve their full sentences (Cass, 1941).

Despite its rocky beginnings, parole, as a correctional concept, has demonstrated its usefulness. Every state in the union has passed laws authorizing its use. Indeed, a few states are now extending the principle of parole to include all prisoners under mandatory conditional release programs, generally three months prior to the sentence expiration date. Presently mandatory conditional release is granted by "gain time" (reduction in sentence through good behavior) or expiration of sentence. Like parole, *MCR* is release under supervision. Parole authorities release the "best risks" with plans for employment and supervision. Those who serve to the expiration of their sentences, generally considered the greatest threat to society, are made to shift for themselves. One Mississippi parole officer told the authors, of often watching prisoners from Parchment Farm (a maximum security institution) cross the road to hitchhike in a southerly direction. If we were passed by, the ex-convict would simply re-cross the road and attempt to hitch a ride north—thus

---

[9]According to an unpublished survey by the Connecticut Department of Corrections (1970), the average case load per parole officer in the United States is 67, with a range of 157 (Louisiana) to 32 (South Dakota).

demonstrating the extent to which he was adrift in society. According to the *UCR* (1970), 75 percent of the men released without supervision will be re-arrested within four years. In the interest of both individual rehabilitation and societal protection, it is imperative that all prisoners released from our institutions be given some form of supervision.

The Parole Board

American penal systems have devised a separation of powers over the destiny of the offenders under their jurisdiction. The courts determine the guilt or innocence of the offender and may place limits on the time the convict must serve. Departments of correction are invested with the custody and care of the inmate. Boards of parole determine if and when a prisoner should be released to the community prior to the expiration of his sentence. Parole boards are organized according to three principal models: (1) a board composed of personnel from within a particular institution,[10] (2) a state parole board housed within the division of correction with authority to release from all state institutions, and (3) a parole board administratively independent from the division of corrections with power to release from any state institutions.

Abuses and favoritism in the early days of parole, under the Elmira system, have led increasingly to the establishment of parole boards independent of the department of correction. This trend, however, has created a situation in which the men who know the prisoner best, the custodial officer and correctional social worker, have little or no control over the release of the men with whom they work day after day. Boards must lean heavily on the sterile information contained in the convict's "record jacket" and perhaps a brief interview with the prospective parolee.[11] Necessarily, their judgements are largely intuitive.

Selection for parole and subsequently release from prison in-

[10]This arrangement is now something of an antique, except for some juvenile institutions.

[11]The authors have witnessed the pathos of men who wait anxiously for a non-professional parole board (businessmen who took a day off once a month from their occupations to fly to the state prison), watch as all sixty interviews are accomplished in two hours (two minutes per man), and then stare unbelievingly as these men, who hold the power of freedom, disappear into the sky which brought them.

volves an interplay between a formal system of rules and the informal system of attitudes (predispositions to act) of parole board members. Thomas (1963) analyzed this process as exhibited by the Indiana parole board. (Thomas was himself a member of this board).

Parole hearings, during this period, were held two months prior to the earliest release date.[12] One month prior to the hearing, each board member received copies of the classification summaries for the men to be considered. The monthly total of these summaries in Indiana averaged about 500. The Indiana parole board, during Thomas' tenure, consisted of three men. To be considered for parole each applicant must have been on "good behavior" for a year. Two votes for or against an applicant determines the decision.

Other than the inmate and the board members, the only other persons present at the formal hearing is the institutional parole officer. The basic consideration in the parole process, from the point of view of the parole board members, is the protection of society. Factors considered by the board included: (1) the nature of the inmate's offense; (2) his criminal record; (3) psychological reports; (4) institutional conduct; (5) parole plan; and (6) community sentiments, and perhaps a prediction table.

Board members may disagree with the recommendations of the institutional recommendations and may have firm opinions about releasing persons guilty of a particular crime, e.g. rape or homicide. Community pressures, e.g. "Does anyone on the outside want this man kept inside?," is also a consideration.

Thomas did not see the parole selection process as a scientific endeavor but rather a "guessing game" in which the members of the board tried to ascertain if the time were right to take a chance on the potential parolee "making it on the streets."

Gottfredson and Ballard (1966), in an attempt to discover if differences in parole decisions were associated not only with the characteristics of the offenders themselves, but also with the persons responsible for the decisions, analyzed 2,053 cases in which parole

---

[12]In many states, the inmates must serve one-third of his maximum sentence before he is eligible for parole. Perhaps the lowest mimimum requirement is Florida where an inmate may be eligible for parole after only six months confinement.

was granted over a one-year period. They concluded that the paroling authority members tended to make similar sentencing decisions when the different kinds of offenders considered were taken as a group. This result does not make the decision making criteria a scientific one, but it does indicate consistency and uniformity.

Most parole boards in the United States find themselves in the position of the one in Connecticut which has recently been described by Jackson (1970). The Connecticut board has nine members, each appointed by the Governor; only three sit at a time. None are professional penologists; they include people of such diverse occupations as a retired minister, a dentist, and the dean of the University of Connecticut law school. Decisions are made on what appear to the board to be appropriate responses to their questions. Any candidate for parole who is belligerent (humility is a great virtue in this situation) or who shows resentment that society has locked him in a cage will jeopardize his chances. The smart inmate will attempt to convince the board that he is grateful for the opportunity to learn to be a "Square John." The situation is thus aptly summed up: "With little to guide them three good men must say 'yes or no' as convicts plead for freedom" (Jackson, 1970).

Four inmates of the Indiana State Penitentiary have described how parole candidates resent at least three aspects of the parole-decision process (Griswold, *et al.,* 1970). First, the tendency of parole boards is to place great emphasis on the candidate's prior record:

> What is so frustrating to men who keep getting rejected for parole because of 'past record' is that there is obviously nothing that the individual can do about it. It cannot be changed, it cannot be expunged. It therefore generates a feeling of helplessness and frustration, especially in men who take seriously what they are told about rehabilitation and perfect institutional records. These men cannot understand the rationale behind parole denials based on past records if the major goal of the correctional system is rehabilitation and if they have tried to take advantage of every rehabilitation program offered by the institution. The men know that merely serving another two or five years is not going to further the 'rehabilitation' process (Griswold, *et al.,* 1970).

The second source of resentment comes from the attitude of parole boards that their principal responsiblity is to protect society and that the rehabilitation of the offender is secondary. With this as their guide, parole boards are reluctant to release offenders who are considered "risks," preferring to let them serve day-for-day and return to the community without supervision. This practice undoubtedly reduces the recidivism rate for men on parole and enhances the public image of parole boards. Its impact on the over-all recidivism rate, however, should be the paramount consideration. "If the parole principle be sound for one prisoner," wrote James V. Bennett, "it is sound for all" *(Of Prisons and Justice, 1964)*. The issue is: whether keeping a poor parole risk in prison for a longer period of time makes him a better parole risk. The answer for some is "yes." The passage of time, more than anything about the dehumanizing prison atmosphere, seems to mature a few men. But for most, the longer an offender is subjected to the crimeogenic environment of a penitentiary, the more likely he is to absorb the values, techniques, and rationalizations of the criminal sub-culture.

Lastly, inmates are convinced that parole boards are more responsive to public opinion and political pressures than to the fact-situation and record of the individual applicant. This feeling on the part of prisoners only adds to their cynicism toward the entire parole process.

Federal *parole* procedures have traditionally been secret procedures. Prisoners are usually not told upon what basis the parole decision is made, nor are they given any detailed explanation when they are denied parole.[13] This mandarin-like stance has been challenged in a suit by a prisoner at the Lewisburg Federal Penitentiary *(Washington Post, 1972)* which has been extended into a class action suit on behalf of all federal prisoners. Among the changes in parole procedure which the prisoners ask are:

—The board give some sort of explanation for its actions, based on the facts in each individual case.
—The board establish general standards on which it makes individual decisions.

---

[13]The federal courts have traditionally taken a "hands off" stance toward parole procedures reasoning that, as an individual has no constitutional right to parole, the courts possess no authority to review parole board actions. A major source of grievance among prisoners from Angola to Attica has been the policy of boards of parole to refuse to adequately explain their decisions in more detail than the observation that refused prisoner exhibits "an antisocial attitude."

—The board allow each prisoner to have a representative (not necessarily an attorney) who may look at the information submitted to the parole board and may then respond to it.

At this point, it should be said that parole procedures are a constant source of grievance from both prisoners (too vague and strict) and the community (too lenient).

To create a balance between an authonomous external parole authority and the institutional workers who see the inmate on a day-to-day basis, the authors suggest the following five-man model parole board. From outside the paroling institution, two men would serve statewide; one would be a psychiatrist who is conversant with the use of sodium pentothol and another would be a clinical psychologist whose specialty is criminology. Within each institution would be an institutional parole officer, whose job it would be to prepare pre-parole reports and sit as a voting member of the board. The other two members of the board would be the correctional case worker assigned to the inmate and the custodial officer in charge of the cell block or dorm where the inmate lives. This board should make extensive use of parole prediction tables, and when a man is turned down for parole, he should be told specifically the reason. He should then be given an outline of specific activities in which to engage before the next parole meeting to show that he is trying to rehabilitate himself.

Parole Supervision

Because of the size of his case load, or an assignment which covers a large geographic area, it may become necessary for a probation or parole officer to utilize a case classification system. To facilitate the prediction of parole adjustment, the Research Division of the California Department of Corrections developed a device known as the Base Expectancy Scoring System (BESS). This instrument was constructed on the basis of differences found to exist among parolees who made favorable community adjustments and those who made unfavorable ones. The differences were assigned weights calculated by multiple correlation. Field studies validated the instrument, i.e. parole adjustments did increase with high BESS scores. With a few modifications, the instrument can be used to predict the outcome of male probationers as well (Nicholson, 1968):

Scoring Form

Characteristic	Points
A. Arrest-free period of 5 or more consecutive years	12____
B. No history of opiate usage	9____
C. Few jail commitments (none to two)	8____
D. Most recent conviction or commitment does not include checks, forgery, or burglary	7____
E. No family criminal record	6____
F. No alcohol involvement	6____
G. First arrest not for auto theft	5____
H. Twelve months steady employment within one year prior to arraignment for present offense	4____
I. Four to eleven months steady employment prior to arraignment for present offense (If given 6 points on Item H, add also 4 points for this item)	4____
J. No alias	4____
K. Favorable living arrangement	4____
L. Few prior arrests (none to two)	4____
Sum of points	76____

Scale for potential adjustment: A=76-57, B=56-37, C=63-).

"A" rating suggests high potential for favorable adjustment, "B" for medium potential, and "C" for low potential. The ratings are useful both for the effective management of cases under supervision and for making recommendations to the court in the presentence report. "A" cases should need minimal supervision, while the greatest efforts should be directed toward "B" and "C" groups.

West Germany has developed a "1984ish" mechanism for monitoring parolees in which an electronic device is buried under the parolee's skin. The device sends out a "beep-beep" signal that can be picked up through walls of any construction. Called "anthropotelemetry," these battery units last two years (which is the longest period Germans are placed on parole). Each transmitter emits a signal coded to the individual carrying it. The signals are transmitted at thirty second intervals to central monitoring stations where the parolees are plotted on a radar-like screen. The invention is unpopular with the ex-convicts. Said one: "At least when I was in my cell at night I could put my head under the blanket and feel that I had some privacy, but not with this box actually inside of me, I'm never alone. Some one is always watching. It gives me the creps. I feel like a robot." (Daniels, 1969). But the device fascinates West Germany Director of Prisons Erik Horzberger who predicted: "By 1971, no one will get out on parole in this country unless he first submits to an operation and has a monitor implanted under the skin" (Daniels, 1969).

Parole is more effective and less expensive to society than imprisonment. Canada, for instance, spends 65 million dollars a year to keep 7,000 prisoners locked up. The Canadian parole commission supervises 2,700 on parole, plus its prison services, for only 2 million dollars. In addition to not being tax burdens, these parolees were earning 673,371 dollars a month. Canada's National Parole Board Chairman, T.G. Street, estimates that "over 60 percent of inmates are not dangerous or vicious or violent. Most of them could or should be on parole" *(Federal Probation,* 1969).

Special Problems in Probation and Parole Supervision: The Sex Offender

The typical response of the layman to the term "sex offender" is an immediate shudder of revulsion. There has been a popular myth that violence is always linked with sex crimes. Thus, the general society responds with fear, anxiety, shame, and disgust to this category of offender.

The number of male sex offenders on probation is relatively small and comprises a little more than 4 percent of the total general probation population. The three types of sexual offender found most frequently in probation caseloads are the exhibitionist, the pedophile, and the homosexual. Together, they account for more than three-quarters of all sex offenders who appear in court. Gigeroff, Mohr, and Turner (1968) define exhibitionism as the exposure of the male genital organ to a female at inappropriate times and places. The victim is usually a stranger who has no reason to expect that the act will occur. In many cases, the motive seems to be to evoke fear and shock. Psychiatrists generally agree that the exhibitionist does not seek further contact with the victim—indeed he may actually fear it. Exhibitionists are neither mentally ill nor retarded; rather, this response to stress tends to come from a male reared in a family where sex was taboo and who is currently experiencing a frustrating situation with a female, such as early marital adjustment or the wife's pregnancy. As a group, exhibitionists are young. The average age centers around twenty-five. The recidivism rate is about 10 percent; this indicates a good probation risk. Since the exhibitionist seldom causes personal injury, his behavior should be viewed as a social nuisance. Probation services are the most humane and sensible method of dealing with this relatively harmless social problem.

Pedophilia (literally "love of children") is defined by Gigeroff, *et al,* (1968) as "the expressed desire for immature sexual gratification with a prepubertal child." Such a perversion may be classified according to the object of the sexual impulse: (1) heterosexual pedophilia (female children), (2) homosexual pehophilia (male children), (3) and undifferentiated pedophilia (both sexes). Pedophilia should not be confused with aggressive acts on children but rather is characterized by immature acts of fondling.[14] The majority of victims in heterosexual pedophilia fall between the ages of six and eleven. Offenders may be divided into three groups by stage of life: the adolescent, characterized by a general immaturity and a retarded psychosexual development; the middle-aged (35-39), for whom the pedophilic response is a regression from a frustrating adult life; and the senescent (mid-fifties to mid sixties) when loneliness and social isolation may lead to a desire for intimate contact with children. The recidivist rate for first offenders of this type is low (clusters around 8 percent), which indicates that pedophiles, especially the heterosexual variety, make good probation risks. However, there is a small group of chronic offenders about 3 percent) who remain prone to pedophilic acts throughout their lives. Probation officers should not attempt to treat this category and should refer them for specialized treatment.

---

[14]Convicts hold pedophiliacs in special contempt, and refer to them derisively as "kiddy fondlers."

Homosexuality is considered deviation for it deals with the misdirection of the libidinal energy. It is by far the most common sexual deviation (Gigeroff, *et al.,* 1969). The law does not list "homosexuality" per se as a crime but prohibits sodomy—a generic term which includes bestiality and buggery. Acts between consenting adults are rarely prosecuted.

Homosexual acts which typically are prosecuted include adult homosexual acts in public. Gigeroff, *et al.* (1969) state that the research reveals a high degree of compulsion in these publically executed acts (bus station restrooms) and say of the background of the offender:

> Frequently, married persons or those who are in positions with specific social expectations arising out of their profession or community leadership are involved. It would seem that for these the whole social context of their lives does not allow them to choose their relationship freely and they are driven to public places and picking up strangers.

A second type of homosexuality which is of a more serious nature involves young male prostitutes and older males. Most often it is the older male who is charged by the police. A third and most serious type involves younger children. In some cases a fine and supervision is sufficient to control the offender's behavior. In others, psychiatric referrals may be advisable. Sending a homosexual to prison for treatment is like sentencing an alcoholic to a brewery for therapy.

Success on Parole

While a parolee may be discharged from supervision prior to the date of his maximum prison sentence, he cannot be kept on parole beyond his mandatory release date. Violations of parole conditions tend to occur in the first months after release. Giardini and Farrow (1952) state: "It has been shown time and again that more than 95 percent of violations occur within the first three years of parole." Those crucial days just after release are described by one female parolee: "The one thing I hadn't counted on was being afraid! As I walked down the street amid crowds of people on their way to work, it seemed to me that every eye was upon me. Every face seemed ready to shout, 'get back in prison where you belong' (Tyler, 1968).

Civil rights are restored in some states upon release from prison on parole; in other states rights are restored after satisfactorily completing parole. Certain other states restore citizenship only after a full pardon from the governor. This loss of citizenship is a source of great resentment on the part of parolees. As one college student (a criminology major) who has served time for marijuana possession put it: "I'll be a college graduate, and I can't even vote!"

Parole commissions report a success rate on a national average of around 75 percent. Local rates of success range from 60 to 90 percent. The Florida Probation and Parole Commission Report for 1968 stated: "The Commission proudly reports a current success ratio of 78.5 percent while under supervision, based on the release of 19,222 parolees since 1941, with revocation necessary in only 4,275 instances." The parole violation rate refers only to the period of parole and does not include the possible return to a criminal career or the offender after termination of supervision. The F.B.I. Uniform Crime Report (1970) reports that 61 percent of inmates paroled will be rearrested within six years.

Glaser (1966) analyzed six factors as being associated with the probability of an offender's return to prison: age, offense, criminal record, race, IQ, and physique.

1. *Age.* There is an inverse relationship between crime and recidivism. The older a man is when released from prison, the less likely he is to return to crime. Inmates released after the age of fifty are more likely to commit misdemeanors than felonies should they return to crime, with the exception of alcoholics. Further, the younger an offender is at first arrest, or confinement, the more likely he is to persist in a criminal career.

2. *Offense.* Over 90 percent of the felony crimes reported to the police are economic offenses. Larceny, forgery, and auto thieves are high risks on parole.

Murderers and sex offenders, however, are better risks than other types of parolees (Federal Probation, 1969). A ten year study (1947-1957) conducted by the Pennsylvania Board of Parole compared the success rate of all sex offenders released on parole with other parolees and checked the likelihood of sex offender's repeating the same type of crime. The results revealed that the percent of sex offenders returned as parole violators (18%) was much lower than the percent of returns for the parole populations as a whole (29%). Further, when violators of the rules of parole were compared with convicted violators, it was shown that the sex offender is less likely to commit a new crime on parole than other parolees in general. Only twenty-one (less than one percent) of 2,154 cases in the sex offender file repeated sex crimes of violence.

A study conducted by the Virginia Probation and Parole Board (Federal Probation, 1969) showed "lifers" to be good parole risks. In 1958 Virginia law was amended, allowing prisoners with life sentences parole eligibility after fifteen consecutive years of confinement. Of these 196 "lifers" paroled in the ten year period (1958-1968), thirty-four were returned to prison. Only seven, however, (3.5%) were recommitted for the commission of new felonies.

Stanton (1969) directed a study to compare the success rate of paroled murderers with that of all other types of parolees released from prison in New York during the period 1948 to 1957. During parole supervision, 7.2 percent of the murderers were guilty of committing a subsequent offense, while 20.3 percent of the other offenders were guilty of a new offense while under supervision. Stanton concluded that the murderer is a better risk on parole because the majority of murderers are first-felony offenders. Also, the average age of the convicted murderer is forty-five. When compared with the average age of twenty-six for all persons paroled, this difference becomes more revealing: Delinquency rates for parolees are highest for that age group under forty-one.

3. *Prior Criminal Record.* All we know of the future is what we know from the past. If an offender has perpetrated a number of crimes, it is not unreasonable to assume that he is committed to a life of crime and will repeat his past behavior. The extent of an offender's criminal record will indicate the probability of his committing more crimes. The exception to this is the four or five time "loser" who has reached the age of "criminal menopause." He has either outgrown his desire to commit crimes or simply is too old and tired to stand the stress of that type of life.

4. *Race, IQ, and Physique.* Although significant differences exist between Negroes and whites in overall crime rates, these same differences are almost non-existent among released prisoners. Race seems to be a greater factor in the commission of original crimes

than in recidivist offenses.

I.Q. has not been found to be a predictive factor with parole violation, and while a husky body build has been found to be related to delinquency, no such research exists on released prisoners.

Ultimately, the success or failure of a person on parole depends largely upon the type of people with whom he or she interacts. As one successful parolee put it: "If I hadn't a mother who could forgive and forget, or an employer who graciously told me we all make mistakes, what might have happened to me? Without encouragement from society and from those I love, no doubt I would have ended up a repeater" (Tyler, 1968).

Pardon

Scott (1952), in his review of pardoning powers, points out that all western nations make use of some form of pardon as a means of lending flexibility to the disposition of criminal cases. England, historically, has vested this power in the Crown. But in the United States, power is vested in the people, who can delegate it to whomever they please. On the Federal level, the President holds this power, and the states normally invest the governor along with a group of advisors. Pardon boards in the United States follow three models: (1) In about one-fourth of the states this power is given to the governor alone, who may appoint a pardon attorney to aid him; (2) half of the states have advisory boards who recommend pardons to the governor who then has the final decision; (3) and another one-fourth of the states invest the pardon board with final authority, and the governor sits as an ex-officio member.

A pardon does not, as Cozard (1958) points out, expurge the record of a conviction and establish the innocence of the person pardoned. A pardon granted specifically on the ground of innocence usually in effect removes the guilty stigma, but the record of the conviction remains.

A pardon really indicates guilt, followed by forgiveness. The purpose of the pardoning power is to return convicted felons to the status they held prior to conviction. In some states, no rights are lost by conviction, so clemency is unnecessary.

There are three types of pardon in capital cases: (1) full, (2) commutation to life or a term of years, and (3) reprieve or stay of execution. Full pardons are generally given only when the person was wrongfully convicted. Although there are many safeguards in our criminal justice system to insure this does not happen, factors can develop—i.e. mistaken identity, perjured testimony of hostile witnesses, public pressures upon a district attorney, or the failure of an individual to testify on his own behalf for fear the jury could learn of previous records—which could contribute to errors in justice.

In most cases of innocence established some time after conviction, a pardon is the only effective way to rectify the wrong; courts generally have no power to grant new trials because of newly-discovered evidence.

Commutation is the substitution of a lighter for a heavier punishment. Unlike pardon, it does not mean forgiveness and does not effect a restoration of civil rights. Generally, the authority to commute a sentence is assumed in the authorization of the pardoning power. The greater power (to pardon) by definition includes the lesser power (to commute). The power to commute is most often used to make a prisoner eligible for parole. Politically, it is a middle road and shifts the responsibility for release from the governor's office to the parole board.

Commutation is appropriate to lend spirit to the letter of the law when there are extenuating circumstances which do not affect the technical, legal question of guilt or innocence of a capital crime. The classical illustration in law *(Regina v. Dudley and Stephens,* 1884) concerned two men and a cabin boy cast adrift in a life boat with almost no food, 1,600 miles from the Cape of Good Hope. After eighteen days, having been without food and water for a week, the two men killed and cannabalized the cabin boy. Four days later, they were rescued. All three would have perished had not the men resorted to "survival of the fittest." The jury convicted them of murder, and they were sentenced to death. Their sentences were, however, commuted because of the unusual circumstances.

Scott (1952) estimated that of those who are sentenced to die, about one in four or five obtains a commutation to life imprisonment. Reprieves are used if new evidence is under consideration: if a woman prisoner is pregnant, if an inmate on death row becomes insane, or if a holiday season is approaching. At present (1974) there are over 600 men on "death row" in the United States.

Amnesty is a general pardon. Literally translated, the word means "removal from memory." Historically, it has been used to restore citizenship to those who have taken part in a rebellion. Lincoln issued two such proclamations after the American Civil War. It is generally held that the power to grant individual pardons includes the power to grant general pardons.

Summary

A number of devices have been incorporated into the criminal justice system of the United States to lend flexibility to the rigid requirement of the criminal code. These measures typically reflect a desire to combine the twin goals of: (1) protection of society and (2) the rehabilitation of the offender to a useful role in society. The older view that justice simply meant extracting exactly the amount of pain from the offender as he had inflicted upon society, i.e. "making the punishment fit the crime." This doctrine survives but is declining with the increasing impact of the behavioral sciences upon the law. Treatment of the offender takes place within the framework of criminal law, and inevitably, conflicts arise between the goals of absolute protection of society and what is therapeutic for the individual.

REFERENCES

Bassin, A.: Daytop Village. *Addictions, Summer:* 42-48, 1970.

Bates, S.: When is probation not probation? *Federal Probation, 24:*13-20, 1960.

Carter, R.M. and Wilkins, L.T.: *Probation and Parole.* New York, John Wiley and Sons, 1970.

Cass, E.: De-bunking the parole experts. *The Prison World, 3:*4-6, 1941.

Cozart, R.: Pardons: their place in correctional procedure. *American Journal of Corrections, 20:*12-15, 1958.

Crossley, R.: The killer had been paroled. *Reader's Digest, 83:*105-108, 1963.

Czajkoski, E.: Department of Criminology, Florida State University, 1972. Personal communication.

Daniel, K.: Parolees controlled by electricity. *Midnight, 16:*4-5, 1969.

Diana, L.: Is casework in probation necessary? *Focus, 34:*1-8, 1955.

Dicerbo, E.: When should probation be revoked? *Federal Probation, 30:*11-17, 1966.

England, R.W.: What is responsible for satisfactory probation and post-probation outcome? *Journal of Criminal Law, Criminology, and Police*

Science, 47:667-676, 1957.

Fant, F.: Impact of the Gault decision on probation practices in juvenile courts. *Federal Probation, 33*:14-18, 1969.

Giardini, G. and Farrow, R.: The paroling of capital offenders. *Annals of the American Academy of Political and Social Science, 284*:85-94, 1952.

Giegeroff, A., Mohr, J., and Turner, R.: Sex offenders on probation: heterosexual pedophiles. *Federal Probation, 32*:17-21, 1968.

Gigeroff, A., Mohr, J., and Turner, R.: Sex offenders on parole: the exhibitionist. *Federal Probation, 32*:17-21, 1968.

Glaser, D.: *The Effectiveness of a Prison and Parole System.* Indianapolis, Bobbs-Merrill, 1966.

Griswold, H.J., Misenheimer, M., Powers, A., and Tromanhauser, E. (Eds.) : *An Eye for an Eye.* New York, Holt, Rinehart and Winston, 1970.

Jackson, D.: A say at the parole board. *Life, 70*:54-64, 1970.

Joseph, H. and Dole, V.D.: Methadone patients on probation and parole. *Federal Probation, 34*:42-48, 1970.

Machlin, M. and Woodfield, W.R.: *Ninth Life.* New York, G.P. Putnam's Sons, 1961.

Newman, C.L.: *Sourcebook on Probation, Parole, and Pardons.* Springfield, Illinois, Charles C Thomas, 1968.

News from the field. *Federal Probation,* (June) *33*:79, 1969.

News from the field. *Federal Probation,* (December) *33*:79, 1969.

Nicholson, R.: Use of prediction in caseload management. *Federal Probation, 32*:54-58, 1968.

Parsons, J.: The presentence investigation report must be preserved as a confidential document. *Federal Probation, 28*:3-7, 1964.

Probation Division, Administrative Office of the United States Courts: *The Presentence Investigation Report.* Washington, D.C., U.S. Government Printing Office, 1958.

Scott, A.: The pardoning power. *Annals of the American Academy of Political and Social Science, 284*:95-100, 1952.

Stanton, J.: Murderers on parole. *Crime and Delinquency, 15*:149-155, 1969.

Sutherland, E.H. and Cressey, D.R.: *Principles of Criminology.* Philadelphia, J.B. Lippincott, 1970.

Twenty-Eighth Annual Report, Florida Probation and Parole Commission, June 30, 1968.

Tyler, Betty: A parolee tells her story. *Federal Probation, 32*:54-56, 1968.

Unkovic, C. and Davis, J.: Volunteers in probation and parole. *Federal Probation, 33*:41-45, 1969.

Vasoli, R.: Some reflections on measuring probation outcome. *Federal Probation, 31*:24-32, 1967.

The Washington Post, February 18, 1972.

Wright, R.: Wanted—a clear understanding of parole. *Jail Association Journal, 1*:8-12, 1939.

NAME INDEX

A

Aaron, T. J., 426, 449
Abarbanel, A., 269, 296
Abrahamsen, D., 275, 296
Accord, L. D., 301, 311, 313, 332
Acton, Lord, 391
Adams, L. R., 189
Adams, Reed, 174 ftn., 182-184
Addonizio, Hugh, 388
Agras, S., 294, 296
Akers, Ronald L., 114, 131, 175-176, 179-180, 182-184, 190, 279 ftn.
Akman, D. D., 108, 131
Albert, R. S., 300, 333
Alexander, J. D., 152, 155
Alexander, M. E., 522, 544
Allen, H. E., 134, 150, 155, 305, 322-323, 333-334
Amir, M., 277-278, 296
Amos, W. E., 217-219
Anant, S., 242-243, 263
Anant, S. S., 293-294, 296
Anderson, R. T., 391, 418
Androes, L., 246, 263
Anthony, 469
Arbitt, J., 505
Arenberg, D., 190
Arnold, Edward, 488
Arnold, Thurman, 472
Atchley, R. C., 537, 544
Augustus, John, 548, 560

B

Bacon, M. K., 108, 131
Bain, Read, 429
Bakan, D., 34-35, 59
Baker, 141, 144, 368
Baldwin, James, 12 ftn.
Ball, R. B., 283, 285, 297
Ballard, 570
Ballin, 150
Banay, R. S., 352, 378

Bandura, A., 210-211, 218, 226, 247, 263, 370-372, 367-378
Banks, L., 457, 484
Banton, M., 430-431, 449
Barbara, Joseph, 388
Barker, J. C., 290-292, 296
Barker, L. J., 472, 484
Barker, R. G., 378
Barker, T., 443, 449
Barker, T. W., 472, 484
Barlow, D. H., 294, 296
Barnes, H. E., 436, 449
Barnes, Marian Q., 23, 26
Barry, H., 108, 131
Bartholomew, 144
Bartlett, D. J., 147, 155
Baruch, Bernard, 396
Bassin, A., 259, 263, 582
Bates, S., 550, 582
Bateson, G., 368, 378
Bayley, D. H., 435, 449
Beattie, R. H., 80, 88
Beccaria, Cesare, 515
Bell, Daniel, 381-382 ftn., 385, 396, 418
Bell, K. G., 236, 263
Belli, Melvin, 17
Bender, Lauretta, 351, 356, 378
Bennett, James V., 572
Bensing, R. C., 363, 378
Bentham, Jeremy, 522
Berk, B. B., 528, 543-544
Berkowitz, L., 369, 378
Bernard, J. L., 305, 310, 314, 333
Berne, Eric, 246, 263
Bernstein, George, 79
Bernstein, I. H., 310, 335
Bertrand, A. L., vii, xi
Biderman, 83
Biggs, J., Jr., 487-490, 498, 505
Biggs, John, 497
Billet, S. L., 244, 263
Black, Justice, 468

585

Hickcock, Dick, 512
Hirning, L. C., 282, 296
Hirsch, J., 138, 140, 155
Hobbes, 7
Hoch, E. L., 505-506
Hohenstein, W., 201, 219
Holmes, Oliver Wendell, 116
Holt, D., 418
Holt, David, 383 ftn.
Hooten, 405
Hooton, 134
Hoover, J. Edgar, 61, 88
Hope, K., 146, 155
Horter, 152
Horzberger, Erik, 575
Hostetter, R. C., 138, 140, 155
Howard, C. G., 15, 26
Hsu, J. J., 242, 264
Hudson, 144
Hugo, Victor, 566-567 ftn.
Hugon, Daniel, 133
Hull, Clark, 177-178
Hunt, W. A., 309, 335
Hunter, 141
Hutson, 372
Hymes, J. P., 314, 334

I

Irving, Clifford, 511 ftn.
Irwin, J., 526-527, 545
Isbell, 248
Ishihara, 142

J

Jackson, D., 571, 583
Jacobs, Patricia A., 141, 144-145, 156
James, Jesse, 394
Jeffery, C. R., 51, 59, 114, 132, 175-176, 179-181, 189-190
Jeffrey, R., 500 ftn., 506
Jellinek, E. M., 225, 230-231, 233, 236, 238, 264
Jenkins, R. L., 207, 219
Jerry, M., 282-283, 285, 287-288, 297
Johns, J. H., 304 ftn., 308-309, 312, 334
Johnson, E. H., 462, 484
Johnson, Lyndon B., 23, 397
Jones, M. C., 232, 264, 532

Joseph, H., 260-262, 264, 583
Jung, 185

K

Kagan, J., 32, 59
Kandel, A., 333
Kant, F., 264
Kapche, R., 309, 312, 333
Kaplan, H. I., 263-264
Karen, R. L., 190
Karpman, B., 238, 264, 268, 276, 284-285, 297, 299, 302-303, 317, 334
Karson, S., 506
Kates, 429
Katz, J., 488, 501, 505
Kay, Barbara, 523, 545
Kazdin, P., 151, 156
Keeler, W. J., 497, 500-501, 506
Kefauver, 385, 428
Kelley, Clarence, 445
Kendler, Tracy S., 506
Kenefick, D., 337, 373, 379
Kennedy, Robert F., 336, 396
Kilburn, K. L., 190
Kinch, J. W., 207, 219
King, Martin Luther, 336, 511
Kinsey, A. C., 12, 23, 267, 269, 297
Klinefelter, 143
Kobrin, S., 105, 132
Koella, W. P., 156
Koepf, 142, 144
Kohlmeyer, W. A., 334
Kolvin, I., 293-294, 297
Korn, R., 518, 537-538, 545
Korsakoff, 237
Kraft-Ebbing, 282
Kramer, W. D., 445, 449
Krantz, S., 445, 449
Krasner, 227
Kretschmer, 134

L

Lacey, Beatrice C., 156
Lacey, J. P., 156
Lacey, 149
Lachenmeyer, C., 37 ftn., 59
Lackin, 236
La Fave, W. R., 426, 449

SUBJECT INDEX

A

Abnormal behavior from chromosomal anomalies, 145-148
Abnormal socialization, 207
Abortions, illegal, 339
Accident, criminal intent in, 21
Accommodations, 80
  defined, 85
Acquisition, 178
Acquittals in aggravated assault cases, 68
Activism, 161
Adaptation to stress, 161-167
Addict defined, 247-248
Addiction defined, 247-248
Addictive alcoholic, 232 (*See also* Alcoholics)
Addictive behavior, 221-266 (*See also* Alcoholism; Drug addiction)
Administration of justice (*See* Justice, administration of)
Adolescent-crisis theory, 101
Adolescent status deprivation, 101
Adult status, frustrated access to, 101-102
Adultery, 24, 268-269
Advertising, misrepresentation in, 398
Age factor
  crime rate, 73-74
  parole, 578
  pedophilia, 284-287
Aggravated assault, 336-337
  alcohol involvement, 359-360
  Blacks, 75
  crime clock, 82 fig.
  crime rate, 67-68
  defined, 64, 339-340, 358
  frequency, 340, 343 fig.
  geographical distribution, 346 (Table)
  home as situs, 78
  homicide distinguished, 358, 360-361

location of offense, 358-360
offender-victim relationship, 359-360
police processing of, 359-360
prior arrest records, 359-360
situational context, 359-360
time of occurrence, 358-359
typical case, 358-360
weapon used, 358-360
Aggression, 121, 375-378
  angry, 369
  chromosomal anomalies, 141
  defined, 366
  delinquency theory, 210-211, 214
  frutration-aggression hypothesis, 366-371, 377
  frustration in relation to, 372-373
  instrumental learning, 368-371, 376
  norms of, 10
  noxious stimuli, 370
  role-models, adults as, 372
  socially learned (modeled) response, 371-373, 376
  theories, 364-373
Aggressive behavior (*See* Aggression)
Aggressive criminals, 277
Al-Anon Family Group, 242
Alateen, 242
Alcohol (*See also* Alcoholics; Alcoholism; Drunkenness)
  caliber of people using, 229-230
  cortical depressant, 227
  creativity, promotion of, 228
  depressant action of, 227
  discrimination, loss of, 227
  increase in number of users of, 229
  intellectual functioning, 228
  judgment loss, 227
  non-emotional effects of, 227
  physiological effects, 227-230
  properties of, 227
  sexual impotence produced by, 227

597